Basics of Financial Management

Basics of Financial Management

Robert Hartl
Indiana State University

wcb
Wm. C. Brown Publishers
Dubuque, Iowa

Book Team

John Stout   Executive Editor
Linda M. Galarowicz   Editor
Kathy Law Laube   Editorial Assistant
Colleen A. Yonda   Production Editor
Lisa Bogle   Designer
Carla D. Arnold   Permissions Editor

wcb group

Wm. C. Brown   Chairman of the Board
Mark C. Falb   President and Chief Executive Officer

wcb

Wm. C. Brown Publishers, College Division

James L. Romig   Vice-President, Product Development
David A. Corona   Vice-President, Production and Design
E. F. Jogerst   Vice-President, Cost Analyst
Bob McLaughlin   National Sales Manager
Catherine M. Faduska   Director of Marketing Services
Craig S. Marty   Director of Marketing Research
Eugenia M. Collins   Production Editorial Manager
Marilyn A. Phelps   Manager of Design

Cover photo: House at Minami-Aoyama by Kunihiko Hayakawa

Cover and interior design by M. B. Tauke

Library of Congress Catalog Card Number: 85–73278

ISBN 0–697–08258–X

Printed in the United States of America
10   9   8   7   6   5   4   3   2   1

To Coral, Caroline, and Tom

Contents

Preface

Several years ago I undertook the serious and challenging task of developing a concise yet thorough text in managerial finance. During the process I was guided by three goals: (1) to provide students with a broad survey of financial management topics; (2) to avoid "mind-numbing" details and unnecessarily advanced topics; and (3) to motivate students to learn finance. I made a concerted effort to write the book in a style and format conducive to student interest and understanding. Terms are, for the most part, consistent throughout the text. Chapters and topics are arranged in a systematic manner. The writing style is conversational and, on occasion, humorous. Furthermore, many of the examples and illustrations are related to the service sector of the economy (e.g., movie theaters, newspapers, vacation resorts) with which students are generally familiar.

This text is designed primarily for the one-semester introductory course at the undergraduate level. Its eighteen chapters present the basics of financial management in cogent, easily digestible units of study. The topics are presented as a cohesive body of knowledge, rather than as a series of seemingly unrelated pieces of information. As a result, students obtain a thorough survey of the subject matter.

Basic Approach

This text utilizes a building block approach by starting out with foundation concepts in Section 1 (chapters 1–4): financial statement analysis, compound interest mathematics, risk measurement, and the important concept of a required rate of return. Sections 2 and 3 build upon the foundation concepts and contain the core material of the text. Section 2 deals with all aspects of asset management and *only* asset management. Section 3 is devoted solely to a discussion of liability and equity management. While there are, admittedly, some advantages to mixing investment and financing decisions together in an advanced level book, in an elementary text this creates considerable confusion as one jumps back and forth. Therefore, the stage is set in Section 1 to allow for a separate discussion of asset management and liability and equity management. By discussing these topics separately, this text is couched in the framework of a balance sheet, thereby capitalizing on the students' familiarity with accounting. Specialized topics, such as international finance, are covered in the last section, Section 4.

Although the book follows the topical structure of the balance sheet, it does not present merely a descriptive view of finance. Rather, I have tried to repeatedly relate concepts to the premise of financial theory. That premise is that stockholder well-being should be the major goal of corporations and their employees.

Highlights   To highlight some of the significant features of the text I have summarized them below.

1. Service organizations are used in many of the examples throughout the text. These firms deserve to be included because they are an increasingly important part of the U.S. economy. Furthermore, college students can relate to these businesses more so than they can to manufacturing enterprises.
2. Personal finance illustrations are employed whenever the situation lends itself. Personal finance is also well represented in the end-of-chapter problems.
3. A separate chapter on financial markets and institutions enhances the teaching effort in financial management.
4. Various kinds of capital asset proposals, including nonfinancial considerations, are delineated in chapter 10 to provide a practical approach to understanding the applications of capital budgeting.
5. Unnecessary details and esoteric topics are eliminated to allow a more concise and understandable survey of financial management.
6. Financial decisions are organized as closely as possible around the balance sheet.
7. End-of-chapter problems are numerous and varied in terms of originality and degree of difficulty.
8. Examples and applications are used liberally throughout the text. Both amplify concepts by providing a "real-world" emphasis to the information presented.
9. Numerous diagrams, figures, and exhibits are included to help students understand difficult concepts and prepare for exams. All of them serve a functional purpose; they are not simply "window dressing."
10. The writing style is conversational, presenting the material at a level appropriate for introductory students.
11. The treatment of compound interest has been greatly expanded relative to other texts in an effort to provide more in-depth coverage of a critical topic and to aid student learning in a difficult subject area.

Textual Learning Aids

Behavioral Objectives   Each chapter is introduced with a chapter overview and a set of behavioral objectives. The objectives provide learning goals for the students and are tied to the test bank as well as to the self-tests in the study guide.

Applications/Examples   Concepts are explained using both *applications* and *examples*. Applications are realistic case-type illustrations of concepts and formula usage; they can be several paragraphs or pages in length. Examples are either simple numeric illustrations showing students how to correctly use equations, or short (one or two sentences) explanations of selected principles.

Finance in the News   Most chapters have a short feature, taken directly from a current news periodical, called *Finance in the News*. These featured readings serve two purposes: (1) "real-world" implications of the concepts in the chapter, and (2) financial topics of current interest to motivate students.

Summaries   Each chapter concludes with a summary that includes tables of formulas where appropriate. By reviewing the summary students can actively focus on the key concepts of each chapter.

Discussion Questions   Each chapter ends with several questions. Although some questions focus on reviewing chapter material, others are more thought-provoking and can serve as vehicles for classroom discussion.

Problems   There are over three hundred problems in the text. These problems were written and solved by the author, and are varied in the terms of originality and degree of difficulty.

End-of-Chapter Appendixes   To provide flexibility for the instructor, in certain chapters some of the more difficult material has been put into an end-of-chapter appendix rather than being incorporated into the chapter.

Careers in Finance Appendix   Several job descriptions have been excerpted from the Financial Management Association's booklet "Careers in Finance." These descriptions provide information on basic functions, primary responsibilities, organizational relationships, required education and experience, and representative skills and knowledge for a variety of occupations in finance.

Supplementary Materials

Instructor's Manual   The instructor's manual is designed to help the user take advantage of the special features of the text. Chapter outlines, with teaching tips and extensive answers to end-of-chapter questions and problems, provide a solid framework for instruction. Two quizzes, designed to easily test students' comprehension of content, are provided for each chapter. These quizzes are in the form of masters that can be directly duplicated for the students. A checklist of answers to selected EOC problems is also provided in the instructor's manual.

Test Bank   A computerized test bank is available to those adopting the text. It contains over one thousand questions that have been designed to test students' achievement of the behavioral objectives in the chapters.

Study Guide   The study guide has been written by the test bank author to ensure consistency in question content and structure. Each chapter contains: (1) suggestions for chapter study, (2) a summary of key concepts, (3) an illustrative example, where appropriate, (4) multiple-choice and true-false questions keyed to chapter objectives in the text, (5) annotated answers to preceding questions, (6) problems keyed to objectives, and (7) answers to problems.

ωⅽⱨ StudyPak   StudyPak provides an alternative to the manual study guide. It contains a sequential, guided review consisting of multiple-choice and true-false questions. Students receive immediate feedback on the accuracy of their answers. After students complete the guided review, diagnostics appear on the screen describing which objectives were most often missed. After the diagnostics, students are given a second chance to answer the questions missed.

ωⅽⱨ QuizPak   QuizPak is a student self-testing program on the microcomputer. Quizpak lets students choose a chapter to review then the computer quizzes them with questions selected from the chapter.

Transparencies   A set of one hundred acetate transparencies will be provided to adopters of the text. These transparencies facilitate instruction and learning by making it easy for instructors to present key concepts from the text.

Templates   Computer templates for solving standard finance problems will be available to those adopting the text. The templates will be available in IBM Lotus 1–2–3, IBM VisiCalc, and Apple VisiCalc versions. All templates will have the terminology, symbols, and format contained in the text, yet each one can be used to solve a variety of end-of-chapter problems in the respective chapters.

Acknowledgements

The following critical reviewers have provided in-depth analyses of individual chapters and many valuable suggestions concerning the final shape and content of the text:

Jerry Hunt, East Carolina University
Arthur Klein, Loma Linda University
Linda Martin, Arizona State University
Larry Guin, Murray State University
Kenneth Crepas, Illinois State University
Peter Goulet, University of Northern Iowa
Abu Selimudden, Berkshire Community College

  I would also like to acknowledge the help of Max Douglas, Kwang-Soo Lee, Steve Lamb, Sam Certo, and Herschel Chait, for their help during the writing of this manuscript. Special thanks to Janet Brown for lending me her typing skills.

Robert Hartl

Foundations of Financial Management

Section 1 of this textbook contains essential background information for the core material coming later in the book. Chapter 1 introduces the subject matter and goals of Financial Management. Chapter 2 takes a close up view of accounting financial statements and reviews accounting terminology. Chapter 3 is concerned with the mathematical properties of interest rates. And, to emphasize the importance of interest rates to Financial Management, chapter 4 examines the economic factors that underlie interest rates, with particular emphasis on risk ■

1

Introduction

Overview

The purpose of this book is to introduce the reader to the many financial decisions faced by a modern business, along with the analytical tools and concepts necessary for an evaluation of these decisions. Although the presentation will be oriented toward the financial decisions of large business corporations, most of the material is applicable to small businesses, nonprofit organizations and, in some instances, consumers.

This chapter provides an overall perspective on the text. It begins with a definition of financial management, followed by a brief history of how this subject of study evolved. The corporate form of business organization is also reviewed here. The central feature of this chapter is the discussion dealing with the objectives of financial management, and the important role played by common stockholders. A preview of the remainder of the text closes out the current chapter■

Objectives

By the end of the chapter the student should be able to:

1. Define financial management
2. Discuss the current impact of financial management on businesses from an historical perspective
3. Explain the role of finance in a business, relating it to other functional areas of the firm
4. Distinguish among proprietorships, partnerships, and corporations
5. List and discuss the goals of financial management, explaining the impacts of risk and timing
6. Define and distinguish between asset management and liability/equity management
7. Relate financial decisions (i.e., asset and liability decisions) to profitability and shareholder satisfaction

Definition of Financial Management

Financial management (also called business finance) is the process of evaluating assets, liabilities, and equity, and making decisions based on this analysis. The emphasis is on financial management of profit oriented business organizations as opposed to consumers and government institutions. It must be said, however, that many of the tools and concepts used in financial management can be readily applied to consumer finance and government finance.

The individual charged with financial management issues is the financial manager.

History of Financial Management

The study of financial management originally centered on the acquisition of funds and the problems encountered when financial obligations could not be met on schedule. As a result, financial articles and texts were replete with information on the liability and equity portions of the balance sheet. Very little attention was paid to assets. Various sources of funds (i.e., trade credit, bank loans, bonds, common stock) were written about in great detail.[1] For example, discussion went on and on about how loan contracts should be written, or the advantages and disadvantages of, say, serial debenture bonds. Unfortunately, there was little underlying economic theory to help in determining the optimal type or mix of financing. As a result, it was easy to become bogged down in vast amounts of detail.

The same thing can be said about financial solvency problems. Here the discussion was primarily legal in nature and also in great detail. A typical textbook section might elaborate at great length about proper disposition of funds in a bankruptcy liquidation.

After World War II the subject of business finance began to include the study of working capital management (e.g., the management of current assets such as cash and accounts receivable). Although the discussion of working capital management was lengthy, it too was absent of an underlying economic theory to allow managers to cut through the mass of detail and get to the heart of problems.[2]

Toward the late 1950s two things occurred more or less simultaneously within the field of finance. In the first instance, financial management began to get involved seriously in the analysis of fixed asset acquisitions (i.e., plant, machinery, etc.). This brought into its jurisdiction the entire balance sheet of the firm. The second thing that happened was the development of an economic theory applied to financial management.[3] This theory has been

---

[1]For example, see Arthur S. Dewing, *The Financial Policy of Corporations* (New York: Ronald Press, 1920), and W. H. Lyon, *Capitalization: A Book on Corporation Finance* (Boston: Houghton Mifflin Company, 1912).

[2]For example, see Raymond P. Kent, *Corporate Financial Management* (Homewood, Illinois: Richard D. Irwin, Inc., 1960), and P. Hunt, C. Williams and B. Donaldson, *Basic Business Finance* (Homewood, Illinois: Richard D. Irwin, Inc., 1958).

[3]Three classics that should be mentioned here are: Harry M. Markowitz, *Portfolio Selection* (New Haven: Yale University Press, 1959), F. Modigliani and M. H. Miller, "The Cost of Capital, Corporation Finance and the Theory of Investment," *American Economic Review* 48 (June 1958), pp. 261–97, and "Dividend Policy, Growth and the Valuation of Shares," *Journal of Business* 34 (October 1961), pp. 411–33.

Figure 1.1   Role of finance in a hypothetical business organization

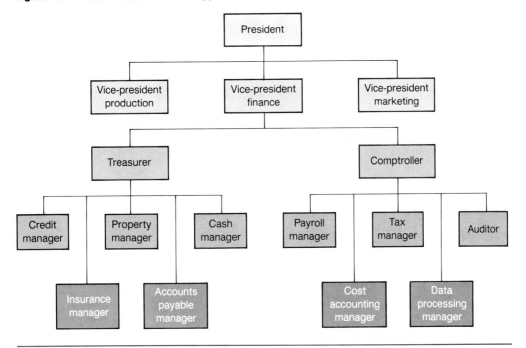

augmented since then and today provides financial management with a conceptual frame-work and related tools that allow it to systematically address problems encountered in managing assets, liabilities, and equity.

    Thus, the study of financial management today and, therefore, the job of the financial manager, is much broader than forty or fifty years ago. In addition, a conceptual framework has been developed along with related models to aid the financial management process.

The Study of Business Finance

Finance is one of the four major functional areas of a business; the other three being production or operations, marketing, and management. Production deals with the design and manufacture of a product. Marketing involves the selling and promotion of a product, as well as its physical distribution. Management relates to the persons in a company: hiring them, motivating them, organizing them, and the like. While normally not singled out in a company organization chart as a functional area, management nevertheless permeates an entire business enterprise. Finance is concerned with all of the monetary aspects of a business, such as: expenditures on plant and equipment, fund raising, dividend payments, checking account control, credit sales, and stockholder relations. The importance of finance to a company can be seen in figure 1.1.

    Students who are not finance or accounting majors quite often wonder why they must take a course in business finance. Their feeling runs something as follows: I will never work in a bank or manage investments, my business career is going to be in sales, personnel, or "management." When am I ever going to be involved with loans, interest rates, or cash budgets? It is quite true that they may never get involved directly in financial problems. However, career paths change. If an individual aspires to move into upper management, then knowledge of financial matters will prove worthwhile. More likely, the nonfinancial person will be working in connection with financial persons from time to time and it would be helpful if both parties know something of the other's area of specialization so that they can communicate.

The study of financial management (as with the study of all business areas) provides a better understanding of how a total business operates, thereby contributing to overall organization goals.

There are two additional reasons why the study of financial management can be helpful for those not planning to work directly with it. First, it provides an individual with additional insight into the functioning of our economy, thus making him or her a better citizen. Second, it can be helpful in the solution of personal financial problems such as: buying a home, financing a car, or purchasing insurance.

Corporate Financial Management

There are basically three types of for-profit business organizations in the United States: proprietorships, partnerships, and corporations. Proprietorships are single owner businesses that are generally small organizations centered in the retail trades. Although small in size, they make up a sizeable percentage of all businesses. Partnerships are business associations of two or more owners, with some partnerships having over a thousand owners. Generally speaking, they are somewhat larger than proprietorships and are prominent in the professional service trades such as law, stockbrokerage, and architecture.

The emphasis in this text will be upon the corporate form of business. Corporations make up the majority of medium- and large-size businesses. However, it is possible to have a small one-owner corporation; they are involved in all types of business, and they account for the bulk of private assets, sales, and employment in the United States. Unlike proprietorships and partnerships, the owners of a corporation are issued shares of stock to show their equity interest. These owners are therefore referred to as stockholders or shareholders. By having shares of stock it is relatively easy to determine an owner's proportional interest in a firm. This in itself makes corporations conducive to the study of financial management. Due to their size, scope, and use of common stock, the discussion of financial management will therefore be aimed at corporations. (However, most of the material could be readily applied to other forms of business organization.)

Since corporations will be the center of discussion, it should be mentioned at the outset that there are five important legal distinctions between them and proprietorships and partnerships. The five differences have to do with taxes, transfer of ownership, life of the business, owner liability, and securities law.

1. *Corporations are the only type of business organization that must have their income taxed twice.* This occurs because the corporate income is taxed at corporate income tax rates and the remaining income (net income) that is returned to the stockholders in the form of dividends will be taxed to them at personal income tax rates.

Figure 1.2   Unique characteristics of the corporate form of business organization

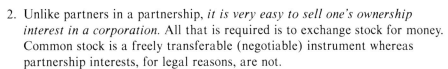

2. Unlike partners in a partnership, *it is very easy to sell one's ownership interest in a corporation.* All that is required is to exchange stock for money. Common stock is a freely transferable (negotiable) instrument whereas partnership interests, for legal reasons, are not.
3. *Corporations, technically, can remain in existence forever.* They are normally only extinguished through a voluntary act of the owners. Partnerships, on the other hand, are dissolved upon the death of one of the partners unless carefully provided for in the original partnership agreement.
4. *A tremendous advantage of corporate ownership is what is referred to as limited liability.* This refers to the fact that the maximum a corporate owner can lose is the amount he or she invested in the particular corporation. No other stockholder assets can be used to cover the corporation's losses. This provision is of particular interest to an investor who has sizeable personal assets that he or she wants to protect.[4] On the other hand, a proprietor or partner could suffer unlimited losses if their businesses went under.
5. The final unique characteristic of corporations arises from the nature of corporate financing, which is done through the sale of securities (e.g., stocks and bonds), and the related social goal of investor protection. Very simply, publicly held corporations (i.e., those with many security investors) *must contend with a vast body of securities law.* This law has developed over the years with the primary purpose of protecting securities investors from unscrupulous management and from other investors. More will be said about this subject later in the book.

There is an additional characteristic of corporations that has occurred *out of practice, not law,* and will be assumed throughout the text: *separation of ownership and control.* In most of today's modern, large corporations the majority of owners do not directly run the company, but instead select others (managers) to run the firm for them. Without getting

---

[4]Limited liability can be, and often is, waived by stockholders.

into a debate about the merits of such practices, and there is considerable debate, it is mentioned here only because the approach taken in this book will be that the management of a corporation, financial management in particular, is distinct from the ownership.

Goal of Financial Management

In the conduct of corporate financial management, it is necessary for the financial manager to have some goal or objective to aim for when managing assets, liabilities, and equity. Without some objective in mind, it becomes nearly impossible to perform analysis properly and to make good financial decisions. The goal of a defense lawyer is to get his or her client off, the goal of a basketball coach is to win; what is the goal of a business? Not everyone is in agreement here. Some feel that sales volume is most important (chief marketing executive); some see customer satisfaction as overriding (Ralph Nader); there are those who claim good labor relations are the reason for having business (AFL–CIO); others see business as a source of charitable contributions and provider of community service (museums); still others feel they should be the guardians of the environment (Sierra Club); at least one organization looks upon business as a large source of public revenue (U.S. Government); and there are those who claim that business should be run in their interest, because they provide most of the money (stockholders).

Does the financial manager possess one or possibly all of the aforementioned goals or does he or she dance to a different tune? It would be foolish to say that all employees or even all managerial employees in a business would possess the same objective if free to choose. But it should not seem foolish to you that a business would function better if all workers were trying to achieve the same goal. One of the principle functions of management in general is to try and get as many employees as possible to strive for the central objective of the business, whatever that goal is stated to be.

But what should an overall corporation goal be? Is there one that is superior to others? *It is the premise of financial theory that stockholder well-being should be the major goal of corporations and their employees.* This premise will be followed throughout the text. Stockholder well-being is not always achieved by greater profits. Financial decisions based on simple profit maximization can be assured of pleasing the owners only if two rare conditions hold. First of all, simple profit maximization assumes that risk is of no concern to stockholders. Furthermore, owners must be indifferent as to when they obtain profits. In other words, they would not care whether they received their money in five years or one year. Examples would be helpful here to describe the implications from discarding these two conditions.

Application: In the first case, shown in table 1.1, we will look at a decision where simple profit maximization is appropriate. Management must decide between two alternative assets whose risk and timing are equal but their profitability is not. Given the choice of these two opportunities, it should be obvious that B is preferable because its profit is larger while it is no more risky than A. In this instance, the proper selection would also be the one that provides the greatest amount of profit. Shareholders are right to be indifferent to timing and risk in this example, because they are irrelevant to the decision.

Table 1.1 A Financial Decision Solely Based on Profit

	Expected Profit	Time Period Received	Risk of Receiving Profit
Opportunity A	$1,000	In 2 years	Zero risk
Opportunity B	$1,500	In 2 years	Zero risk

The second case, displayed in table 1.2, will hold risk constant, but allow profits and timing to vary. Here again, management must decide between two alternatives. Opportunity B has the greatest profit, but it is received much later than A's profit.

Table 1.2 A Financial Decision Based on Profit and Timing

	Expected Profit	Time Period Received	Risk of Receiving Profit
Opportunity A	$1,000	In 2 years	Zero risk
Opportunity B	$1,500	In 8 years	Zero risk

Consequently, in this case it is not immediately clear that B is superior to A. A's profit is received earlier and therefore can be put to use sooner than B's. As long as the owners can earn a positive interest rate on funds, then the $1,000 from A can be invested at interest for six years while they wait for the payoff from B to occur. Whether or not the $1,000 from A plus interest would be greater than the $1,500 from B by the time the eighth year rolls around will depend upon the interest rate. If the rate is 10%, the $1,000 would grow to $1,772, which is clearly better than B.[5] Basing this decision upon simple profit maximization would therefore be wrong. The process of adjusting for timing differences by the use of interest rates is referred to as the *time value of money,* about which much more will be said later.

In the third case, shown in table 1.3, risk will be allowed to vary, but timing and profit will be identical for each opportunity so that we may isolate on risk. As before, one of two alternatives must be selected.

Table 1.3 A Financial Decision Solely Based on Risk

	Expected Profit	Time Period Received	Risk of Receiving Profit
Opportunity A	$1,000	In 2 years	High risk
Opportunity B	$1,000	In 2 years	Low risk

Here we have a situation where the expected profit from each opportunity is the same, and they are to be received at the same point in time. According to profit maximization and adjustment for the time value of money, they are equally good. However, the element of risk has entered the picture, because there is no longer an equal chance of obtaining the profits. We will avoid a detailed discussion for now about the definition and measurement of risk and simply state that A is a high-risk choice and B a low-risk choice. For instance, A could be a new product addition and B an expansion of a familiar, old product line. Since most persons (business owners included) tend to avoid unnecessary risk, at least where money is concerned, we can safely say that B is preferable to A when risk is taken into account.

---

[5]This was computed with the use of the compound interest formula that will be taken up in chapter 3.

Table 1.4   A Financial Decision Based on Profit and Risk

	Expected Profit	Time Period Received	Risk of Receiving Profit
Opportunity A	$1,500	In 2 years	High risk
Opportunity B	$1,000	In 2 years	Low risk

In the fourth case, shown in table 1.4, a more difficult situation presents itself. Asset alternative A has the higher profit while B has lower risk. In cases of this sort, the decision will depend on the shareholders' *tradeoff between profit and risk.* ∎

The important thing to remember is that financial analysis and decision making can be based solely on profit only when risk and timing are of no consequence. Rarely do we find this to be the case.

Hopefully, we can now come to some conclusion about what the financial manager should use as a goal. As stated earlier, the goal of the financial manager should be identical with the goal of the corporation. Furthermore, the overriding goal of the corporation is to please its owners. The financial manager can achieve this by evaluating asset, liability, and equity decisions on the basis of profitability, risk, and the time value of money.

How does the financial manager know that he or she has performed satisfactorily? Fortunately, there is an economic variable that provides a composite picture of risk and profitability, and it is intertwined with the owners' interests. We are speaking here of the market price of a company's common stock.[6] Stock prices are a function of a corporation's profitability and riskiness. Imagine the stock market as a large voting booth where investors vote with dollars for their favorite companies. Should management make a financial decision having a particular impact on a firm's time-adjusted profit and risk that is not agreeable with investors, then they will react by driving down the price of the firm's stock. If they more than approve of management's decision, then they will bid up the stock price in an attempt to get a share of the benefits. Since we would prefer to know the impact on stock prices prior to a decision rather than after, the financial manager must spend the better part of his or her time doing profitability and risk analysis. *Thus, improving the market price of the stock will be the financial manager's primary goal for taking actions and measuring results. His or her long-term goal is to make that market price as high as possible.* This goal is commonly referred to as *wealth maximization,* due to the fact that stock is an asset of the owners and raising its price will increase their wealth. To try and achieve wealth maximization the financial manager must try to put himself or herself in the owners' shoes in an attempt to anticipate their reactions to the firm's financial decisions. Obviously, this problem would not be so taxing if the management and the owners were the same. The relationship between financial management and stockholder satisfaction is displayed in figure 1.3.

---

[6]Not all stocks are traded on the stock market. These would include stocks of very small corporations or closely held large corporations consisting of only a few stockholders.

Figure 1.3   Linkage between financial management decisions and stockholder well-being

Asset, liability, and equity decisions	→	Impact on profit and risk	→	Market price of common stock	→	Shareholder wealth	→	Shareholder satisfaction

Preview of the Text

The typical issues encountered in financial management can be framed around a balance sheet. As was defined earlier, financial management is the process of evaluating assets, liabilities, and equity and making decisions about them. The evaluation encompasses an analysis of profitability and risk. Financial decision making is based upon the profitability and risk analysis as well as owner attitudes toward profit and risk.

Assets are extremely important to a business. Because they are so important, management must pay close attention to them. Assets are purchased, sold, stored, maintained, repaired, used, and insured. Financial management is involved in all of these issues and more. And there are right ways and wrong ways to handle them. Analysis of and decisions on each of these issues can be very complex. Consider the seemingly simple example of acquiring furniture for a new office. What kind should be acquired, how much, new or used, from which vendor and when should it be acquired? Each one of these questions should be answered in the context of profit and risk and, accordingly, the stockholders' reactions. A financial manager's responsibilities for assets is described by the term *asset management*. Since current assets and fixed assets have distinctive characteristics, we will discuss them separately.

While assets truly are critical for a business they could not exist without funds to support them. This brings us to liabilities and equity. Financial management must contend with many dilemmas related to these items. Important considerations for any business are: whether to use debt or equity financing; should debt be short- or long-term; will equity be raised internally or externally; how to get the best loan terms; whether or not to pay off a loan prior to maturity; and how to handle a financial crisis. These issues fall under the category of *liability and equity management*. They are difficult questions and must be dealt with in terms of their profit and risk consequences and, ultimately, their impact on the market price of the common stock.

Asset management is covered in section 2 of the book and liability and equity management in section 3. Prior to tackling those two subjects, we will go over some necessary background material in section 1. Figure 1.4 presents a detailed preview of the material to come.

Figure 1.4   Preview of text subject matter

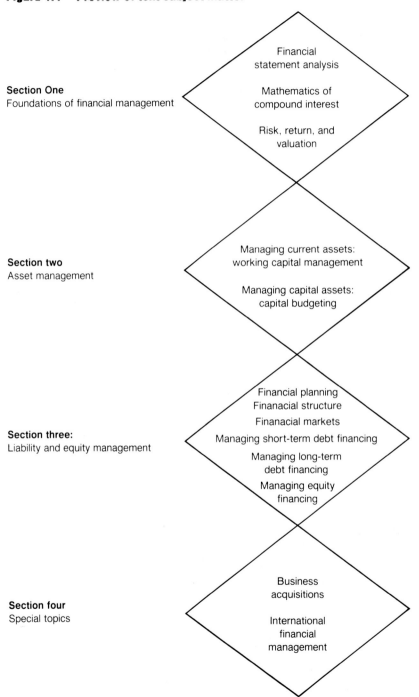

Section One
Foundations of financial management

Financial
statement analysis

Mathematics of
compound interest

Risk, return, and
valuation

Section two
Asset management

Managing current assets:
working capital management

Managing capital assets:
capital budgeting

Section three:
Liability and equity management

Financial planning
Finanacial structure
Finanacial markets
Managing short-term debt financing
Managing long-term
debt financing
Managing equity
financing

Section four
Special topics

Business
acquisitions

International
financial
management

Key Terms/Concepts

Asset management
Corporation
Financial management
Liability and equity
  management

Profit maximization
Separation of ownership and
  control
Stockholder

Time value of money
Tradeoff between profit and
  risk
Wealth maximization

Questions

1. What are the weaknesses of profit maximization when used as the objective of financial decision making?

2. In a capitalistic society, the number one priority of a corporation is to please its common stockholders. Why is this so?

3. Explain why corporations became the dominant form of business enterprise in the United States.

4. Describe, in your own words, what risk means to common stock investors.

Selected References

Donaldson, G., "Financial Goals: Management versus Shareholders," *Harvard Business Review* (May–June 1963), pp. 116–29.
Financial Management, Tenth Anniversary Edition (1981).
Haley, C. W., "A Theoretical Foundation for the Basic Finance Course," *Journal of Financial and Quantitative Analysis* (November 1975), pp. 691–94.
Hill, L. W., "The Growth of the Corporate Finance Function," *Financial Executive* (July 1976), pp. 38–43.
Weston, J. F., *The Scope and Methodology of Finance*, Englewood Cliffs, N.J.: Prentice-Hall, Inc., 1966.

▮ Finance in the News

As financial management becomes more complex, corporations frequently find it necessary to obtain advice from outside consultants. These consultants help achieve the goal of financial management—maximizing the financial well-being of a company—by determining what actions will most benefit its financial statements. The following article describes one such consulting operation.

It's 2 A.M.—Do You Know Where Your CPA Is?

It's 11 p.m. in Los Angeles. An investment banker is in his hotel room, working out a merger for a prospective client. The transaction makes sense, but he's worried that the client's outside auditors—who will be in on a crucial meeting first thing in the morning—will kill the deal, saying it would look bad on the books. He shuffles through his briefcase and finds a telephone number in New York, where it is already 2 a.m. Even so, within minutes he was speaking with a Touche Ross & Co. accountant, who immediately confirmed his fears. The deal, instead of being signed on Oct. 25, was put off indefinitely.

Such high-pressure decisions are nightmarish for most CPAs, who normally would want plenty of time to pore over each nuance. But the proliferation of new financing instruments and exotic merger deals—along with the typical investment banker's frantic work schedule . . .—has created a growing demand for accounting firms that can provide commensurately fast advice on the tax and financial statement aspects.

Touche Ross, the youngest and smallest of the Big Eight, appears to be the nimblest. It has a bustling special unit ensconced at the top of the World Trade Center, complete with a hotline through which dealmakers can reach—and rouse—a crack team of accountants at any hour of the night. "While we're not investment bankers ourselves, we have tried to gear ourselves to their kind of business: deals, rush-rush, keep it quiet," says Robert S. Kay, a top Touche Ross partner.

Getting involved in such snazzy consulting was a culture shock. "In a profession not noted for entrepreneurial behavior, we spent money and took risks," says J. Thomas Presby, the partner in charge of the 24-hour unit that Touche calls its Financial Services Center. It was also a good opportunity for the firm to pick up some audit clients among New York's banks and securities firms, a market it admits has been difficult to crack. Despite his long tenure with the firm, Presby says, a failure on Wall Street would have meant "my partners would find a nice place for me in the Timbuktu office."

Tremendous Benefits

Fortunately for him, the Financial Service Center's revenues have grown briskly since it opened in 1981. Touche consultants made the accounting judgments that cleared the way for a number of pioneering transactions, including Morgan Guaranty's European bond arbitrage deals that gave Sterling Drug, Baxter Travenol, and PepsiCo tremendous accounting benefits atop the cash flow (BW—Apr. 2).

Since then, more corporations have become more aware that a financing is not only a way to raise funds. It also is something that can needlessly damage a balance sheet or—thanks to accounting vagaries—can let a company gain cosmetic benefits. "A lot of my work has to do with esoteric financings, deals that have never been done before," says Kathleen E. O'Kain, a vice-president at Prudential-Bache Securities Inc. "It's helpful to be able to find out whether an instrument would be classified as debt or equity," she says. "Sometimes the line is blurred."

Just as often, CPA firms have no ready answers. The Financial Accounting Standards Board—the rule-making body—has frequently lagged behind Wall Street, offering no guidance on the latest deals. CPA firms are reluctant to provide consultation on such uncharted waters. Touche Ross may be the only firm that has marshalled enough resources to keep up. "What they have done is to set up a group whose only mission in life is to respond to questions that are driven by a financing transaction," says a top investment banker. "They are not audit people doing this on the side."

The latest transaction to set Wall Street abuzz was a Citibank move, which came to light in mid-September. It sold some loans to a new company it had created, Chatsworth Funding, Inc., which financed the deal by issuing commercial paper. The bank treated the transaction as a sale, not a borrowing, and the Securities & Exchange Commission as well as the FASB have yet to decide whether the accounting treatment was proper. Touche was not involved with this deal, but the accounting firm has since received calls from other financial institutions, asking if they, too, could treat such an arrangement as a sale. Touche said it looks O.K., but warned "it's a hot subject"—just the kind Touche likes.

By Stuart Weiss in New York

Financial Statement Analysis

Overview

Accounting terminology is prevalent within the field of financial management. Accounting financial statements are the source of much valuable information about a company's health and prospects. This is particularly true of balance sheets and income statements. The information derived from financial statements can be used to identify financial strengths and weaknesses, and thereby aid in financial decision making. This chapter is devoted primarily to the analysis of financial statements: we will learn the reasons for financial statement analysis, how to prepare for it, how it is conducted, and what it can mean ■

Objectives

By the end of the chapter the student should be able to:

1. Define and explain the uses of Financial Statement Analysis (FSA)
2. Classify users of financial statements and describe their information needs
3. Define income statement and relate it to FSA
4. Define balance sheet and relate it to FSA
5. Discuss the preparatory steps an individual must complete prior to FSA
6. Describe liquidity analysis, and construct and interpret ratios that measure liquidity
7. Describe solvency analysis, and construct and interpret ratios that measure solvency
8. Describe profitability analysis, and construct and interpret ratios that measure profitability
9. Explain how management can use FSA as an aid in fund raising and in problem solving
10. Define and calculate activity ratios
11. Evaluate financial ratios through (a) industry comparisons, (b) time series analysis, and (c) decomposition analysis
12. Apply FSA to a given situation

Introduction

Financial statements, in particular the balance sheet and income statement, are important sources of business information. There is a great deal of interest in them. An entire subject of study has evolved around the interpretation and evaluation of them. The name given to this subject is Financial Statement Analysis (FSA).

There are several reasons why it is useful to analyze financial statements. In their raw form, balance sheets and income statements can provide useful information for decision-making purposes. But much additional information can be obtained from them through the application of some relatively simple mathematical computations. For instance, the income statement will tell us what a corporation's net income was for a particular period of time. This is a total figure, however, and a decision maker may also wish to have the net income per share of common stock. Such a number can be obtained easily, thus increasing the usefulness of the income statement for this particular analyst.

A second reason for analyzing financial statements is to find clues to problem areas and strengths that the firm in question might have. Balance sheets and income statements taken at face value can hide some very interesting bits of information that could prove useful to an examiner. Many times this information can be filtered out through some elementary computations. These computations may take, for example, the form of finding the ratio of sales to inventory. This computation can tell the analyst more about the inventory situation than simply using the inventory by itself. If done properly, FSA will generate more in-depth knowledge about a company's financial situation than the financial statements.

Finally, examination of a particular corporation's assets, revenues, expenses, and liabilities at a particular time and isolated from everything else is of limited value. How can you evaluate something unless there is something else to compare it to? We judge a basketball player's performance based upon how he compares with other players in the game or what he has done in the past. The same holds true of a business. If AT&T makes two billion dollars in net income this year is that good or bad? By itself, this number is practically meaningless. If it is less than last year's profit, small in relation to the investment in the firm, or relatively inferior to competitors, many persons might well consider it to be bad. The point is, we need to have standards of comparison, for business, like everything else, is relative. One of the primary purposes of FSA is to convert financial statement figures into a form that is conducive to making comparisons.

In summary, FSA provides us with financial statement information that is more complete, in greater depth, and easier to compare ■

Users of Financial Statements

It is easy to get caught up in the complexities of preparing financial statements and lose sight of the fact that others will be using the statements to make important decisions. Balance sheets, income statements, and all of the other subsidiary documents falling under the general category of financial statements are not ends in themselves. They are prepared because many persons feel they contain valuable information that could be helpful in making important business decisions. It is not carved in granite that corporations must prepare financial statements. If analysts would one day decide that financial statements were useless, then, eventually, we would see statements disappear. As a matter of fact, widespread preparation and use of balance sheets and income statements is a relatively recent phenomenon.

Just who are these users of financial statements? For descriptive purposes it is useful to classify them into five groups: short-term creditors, long-term creditors, stockholders, management, and others.

Short-Term Creditors   Short-term credit is the acquisition of funds (loans) or goods (accounts payable) that must be paid for within a short period of time, usually defined as less than one year. Providers of such credit are short-term creditors and those who obtain this credit are short-term debtors. Most business firms simultaneously fill the roles of both short-term creditor and debtor. They are debtors when they acquire a loan from a bank or purchase materials from a supplier on credit. They become creditors when they sell *their* merchandise to customers and wait for payment (e.g., accounts receivable).

Creditors want to be paid, and they are not usually willing to rely solely upon a borrower's claims and promises to get their money back. The debtor's financial situation will determine to a large extent its ability to repay. Therefore, an analysis of the borrower's financial statements can help tremendously with short-term credit decisions.

Long-Term Creditors   Long-term credit represents money extended to a business for which repayment is spread over a considerable period of time, perhaps ten to thirty years. This particular type of financing is obtained in the form of bonds and mortgages and the buyers of these securities are long-term creditors. A list of potential long-term creditors would include: individuals, life insurance companies, pension funds, and bank trust departments. All of these long-term business lenders are very concerned about getting their money back plus interest. To help them in deciding whether or not a business qualifies as an acceptable credit risk they spend a great deal of time examining the credit applicant's financial position and earnings record. This analysis is not only done prior to making the loan, but also after the securities are purchased to make sure the borrower remains financially sound.

Common Stockholders   Prior to the 1930s, corporate financial statements were few and far between. Those that were prepared were often incomplete, incorrect, and, in some cases, fraudulent. As a result, owners of a firm who were not in management often had to live in the dark when it came to knowledge about their companies. Prodded by stockholders, mandated by governments, and carried out by the accounting profession, financial statement preparation blossomed.

Current owners want to know the condition of their business and how it is progressing. Potential owners wish to know the company's prospects before they buy into it. Balance sheets and income statements may be able to provide them with much of this information if they are analyzed intelligently.

Management   Corporate management becomes involved in FSA for three basic reasons. In the first place, the company functions as a creditor if it sells to customers on credit. This places the firm in the category of short-term creditor discussed above. Secondly, because creditors and stockholders are analyzing the company's financial statements, it behooves management to do likewise since it is in their interest to understand and please these outsiders who provide them with financing. Finally, there are many internal uses of FSA in such areas as control and decision making.

Others   Although we are going to be mainly concerned with the financial statement uses of creditors, owners, and management, there are many other groups who examine them. Included in the *other* category are: labor unions, customers, tax authorities, government regulators, and, last but not least, competitors.

Since FSA revolves around the income statement and balance sheet, it is worthwhile to describe briefly *what they are* and, just as importantly, *what they are not*.

Income Statement

The profitability of a business is revealed by an income statement. An income statement is designed to show how profitable a business has been over a given period of time (i.e., three months, a year, etc.). For example, the income statements in table 2.2 show the costs and revenues of Richardson Marine, Inc., in 1985 and 1986, and the resulting net incomes.

In the production and sale of a product a firm uses the three economic resources of land (including raw materials and energy), labor, and capital. The revenue from the sale of a product must be sufficient to cover the cost of these factors of production, if the firm wishes to remain in business. Any revenue over and above these costs is profit. The accounting profession follows a set of guidelines, *Generally Accepted Accounting Principles (GAAP)*, with the intent of obtaining such a measure of profit. However, profit is often difficult to measure, because of changing prices for the factors of production, combined with an accounting rule that was designed to provide objectivity to accounting practice. The accounting rule is the *original cost rule*, which maintains that the resources used up in the production and sale of a product should be expensed at their original or historical costs. This is an objective method to measure costs. Unfortunately, the prices of these resources can change over time. By attributing historical cost to a resource whose replacement or current cost is higher (or lower) will have the effect of overstating (or understating) profit. In other words, a firm's productive capacity would be altered if these erroneous profits were paid to stockholders in the form of dividends. Two resources are of special significance here: (1) raw materials and (2) plant and equipment. *Inflation* in particular can have a tremendous impact on the cost of these two items. Imagine the distortion brought about by depreciating an old building based on its original cost of $1,000,000 when it would cost $8,000,000 to replace that same building today.

Economists, investment analysts, and others criticize this accounting rule for distorting corporate profits; but accountants counter that they are justified, given the complexities of business and the objectivity they get by using documented historical cost. Some improvements have been made with the increasing use of Lifo inventory costing and, in a few instances, the provision of supplementary inflation-adjusted income statements. The fact remains, however, that one must be careful when evaluating the reported net income of a corporation, particularly during inflationary times.

Balance Sheet

Financial position of a corporation is measured by the firm's balance sheet. The balance sheet lists the kinds and amounts of a firm's assets (what it owns) as well as liabilities and equity (what it owes) as of a given date. (For example, table 2.1 shows the assets and liabilities of Richardson Marine, Inc. on December 31, 1986 and on December 31, 1985.) A GAAP requires accountants to record asset values at their original acquisition cost and liabilities at what they were when originally incurred. Such figures are normally referred to as *book values.* These dollar amounts are maintained on the books as long as the corresponding assets and liabilities remain in existence, with two exceptions: (1) depreciable assets, such as buildings, are reduced in value each year by the amount of depreciation taken; (2) loans are reduced for partial payment (e.g., installment payments).

Problems with the original cost rule occur because many assets and liabilities are held for a considerable period of time, during which prices can and do change. If they change significantly, then the historical figures shown on the balance sheet can be very misleading indeed. For example, a piece of land purchased in 1960 for $800,000 could, as a result of inflation, easily be sold today (current liquidation value) for $3,000,000. The $800,000 figure shown on the balance sheet is, for all practical purposes, useless.

Some assets can change in price in only a short time, due to supply and demand shifts, such as agricultural commodities held in inventory. Although often overlooked, liabilities can also change in value from the time they were first incurred. For example, a twenty-year bond issue sold originally (five years ago) for $10,000,000 could possibly be paid off (liquidated) today for $7,000,000. The reason for such a change in liability value is rather complicated to explain at this point in the text, suffice it to say that it can be caused by a change in interest rates.

To reiterate, prices of assets can change, principally because of inflation or deflation, thus causing "old" assets recorded at historical or original cost to be misstated on the balance sheet. In addition, "old" liabilities can change in value primarily due to interest rate movements. Thus, their balance sheet values can also be misleading. *If a major purpose of balance sheets is to reveal the liquidating value of assets and liabilities, then that objective can be significantly harmed by changing prices.*

Financial Statement Analysis: Preparation

There are three basic steps involved in Financial Statement Analysis: (1) preparation, (2) computation and interpretation, and (3) evaluation. We will cover each in turn.

Before an individual performs FSA, he or she must go through some preparatory steps that will make the analysis more efficient and effective. This preparation involves answering the following five questions:

1. What objective do you have in mind? What is the purpose of the examination: determining credit worthiness, whether to buy the company's stock, etc.? The answer provided here will dictate the *type* of analysis one should perform.
2. Are the financial statements complete and detailed? The more, the better.
3. Have the financial statements been audited (i.e., given the stamp of approval) by a reputable accounting firm? If they have not, you will not be able to put much confidence in the figures presented. They might be honestly biased, made up with the intent to defraud, or quite possibly done in error.
4. Is the income statement unduly distorted by price changes? If the answer is yes, is it feasible to reconstruct the statement devoid of these distortions?
5. Are the book value figures for assets and liabilities shown on the balance sheet reasonable approximations of their liquidating values? If not, is it possible to get such figures?

It is beyond the scope of an introductory financial management course to delve into the complexities that occur when one tries to reconstruct balance sheets and income statements for price changes. For that reason, we will make the heroic assumption throughout the text that no financial statement corrections are necessary. In other words, we will assume that the figures shown in income statements and balance sheets are meaningful.

Financial Statement Analysis: Computation and Interpretation

When the purpose of financial statement analysis is determined and complete, accurate, and meaningful financial statements are gathered, we are ready to begin the computational and interpretation phase of the analysis. During this phase we will construct various financial statement relationships, or ratios. For this purpose we will employ the most recent audited financial statements of Richardson Marine, Inc., shown in tables 2.1 and 2.2.

General Overview   Before entering into a specific type of analysis, it is helpful to get an overall perspective of Richardson Marine's financial situation.

Table 2.1   Richardson Marine, Inc. Balance Sheets as of December 31

Assets	1986	1985
Cash	$ 774,000	$ 710,000
Marketable securities	1,806,000	1,800,000
Accounts receivable	3,354,000	3,580,000
Inventory	4,386,000	3,800,000
Current assets	$10,320,000	$ 9,890,000
Equipment	6,966,000	6,500,000
Plant and office	6,450,000	4,300,000
Land	2,064,000	2,064,000
Long-term assets	$15,480,000	$12,864,000
Total assets	$25,800,000	$22,754,000

Liabilities and Stockholder's Equity		
Accounts payable	$ 1,548,000	$ 522,000
Accrued wages	1,548,000	1,400,000
Taxes payable	1,290,000	1,310,000
Notes payable	1,806,000	1,715,000
Current liabilities	$ 6,192,000	$ 4,947,000
Bonds	4,128,000	4,919,000
Mortgages	3,096,000	3,096,000
Long-term liabilities	$ 7,224,000	$ 8,015,000
Common stock (645,000 shares par value $4)	2,580,000	2,580,000
Common stock surplus over par value	3,354,000	3,354,000
Retained earnings	6,450,000	3,858,000
Stockholder's equity	$12,384,000	$ 9,792,000
Total liabilities and stockholder's equity	$25,800,000	$22,754,000

Table 2.2   Richardson Marine, Inc. Income Statements for Years Ended December 31

	1986	1985
Sales (90% on credit)	$48,000,000	$43,200,000
Cost of goods sold	20,640,000	18,860,000
Selling and administrative expenses	7,200,000	7,100,000
Depreciation	10,560,000	9,680,000
Total operating expenses	$38,400,000	$35,640,000
Earnings before interest and taxes	$ 9,600,000	$ 7,560,000
Interest expenses	1,440,000	1,350,000
Earnings before taxes	$ 8,160,000	$ 6,210,000
Income taxes	3,840,000	3,750,000
Net income (loss)	$ 4,320,000	$ 2,460,000

Additional Information:		
Dividends paid	$ 1,728,000	$ 1,680,000
Dec. 31 market price of stock	$ 33.50	$ 28.00
Purchases on account	$13,932,000	$12,200,000

Richardson Marine has been in the leisure boat manufacturing business for ten years. From its financial statements we can see that the accounts are fairly standard. That is, there are no strange entries, such as, "Advance from Sale of Uraguay Mineral Rights." The firm makes 90% of its sales on credit. Part of its operations have been financed with debt, and it is solvent. Furthermore, it was profitable during the last two years. Without further home- work we cannot really say much more about this firm's financial situation. *We will now conduct an analysis of the 1986 financial statements.*

A valuable starting point in an analysis is to convert all of the balance sheet and income statement dollar amounts to percentages. This will put all of the figures in perspective and may also be of use later. Converting dollar amounts to percentages is referred to as creating *common size statements,* and it is quite simple to perform. Simply divide each asset amount by total assets, each liability and equity figure by their sum, and each income statement item amount by sales. Take the balance sheet, for example: the cash proportion of total assets is equal to cash of $774,000 divided by total assets of $25,800,000, or 3%. In other words, on December 31, 1986, cash made up 3% of Richardson's assets. Going through the same pro- cess for the income statement we see, for example: the cost of goods sold proportion of sales amounts to cost of goods sold of $20,640,000 divided by sales of $48,000,000, or 43%.

This process is repeated for every item in the financial statements. After this is accom- plished, the financial statements are drawn up again showing percentages and dollars as revealed in tables 2.3 and 2.4.

Table 2.3   Richardson Marine, Inc. Common Size Balance Sheet as of the Year Ended Dec. 31, 1986

Assets

Cash	$ 774,000	3%
Marketable securities	1,806,000	7%
Accounts receivable	3,354,000	13%
Inventory	4,386,000	17%
Current assets	$10,320,000	40%
Equipment	6,966,000	27%
Plant and office	6,450,000	25%
Land	2,064,000	8%
Long-term assets	$15,480,000	60%
Total assets	$25,800,000	100%

Liabilities and Stockholder's Equity

Accounts payable	$ 1,548,000	6%
Accrued wages	1,548,000	6%
Taxes payable	1,290,000	5%
Notes payable	1,806,000	7%
Current liabilities	$ 6,192,000	24%
Bonds	4,128,000	16%
Mortgages	3,096,000	12%
Long-term liabilities	$ 7,224,000	28%
Common stock (645,000 shares par value $4)	2,580,000	10%
Common stock surplus over par value	3,354,000	13%
Retained earnings	6,450,000	25%
Stockholder's equity	$12,384,000	48%
Total liabilities and stockholder's equity	$25,800,000	100%

Table 2.4   Richardson Marine, Inc. Common Size Income Statement for Year Ended Dec. 31, 1986

Sales (90% on credit)	$48,000,000	100%
Cost of goods sold	20,640,000	43%
Selling and administrative expenses	7,200,000	15%
Depreciation	10,560,000	22%
Total operating expenses	$38,400,000	80%
Earnings before interest and taxes	$ 9,600,000	20%
Interest expense	1,440,000	3%
Earnings before taxes	$ 8,160,000	17%
Income taxes	3,840,000	8%
Net income (loss)	$ 4,320,000	9%

Should we need any of these percentages later, it will be easy to refer to them.

A statement of changes in financial position shows the changes that have taken place in a firm's assets, liabilities, and equity over a given period of time. The time period covered is normally one year.

It is relatively easy to draw up a statement of changes in financial position. Two balance sheets, one for each year, are placed side by side. Each of the accounts are then netted (the older figures are subtracted from the more recent figures). These differences are the changes that have taken place over the year. Those accounts that have experienced a change are then placed in a table along with their respective increases and decreases. The result is a statement of changes in financial position. These statements are useful in financial planning and loan evaluation.

Such a statement can be generated for Richardson Marine using the firm's balance sheets shown in table 2.1. The 1986 statement of changes in financial position is presented in table 2.5.

Table 2.5   Richardson Marine, Inc. 1986 Statement of Changes in Financial Position

Assets			**Liabilities and Equity**		
Account	*Increase*	*Decrease*	*Account*	*Increase*	*Decrease*
Cash	$ 64,000		Accounts payable	$1,026,000	
Marketable securities	6,000		Accrued wages	148,000	
Accounts receivables		$226,000	Taxes payable		$ 20,000
Inventory	586,000		Notes payable	91,000	
Equipment	466,000		Bonds		791,000
Plant and office	2,150,000		Retained earnings	2,592,000	

Some notable changes have occurred. Accounts payable, a short-term method of debt financing, have replaced bonds, a long-term source of debt financing. Furthermore, there has been a very large increase in capital assets (plant, office, and equipment) funded, for the most part, by retained earnings.

Liquidity Analysis   *Liquidity* refers to a firm's capability to pay short-term bills as they come due. Liquidity analysis, therefore, includes techniques that measure cash, as well as assets that can be converted easily to cash, relative to a firm's current liabilities. *It also refers to the work done by short-term creditors when they are evaluating a loan request or credit sale.* To understand exactly what short-term creditors want from financial statements, remember: they are thinking about making a loan that they want repaid in a short period of time. How can financial statements help them with this decision? They are useful because they can help in answering the following question: where will the money come from in say, four months, to pay this liability, as well as any other short-term liabilities the firm has? It is tempting to say that the cash will come from revenue over the next four months. Because of accruals, deferrals, and cash expenses, however, it is quite possible for a company to show a large increase in sales over a four month interval but not have the cash to pay bills. For that reason short-term credit analysts look to those assets in the firm's possession that can and probably will be turned into cash in a very short period of time.

That brings us to current assets. Cash balances are already in the most liquid state and marketable securities are the next best thing to cash. Accounts receivable are past sales that should be collected soon and inventory is waiting to be sold, albeit, probably on credit. However, the cash derived from current assets must also be sufficient to cover current liabilities. Current liabilities are payments the firm will have to make in a short time. Furthermore, they will compete for payment with the loan under consideration.

There are two popular methods used to measure liquidity: the *current ratio* and the *quick ratio*. Both measure the degree to which current assets are sufficient to pay current liabilities.

The current ratio computational method and its 1986 value for Richardson Marine are:

$$\text{Current Ratio} = \frac{\text{Current Assets}}{\text{Current Liabilities}}$$

$$\text{Richardson Current Ratio} = \frac{\$10,320,000}{\$\ 6,192,000} = 1.67$$

This indicates that Richardson's current assets are 67% greater than the current liabilities they are required to cover. Thus, there is some extra coverage available. Some analysts prefer *net working capital* over the current ratio. Net working capital is current assets minus current liabilities, or $4,128,000.

The quick ratio is identical to the current ratio with the exception that inventory is subtracted from current assets. Such an adjustment is made because not all of the inventory may be converted into cash in time to cover scheduled payments. That is, inventory is not normally as liquid as the other current assets. If the inventory figure is relatively large the quick ratio will differ significantly from the current ratio.

The quick ratio computational method and its 1986 value for Richardson are:

$$\text{Quick Ratio} = \frac{\text{Current Assets} - \text{Inventory}}{\text{Current Liabilities}}$$

$$\text{Richardson Quick Ratio} = \frac{\$5,934,000}{\$6,192,000} = .96$$

According to this computation, Richardson has very liquid assets that are 4% below current obligations.

Further evaluation is required before we can say whether Richardson's liquidity ratios are high enough for short-term creditors.

Solvency Analysis   *Solvency analysis is the investigation that long-term creditors perform prior to extending a loan.* Corporations wish to acquire funds from them, the payment for which will extend over a very long period of time, possibly thirty years. Given the long-term nature of such loans (e.g., bonds and mortgages), what could prospective lenders get from financial statements that would help them with these decisions? Stockholders are also concerned about the solvency of their business. After all, they will be the first to suffer if the firm encounters financial difficulties.

Solvency analysis trys to determine the ability of the borrower to stay in business for many years to come. The overriding question is: what is the likelihood that the credit applicant will be able to make interest payments on all of its debt for an extended period of time? The capacity of a firm to stay in business and pay its debts for many years is determined primarily by profitability. There is little value in basing a thirty-year loan decision upon current assets; and the value of fixed assets will not tell us much about a corporation's staying power.

Now that we have decided long-term creditors are concerned about profits, just which profit figure is most relevant: earnings before interest and taxes, earnings before taxes, or net income? The overwhelming preference of practitioners and financial experts is for *earnings before interest and taxes (EBIT)*. The reason for this preference is that, if need be, a firm can apply all of its earnings before interest and taxes to the payment of interest charges. Long-term creditors want a borrower to have significantly large EBIT. The significance of earnings before interest and taxes is measured by comparing it to interest charges. This is done by dividing the former by the latter and we call the result *times interest earned*. The larger this figure is, the better off creditors will be. The formula for times interest earned and the corresponding 1986 computation for Richardson Marine are as follows:

$$\text{Times Interest Earned} = \frac{\text{Earnings Before Interest and Taxes}}{\text{Interest Charges}}$$

$$\text{Richardson Times Interest Earned} = \frac{\$9,600,000}{\$1,440,000} = 6.67$$

According to this computation Richardson has 1986 profit available for the payment of interest charges that is six and two-thirds times as large as the interest charges. Therefore, Richardson could suffer a sizeable decline in its EBIT and still maintain interest payments. This is not to say that a firm would be unable to make interest payments were profits negative for one year or even two years. It simply means that this is a condition that should be minimized.

When lenders invest in a business for twenty years they hope and expect to get their principal back with interest in a timely and orderly manner. That is why they lend money only to businesses they believe to have excellent long-run profit potential. Nevertheless, firms that once looked unshakeable can encounter overwhelming financial problems within a few years that threaten their survival. To protect against such an unlikely event the lender will look to the corporation's assets to satisfy its debts. Creditors not only get a claim on earnings ahead of stockholders, they also have a prior claim on assets if the firm becomes bankrupt. For this reason, asset values can be important to them and the more assets the better the protection. The two most popular methods used to compare the adequacy of asset values with debt obligations are the *debt-to-equity* ratio and the *debt-to-assets* ratio. Formulas for their computation and the corresponding 1986 calculations for Richardson Marine are as follows:

$$\text{Debt-to-Equity} = \frac{\text{Total Liabilities}}{\text{Stockholder's Equity}}$$

$$\text{Richardson Debt-to-Equity} = \frac{\$13,416,000}{\$12,384,000} = 1.08$$

$$\text{Debt-to-Assets} = \frac{\text{Total Liabilities}}{\text{Total Assets}}$$

$$\text{Richardson Debt-to-Assets} = \frac{\$13,416,000}{\$25,800,000} = .52$$

Since, by definition, debt plus equity equals total assets, the above two ratios provide essentially the same information, but from different angles. Financial analysts often prefer one to the other for personal reasons. In the case of Richardson Marine we see that debt is 1.08 times as large as equity. From another viewpoint, debt is 52% of total assets, thereby signifying that equity is 48% of total assets. A potential lender can tell from these ratios that creditors are supplying 52% of the financing for this corporation. If the firm becomes bankrupt the assets would only have to be liquidated for fifty-two cents on the dollar for all of the debts to be satisfied. Thus, there is some cushion. But cushions should be substantial because liquidation values for bankrupt firms can be significantly different from their book values. In addition, bankruptcy legal fees will further reduce the creditor's receipts.

Further evaluation is necessary before we can make any judgment about whether Richardson's times-interest-earned and debt ratios are acceptable to long-term creditors.

A warning is in order here. Generally Accepted Accounting Principles do not require all lease obligations and leased property to be shown on the balance sheet. These liabilities and assets are important considerations and they are becoming more numerous. Excluding them from solvency ratios may seriously distort the ratios' meaning. The analyst must be on guard for lease obligations. (Also be on the lookout for pension liabilities, another troublesome factor.)

One final calculation that many find interesting is the *average cost of debt,* which is simply the interest charges divided by total debt. For Richardson Marine it is $1,440,000 divided by $13,416,000, or 10.7%. This company pays an average interest rate of 10.7% on borrowed funds.

Profitability Analysis   Current owners of the corporation as well as prospective stockholders are routinely involved in profitability analysis. Current stockholders wish to know how well the company has performed in the past and how profitable it will be in the future. Their assessment of profitability will influence their evaluation of management (past profits) and whether or not to remain owners (future profits). Potential stockholders desire information on future profitability as they make up their minds to become owners.

Can financial statement analysis help owners (current or prospective) to evaluate profitability? The intelligent use of valid, meaningful financial statements *can* definitely tell us how well the firm has performed and *might* help us to assess future profitability. Different persons emphasize different measures of profitability and a given analyst may vary his or her profit measures based upon the type of business being evaluated and when it is evaluated (i.e., during recession or inflation).

Corporate profitability can be measured in absolute terms (dollars) and in relative terms (percentage).

Dollar Profitability Analysis   There are four popular measures of dollar profitability: *net income (NI), earnings per share (EPS), dividends (D),* and *dividends per share (DPS).* Their computational methods and the 1986 values for Richardson Marine are as follows:

$$\text{Net Income} = \text{Taken Directly from Income Statement}$$

$$\text{Richardson NI} = \$4,320,000$$

This is the key figure on the income statement. It is the earnings that are available for payment to the owners of a business, as the result of operations over a prior period of time (in this case, one year). Under no circumstances does it tell us for certain that future net income will be $4,320,000 a year. However, it is an excellent start in that direction.

$$\text{Earnings Per Share} = \frac{\text{Net Income}}{\text{Common Stock Shares Outstanding}}$$

$$\text{Richardson EPS} = \frac{\$4,320,000}{645,000} = \$6.70$$

EPS simply converts the NI into a per share figure, which is generally a more useful number to stockholders who wish to know their proportional interest in the company.

$$\text{Dividends} = \text{Amount of Money Paid to Stockholders}$$

$$\text{Richardson D} = \$1,728,000$$

Richardson's owners received $1,728,000 in cash dividends. The importance of dividends cannot be overemphasized, because they are the only concrete benefit of being a stockholder.

$$\text{Dividends Per Share} = \frac{\text{Dividends}}{\text{Common Stock Shares Outstanding}}$$

$$\text{Richardson DPS} = \frac{\$1,728,000}{645,000} = \$2.68$$

As with the case of EPS, DPS is simply a conversion of the total figure into a per share figure, which allows stockholders to more readily examine their personal situations. Richardson stockholders received $2.68 for each share they owned. As a percentage of earnings, the 1986 dividends amounted to 40%. This is commonly referred to as the *payout rate.*

Relative Profitability Analysis   Relative profitability measures are generally superior to dollar measures, because they put profit into a better perspective. There are five such measures that are widely used by analysts: *return on assets (ROA), return on equity (ROE), return on sales (ROS), earnings-price ratio (E/P),* and *dividend yield (DY).* The first three of these make use of financial statement information only; whereas, the last two combine income statement data with stock market information. Methods to calculate each of these and the corresponding 1986 values for Richardson Marine follow:

$$\text{Return on Assets} = \frac{\text{EBIT}}{\text{Total Assets}}$$

$$\text{Richardson ROA} = \frac{\$9,600,000}{\$25,800,000} = .372$$

Thus, Richardson earned 37.2% during 1986 on the assets at its disposal. This is an excellent measure of how well a business uses its assets. Most analysts prefer to use earnings before interest and taxes instead of net income to calculate ROA. Their reasoning runs as follows: EBIT represents the profitability of the business and this profit is divided among three parties: (1) creditors (interest), (2) government (taxes), and (3) owners (net income).

$$\text{Return on Equity} = \frac{\text{Net Income}}{\text{Stockholder's Equity}}$$

$$\text{Richardson ROE} = \frac{\$4,320,000}{\$12,384,000} = .349$$

This tells us that Richardson's owners have earned a 34.9% return on the book value of their investment in the firm. ROE is also frequently referred to as *return on investment.*

$$\text{Return on Sales} = \frac{\text{EBIT}}{\text{Sales}}$$

$$\text{Richardson ROS} = \frac{\$9,600,000}{48,000,000} = .20$$

Richardson earned a 20% return on sales. Another name for this is *profit margin.* Note that each of the three returns is different. Such a result is to be expected of a typical corporation.

$$\text{Earnings Price Ratio} = \frac{\text{Earnings per Share}}{\text{Current Market Price of Common Stock}}$$

$$\text{Richardson E/P} = \frac{\$6.70}{\$33.50} = .20$$

Stockholders earned 20% on the market value (i.e., what they could sell their stock for) of their investment. The inverse of this figure is called the *price-earnings ratio (P/E)* and it is very popular with stock investors. Richardson's P/E is 5. In stock market parlance this means that investors are willing to pay five times current earnings for this stock.

$$\text{Dividend Yield} = \frac{\text{Dividends per Share}}{\text{Current Market Price of Common Stock}}$$

$$\text{Richardson DY} = \frac{\$\ 2.68}{\$33.50} = .08$$

Owners wish not only to know what they earned on the market value of their investment, but also to know what they were paid. This answer is provided by the dividend yield of 8%.

Through careful evaluation of these profit measures, a stock investor will determine the company's past performance and try to estimate its future profitability. The techniques of evaluation will be discussed shortly.

Stockholders' equity is also of interest to stockholders. Not only does it tell them what they have invested in the firm by way of stock purchases and retained earnings, but also what they might obtain if the firm were liquidated. Stockholder's equity is equal to assets minus liabilities, or, alternatively, the sum of common stock par value, surplus over par value and retained earnings. The 1986 stockholders' equity for Richardson Marine is:

Richardson Stockholder Equity = $12,384,000

Should one want a per share figure, simply divide stockholder's equity by the number of shares of common stock outstanding. For Richardson Marine the 1986 per share figure is $19.20, and it is called *book value per share*. If Richardson's balance sheet figures are close approximations of liquidation values, then we can say that Richardson's stockholders would receive about $12,384,000 from a liquidation of the business, or $19.20 per share.

There are many situations that can arise to make profitability analysis more complicated than shown here. We will discuss three of these situations.

If *preferred stock* exists, then the analyst must adjust most income and equity figures accordingly. Income can be adjusted by deducting preferred stock dividends from net income to obtain net income available for common stockholders. Equity is adjusted by subtracting the par value of preferred stock from stockholder's equity to obtain common stockholder's equity. As a matter of fact, howeve., preferred stock is seldom encountered today.

Another problem arises when a corporation shows extraordinary gains or losses on the income statement. *Extraordinary items* occur, for example, from lawsuits or the sale of part of the business. When these items exist, they should not be figured into the net income for a single year, but instead averaged over several years. Extraordinary gains and losses are nonrecurring items that are difficult to associate with a particular time period.

A final complexity involves companies that have changed the number of shares of stock outstanding over the years through *stock splits and stock dividends*. If they have, and should an analyst be interested in per-share figures over the period of time when the stock splits occurred, then he or she must adjust the outstanding shares to account for this. For instance, a company doubled its shares of stock by a two-shares-for-one split three years ago. One cannot measure its EPS using the old number of shares before the split and the new number after the split. To do so would make any comparison of the figures meaningless. An easy way around this is to double the shares outstanding before the split. EPS can then be computed with a common denominator.

Managerial Analysis   We have presented various financial statement computations useful to outside suppliers of financing. Insiders (management) can also make use of FSA.

Aid in Fund Raising   One of the important jobs of management is to take care of the corporation's financial needs. Because creditors and stockholders provide most of the firm's financing and since they rely heavily upon FSA to make their investment decisions, it behooves management to understand how they use FSA. *Management must be thoroughly familiar with the type of FSA these outsiders perform.* In a sense, they should try to put themselves in the creditors' shoes so as to pave the way for financing. Not only should management do everything in its power to see to it that such computations as the current ratio and EPS come up to investor's standards, but they should also be prepared to explain why they may not. This will require a considerable amount of work on management's part, but the rewards can be substantial. Unfortunately, in their enthusiasm to make a good showing to investors, management has been known to doctor financial statements. Such doctoring, while not entirely ethical, is normally legal and can have a sizeable influence on many ratio computations.

Aid in Problem Solving   Internal problem solving can often be aided by the computation and evaluation of financial statement relationships. The problem-solving relationships management is most often interested in are commonly referred to as *activity or turnover ratios.* Although there are many activity ratios that could be calculated, only the three most relevant to financial management are considered here: *accounts receivable turnover (ART), inventory turnover (IT), and accounts payable turnover (APT).*
    The calculation procedure for accounts receivable turnover and the associated 1986 value for Richardson Marine are as follows:

$$\text{Accounts Receivable Turnover} = \frac{\text{Credit Sales}}{\text{Accounts Receivable Balance}}$$

$$\text{Richardson ART} = \frac{\$43,200,000}{\$\ 3,354,000} = 12.88$$

This indicates that Richardson's accounts receivable turnover (i.e., old receivables are replaced by new receivables) 12.88 times each year. Why do we say each year? Because the credit sales figure is an annual number. Turnover can be easily converted into days by dividing the turnover into 360. (Note: We will assume a 360 day year throughout the book.) In this case, we see that, on the average, receivables turn over approximately every twenty-eight days. In other words, Richardson's average credit customer has paid his or her bill in twenty-eight days, which we will hereafter refer to as *average collection period.* Another useful figure related to accounts receivable is *average daily credit sales,* which is annual credit sales divided by 360 days. Richardson's average daily credit sales figure is $120,000, which, when multiplied by the average collection period of twenty-eight days, equals the receivables balance of $3,360,000.[1] It is important that you understand the relationship between credit sales, collection period, receivables balance, and turnover. Such relationships are very helpful in managing a firm's credit program, as we shall see in the chapter covering accounts receivable management.

Notice that credit sales are used rather than total sales to compute accounts receivable turnover. Credit sales are preferred, but if one only has access to total sales then it will suffice.

Financial managers find a great many uses for the inventory turnover. The formula for such a computation and the related 1986 figure for Richardson Marine are:

$$\text{Inventory Turnover} = \frac{\text{Cost of Goods Sold}}{\text{Inventory Balance}}$$

$$\text{Richardson IT} = \frac{\$20,640,000}{\$\ 4,386,000} = 4.70$$

Richardson's inventory is turned over, or rotated, 4.7 times a year. As with receivables, we can convert this to days by dividing the turnover into 360 days, or approximately 76.6 days. This states that the average inventory item is on hand for about 77 days, which we will hereafter refer to as *average holding period.* Cost of goods sold is preferred over sales for this computation because inventory is recorded at cost and, therefore, is more closely linked to cost of goods sold. Also, when dealing with a manufacturing firm we can derive the *average daily production rate:* it is cost of goods sold divided by 360 days. Richardson's is $57,333. When this figure is multiplied by average holding period, we arrive at the inventory balance.[2]

Now that we have computed the receivables and inventory turnovers, we can state that an *average* unit in Richardson's inventory will be turned into cash in 76.6 + 28 = 104.6 days, *if,* that is, the goods are sold on credit. On cash sales, Richardson only needs to wait 76.6 days.

The final turnover we will look at is accounts payable turnover. Its computational method and the corresponding 1986 value for Richardson Marine are as follows:

$$\text{Accounts Payable Turnover} = \frac{\text{Credit Purchases}}{\text{Accounts Payable Balance}}$$

$$\text{Richardson APT} = \frac{\$13,932,000}{\$\ 1,548,000} = 9$$

Richardson turns over its payables nine times a year, for an *average payment period* of 40 days. In other words, on average, it pays for its purchases 40 days after delivery. Credit purchases divided by 360 days equals *average daily purchases on account,* which, for Richardson, is $13,932,000 ÷ 360 = $38,700. Average daily purchases multiplied by the average payment period is equal to the accounts payable balance. Knowledge of these relationships can be useful to management in planning short-term financing, as we shall see in chapter 13.

---

[1] The figures will not come out exactly due to rounding.

[2] The figures are not exact due to rounding.

Table 2.6   Richardson Marine Accounts Receivable Month Ending Balances 1986

Month	Receivables Balance
January	$2,422,000
February	1,312,000
March	725,000
April	380,000
May	1,300,000
June	1,936,000
July	3,250,000
August	4,215,000
September	5,005,000
October	3,725,000
November	3,500,000
December	3,354,000
Twelve month average	**$2,593,667**

Notice that credit purchases are used to compute accounts payable turnover. If this figure is not available, which is often the case, one may approximate it with total purchases. Should it not be feasible to acquire a reasonably good purchases figure, then the accounts payable turnover cannot be computed.

A potential problem faces all of the turnover ratios when a business's operations are seasonal. The denominators of each ratio are balance sheet numbers, or, in other words, figures taken at a specific point in time. Businesses with seasonal operations can experience dramatic changes in their receivables, inventory, and payables balances over the year. Take for example accounts receivable. If Richardson's sales are seasonal, as you would expect of a boat manufacturer, then selecting an accounts receivable balance as of a single date (i.e., December 31) may be misleading. Look at table 2.6. Here is a firm whose receivables fluctuate dramatically over the year. Selection of any one date would be misleading, so would an average of receivables for two dates if they are in the same season (beginning and end of year). Based upon the receivables balance selected and given an annual credit sales figure, drastically different turnovers can be computed. What we would like to have in this case is the monthly average. The monthly average accounts receivable balance for Richardson Marine is shown in table 2.6 as $2,593,667. This will provide an accounts receivable turnover of 16.66, which differs markedly from the 12.88 computed earlier. The point is, if you are attempting to compute turnover ratios and the only balance sheet values available are totally misleading, then you probably should not exert the effort. Unfortunately, an analyst who is outside the company and unfamiliar with its operations may not know if the figures are misleading.

One final note about turnover ratios. Due to the fact that each of these turnover ratios deals with a current asset or current liability, they are often used by short-term creditors in liquidity analysis.

DuPont System   A great many businessmen feel the return on assets is the best overall measure of a company's performance that can be obtained from financial statements. As you recall, ROA is EBIT divided by total assets, and it signifies how well management uses the assets at its disposal.

It is not surprising then, that a method was devised to delve more deeply into the ROA. This method is commonly known as the DuPont System, named after the firm that developed it. The DuPont System separates the ROA into two basic elements: (1) return on sales (profit margin) and (2) *total asset turnover.* The former was defined earlier as EBIT divided by sales. The latter is found by dividing sales by total assets.

The basic DuPont System is:

$$\text{ROA} = \frac{\text{EBIT}}{\text{Sales}} \times \frac{\text{Sales}}{\text{Assets}} = \text{Profit Margin} \times \text{Asset Turnover}$$

Presented in this way, we can see that the rate of return on a company's total assets is determined by the profit margin on a dollar of sales and the speed at which assets are replaced. A high profit margin and rapid asset turnover will therefore generate a large return on assets. Each of these two ratios can in turn be analyzed further.

Here is a DuPont analysis for Richardson Marine:

$$\text{ROA} = \text{Profit Margin} \times \text{Asset Turnover} = .20 \times 1.86 = 37.2\%$$

Summary   In this section of the chapter several financial statement relationships have been defined and discussed. Needless to say, there are many other computations that could be made. Those presented here are sufficient in scope for a first course in financial management. Moreover, they are the most widely accepted and used by financial analysts.

Often the analyst is not able to calculate a relationship in the most appropriate manner and must use the next best alternative (e.g., using sales, when cost of goods sold is not available, for inventory turnover). In other instances, the data the analyst has to work with is so deficient that some ratios or calculations are just not possible (e.g., cannot find a reasonable purchases figure for accounts payable turnover). Of course, analysts inside the company have more financial data at their disposal than outsiders. Table 2.7 summarizes Richardson Marine's financial ratios.

Table 2.7   Summary of Richardson Marine's 1986 Financial Ratios

Liquidity Ratios

Current ratio
$$= \frac{\text{Current Assets}}{\text{Current Liabilities}} = \frac{\$10,320,000}{\$\ 6,192,000} = 1.67$$

Quick ratio
$$= \frac{\text{Current Assets} - \text{Inventory}}{\text{Current Liabilities}} = \frac{\$5,934,000}{\$6,192,000} = .96$$

Solvency Ratios

Debt-to-equity
$$= \frac{\text{Total Liabilities}}{\text{Stockholder's Equity}} = \frac{\$13,416,000}{\$12,384,000} = 1.08$$

Debt-to-assets
$$= \frac{\text{Total Liabilities}}{\text{Total Assets}} = \frac{\$13,416,000}{\$25,800,000} = .52$$

Times interest earned
$$= \frac{\text{Earnings before Interest and Taxes}}{\text{Interest Charges}} = \frac{\$9,600,000}{\$1,440,000} = 6.67$$

Average cost of debt
$$= \frac{\text{Interest Charges}}{\text{Total Liabilities}} = \frac{\$\ 1,440,000}{\$13,416,000} = 10.7\%$$

Profitability Ratios

Earnings per share
$$= \frac{\text{Net Income}}{\text{Common Stock Shares Outstanding}} = \frac{\$4,320,000}{645,000} = \$\ 6.70$$

Dividends per share
$$= \frac{\text{Dividends}}{\text{Common Stock Shares Outstanding}} = \frac{\$1,728,000}{645,000} = \$\ 2.68$$

Dividend payout rate
$$= \frac{\text{Dividends}}{\text{Net Income}} = \frac{\$1,728,000}{\$4,320,000} = .40$$

Return on equity
$$= \frac{\text{Net Income}}{\text{Stockholder's Equity}} = \frac{\$\ 4,320,000}{\$12,384,000} = 34.9\%$$

Return on sales
$$= \frac{\text{Earnings before Interest and Taxes}}{\text{Sales}} = \frac{\$\ 9,600,000}{\$48,000,000} = 20\%$$

Return on assets
$$= \frac{\text{Earnings before Interest and Taxes}}{\text{Total Assets}} = \frac{\$\ 9,600,000}{\$25,800,000} = 37.2\%$$

Earnings-price ratio
$$= \frac{\text{Earnings per Share}}{\text{Market Price of Common Stock}} = \frac{\$\ 6.70}{\$33.50} = 20\%$$

Price-earnings ratio
$$= \frac{\text{Market Price of Common Stock}}{\text{Earnings per Share}} = \frac{\$33.50}{\$\ 6.70} = 5$$

Dividend yield
$$= \frac{\text{Dividends per Share}}{\text{Market Price of Common Stock}} = \frac{\$\ 2.68}{\$33.50} = 8\%$$

Book value per share
$$= \frac{\text{Stockholder's Equity}}{\text{Common Stock Shares Outstanding}} = \frac{\$12,384,000}{645,000} = \$19.20$$

From the book *Almanac of Business and Industrial Financial Ratios*, 1984 edition, by Leo Troy. Copyright © 1984 by Prentice-Hall, Inc. Published by Prentice-Hall, Inc., Englewood Cliffs, N.J. 07632.

Activity Ratios

Accounts receivable turnover	$= \dfrac{\text{Credit Sales}}{\text{Accounts Receivable Balance}}$	$= \dfrac{\$43,200,000}{\$\ 3,354,000}$	$= 12.88$
Average collection period	$= \dfrac{360\ \text{Days}}{\text{Accounts Receivable Turnover}}$	$= \dfrac{360}{12.88}$	$= 28\ \text{days}$
Inventory turnover	$= \dfrac{\text{Cost of Goods Sold}}{\text{Inventory Balance}}$	$= \dfrac{\$20,640,000}{\$\ 4,386,000}$	$= 4.70$
Average holding period	$= \dfrac{360\ \text{Days}}{\text{Inventory Turnover}}$	$= \dfrac{360}{4.70}$	$= 77\ \text{days}$
Accounts payable turnover	$= \dfrac{\text{Credit Purchases}}{\text{Accounts Payable Balance}}$	$= \dfrac{\$13,932,000}{\$\ 1,548,000}$	$= 9$
Average payment period	$= \dfrac{360\ \text{Days}}{\text{Accounts Payable Turnover}}$	$= \dfrac{360}{9}$	$= 40\ \text{days}$
Total asset turnover	$= \dfrac{\text{Sales}}{\text{Total Assets}}$	$= \dfrac{\$48,000,000}{\$25,800,000}$	$= 1.86$

Financial Statement Analysis: Evaluation

Now that we have gone through all of these financial statement relationships and have a basic understanding of what they mean, we are ready for the final step in FSA. We must decide if these calculations are good or bad, informative or not informative. This is the evaluation stage of financial statement analysis.

Before we begin the evaluation process let us point out that different classes of analysts may have different opinions about the meaning of a particular ratio. Management, for example, may look favorably upon a current ratio if it is low, whereas short-term creditors would prefer a high current ratio. With this in mind, let us begin the evaluation.

Evaluation normally has three stages. In stage one, the analyst compares a firm's relevant ratios to standard or benchmark ratios. If a decision cannot be made based upon findings in stage one then stage two comes into play. Stage two looks at changes in a firm's ratios over time in an attempt to discern any patterns that have developed or may be developing. This is known as time series analysis. If an answer is still not in sight, the analyst can move to stage three. This final stage involves an in-depth examination of each financial relationship, which we will call decomposition analysis. Moving from one stage to the next requires the expenditure of time and money, so they should not be made capriciously.

Comparison to Industry Averages   How do we know if a financial ratio is good or bad, high or low? For that matter, how do we judge the size or amount of anything? Consciously and unconsciously, most persons make decisions about whether something is high or low by comparing it to an average. A follower of the game of baseball determines if a baseball player is a good hitter by comparing his or her hitting percentage with the average percentage of other players, even if it is a "ballpark" average. By the same token, a given financial ratio for a firm can be compared with the average of that ratio for other firms. To continue with our baseball example, if a player is in little league it would not make much sense to compare his or her hitting statistics to the average hitting statistics of the major leagues. This reasoning also holds true for business. For example, we do not compare the financial ratios of a grocery store chain to the average ratios of all businesses. Not that such comparisons would be totally meaningless, but better contrasts can be made with ratios of similar businesses. Thus, *a given business's financial ratios should be compared to the average ratios of firms in its industry.* By using industry averages as standards of reference we are implicitly assuming that the "industry" is correct.

Industry averages can be obtained for many ratios and most industries from credit reporting firms such as Robert Morris Associates and Dun and Bradstreet. As an example, exhibit 2.1 contains published ratios for the radio and television broadcasting industry. Should the analyst be unable to obtain a particular ratio or a specific industry's ratios from a published source, then he or she can always compute them. This is a relatively simple task. A sample is selected (preferably random) of businesses in an industry, their financial statements obtained, ratios computed, and then averaged. Regardless of whether one uses published industry averages or computes one's own, it is of the utmost importance that they are computed the same way as those for the firm that is to be evaluated. Recall that there is more than one way to compute many ratios. Comparing ratios that have been calculated differently is a meaningless exercise. One other thing to keep in mind: although most firms in an industry use the same accounting practices, the student should be aware that Generally Accepted Accounting Principles allow for some latitude.

Application: It is helpful at this point to look at an example ratio comparison. In this example, we are concerned with a potential short-term lender to Richardson Marine. This creditor (a commercial bank) is trying to determine the credit-worthiness of Richardson for a $300,000 loan to be repaid in four months. A significant part of the bank's credit evaluation is financial statement analysis, more specifically, liquidity analysis.

The bank's commercial loan officer determines Richardson's most recent current and quick ratios to be 1.67 and .96 respectively (refer to the liquidity analysis section to see how these numbers were btained). Richardson's liquidity ratios reveal that the firm has total current assets in excess of current liabilities, but current debts slightly exceed the more liquid assets. To determine whether Richardson's liquidity ratios provide sufficient protection for the bank, they are first compared to the corresponding averages of the Pleasure Boat Industry.

	Richardson Marine	Pleasure Boat Industry
Current Ratio	1.67	2.2
Quick Ratio	.96	1.4

As you can see, Richardson's liquidity ratios are lower than the industry's.[3] From the bank's point of view this is not good. Based upon this information the bank may deny the loan. In all probability, however, it would carry the evaluation further. It might do so for several reasons: the liquidity ratios are not significantly deficient, Richardson has been a good customer in the past and deserves extra attention, or, another possibility, Richardson's management may have presented a reasonable defense for their relatively poor ratios ▪

---

[3]Ratio comparisons such as this are very conducive to statistical hypothesis testing. In this case the test would be: are Richardson's ratios statistically, significantly different from the industry ratio or are the differences due to chance?

Exhibit 2.1   Communication: Radio and Television Broadcasting (Corporations With and Without Net Income, 1984 Edition)

Item Description For Accounting Period 7/79 Through 6/80	A Total	B Zero Assets	C Under 100	D 100 to 250	E 250 to 500	F 500 to 1,000	G 1000 to 5,000	H 5,000 to 10,000	I 10,000 to 25,000	J 25,000 to 50,000	K 50,000 to 100,000	L 100,000 to 250,000	M 250,000 and over
						Size of Assets in Thousands of Dollars (000 Omitted)							
1 Number of enterprises	4573	8	1260	1004	1039	551	523	81	57	27	9	4	10
2 Total receipts (in millions of dollars)	12891.3	29.2	134.5	289.6	394.9	584.4	1222.4	445.6	808.0	675.4	366.2	408.0	7533.0

Selected Operating Factors in Percent of Net Sales

Item	A	B	C	D	E	F	G	H	I	J	K	L	M
3 Cost of operations	54.3	53.3	50.1	46.6	48.5	42.7	46.1	42.8	52.4	46.4	56.2	37.3	59.4
4 Compensation of officers	2.4	4.4	5.5	11.7	9.5	9.5	4.6	3.4	2.8	2.3	1.8	1.2	0.7
5 Repairs	0.1	–	–	–	0.1	–	0.1	–	0.2	0.1	0.2	0.5	0.1
6 Bad debts	0.7	–	1.0	1.3	0.8	1.0	1.1	0.9	0.7	0.7	0.5	0.7	0.6
7 Rent on business property	1.3	2.0	2.7	1.5	1.9	1.4	2.3	1.0	1.7	1.4	1.1	0.6	1.2
8 Taxes (excl federal tax)	3.2	2.3	5.9	4.1	5.4	4.1	4.0	4.5	3.8	5.6	4.4	3.2	2.4
9 Interest	2.9	6.9	5.6	3.4	2.9	2.6	5.0	5.9	4.5	6.1	4.6	3.0	1.8
10 Deprec/deplet/amortiz*	5.5	5.3	5.0	4.4	6.1	4.8	8.0	10.1	6.5	8.6	5.4	5.6	4.5
11 Advertising	1.8	2.5	0.2	–	0.2	0.6	0.9	0.2	0.6	0.7	0.7	0.1	2.7
12 Pensions & other benef. plans	1.6	0.8	1.5	–	0.5	1.8	0.8	1.9	1.2	1.6	1.2	1.9	1.8
13 Other expenses	18.8	27.4	31.1	22.4	26.4	27.8	27.0	27.1	21.2	21.1	19.7	21.8	14.9
14 Net profit before tax	7.4	*	*	4.6	*	3.7	0.1	2.2	4.4	5.4	4.2	24.1	9.9

Selected Financial Ratios (number of times ratio is to one)

Item	A	B	C	D	E	F	G	H	I	J	K	L	M
15 Current ratio	1.4	–	–	2.1	1.4	1.7	1.1	1.1	1.4	1.7	1.5	1.7	1.4
16 Quick ratio	0.9	–	–	2.0	1.3	1.4	1.0	0.9	1.0	1.1	0.9	1.2	0.9
17 Net sls to net wkg capital	10.4	–	–	9.5	14.1	9.4	34.6	35.1	9.5	5.4	5.3	5.7	10.2
18 Net sales to net worth	2.1	–	–	4.2	3.2	3.4	3.0	2.4	2.0	1.7	1.3	0.9	2.1
19 Inventory turnover	–	–	–	–	–	–	–	–	–	–	–	–	–
20 Total liab. to net worth	1.2	–	–	1.5	2.0	1.4	1.9	2.0	1.4	1.6	1.5	0.5	1.0

Selected Financial Factors in Percentages

Item	A	B	C	D	E	F	G	H	I	J	K	L	M
21 Current liab. to net worth	53.3	–	–	41.0	61.7	56.4	74.0	63.5	50.1	46.5	50.3	21.3	53.4
22 Inventory to curr assets	9.1	–	–	–	–	4.3	1.9	1.1	7.8	5.8	15.7	6.4	11.5
23 Net income to net worth	13.7	–	–	36.2	–	14.4	15.0	3.1	11.5	13.7	8.7	14.4	14.8
24 Retained earn. to net inc.	70.3	–	–	92.5	–	89.6	85.0	39.5	77.1	83.8	79.7	52.0	71.2

*Depreciation largest factor

Source: Almanac of Business and Industrial Financial Ratios. Leo Troy. 1984. Prentice-Hall, Inc

Time Series Analysis   In addition to comparing a company's ratios with those of other firms in its industry, it is helpful to compare the same firm's ratios over time. This allows the analyst to examine any patterns that may exist. The popular name for the examination of data over time is time series analysis.

To perform time series analysis on financial ratios, all one needs are several years (quarters if available) of ratios. They should all be computed the same way and the period of time should be long enough to cover at least one complete business cycle.

Application: Let us return to the Richardson Marine loan application example and see how time series analysis can be applied to Richardson's liquidity ratios. Remember that the bank loan officer found Richardson's liquidity ratios to be deficient when compared to industry averages. The loan was not turned down right away, let us assume, because Richardson's management told the bank that the poor ratio showing was temporary. The loan officer can substantiate this claim by the use of time series analysis. The officer first requests and obtains financial statements for the last, perhaps, ten years and uses them to calculate current and quick ratios for each year. The resulting ratios are shown in table 2.8. These figures are then plotted on a graph such as figure 2.1. Each x represents an observed current ratio and each o is an observed quick ratio. The dotted lines drawn through the points are *trend lines*[4] ■

Table 2.8   Richardson Marine Liquidity Ratios Computed at Year-End

Year	Current Ratios	Quick Ratios
1977	2.83	2.58
1978	2.60	1.65
1979	2.31	1.90
1980	2.45	1.80
1981	2.08	1.52
1982	1.80	1.47
1983	1.85	1.15
1984	1.78	1.10
1985	1.70	.98
1986	1.67	.96

Figure 2.1   Time series analysis of Richardson Marine's liquidity ratios

Current and quick
ratios

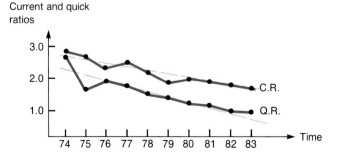

[4]The trend line shown in figure 2.1 is simply a visual connection of the plotted points. A superior method is to use statistical regression techniques.

An observation of the data points reveals that both ratios have been somewhat erratic, which tends to support Richardson's contentions. However, the trend lines show a definite downward movement. As far as the banker is concerned, Richardson's liquidity ratios are not only currently unsatisfactory (i.e., below industry averages), but they have been getting progressively worse. Contrary to what its management says, Richardson's liquidity problems are apparently not temporary.

Based upon industry comparisons and time series analysis, Richardson now has two strikes against it. The analysis up to this point indicates Richardson to be a below average and deteriorating credit risk. The loan officer could turn down the loan request now or grant it accompanied by strict loan terms. Before taking such actions, however, the loan officer may want to make one final evaluation to verify the earlier work. This takes us to decomposition analysis.

Decomposition Analysis   Decomposition generally means to separate something into its constituent parts or elements. As applied to FSA it can be used to mean the careful examination of financial ratios. Decomposition analysis of financial relationships involves breaking the ratios down into their individual components and examining each in detail. The purpose of this is to determine the quality of a ratio. Since ratios are comprised of so many different elements, it is quite possible for two ratios of equal size to be unequal in other respects. Such an analysis can become quite involved, but the intent here is simply to acquaint the student with the procedure.

The bank loan officer investigating Richardson Marine's credit rating can apply decomposition analysis to Richardson's liquidity ratios. Take the current ratio for example. The loan officer knows that it is low by industry standards and that it has been trending downward. Decomposition can provide further insight into Richardson's liquidity position by helping to answer the question: how current is the current ratio?

To try and answer this question, the current ratio is separated into its various components (i.e., cash, receivables, inventory, payables, accruals, etc.) and a detailed investigation is made of each one. The investigation will attempt to find if these items are more or less than what the financial statements say they are. Unfortunately, to be able to do this in depth often requires more information than is provided in standard financial statements.

Application: Let us observe the outline of an in-depth analysis of accounts receivable. From Richardson's balance sheet we see that receivables are $3,354,000. At least three useful analyses of receivables can be made if adequate information is available. (1) The banker can compute the receivables turnover and associated average collection days. Receivables with high turnover are more liquid (i.e., can be converted into cash more quickly) than those with low turnover. (2) If the loan officer knows Richardson's bad debt experience (i.e., those credit sales that are not collectable) the officer could calculate the *bad debt proportion* of credit sales. Applying this percentage to the current receivables balance will provide an estimate of uncollectable accounts. The lower this proportion, the better quality the receivables. (3) An aging schedule of receivables can be drawn up to provide even more information. Should the loan officer be able to obtain Richardson's account files, an *aging schedule* can be constructed. It simply shows what proportion of receivables are, for example, 0 to 15 days old, 16 to 30 days old, 31 to 45 days old, and so on. The banker would like to see a large percentage in the early stages, as this would indicate they have not become tainted.

This process can be carried even further by doing industry comparisons and time series analysis for these secondary computations. There are also sophisticated statistical models that can be applied here. After similar examinations are performed on other current assets and liabilities, the loan officer will be able to make a *qualitative judgement* with regard to Richardson's current ratio ∎

Conclusion   Even though the loan officer conducts a complete financial ratio evaluation and all signs point in the same direction, he or she still cannot be sure of the correct loan decision. FSA is only part, albeit an important part, of a much broader analysis. Suppose the comparison to industry averages, time series analysis, and decomposition analysis all said, in effect, do not make the loan, it is too risky. The banker might decide to approve the loan anyway, based on such considerations as the quality of management, competition in the industry, government regulation, or debt payment history. In total, these other factors could outweigh the findings of financial statement analysis.

Summary

Corporate financial statements (principally the income statement and balance sheet) contain valuable information for a company's creditors, stockholders, management, and others. Financial statement analysis is a formalized, systematic process that has been developed to derive the greatest quantity and quality of information from income statements and balance sheets. There are three distinct stages to financial statement analysis: preparation, measurement, and evaluation. In the preparation stage, the analyst requires assurance that a firm's financial statements are in accordance with Generally Accepted Accounting Principles and are not unduly distorted by inflation. This is also the time to decide what type of analysis is needed. The measurement stage consists of various calculations and relationships (i.e., ratios) involving a firm's balance sheet and income statement data (see table 2.7 on pages 34–5.) These financial ratios are considered to be more enlightening than financial data read directly from financial statements. Financial ratios for a company are compared to the company's past ratios as well as average industry ratios in the evaluation stage.

Financial statement analysis is usually classified in one of four ways. Liquidity analysis looks into a firm's ability to meet near-term financial obligations, such as trade credit. Solvency analysis attempts to answer the question: is a firm making intelligent use of debt financing? Profitability analysis examines a business's earnings performance, both current and past, with emphasis on stockholder results and prospects. Finally, activity ratios measure how well a firm uses such resources as accounts receivable, inventory, and accounts payable.

No one claims that financial statement analysis will answer all of the questions about a firm's financial health. As a matter of fact, there are times when the analysis of financial statements can be inappropriate. Nevertheless, it can be a powerful tool if used with care and intelligence.

Key Terms/Concepts

Accounts payable turnover
Accounts receivable turnover
Activity ratios
Aging schedule
Average collection period
Average cost of debt
Average daily credit sales
Average daily production rate
Average daily purchase on
  account
Average holding period
Average payment period
Bad debt proportion of credit
  sales
Balance sheet
Book value
Book value per share
Common size statement
Current ratio
Debt-to-assets
Debt-to-equity

Decomposition analysis
Dividends
Dividends per share
Dividend yield (DY)
Dollar profitability analysis
DuPont System
Earnings before interest and
  taxes (EBIT)
Earnings per share (EPS)
Earnings-price ratio (E/P)
Financial Statement Analysis
  (FSA)
Generally accepted
  accounting principles
  (GAAP)
Income statement
Industry averages
Inventory turnover
Liquidity
Liquidity analysis

Net income (NI)
Net working capital
Original cost rule
Payout rate
Profitability analysis
Profit margin
Quick ratio
Relative profitability analysis
Return on assets (ROA)
Return on equity (ROE)
Return on investment (ROI)
Return on sales (ROS)
Solvency analysis
Statement of changes in
  financial position
Stockholders' equity
Time series analysis
Times interest earned
Total asset turnover
Users of financial statements

Questions

1. List three situations in which liquidity analysis can be useful?

2. The market value of a corporation's common stock is seldom the same as the book value. What is (are) the reason(s) for this?

3. Would you expect to find every firm in an industry following identical accounting practices and procedures? Why or why not?

4. Why are audited financial statements preferred over unaudited financial statements in the conduct of financial statement analysis?

5. What is the justification for separating current assets from capital or long-term assets on the balance sheet?

6. All other things being the same for a given business, what would you expect to coincide with a low dividend payout rate?

7. Of what relevance is the accounting entry "Par Value of Common Stock?"

8. Could inventory ever be more liquid than accounts receivable? If the answer is yes, provide some examples.

9. What is the relationship between the return on assets and the return on equity?

Problems

1. Indicate whether the following transactions would increase (+), decrease (−), or not affect (0) the current ratio. You may assume that the ratio is currently greater than one.
    A. Notes payable are paid for with cash
    B. Common stock is sold for cash
    C. Goods are sold on credit, at a profit
    D. Workers are partially compensated for back wages with common stock
    E. A short-term loan is taken out to pay income taxes

2. XYZ Corporation paid a $2 per share dividend on 2,000 shares of common stock and a $4 dividend on 1,000 shares of preferred stock. Net income for the year was $10,000. What were the earnings per share of common stock?

3. A firm with annual sales of $4.8 million has an average collection period of 20 days. Accounts receivable are 40% of total current assets and the current ratio is 2.4 to 1. Assuming a 360 day year and that all sales are on credit, determine this firm's total current liabilities.

4. A clothing retailer started 1984 with $360,000 in merchandise inventory. During the year it purchased $1,840,000 worth of goods and incurred a cost of goods sold equal to $2,100,000. What is the 1984 ending inventory?

5. A firm's average collection period is 45 days, but it requires payment in 30 days. Its balance sheet shows outstanding accounts receivable of $3,900,000. How much of the receivables balance is past due?

6. The sale of bonds to finance an increase in inventory would have what kind of *immediate* impact (increase, decrease, or no affect) on the following items?
    A. Current ratio
    B. Net income
    C. Debt-to-equity ratio
    D. Dividends per share
    E. Return on assets

7. A debt-to-asset ratio of .40 would translate into a debt-to-equity ratio of what?

8. Determine the cost of goods sold for a company under the following circumstances: quick ratio is 2.5, current ratio is 4, total current liabilities are $620,000, and the inventory turnover is six times.

9. Determine on your own the average liquidity ratios for the airline industry.

10. ABC Corporation's audited 1986 income statement and balance sheet are displayed below. Using these financial statements, calculate all of the ratios for which data is available. If there is more than one way to compute the ratio, select the method that is most appropriate.

ABC Corporation Balance Sheet Year Ending June 30, 1986

Assets		Liabilities and Equity	
Cash	$ 90,000	Accounts payable	$180,000
Accounts receivable	150,000	Accrued wages	240,000
Inventory	210,000	Bonds	240,000
Plant & equipment	450,000	Common stock (40,000 shares	
Total assets	$900,000	outstanding)	180,000
		Retained earnings	60,000
		Total liabilities & stockholder	
		equity	$900,000

ABC Corporation Income Statement For the Fiscal Year Ending June 30, 1986

Sales	$1,200,000
Cost of goods sold	900,000
Selling and admin. expense	90,000
Earnings before interest and taxes	$ 210,000
Interest expense	60,000
Earnings before taxes	$ 150,000
Income taxes	75,000
Net income	$ 75,000

11. The average (daily) collection periods of the last ten quarters for Wilson Drug, Inc., and the Pharmaceutical Industry are listed below.

		Wilson Drug	Drug Industry
1985	Quarter IV	33 Days	40 Days
	Quarter III	33 Days	41 Days
	Quarter II	36 Days	40 Days
	Quarter I	37 Days	38 Days
1984	Quarter IV	40 Days	40 Days
	Quarter III	42 Days	41 Days
	Quarter II	44 Days	39 Days
	Quarter I	47 Days	39 Days
1983	Quarter IV	47 Days	38 Days
	Quarter III	52 Days	39 Days

Required:
   A. On the same diagram, perform a time series analysis on each set of collection periods
   B. Based upon the time series analyses, contrast Wilson Drug's collection period with the industry's
   C. What factors might cause such divergent behavior

12. Velcro Incorporated is a medium-sized clothing manufacturer located in Massachusetts. Shown below are selected 1986 financial statistics for the clothing and textile industry. Using Velcro's accompanying financial statements, compute the firm's comparable financial ratios and contrast them with the industry averages.

Industry Average	
Return on sales	5%
Return on equity	12%
Return on assets	9%
Current ratio	2.3 $\times$
Quick ratio	1.6 $\times$
Inventory turnover	3.8 $\times$
Average collection period	62 Days
Debt-to-equity ratio	1.35 $\times$
Average cost of debt	15%
Times interest earned	3.2 $\times$

Velcro Incorporated Statement of Financial Position March 31, 1986

Assets

Cash	$ 1,500,000
Marketable securities	2,000,000
Accounts receivable (net)	4,000,000
Inventory	5,000,000
Total current assets	$12,500,000
Land	2,500,000
Plant and office building (net)	8,800,000
Machinery and equip. (net)	10,000,000
Investment in subsidiary	1,200,000
Total long-term assets	$22,500,000
Total assets	$35,000,000

Liabilities and Equity

Accounts payable	$ 3,000,000
Taxes payable	1,000,000
Accrued wages	1,500,000
Notes payable	2,500,000
Total current debt	$ 8,000,000
First mortgage bonds	4,000,000
Debenture bonds	6,500,000
Total long-term debt	$10,500,000
Common stock (2,000,000 shares @ $3.75)	7,500,000
Paid in surplus over par value	2,700,000
Retained earnings	6,300,000
Total owners' equity	$16,500,000
Total debt and owners' equity	$35,000,000

Velcro Incorporated Statement of Income For the Year Ended March 31, 1986

Sales	$52,500,000
Cost of sales	27,500,000
Selling and promotion expense	2,000,000
Administrative expense	3,500,000
Depreciation expense	11,000,000
Gross earnings	$ 8,500,000
Interest expense	2,250,000
Taxable earnings	$ 6,250,000
Income taxes	3,150,000
Net earnings	$ 3,100,000

13. The Rand Corp. chain of department stores had a 1986 cost of goods sold equal to $92,000,000. The firm's 1986 monthly inventory count was as depicted in the following table:

Date		Inventory
January	15	$22,250,000
February	13	15,100,000
March	15	13,230,000
April	14	13,920,000
May	16	15,005,000
June	15	16,880,000
July	15	18,950,000
August	16	19,975,000
September	16	20,000,000
October	15	24,020,000
November	14	28,500,000
December	15	29,350,000

Calculate Rand's 1986 Inventory Turnover using:
   A. Beginning of the year inventory
   B. End of the year inventory
   C. An average of the beginning and ending inventories
   D. An average monthly inventory

14. Shown below are the audited 1987 financial statements for Anatex Company. Using these statements, calculate (where possible) all of the ratios that were described in this chapter. If there is more than one way to calculate a ratio, select the method that is most appropriate. In addition, interpret the meaning of Anatex's ratios.

Anatex Company Balance Sheet As of December 31, 1987

Assets		Liabilities and Equity	
Cash	$ 9,000	Accrued wages	$ 16,000
Marketable securities	9,000	Taxes payable	8,000
Accounts receivable (net)	27,000	Notes payable	12,000
Inventory	40,000	Accounts payable	24,000
Prepaid insurance	5,000	Rent payable	12,000
Total current assets	$ 90,000	Total current liabilities	$ 72,000
Land	20,000	Mortgage on office building	12,000
Plant (net of depreciation)	80,000	Debenture bonds (11%)	30,000
Equipment	110,000	Sub. debenture bonds (13%)	30,000
Accumulated depreciation	(60,000)	Total long-term liabilities	$ 72,000
Total capital assets	$150,000	Preferred stock (10%)	12,000
Total assets	$240,000	Common stock (4,000 shares at $5 par value)	20,000
		Common stock in excess of par value	15,000
		Retained earnings	49,000
		Total stockholders' equity	$ 96,000
		Total liabilities and stockholders' equity	$240,000

Anatex Company Statement of Earnings For the Year Ending December 31, 1987

Sales (80% on credit)	$300,000
Cost of goods sold	170,000
Depreciation	16,000
Selling and administrative expense	54,000
Earnings before interest and taxes	$ 60,000
Interest expense	9,000
Earnings before taxes	$ 51,000
Income taxes	21,400
Net income	$ 29,600
Additional information:	
Preferred stock dividends	$ 1,600
Common stock dividends	$ 14,000
Most recent market price of common stock	$ 56

15. Displayed below are selected financial ratios for El Cheapo airlines and the airline industry.

Financial Ratio	El Cheapo Airlines	Airline Industry
Current ratio	1.80	2.60
Quick ratio	1.60	2.50
Debt-to-assets	.65	.55
Times interest earned	18 ×	15 ×
Average cost of debt	8.5%	10.5%
Receivables turnover	60 ×	48 ×
Payables turnover	4.5 ×	8 ×
Inventory turnover	50 ×	45 ×
Return on sales	4.2%	6.0%
Return on equity	22.0%	15.0%
Return on assets	16.5%	12.0%
Price-earnings ratio	8 ×	13 ×

Required:
   A. Describe El Cheapo's financial situation in general
   B. Contrast El Cheapo's financial situation with that of the industry from the perspective of:
      1. Owners
      2. Short-Term Creditors
      3. Long-Term Creditors

16. Digitum Computer's 1986 and 1987 audited financial statements are reproduced below:
   Required:
   A. Calculate Digitum's financial ratios (where possible and in the most appropriate way)
   B. Draw up a statement of changes in financial position for 1987
   C. Discuss the changes that have taken place during 1987

Digitum Computer Consolidated Earnings Reports* For the Years Ended, December 31, 1986 and 87

	1987	1986
Net sales	$82,600	$75,000
Other income	4,400	3,500
Total revenues	$87,000	$78,500
Operating expenses:		
Cost of goods sold	36,800	29,400
Research and development costs	15,500	15,000
Selling expense	10,000	6,800
Administrative and general expense	7,300	4,900
Total operating expenses	$69,600	$56,300
Earnings before interest and taxes	$17,400	$22,200
Interest charges	5,200	3,000
Earnings before income taxes	$12,200	$19,200
Taxes on income	4,800	7,200
Net earnings	$ 7,400	$12,000
Per share figures:		
Net earnings	$ 4.00	$ 7.50
Cash dividends	$ 2.00	$ 2.50
Shares outstanding at year end	1,850	1,600

*With the exception of per share figures, all amounts are in thousands.

Digitum Computer Consolidated Balance Sheets as of December 31*

Assets	1987	1986
Current assets:		
Cash and marketable securities	$ 2,875	$ 3,550
Notes and accounts receivable	10,450	5,500
Inventories		
Finished goods	13,000	12,950
Work in process	6,500	7,000
Raw materials	8,025	7,350
Prepaid expenses	2,800	1,750
Total current assets	$ 43,650	$38,100
Property, plant, and equipment:		
Land	4,500	4,500
Buildings and improvements	24,750	21,000
Machinery and equipment	22,675	10,650
Leaseholds and improvements	10,300	-0-
Construction in progress	5,000	6,500
Less accumulated depreciation	(12,450)	(10,000)
Total property, plant, and equip.	$ 54,775	$32,650
Other assets		
Investment in French affiliate	8,000	8,000
Patents and other intangibles	8,500	9,500
Total assets	$114,925	$88,250

Digitum Computer Consolidated Balance Sheets as of December 31* _Continued_

Liabilities and Stockholders' Equity	1987	1986
Current liabilities:		
Notes payable	$ 20,500	$15,750
Commercial paper	10,000	–0–
Accounts payable	18,800	12,000
Accrued expenses	6,750	6,200
Income taxes payable	5,250	6,550
Total current liabilities	$ 61,300	$40,500
Long-term debt:		
Term loan	8,000	17,000
Bonds	15,000	15,850
Long-term lease obligations	7,775	–0–
Total long-term debt	$ 30,775	$32,850
Stockholders' equity:		
Common stock, par value $1	1,850	1,600
Common stock in excess of par	14,000	10,000
Retained earnings	7,000	3,300
Total stockholders' equity	$ 22,850	$14,900
Total liabilities and equity	$114,925	$88,250

*All amounts are in thousands.

17. Stock prices and per share earnings of Ferguson Trucking Company over the last eight years are displayed below.

	1979	1980	1981	1982	1983	1984	1985	1986
Earnings per share	$.25	$.50	$.60	$.15	$.60	$.90	$.55	$1.10
Dividends per share	$.10	$.10	$.15	$.15	$.15	$.20	$.20	$.25
Stock price (these are year ending stock prices)	$3	$8	$7	$4	$8	$12.60	$7	$11
Price-earnings ratio	12 ×	16 ×	11.7 ×	NA	13.3 ×	14 ×	12.7 ×	10 ×

Required:
   A. Perform a time series analysis on each of the above four series
   B. Based on the time series analysis performed in A, what conclusions and observations can be made about the trend and stability of Ferguson Truckings earnings and dividends
   C. Discuss the stock market's reaction to this company's performance

18. The most recent earnings reports and balance sheets of XYZ Corporation are displayed below. Based upon these financial statements, answer the following questions:

   A. Is XYZ Corporation profitable? What direction are its profits moving?
   B. Explain the rationale behind the "other income" category on the income statements.
   C. What would the owners of XYZ receive, per share of stock owned, if the assets were liquidated today for $27,000,000 and all debts retired? Explain the difference between this figure and the 1987 book value per share and most recent market value of $19.
   D. What would be the effect on XYZ's debt-to-asset ratio (degree of financial leverage) for 1987, if leased assets and corresponding lease obligations of $3,200,000 are included in the balance sheet?

XYZ Corporation Income Statements For Fiscal Years Ending June 30

	1987	1986
Net sales	$15,960,000	$17,600,000
Cost of sales	10,815,000	10,840,000
Gross margin	$ 5,145,000	$ 6,760,000
Selling, general and administration expenses	2,580,000	2,300,000
Operating income	$ 2,565,000	$ 4,460,000
Other income (expense):		
Interest income	130,000	125,000
Interest expense	(735,000)	(305,800)
Foreign currency gains (losses)	100,250	(115,000)
Earnings before taxes	$ 2,060,250	$ 4,164,200
Provision for income taxes	605,000	1,505,000
Net income	$ 1,455,250	$ 2,659,200
Earnings per share	$2.91	$5.32
Dividends per share	$ .80	$1.00

XYZ Corporation Statements of Financial Position

Assets	June 30, 1987	June 30, 1986
Current assets:		
Cash	$ 138,000	$ 250,000
Certificates of deposit	210,000	1,255,000
Receivables (less allowance for bad debts)	3,150,000	3,605,000
Inventories	7,800,000	5,600,000
Prepaid expenses	95,000	120,000
Total current assets	$11,393,000	$10,830,000
Fixed assets:		
Land	275,000	215,000
Buildings and improvements	2,225,000	1,420,000
Machinery and equipment	9,830,000	6,950,000
Construction in progress	900,000	1,400,000
Less accumulated depreciation	(3,150,000)	(2,175,000)
Total net fixed assets	$10,080,000	$ 7,810,000
Other long-term assets:		
Patents (less accumulated amortization)	880,000	735,000
Investments in affiliates	355,000	290,000
Miscellaneous assets	790,000	595,000
Total other assets	$ 2,025,000	$ 1,620,000
Total assets	$23,498,000	$20,260,000

XYZ Corporation Statements of Financial Position

Liabilities and owners' equity	June 30, 1987	June 30, 1986
Current liabilities:		
Notes payable to banks	$ 720,000	400,000
Current portion of long-term debt	105,000	285,000
Accounts payable	825,000	1,635,000
Accrued income taxes	185,000	580,000
Accrued salaries and wages	550,000	415,000
Accrued interest	245,000	80,000
Accrued rent	90,000	90,000
Other	415,000	350,000
Total current liabilities	$ 3,135,000	$ 3,835,000
Long-term debt	6,630,000	4,050,000
Deferred income taxes	1,250,000	1,000,000
Total long-term liabilities	$ 7,880,000	$ 5,050,000
Stockholders' equity:		
Common stock (500,000 shares @ $1 par)	500,000	500,000
Additional paid-in capital	4,935,000	4,885,000
Retained earnings	7,048,000	5,990,000
Total stockholders' equity	$12,483,000	$11,375,000
Total liabilities and owners' equity	$23,498,000	$20,260,000

Selected References

Altman, E. I., "Financial Ratios, Discriminant Analysis and the Prediction of Corporate Bankruptcy," *Journal of Finance* (September 1968), pp. 589–609.

Helfert, E. A., *Techniques of Financial Analysis,* 5th ed. Homewood, Ill.: Richard D. Irwin, 1982.

Horrigan, J. O., "A Short History of Financial Ratio Analysis," *Accounting Review* (April 1968), pp. 284–94.

Jaedicke, R. K., and R. T. Sprouse, *Accounting Flows: Income, Funds, and Cash,* Englewood Cliffs, N.J.: Prentice-Hall, 1965.

Lev, B., *Financial Statement Analysis: A New Approach,* Englewood Cliffs, N.J.: Prentice-Hall, 1974.

Pohlman, R. A., and R. D. Hollinger, "Information Redundancy in Sets of Financial Ratios," *Journal of Business Finance and Accounting* (Winter 1981), pp. 511–28.

▮ Finance in the News

When evaluating financial statements, creditors and investors should be able to compare liquidity, solvency, profitability, and activity ratios. Some of this information, hopefully, can be inferred from annual reports. Unfortunately (or fortunately, for some?) stories of tomatoes, pictures of swimsuit-clad women, and scented reports may somehow obscure the issues, as indicated in the following article.

The Creative Writing in This Year's Annual Reports

Is Harry J. Gray a team player? Robert J. Carlson, who quit his job as United Technologies Corp.'s president after a power struggle with Chairman Gray, might not think so. But judging from UTC's new annual report, that is what Gray wants investors to believe. All three photographs of Gray—including the cover shot—show him with teams of managers and workers.

It's hardly novel for annual reports such as UTC's to contain self-promotion. This year, steelmakers again bemoan imports, phone companies tell regulators how to act, and T. Boone Pickens Jr., chairman of Mesa Petroleum Co. and king of the raiders, preaches the virtues of his takeover crusade.

But in this year's batch of reports, companies also strive to convince shareholders that they have the skills to succeed in today's tough world. TRW Inc.'s report is entitled *Competitive Innovation* and deals with its plans to emerge a winner in "the world trade olympics." The theme of Crown Zellerbach Corp.'s opus is "keeping pace with changing markets." And companies ranging from Burlington Industries Inc. to Eastman Kodak Co. suddenly are inundated with entrepreneurs, in love with their customers, or riding the technology boom.

Some executives seem to believe that brutal honesty is the way to convince shareholders that they know what they're doing. Cleveland's Parker Hannifin Corp. prominently lays out in a chart how its performance compared with management's goals: It largely fell short. After gambling millions of dollars that a polyvinyl chloride shortage would materialize, B. F. Goodrich Co.'s leaders admit: "Many of these forecasts were wrong."

Why did General Electric Co.'s industrial electronics business fail to translate record sales into any earnings? "A management execution miss," write GE's top brass, who have since reorganized that unit and installed a new chief. And lest his shareholders get carried away by his financial services company's seemingly stellar gain in net worth, Berkshire Hathaway Inc. Chairman Warren E. Buffett . . . tells them: "This sounds pretty good, but actually it's mediocre."

Thanks a Lot

Many chief executives apparently still believe that there's nothing to be gained from dwelling on bad news. Mattel Inc., the big toy company, buries in its accounting explanations the fact that it had to sell off its electronics business because of heavy losses. United Technologies notes that it elected a new president but neglects to say what happened to the old one, Carlson.

But perhaps nobody tries harder to play down trouble than Continental Illinois Corp. While noting the bank lost $1.1 billion in 1984, its new leaders—John E. Swearingen and William S. Ogden—only hint that Continental's survival was so costly: The Federal Deposit Insurance Corp. bailed out the bank and installed new management. They even express their appreciation "to those board members who are not standing for reelection"—without noting that the government forced the directors out.

The thickness and glossiness of annual reports seem directly related to the company's fortunes—or lack thereof. Phelps Dodge Corp.'s report again has no photographs and is four pages shorter than last year's. The annual report of Public Service Co. of New Hampshire, the largest owner of the unfinished Seabrook nuclear power plant, looks as if it had been photocopied. But Wheeling-Pittsburgh Steel Corp. has the skimpiest thus far: none. The steelmaker is more preoccupied with hammering out a survival plan with its union and lenders than putting out an annual report, a company spokesman explains. . . .

Computer Caper

Besides being able to brag about record earnings, H. J. Heinz Co. can lay claim to having one of the slickest reports. Its 96-page opus includes a 46-page celebration of—yes—the tomato, which is a key ingredient in more than 500 Heinz products. Grumman Corp's report looks like a tabloid newspaper. The lead story: Grumman's $1.14 billion contract to upgrade Navy F-14 fighter and A-6 attack planes.

Apple Computer Inc.'s missive features photographs of media magnate Ted Turner, Chrysler Corp. Chairman Lee A. Iacocca, San Francisco Mayor Dianne Feinstein, David Rockefeller, and other "outstanding" people who supposedly use its Macintosh personal computer to do their jobs. Why supposedly? Because Mayor Feinstein, it turns out, uses a Wang computer to keep track of her schedule—not an Apple. And *Technology News of America* reports that Turner, Iacocca, and Rockefeller are not regular Mac users, either.

But Warnaco Inc., a maker of intimate women's apparel and swimsuits, may win the prize for the sexiest report. It features beautiful models in scanty examples of the company's products. And by scenting its report with allspice, McCormick & Co. wins top honors for the most aromatic offering. The big spice maker's report smelled so good that one shareholder claims his dog ate it.

By Steven E. Prokesch in New York, with bureau reports

Compound Interest and the Time Value of Money

Overview

The mathematics of compound interest is concerned with the mathematical properties of interest rates, in particular, compound interest. After completing the present chapter we will be prepared to calculate interest rates on such things as loans, savings accounts, and securities. Moreover, we will understand and be prepared to measure the impact that interest rates have on a number of financial variables.

The material in this chapter is invaluable to an understanding of and involvement with many of the issues that arise throughout the book ▪

Objectives

By the end of the chapter the student should be able to:

1. Explain why interest "rates" are used to evaluate investments
2. Distinguish between simple interest and compound interest
3. Explain why investments with compound interest grow geometrically
4. Distinguish between compounding and discounting
5. Solve compound interest problems to find (a) future value, (b) cash flows, or (c) interest rate
6. Solve discounting problems to find (a) present value, (b) cash flows, or (c) interest rate
7. Explain how changing interest rates and/or time periods influence future value and present value
8. Convert annual interest rates to their less-than-annual equivalent and vice versa
9. Solve annuity compounding problems to find (a) future value, (b) amount of annuity, (c) interest rate, or (d) life of annuity
10. Solve annuity discounting problems to find (a) present value, (b) amount of annuity, (c) interest rate, or (d) life of annuity
11. Solve perpetuity problems and explain when it is appropriate to use a perpetuity formula
12. Explain the concept and importance of time value of money
13. Apply various compound interest principles and formulas in given situations

Introduction

A great deal of the subject matter of financial management revolves around interest rates. Almost all debt financing (liabilities) is acquired at a cost, that cost being the interest rate. Furthermore, the majority of investments (assets) are evaluated according to the rate of interest that they earn.[1] Some of you are probably asking yourselves why we need a "rate" of interest paid or earned? Why can we not work with dollars of interest paid or dollars of interest earned? As a matter of fact, you can use interest "dollars" for some types of analysis, but to do so can be very cumbersome. Consider the following example: your company wishes to raise funds by selling a bond issue. Prior to doing so you would obviously like to know what such funds are going to cost, just as you would want to know the cost of a machine before buying it. A glance at the latest edition of the *Wall Street Journal* indicates that IBM just sold bonds on which interest charges are to be $1,620,000 per year. Is that high or low? It depends to a large extent upon how much money they raised, or in other words, the relative cost. To determine this, you must find the amount of money they borrowed and compare it to the dollar amount of interest in such a way as to get a relative cost, i.e., an interest rate. Rates of interest are much easier to evaluate than dollars of interest because they are directly comparable to each other. For that reason the *Wall Street Journal* and other financial publications normally just quote interest rates.

There are also occasions when dollars of interest just will not do. What of an investment of $5,000 that returns $6,000 in two years (interest of $1,000) and an alternative investment for the same amount that pays $6,700 in three years (interest of $1,700)? Because they payoff at different points in time, they are not directly comparable when dollars are used. This is the problem discussed in chapter 1 that we labeled the time value of money. Proper use of interest rates, however, will allow us to evaluate these two alternatives even though interest dollars will not.

Hopefully you are now sold on the value of interest rates and are ready to work with them. Later in the text we will discuss why there is such a wide variety of interest rates and what causes them to change over time. For right now, we are only concerned with questions surrounding their use: how to compute them, when to use them, how to use them, and the effects of using them. The discussion will be primarily mathematical in nature.

It will greatly facilitate our discussion of interest rate mathematics if we recognize at the start that all of the factors having a bearing on the subject are cash flows of one sort or another. Not only the size of cash flows but also when they occur. To mention just a few examples of cash flows: loans are obtained in cash; dividends and interest charges are paid in cash; stocks are purchased with cash; construction costs of buildings are paid in cash; savings deposits/withdrawals are made by cash; and taxes are dispensed with in cash. In general, a cash flow is an expenditure (outflow) or receipt (inflow) of money. All business transactions are ultimately finalized by cash flows, although they take place under many different names. Rather than become confused by the terminology (par values, coupons, amortizations, dividends, deposits, sales, wages, and the like) for our present discussion we will use the term "cash flow" to represent all of them ■

---

[1] In practice, most businesspersons refer to the rate of interest earned on assets as a rate of return.

Interest: Compound or Simple

Even though persons agree that interest rates are useful, they may not completely agree on how they should be calculated or applied. Disagreement arises over what base the interest rate should be applied to. Many loans and investments change in amount from when they are first entered into. Should the interest rate be applied to the beginning balance (principal) or the changing balance? According to those who use *simple interest,* the rate is applied to the initial balance regardless of whether it increases or decreases in amount. Patrons of *compound interest,* however, believe that interest rates should be figured on the changing balance. Experts overwhelmingly consider the compound interest method superior, both from a mathematical standpoint and in line with economic theory. Their reasoning runs as follows: if an amount of money is borrowed and then repaid a portion at a time, interest should only apply to the reduced balance because the lender has recouped the paid-off portion to relend to someone else, while the borrower has use of only a segment of the original loan. By the same token, if a saver places money in a savings account on which interest is accrued at regular intervals, but not withdrawn, he or she deserves to earn interest on not just the initial balance but also on the accrued interest (which could have been withdrawn). Subsequent deposits should also earn interest. Such a method of figuring interest not only makes economic sense, it is completely fair. *It is often said that compound interest is "interest on interest." A more general and accurate statement would be that it is "interest on the changing balance."*

Compound Interest Model   It is normally easier to develop the mathematics of compound interest if one applies it to a simple financial problem such as a savings account. The derivation of the compound interest formula can also be simplified if an interest rate is given at the start. Such a methodology is employed here.

Application: Let us assume that a local savings and loan association is paying a 12% compound annual rate of interest on savings accounts. (Note: interest rates are almost always quoted on an annual basis.) A depositor places $1,000 of cash into this account on January 1 and plans to leave it in for three years. How much money will be in the account in three years? On December 31 one year later, the savings and loan credits the depositor's account for the full 12% or .12 × $1,000 = $120. This leaves an ending balance in the account of $1,000 + $120 = $1,120. Should the entire $1,120 balance be left in for a second year, the amount of interest earned would be .12 × $1,120 = $134.40. The balance in the account after two years is $1,120 + $134.40 = $1,254.40. If this figure is invested for a third full year, interest earnings would amount to .12 × $1,254.40 = $150.53, leaving an ending deposit balance after three years of $1,404.93. This ending balance consists of the original $1,000 principal and interest income of $120 + $134.40 + $150.53 = $404.93. Note that the interest dollars are growing even though the interest rate remains constant. This occurs because the constant interest rate is applied to a changing (growing) balance. The balance is changing, in this case, due to the reinvestment of interest earnings each year. This is compound interest in action. This relationship is shown mathematically in table 3.1.

Table 3.1   Derivation of Compound Interest Formula

Part A:

Year 1 $1,120.00 = $1,000.00 + $1,000.00(.12)
Year 2 $1,254.40 = $1,120.00 + $1,120.00(.12)
Year 3 $1,404.93 = $1.254.40 + $1,254.40(.12)

Part B: Rewrite after Factoring

Year 1 $1,120.00 = $1,000.00(1.12)
Year 2 $1,254.40 = $1,120.00(1.12)
Year 3 $1,404.93 = $1,254.40(1.12)

Part C: Rewrite after Substitution

Year 1 $1,120.00 = $1,000.00(1.12)

Year 2 $1,254.40 = $1,000.00(1.12)(1.12)

Year 3 $1,404.93 = $1,000.00(1.12)(1.12)(1.12)

Part D: Rewrite after Simplifying

Year 1 $1,120.00 = $1,000(1.12)^1
Year 2 $1,254.40 = $1,000(1.12)^2
Year 3 $1,404.93 = $1,000(1.12)^3

As you can see in Part D of table 3.1, a pattern has developed. This can be generalized in the following way.

If we let:

C = Cash flow (principal)
t = Total number of times interest is applied
i = Rate of interest per period of time
FV = Future value or ending balance

we obtain:

Equation 3.1 $FV = C(1+i)^t$

This equation is a generalized model for the equations developed in table 3.1, Part D. It also introduces the term *future value* (*FV*) as a replacement for ending balance. For example, if C is $1,000, t is 2 years and i equals 12% per year, then plugging into equation 3.1 we can compute FV as follows:

$$\$1,254.40 = \$1,000(1.12)^2$$

that is exactly the two-year savings result developed previously. Equation 3.1 is the fundamental equation of compound interest and the basis for all of the other compound interest formulas.

Simple Interest Model   Simple interest is figured on only the beginning balance, thereby making for a much easier computation. Ease of computation is its only redeeming quality, however, since it is inferior in every other respect to compound interest. Despite its weaknesses, one must be on guard because it continues to be used in some instances. Simple interest used in connection with the preceding problem would provide a future value in three years of: $1,000 principal + ($1,000 × 12% × 3 years) = $1,360. In general terms this equation is $FV = C(1+it)$. This corresponds to the $1,404.93 computed by using compound interest. As you can see, simple interest generates a smaller future sum than compound interest and will always do so. The difference does not appear to be significant in this example, but it grows dramatically as the number of years increases. Figure 3.1 clearly demonstrates the difference between compound interest and simple interest.

In figure 3.1 we have an initial sum of $1,000 invested at 12% annual compound interest and 12% annual simple interest. The bottom curve shows the initial $1,000 principal growing at simple interest and the top curve represents growth at compound interest. Note how the curves widen dramatically as t increases. After three years we saw a difference of only $1,404.93 − $1,360.00 = $44.93. But in 20 years the difference would amount to $9,646 − $3,400 = $6,246. Such a great discrepancy shows the dangers in using simple interest.

Figure 3.1   Future value of $1,000 at 12% compound interest and 12% simple interest

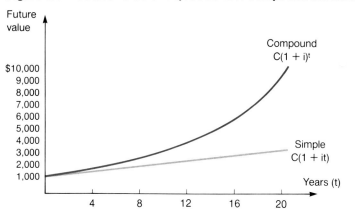

There is one other interesting observation that can be made about the FV curves in figure 3.1. The simple interest curve is linear with a constant upward slope. On the other hand, compound FV is represented by a curvilinear line whose slope rises at increasing rates. Such a curve is said to be a geometric mathematical function. *When dealing with geometric as opposed to linear mathematical functions be very careful about making approximations.* In other words, no longer can we assume that $2 + 2 = 4$. When interest is compounded, one cannot say, for example, that a doubling of interest rates will double interest dollars. The fact of the matter is, interest could very well be several times as large.

Now, before we get into the details of compound interest, an important distinction needs to be made. *Compound interest problems can be approached from two different perspectives: compounding and discounting.* In most situations, either approach can be used, but typically one will be superior because it is easier to use and/or it makes more intuitive sense. With some practice an individual can usually determine the best method. However, in the initial stages it is helpful to have guidelines. Guidelines will therefore be provided later in the chapter.

Compounding

General Model   Compounding means to grow or expand, to move forward. It is a future-oriented concept. Equation 3.1 was developed from a problem that was future- or growth-oriented. A saver wished to know the amount of money in his or her savings account in three years. An examination of equation 3.1 reveals this to be the case.

Equation 3.1 repeated: $FV = C(1+i)^t$

The formula shows us that a cash flow (C) expands over time (t) due to the application of interest (i) to arrive at an eventual sum of money (FV). If we know any three of the four variables in equation 3.1, we can solve for the unknown. Not only is this the basic equation of compound interest, as stated earlier, it is also the fundamental formula used for compounding. However, it was derived from a situation that involved only one cash flow, namely, the $1,000 savings account deposit. Most investments and loans involve more than one cash flow, so what is needed is a more general expression to account for this fact.

Such an expression is equation 3.2 shown below:

Equation 3.2 $\quad FV = C_1(1+i)^{t_1} + C_2(1+i)^{t_2} + \ldots + C_n(1+i)^{t_n}$

Where:

C_j = Cash flows such that C_1 is the first cash flow to occur, C_2 is the second, and so on; there can be $j=1$ to n cash flows

t_j = The number of times (i.e., number of time periods) that interest is applied to the j_{th} cash flow

FV = Future value

Furthermore, i and t_j should be on the same basis. That is, if the time periods are months then we should use a monthly rate of interest. We shall hereafter refer to equation 3.2 as the *compounding model*.

This equation is not as difficult as it looks. In words, it says that cash flow C_1 earns interest rate i for t_1 periods of time, followed by a second cash flow C_2 earning interest rate i for t_2 periods and so on. They are then summed to obtain their combined future value. Since C_1 is the first cash flow, by necessity it will earn interest for more periods (i.e., interest will be compounded more times) than cash flow C_2, and C_2 more than C_3.

The subscripts on the variables allow this general model to be very flexible. They also make it conducive to computer programming. Equation 3.2 can be used with a single cash flow, in which case n would be 1, or hundreds of them. The cash flows can be of any size and include expenditures (cash outflows) and/or receipts (cash inflows). *When a problem includes both cash inflows and outflows it is necessary to place different signs (+ or −) on them.* The time periods can be of any length, including days, months, quarters, or years. The generality of this model will allow us to handle a variety of problems.

In the earlier illustration used to develop the formula of compound interest, we solved for the final balance in a savings account, or future value. But much more than that can be done. Equation 3.2 contains many variables: all of the Cs, and t_js as well as FV and i. If we know all but one of these variables we can solve for the unknown. Although any one of the variables in equation 3.2 could be derived, there are certain ones that are of more interest to financial management than the others. The interest rate and FV fall into this category, as well as cash flows that often have to be derived for loans and investments. While time periods (t_j) are very important in compound interest, only rarely in financial management do we need to solve for them directly. Therefore, the variables that we will derive from equation 3.2 are limited to the following list: (1) Future value (FV); (2) Specific cash flow (C_j); (3) Equal cash flows (C); (4) Interest rate (i).

Equation 3.2 is a rather cumbersome formula to work with. The computations can be lengthy and the algebra formidable. Thus, using it to find future value, cash flows, and the interest rate can best be accomplished (i.e., faster) if it is programmed for a computer. This is especially true for long and involved problems.

Use of Interest Tables   When computers (or sophisticated calculators) are not available, our only choice is to wrestle personally with equation 3.2. However, this is anything but a fruitless exercise, since it contributes to a much greater understanding of compound interest. Nevertheless, any help with this task is greatly appreciated. Referring to equation 3.2, we can see that the term $(1+i)^{t_j}$ occurs several times. Raising any number to a power is a troublesome task. When that number contains a decimal (as interest rates are inclined to do) the task can be excruciating, even when a calculator is used. Consider the work involved in solving for X when $X = (1.07)^{55}$. To help us in this ordeal, a number of such computations have already been done and placed in easy-to-use tables for our convenience. These calculations can be found in appendix A on pages 513–15. The tables in appendix A have the number of time periods (t_j) listed down the far left side and interest rates (i) recorded along the top. In the bodies of the tables can be found mathematical derivations of $(1+i)^{t_j}$. For example: an i of 8% and a t of 4 periods would intersect at 1.3605 in the body of the table. This number is equal to $(1.08)^4$ or $(1.08) \times (1.08) \times (1.08) \times (1.08)$. It would be helpful to have a name for these computations, so we will give them one. They will be called *compound factors* (*CF*) and appendix A is entitled the *compound factor table*. In equation form, a compound factor would be written as follows:

Equation 3.3 $CF = (1+i)^{t_j}$

The compound factor notation for a specific interest rate-number of time periods combination is CF_{i/t_j}. Thus, the compound factor notation for 8% interest and four time periods is $CF_{.08/4}$ and it equals 1.3605. Note: If no time passes for a particular cash flow, then $t = 0$ and the CF is $(1+i)^0 = 1$.

Because compound factors are so helpful it would be useful to rewrite equation 3.2 in an operational form, as shown below:

Equation 3.4 $FV = C_1(CF_{i/t_1}) + C_2(CF_{i/t_2}) + \ldots + C_n(CF_{i/t_n})$

Now we are ready to observe some relatively straightforward problems. The primary intent of this section is to demonstrate the mechanics of using the compounding model, equation 3.2, to solve compound interest problems.

Example: What is the combined FV of $5,000 invested for 3 periods, $10,000 for 2 periods and $15,000 for 1 period given a 12% interest rate per period? Thus, $C_1 = \$5,000$, $C_2 = \$10,000$, $C_3 = \$15,000$, $t_1 = 3$, $t_2 = 2$, $t_3 = 1$ and $i = .12$. Inserting this information into equation 3.2 we obtain:

$FV = \$5,000(1.12)^3 + \$10,000(1.12)^2 + \$15,000(1.12)^1$

In operational form it becomes:

$FV = \$5,000\ CF_{.12/3} + \$10,000\ CF_{.12/2} + \$15,000\ CF_{.12/1}$

Therefore:

$FV = \$5,000(1.4049) + \$10,000(1.2544) + \$15,000(1.120) = \$36,368$

The solution to this problem can be shown graphically on a time line as follows ■

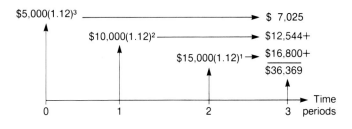

$5,000(1.12)^3$ ───────────────▶ $ 7,025

$10,000(1.12)^2$ ────────────▶ $12,544+

$15,000(1.12)^1$ ─▶ $16,800+

$36,369

0   1   2   3   Time periods

Example: What are the three equal cash flows (i.e., $C_1 = C_2 = C_3 = C$) necessary to accumulate a FV of $27,300? The first will earn interest for three periods, the second for two periods, and the last for one period, all at a 10% interest rate per period.

Inserting the information into equation 3.2 we obtain:

$$\$27,300 = C(1.10)^3 + C(1.10)^2 + C(1.10)^1$$

In operational form it becomes:

$$\$27,300 = C(CF_{.10/3}) + C(CF_{.10/2}) + C(CF_{.10/1})$$

Solving for C:

$$C = \frac{\$27,300}{CF_{.10/3} + CF_{.10/2} + CF_{.10/1}}$$

Therefore:

$$C = \frac{\$27,300}{1.331 + 1.21 + 1.10} = \$7,498 \ ■$$

Example: What interest rate is implied by cash flows ($C_1 = \$20,000$, $C_2 = \$15,000$, $C_3 = \$10,000$ and $C_4 = \$5,000$) invested for time periods ($t_1 = 4$, $t_2 = 3$, $t_3 = 2$ and $t_4 = 1$) that generate an FV of $70,000?

Substituting into equation 3.2:

$$\$70,000 = \$20,000(1+i)^4 + \$15,000(1+i)^3 + \$10,000(1+i)^2 + \$5,000(1+i)^1$$

In operational form:

$$\$70,000 = \$20,000(CF_{i/4}) + \$15,000(CF_{i/3}) + \$10,000(CF_{i/2}) + \$5,000(CF_{i/1})$$

Unlike FV and cash flow, it is not mathematically possible to solve directly for the interest rate in this problem. *Trial and error is the only way this equation can be solved for in terms of i.* Specifically, we are looking for the i that equates the right hand side of the equation to the left side (i.e., $70,000). The easiest way to accomplish this (without the aid of a computer) is to solve the equation with different interest rate CFs until the right-hand side equals the $70,000 FV. When this occurs, we will have found our interest rate.

What interest rate should we start with? Let us use a nice round number like 10%. First Trial:

Trial .10 = $20,000(1.4641) + $15,000(1.331) + $10,000(1.210) + $5,000(1.100)
Trial .10 = $66,847

This is quite a bit less than $70,000. Now try a larger interest rate, say 20%.
Second Trial:

    Trial .20 = $20,000(2.0736) + $15,000(1.728) + $10,000(1.440) + $5,000(1.200)
    Trial .20 = $87,792

Since $87,792 is much larger than $70,000, obviously 20% is too great. Because the 10% interest rate came closer to $70,000 than the 20% rate, it is likely that the correct interest rate is closer to 10% than to 20%. What about 12%?
Third Trial:

    Trial .12 = $20,000(1.5735) + $15,000(1.4049) + $10,000(1.2544) + $5,000(1.120)
    Trial .12 = $70,688

This is much closer. If a fourth trial of 11% were used, we would get a figure of $68,750. Therefore, the exact rate lies somewhere between 11% and 12%. For many purposes, an answer like this would be adequate. If more accuracy is desired, one may interpolate using the compound factor tables or, better yet, program the equation on the computer and let it solve for any degree of precision desired. As a matter of fact, a computer goes through much the same trial and error search that we just performed. Of course, it would be much faster ∎

A sampling of compound interest problems have been presented along with the mathematical mechanics necessary for their solutions. They were designed for and solved with the compounding method of compound interest. The emphasis was not on real-world problems that one might encounter, but rather on mechanics. Real-world examples will follow later in the chapter.

Effect of Changing Interest Rates and Time Periods   We often fail to appreciate the influence that interest rates and time can have on compound interest problems. Due to the geometric nature of the compound interest formula, a change in interest rates or the number of times interest is compounded can have an impact out of all proportion to the amount of change. The influence of differing interest rates on compounding and FV is illustrated by figure 3.2.

Figure 3.2 reveals the future values one would obtain by investing a single $5,000 sum of cash for 10 years compounded at annual interest rates of 6%, 12%, and 18%. The lightly shaded area in each bar represents the accumulated interest earned over the ten years and the balance represents the $5,000 cash flow. The FV at 18% is nearly three times as large as the FV at 6%. The increase in interest is even more striking. An interest rate of 6% generates $3,955 in interest, whereas the 18% rate provides for $21,170 in interest or 5.4 times as much. The growth in interest is geometric. This can be shown by the fact that a doubling of interest rates from 6% to 12% causes interest to be $10,530 ÷ $3,955 = 2.7 times as large, whereas a tripling of interest rates from 6% to 18% leads to a multiple of $21,170 ÷ $3,955 = 5.4 times.

The impact of differing time periods can be equally dramatic, as shown in figure 3.3.

Figure 3.3 shows the FVs one would obtain by investing a single $5,000 sum of cash at 15% annual interest for 5, 10, and 15 years. The lightly shaded area in each bar represents accumulated interest and the dark areas signify cash flow (i.e., principal or initial investment). One cannot help but notice the dramatic impact that time has on compound interest.

Figure 3.2   Future value of $5,000 in ten years

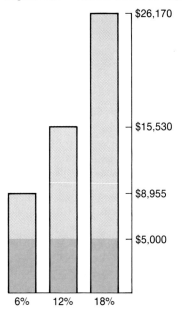

$26,170

$15,530

$8,955

$5,000

6%   12%   18%

Figure 3.3   Future value of $5,000 at 15% interest

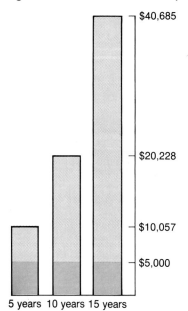

$40,685

$20,228

$10,057

$5,000

5 years 10 years 15 years

A doubling of time (from 5 years to 10 years) generates not only a doubling of FV but a tripling of interest (i.e., $15,228 \div $5,057 = 3$). The geometric nature of the formula shows up when the time interval is tripled to 15 years. Here we see that the FV is more than four times as large and the interest is a multiple of $35,685 \div $5,057 = 7.06$ times. It should be noted, however, that the dramatic differences shown in figure 3.3 are due in part to using a 15% interest rate. Smaller rates would have less of an impact, as we saw in figure 3.2.

Discounting

Discounting is an alternative method of solving compound interest problems. In order to make the transition from compounding to discounting we must reverse our thinking about compound interest problems. *Whereas compounding is centered around future value (FV) discounting is oriented toward present value (PV).* Rather than asking, "what are cash flows going to be worth in the future," we will instead ask, "what are cash flows worth today?" In other words, we are now going to be working compound interest problems in reverse order. Reverse, that is, in terms of time.

General Model   The basic equation of compound interest, equation 3.1, was formulated in terms of future value. It was then used to develop the compounding model, equation 3.2. A very simple alteration of equation 3.1 will allow us to convert compound interest from compounding to discounting. For ease of comparison, both equations are shown below:

Equation 3.1 $FV = C(1+i)^t$ (Compounding)

Equation 3.5 $PV = \dfrac{C}{(1+i)^t}$ (Discounting)

A glance at these two equations reveals their fundamental difference. The compounding formula has cash growing (multiplied) by compound interest, but the discounting equation requires cash to be reduced (divided) by compound interest. Interest rates are also interpreted differently for the two methods. The difference is semantic, but, nonetheless, revealing. Compounding implies that interest "will" be earned whereas discounting implies that it "could" be earned.

Let us say, for example, that we wish to know the present value (current worth) of a $10,000 cash flow occurring 10 periods in the future given that money can earn 12% compound interest per period. Inserting these figures into equation 3.5 we obtain:

$$PV = \frac{\$10,000}{(1.12)^{10}}$$

The PV can be easily obtained by dividing the $10,000 by the $CF_{.12/10}$. Thus,

$$PV = \frac{\$10,000}{3.1058} = \$3,220$$

Of what economic significance is this number? It means that if an individual can earn 12% compound interest on money over the next 10 periods, then that person would be indifferent between $3,220 in cash today and $10,000 in 10 periods. That is because $3,220 would accumulate to $10,000 in 10 periods if invested at 12% compound interest. In other words, the two dollar figures are equivalent and they are made equivalent by an interest rate. This principle will prove extremely valuable to us later.

Equation 3.5 can be generalized to handle more than one cash flow. Such a model would be the counterpart of equation 3.2 and is shown below:

Equation 3.6 $$PV = \frac{C_1}{(1+i)^{t_1}} + \frac{C_2}{(1+i)^{t_2}} + \ldots + \frac{C_n}{(1+i)^{t_n}}$$

The variables have the same meaning as they did for equation 3.2. Here, as before, C_1 is the first cash flow to occur, C_2 the second, and so forth. Also, t_1 is the number of time periods that interest is applied to cash flow C_1, t_2 the number of time periods applied to cash flow C_2, etc. Because we are bringing cash flows back to the present, t_1 is always less than t_2 and t_2 less than t_3, etc. This is just the reverse of compounding, where we were working cash flows forward. Although this might appear contradictory, such is not the csae. When going forward, the earliest cash flow should benefit the most from interest (i.e., $t_1 > t_2$); whereas with discounting, the earliest cash flow should be penalized the least (i.e., $t_1 < t_2$). We shall hereafter refer to equation 3.6 as the *discounting model*.

Use of Interest Tables   Equation 3.6 can be used to find a single cash flow (C_j), the interest rate (i), equal cash flows (C), and present value (PV). Unfortunately, it is just as cumbersome to work with as the compounding model. As a result, computers and sophisticated calculators can be of tremendous help. But these may not be available. To aid us with the compounding model, equation 3.2, we were provided with tables of many $(1 + i)^{t_j}$ values that we named compound factors. We can use these same tables when applying the discounting model. But, whereas they are multiplied by cash flows in the compounding model $(C(1+i)^{t_j})$, they are divided into cash flows in the discounting model $\left(\frac{C}{(1+i)^{t_j}}\right)$. Division is not quite as easy to work with as multiplication. Therefore, we are provided with a second set of tables that are comprised of compound factor reciprocals (i.e., they have all been divided into one). These tables are found in appendix B. In order to differentiate these numbers from those in appendix A, we will refer to them as *discount factors* (*DF*). The discount factor notation for a specific interest rate–time periods combination is DF_{i/t_j}. In equation form, a discount factor would appear as follows:

Equation 3.7 $$DF = \frac{1}{(1+i)^{t_j}}$$

Appendix B can be used in exactly the same way as appendix A. Thus, we can look up a DF if we know the interest rate and the number of time periods. As an example, the discount factor for an i of 15% and a t_j of 10 is .2472. This situation can be written mathematically as follows:

$$DF_{.15/10} = \frac{1}{(1.15)^{10}} = \frac{1}{4.0456} = .2472$$

Equation 3.6 is rewritten below in *operational form:*

Equation 3.8 $PV = C_1(DF_{i/t_1}) + C_2(DF_{i/t_2}) + \ldots + C_n(DF_{i/t_n})$

We are now ready to work some example compound interest problems by the discounting method. As before with compounding, our primary concern in this section is to learn mechanics. More practical problems will follow later in the chapter.

Example: What is the combined present value of $1,000 received in one period, $2,000 received in three periods, and $3,000 received in five periods, given an interest rate of 12% per period? Substituting into equation 3.6 we obtain:

$$PV = \frac{\$1,000}{(1.12)^1} + \frac{\$2,000}{(1.12)^3} + \frac{\$3,000}{(1.12)^5}$$

In operational form:

$$PV = \$1,000DF_{.12/1} + \$2,000DF_{.12/3} + \$3,000DF_{.12/5}$$

Therefore:

$$PV = \$1,000(.8929) + \$2,000(.7118) + \$3,000(.5674) = \$4,019$$

The solution to this problem can be shown graphically on a time line as follows

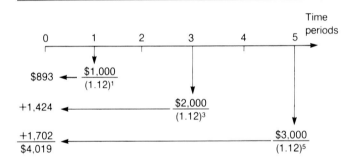

Example: The present value of four future cash outlays is $25,000. The first three consist of $4,000 expenditures in one, two, and three periods. A final cash flow occurs in four periods. Given that a 13% interest rate could be earned during each of the four periods, what is the final cash flow?
Substituting into equation 3.6 we obtain:

$$\$25,000 = \frac{\$4,000}{(1.13)^1} + \frac{\$4,000}{(1.13)^2} + \frac{\$4,000}{(1.13)^3} + \frac{C_4}{(1.13)^4}$$

In operational form:

$$\$25,000 = \$4,000DF_{.13/1} + \$4,000DF_{.13/2} + \$4,000DF_{.13/3} + C_4(DF_{.13/4})$$

Solving for C_4:

$$C_4 = \frac{\$25,000 - \$4,000DF_{.13/1} - \$4,000DF_{.13/2} - \$4,000DF_{.13/3}}{DF_{.13/4}}$$

Therefore:

$$C_4 = \frac{\$25,000 - \$4,000(.885) - \$4,000(.7832) - \$4,000(.6931)}{.6133} = \$25,363$$

Example: What is the compound rate of interest that equates cash flows of $9,000 in one period, $6,000 in two periods, and $3,000 in three periods to a $13,400 present value?

Substituting into equation 3.6:

$$\$13,400 = \frac{\$9,000}{(1+i)^1} + \frac{\$6,000}{(1+i)^2} + \frac{\$3,000}{(1+i)^3}$$

In operational form:

$$\$13,400 = \$9,000DF_{i/1} + \$6,000DF_{i/2} + \$3,000DF_{i/3}$$

Trial and error is the only way this equation can be solved in terms of i. The procedure is identical to that used earlier for compounding. Specifically, we are looking for the i that equates the right side of the operational equation to the left side (i.e., $13,400). For the first trial we will use 12%.

First Trial:

Trial .12 = $9,000(.8929) + $6,000(.7972) + $3,000(.7118)
Trial .12 = $14,955

The 12% rate generated a sizeable error of $14,955 − $13,400 = $1,555. A larger interest rate should be selected for the next trial because 12% erred on the high side. (Recall that the interest rate and PV are inversely related.) An 18% rate will be used for the second trial.

Second Trial:

Trial .18 = $9,000(.8475) + $6,000(.7182) + $3,000(.6086)
Trial .18 = $13,763

This is much closer. The correct interest rate is close at hand and it is slightly larger than 18%. For the third trial we will use 20%.

Third Trial:

Trial .20 = $9,000(.8333) + $6,000(.6944) + $3,000(.5787)
Trial .20 = $13,402

It is clear that the exact interest rate is very near 20%. An error of $2 exists compared with a PV of $13,400, or less than one tenth of one percent. Little would be gained by pursuing this. Consequently, we can state that the interest rate is 20% ■

Effect of Changing Interest Rates and Time Periods   Earlier, we saw the enormous influence that differing interest rates and time periods can have on compounding and FV. It would be worthwhile at this stage to perform a similar analysis on discounting and PV. The results of this analysis are displayed in figures 3.4 and 3.5.

Figure 3.4 reveals the PV of an $80,000 cash flow occurring in 15 years discounted at annual interest rates of 5, 10, and 15 percent. These bar charts are read differently than those constructed for compounding. The height of each bar indicates the cash flow and the dark shaded area measures present value. This is a reversal of the compounding charts, which is to be expected since compounding and discounting are reversals of each other. The lightly shaded area represents interest. However, this is not accumulated interest that has been added, as in the case of compounding, but rather accumulated interest that has been subtracted. In other words, the lightly shaded area measures the amount of interest "taken out of" the $80,000 cash flow. Figure 3.5 can be portrayed in the same way.

Two important principles are displayed in figure 3.4. In the first instance, it is very apparent that interest rates and PV are inversely related. This property will be very important to us in subsequent discussions. Secondly, the inverse relationship between rates and PV is

Figure 3.4   Present value of $80,000 in fifteen years

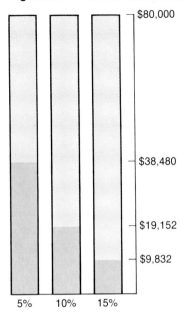

			$80,000
5%	10%	15%	$38,480
			$19,152
			$9,832

Figure 3.5   Present value of $30,000 at 16% interest

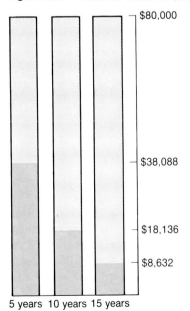

			$80,000
			$38,088
			$18,136
5 years	10 years	15 years	$8,632

geometric in nature. That is, a tripling of interest rates cause PV to fall by more than three times. In this example, an increase from 5% to 15% leads to a decline in PV from $38,480 to $9,832, which is only about one-fourth as large.

Figure 3.5 exhibits the PV of an $80,000 cash flow that has been discounted at an annual interest rate of 16% for 5, 10, and 15 years. The same two principles are displayed in figure 3.5 that were shown in figure 3.4. Namely, there is an inverse relationship between time and PV, and it is geometric in nature.

Combining these two analyses leads one to conclude that cash flows will have relatively little present value when interest rates are high and the cash flows are far into the future, and vice versa.

Compounding vs. Discounting

With the availability of computers, calculators, and detailed interest tables the arithmetic in compound interest problems is manageable. The difficulty comes in the initial stages when compound interest problems are interpreted and set up. The nature of the problem, business jargon, laws, and the objective of the decision maker all combine to produce complications. A frequent complication is whether to use the compounding or discounting model. Some clues are provided below to help us make this distinction.

Discounting and compounding are alternative methods for dealing with compound interest problems. Whereas compounding is centered on future value, discounting is oriented toward present value. Thus, compounding is primarily concerned with some future objective, whereas discounting is used when the center of attention is on the present. The proper method to use depends upon the nature of the problem. A problem that is "focused" on some future date would more sensibly be analyzed by compounding. As an example of such a problem, consider a 50-year-old worker who wishes to know how much money will be in his or her pension fund at age sixty-five. On the other hand, it would be easier and more meaningful to use discounting for a problem that is primarily "focused" on the present. The maximum price one should pay today for an apartment building is an example of a problem focused on the present. Unfortunately, there are many instances when it is difficult to tell exactly where the focus of a problem lies. As a result, it is not obvious if we should use discounting or compounding. *Common practice is to use discounting for all problems that are not clearly designated as future oriented. The remainder of the text will do likewise.*

Figure 3.6 will provide additional insight into the workings of compound interest and help to clarify the relationship between compounding and discounting.

Value (i.e., PV and FV) is plotted along the vertical axis and time periods (t) is plotted on the horizontal axis. The curve plotted on the graph is based upon a single cash flow that is compounded (moving to the right) and discounted (moving to the left) at 8% interest. Take careful note of the fact that FV and PV are on the same curve (i.e., the same functional relationship), they just move in opposite directions. Given that 8% truly will be earned (compounding) or could be earned (discounting), we can say that any cash flow on this curve is equally good. For example, $6,000 in cash today (t = 0) is as good as $12,000 in cash in 9 periods. Why? Because the FV of $6,000 compounded at 8% for 9 periods is approximately equal to $12,000. Conversely, the PV today of $12,000 discounted at 8% for 9 periods is $6,000. The same is true of any two dollar amounts on the curve. We shall refer to diagrams such as this as *cash equivalent curves.*

Figure 3.6   Relationship between present value and future value

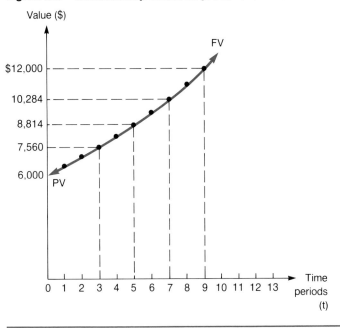

As a further example, we can say that $7,560 in 3 periods is equivalent to $6,000 today and $12,000 in 9 periods. This last example highlights an important principal. Cash flows can be discounted back to points in time other than today (t = 0), and compounding can begin at a future date as well as today. Consider the $7,560. It is the PV 3 periods hence of $12,000 in 9 periods and is computed as follows: $7,560 = $\dfrac{\$12{,}000}{(1.08)^6}$. Conversely, $12,000 is the FV of $7,560 compounded at 8% interest from time period 3 to time period 9 and is calculated as follows: $12,000 = $7,560(1.08)^6$. Neither one of these calculations directly involved the present, (i.e., t = 0). Only the time interval from 3 to 9 periods (i.e., 6 periods) had a direct bearing on the calculations.

It may seem confusing to say "present value three periods hence," since most of us consider the word "present" to mean now or today. Although most financial management problems are focused on the here-and-now, there are instances when we need to know PV for a point in time other than today.

Special Topics in Compound Interest

Intra-Year Compounding   In the earlier discussion of compound interest it was mentioned that the interest rate (i) and time periods (t_j) should be on the same basis. Thus, if the time periods of concern are months, then the interest rate should be a monthly rate. However, it is common practice to quote interest rates on an annual basis. The previous examples obscured this fact so that we could focus on mechanics. There, we simply assumed that i and t_j were already consistent. Many cases arise, however, where we must solve problems that combine annual interest rates and less than annual time periods. In order to proceed with these problems we must adjust the annual interest rate to correspond to the different time period. This simply requires that the annual rate be divided by the number of relevant time periods in the year. For instance, an annual rate of 16% and quarterly time periods would generate a quarterly interest rate of $.16 \div 4$ quarters $= 4\%$. Failure to make such an adjustment could lead to serious error. An adjustment is necessary when an annual rate of interest is given and (a) interest is compounded more than once a year and/or (b) cash flows occur more than once a year.

Example: As an example of case a, consider a single $1,000 cash deposit in a savings institution that pays interest at the rate of 12% per year. What is the ending balance (FV) in the account one year later assuming the following compounding frequencies?

Annual: $C_1(1+i)^{t_1} = \$1{,}000(1.12)^1 = \$1{,}000 \, CF_{.12/1} = \$1{,}120.00$

Semi-Annual: $C_1(1+i)^{t_1} = \$1{,}000(1.06)^2 = \$1{,}000 \, CF_{.06/2} = \$1{,}123.60$

Quarterly: $C_1(1+i)^{t_1} = \$1{,}000(1.03)^4 = \$1{,}000 \, CF_{.03/4} = \$1{,}125.50$

Monthly: $C_1(1+i)^{t_1} = \$1{,}000(1.01)^{12} = \$1{,}000 \, CF_{.01/12} = \$1{,}126.80$

Continuous compounding, which requires the use of logarithms, would generate a FV of $1,127.50. Observe how i goes down as t_j goes up when the frequency of compounding increases. Also note the increase in FV as the compounding frequency rises. Although this particular example concerns compounding, one could also be developed for discounting. As discounting is the reverse of compounding, discounting would generate smaller and smaller PVs as the frequency of intrayear compounding increased.

Case b, more than one cash flow per year, occurs many times in finance. The following statements, while not always true, are safe generalizations: dividends on common stock are paid quarterly; rent is due monthly; bond interest is paid semiannually; home mortgages are paid monthly; and revenue and expenses for most firm's occur daily ■

Example: Consider the cash rental receipts to the owner of real estate. What is the present value of a series of $500 monthly rental receipts for 10 years given an 18% annual rate of interest? This problem should be solved through discounting each rental receipt by an interest rate of $.18 \div 12$ months $= .015$ and would appear as follows:

$$PV = \frac{\$500}{(1.015)^1} + \frac{\$500}{(1.015)^2} + \ldots + \frac{\$500}{(1.015)^{119}} + \frac{\$500}{(1.015)^{120}} = \$27{,}749$$

Observe that although the rentals last for ten years, the relevant time periods are months and there are up to 120 of them. An approximation to the correct procedure is to sum the monthly rentals to obtain an annual rental and then apply the 18% annual rate, as follows:

$$PV = \frac{\$6{,}000}{(1.18)^1} + \frac{\$6{,}000}{(1.18)^2} + \ldots + \frac{\$6{,}000}{(1.18)^{10}} = \$26{,}964$$

At first glance, it might appear as though you would get identical answers from these two methods. Such is not the case, however, as the answer from the correct method is $27,749, while the alternative provides a PV of $26,964. In many situations, this relatively small difference permits us to use either method. Under no circumstance, however, could we justify discounting each of the $500 cash flows by 18%. Similar adjustments would be necessary if we were compounding ■

Converting Interest Rates Financial managers are often faced with a less-than-annual interest rate that they prefer to convert to a standard *equivalent annual rate.* For the sake of convenience, one may also wish to convert from an annual rate to an *equivalent less-than-annual rate.* (Daily interest rates will be much in evidence in the chapters on working capital.) A *simplistic approach* would be to say that 1% per month is equivalent to 12% per year or conversely, that 18% per year is equivalent to 1.5% per month. These statements are correct only if intrayear compounding does not apply.

There exists a more *sophisticated approach* that does consider intrayear compounding. *The sophisticated approach is more accurate than the simplistic approach.* Refer, if you will, to the example of intrayear compounding in the preceding section. Specifically, the monthly compounding of $1,000 at 1% per month for one year that generated a future value of $1,127 (rounded up from $1,126.80). The difference between the $1,000 cash flow and the FV of $1,127 is the interest, or $127. Dividing the $127 by $1,000 provides an equivalent annual interest rate of 12.7%. Equivalent is the key word here and it means that 1% compounded monthly is equal to 12.7% compounded annually. That is, $1,000(1.01)^{12} = $1,000(1.127)^1 = $1,127$. By the same token, 18% per year converts to an equivalent monthly rate of 1.39%. This means that 1.39% compounded monthly would generate as much interest income as 18% compounded annually.

The sophisticated approach for making interest rate conversions can be accomplished as follows:

Equation 3.9   Equivalent annual rate $= (1 + i_p)^m - 1$

Equation 3.10   Equivalent less-than-annual rate $= \sqrt[m]{1 + i_a} - 1$

Where:

i_p = Interest rate per less-than-annual time period
i_a = Interest rate per year
m = Number of time periods (compoundings) per year

Example A:
Convert a quarterly rate of 5% to an equivalent annual rate:
Equivalent annual rate $= (1.05)^4 - 1 = 21.6\%$ ■

Example B:
Convert an annual rate of 21% to an equivalent semiannual rate:
Equivalent semiannual rate $= \sqrt[2]{1.21} - 1 = 10\%$ ■

Despite its greater accuracy, we will seldom use the sophisticated approach for equivalent interest rates in this text for three reasons: (a) Conversion is rather difficult to perform unless one has a fairly sophisticated calculator; (b) the difference between sophisticated equivalent rates and those obtained with the simplistic approach are normally small, less than 1% on an annual basis; and (c) it is common practice to use the simplistic approach in business, tempered by the knowledge that such figures are only approximations.

For these reasons, we will usually rely upon simple multiplication and division to make our conversions. Thus, 1% a month will be 12% a year and 18% a year will be 1.5% a month.

Nevertheless, you should now realize that when, for instance, credit card charges of 1.5% are stated to be 18% per year, this is an oversimplification. It would be more accurate to say they are 18% a year before compounding. Actually, the sophisticated equivalent annual rate is about 19.6%. *In discussions throughout the remainder of this text all interest rate conversions will be simplistic unless otherwise indicated.*

Annuities   A term used often in connection with compound interest is *annuity. For the purposes of this text, we will define an annuity as a series of two or more equal cash flows that begin one period hence and recur regularly (e.g., every month, quarter, year, etc.) for a given length of time.*[2] Consider, for example, a five year, $4,000 annual annuity. This should be read as follows: a cash flow of $4,000 occurs one year from now, followed by $4,000 in two years, $4,000 in three years, $4,000 in four years, and $4,000 in five years. Carefully note that there are five cash flows in a five year annual annuity. Furthermore, the cash flows are equal ($4,000 each), they arise at the end of a period, and they are all separated by the same amount of time (one year). If any one of these conditions is not met, then we are not dealing with an annuity as defined earlier. A further example would be a two-year, $300, quarterly annuity. This would consist of eight $300 cash flows that begin in three months and recur every three months thereafter for two years.

There are many situations in finance and business that give rise to annuities. These would include installment loans, some insurance premiums, pension benefits, and preferred stock dividends. Furthermore, a cash flow sequence does not have to be called an annuity to be treated like one.

The compounding model (equation 3.2) and the discounting model (equation 3.6) can be simplified considerably when cash flows are in the form of an annuity. It is to our benefit to use these formulas because they are much easier to work with, and, in addition, we will encounter many annuities throughout the book.

Annuity Compounding   The annuity compounding formula is:

Equation 3.11 $FV = C\left[\dfrac{(1+i)^n - 1}{i}\right]$

Where C is the annuity cash flow and n is the life of the annuity or number of periods it lasts. Although this formula may not appear to be a great improvement, it becomes one when tables are provided for the values inside the brackets. Tables such as this are in appendix C, entitled annuity compound factor tables. The figures in the bodies of these tables are computations of $\dfrac{(1+i)^n - 1}{i}$ for many different values of i and n. These computations will hereafter be referred to as *annuity compound factors (ACF)* and they are used in much the same way we used CFs. In equation form, an ACF can be written as follows:

Equation 3.12 $ACF_{i/n} = \dfrac{(1+i)^n - 1}{i}$

---

[2]This particular annuity is often referred to as an "ordinary annuity." A less-common variety is the "annuity due." The only difference is that an annuity due has cash flows starting at the beginning of the period (immediately) and ending with a period to go.

Example: The ACF for 6 periods and an interest rate of 12% is found in appendix C to be 8.1152. This example can be written out mathematically as follows:

$$ACF_{.12/6} = \frac{(1.12)^6 - 1}{.12} = 8.1152$$

In operational form the annuity compounding equation 3.11 becomes:

Equation 3.13 $FV = C\,(ACF_{i/n})$

By using ACFs we can easily determine the FV of an annuity, amount of an annuity (C), interest rate, and even the life of an annuity (n) ■

Example: What is the FV of twenty $2,000 cash flows invested successively at the end of each of the next 20 years given an annual interest rate of 13%? This is definitely an annuity compounding problem and it can readily be solved with the aid of equation 3.13 as follows:

$$FV = \$2,000(ACF_{.13/20}) = \$2,000(80.947) = \$161,894$$

This is considerably faster than using the compounding model of the previous chapter and CFs. The use of ACFs to solve for interest rates can save even more time ■

Example: Suppose an individual wished to know the interest rate needed to convert an eight-year annual annuity of $5,000 to a FV of $61,500. Substituting into equation 3.13 we get:

$$\$61,500 = \$5,000\ ACF_{i/8}$$

Solving for $ACF_{i/8}$:

$$ACF_{i/8} = \frac{\$61,500}{\$5,000} = 12.3$$

We now know the ACF is 12.3 and we also know that it is for 8 periods. All we have to do now is find the interest rate in appendix C that corresponds to n = 8 and ACF = 12.3. First, locate 8 periods and move across the table until an ACF of 12.3 (or close to it) is located. The interest rate in question will be directly above this ACF. As you can see, it is 12% ■

Annuity Discounting   The annuity discounting formula is:

Equation 3.14 $PV = C \left[\dfrac{1 - \dfrac{1}{(1+i)^n}}{i} \right]$

Here again, C is the annuity cash flow and n is the life of the annuity, or number of periods over which it occurs. Appendix D contains tables with calculations of $\left[\dfrac{1 - \dfrac{1}{(1+i)^n}}{i} \right]$

for many different values of i and n. These computations will henceforth be called *annuity discount factors (ADF)*. Appendix D is used similarly to appendix C.

In equation form, an ADF can be written as follows:

Equation 3.15 $ADF_{i/n} = \dfrac{1 - \dfrac{1}{(1+i)^n}}{i}$

For instance, an ADF for 10 periods and an interest rate of 8% can be found in appendix D to equal 6.7101. This example can be written mathematically as follows:

$$\text{ADF}_{.08/10} = \frac{1 - \frac{1}{(1.08)^{10}}}{.08} = 6.7101$$

We can now develop an operational form of the annuity discounting equation 3.14 as follows:

Equation 3.16 $\text{PV} = \text{C(ADF}_{i/n})$

ADFs can be very helpful in solving for PV, i, C, and n. As an illustration, what is the PV of a ten-year, $3,500 quarterly annuity given an annual interest rate of 12% (3% per quarter)? This can easily be solved with the help of equation 3.16 as follows:

$$\text{PV} = \$3,500(\text{ADF}_{.03/40}) = \$3,500(23.1148) = \$80,902$$

As a further illustration, calculate the five-year, annual annuity cash flow that has a PV of $38,900, given an interest rate of 9%. Substituting into equation 3.16 we obtain:

$$\$38,900 = \text{C(ADF}_{.09/5})$$

Solve for C:

$$C = \frac{\$38,900}{\text{ADF}_{.09/5}} = \frac{\$38,900}{3.8897} = \$10,000$$

Interest rates and annuity life can be found just as easily as PV and C.

Perpetuities   Perpetuities are infinite-lived annuities. In other words, they meet all of the conditions for an annuity plus an additional requirement: that they go on forever. A monthly perpetuity of $500, for example, would consist of $500 cash flows occurring at the end of each month until the end of time. The FV of such a cash flow stream, compounded at any interest rate, would be infinitely large. However, discounting a perpetuity is a different matter. The discounting model applied to a perpetuity would look, in general, as follows:

$$\text{PV} = \frac{C}{(1+i)^1} + \frac{C}{(1+i)^2} + \frac{C}{(1+i)^3} + \ldots + \frac{C}{(1+i)^\infty}$$

By setting the last term, $\frac{C}{(1+i)^\infty}$, equal to zero and going through the appropriate mathematical operations, this formula can be simplified to:

Equation 3.17 $\text{PV} = \dfrac{C}{i}$

Equation 3.17 is the perpetuity discounting formula. As an illustration, what is the PV of an annual perpetuity of $2,000 given an annual interest rate of 8%? Substituting into equation 3.17 we get:

$$\text{PV} = \frac{\$2,000}{.08} = \$25,000$$

One can also solve for the C and i of a perpetuity.

There are very few loans and investments that qualify as perpetuities. There are, however, two good reasons for discussing perpetuities. First of all, an annuity does not always have to go on forever to use the perpetuity formula. At high interest rates and relatively distant time periods, cash flows will not have much PV anyway. For example, the discount factor for 15% and 40 periods, $DF_{.15/40}$, is only .0037. A sum of $1,000,000 in conjunction with such a small DF would only generate a PV of $3,700. Therefore, the perpetuity equation can provide very close approximations in cases where interest rates are high and the annuity extends relatively far into the future. An interest rate of 15% and a life of 40 years would certainly qualify here.

Time Value of Money   The time value of money was discussed briefly in chapter one. After having been exposed to compound interest it is easier to appreciate this concept. In general, the time value of money states that the timing of cash flows is very important. More specifically, it means that a dollar received today is superior to a dollar received in one year and the dollar received in one year is preferred to a dollar received in five years. The faster money is received, the sooner it can be invested. Viewed in a different way, a dollar paid today is inferior to a dollar paid in one year. In other words, interest can be earned on the delayed payment. The premise underlying these statements is the realistic assumption that interest rates are positive.

Time value of money is fundamentally related to compound interest. When compounding, the earlier cash flows will grow relatively more in value than later cash flows because they benefit from more compoundings (i.e., t is larger). By the same token, discounting reduces the value of earlier cash flows less than the value of later cash flows.

Applications of Compound Interest

The purpose of this section is twofold: 1) to show the numerous practical uses of compound interest and 2) to provide a system to facilitate compound interest problem solving.

All of the examples we will look at below involve contractual arrangements. They were selected for use in this introductory section due to their familiarity to students and relatively straightforward nature. In particular, the examples do not consider such complicating factors as taxes, uncertainty, and transactions costs.

When working with compound interest problems it is helpful to have a system or plan of action. Such a system will make the problems easier to solve and reduce the chance of careless errors. The plan of action to be used consists of four steps: problem orientation, translation, organization, and mathematics.

The first thing we need to ask is whether the situation is future or present oriented. This will indicate whether we should use the compounding model or the discounting model to solve the problem. As indicated earlier in the chapter, we will use discounting for all problems not clearly designated as future oriented. *Next, we must translate from the terminology used in the problem to the terminology used in the compound interest models.* For instance, what name or names within the problem are used for what we have been calling cash flows. *The third step is organizing the problem.* Included here are: setting up the equation, placement of the proper signs $(+, -)$ on the cash flows, and making certain that interest rates and time periods are consistent. *The final step in the solution to the problem rests with mathematics.*

Application A: Savings Accounts   George Myers and his wife Ann hope to have enough money saved in five years to be able to make a down payment on a house. They estimate that a suitable house will cost them $70,000 in five years. The Credit Union where Ann works has an account that pays 9% compound annual interest on funds left in for a minimum of one year. Their budget makes it most convenient for them to make deposits once a year and preferably in equal amounts. Furthermore, they wish to make only five deposits. Recognizing that they will need a down payment of at least 20%, what will the equal deposits have to be if they begin immediately?

Since the down payment is the focus of the problem and because it will take place later, we can safely assume a future orientation and will therefore use the compounding model.

We are trying to find five equal, annual deposits. Deposits are cash flows and in this case $C_1 = C_2 = \ldots = C_5 = C$. In order to solve for C we must have i, FV, and time periods (t_is). The down payment of $14,000 can serve as the FV because it is an objective future amount. C_1 will earn interest for five years ($t_1 = 5$), C_2 for four years ($t_2 = 4$), C_3 for three years ($t_3 = 3$), C_4 for two years ($t_4 = 2$), C_5 for one year ($t_5 = 1$), and i = 9%.

The time periods and interest rate are already consistent and all of the cash flows are in the same direction (i.e., outflows), which allows us to disregard signs.

Substituting into the compounding model we obtain:

$$\$14,000 = C(1.09)^5 + C(1.09)^4 + C(1.09)^3 + C(1.09)^2 + C(1.09)^1$$

In operational form:

$$\$14,000 = C(CF_{.09/5}) + C(CF_{.09/4}) + C(CF_{.09/3}) + C(CF_{.09/2}) + C(CF_{.09/1})$$

Through appropriate mathematical procedures the deposits are found to be equal to $2,146 ■

Application B: Stocks   A recent common stock analysis report prepared by the Buy Low–Sell High Investment firm includes a forecast for the shares of Consolidated Products, Inc. Buy Low's researchers predict that Consolidated's DPS will be $1.25, $1.50, $1.75, and $2.00 for each of the next four years, respectively. They go further and estimate a market price for the stock in four years of $20 per share. This is a sizeable increase over the current market price of $13. Putting aside the fact that such estimates are often unreliable, what compound annual rate of return would an investor earn on a share of Consolidated common stock if it were purchased for cash today and held for four years?

This particular problem does not have a clear focus on the present or future. As a matter of fact, situations calling for interest rates are often like this. As stated earlier, when facing a dilemma such as this we will proceed with the discounting model. We need to compute a rate of return (i.e., interest rate). Interest rates can be calculated with the discounting model if one knows PV, cash flows, and time periods. The current market price of $13 is a cash flow that can serve also as the PV because the PV of $13 paid today is $13. All four dividends and the selling price are cash "inflows" to the investor. The $1.25 cash flow ($C_1$) will be received in one year (t_1), followed by $1.50 ($C_2$) in two years ($t_2$), $1.75 ($C_3$) in three years ($t_3$), and $2.00 + $20.00 = $22.00 ($C_4$) in four years ($t_4$). No adjustments need to be made to the interest rate or time intervals since they are both annual. Furthermore every cash flow is a receipt so there is no problem with signs.

Substituting into the discounting model we obtain:

$$\$13 = \frac{\$1.25}{(1+i)^1} + \frac{\$1.50}{(1+i)^2} + \frac{\$1.75}{(1+i)^3} + \frac{\$22.00}{(1+i)^4}$$

In operational form:

$$\$13 = \$1.25\, DF_{i/1} + \$1.50\, DF_{i/2} + \$1.75\, DF_{i/3} + \$22.00\, DF_{i/4}$$

Following proper mathematical operations would show that the rate of return is approximately 22% ■

Application C: Bonds   A security salesperson has just contacted Mr. Wertheimer about the purchase of some corporate bonds due to be issued in a few days. The selling price would be determined at that time. The bonds pay a 12% coupon semiannually for 20 years. The par value of each bond is $1,000. Mr. Wertheimer considers these bonds to be sound investments, but would only purchase them if the price is low enough to provide an annual yield of 14%. What is the maximum price he should pay for a single bond?

Mr. Wertheimer's main concern is how much to pay for these bonds. Since he would pay for them today, his focus is on the present, thus discounting.

The maximum price to pay for a bond today is a present value. PV can be determined if we know cash flows, time periods, and interest rate. Cash flows include the interest coupon payments and the par value. The former are $.12 \times \$1,000 = \$120$ per year or $60 every six months and the latter is given as $1,000. The first coupon receipt (C_1) will be in one six-month period (t_1), the second (C_2) in two six-month periods (t_2), and so on until the last interest payment *and* par value (C_{40}) are obtained in 40 periods (t_{40}). The appropriate interest rate is 14%, not the 12% coupon, because this is what Mr. Wertheimer requires.

Mr. Wertheimer will be receiving all of the cash flows, thus making them inflows. Since they are all in the same direction, signs are not an issue. However, we must convert the 14% annual interest rate to a semiannual rate to coincide with the semiannual time periods. As a result, i will be 7%.

Substituting into the discounting model we obtain:

$$PV = \frac{\$60}{(1.07)^1} + \frac{\$60}{(1.07)^2} + \ldots + \frac{\$60}{(1.07)^{40}} + \frac{\$1,000}{(1.07)^{40}}$$

In operational form:

$$PV = \$60\, DF_{.07/1} + \$60\, DF_{.07/2} + \ldots + \$60\, DF_{.07/40} + \$1,000\, DF_{.07/40}$$

If computations are done correctly, the maximum purchase price (PV) should be $867. Note: appendix D, annuity discount factors, can be used to find the PV of the coupon payments ∎

Application D: Pensions   Mrs. Paultz, a widow who recently celebrated her 49th birthday, is planning her retirement. Even though she owns her house and is eligible for social security benefits, her present employer does not have a pension plan. Mrs. Paultz would like to receive an additional pension benefit of $6,000 per year beginning at age 65 and continuing through age 74. The $6,000 is to be received on her birthday each year. She could buy an annuity from a life insurance company, but prefers to set up her own plan at a local savings and loan that is paying 8% on retirement accounts. Assuming that she can begin the plan in one year (at age 50), what equal annual deposits must she make in order to carry out her plan? The last deposit is on her 64th birthday.

Here we have a problem that could be just as easily aproached with either compounding or discounting. There is no clear-cut focus. Therefore, following our previous guidelines we will solve it within a discounting framework.

Deposits are cash flows that can be calculated if we know the present value, time periods, and interest rate. It is not obvious from this problem as to what should serve as the PV. Note that the deposits plus compound interest should be just sufficient to cover the pension withdrawals. This means that the present value of these two offsetting series of cash flows must be *zero*. Therefore, the PV to be used is zero. We face two series of equal cash flows. The first series includes the unknown annual deposits ($C_1 = C_2 = \ldots = C_{15} = C$) that begin in one year ($t_1 = 1$) and end in fifteen years ($t_{15} = 64 - 49 = 15$). The second series consists of the annual $6,000 withdrawals ($C_{16}$ through C_{25}) that start in sixteen years ($t_{16} = 16$) and end in 25 years ($t_{25} = 74 - 49 = 25$). Interest rate i equals 8% per year.

Time periods and the interest rate are both in terms of years and therefore consistent. Cash flows, however, are mixed. To Mrs. Paultz the deposits are cash outflows and the pension withdrawals are inflows. As a consequence, they must have different signs. We will place negative signs on the cash outflows and positive signs on the cash inflows. This practice will be followed throughout the text when these situations arise.

Substituting into the discounting model we obtain:

$$0 = -\frac{C}{(1.08)^1} - \ldots - \frac{C}{(1.08)^{15}} + \frac{\$6,000}{(1.08)^{16}} + \ldots + \frac{\$6,000}{(1.08)^{25}}$$

In operational form:

$$0 = -C(DF_{.08/1}) - \ldots - C(DF_{.08/15}) + \$6,000\,DF_{.08/16} + \ldots + \$6,000\,DF_{.08/25}$$

Performing the necessary mathematics to solve for C would indicate that the annual deposits must be $1,483 ∎

Application E: Insurance   Upon graduating from college a student is contacted by a life insurance agent. The agent shows her a whole-life insurance plan that contains a number of different monetary series: premiums, paid-up insurance, cash values, face amount of insurance, dividends, etc. Special emphasis is placed on a particular cash value at age 62 (the student is currently age 22): there in boldface type is the number $200,000. This represents the amount the policyholder can obtain from the plan at that time without having to die. The agent says that this cash value can be obtained along with (but *not* in addition to) insurance for the paltry sum of $1,200 per year in premiums for forty years. In other words, the cash value at age 62 exceeds the premiums by $200,000 − 40 × $1,200 = $152,000. The student would get back over four times what she put in.

This particular student, however, is nobody's fool. After all, she has taken a course in financial management. Having some compound interest tables handy, the student proceeds to figure the compound annual rate of interest implied in the insurance plan. If we assume the premiums begin in one year (age 23) and stop at age 62, what is the annual interest rate she would earn? Since the insurance agent is emphasizing the cash value in the future, we will do likewise and work the problem with the compounding model.

Interest rate calculations require three things: (1) a future value, (2) cash flows, and (3) time periods. Let us make the $200,000 future cash value our FV. The premiums are the cash flows, and they are each $1,200. C_1 will earn interest for thirty-nine years ($t_1 = 62 - 23 = 39$), C_2 for thirty-eight years ($t_2 = 38$), and so on, ending with C_{40} earning interest for zero years ($t_{40} = 0$).

The periods are years and the interest rate is annual, so no adjustment is necessary here. From the student's standpoint, the cash flows are all expenditures, thus permitting us to disregard signs.

Substituting into the compounding model we obtain:

$$\$200,000 = \$1,200(1+i)^{39} + \$1,200(1+i)^{38} + \ldots + \$1,200(1+i)^0$$

In operational form:

$$\$200,000 = \$1,200CF_{i/39} + \$1,200CF_{i/38} + \ldots + \$1,200CF_{i/0}$$

Following correct mathematical procedures would generate an interest rate of about 6¼%. Note: the insurance premiums are a forty-year annuity, consequently we may use appendix C and equation 3.13 to solve this problem ∎

Application F: Loans   A prospective house buyer needs to borrow $75,000 in order to purchase a $100,000 house. American General Savings Association has agreed to loan the money with the following terms: twenty-five year maturity, 12% compound annual interest rate, and paid with equal monthly installments. What should the savings association require the payments to be? They will begin one month after the loan is made, which is typical for loans of this nature.

A case could be made that the loan negotiation is the focus of this problem. However, not everyone would agree to such an interpretation. We will conclude, therefore, that there is no focus and attack the problem with discounting.

Loan payments are cash flows. Cash flows can be readily found if one has a PV, time periods, and an interest rate. From the standpoint of the savings association, the monthly installment payments are receipts or cash inflows and there will be 12 months × 25 years = 300 of them. As a result of the cash flows being equal, $C_1 = C_2 = \ldots = C_{300} = C$. The $75,000 loan, even though it too is a cash flow, can take the role of PV because it is an objective current amount. The first installment will be received in one month ($t_1 = 1$), the second in two months ($t_2 = 2$) and so on, until the final one is received in three hundred months ($t_{300} = 300$). The annual interest rate required on the loan is 12%.

We need to convert the annual rate of interest to a monthly rate so that it will conform with the monthly cash flows. Twelve percent a year will then become 1% a month. Affixing the proper signs to the cash flows is of no concern since they are all receipts (to the lender).

Substituting into the discounting model we obtain:

$$\$75,000 = \frac{C}{(1.01)^1} + \frac{C}{(1.01)^2} + \ldots + \frac{C}{(1.01)^{299}} + \frac{C}{(1.01)^{300}}$$

In operational form:

$$\$75,000 = C(DF_{.01/1}) + C(DF_{.01/2}) + \ldots + C(DF_{.01/299}) + C(DF_{.01/300})$$

By performing the necessary mathematical operations to solve for C, we would determine a monthly loan payment of $790. Appendix D and equation 3.16 can be used here due to the fact that the loan payments are an annuity ∎

Conclusion

With a few exceptions, we are finished with the discussion of compound interest. However, we have only just begun our use of it. A knowledge of compound interest is fundamental to understanding much of the remaining text material.

It should be emphasized that most of the problems encountered in financial management that have to do with interest rates are handled with the discounting model. This results from the fact that most financial questions are either present oriented or there is no clear cut orientation. Compounding is more applicable to compound interest problems encountered with setting up savings plans, as the previous examples have shown. Accordingly, you should become well acquainted with the discounting model.

Summary

Interest rates are extremely important within the world of finance and in financial management decision making. It is a rare occasion that one can make a wise financial decision without some consideration of interest rates. The measurement of interest rates and the impact they have on other financial variables is accomplished with two models: simple interest and compound interest. Compound interest is the superior method and the one that is most accepted in the business and financial communities. Although often defined as "interest on interest," it is more accurate to describe compound interest as "interest on the outstanding balance."

There are two ways to apply compound interest: compounding (or future value) and discounting (or present value). However, the discounting approach is employed in the majority of cases where compound interest is called for. Not only can compound interest be used to compute interest rates, but also future values, present values, cash flows, and time periods. There are several special applications requiring compound interest, the most important of which is the annuity. There are a number of mathematical equations associated with interest rate computations. All of the key compound interest equations are summarized in table 3.2.

Table 3.2   Summary of Key Compound Interest Formulas

Future Value

General model

$$FV = C_1(1+i)^{t_1} + C_2(1+i)^{t_2} + \ldots + C_n(1+i)^{t_n}$$

or

$$FV = C_1(CF_{i/t_1}) + C_2(CF_{i/t_2}) + \ldots + C_n(CF_{i/t_n})$$

Single cash flow

$$FV = C(1+i)^t \quad \text{or} \quad FV = C(CF_{i/t})$$

Annuity cash flow

$$FV = C\left[\frac{(1+i)^n - 1}{i}\right] \quad \text{or} \quad FV = C(ACF_{i/n})$$

Present Value

General model

$$PV = \frac{C_1}{(1+i)^{t_1}} + \frac{C_2}{(1+i)^{t_2}} + \ldots + \frac{C_n}{(1+i)^{t_n}}$$

or

$$PV = C_1(DF_{i/t_1}) + C_2(DF_{i/t_2}) + \ldots + C_n(DF_{i/t_n})$$

Single cash flow

$$PV = \frac{C}{(1+i)^t} \quad \text{or} \quad PV = C(DF_{i/t})$$

Annuity cash flow

$$PV = C\left[\frac{1 - \dfrac{1}{(1+i)^n}}{i}\right] \quad \text{or} \quad PV = C(ADF_{i/n})$$

Interest rates give rise to the economic phenomenon of time value of money. The time value of money states that a dollar received today is more valuable than a dollar received in the future, because interest can be earned during the intervening time period ■

Key Terms/Concepts

Annuity	Compound interest	Intrayear compounding
Annuity compound factors	Discounting	Perpetuity
Annuity discount factors	Discount factors	Present value
Cash equivalent curves	Equivalent interest rates	Simple interest
Compounding	Future value	Time value of money
Compound factors		

Questions

1. Considering that compound interest is universally acknowledged to be a superior technique to simple interest, why would anyone knowingly use simple interest?

2. What is meant by the time value of money?

3. In what situations is compounding more suitable than discounting?

4. Explain the following description of a savings account, "interest is compounded daily and paid quarterly."

5. Under what circumstances must trial-and-error be used to solve for an interest rate?

6. Explain the difference between a perpetuity and an annuity.

7. Under what circumstances would a future cash flow and a present value produce a negative interest rate?

8. What is the relationship, if any, between the annuity discount factor table and the discount factor table?

9. Derive a compound interest formula that allows interest rates to vary from period to period.

10. What is the meaning of present value?

Problems

1. What will $5,000 invested today accumulate to in 8 years, given an interest rate of 8%?

2. Calculate the FV of $20,000 deposited in a savings account for five years at 9% interest. Recompute, assuming $8,000 is withdrawn from the account after two years.

3. How much must be invested at an interest rate of 8% in order to arrive at a future value of $10,000 in ten years?

4. A savings deposit of $4,000 must earn what interest rate to be able to grow to $12,000 in ten years?

5. How long will it take for $10,000 to accumulate to $50,000 if the interest rate is 10%? If the interest rate is 15%?

6. What is the FV of $12,000 invested for four years plus $9,000 invested for three years plus $6,000 invested for two years plus $3,000 invested for one year, all at 10% interest?

7. A cash flow of $10,000 invested for three years plus $15,000 invested for two years plus $20,000 invested for one year will accumulate to $57,100. What interest rate will make this possible?

8. What will two $10,000 cash flows accumulate to in ten years (combined total), if the first is invested today and the second is invested five years later? The interest rate is 6%.

9. What constant amount will have to be invested each year, beginning in one year, for six years, if a sum of $20,000 is to be accumulated at the end of that time? The applicable interest rate is 5%.

10. At simple interest, what is the future value of $50,000 invested for ten years. The applicable interest rate is 12%.

11. Determine the present value of a $25,000 cash flow to be received in fifteen years, given the following interest rates:

    a) 5%, b) 10%, c) 15%.

12. What is the present value of the following: $5,000 received in one year plus $10,000 received in two years plus $15,000 received in three years. The applicable interest rate is 12%.

13. A cash payment that must be made in six years has a current value of $1,500 based on an assumed interest rate of 13%. What is this cash payment?

14. What is the PV of $200 received at the end of each year, for the next five years, given an interest rate of 16%?

15. Calculate the interest rate to be earned on an investment of $50,000 that will generate cash receipts of $30,000 in one year plus $40,000 in two years.

16. Given an interest rate of 8%, what is the PV of the following cash flow stream: $25,000 *received* in two years plus $50,000 *paid* in four years plus $75,000 *received* in six years?

17. What rate of interest is necessary to equate cash receipts of $2,315 per year, for four years, to a $6,000 investment made today. You may assume that each of the $2,315 receipts occur at year end.

18. Six equal, annual cash flows are worth $5,000 today when discounted at an 18% rate of interest. What are these cash flows?

19. What is the present value of a $50 annual annuity for twenty-five years, using a 6% interest rate? Recompute using a rate of 10%.

20. An investor who receives a $14,860 cash flow in five years will earn what quarterly rate of return on an initial investment of $10,000? What is the equivalent annual rate of return?

21. Calculate the FV of $2,000 remaining in a savings account for five years, assuming that the interest rate will be 12% a year, but compounded: quarterly, semiannually, monthly.

22. Two percent a month is a sophisticated equivalent annual interest rate of what?

23. What equal annual payments are necessary to pay off a $1,000,000 loan over ten years, given an interest rate of: 15%, 12%, 18%?

24. Cash flows of $27,175 for ten years will provide what rate of return on an investment of $200,000?

25. A car that sells for $11,000 today, will cost approximately how much in five years if the inflation rate turns out to be 8%?

26. Based on an annual interest rate of 15%, figure the equal monthly savings deposits necessary to accumulate $8,000 in five years.

27. A $15,000 savings deposit would benefit the most from which of the following: 20% simple interest for five years or 12% compound interest for the same time span?

28. The earnings per share on U.S. Paper Company's common stock have grown from $1.20 to $3.00 over a six year period. This translates into what compound annual growth rate?

29. An investment of $500,000 is expected to provide cash benefits of $49,707 per year. How many years must this annuity be realized before the investment will earn a rate of return equal to 7%?

30. Determine the interest rate that equates a present value of $4,360 to cash flows of $1,000 in one year plus $2,000 in five years plus $1,000 in seven years plus $4,000 in nine years.

31. A local bank is offering certificates of deposit that pay 16% annual interest, compounded quarterly. What is the sophisticated equivalent annual interest rate on these certificates?

32. Find the present value (today) of $1,000 received each year, beginning in ten years and lasting for five years. There are a total of six cash flows and the applicable interest rate is 10%.

33. Calculate the equal monthly payments on a five year, $12,000 car loan. The interest rate is 15% per annum.

34. An individual can invest $50,000 today and would like to have $70,000 in four years. Given an interest rate of 15%, how much money can this investor withdraw from the investment in two years and still have $70,000 left two years later?

35. What is the most you would be willing to pay for the right to receive $1,000 per year, for twelve years, plus a $10,000 lump sum at the end of the twelfth year? You could earn 8% on your money elsewhere.

36. Given an annual interest rate equal to 18%, compute the present cost of sixty consecutive $300 monthly rental payments.

37. An annual interest rate of 18% is what sophisticated equivalent semiannual rate?

38. Determine the final payment on a $3,000,000 loan that is to be repaid over seven years. The first six payments will be $545,000 each and the interest rate on the loan is 14%.

39. A local savings and loan association is paying 8% interest on passbook savings accounts. A depositor can place $500 in this account today, $1,000 in one year, and $1,500 in two years. How much money will be in the account in five years, assuming there are no withdrawals? How much of this total is interest?

40. Fifth National Bank has agreed to lend Hopeful Cosmetics $1,450,000 at an annual interest rate of 20%. The loan is to be repaid in equal quarterly installments over six years. What are these payments? How would a loan maturity of eight years affect the loan payments?

41. The cash flows shown below are to be discounted back to the present (time period 0) at an interest rate of 10%.

Time period	1	2	3	4	5	6	7	8	9	10
Cash flow	$1,000	$1,000	$1,500	$1,500	($4,000)	$2,000	$2,000	$1,500	$1,500	$5,000

42. Derive a cash equivalent curve for a current cash flow of $25,000 and an interest rate of 12%. The time span to be covered by the curve is zero to ten years.

43. Mr. Wilson is planning his retirement. Currently 54 years of age, he plans to retire at age 65 and would like to draw a pension of $12,000 per year until the age of 80, should he live so long. Assuming a guaranteed interest rate of 10%, find the savings annuity that will assure Mr. Wilson of his pension. The savings will begin on his 55th birthday and end on his 64th birthday. The pension annuity will begin on his 65th birthday and end on his 79th birthday.

44. Find the simple annual interest rate that would generate the same monthly car payment as a 12% compound annual interest rate. The loan is for $10,000 and is to be repaid in 60 monthly installments.

45. A bond is an investment that pays a regular cash flow (interest coupons) and a lump sum cash flow (par value) at maturity. The coupon interest, par value, and maturity are contractual. Therefore, only the price of the bond can change. What price would a bond have to sell for to provide a buyer with a 14% annual rate of return. The bond has a $10,000 par value and pays $450 in interest semiannually until it matures in 20 years.

46. It is often necessary to convert lump sum cash flows or irregular cash flow series into annuities. Convert the following irregular cash flow series into an annuity using a 12% interest rate.

Time period	1 year	2 years	3 years
Cash flow	$10,000	$50,000	$100,000

47. J. M. Enterprises is a small real estate developer. The company needs to acquire, without undue delay, a $320,000 loan to purchase part interest in a lucrative real estate venture. Due to the nature of the venture, J. M. would prefer to repay the loan and interest with graduated payments. A request for the funds has been made from a wealthy local financier. J. M. says that in return for a $320,000 loan they are prepared to pay the financier $100,000 in one year, $200,000 in three years, and $300,000 in five years. Before accepting the deal, the financier wants to compute the compound annual interest rate he would earn. a) Solve for this interest rate, and b) turn this unusual cash flow stream into a five-year annuity.

48. Ms. Myers, a university student, has just inherited $15,000 from her uncle. Her business professor has advised her to place the money in a bank certificate of deposit. She will graduate in two and one-half years and would like to use the principle plus interest for traveling. Metropolitan First State Bank is offering 30 month C.D.s that pay 15% annual interest, compounded monthly. If Ms. Myers buys one of these today, how much can she expect to have available for traveling after graduation? If, after 18 months, she found that she could earn 20% on money market funds, would it be wise for her to cash in her C.D. at a penalty of $1,000?

49. Mr. Valero recently won $200,000 in the Kansas Lottery. After some deliberation, he has decided to purchase a guaranteed annuity from a life insurance company. Currently 50 years old, Mr. Valero would like to begin receiving the annuity at age 60 and annually thereafter up to and including his 73d birthday. Based upon a guaranteed interest rate of 8%, how much can the insurance company promise Mr. Valero? He will turn the entire $200,000 over to the insurance company today and will make no further payments.

50. If you sold a share of stock today for $56 that was purchased for $13 six years ago, what annual rate of return did you earn?

51. What is the present value of a perpetual, annual cash flow of $2,000 given an interest rate of: 5%, 10%, 15%, and 20%?

52. The present value of a $10,000 annual annuity is $61,445 when discounted at an interest rate of 10%. How many years will this annuity last?

53. In order to accumulate $141,930 in nine years, what interest rate would a saver need to earn on nine annual savings deposits of $10,000 each?

54. Would you be willing to pay $5,000 today for the right to receive $100,000 in forty years, given that you could earn 12% interest during the intervening period of time? You may assume that there is no risk associated with receiving the $100,000.

55. A business loan of $50,000 is to be repaid (principal plus interest) in equal annual installments of $6,900 for ten years. What interest rate is being charged on this loan? Recompute, assuming the payments are for fifteen years instead of ten.

56. When an installment loan was originally extended, it had a face value of $30,000. It carries an interest rate of 15% and requires equal annual payments of $5,000. There are four payments remaining on the loan with the next payment due in one year. Based upon this information, compute the current loan balance.

57. Mr. and Mrs. Oser would like to begin a college fund for their daughter, who just turned eight years old. They estimate annual college expenses of $7,500 for four years. Furthermore, all of the expenditure will be made at the beginning of each school year. Assuming they will be able to earn 10% on their money, how much must they set aside each year, starting today and continuing through their daughter's 18th birthday (which just happens to coincide with the first day of her freshman year).

58. A loan of $25,000 is to be repaid over 15 years in equal monthly installments of $350. (a) Determine the monthly interest rate on this loan. (b) Convert the monthly rate to an equivalent annual interest rate.

59. The annual interest rate on a $50,000 loan is 18%. The loan is to be repaid in equal monthly installments over 5 years. What are these payments?

60. An $80,560 investment is expected to generate the following sequence of cash inflows:

Year 1	Year 2	Year 3	Year 4	Year 5	Year 6
$9,000	$9,000	$9,000	$9,000	$9,000	$109,000

What is the expected rate of return on this investment?

Selected References

Bierman, Harold, Jr., and Seymour Smidt, *The Capital Budgeting Decision,* 6th ed. New York: Macmillan, 1984.
Cissell, Robert, and Helen Cissell, *Mathematics of Finance,* 5th ed. Boston: Houghton Mifflin, 1978.
Clayton, Gary E., and Christopher B. Spivey, *The Time Value of Money,* Philadelphia: W. B. Saunders Company, 1978.
Hart, William, *Mathematics of Investment,* Lexington, Mass.: D. C. Heath, 1975.

Finance in the News

If you had $1,000 to invest, would you prefer to obtain five percent compound interest for three years or six percent for two years? It all depends on which would give you the higher return, and to calculate the return you need to have an understanding of compound interest. The following Wall Street Journal article explains the importance of compounding to savers and investors.

Compounding: It's Boring But a Wonder

John Maynard Keynes supposedly called it magic. One of the Rothschilds is said to have proclaimed it the eighth wonder of the world. Today people continue to extol its wonder and its glory.

The object of their affection: compound interest, a subject that bores or confuses as many people as it impresses.

Yet understanding compound interest can help people calculate the return on savings and investments, as well as the cost of borrowing. These calculations apply to almost any financial decision, from the reinvestment of dividends to the purchase of a zero-coupon bond for an individual retirement account.

Simply stated, compound interest is "interest on interest." Interest earned after a given period, for example, a year, is added to the principal amount and included in the next period's interest calculation.

"With all the time you spend working, saving, borrowing and investing," says Richard P. Brief, a New York University business professor, "one could argue that the calculations (of compound interest) ought to be understood by most people. And it is within reach of most people."

The power of compound interest has intrigued people for years. Early in the last century, an English astronomer, Francis Baily, figured that a British penny invested at an annual compound interest of 5% at the birth of Christ would have yielded enough gold by 1810 to fill 357 million earths. Benjamin Franklin was more practical. At his death in 1790, he left 1,000 pounds each to the cities of Boston and Philadelphia on the condition they wouldn't touch the money for 100 years. Boston's bequest, which was equivalent to about $4,600, ballooned to $332,000 by 1890.

But savers and investors don't have to live to 100 to reap its benefits.

Consider an investment with a current value of $10,000 earning annual interest of 8%. After a year the investment grows to $10,800 (1.08 times $10,000). After the second year it's worth $11,664 (1.08 times $10,800). After three more years, the investment grows to $14,693.

The same concept applies to consumer borrowing. A $10,000 loan, with an 8% interest charge compounded annually, would cost $14,693 to repay in a lump sum after five years.

More-frequent compounding also results in higher annual yields. For instance, if an 8% annual interest rate is compounded quarterly, the principal would grow by 2% compounded every three months. Using the earlier example, the $10,000 investment that grew to $14,693 after five years of annual compounding would grow to $14,859 with quarterly compounding. Monthly compounding would give $14,898 and weekly compounding would result in $14,914. This helps explain why, for example, one bank can offer a savings product with a higher nominal interest rate than the competition, but a lower effective annual yield. It simply compounds less frequently.

Computers and calculators with built-in formulas make solving compound-interest problems relatively easy. Calculators without the built-in formula ought to have an exponent key (see table). People can also use compound-interest tables, which, along with explanations of interest-rate calculations, can be found in a free booklet published by Federal Reserve Bank of New York's public information department, 33 Liberty St., New York, N.Y. 10045.

Figuring the Return

The formula for annual compound interest is $P \times (1 + r)^n$. P is the principal, r is the interest rate and n is the number of years.

Here are the values of $10,000 invested at 8% or 12% over various periods:

Years	8%	12%
5	$ 14,693	$ 17,623
10	21,589	31,058
20	46,610	96,463
40	217,245	930,510
100	21,997,613	835,222,660

Investors and savers can also take a rule-of-thumb shortcut to determine how long it would take to double a sum of money at a given interest rate with annual compounding: Divide 72 by the rate. For example, the $10,000 investment yielding 8% a year would double in about nine years (72 divided by eight).

But people should be aware that inflation compounds, too. Unless inflation disappears, that projected $20,000 investment nine years from now will be worth something less than that in today's dollars.

4

Risk, Return, and Valuation

Overview

In the preceding chapter we discussed the mathematical properties of interest rates. However, a knowledge of interest rate mathematical properties and derivations is not sufficient for a complete understanding of this important topic. The major objective of this chapter is to go behind the scenes and explore in detail the economic forces that determine the overall level of interest rates as well as the differences among rates. In the process, we will discover the important role that risk plays in interest rate determination. We will also spend a considerable amount of time discussing the meaning of risk and ways to measure it. The chapter concludes with a description of common stock valuation; that is, how the market price of a corporation's common stock is determined ■

Objectives

By the end of the chapter the student should be able to:

1. Explain how the interest rate is the link between assets and liability/equity claims
2. Discuss the determinants of interest rates, including inflation premium, time preference premium, tax premium, and risk premium
3. Explain how the demand for and supply of funds determine the interest rate
4. Provide a financial definition of risk
5. Discuss the trade-off or association between risk and return
6. Explain how the standard deviation of IRR and risk are related, and be able to calculate standard deviations, expected values, and probabilities
7. Discuss the meaning and implications of portfolio risk
8. Calculate expected values and standard deviations of portfolios, and managerially interpret the results
9. Explain the relationships between the capital asset pricing model, market risk, Beta, and the security market line
10. Compute and interpret CAPM problems
11. Explain how the risk-profit ratio is used
12. Explain the basic concept of security valuation and calculate common stock value using the stock valuation model

Introduction

To carry out its role as a provider of products and/or services, a corporation will find it necessary to have the use of various kinds of assets, such as: inventory, equipment, and buildings. Asset management is the process of acquiring, modifying, and combining assets, and the subject of much of this text. It is a fact of corporate life that no assets can be acquired without financing. In balance sheet terminology, this financing is described with rather impersonal names, such as: accounts payable, bonds, retained earnings, and common stock. Behind these balance sheet names, however, stand a wide array of investors who have entrusted their money to corporate management. For a corporation to survive, its management should see that these investors are taken care of. For a corporation to prosper, common stock investors (owners) must be especially well taken care of. It is the premise of this text, and financial management in general, that corporations and corporate assets are created and managed solely for the benefit of investors, the owners in particular. To summarize, corporations obtain financing from investors for the purpose of acquiring assets. These assets, in turn, are to be used in the interest of investors.

The link between assets and the liability and equity claims of investors is the interest rate.[1] Investors place their money in the care of corporate management because they expect to be compensated for doing so. Or, to use a popular phrase, they expect a return on their investment. Investor compensation comes in the form of an interest rate or a rate of return. For their part, assets must generate sufficient earnings to pay these interest rates. In more general terms, we can make the following statement: *corporate management should take interest rates into account when making decisions about the acquisition, modification, or combination of assets.*

Given the central importance accorded to interest rates in financial management, it is well worth our while to examine them in more detail. Two interest rate related topics will be examined at length in this chapter: risk and valuation. Risk is a determinant of interest rates while interest rates are a factor in security (e.g., common stock) valuation ■

Determinants of Interest Rates

To a corporation or other borrower, an interest rate is the cost of financing. From an investor's standpoint, an interest rate is the price that is charged for invested funds. Of course, the interest rate itself is not a monetary figure but simply a percentage. However, it becomes a monetary figure when multiplied by a monetary value (i.e., principal of a loan).

A question that persons in finance often encounter is, why are interest rates so "high"? It should be noted that rarely is one ever asked to explain "low" interest rates. Another question that arises often is, why are there so many different interest rates in existence? In very general terms, interest rates are determined in the financial marketplace just as prices of goods are determined in the marketplace for goods and services, by the forces of supply and demand. But this statement is too general for our purposes. What are the specific underlying determinants? It will be easier to answer this question if we approach it from the investor's viewpoint.

---

[1] In actuality, there will be several interest rates because there are several investors. Interest rates is used here in the broad sense to include stock dividends.

Investors advance money to corporations, governments, and consumers through such devices as loans and common stock, with the expectation that they will be repaid at some future date or dates. For providing this valuable service, what do investors require in return? They certainly do not expect to be worse off when they get their original investment back than when it was first advanced. One thing that can cause them to be worse off would be a reduction in the purchasing power of money (inflation) while the investment is outstanding. For instance, a loan of $10,000 that is repaid after prices have increased 8%, would only buy about 92% as much as it could have when the loan was first extended. An investor who anticipates the 8% inflation in advance will try to offset it with an 8% interest rate. This is called an *inflation premium*.

In addition to an inflation premium, most investors would demand some compensation for having to wait to spend their money. Economists often refer to this behavior as "sacrificed consumption." The theory being, that most persons prefer current consumption to saving and consuming later. Therefore, they must be induced to save (i.e., invest) by a monetary reward. We will refer to this reward as a *time preference premium*. Although it is impossible to measure the time preference premium exactly, most experts are of the opinion that it has historically varied between 1% and 4%. The underlying forces that bring about change in this premium are rather complex and much in dispute. Included among them are: Federal Reserve monetary policy, economic growth, and the national savings rate. This premium is also often referred to as the "real interest rate."

So far we have learned that investors want an interest rate that includes an inflation premium and a time preference premium. Due to the fact that these are positive, a further complication arises. Federal income tax law states that, in most cases, interest income is also taxable income. Consequently, if an investor requires an interest rate of 12% to compensate for time preference and expected inflation, he will have to bargain for even more in order to pay income taxes. In other words, a *tax premium* is now required. For instance, if that same investor's tax rate is 20% then he will need an interest rate of 15% before taxes in order to receive 12% after taxes (the 3% tax premium going to the government).[2]

To ask an investor to take an interest rate that is less than what he requires for sacrificed consumption, inflation, and taxes, would be asking him or her to invest at a loss.

At any given point in time, individual investors will hold a wide range of views about the inflation outlook. Moreover, they can be expected to have differing time preferences and a multitude of income tax rates. Despite these varied circumstances and different outlooks, a consensus will be reached as to the size of each of these premiums. This consensus will be worked out through the interaction of supply and demand forces in the financial marketplace; investors comprise the supply of investable funds while corporations and other borrowers make up the demand for funds. Using a bit of imagination, this situation would appear as shown in figure 4.1.

---

[2]The interest rates on tax-free securities, such as municipal bonds, would not contain a tax premium and, all other things being equal, are noticeably lower than other rates.

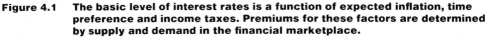

Figure 4.1   The basic level of interest rates is a function of expected inflation, time preference and income taxes. Premiums for these factors are determined by supply and demand in the financial marketplace.

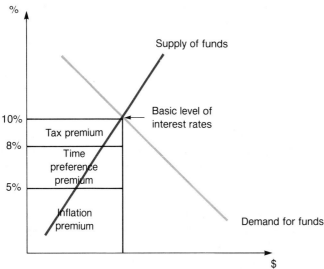

According to the hypothetical situation depicted in figure 4.1, investors have the market-determined right to receive a time preference premium of 3%, an inflation premium of 5%, and a tax premium of 2%, for a combined market interest rate of 10%. Unfortunately, no one can tell exactly what each of these premiums are in an actual situation since they are lumped together in an interest rate. The important thing to know is that they do in fact exist and they are applicable to almost all loan and investment interest rates.

Together, these three premiums comprise the base or minimum interest rate upon which all interest rates are built. A rational investor would not be satisfied with a lower rate, and any borrower could not pay less than this rate. Furthermore, a change in any one of these premiums could lead to a change in the overall level of interest rates. Should the market reach a consensus that inflation will be higher than previously thought, for example, the inflation premium will rise thereby pushing up all interest rates. *Moreover, this most basic of all interest rates should be used to measure and account for the time value of money.*

There is one other major determinant of interest rates—risk. Should there be any uncertainty that the original investment and/or interest will not be repaid in full, the typical investor will demand some further compensation, that is, a *risk premium*. This premium is added onto the three previously mentioned premiums. The greater the risk or uncertainty, the larger the risk premium must be. This is shown in figure 4.2.

Figure 4.2   In perfect financial markets, interest rates should vary only with respect to an investment's degree of risk.

Interest rate

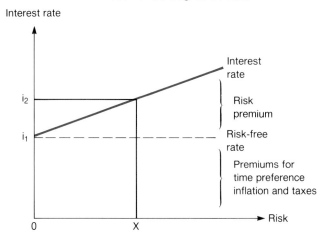

An examination of figure 4.2 shows that when risk is zero, investors only require compensation for time preference, expected inflation, and income taxes, or interest rate i_1. In other words, the base interest rate is also the *risk-free interest rate.* As risk increases, say to point X, the interest rate increases to i_2 because of the additional risk premium (i_2 minus i_1).

Investments and loans possess varying degrees of risk. Government bonds, for example, are less risky than corporate bonds, which are less risky than common stocks. Consequently, different risk premiums would be required on these securities and, thus, different interest rates. *In perfectly competitive financial markets, one could say that interest rates should differ from one investment to another strictly on the basis of risk premiums.*[3]

In summary, interest rates are determined by the supply and demand interaction of investors and borrowers in the financial markets. Four major economic factors influence interest rates: inflation expectations, time preference, income tax rates, and risk. Premiums for the first three determine the base (risk-free) "level" of interest rates, whereas risk premiums explain most of the "variation" in rates.

Another popular name for interest rates, and one that emphasizes the demands that investors make upon assets, is *required rate of return* (*RRR*). We will use this term extensively throughout the asset management section of the text. In the liability and equity management portion of the text it is important that we look upon interest rates as a cost to the corporation. Therefore, we will use the phrase *cost of financing* as a substitute for interest rates on many occasions.

All of these various relationships are displayed in table 4.1.

---

[3]Financial markets are not completely perfect. Tax laws, transactions costs, and government regulations all create havoc with interest rates. However, such distortions do not significantly alter the basic premise that interest rate differences are mainly attributable to risk.

Table 4.1 Interest Rate Terminology

Interest rate = Time preference premium + Expected inflation premium + Income tax premium + Risk premium

Interest rate = Risk-free interest rate + Risk premium

Interest rate = Required rate of return = Cost of financing

We now know that an investor's required rate of return (interest rate) is comprised of the risk-free interest rate and a risk premium.[4] What we do not know, yet, is how an investor goes about assigning numerical values to these two items. With regard to the risk-free interest rate, this is a relatively easy task. On any given date, the risk-free interest rate can be approximated reasonably well by the interest rate on U. S. Government Treasury Bills. These investments are probably the safest in the world. Assigning numerical values to risk premiums is much more difficult to do, simply because one must first define and measure risk. It is this topic to which we now turn.[5]

Risk

Corporate managers, and financial managers in particular, would be well advised to gain an understanding of investment risk. A survey of investment risk follows.

Risk Defined There is no disputing the fact that risk is brought about by uncertainty. Beyond this basic agreement, however, risk often means different things to different persons. To some, it is simply the fear of the unknown. To others, it comes about through change or instability. Risk to many persons is the danger of losing something of value, such as money. Fear of the unknown, danger of loss, and instability are all useful descriptions for the topic we will now cover. There are doubtless other ways to define risk, but these terms should provide us with a basic understanding.

It is difficult to discuss the concept of risk without also mentioning the persons who are involved with it. We have already learned that risk means different things to different persons, but there are further complications. Individuals are not only affected psychologically

[4]The marketability of an investment could also be included among the list of interest rate determinants. Many investors value the ability to liquidate their investments as the need arises. Consequently, they demand a marketability premium for investments that are not readily marketable, such as common stock in a small, obscure corporation.

[5]The required rate of return is the minimum that an investor will expect from an investment. A higher interest rate would certainly be much better.

by risk, they are often in a position to create it by their actions. For example, many persons are afraid of being in an automobile accident. However, they can avoid this risk by deciding never to ride in automobiles. The complex relationship between risk and persons does not end here.

Let us assume that there are two investors who are faced with the same investment decision. They have been given equal information and they define risk in the same way. It is quite possible that these two investors would not measure the same degree of risk in connection with the investment. In fact, one of them may see no risk at all, while the other perceives a substantial element of risk. Such a divergence of opinion could happen because of differences in intelligence, method of risk measurement, personal experience, or intuition. Moreover, even if these two investors do measure the same amount of risk, they may react differently. Differences in age, wealth, job security, or personality can all lead to such behavior. The point is, risk is a very complex subject. The present discussion will only touch on the major risk issues. The psychological and sociological factors are left to be explained by experts in those fields. As you read the material in this section, keep in mind that the subject matter is the object of much controversy.[6]

Risk-Return Trade-Off   Risk is very much a personal matter. Nevertheless, there appear to be some predominant human characteristics that will allow us to generalize about risk and deal with it. The most important of these are: 1) intelligent persons are, as a rule, averse to risk. In other words, the less risk they are exposed to the better off they are, all other things the same; 2) an attempt is usually made, either objectively or subjectively, to measure risk; 3) a potential reward must be offered to these rational, risk-averse individuals before they will accept risk—the size of the reward will vary with the degree of risk; 4) a potential increase in wealth is a generally accepted reward for encountering risk. We are concerned here with the risk behavior of a particular group of persons (corporate investors) to a particular type of risk (investing in corporations).

Investors, being *risk-averse,* demand to be rewarded for incurring risk. This reward is in the form of an interest rate risk premium that, when combined with the base or risk-free interest rate, becomes the required rate of return (RRR). An increase in the degree of risk will lead to a higher RRR as investors raise their risk premiums. *Thus, there exists a trade-off between risk and required rate of return.* What is the nature of this trade-off that investors make between risk and return? The risk-return trade-off depends to a large extent upon investor attitudes toward profits and losses (i.e., changes in investor wealth).[7] Considering that these attitudes often vary from one investor to another, we can expect risk-return trade-offs to do likewise. Figure 4.3 reveals the risk-return trade-offs of two common stock investors (A and B). When risk is zero, both investors are willing to accept the market-determined risk-free rate of interest (in this case 8%). As risk increases from left to right, each investor's RRR rises as they demand more return in exchange for accepting more risk. However, their

---

[6]A reading list at the end of this chapter contains several references to the subject of risk.

[7]Investor attitudes toward risk and return fall under the subject of utility theory. For additional insight into this issue see M. Friedman and L. J. Savage, "The Utility Analysis of Choices Involving Risk," *The Journal of Political Economy* (August 1948), pp. 279–304 and James C. Van Horne, *Financial Management and Policy,* 6th ed., Prentice-Hall, Inc. Englewood Cliffs, New Jersey, 1983.

Figure 4.3   Risk-return trade-offs for investors with different attitudes toward risk

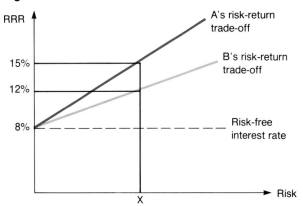

attitudes toward profits and losses are not identical. Investor A is more risk averse than investor B, as indicated by the greater slope of A's risk-return trade-off line. For example, at a risk level of X, A has an RRR of 15% (a risk premium of 7%) while B demands an RRR of 12% (a risk premium of only 4%). Of course, they would each gladly accept higher returns.

We will make two final observations about the RRR before moving on. *Just because investors demand or require a specific interest rate is no guarantee that they will receive it, as long as risk is involved.* A risk premium is more like a promise or expectation than a guarantee. *In fact, common stock investors may realize a rate of return far in excess of their required rate of return.* On the other hand, a company that fails to meet the RRRs of its investors is asking for serious trouble.

The idea that investors account for risk by means of an interest-rate risk premium is not a universally held opinion. Some financial experts find conceptual flaws with this approach.[8] While this may be true, the other methods of risk adjustment have even more shortcomings.

We will now turn our attention to the measurement of risk.

Risk Measurement

When investors advance funds to a corporation, they are really investing in the firm's assets. Consequently, investors look to these assets, either singly or in combination, for their salvation. The future cash flows generated by the turnover of current assets and the depreciation on capital assets is used, by and large, to repay the investments in those assets. The future profits that are earned on assets are used to pay investors' required rates of return. Operating under the reasonable assumption that profitable assets are also being turned over, it follows that investors should focus their attention on asset earnings potential. (It will simplify our discussion of risk measurement if, rather than using dollars of profit, we instead

---

[8]See Alexander A. Robichek and Stewart C. Myers, "Conceptual Problems in the Use of Risk-Adjusted Discount Rates," *Journal of Finance* (December 1966), pp. 727–30.

use rates of profit so as to correspond with investor required "rates" of return.) The rate of profit from assets shall henceforth be called *internal rate of return* (*IRR*).

In the unlikely event that asset profitability could be estimated with 100% accuracy, there would be no risk for investors. They would therefore be content with an IRR equal to the risk-free rate of interest. Most of the time, however, investors are uncertain as to how lucrative an asset or assets will be. Competition, government regulation, business cycles, and labor relations, among other factors, can affect earnings in unpredictable and important ways. It is not at all rare to find, for example, an asset with potential internal rates of return that range from a -100% to a $+100\%$. Asset IRRs are, thus, in the words of a statistician, random variables. *It is the uncertainty of, or variability in, asset profitability that creates risk for investors, and the greater the uncertainty, the greater the degree of risk.* Investments are risky because assets are risky. *It is also generally true that, asset profitability becomes more difficult to estimate as we look further into the future.*

The risk measurement techniques presented in the next section are generalized so that we may focus on the overall aspects of this topic. In particular, risk measurement will be affected by whether or not an investor is examining common stock or debt securities, long-term or short-term debt instruments, or loans backed by collateral or not backed by collateral, to name a few factors. These particulars will be overlooked for the time being.

Asset Risk in Isolation   Many financial experts believe that the risk of a business asset can be measured with the *variance* (*Var*) or *standard deviation* (*SD*) of the asset's IRR.[9] The same can be said for a group of assets or even an entire company of assets. The variance is a statistical measure of the variability (i.e., uncertainty) of a random variable around the variable's average or *expected value* (*E*). The standard deviation is the square root of the variance, making it a more practical statistic. When the different outcomes of a random variable are given in the form of a probability distribution, the standard deviation can be calculated by means of the following three equations:

Equation 4.1 $$E(X) = \sum_{i=1}^{n} P_iX_i = P_1X_1 + P_2X_2 + \cdots + P_nX_n$$

Equation 4.2 $$Var(X) = \sum_{i=1}^{n} P_i[X_i - E(X)]^2 = P_1[X_1 - E(X)]^2$$
$$+ P_2[X_2 - E(X)]^2 + \cdots + P_n[X_n - E(X)]^2$$

Equation 4.3 $$SD(X) = \sqrt{Var(X)}$$

Where:

$E(X)$ = the expected value, mean, or average of the variable X
$Var(X)$ = Variance of X
$SD(X)$ = Standard deviation of X
n = Total number of outcomes
X_i = Value of the i_{th} outcome
P_i = Probability of the i_{th} outcomes

---

[9]The material in this section assumes the reader is knowledgeable in elementary statistics.

Application: Ace Office Furniture, Inc., sells office furniture in the Cleveland area. Management wishes to add personal computers to the product line, but to do so would require an $800,000 inventory of computers and spare parts. Based on the computer inventory's IRR probability distribution displayed below, what level of risk would an investor in this asset face?

Table 4.2   IRR Probability Distribution of Computer Inventory

Outcome	IRR	Probability
A	−20%	.05
B	−10%	.10
C	0%	.10
D	+10%	.25
E	+25%	.30
F	+35%	.20

There are six potential IRRs associated with the computer inventory. Outcome E has the greatest probability of occurring and A the lowest. It is possible to calculate the standard deviation of these IRRs with equations 4.1, 4.2, and 4.3 by substituting IRR for X.

$$E(IRR) = \sum_{i=1}^{n} P_i IRR_i = .05(-.20) + .10(-.10) + .10(0) + .25(.10) + .30(.25)$$
$$+ .20(.35) = .15$$

$$Var(IRR) = \sum_{i=1}^{n} P_i [IRR_i - E(IRR)]^2$$

$$Var(IRR) = .05(-.20-.15)^2 + .10(-.10-.15)^2 + .10(0-.15)^2 + .25(.10-.15)^2$$
$$+ .30(.25-.15)^2 + .20(.35-.15)^2$$

$$Var(IRR) = .05(.1225) + .10(.0625) + .10(.0225) + .30(.01) + .20(.04) = .02625$$

$$SD(IRR) = \sqrt{var(IRR)} = \sqrt{.02625} = .162$$

We now have a measure of profitability: $E(IRR) = 15\%$ and risk: $SD(IRR) = 16.2\%$ for Ace Office Furniture's computer inventory. Much more information can be obtained from these two figures if we can assume that the inventory IRRs are represented by a continuous normal probability distribution, as shown in figure 4.4.

Here we have a normal probability distribution of the variable IRR with an expected value of .15 and a standard deviation of .162. According to the standardized normal curve $\left[Z = \dfrac{X - E(X)}{SD(X)} \right]$, 68% of all possible IRRs are within one standard deviation (above and below) the average and 95% fall within two standard deviations.

A normal probability distribution curve, such as the one shown in figure 4.4 is, in and of itself, an excellent picture of the degree of risk. This can be seen more clearly if we compare it to another normal probability distribution that has the same $E(IRR)$ of .15, but a much lower $SD(IRR)$ of .04, as shown in figure 4.5.

Figure 4.4   Normal probability distribution

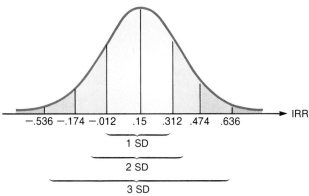

Figure 4.5   A comparison of two assets having equal profitability, but unequal risk.

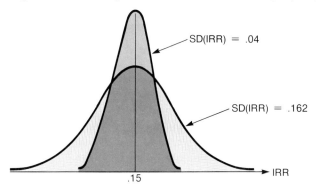

It is obvious that the second IRR probability distribution is much more compact. There is a probability of 95% that the IRR will fall between −17.4% and +47.4% in the first case, but within a much narrower range of +7% to +23% in the second case. Hence, there is less uncertainty and, thus, less risk associated with the business asset that it represents.

Given an E(IRR), a SD(IRR) and assuming a normal probability distribution, one can also obtain probabilities of various outcomes. This can be shown in connection with the computer inventory. We know E(IRR) = .15 and SD(IRR) = .162. If we further assume that IRR is normally distributed, it is possible to compute the probability of loss. Loss in one sense is earning less than the risk-free interest rate, which is assumed here to be 8%. Obtaining an IRR of less than zero would be an even more severe outcome.

Figure 4.6   Probability that an asset's IRR will be less than a given amount

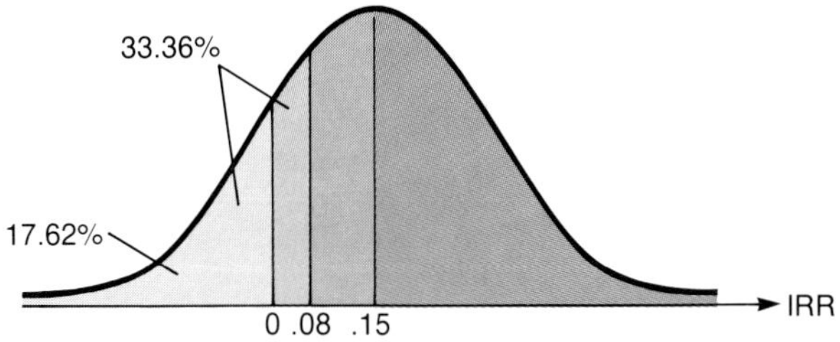

Making use of the standardized Z statistic and a normal probability table (appendix E) we can calculate: 1) the probability that IRR will be less than or equal to the risk-free interest rate, and 2) the probability that IRR will be less than or equal to 0. Thus,

$$Z = \frac{X - E(X)}{SD(X)} = \frac{IRR - E(IRR)}{SD(IRR)} = \frac{.08 - .15}{.162} = -.43 = 33.36\%$$

$$Z = \frac{X - E(X)}{SD(X)} = \frac{IRR - E(IRR)}{SD(IRR)} = \frac{.0 - .15}{.162} = -.93 = 17.62\%$$

There is a 33.36% probability that the added inventory's IRR will be less than or equal to 8% and a 17.62% probability that it will be less than or equal to 0%. This is pictured in figure 4.6 ∎

Portfolio Risk   The standard deviation of an individual business asset's IRR has just been presented as a measure of its risk. *However, the risk of the firm is more important than the risk of an individual asset. What we would prefer to know, therefore, is how a single asset will contribute to the risk of the total business.* This involves an analysis of the interrelationships between an individual asset's risk and the current risk of the firm. Due to these interrelationships, a particular purchase could increase, decrease, or leave unchanged the riskiness of the firm. The impact cannot be ascertained by simply looking at the individual asset's SD(IRR). It also depends upon how the asset's SD(IRR) meshes with the firm's SD(IRR). This is risk measurement in a *portfolio context,* where the firm and proposed asset comprise the portfolio.

Under these circumstances, a portfolio SD(IRR) is required. The risk contribution of the new asset to the firm is the difference between the portfolio SD(IRR) and the firm SD(IRR). On the other hand, an asset's contribution to a corporation's profit is the difference between the firm's current E(IRR) and the portfolio E(IRR). It might appear as though we could obtain a portfolio SD(IRR) by simply taking a weighted average of the asset's SD(IRR) and the firm's SD(IRR). This is not the case, however, as shown in equations 4.4 and 4.5:

Equation 4.4 $Var(IRR_p) = W_a{}^2 Var(IRR_a) + W_f{}^2 Var(IRR_f)$
$$+ W_a W_f 2Cov(IRR_a, IRR_f)$$

Equation 4.5 $SD(IRR_p) = \sqrt{Var(IRR_p)}$

Where:

$$Var(IRR_p) = \text{Variance of portfolio IRR}$$
$$SD(IRR_p) = \text{Standard deviation of portfolio IRR}$$
$$IRR_a = \text{Internal rate of return from the asset}$$
$$IRR_f = \text{Internal rate of return from the firm}$$
$$IRR_p = \text{Internal rate of return from the portfolio}$$
$$W_a = \text{Proportion of funds invested in asset}$$
$$W_f = \text{Proportion of funds invested in firm}$$
$$Var(IRR_a) = \text{Variance of asset IRR, found from equation 4.2}$$
$$Var(IRR_f) = \text{Variance of firm IRR, found from equation 4.2}$$
$$Cov(IRR_a, IRR_f) = \text{Covariance of asset IRR and firm IRR}$$

Furthermore:

Equation 4.6

$$Cov(IRR_a, IRR_f) = \sum_{i=1}^{n} JP_i[IRR_{a_i} - E(IRR_a)] \times [IRR_{f_i} - E(IRR_f)]$$

Where:

$$JP_i = \text{Joint probability that a particular combination of } IRR_a \text{ and } IRR_f \text{ will occur}$$
$$n = \text{Total number of joint outcomes}$$
$$IRR_{a_i} = \text{Possible IRRs generated by the asset}$$
$$IRR_{f_i} = \text{Possible IRRs generated by the firm}$$
$$E(IRR_a) = \text{Expected IRR earned by asset}$$
$$E(IRR_f) = \text{Expected IRR earned by firm}$$

A key item in equation 4.4 is the *covariance,* $Cov(IRR_a, IRR_f)$. The covariance is a measure of the interrelationship, comovement, or association of two variables. In this case, the two variables happen to be internal rates of return. A positive covariance indicates that two variables, on average, move in the same direction. A negative covariance, on the other hand, implies the variables move in opposite directions, or offset each other. Zero covariance implies no relationship (i.e., independence). There are also different degrees of positive and negative covariance. Weights W_a and W_f are also important in this measure of risk.

According to equation 4.4, an asset can influence a business's risk in relation to the individual riskiness of the asset ($Var(IRR_a)$), the proportional investment placed in the asset (W_a) and the covariance ($Cov(IRR_a, IRR_f)$).

On the other hand, an asset's contribution to the firm's IRR is much more straightforward. It is determined solely by the asset's E(IRR) and the proportional investment in the asset (W_a). This can be seen below in the equation used to compute the portfolio E(IRR).

Equation 4.7 $\quad E(IRR_p) = W_aE(IRR_a) + W_fE(IRR_f)$

Application: These concepts can be better understood if they are used in an example. Previously, we considered the individual risk and profitability of a computer inventory decision by Ace Office Furniture, which requires an investment of $800,000. Let us say that the business presently has assets with a total current value of $1,200,000. Therefore, a combination of the two would furnish a portfolio of $2,000,000. Therefore, W_a = $800,000/$2,000,000 = .40 and W_f = $1,200,000/$2,000,000 = .60.

We should begin our analysis by measuring the firm's current risk and profitability. To accomplish this, we must have Ace Furniture's IRR probability distribution, which is provided in table 4.3:

Table 4.3   IRR Probability Distribution of Ace Office Furniture

IRR	Probability
−30%	.10
−10%	.15
5%	.25
15%	.25
30%	.15
50%	.10

With the aid of equations 4.1, 4.2, and 4.3, Ace Furniture's E(IRR) and SD(IRR) can be computed as follows:

$$E(IRR_f) = .10(-.30) + .15(-.10) + .25(.05) + .25(.15) + .15(.30) + .10(.50) = .10$$

$$Var(IRR_f) = .10(-.30-.10)^2 + .15(-.10-.10)^2 + .25(.05-.10)^2 + .25(.15-.10)^2$$
$$+ .15(.30-.10)^2 + .10(.50-.10)^2$$

$$Var(IRR_f) = .10(.16) + .15(.04) + .25(.0025) + .25(.0025) + .15(.04) + .10(.16)$$
$$= .04525$$

$$SD(IRR_f) = \sqrt{.04525} = .2127$$

The profitability and risk of Ace Office Furniture are: $E(IRR_f)$ = 10% and $SD(IRR_f)$ = 21.27%. Corresponding figures for the computer inventory are $E(IRR_a)$ = 15% and $SD(IRR_a)$ = 16.2%. The portfolio profitability is derived from equation 4.7 as shown below:

$$E(IRR_p) = .40(15\%) + .60(10\%) = 12\%$$

The portfolio risk is calculated with equations 4.4 and 4.5. All of the necessary ingredients for this computation are available with the sole exception of covariance. As equation 4.6 indicates, covariance requires the *joint probabilities* (*JP*) of the two variables under consideration, namely IRR_a and IRR_f. The joint probability distribution of IRRs for the computer inventory and Ace Office Furniture is displayed in table 4.4.

Table 4.4   IRR Joint Probability Distribution

IRR$_a$	IRR$_f$	Joint Probability
−20%	+50%	.05
−10%	−10%	.05
−10%	+15%	.05
+ 0%	−10%	.10
+10%	+ 5%	.10
+10%	+30%	.15
+25%	−30%	.10
+25%	+ 5%	.15
+25%	+50%	.05
+35%	+15%	.20

This joint probability distribution indicates, for example, that there is a 5% probability that when the asset IRR is −20% the firm IRR is +50%. Now that we have the joint probabilities, equation 4.6 can be used to calculate the covariance. Due to the number of computations involved, all of the work is presented in table format. This is shown in table 4.5.

Table 4.5   Derivation of the Covariance

IRR$_a$	IRR$_f$	JP	IRR$_a$ − E(IRR$_a$)	IRR$_f$ − E(IRR$_f$)	[IRR$_a$ − E(IRR$_a$)] × [IRR$_f$ − E(IRR$_f$)]	JP[IRR$_a$ − E(IRR$_a$)] × [IRR$_f$ − E(IRR$_f$)]
−.20	.50	.05	−.35	.40	−.1400	−.0070
−.10	−.10	.05	−.25	−.20	.0500	.0025
−.10	.15	.05	−.25	.05	−.0125	−.000625
0	−.10	.10	−.15	−.20	.0300	.0030
.10	.05	.10	−.05	−.05	.0025	.00025
.10	.30	.15	−.05	.20	−.0100	−.0015
.25	−.30	.10	.10	−.40	−.0400	−.0040
.25	.05	.15	.10	−.05	−.0050	−.00075
.25	.50	.05	.10	.40	.0400	.0020
.35	.15	.20	.20	.05	.0100	.0020
						Cov = −.004125

The covariance of the two IRRs is a negative .004125. This implies that a slight inverse relationship exists between the asset IRR and the firm IRR. More than likely though, they are unrelated to each other. The significance of this will be addressed shortly.

We are now ready to compute the standard deviation of the portfolio. This requires the use of equations 4.4 and 4.5 that are repeated below:

Equation 4.4 $Var(IRR_p) = W_a^2 Var(IRR_a) + W_f^2 Var(IRR_f) + W_a W_f 2Cov(IRR_a, IRR_f)$

Equation 4.5 $SD(IRR_p) = \sqrt{Var(IRR_p)}$

Plugging in the known values of $W_a = .40$, $W_f = .60$, $Var(IRR_a) = .02625$, $Var(IRR_f) = .04525$ and $Cov(IRR_a,IRR_f) = -.004125$ we obtain:

$$Var(IRR_p) = (.40)^2(.02625) + (.60)^2(.04525) + (.40)(.60)(2)(-.004125)$$

$$Var(IRR_p) = (.16)(.02625) + (.36)(.04525) + (.48)(-.004125)$$

$$Var(IRR_p) = .00420 + .01629 - .00198 = .01851$$

$$SD(IRR_p) = \sqrt{.01851} = .136$$

The risk of the portfolio as measured by the standard deviation is 13.6%, while the portfolio profit, as measured by expected value, is 12%. Before going any further, it is beneficial to combine all of the risk and profit measures encountered up to this point.

	Asset	Firm	Portfolio
E(IRR)	.15	.10	.12
SD(IRR)	.162	.213	.136

The question posed earlier was: in what way would the purchase of an asset affect a firm's riskiness? With the information shown above, it is possible for a concerned investor to evaluate the inventory's contribution to Ace's profit and risk.

If Ace Furniture purchases this asset it can expect an *increase* in internal rate of return (from an E(IRR) of 10% to an E(IRR) of 12%) and a *decrease* in risk (from a SD(IRR) of 21.3% to an SD(IRR) of 13.6%). The fact that the firm's profit may increase should not come as a great surprise. After all, adding an asset with a 15% expected return to a firm currently earning 10% has to make a positive contribution to the business's profitability.

An analysis of the change in risk is more complex. Some risk reduction is to be expected because the new inventory's SD(IRR) is lower than the firm's. But the decline in risk greatly exceeds what could be attributed to this factor. As a matter of fact, a portfolio consisting of the asset and firm has less risk than either one of them separately. This apparently magical outcome results from one of the most important concepts in finance, *diversification* ∎

The concept of diversification is understood by most persons. Phrases such as "spread the risk" and "don't put all your eggs in one basket" exemplify this basic understanding. They do not, however, get to the heart of the matter and that heart is covariance.

Covariances can be high or low, positive or negative. A high, positive covariance indicates a close relationship between two variables. That is, they tend to reinforce one another. Consequently, little diversification and risk reduction is possible under these circumstances. A high, negative covariance signifies a diametrically opposite movement of two variables, whereby they offset each other. In this case, it is very easy to obtain diversification, and to such a degree that risk can be practically eliminated. The profitability of most business-related assets exhibit covariances between these two extremes. In the preceding example, the computer inventory IRR and Ace Office Furniture IRR exhibited a negative covariance. As a result, there is risk reduction when the computer inventory and firm are combined. Unfortunately, most business assets are positively related to each other by the general economy. It is not necessary to have negative covariances, however, to obtain some risk reduction. Low, positive covariances provide excellent opportunities for risk improvement. Assets possessing such cash flow covariances, are said to be more or less independent of one

Figure 4.7a   Negative covariance of variables X and Y

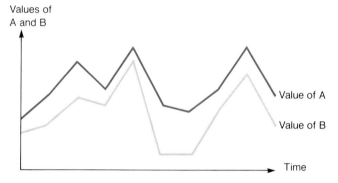

Values of X and Y

Value of X

Value of Y

Time

Figure 4.7b   Positive covariance of variables A and B

Values of A and B

Value of A

Value of B

Time

another. To benefit from these opportunities a business must combine many low covariance assets in its portfolio, and, within limits, the more the better. Insurance companies do this when they use the "law of large numbers" to narrow their underwriting risk. The egg carrier does likewise by using several baskets. This is not to say, that every business should possess a large variety of assets. After all, risk is only one aspect of asset management. Profit is equally important and it should not be unduly sacrificed to reduce risk.

Market Risk: The Capital Asset Pricing Model   The principle has just been established that an asset's risk should be measured in conjunction with the firm's risk. The portfolio approach to risk measurement specifically considers diversification benefits. Portfolios can be composed of an asset and a business, as we discussed earlier, but a great many financial experts believe the relevant portfolio should be much broader. Their argument begins by stating that investors are concerned about a firm's degree of risk. However, for most of them, the money they have invested in a business is but a fraction of their total investment portfolios. An investor's portfolio might include any number and kinds of assets from a wide variety of businesses, not to mention consumer goods. It is this portfolio that is of primary interest to the investor. *As the result, the riskiness of an individual asset should be evaluated within the context of the entire array of assets or the market portfolio.*

A major difficulty for an investor in applying this concept is the lack of any identity for the market portfolio, which exists only in theory. To circumvent this problem, it is recommended that a proxy be used to represent the market portfolio. The stock market (as represented by a broad stock market index, such as the Standard and Poor's 500 stock index) is typically prescribed for this purpose. This choice is based on the presumption that the stock market is a reasonable representative for all assets; that is, the stock market will tend to mimic what is happening to most business assets. There is a great deal of logic in this argument. After all, common stocks represent ownership in corporations that use a wide variety of assets, and, because the stocks in the stock market are so diverse, the market possesses great diversification.

A very good way to measure the risk contribution of an asset to the market portfolio, as represented by the stock market, is the statistic *Beta* (β). The value of Beta can be computed as follows:

Equation 4.8 $$\beta = \frac{\text{Cov}(\text{IRR}_a, \text{IRR}_m)}{\text{Var}(\text{IRR}_m)}$$

Where:

$$\beta = \text{Risk measure Beta}$$
$$\text{Var}(\text{IRR}_m) = \text{Variance of stock market index IRR}$$
$$\text{Cov}(\text{IRR}_a, \text{IRR}_m) = \text{Covariance of asset IRR and stock market index IRR}$$

β is not a variance or standard deviation, but rather the ratio of two variances. It measures the risk of each individual business asset in relation to the risk of the stock market. The risk of the market ($\text{Var}(\text{IRR}_m)$) serves as a common denominator. A β of 1 indicates a one-to-one relationship between the asset and the market; a $\beta > 1$ implies the asset is riskier than the market and a $\beta < 1$ implies the asset is less risky than the market. Beta is very useful when making risk comparisons. For example, an asset with a β of 2 would be riskier than one with a β of 1.40.

Beta has a rather large following in the investment and financial community, particularly in the securities markets. It is also the centerpiece of a sophisticated theory of risk, return, and asset valuation called the *capital asset pricing model (CAPM)*.[10]

Reduced to its bare essentials, the capital asset pricing model states that there are two kinds of risk associated with an asset: *unsystematic risk* and *systematic risk*. Unsystematic risk is the unique risk of an asset and it is measured by the $\text{Var}(\text{IRR}_a)$. This risk can be eliminated or "averaged out" by investors through diversification. Examples of this type of risk include random events such as strikes and lawsuits. Systematic risk is the risk that an asset has in common with the market portfolio and is measured by the $\text{Cov}(\text{IRR}_a, \text{IRR}_m)$. The risk of the market portfolio, or $\text{Var}(\text{IRR}_m)$, cannot be eliminated through diversification because it already contains all available assets. For example, inflation and national political events can potentially affect *all* assets in a market portfolio. Since an investor cannot diversify away this type of risk (the systematic risk), it is the only risk relevant to the CAPM.

---

[10]Turn to the reading list at the end of this chapter for further information concerning the capital asset pricing model.

The source of an asset's systematic risk is the market risk. Due to the fact that some assets are more closely related to the market than others, systematic risk will vary accordingly. Beta is the ratio of systematic risk to market risk and, as such, it measures the relative risk of an asset to the market. Since an asset's unsystematic risk can be eliminated through adequate diversification, the market will not compensate investors for incurring it. However, the market does compensate investors for systematic risk or Beta with a market-determined risk premium. The implications of this for investors in asset-backed securities is demonstrated graphically by the *security market line (SML)*. The security market line is represented by equation 4.9:

Equation 4.9 $E(R_j) = R_f + \beta\,[E(R_m) - R_f]$

Where:

$E(R_j)$ = Expected rate of return on security j
R_f = Risk-free interest rate
β = Relative systematic risk or Beta
$E(R_m)$ = Expected rate of return on the market portfolio

According to equation 4.9, the expected rate of return $E(R_j)$ on a given security (j), is equal to the risk-free rate of interest (R_f) plus the security's relative systematic risk (β) multiplied by the risk premium $[E(R_m) - R_f]$ that is demanded on the market portfolio. *In market equilibrium, the two expected rates of return are equal to required rates of return.*

A diagram of the security market line is shown in figure 4.8. As demonstrated in figure 4.8, the SML is simply a graphical representation of equation 4.9. According to the CAPM, all security RRRs should lie on the security market line. The exact position on the line is determined by a security's β, and nothing more. A security with a β of 1.75, for instance, will have a higher RRR than a security with a β of .90. It is noteworthy that the slope of the SML is the risk premium required on the market portfolio, or $E(R_m) - R_f$.

Figure 4.8   **The security market line (SML) represents the trade-off between systematic risk (β) and security returns (R_j). Note that the risk premium for a relatively safe stock (i.e., $\beta < 1$) is lower than the risk premium for a riskier stock (i.e., $\beta > 1$).**

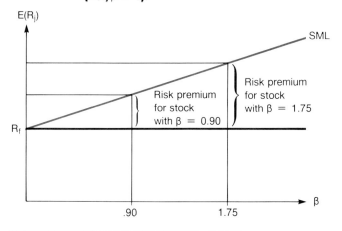

The CAPM theory rests on some rather strong economic assumptions. For example, it assumes that the marketplace is highly efficient, that investors have "perfect information," and that there are no barriers to information transfer. It also assumes that investors are "reasonable," i.e., they prefer high returns with low risk and can objectively measure risk. These assumptions, although they do not fit the real world perfectly, are necessary for the CAPM to be of practical value. Research to date on the usefulness of the theory is mixed, but on balance tends to support the CAPM.

Risk-Profit Ratio   When comparing the risk of different assets, a useful device is the *risk-profit ratio*. This is simply a risk measure divided by a profit measure, such as, SD(IRR) / E(IRR) or Beta / E(IRR).[11] Consider, for instance, two assets, A and B. A has an E(IRR) = .18 and a SD(IRR) = .045, while B has an E(IRR) = .21 and a SD(IRR) = .07. Taking into account both profit and risk, which of these assets is superior? The answer can be found by comparing their risk-profit ratios, as follows:

$$\text{Risk-profit ratio (A)} = \frac{.045}{.18} = .25$$

$$\text{Risk-profit ratio (B)} = \frac{.07}{.21} = .333$$

In this case, alternative A is superior because it has less risk per unit of return.

Security Valuation

The material presented in chapter 3 and the first portion of this chapter have prepared us for our next topic, security valuation. *Security valuation is the process of pricing (i.e., valuing) securities, such as stocks and bonds, in the financial marketplace.* Our primary concern at the moment is with the valuation of common stocks, simply because the stated goal of financial management is the maximization of stockholder wealth.[12]

Essentially, a share of common stock has value because its owner may receive future cash dividends. The fact that dividends are paid in the future means that an investor will require the risk-free rate of interest for expected intervening inflation, sacrificed consumption, and, quite possibly, taxes. The fact that dividends are a function of the earnings from corporate assets means that they are unpredictable (some corporate dividends more so than others, of course). Therefore, an investor in common stock will require a risk premium on top of the risk-free interest rate. *In general, then, we may say that the current value of a share of common stock is equal to the present value of expected annual dividends per share, discounted at the required rate of return.*[13] This is stated in the *stock valuation model,* equation 4.10.

---

[11]Coefficient of variation is the formal name for standard deviation divided by expected value.

[12]Bond valuation will be taken up in chapter 14.

[13]In reality, common stock dividends are normally paid quarterly. However, such an adjustment to the stock valuation model would not alter to any great degree the basic meaning or use of the model.

Equation 4.10

$$\text{Stock value} = \frac{\widetilde{DPS}_1}{(1+RRR)^1} + \frac{\widetilde{DPS}_2}{(1+RRR)^2} + \ldots + \frac{\widetilde{DPS}_n}{(1+RRR)^n}$$

where:

$\widetilde{DPS}_i$ = Estimated ($\sim$) dividends per share in year i
RRR = Required rate of return
n = Life of the corporation

Example: Given an RRR equal to 12% and estimated, annual dividends per share of $5 for each of the next 20 years, what is the current stock value? Inserting the information into the stock valuation model, we find the answer to be:

$$\text{Stock value} = \frac{\$5}{(1.12)^1} + \frac{\$5}{(1.12)^2} + \ldots + \frac{\$5}{(1.12)^{20}}$$

Converting to operational form using annuity discount factors:

$$\text{Stock value} = \$5(ADF_{.12/20}) = \$5(7.4694) = \$37.35 \blacksquare$$

At this point in the discussion, a distinction needs to be made between market valuation and individual valuation. Individuals value common stocks based upon their personal views as to the level of future dividends, degree of risk, and desired risk premium. The stock market, on the other hand, is made up of many investors, some of whom own stock and some who do not. These investors come together in the marketplace and, despite often widely divergent views and values, strike a balance between supply and demand to arrive at a price for each stock.[14] This market-determined price is the market value of the stock and the value that financial managers are most concerned with. For all practical purposes, we can think of market valuation as if it were a group decision, whereby a market estimate of dividends is discounted by the market's RRR.

Application: Tytex Corporation was formed very recently by two environmental engineers. According to the company's stock offering prospectus, the firm will engage in hazardous waste clean-up at corporate sites around the country. All of the work should be completed within five years, at which time the remaining assets, if any, will be liquidated. The company wishes to sell 1,000,000 shares of common stock to finance its asset requirements. The stock market has forecasted annual dividends per share from this venture in accordance with the probability distribution shown in table 4.6.

---

[14]As with any market-determined price, some investors will consider the price more than satisfactory, while others will feel just the opposite, depending upon their individual valuations.

Table 4.6   Tytex Corporation Dividends per Share Probability Distribution

Event	Year 1	2	3	4	5	Probability
A	$ 1.50	$ 1.50	$ 1.50	$ 1.50	$ 1.50	.10
B	$ 4.00	$ 4.00	$ 4.00	$ 4.00	$ 4.00	.20
C	$ 7.00	$ 7.00	$ 7.00	$ 7.00	$10.60	.40
D	$ 6.00	$ 8.00	$10.00	$12.00	$15.70	.20
E	$12.00	$12.00	$12.00	$12.00	$17.25	.10
E(DPS)	$ 6.15	$ 6.55	$ 6.95	$ 7.35	$10.07	

There are five possible dividend streams, with C being the most probable. Listed in the final row of the table are the expected (or average) dividends for each year, as calculated with equation 4.1. The stock market's required rate of return on this investment is 16%, which consists of a risk-free interest rate of 6% and a risk premium equal to 10%. What will a share of this stock sell for on the market? Inserting this information into the stock valuation model, equation 4.10, we find the answer to be:

$$\text{Stock value} = \frac{\$6.15}{(1.16)^1} + \frac{\$6.55}{(1.16)^2} + \frac{\$6.95}{(1.16)^3} + \frac{\$7.35}{(1.16)^4} + \frac{\$10.07}{(1.16)^5}$$

Converting to operational form:

$$\text{Stock value} = \$6.15DF_{.16/1} + \$6.55DF_{.16/2} + \$6.95DF_{.16/3}$$
$$+ \$7.35DF_{.16/4} + \$10.07DF_{.16/5}$$

Therefore:

$$\text{Stock value} = \$6.15(.8621) + \$6.55(.7432)$$
$$+ \$6.95(.6407) + \$7.35(.5523)$$
$$+ \$10.07(.4761) = \$23.47 \blacksquare$$

The stock valuation model has a lot to tell management about stock prices. *First of all, stock values are heavily influenced by the level of estimated dividends.* As the stock market raises its expectations of a company's dividends, the stock price will be bid up on the market to a new, higher value. Although this is no earthshaking discovery, it is nice to see it formalized. *Secondly, the RRR is inversely related to stock prices.* Thus, a lower RRR will lead to a higher stock value and vice versa. *Finally, a change in dividend expectations can, in some instances, be offset by a change in RRR, while at other times changes in both can complement each other.*[15]

A financial manager's job is to manage his company's financial affairs so as to maximize the market price of its common stock. As the stock valuation model shows, this can be accomplished in several ways: 1) increasing profitability and, thus, dividends; 2) reducing the market RRR applied to dividends by reducing risk; 3) accomplishing both 1 and 2; and 4) capitalizing on advantageous trade-offs between profits and RRR (for instance, following a course of action that increases profitability more than it increases risk). Much of this text will concern itself with these situations.

---

[15]For a more in-depth discussion see Long, John B., Jr. "The Market Valuation of Cash Dividends: A Case to Consider," *Journal of Financial Economics* (June–September 1978), pp. 235–64.

Summary

Interest rates are the link between the liability and equity claims of investors and the asset holdings of corporations or other borrowers. Investors demand an interest rate as compensation for providing funds to a corporation. Assets are not only purchased with these funds, but they must also provide the wherewithal to repay the principal, with interest. From the company's standpoint, the interest rate demands of investors represent costs.

Three basic elements or premiums are factored into most interest rates: compensation to investors for sacrificed consumption (time preference premium); compensation to investors for expected future inflation (inflation premium); and compensation to investors for having to pay income taxes on interest income (tax premium). When combined, these three premiums constitute what is commonly referred to as the risk-free interest rate. The risk-free interest rate, in turn, is used to measure the time value of money. In addition to demanding compensation for time preference, taxes, and expected inflation, investors, being risk-averse, also require compensation for bearing risk. This gives rise to a risk-premium. Since investments vary in degree of riskiness, so will risk-premiums and, thus, interest rates. To emphasize the requirements of investors, interest rates are often referred to as required rates of return. From the firm's standpoint, however, interest rates represent the costs of financing asset acquisitions. Interest rates are also important in security valuation.

It is the uncertainty of, or variability in, asset profitability that creates risk for investors, and the greater the degree of uncertainty, the greater the degree of risk. In other words, corporate securities are risky because corporate assets are risky. Many experts believe that the risk associated with a business asset can be measured with the variance and standard deviation of the asset's internal rate of return. However, the risk of the *firm* is more important to investors than the risk of a single asset. Assessing the risk of an entire company of assets is risk measurement in a portfolio context. Portfolio risk measurement takes into account diversification properties and makes use of the statistical covariance. In fact, many financial experts believe that the relevant standard for risk evaluation should be the market portfolio, as expressed in the capital asset pricing model and the statistical Beta. The various statistical measures of risk are displayed in table 4.7 ■

Table 4.7   Summary of Key Statistical Formulas

Risk and Return Measures for a Single Asset

$$E(IRR) = \sum_{i=1}^{n} P_i IRR_i = P_1 IRR_1 + P_2 IRR_2 + \cdots + P_n IRR_n$$

$$Var(IRR) = \sum_{i=1}^{n} P_i[IRR_i - E(IRR)]^2 = P_1[IRR_1 - E(IRR)]^2 + P_2[IRR_2 - E(IRR)]^2 + \cdots + P_n[IRR_n - E(IRR)]^2$$

$$SD(IRR) = \sqrt{Var(IRR)}$$

Risk and Return Measures for a Portfolio of Two Assets

$$E(IRR_p) = W_a E(IRR_a) + W_f E(IRR_f)$$

$$Var(IRR_p) = W_a^2 Var(IRR_a) + W_f^2 Var(IRR_f) + W_a W_f 2Cov(IRR_a, IRR_f)$$

$$Cov(IRR_a, IRR_f) = \sum_{i=1}^{n} JP_i [IRR_{a_i} - E(IRR_a)][IRR_{f_i} - E(IRR_f)]$$

$$SD(IRR_p) = \sqrt{Var(IRR_p)}$$

Key Terms/Concepts

Beta (β)	Joint probabilities	Security market line (SML)
Capital asset pricing model (CAPM)	Market risk	Security valuation
	Portfolio risk	Standard deviation
Cost of financing	Required rate of return (RRR)	Stock valuation model
Covariance	Risk	Systematic risk
Diversification	Risk averse	Tax premium
Expected value	Risk premium	Time preference premium
Inflation premium	Risk-profit ratio	Unsystematic risk
Interest rate	Risk-return trade-off	Variance
Internal rate of return (IRR)		

Questions

1. What three factors make up the risk-free interest rate?

2. Define the term "systematic risk."

3. Diversification is often described with the phrase "don't put all your eggs in one basket." Would this remain applicable if six baskets are used and they are all transported on the same bicycle? Explain why or why not.

4. What is the source of risk for investors in corporate securities?

5. Why are corporate creditors exposed to less risk than corporate stockholders?

6. Why might investors find it difficult to measure risk with Beta or the standard deviation of internal rate of return?

7. Holding other factors constant, what would happen to the market price of a given firm's common stock if investors lowered their assessment of its risk?

8. Are investors in a risky venture exposed to risk, even if they are unaware of its existence?

9. Does the risk-free interest rate change over time? Explain why or why not.

10. Diagram a probability distribution with E(IRR) = 13% and SD(IRR) = 0%.

Problems

1. Compute E(IRR) from the following probability distribution:

IRR	Probability
−100%	.10
0%	.20
10%	.30
20%	.30
40%	.10

2. The IRR probability distribution for a business asset is shown below:

IRR	Probability
10%	.40
9%	.20
8%	.10
− 5%	.30

Derive the E(IRR) and SD(IRR) from this probability distribution.

3. The market price of a share of common stock in one year is described by the following probability distribution:

Market Price	Probability
$74	.30
$76	.10
$78	.20
$80	.10
$82	.10
$86	.10
$88	.10

Find the E(Market Price) and the SD(Market Price) for this common stock.

4. The internal rate of return from a particular asset is heavily influenced by the state of the economy. This is demonstrated in the asset's IRR probability distribution, shown below.

State of Economy	IRR	Probability
Boom	50%	.10
Above normal	30%	.25
Normal	15%	.40
Below normal	− 5%	.20
Recession	−30%	.05

Required:
   A. Calculate E(IRR) and SD(IRR).
   B. What is the probability that the IRR will be less than a risk-free interest rate of 8%? Assume a normal distribution.
   C. What is the probability that the IRR will be less than 0%?

5. A firm is considering the purchase of a piece of land. A real estate appraiser has estimated that the land can be sold in five years for the following prices and associated probabilities:

Selling Price	Probability
$10,000	.30
$15,000	.25
$20,000	.25
$25,000	.20

Required:
   A. Compute the E(Selling Price) and SD(Selling Price) of the land.
   B. Assuming a normal distribution, what is the probability that the land will sell for less than $10,000?

6. Given a time preference premium of 3%, expected inflation of 6% and a 50% income tax rate, derive the risk-free interest rate.

7. A company is evaluating two alternative (i.e., mutually exclusive) assets. The IRR probability distributions for both of these assets are displayed below.

Asset A		Asset B	
IRR	Probability	IRR	Probability
25%	.05	60%	.10
20%	.25	40%	.20
15%	.40	30%	.40
10%	.25	0%	.20
5%	.05	-20%	.10

Required:
   A. Calculate E(IRR), SD(IRR), and Risk-Profit ratio for each of the two alternatives.
   B. In terms of SD(IRR), which asset is the riskiest?
   C. In terms of the Risk-Profit ratio, which asset is the riskiest?

8. Shown below are the IRR probability distributions for two assets, X and Y. An investor has the choice of putting all of his or her money in one of the assets or of dividing it equally between the two.
Required:
   A. Calculate E(IRR) and SD(IRR) for each asset.
   B. Calculate the E(IRR) and SD(IRR) for a portfolio of these two assets (with 50% of the portfolio allocated to each).
   C. What conclusions can be drawn from the answers to A and B?

Asset X		Asset Y	
IRR	Probability	IRR	Probability
-25%	.20	-10%	.15
- 5%	.30	10%	.40
35%	.30	20%	.30
55%	.20	30%	.15

Joint Probability Distribution of X and Y

IRR_x	IRR_y	Joint Probability
−25%	10%	.20
− 5%	20%	.30
35%	−10%	.05
35%	10%	.15
35%	30%	.10
55%	−10%	.10
55%	10%	.05
55%	30%	.05

9. A firm that currently has $8,750,000 in assets, can acquire a new asset costing $1,250,000. The new asset's SD(IRR_a) is .20 while the firm's SD(IRR_f) equals .14. Furthermore, Cov(IRR_a, IRR_f) is 0. If the new asset were combined with the firm, would the resulting company (i.e., portfolio) be more or less risky than without the asset?

10. An investor requires a risk premium of 1% for each 2% in SD(IRR) that he or she is exposed to. Given a risk-free interest rate of 12%, determine this investor's RRR for an asset that has a SD(IRR) of 16%.

11. Given a risk-free interest rate (R_f) of 6% and an expected market rate of return $E(R_m)$ of 11%, calculate the market's RRR on an asset whose β is 1.60.

12. The stock market's IRR probability distribution is presented below along with the IRR probability distribution of a particular asset and the IRR joint probability distribution for the market and the asset. From this information, compute the asset's Beta.

Asset IRR Probability Distribution		**Market IRR Probability Distribution**	
IRR_a	Probability	IRR_m	Probability
−25%	.10	−20%	.05
0%	.20	−10%	.10
25%	.40	0%	.25
35%	.20	10%	.30
55%	.10	20%	.20
		30%	.10

IRR Joint Probability Distribution

IRR_a	IRR_m	Probability
−25%	0%	.10
0%	−10%	.10
0%	10%	.05
0%	20%	.05
25%	−20%	.05
25%	10%	.20
25%	20%	.15
35%	0%	.15
35%	10%	.05
55%	30%	.10

13. Derive the market value of a share of common stock in a firm that is expected to pay annual dividends of $4.25 per share for thirty years. The market's RRR is 20%.

14. What is the market value of a share of common stock in a firm that is expected to pay annual dividends of $3 per share indefinitely. The market-determined RRR is a) 15% and b) 10%.

15. Ellis Company is and has been quite profitable, but it has never paid any dividends. Nevertheless, the company's common stock has steadily increased in price on the stock market. What is the explanation for this phenomenon?

16. The stock market is predicting that MCT Corporation will pay a single dividend of $10,000 per share in forty years. Due to the high uncertainty surrounding this prediction, the market's RRR is a substantial 20%. What is the market price of MCTs common stock?

17. Hyway Enterprises was formed to conduct business for only a relatively short period of time. Per share dividend estimates on its common stock are presented below in the form of a probability distribution.

	Year 1	2	3	4	5	6	7	Probability
Event								
A.	$1.25	$1.25	$1.25	$1.25	$1.25	$1.25	$1.25	.30
B.	$1.00	$1.25	$1.50	$1.75	$2.00	$2.25	$2.50	.40
C.	$1.50	$2.00	$2.50	$3.00	$3.50	$4.00	$4.50	.30

Required:
   A. Calculate the E(DPS) for each year.
   B. Given a market-determined RRR of 16%, find the market price of Hyway Enterprises common stock.

Selected References

Fisher, L., and J. H. Lorie, *A Half Century of Returns on Stocks and Bonds,* Chicago: University of Chicago Graduate School of Business, 1977.

Freund, John E., and Frank J. Williams, *Elementary Business Statistics: The Modern Approach,* 4th ed., Englewood Cliffs, N.J.: Prentice-Hall, Inc., 1982.

Rosenberg, Barr, "The Capital Asset Pricing Model and the Market Model," *Journal of Portfolio Management* (Winter 1981), pp. 5–16.

Sharpe, W. F., *Investments,* 2nd ed., Englewood Cliffs, N.J.: Prentice-Hall, Inc., 1981.

Tobin, James, "Liquidity Preference As Behavior towards Risk," *Review of Economic Studies* (February 1958), pp. 65–86.

Van Horne, James C., *Financial Management and Policy,* 6th ed., Englewood Cliffs, N.J.: Prentice-Hall, Inc., 1983, pp. 13–76.

Van Horne, James C., *Function and Analysis of Capital Market Rates,* Englewood Cliffs, N.J.: Prentice-Hall, Inc., 1970.

Wagner, W. H., and S. C. Law, "The Effect of Diversification on Risk," *Financial Analysts Journal* (November–December 1971), pp. 48–53.

Finance in the News

Risk is generally reduced with proper portfolio management. Portfolios should provide a hedge against both inflation and falling interest rates. Following is a scenario of a Florida couple who received financial advice to build a portfolio to achieve both goals.

An Early Retirement Is the Goal of Two Young Floridians

David Parkinson, 32, believes in postponing life's pleasures—but not forever. "I'd like to quit work when I'm 50. We want to travel," says Parkinson. "And we would like to live on the beach eventually," adds his wife Jan, 31. The Tampa, Fla. couple already own their retirement retreat, a shore house on nearby Anna Maria Island, and although they are a long way from realizing the rest of their plan, they have saved $50,000.

They have built this nest egg mostly by holding down their housing expenses. While young people typically devote 25% or more of their income to mortgage or rental costs, the Parkinsons have spent much less. The six-room house they owned for nine of their 10 years of marriage had a mortgage of just $240 a month. This, together with the fact that they have no children and live frugally, enabled them to make regular additions to their investments.

Their combined salary from Dave's job as a contract administrator for the Tampa department of public works and Jan's as a director of planning at St. Joseph's Hospital is $70,000, up from $20,000 10 years ago. Rental of the beach house adds $10,800. With last year's move into a new townhouse, their mortgage costs ballooned to $1,394 a month, so a well-considered investment plan is more important than ever.

Right now, the Parkinsons own 100 shares of Hillenbrand Industries (recently traded on the New York Stock Exchange at $26), 104 shares of Jaclyn Inc. (American Stock Exchange, $14.50) and 600 shares of Claires Stores (over the counter, $18.25). The stocks, bought last year with the advice of Laura Waller, a financial planner in Tampa, are now worth about $15,000. In 1982, Waller also got the couple to open Individual Retirement Accounts invested in the FPA Paramount Fund, a growth and income fund with an 8% load. Their $10,000 contribution is now worth about $10,500. The couple put another $12,550 in the same fund outside the IRA and $13,300 in a money-market fund.

Present Holdings		Recommendations	
During their 10-year marriage, the Parkinsons have amassed a portfolio worth about $50,000.		Financial planner Colin Benjamin Coombs would sell the stocks and use the proceeds to diversify the portfolio.	
Stocks	29%	Growth and income fund	32%
Money-market fund	26%	Money-market fund	26%
Growth and income fund	24%	IRA (government bond fund)	21%
IRA (growth and income fund)	21%	Oil and gas limited partnership	21%

The Parkinsons are receiving tax shelter not only from their IRAs but also from their real estate. The mortgage interest and property tax deductions from their two houses—plus the upkeep on the beach house—will amount to $23,000 this year. What the Parkinsons lack, according to two other financial planners *Money* consulted, is sufficient diversification of their portfolio. The planners maintain that the potential yields of the investments they recommend are high enough to justify their sales charges.

Colin Benjamin Coombs of Polycomp Financial Group in Woodland Hills, Calif. would sell the Parkinsons' individual stocks and invest the proceeds partly in FPA Paramount (now open only to current shareholders) and partly in an oil and gas income partnership, which would give them a hedge against inflation. He recommends the 8½% load HCW Income Fund (Church Green Bldg., 101 Summer St., Boston, Mass. 02110), whose current yield of about 10% a year could increase if energy prices rise.

To protect the portfolio against possible falling interest rates, he would take the IRA dollars out of their stock fund and invest them in a government securities fund. His choice would be American Capital Government Securities Fund (713–993–0500), a low-risk 6¾% load fund recently yielding 12½%.

Withdrawing without Penalty

Coombs believes that Jan should be investing in a tax-sheltered annuity—offered by her hospital and other nonprofit institutions—rather than in an IRA. While IRAs limit annual contributions to $2,000, Jan could invest up to 16⅔% of her gross income in a tax-sheltered annuity. What's more important to the Parkinsons' retirement plans, Jan could make early withdrawals from the annuity, unlike the IRA, without penalty.

Venita VanCaspel of Houston, a financial planner with her own practice, urges the Parkinsons to take $4,000 from the money-market fund and make their 1985 IRA contributions into FPA Paramount as soon as possible. She also advises them to put $10,000 from the money-market account and stock sales into a real estate limited partnership, which, she says, could appreciate more than an equity holding would. She likes Century Property Growth Fund 22 (Fox Capital Corp., 2755 Campus Dr., Suite 220, San Mateo, Calif. 94403), a buyer of rental properties in the sunbelt that she expects to yield an average after-tax annual return of 19% over the five- to eight-year life of the partnership. "Rents will go up," says VanCaspel, "because new families can't afford to buy homes."

Writer: Robert McNatt

Reprinted from the April 1985 issue of *Money Magazine* by special permission; © 1985, Time, Inc.

Asset Management

Throughout the next six chapters we will discuss the principles, practices, and procedures involved with the management of corporate assets. Corporate assets are managed because many important decisions must be made in connection with them. Decisions such as whether to: sell or keep an obsolete asset; repair or replace a worn-out asset; increase or decrease the level of a current asset; purchase or reject a new asset; and determine the appropriate combination of assets. We will examine in considerable detail how decisions such as these are analyzed and evaluated. Decisions regarding assets should be based upon an analysis and evaluation of the decision's effect on stockholder earnings and risk exposure. By following this course of action, we will be proceeding in a manner that coincides with shareholder wealth maximization (i.e., maintaining or increasing the market price of common stock).

Working capital management is presented in chapters 5, 6, and 7. Capital budgeting (the popular phrase used to describe the management of capital assets) is covered in chapters 8, 9, and 10■

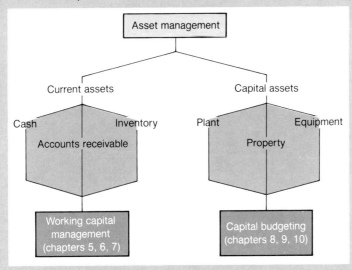

5

Working Capital Management: Overview

Overview

Working capital is used to describe the combined total of a company's current assets.[1] For most corporations, working capital consists primarily of cash, marketable securities, accounts receivable, and inventory. This chapter and the next two chapters are concerned with working capital and its management. Working capital management involves the various decisions a firm makes with regard to its current assets.

The present chapter should give us an overall perspective into the nature of current assets, their relationship to one another, and a preview of working capital management. The latter topic will be examined in much more detail in chapters 6 (management of cash and marketable securities) and 7 (management of inventory and receivables)■

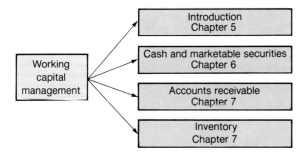

---

[1]By definition, net working capital is current assets minus current liabilities.

Objectives _____

By the end of the chapter the student should be able to:

1. List the major categories of working capital and explain the basic concepts of working capital management
2. Discuss the need for and relative riskiness of current assets
3. Explain how marginal costs and marginal benefits are related to the optimal current asset level
4. Explain the importance of managing current assets
5. Explain how variations in sales activity affect the optimal level of working capital
6. Plot working capital behavior over time and identify seasonal, cyclical, and trend patterns
7. List and explain the causes of discrepancies between optimal and actual levels of working capital
8. Describe the cash conversion cycle and apply it to given situations

Introduction

Working capital management, also known as current asset management, involves the determination of the appropriate levels for each current asset and the day-to-day administration and control of those assets. The objective in managing working capital is to maximize shareholder wealth. This implies that decisions concerning current assets will be based upon an evaluation of profitability and risk.

Current assets are sufficiently different from capital assets as to require separate coverage. As a rule, capital assets are more affected by income taxes, necessitate larger sums of money, involve more risk, and require less day-to-day attention. The constant attention required of current assets is due in large part to their more frequent turnover.

There are three major categories of working capital: cash and marketable securities, accounts receivable, and inventory. Cash and marketable securities should really be considered as a package since marketable securities are held for the same reasons that cash is held. They are simply substitutes for one another. It is common practice today to refer to the management of cash and marketable securities as *cash management*. Cash management is of such importance to business that an entire chapter (chapter 6) will be devoted to it. Management of accounts receivable is typically known by the more concise phrase *credit management.* The other current asset that will be considered is inventory. *Inventory management* is covered in substantially less detail than the other two topics. This in no way is meant to imply that inventory is of less significance than cash or receivables. The fact of the matter is, inventory is so heavily involved with production and marketing that it would be better to turn the subject over to those disciplines. Therefore, our interest in inventory will be limited to financial considerations. Credit management and inventory management are covered in chapter 7. The importance of working capital to business can be gleaned from table 5.1, which shows the relative size of each asset category for nonfinancial United States corporations ■

**Table 5.1   Current Assets of Nonfinancial Corporations As of June 1984
(Billions of Dollars)**

Cash and marketable securities	$ 192.3
Notes and accounts receivable	612.6
Inventories	633.3
Other	192.5
Total current assets	$1,630.8

Source: Federal Reserve Bulletin, Board of Governors of the Federal Reserve System, Washington, D.C. (January 1985).

Nature of Current Assets

Current assets are a necessary evil for business. It is impossible to run most businesses today without cash or inventory and, in some industries, accounts receivable are mandatory.

Cash holdings are necessary to pay for many bills that come due, because cash inflows from operations do not always match cash outflows. Theoretically, a firm could pay for wages, supplies, and interest charges with inventory or machinery. However, workers, suppliers, and creditors would find such methods of payment rather inconvenient and would only approve of them under adverse conditions (i.e., bankruptcy). Consequently, some minimum cash holdings are necessary.

Inventory stocks of materials and finished goods are important for several reasons: they allow for smooth production activity; the frequency of ordering is reduced and, therefore, ordering cost is minimized; and inventory stocks will assure that customers can be satisfactorily serviced. Inventory could be dispensed with if it were possible to have goods delivered or produced instantaneously at zero cost and customers had no desire to examine merchandise or do comparison shopping. These conditions, obviously, do not exist.

In many instances accounts receivable are an important factor in the success or failure of a firm. Receivables exist as a result of sales on credit and credit sales make up a significant portion of total sales for many companies. Theoretically, manufacturing and commercial enterprises would not need to be in the lending business if specialized lending institutions (e.g., banks, savings and loans, etc.) adequately took care of credit needs. For various reasons, however, they do not.[2] Many firms also use credit as a marketing device to generate or maintain sales.

Given that current assets are so necessary, why are they also considered to be an evil? Current assets, like all assets, must be financed, and financing, as we all know, is not usually free. Furthermore, the day-to-day control and maintenance of working capital is very time consuming and costly. *A major criticism of working capital and something that frustrates management is its low rate of profitability in relation to capital assets.* But it is very difficult to measure the contribution from current assets. Their value often is not recognized until they are gone. In any event, checking accounts and stocks of inventory are not very creative or risky ventures and consequently should not be expected to provide large profits; but note that *current assets do not expose a business to a high degree of risk and, in some cases, may actually reduce it.*

To summarize, current assets are indispensable, and while they may not generate terrific earnings they are also relatively safe. Having said this, one should not conclude that current asset management is a simple task. Quite the contrary. It requires many tough decisions and a great deal of supervision as we will see in the remainder of this chapter and in the next two chapters.

Managing Current Assets

Managing working capital essentially involves two issues: 1) determination of the optimal level for each current asset and 2) development of policies and practices to effectively administer current assets.

Optimal Level of Current Assets   Current assets are optimal when stockholders would not gain in terms of profit or risk from a change in their amounts. The optimal amounts of cash/marketable securities, receivables, or inventory to hold at any given point in time depends upon many factors. Sales volume is generally the most important determining factor for all of them. *All things being equal, the greater the sales volume, the greater the quantity of inventory, receivables, and cash a firm must have on hand.* But there are other important considerations in addition to sales volume. Most of these determining factors can and do change, and, as a consequence, there will be changes in the optimal level of current assets.

---

[2]Government regulations and tradition can lead to such behavior.

Figure 5.1   The optimal level of a current asset is determined by a comparison of marginal costs and marginal benefits.

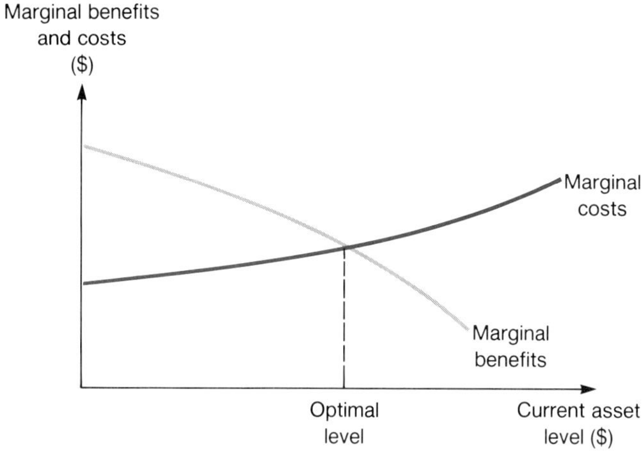

The current assets one observes on a corporation's balance sheet did not get there by accident. If they did, then that business would be in for some trouble. Preferably, the amount of money tied up in each current asset should be the result of a conscious decision on the part of management. Within rather wide limits, businesses have considerable discretion as to how much cash to hold, inventory to stock, and receivables to carry. But at any given point in time, there is only one amount for each that is optimal. Generally speaking, a search for the optimal quantity of a particular current asset begins with an estimate of sales volume. For that given sales volume, *the optimal current asset level is found by comparing the marginal benefits and marginal costs of different asset levels.* The optimal level is at the point where marginal benefits equal marginal costs. This is exhibited in figure 5.1.

According to figure 5.1, any firm can benefit from some amount of working capital, thus the high marginal benefit at very low current asset levels. However, as the current asset balance rises, the marginal benefit declines due to diminishing returns. Marginal costs start out at a lower level and usually increase at a somewhat slower rate, if at all.[3] As long as marginal benefits exceed marginal costs it pays to increase the current asset. The optimum is found where the two intersect. In addition to sales, a change in costs or benefits (i.e., a shift of the curves) will lead to an alteration in the optimal level of a current asset.

It is difficult to generalize about specific costs and benefits at this stage since each current asset is unique. There are, however, two universal elements: risk and interest expense on the money tied up in working capital.

---

[3]The shapes of the curves shown in figure 5.1 are merely illustrative. The exact configurations for a particular company could be noticeably different.

Administration of Current Assets It is not sufficient to calculate an optimal level for each current asset. Knowing what is appropriate and actually attaining it can be difficult and time consuming. Therefore management must develop a plan of action designed to achieve or maintain the optimal level. This plan should contain controls that monitor each asset and procedures to follow if corrective actions become necessary.

Current assets also require a considerable amount of regular attention. Having determined and achieved the optimal level of cash and marketable securities, for example, does not end the financial manager's job. Cash is constantly flowing into and out of a firm and must be handled in an efficient manner. In the case of marketable securities, the makeup of an optimal securities balance can be just as important as finding the optimal level itself. Many types of marketable securities are available for investment and they are not equally desirable. Consequently, it is important for management to select them carefully.

Working Capital Behavior over Time

The management of current assets can be carried out in a more satisfactory manner if we understand the behavior of these assets over time. At any given point in time, there is an optimal level of working capital desired by each business, as we saw earlier. There are a number of factors that combine to determine this optimal level and they differ somewhat for each current asset. A major, if not *the* major, consideration in deciding the appropriate amount of working capital is a firm's sales volume. The relationship between sales and total current assets differs among industries and even among firms within an industry. Nevertheless, a positive relationship between the two exists. *A variation in sales activity over time would, consequently, bring about a change in the optimal amount of working capital.* The volume of sales can change over time principally due to three causes: growth, seasonal fluctuations, and business cycles. Variations in sales volume brought about by these circumstances will induce changes in the desirable level of working capital as shown in figure 5.2a, b, c, and d. Each of these diagrams is designed to highlight the relationship between sales and working capital. Therefore, all other relevant factors, such as interest rates, are held constant.

Case I: Figure 5.2a exemplifies a firm that is not growing, is not affected by seasonal variations in production or sales and does not feel the impact of business cycles. This is, admittedly, a very unusual firm and probably not a very exciting one. Be that as it may, its desired or optimal amount of working capital is constant over time. This assumes, however, that determining factors other than sales volume are held constant.

Words of caution are in order here. A constant working capital does not require that the individual components (e.g., cash, receivables, and inventory) are always of the same magnitude. It may very well be that increases in one are offset by decreases in the other. In addition, it would be incorrect to assume that there is no asset turnover just because current assets remain unchanged in amount from period to period. In the case of receivables, for example, as old accounts are paid off, new ones take their place, leaving the total unchanged.

Case II: The type of company represented by figure 5.2b differs from the previous one in that its sales are growing.

Figure 5.2a   Working capital behavior for a firm whose sales are nongrowth, nonseasonal, and noncyclical

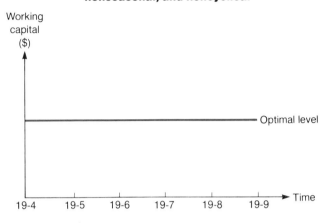

Figure 5.2b   Working capital behavior for a firm whose sales are growing, nonseasonal, and noncyclical

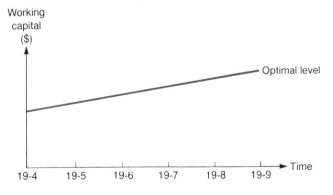

Sales volume is trending upward over time as is the optimal amount of working capital needed to accommodate the sales growth. This is shown by an upward sloping optimal working capital curve. But do not let the straight line mislead you. It is used for this example in the interest of convenience. Actually, it may take any number of shapes depending upon the growth rate of sales and the relationship between current assets and sales. The point is that growing businesses generally require more current assets. Higher sales automatically generate more accounts receivable for businesses that sell on credit. In addition, one would expect a growing company to require more cash on hand as well as larger inventory stocks. By the same token, companies with declining sales can get by with less working capital.

Figure 5.2c   Working capital behavior for a firm whose sales are growing, seasonal, and noncyclical

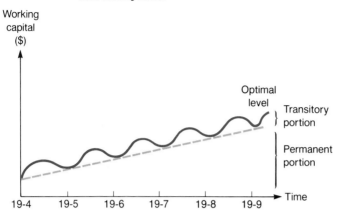

Case III: We now turn to a company with a more complex pattern of sales than the previous two. This firm is not only growing, it is also susceptible to seasonal fluctuations in sales and production. (Actually, seasonal sales may or may not be associated with seasonal production.) The desired working capital of such a company is shown in figure 5.2c.

An inspection of figure 5.2c indicates a growing working capital requirement. The dotted line drawn tangent to the seasonal lows shows a definite upward slope. It also highlights the fact that this company possesses two kinds of working capital: a *transitory* portion brought about by seasonal swings in business activity and a segment that is of a more *permanent* nature (albeit, permanently growing).

The total current assets for this business are increasing steadily over the years, but fluctuating during the year. According to the time scale on the horizontal axis, working capital rises during the spring and summer months and then drops off in the fall and winter. The spring increase could be due to an inventory build-up, followed by greater credit sales and a corresponding rise in receivables in the summer. Receivables are collected in the fall and winter in conjunction with a cut in production and inventories. This up-and-down pattern is very consistent from one year to the next. Therefore, we are able to describe it as seasonal in nature. Firms that contend with transitory working capital requirements, due to seasonal activity, also encounter special financing problems. We will discuss these financing problems in chapter 11.

Case IV: The final situation we will consider involves a company with a very complex pattern of business activity. Here we have a firm whose sales, although definitely growing, are susceptible to both seasonal swings *and* business cycles. That is, business recessions depress sales and inflationary expansions stimulate them. Fortunately or unfortunately, depending upon one's point of view, many companies fall into this classification. Figure 5.2d depicts this situation. Optimal working capital needs for this business are gradually increasing over the years accompanied by steady seasonal fluctuations. As in the previous example, current assets rise in spring and summer and then drop off in fall and winter. Then, about the second quarter of 19–6, a business recession sets in. This is indicated by the left

Figure 5.2d   Working capital behavior for a firm whose sales are growing, seasonal, and cyclical

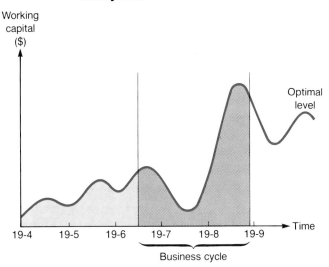

border of the shaded area in figure 5.2d. The typical business would prefer to reduce current assets, particularly inventory, in the early stages of a recession. A popular description of this behavior is "getting lean prior to rough times." Therefore, the optimal level of working capital drops significantly. Around the second quarter of 19–7, business picks up again and, with it, the desired level of working capital. Sales, and thus the optimal build-up of working capital, might then exceed the long run growth trend since business expansions are often inflationary in their latter stages. That is the case here. Eventually, about the third quarter of 19–8, current assets return to their normal pattern (right border of shaded area).

Of course, business cycles are not identical, nor do all firms react the same way to them. This example is merely meant to provide a glimpse into the way in which working capital can be affected by business cycles.

Actual vs. Optimal Working Capital   We have just discussed at some length the behavior of working capital over time in conformance with four different sales activity patterns. The discussion centered upon the optimal or desired amount of working capital a given firm would have under each sales pattern. Not surprisingly, the actual level of working capital often deviates from the desired level either in total or the individual components. Many things can account for such discrepancies, but they can, for all practical purposes, be placed in one of five classifications: forecasting errors, time lags, client behavior, poor management, and other.

Forecasting Errors: No matter how consistent a seasonal sales pattern has been in the past, it rarely repeats in the future exactly the same way. For example, the normal 50% increase in sales at Christmas may turn out to be 25%. As a result, particular current assets may be more or less than optimal for that particular sales level. Forecasting business cycles is especially fraught with error. It is difficult to predict when a cycle will start, how far it will go, when it will reverse or how long it will last. Business expansions and contractions are often upon a company before they know it. Consequently, they have no time to plan and are therefore late in determining the optimal levels for current assets. That is why, for example, a firm may desire to reduce inventory in a downturn, but, due to faulty forecasting, the firm actually encounters a large increase. Sales growth trends are also difficult to predict, with changing consumer attitudes and competition complicating matters.

Time Lags: Forecasting problems could be substantially offset if time lags did not exist. A time lag is the lapse of time that takes place from the moment management decides corrective action is needed and the action is carried out. Most time lags are related to inventory (i.e., delivery time, production time, and liquidation time), but they can also come into play with receivables and cash. Consider, for example, a firm that built up inventory in anticipation of a seasonal sales increase that does not materialize (i.e., a forecasting error). Consequently, inventory exceeds the new optimal amount. A production cutback and inventory liquidation is in order. However, these take time to accomplish (unless, of course, costly layoffs and price cuts are imposed). In the meantime, inventory is too high.

Client Behavior: An accurate forecast of sales volume will not always guarantee an optimal level of current assets. Suppliers and credit customers can cause havoc with the best-laid plans. Suppliers can do this by disrupting deliveries and, therefore, inventory. Customers can do likewise through late payments that will increase accounts receivable.

Poor management: Cash, receivables, and inventory can all drift off course because of poor management. Management must constantly monitor internal operations and deal with clients in an effort to control working capital. While such activities will not assure an optimal level of working capital they can certainly help. Very poor management can even make a bad situation worse.

Other: Included in this category are those nonrecurring events that impact on current assets, such as strikes, lawsuits, and adverse weather conditions.

A combination of bad forecasting, large time lags, adverse client behavior, and poor management can cause actual working capital to differ substantially from what would be optimal. Figure 5.3 shows how far off actual working capital can be from the optimal. Good management will try to keep these problems from occurring or, at least, minimize their impact. Certainly, internal controls and sound forecasting procedures are needed to keep a good working capital plan on course.

Current Assets vs. Capital Assets   Additional insight into current assets can be obtained by comparing their behavior to that of capital assets. For this analysis we will use a hypothetical firm characterized by complex sales activity. That is, a firm whose sales are seasonal, cyclical, and growing. Furthermore, this company has a substantial investment in capital assets. Figure 5.4 describes the situation.

The most striking thing about this comparison is the much greater volatility of current assets. Working capital can change quickly and dramatically, albeit not always according to management's wishes. Capital assets, which are primarily fixed in nature, follow a smooth

Figure 5.3   The actual level of working capital often diverges from that which is desired.

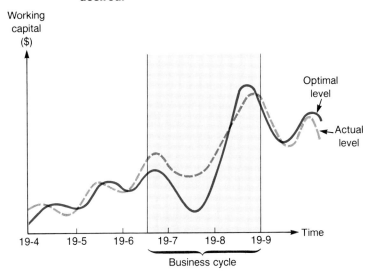

Figure 5.4   Contrasting the behavior of current assets and capital assets over time

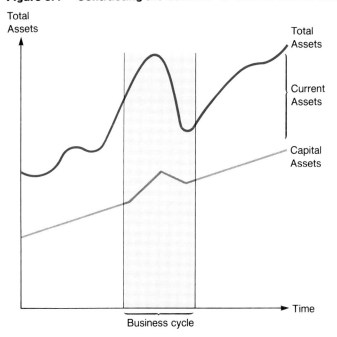

upward movement in line with the trend of sales growth, changing course only during the business cycle.[4] Although businesses would prefer to change capital assets more often and in larger degree to better fit their needs, this is not normally feasible. There are substantial costs involved in changing productive capacity, not to mention time delays. As a consequence, *capital assets are much more stable than current assets.*

Cash Conversion Cycle

So far, we have been mainly concerned with the combined total of working capital. In the subsequent two chapters our attention will be turned to the individual components of working capital. The purpose of the present section is to explain the interrelationships among inventory, accounts receivable, and cash.

Inventory, receivables, and cash form a cycle as one is converted into the other and the process is repeated over and over again. For a manufacturing company the cycle would appear as follows: materials, labor, energy, etc. are acquired with cash; they are then used to produce products; these goods are held in inventory until sold; sales of inventory are made on credit; the credit sales become accounts receivable until collected; and, finally, collections are made in cash. The cycle starts again when the cash inflow is used to acquire more materials, labor, etc. A cycle begins with a decrease in cash balances (cash outflow) and ends with an increase in cash balances (cash inflow). This entire process of going from cash to inventory to receivables and back to cash again is referred to as the *"cash conversion cycle."* A schematic diagram of the cash conversion cycle is shown below in figure 5.5.

Cash conversion cycles are a continual process in the sense that all stages are occurring simultaneously. That is, while some goods are being produced, others are being sold and still others are being paid for. Through it all, the cash, receivables, and inventory balances are never zero. The level of activity can vary, however, due to seasonal fluctuations, business cycles, and sales trends.

A cash conversion cycle can take considerable time to complete. The inventory turnover and accounts receivable turnover are the two key determinants of this time period. As an illustration, a given product with an inventory turnover of 4.8 times (every 75 days) and an accounts receivable turnover of 8 times (every 45 days) would incur a cash conversion cycle of 120 days. In other words, it takes, on average, 120 days to produce, sell, and collect payment for this product. In such a long period of time, receivables and inventory can grow to extraordinarily large amounts. Injecting $100,000 a day into this system would produce an average investment in receivables and inventory of $100,000 \times 120$ days $= $12,000,000.[5] As a result, $12,000,000 in financing is needed to carry these assets. To state the matter another way, the $100,000 spent each day will not be recouped for 120 days.

---

[4]In actuality, large capital asset purchases and sales would not generate such a smooth curve.

[5]In addition to receivables and inventory, most companies also hold substantial amounts of cash transactions balances.

Figure 5.5   Cash conversion cycle

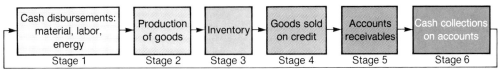

In the first stage of the cash conversion cycle, it is stated that materials, labor, and energy are paid for with cash before they are used in production. As a matter of fact, payment for these services is normally delayed for a period of time, thus giving rise to accounts payable and accrued wages. These current liabilities have the effect of reducing the time needed to complete the cash conversion cycle (i.e., cash outflow to cash inflow). Referring to the previous example where the cycle took 120 days to complete, now let us say that bills and wages are not due for 30 days. This results in a decrease in the cash conversion cycle to 90 days. The net effect is to reduce the amount of financing needed to carry current assets by 30 ÷ 120 = 25%.

Summary

Working capital management involves the determination of the optimal amount of each current asset and the day-to-day administration and control of those assets, with the objective of maximizing stockholder wealth. There are three major categories of working capital: cash and marketable securities, accounts receivable, and inventory. The optimal level for each category of current assets is found by comparing the marginal benefits and marginal costs at different asset levels. The amount of a current asset should be increased as long as the marginal benefits exceed the marginal costs. After a firm has determined an optimal current asset level, administrative practices and procedures must be instituted to achieve and maintain (i.e., control) the level.

A company's sales volume ordinarily has a large, positive impact upon the desired amount of working capital, although the relaltionship is stronger for some firms than for others. A variation in sales activity over time would, therefore, bring about a change in the optimal levels of cash, receivables, and inventory. A company's sales could change over time for one or all of the following reasons: a growth trend, seasonal fluctuations, and business cycles. Variations in sales activity brought about by these factors will induce similar changes in working capital.

Inventory, receivables, and cash form an interrelated cycle as one is converted into the other in a repetitive manner. The entire process of going from cash to inventory to receivables and back to cash again is commonly referred to as the cash conversion cycle ∎

Key Terms/Concepts

Cash conversion cycle	Marginal benefit	Working capital behavior
Cash management	Marginal cost	Cyclical component
Credit management	Optimal level of current assets	Seasonal component
Forecasting errors	Time lags	Trend component
Inventory management		

Questions

1. The four major categories of current assets are cash, marketable securities, accounts receivable, and inventory. List at least three other current assets.

2. The cash conversion cycle can be reduced with the use of current liabilities. How else can a company reduce its cash conversion cycle?

3. What type of business is characterized by the most dramatic changes in working capital over time?

4. Provide the names of three businesses that have little or no need for inventory. Are there any companies with little or no accounts receivable?

5. In what sense is a current asset level "optimum"?

6. Would a firm with seasonal sales find it more difficult to manage its current assets than a firm whose sales are not seasonal? Explain.

7. What is meant by the phrase "cash conversion cycle"?

8. How do you suppose current assets came to be called working capital?

Problems

1. Ralph and Mona's Appliance Store turns over its inventory four times a year, receivables six times a year, and accounts payable twelve times a year. Compute the average holding period, average collection period, and average payment period for this company. Ralph and Mona's Appliance Store experiences a cash conversion cycle of how many days?

2. Given an inventory turnover of 3X, an accounts receivable turnover of 4.8X, and an accounts payable turnover of 8X, find the cash conversion cycle.

3. Bosk, Inc., is experiencing a cash conversion cycle of 115 days. The firm's average daily expenditures for labor, energy, materials, and the like amount to $250,000: (a) determine Bosk's average total investment in inventory and accounts receivable; (b) a reduction in the cash conversion cycle to 100 days would lower the average investment in receivables and inventory to what amount?

4. Nutri-Hygiene's monthly current assets for the last five years are displayed in the table shown below.*

	1982	1983	1984	1985	1986
Jan.	$620	$590	$690	$ 830	$645
Feb.	580	620	690	845	585
Mar.	740	820	840	1000	650
Apr.	770	850	830	970	700
May	785	850	955	1060	730
June	900	910	965	1070	800
July	840	815	875	1105	845
Aug.	685	790	950	980	815
Sept.	610	800	825	815	710
Oct.	720	940	895	920	740
Nov.	535	945	925	890	610
Dec.	605	895	970	875	585

*Figures are in thousands of dollars.

Required: Identify the seasonal, cyclical, and trend patterns.

Selected References

Beranek, William, *Working Capital Management*, Belmont, Calif.: Wadsworth, 1968.

Hauke, John E., and Arthur G. Reitsch, *Business Forecasting*, Boston: Allyn and Bacon, 1981.

Knight, W. D., "Working Capital Management—Satisficing versus Optimization," *Financial Management* (Spring 1972), pp. 33–40.

Mehta, Dileep, *Working Capital Management*, Englewood Cliffs, N.J.: Prentice-Hall, 1974.

Richards, Verlyn D., and Eugene J. Laughlin, "A Cash Conversion Cycle Approach to Liquidity Analysis," *Financial Management* (Spring 1980), pp. 32–38.

Smith, Keith V., *Guide to Working Capital Management*, New York: McGraw-Hill, 1979.

Smith, Keith V., "State of the Art of Working Capital Management," *Financial Management* (Autumn 1973), pp. 50–55.

Welter, Paul, "How to Calculate Savings Possible through Reduction of Working Capital," *Financial Executive* (October 1970), pp. 50–58.

6

Working Capital Management: Cash and Marketable Securities

Overview

The general aspects of working capital management were explored in chapter five. Now it is time to turn our attention to the specifics of managing current assets.

All businesses find it necessary to hold cash and/or marketable securities (i.e., liquid assets) to meet their liquidity needs. Beyond this basic premise, there are several decisions that must be made. In the first place, is there a best or optimal amount of liquid assets for a given firm, and how is it determined? Secondly, how should a company divide its liquid asset holdings between cash and marketable securities? Finally, which marketable securities should be selected from among the many that are available? In addition to wrestling with the decisions mentioned above, a firm will probably find it advisable to manage its cash receipts and disbursements. All of these issues shall be addressed in the current chapter. Chapter 7 will cover the management of accounts receivable and inventory ∎

Objectives

By the end of the chapter the student should be able to:

1. Explain the concept of liquidity, including discussion of transactions demand and precautionary demand
2. Describe the U.S. payments system
3. Explain and give examples of "float"
4. Explain how optimal levels of liquid assets can be estimated
5. Define "compensating balances"
6. Provide examples of situations when liquid assets are used as a "store of value"
7. Assuming a given liquid asset balance, explain how to decide on the allocation of cash versus marketable securities
8. Explain the need for, and provide examples of, maximizing positive float and minimizing negative float
9. List the characteristics of marketable securities
10. Explain and calculate the relationship between interest rates and security prices
11. Calculate yields on marketable securities
12. List and describe various types of securities

Introduction

Cash and marketable securities provide liquidity for a business (medium of exchange) and they can also serve as a temporary haven (store of value). Together, they are the true liquid assets of a firm. Cash consists of checking account deposits, and to a lesser extent, currency and coin. Marketable securities are investments that can be converted into a predetermined amount of cash, on very short notice and at little expense. The major difference between cash and marketable securities is that the latter generates income. Since these two assets are such close substitutes for one another they are often referred to in the same vein. It is fairly common practice today, for example, to use the words "liquid assets" or "cash" in place of cash and marketable securities. In turn, "liquidity management" and "cash management" are the terms often used to describe the management of these assets. However, we will retain the distinction in much of this chapter for explanatory purposes.

The objectives of this chapter are twofold: 1) to explain how a business can determine the optimal quantities of cash and marketable securities to hold; and 2) to describe some principles and procedures that are useful in administering cash and marketable securities. Before engaging these issues, it is important to understand the concept of liquidity and the payments system in the United States ■

Nature of Liquidity

In as much as liquidity is the major motive for holding cash and marketable securities, it is advantageous to investigate this concept in more detail. *Liquidity is the ability to pay bills as they come due.* These bills might be for any or all of the following: wages, supplies, interest, utilities, rent, taxes, or materials. For practical reasons, most individuals and organizations prefer to be paid in cash. This may seem like an obvious statement, but it has not been many generations ago that most transactions were of the barter variety (e.g., chickens traded for shovels). Barter was a very inefficient payment system then and would be worse in our complex economic society of today. Nevertheless, a business could theoretically pay its bills with goods or services and, in fact, they sometimes still do. Without question, however, the overriding preference is for payment in cash. It is much easier to carry, spend, and maintain cash as opposed to, say, bushels of corn.

Companies thus find it necessary to hold cash balances and cash equivalents, such as marketable securities, to meet their future liquidity needs. What is it that gives rise to liquidity needs in the first place? The need for liquidity arises basically from two factors or demands: 1) the uneven nature of daily cash receipts and disbursements, commonly referred to as the transaction demand; and 2) the uncertainty surrounding cash receipts and expenditures that gives rise to a precautionary demand.

Transactions Demand for Liquidity   The daily cash transactions of a typical business seldom exactly match. Cash receipts are either higher or lower than cash expenditures. As a consequence of this lack of synchronization, some days will have a cash surplus and other days a cash deficit. A common occurrence is for several days of surpluses or deficits to be strung together. Seasonal differences in production and sales can account for this phenomenon as well as uneven receipt and expenditure patterns within a month or even a week. With regard to the latter situation, firms that bill their customers monthly can expect to receive payment in a narrow time span (i.e., within 4 to 8 days of due date), but their expenditures for wages, materials, and the like are spread over the month.

Transactions liquidity is needed for those days on which cash expenditures are expected to exceed cash receipts (i.e., the days when deficits occur). It is not at all unusual for several deficit days to run together. Liquidity is already accounted for on those days when receipts equal or exceed expenditures. A business that can forecast a continuous period of daily cash surpluses will have no demand for transactions liquidity during that time span and, therefore, will have no need to hold cash or marketable securities for that purpose.

These concepts can be clarified by two hypothetical situations. Table 6.1 contains forecasts of one month's daily cash receipts and expenditures for two different firms.

Table 6.1   Two Forecasts of Daily Cash Receipts and Disbursements for the Next 30 Days

	Firm A				Firm B		
Day	Receipts	Expenditures	Surplus (Deficit)	Day	Receipts	Expenditures	Surplus (Deficit)
1	$ 4,000	$ 3,500	$ 500	1	$ 20,000	$ 7,000	$13,000
2	6,000	4,500	1500	2	10,000	7,000	3,000
3	3,000	3,000	0	3	0	7,000	(7,000)
4	4,000	3,500	500	4	0	7,000	(7,000)
5	4,000	3,500	500	5	0	7,000	(7,000)
6	3,000	3,000	0	6	0	7,000	(7,000)
7	4,000	3,500	500	7	0	7,000	(7,000)
8	4,000	3,500	500	8	0	7,000	(7,000)
9	6,000	4,500	1500	9	0	7,000	(7,000)
10	3,000	3,000	0	10	0	7,000	(7,000)
11	4,000	3,500	500	11	0	7,000	(7,000)
12	4,000	3,500	500	12	0	7,000	(7,000)
13	3,000	3,000	0	13	0	7,000	(7,000)
14	4,000	3,500	500	14	0	7,000	(7,000)
15	4,000	3,500	500	15	0	7,000	(7,000)
16	6,000	4,500	1500	16	0	7,000	(7,000)
17	3,000	3,000	0	17	0	7,000	(7,000)
18	4,000	3,500	500	18	0	7,000	(7,000)
19	4,000	3,500	500	19	0	7,000	(7,000)
20	4,000	3,500	500	20	0	7,000	(7,000)
21	3,000	3,000	0	21	0	7,000	(7,000)
22	4,000	3,500	500	22	0	7,000	(7,000)
23	6,000	4,500	1500	23	2,000	7,000	(5,000)
24	3,000	3,000	0	24	6,000	7,000	(1,000)
25	4,000	3,500	500	25	14,000	7,000	7,000
26	4,000	3,500	500	26	20,000	7,000	13,000
27	4,000	3,500	500	27	30,000	7,000	23,000
28	3,000	3,000	0	28	38,000	7,000	31,000
29	4,000	3,500	500	29	50,000	7,000	43,000
30	6,000	4,500	1500	30	60,000	7,000	53,000
Total	$122,000	$106,000	$16,000	Total	$250,000	$210,000	$40,000

Assuming that actual cash receipts and expenditures follow true to form, these two firms face significantly different liquidity requirements. Firm A foresees no days of deficits, because receipts always equal or exceed expenditures. Accordingly, Firm A may not need to hold any liquid assets. Firm B, on the other hand, expects to run deficits from days three through twenty-four. Consequently, this business will need to hold some cash and/or marketable securities if it wishes to meet its payments on time. Notice that Firm B faces liquidity requirements even though its total cash surplus for the month ($40,000) exceeds Firm A's ($16,000).

Precautionary Demand for Liquidity   Transactions demand for liquidity is determined by planned or expected cash receipts and expenditures. A daily cash flow forecast for even a month or two into the future can be off mark. Cash receipts can fall below expectations for any number of reasons. Cash expenditures, while generally more predictable than receipts, can increase unexpectedly. As a result, planned surpluses can turn into deficits and small deficits into larger ones. *This uncertainty creates a precautionary demand for liquidity that is over and above the transactions demand.* The precautionary demand can be fulfilled by holding additional quantities of cash and/or securities. *However, some companies meet their precautionary needs by prearranging bank loans that can be drawn down on short notice.* In the earlier discussion on transactions demand, we saw a business, Firm A, that had no need for liquidity. Its planned daily cash receipts always covered expenditures. Nevertheless, a firm in this position would probably hold some liquid assets for precautionary reasons.

Dangers of Inadequate Liquidity   Our discussion of liquidity has emphasized the need for liquid assets to be used to eliminate daily cash deficits. In other words, cash and marketable securities are held for the purpose of paying bills on those days when receipts are insufficient to do so. One may ask, why is it so important to avoid deficits? In a nutshell, it is normally good business practice to pay bills on time. To be even one day late can cause a firm problems. The severity of the problems depends to a large extent upon to whom the payment is due and industry customs. Inability to pay utilities is not usually as severe as missing interest payments. Also, late payments to suppliers are more acceptable in some industries than in others.

At a minimum, late payment can cause a firm embarrassment. However, insolvency and bankruptcy could result at the other extreme. In between these two extremes are a range of difficulties such as: hard feelings on the part of employees; a damaged credit rating; sale of nonliquid assets at distress prices; inability to buy materials and supplies on credit; and higher interest rates on loans. A well-managed business will try to minimize these difficulties.

United States Payments System

All business transactions are ultimately finalized in cash. Expenditures are made with cash and receipts are obtained in cash. Although a business may acquire merchandise on credit, it must eventually be paid for in cash. The same thing is true with regard to credit sales.

While a few businesses, notably small retail and service establishments, handle rather large amounts of currency and coin, the overwhelming payment mechanism is the checking account. There are two primary methods used to transfer funds into and out of checking accounts: wire transfers and checks.

Wire transfers are nothing more than electronic debits and credits to checking accounts stored in computers. Wire transfers are possible in the United States because many bank computers are linked together by the *Federal Reserve Communications System (Fedwire)* and *automated clearinghouses*. An international communications system has also developed. By using wire transfers, funds can be transferred from a New York bank account to a Los Angeles bank account almost instantaneously. The procedure is relatively straightforward, a customer simply instructs its bank to wire funds from its account to another business's bank account. Banks do charge a fee for this service, which tends to restrict its use to relatively large sums of money.

Although wire transfers are increasing in importance, checks remain the most popular means of cash payment. This is particularly true for retail purchases. The interesting thing about checks, from a financial management viewpoint, is that an immediate transfer of funds does not usually occur when a check is written. There are three reasons why this might occur and they all come under the heading of *float*.

Mail Float   Many checks are mailed out of convenience or due to a great distance between the two parties to a transaction. It can take up to a week for a letter to traverse the United States. Checks mailed from or to foreign countries can take much longer than that. In the meantime, the check writer has officially paid the bill even though no funds have been removed from the checking account.

Processing Float   Once the checks have arrived at their destination the customer accounts must be duly credited. Following this, the checks are then transported to the bank for deposit. Allowing time for handling and so forth, this entire process may take as much as two or three days. Consequently, the check writer obtains a free ride for a little while longer.

Clearing Float   Technically, the money from checks deposited in a bank cannot be used until the checks have cleared against the bank they were written on. One reason for the delay is the possibility that there are insufficient funds in the check-writer's account. Clearing float may take several days to complete depending upon the proximity of the two banks involved. However, when the Federal Reserve is involved in the clearing (as it usually is) it artificially limits the clearing time to two days by covering the check itself.

The combination of mail float, processing float, and clearing float can create problems and opportunities for companies as we shall see later.

Figure 6.1   Elements of check float

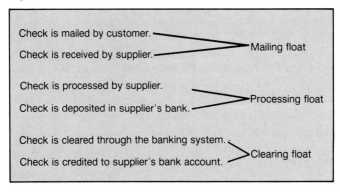

Electronic Funds Transfer System   *Electronic Funds Transfer System (EFTS)* is the general name used to describe the electronic movement of funds. Many experts are of the opinion that in not too many years, the United States, Japan, and Western Europe will be completely wired for a 100% electronic monetary system. Under this system, all transactions will be computerized, and, in place of currency and checkbooks, we will carry debit and credit cards to make all of our purchases. If such a system does materialize then we will witness, among other things, the end of float. The technology for EFTS exists, the major roadblocks are consumer acceptance and some unanswered legal questions.

Optimal Level of Liquid Assets

That most businesses must hold cash and marketable securities for liquidity needs is taken for granted. Difficulties arise when we try to measure the optimal level of liquid assets and, subsequently, divide the optimal balance between cash and securities.

The optimal amount of liquid assets a firm should hold at any given time is determined by a comparison of marginal benefits and costs. More specifically, the optimal level of liquid assets is at the point where the marginal costs of holding liquid assets equals the marginal benefits. This can be seen in figure 6.2.

The major benefit derived from holding liquid assets is the ability to pay bills on time and thus avoid the difficulties posed by late payment. A further benefit is the interest earned on marketable securities. Marginal benefits start out very high and decline continuously up to liquid asset level X. After that point, they are strictly governed by the income from marketable securities. The cost of holding liquid assets is determined by the cost of financing (i.e., the required rate of return) necessary to support these assets. A good example of this would be the interest rate on short-term bank loans. Figure 6.2 assumes that the marginal cost is constant over a given range of financing. Therefore the cost of financing one additional

---

Figure 6.2   Liquid asset balances are determined by marginal benefits and costs.

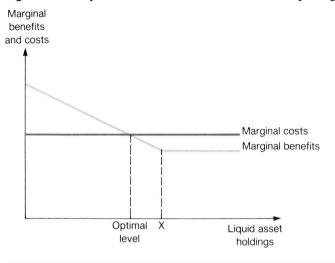

---

dollar of liquid asset is no higher than financing each previous dollar. If the cost increases as additional financing is obtained, the curve would be upward-sloping rather than horizontal. Figure 6.2 is also drawn under the assumption that financing costs exceed the interest rates earned on marketable securities by a consistent amount (note the two horizontal segments).

The preceding discussion was somewhat theoretical. Obviously, no firm can determine *exactly* where marginal benefits equal marginal costs. This does not mean that a company is totally helpless in approximating its optimal liquid asset balance. There are practical methods available to aid management in this regard. A procedure is presented below that is designed around the two factors that give rise to liquidity needs: transactions demand and precautionary demand.

Measuring Transactions Demand for Liquid Assets   A month is a useful time period to measure the transactions demand for liquid assets, as we saw earlier. A company that wishes to estimate transaction needs for the forthcoming month of November can do so by constructing a daily cash receipts and expenditures forecast like those in table 6.1. A very good way to develop such a forecast is to start with the daily cash receipts and expenditures for past Novembers. By averaging these figures, adjusting for trends and unusual events such as holidays, the estimated daily cash receipts and disbursements for next November might appear as in table 6.2.

Table 6.2   A Forecast of Daily Cash Receipts and Disbursements for the Month of November

Day	Cash Receipts	Cash Expenditures	Surplus (Deficit)
1	$47,000	$ 0	$47,000
2	42,000	0	42,000
3	34,000	0	34,000
4	24,000	24,000	0
5	18,000	10,000	8,000
6	10,000	0	10,000
7	2,000	125,000	(123,000)
8	2,000	0	2,000
9	2,000	0	2,000
10	1,000	10,000	(9,000)
11	1,000	0	1,000
12	1,000	0	1,000
13	1,000	0	1,000
14	0	152,000	(152,000)
15	0	10,000	(10,000)
16	0	5,000	(5,000)
17	0	5,000	(5,000)
18	2,000	24,000	(22,000)
19	4,000	10,000	(6,000)
20	8,000	10,000	(2,000)
21	8,000	125,000	(117,000)
22	13,000	0	13,000
23	17,000	0	17,000
24	20,000	0	20,000
25	30,000	10,000	20,000
26	32,000	0	32,000
27	35,000	0	35,000
28	40,000	0	40,000
29	48,000	15,000	33,000
30	50,000	35,000	15,000

It is evident from table 6.2 that this firm's receipts are concentrated at the beginning and end of the month while expenditures occur sporadically. Of primary interest to us are the daily deficits that begin on the 7th. Liquid asset holdings must be at least $123,000 on November 7. Another $9,000 is needed on November 10 and a minimum of $319,000 must be available beginning November 14 to carry the firm through November 21.

Measuring Precautionary Demand for Liquid Assets   The cash receipts and expenditures shown in table 6.2 are only estimates. Although they may be good estimates, it would be only a coincidence if they turned out exactly as forecasted. Given the problems most firms experience when they cannot make their payments on time, it behooves them to hold extra liquid assets. These would be over and above those needed for transactions purposes. Of course, one could take the easy way out and hold balances large enough to cover any and all possible deficits. However, as we saw earlier, it is costly to hold liquid assets. Stockholders might also question the logic of devoting a large percentage of a corporation's assets to liquid assets. Many owners take the attitude that they could invest in marketable securities on their own and see no need to pay corporate managers high salaries for this function. It is good management, then, to hold precautionary balances to a reasonable level. What is reasonable? Unfortunately, there are no hard and fast rules here. One reasonable procedure would be to examine the historical variability of each month's cash receipts and disbursements. The greater the variability, the greater the precautionary balances should be. Statistical measures such as standard deviation can be useful for this purpose. In any event, one should not be surprised to find that some months require higher precautionary balances than others.

Industry Averages   Average industry figures on liquid asset holdings could provide a useful reference for a company's particular situation. The industry figures should be independent of firm size to make them more meaningful. Thus, ratios are in order. Two useful industry average ratios are liquid assets to total current assets and liquid assets to total assets.[1]

Compensating Balances   Most commercial banks require their business customers to maintain noninterest bearing checking deposits. These are more formally known as *compensating balances*. Banks use these in lieu of charging corporations fees for services rendered. Such services include check clearing, payroll processing, foreign exchange transactions, and the like. Depending upon the rules associated with these deposits, a company may be able to use them to cover part or all of their transactions and precautionary needs. *In some instances, compensating balance rules require a minimum absolute balance at all times.* Consequently, these deposits are, for all practical purposes, of limited use as liquid assets. *In other instances, the rules say that the compensating balance should be an average minimum during the month.* Under these circumstances, a company may be able to use these deposits as liquid assets.

Other Reasons for Holding Liquid Assets

In addition to providing liquidity, cash and marketable securities can also serve as temporary repositories. That is, a company may decide to hold liquid assets in excess of near-term transactions and precautionary demands. It is not that the firm has no better use for these funds, but rather that they are targeted for use in the rather distant future.

While it is easy to criticize businesses for these practices with statements like "why are they tying up resources in such low-yielding assets," there are often legitimate reasons for doing so. 1) It may not be the best time to purchase assets. Prices may be expected to decline, and the firm can move more quickly if it has liquid assets available. 2) Funds that are targeted for future use could be paid out to owners in the form of dividends and then retrieved through stock sales. However, the expense of such an undertaking may make it unfeasible. 3) Bank loans and the sale of securities prior to when the funds are needed can be justified if interest rates are down or the stock market is up. 4) It is often better to acquire the financing for a large project (e.g., plant construction) all at once even though the funds are drawn down over a considerable period of time. This is due to the fact that costs are usually incurred each time funds are raised. For these reasons and others, businesses often hold larger liquid asset balances than what it appears they need at the moment.

---

[1]See chapter 2 for sources of industry ratios.

Cash vs. Marketable Securities

After a firm has determined the optimal quantity of liquid assets it should hold, the next problem is deciding how to divide these assets into cash and marketable securities in an optimal manner.[2]

In the earlier section on the U.S. payments system, we saw how easy and fast it is, with the aid of wire transfers, to move from cash to securities and back again. From a technological standpoint, one could use cash receipts to buy marketable securities at 10:00 A.M. then turn around and sell them at 2:00 P.M. to meet a payroll payment. In the four hour interval, interest income is generated and the checking account balance is hardly interrupted. Given these possibilities, what is it that prevents businesses from holding all of their liquid assets in the form of marketable securities? The answer is trading costs. *Trading costs* include paperwork, registration fees, and dealer compensation. *Dealers are security traders who buy at wholesale (bid price) and sell at retail (ask price).* The difference between the ask price and the bid price is their compensation. As you can imagine, frequent buying at retail and selling at wholesale can get to be expensive. As a consequence, trading costs must be balanced against the interest earnings from marketable securities.

The general rule to follow is to continue to invest cash in marketable securities as long as interest income exceeds trading costs. The four key variables in this decision are the interest rate, available cash, number of days the funds can be invested (holding period), and trading costs. Interest income can be calculated with the following equation:

Equation 6.1

Interest Income $=$ Daily Interest Rate $\times$ Holding Period $\times$ Investment

Where the daily interest rate is found by dividing the annual rate by 360 days.

Application: J. M. B. Enterprises has $1,200,000 in a checking account that will not be needed to make transactions for five days. J. M. B. can acquire securities paying an annual rate of interest of 9%, which is an equivalent daily interest rate of .09 $\div$ 360 $=$ .00025. The costs of trading these securities will be $600. Is it worthwhile to make this investment? The interest earnings can be found with equation 6.1 as follows:

Interest Income $=$ (.00025) $\times$ (5 days) $\times$ ($1,200,000) $=$ $1,500

Since the interest income exceeds the trading costs, J. M. B. should buy the securities ■

There is one major flaw in the preceding example. It assumes that the five-day holding period is known with certainty. This may or may not be the case. J. M. B. Enterprises *plans* to use the money to cover a deficit in five days. The situation can be altered considerably if the securities must be turned into cash in only two days. Uncertainty of holding period makes the cash-securities division more difficult. This is especially true if the expected time is very short to begin with. We can now add uncertainty of holding period to trading costs as drawbacks to using marketable securities as liquid assets. By balancing these two factors against interest earnings, firms select the optimal portion of their liquid assets to be held as marketable securities. The difference between this figure and total liquid assets is the optimal

---

[2]As a general rule, corporations cannot have interest paying checking accounts such as NOW accounts.

cash balance. However, the existence of compensating balance requirements could artificially force the cash balance to be higher than what is preferred.

Many firms have found it profitable to invest all of their cash holdings in marketable securities at the close of business and disinvest the next morning. Such transactions are known as "overnight loans." Who, you may be wondering, borrows money at such odd hours? To understand the answer, one must view the financial markets from a global perspective. Although banks and businesses may be closed in the United States, they can be operating at full speed in Asia. After the Asian markets close down, the European banks are open for business. Foreign markets provide much of the demand for overnight loans.

Controlling Cash Receipts and Disbursements

As we saw earlier, the use of checks gives rise to float. Although more and more business transactions are done by wire transfer, the majority are handled with checks. In combination, these two facts point to a world in which float is an ever present reality.

A business faces two kinds of float. *Positive float* arises from disbursements. It is the elapsed time from when a payment is made by check until the funds are deducted from the firm's checking account. *Negative float* is brought about by receipts. It is the interval from when a customer writes a check until it is added to the firm's checking account. *The goal of a firm is to maximize positive float and minimize negative float subject to legal constraints and business custom.*

In attempting to maximize positive float and minimize negative float, management needs a considerable amount of information and at least some imagination. Concerning information, it is imperative that management have estimates of the time it takes to mail checks between different locations as well as the duration for clearing checks through various banks.

Managing float in line with the preceding goal can be very lucrative. A company that can reduce the negative float on incoming checks will have the use of its money sooner. On the other hand, by increasing positive float, a business can use someone else's money longer.

Example: A business has uniform annual sales of $50,000,000. All of its customers pay by check and, on average, these checks are floating in the system for five days. Reducing this negative float to two days will allow for the use of $50,000,000 three days sooner. Given that this firm can earn 13.5% a year on marketable securities, the income attributable to the reduction in float is computed with equation 6.1 as follows:

$$\text{Interest Income} = (.135 \div 360) \times (3 \text{ days}) \times (\$50,000,000) = \$56,250$$

In the preceding example, $56,250 can be earned by reducing the negative float in connection with incoming checks. Yet there are normally costs associated with managing float. As an example, commercial banks usually require some form of compensation when they are hired to help in these situations. As with most other business situations then, proposals to increase positive float or decrease negative float should be evaluated according to their prospective benefits and costs. We will now examine some of the more popular methods used to manage float.

Minimize Negative Float   Negative float can be completely eliminated if customers pay by wire transfer. It is not currently feasible to pay small bills by this means. Large payments, on the other hand, are conducive to wire transfers. Firms that receive large payments may find it worthwhile to require them to be made by wire transfer. However, since the customer would suffer a decline in positive float from this, some inducement may be necessary, such as a lower selling price. Hence, a comparison of benefits and costs is in order.

Another method for speeding the inflow of cash that has gained wide acceptance is *regional banking*.[3] This is used by businesses that have a widely dispersed customer market. Basically, regional banking is a decentralized collection system. The specifics of regional banking systems vary. Nevertheless, it is possible to generalize about their characteristics. Consider a company headquartered in Chicago that has customers in Seattle. Rather than have the Seattle customers send checks all the way to the firm's headquarters in Chicago, they are instructed to send payment to an address in Seattle. A Seattle bank is employed to collect and process the checks and clear them through the banking system. The collected funds are then wired to the company's headquarters bank in Chicago. Not only would this reduce mail and processing float, it would also reduce clearing float because checks are cleared in the vicinity of the Seattle bank.

Regional banking systems can definitely reduce negative float, as shown above, but they are also expensive. Banks charge for collection services, either by requiring noninterest bearing compensating balances or specified fees. Certainly, the cost of maintaining many banks would be prohibitive. A company must be selective in choosing the number and location of banks in a regional collection system to obtain the best results. In addition to mailing and clearing times, one must also consider customer density in an area and each bank's compensation. Lastly, the level of interest rates on marketable securities are important because they affect the earnings to be gained from reduced negative float. In essence, then, a benefit-cost analysis should be applied to each alternative system.

Application: Orion Aluminum, Inc. is a large fabricator of aluminum with headquarters in St. Louis. It ships aluminum products all over the United States and parts of Canada. In a typical year total sales are $200,000,000. At the present time, Orion's customers pay for their purchases by sending checks to the St. Louis headquarters. There they are processed prior to deposit in the firm's St. Louis bank. Before the company can use these funds, the checks must be cleared through the banking system. The average times for each of these activities are respectively: mailing—4½ days; processing—1½ days; and clearing—2 days. On average, the negative float is 8 days.

Orion's management has been studying this situation and has proposed a regional banking system. This system will consist of collection banks in six cities: Toronto, Boston, Baltimore, Atlanta, Denver, and Los Angeles in addition to St. Louis. It is expected that the system will, on average, reduce mail float to 1½ days, processing to 1 day and clearing to 1½ days. Thus, the new float of 4 days would mean that Orion can have the use of its $200,000,000 annual sales four days sooner. As a group, the banks will require Orion to maintain noninterest bearing compensating balances of $3,000,000 for the entire year. These compensating balances are absolute minimums and therefore cannot be used for transactions purposes. Given that Orion can earn 11¼% per year on marketable securities, should it go ahead with the regional banking system?

---

[3]Variants of regional banking are lockbox systems and concentration banking.

The benefits are interest earnings on the earlier cash receipts or:

$$\text{Interest Earnings} = (.1125 \div 360) \times (4 \text{ days}) \times (\$200,000,000) = \$250,000.$$

The cost is the foregone interest earnings on the compensating balances, or $3,000,000 \times .1125 = \$337,500$. Since the costs exceed the benefits, Orion would be better off not to use this regional banking system. However, a different system may be profitable ■

One further procedure used to minimize negative float involves the use of *couriers*. As peculiar as it may sound, there are many instances in which a company can profit by sending a courier to pick up a single check. Since it is rather expensive to use couriers, this procedure is only feasible when the float is long and the check is large. A $50,000,000 check written by the South Korean Government payable to a defense contractor located in Atlanta is a good candidate for courier pick-up. The interest that could be earned by obtaining the use of $50,000,000 just two or three days sooner can be significant. In fact, the earnings could vastly exceed the salary, air fare, and expenses incurred by sending an employee to receive the check. This procedure has become so popular that a number of firms have been established that specialize in providing check courier services to other companies.

Maximize Positive Float   There are a number of ways to increase positive float. The objective of each is to lengthen the time from when a check is written until it is deducted from the checking account.[4] Two of the procedures are discussed here.

Positive float can be increased fairly easily if one is prepared to offend his suppliers and creditors. Simply mail the check on the appointed date, but see to it that it is written on a bank located a great distance from the supplier's bank. Or better yet, have the check mailed from a distant point. By doing this, mailing and clearing float are maximized. For instance, A owes B $1,000,000 on May 31. A and B and their main banks are all located in New York City. However, A also maintains a checking account at a bank in Los Angeles as well as a regional office. The regional office mails the check on May 31 and it is written on the Los Angeles bank. The float generated by such a transaction will greatly exceed what could have occurred. Needless to say, suppliers and creditors do not appreciate such tactics and as a result they can hurt a firm in the long run. Just where to draw the line on this practice is more art than science.

Payroll is another place where positive float can be used advantageously. In this example, however, the intent is not to increase float, but rather to identify and capitalize on it. An examination of cancelled payroll checks often indicates that employees are not depositing their checks immediately. A Friday afternoon payroll will not clear against a firm's account over the weekend even though the payroll checks are deposited on Friday. More interestingly though, many of the payroll checks may be deposited on Monday or Tuesday for one reason or another. Consequently, a company gets additional positive float on some of the payroll. By identifying the additional float, a company can keep a portion of the payroll funds invested for a few more days.

---

[4]A delay in mailing a check does not fall under the category of cash management. This is a financing decision and should be treated accordingly.

Coordinating Bank Accounts   A company that finds it advantageous to use several banks, as opposed to one, must contend with an inherent problem of such a scheme. The problem is one of coordination. That is, funds can be transferred among the banks. How, when, and where these transfers take place are important to the overall management of cash. If not careful, a company can have a Cincinnati bank with a $300,000 balance and no local need for it, while at the same time a New Orleans bank has a zero balance and a need for $300,000. The key to coordination is timely information. Should interstate banking and electronic funds transfer become pervasive, as seems likely, the control of cash receipts and disbursements would be greatly simplified. Not only would float be eliminated, but a company with nationwide operations could get by with one bank.

Investing in Marketable Securities

Once a decision has been made to purchase marketable securities the financial manager is then presented with additional tasks. The securities must be selected from a wide range of alternatives. This selection in turn, depends upon the characteristics of individual securities, their relative yields, and the firm's investment strategy.

Characteristics   Not all securities qualify as marketable securities. To serve as true liquid assets, however, investments should be marketable. *A security is truly marketable if it can be quickly and inexpensively converted into cash, at a predictable price, and with little danger of nonpayment.* To fit this definition, a security must possess three characteristics: safety from default, active resale trading, and short maturity. Investments that are lacking in one or more of these characteristics are, by definition, not marketable and, therefore, will expose the business to an element of risk.

Safety: Standing behind every security is an organization, be it public or private. These organizations have a contractual obligation to repay principal and interest on their debts. In spite of this obligation, a given organization may experience financial problems and be unable to pay its debts. The inability to pay principal and/or interest is more formally known as default. While it is impossible to find securities that are completely safe from default, there are many issues backed by financially strong businesses and governments.

Figure 6.3   Major characteristics of a truly marketable security

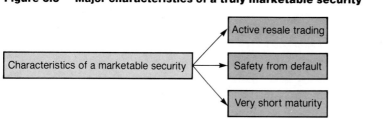

Securities sold by the U.S. Government are considered to be the safest in the world. Large, established, and well-managed corporations and commercial banks are also excellent sources of sound investments. It is these organizations that companies typically look to in their quests for marketable securities.

Some firms choose to bypass high-quality investments in favor of the lower quality and, therefore, higher yielding securities. The risk of such a policy should not be taken lightly. Many experts feel that nonfinancial corporations are better off not speculating in a field outside of their normal business activities.

Trading Activity: If it were possible to predict exactly when cash is needed from marketable securities, one could ignore trading activity. Management could simply buy securities that mature (i.e., payoff) on the future cash deficit dates. Unfortunately, cash needs typically arise without warning. Under such circumstances, marketable securities must be converted into cash prior to their maturities. This requires the existence of an active *secondary or resale market,* and the more active the better. An active resale market is one with a great number of buyers and sellers and continuous trading. The key performers in the secondary markets are the dealers who act as middlepersons in the purchase and sale of securities. They provide investors with the assurance that they can sell their securities quickly. Furthermore, trading costs are lower on active secondary markets precisely because dealers have it so easy finding buyers and sellers.

Not all securities are traded in active secondary markets. As a matter of fact, some securities have no resale market at all. Issues of small businesses and local governments fall in the latter category. A business that invests its liquid assets in securities that are not actively traded on a secondary market, runs the risk of a delayed sale and/or high trading costs.

Maturity: A truly marketable security should have a very short maturity. One year is the standard dividing line between short-term and long-term, but twelve months may be too long for some purposes. It is not at all unusual to find liquid assets invested in securities that mature in less than one month.

As we saw earlier, companies often convert their marketable securities into cash prior to maturity. This is done by selling the securities on a secondary market at market prices. Market prices can vary considerably from the par values of fixed-income securities for a number of reasons. The most common reason is a change in market interest rates. Interest rates can change frequently and, over a period of time, significantly. This has been especially true in recent years (figure 6.4). A basic principle of finance states that *interest rates and fixed-income security prices are inversely related.* In other words, when market interest rates rise, outstanding securities will fall in price and vice versa. The price must change because the coupon, maturity, and par value are fixed by contract. Consider, for example, an investor who purchased a 10% coupon, $10,000 par value bond five years ago. The bond currently has 25 years remaining to maturity. New bonds similar to this one now yield 16% interest on the market. Should the investor decide to sell the bond today, nobody would pay the face value when they can buy many new bonds earning 16%. To make the bond attractive to the market, the investor must sell it at a discount from par value such that the 10% coupon and discount add up to 16%. This discounted price becomes the market price and will be about $6,330.[5] Had interest rates fallen below 10%, say to 8%, then the bond could be sold at a

---

[5]Bond market prices are found by discounting the interest payments and par value back to the present (i.e., PV) at the market rate of interest.

Figure 6.4   Interest rates on long-term U.S. Treasury Bonds, 1979–1983

Source: *Federal Reserve Bulletin*, Board of Governors of the Federal Reserve System, Washington, D.C.

premium over par value or about $12,148. These increases and decreases from par value are capital gains and losses. The main reason this bond's price fluctuated so dramatically is its very long maturity (i.e., 25 years). The price of a short-term bond would not react so drastically, because it does not have as much time left to account for the new interest rates. For example, a 10%, $10,000 par value bond with one year remaining to maturity would sell at prices of $9,465 and $10,189 if interest rates changed to 16% and 8% respectively. It might be helpful to examine figure 6.5.

It is clearly evident that *shorter-term securities can be sold prior to maturity at more predictable prices than longer-term securities.* Moreover, predictability increases as the maturity gets shorter. A business that desires a high degree of certainty in its liquid asset security holdings will hold very short-term instruments, in the neighborhood of three to six months.[6] Most businesses fall in this category on most occasions. There are at least two factors, however, that often entice companies to place a portion of their liquid assets in long-term securities: interest rate speculation and the term structure of interest rates.

---

[6]The development of interest rate futures contracts have reduced the risk of holding long-term securities as liquid assets.

Figure 6.5   Relationship between the market values of bonds and market interest rates

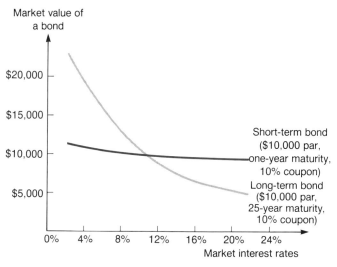

As we have just seen, capital gains can be obtained on securities when interest rates fall. A financial manager who expects interest rates to fall in the near future, can magnify his company's gains by substituting long-term for short-term securities. While both will increase in value, the former will gain the most. This can also be seen in figure 6.5. The danger, of course, is that interest rates might rise instead of fall, in which case long-term securities will suffer more. Interest rate forecasting is a very difficult task, even for an experienced and trained analyst. For that reason, many authorities consider it speculative to purchase long-term securities based solely on interest rate predictions. As with all financial decisions, this involves a tradeoff between profit and risk.

Occasionally long-term securities are selected for liquid assets over their short-term counterparts due to the *term structure of interest rates.* A term structure of interest rates describes the relationship between interest rates and maturity that exists in the financial market at a given point in time. This relationship is normally positive. That is, short-term rates are usually less than longer-term rates. This is exemplified in figure 6.6, which shows the yields (interest rates) on U.S. Government securities of varying maturities. The higher long-term yields surely attracted some short-term investors in spite of these securities having more uncertain market prices.

Yields   It is common practice to refer to the interest rates on securities, marketable or otherwise, as yields. At any given time there normally will be many different yields from which to select. The observed variations are due to difference in safety, trading activity, maturity, and, on occasion, tax status.

Although yields normally are shown in the financial press and freely quoted by security dealers, one should nevertheless be familiar with how they are computed. Marketable securities, by and large, do not pay a contractual rate of interest. Instead, *they trade on a discount basis.* In other words, they are purchased at a price less than par or face value.

Figure 6.6   Yields on selected U.S. Government securities, May 23, 1984

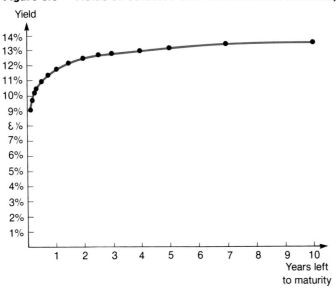

The difference between the purchase price and par value (i.e., the discount) becomes the interest income. Interest income is divided by the purchase price to obtain the yield. The yield on a discounted security can be found with the following equation:

Equation 6.2

$$\text{Yield} = \frac{\text{Par Value} - \text{Purchase Price}}{\text{Purchase Price}}$$

Equation 6.2 is actually a variation of the basic compound interest discounting equation where: purchase price is a present value, par value becomes a cash flow, the time period is one, and yield is used in place of interest rate. Thus,

$$\text{Purchase Price} = \frac{\text{Par Value}}{(1 + \text{Yield})^1}$$

that, when solved for yield, equals equation 6.2.

Since most marketable securities mature in less than one year, *the yield found with equation 6.2 must be converted into a standard annual yield.*

Example: Securities with a face value of $1,000,000 can be purchased for $979,000. They will mature in 60 days at which time the par value will be received. The yield on this investment can be found with equation 6.2 as follows:

$$\text{Yield} = \frac{\$1,000,000 - \$979,000}{\$979,000} = 2.15\% \text{ per 60 days}$$

On an annual basis the yield is (assuming a 360 day year)[7]:

$$.0215 \times (360 \div 60) = 12.9\%$$

An additional adjustment is often made to the yield for income taxes. The purpose of this adjustment is to account for the fact that some marketable securities are exempt from federal or state income taxes; and it is after-tax yields that really matter when comparing alternative securities. The adjustment can be made simply by multiplying the annual yield by one minus the respective income tax rate.

Equation 6.3   After-Tax Yield = Yield (1 − Tax Rate)

For instance, a marketable security pays an annual taxable yield of 15%. Given an income tax rate of 40%, the after-tax yield would be .15 (1 − .40) = 9% ■

Securities   There are a number of securities that possess all or most of the characteristics of marketability. As a rule, these securities have original maturities of less than one year, they are actively traded on a secondary market, and their investment quality is outstanding. Furthermore, they are typically purchased and traded on a discount basis in minimum denominations of $100,000 and more. With the notable exception of U.S. Treasury Bills and Banker's Acceptances, it is possible to tailor the maturity of these securities to the investor's particular needs. A brief description of the more popular types of marketable securities follows.

U.S. Treasury Bills: Treasury Bills or T Bills are obligations of the United States Government. They are issued on a regular basis with standard maturities of 13, 26, 39, and 52 weeks. An excellent secondary market exists for these securities and the fact that they are backed by the Federal Government assures their safety. An additional feature of these securities is their freedom from state and local taxation. Without question, Treasury Bills are the epitome of a marketable security.

Short-Term Agency Securities: Agencies sponsored by the Federal Government sell securities to finance their activities. A portion of their issues have maturities as short as a few days. There is an active secondary market for these securities and, while they are not a formal obligation of the U.S. Government, there is an implicit guarantee behind them. Included among these agencies are the Federal Farm Credit Banks, Federal National Mortgage Association, and the Federal Home Loan Mortgage Corporation.

Banker's Acceptances: A bill of exchange is a device used to pay for goods that must be transported great distances. They are particularly useful in international trade where the shipping time may be several months. An exporter who wishes verification of payment prior to shipment may ask the importer for a bill of exchange equal to the amount of purchase. This is basically a check dated for payment on or about the delivery date of the goods. Verification occurs when the importer's bank "accepts" responsibility for payment, which, in turn, causes the bill of exchange to become a "banker's acceptance." Should the exporter desire not to wait for payment, it can sell the banker's acceptance back to the bank or in the market, but at a discount. The size of the discount depends upon the level of market interest rates and the acceptance's maturity or due date. Safety is accorded banker's acceptances by the bank's guarantee. This combined with a short maturity and an active secondary market make banker's acceptances very good marketable securities.

---

[7]The sophisticated equivalent annual yield is: $(1.0215)^6 - 1 = 13.6\%$.

Commercial Paper: Commercial paper is issued by large commercial corporations and finance companies to raise short-term funds. They vary in quality depending upon the financial strength of the issuing organization. Commercial paper has one drawback as a marketable security and that is its poor secondary market.

Negotiable Certificates of Deposit: Commercial banks raise vast sums of money from the sale of certificates of deposit (CDs). CDs of $100,000 and up are negotiable (i.e., they can be transferred among investors) and generally mature in less than six months. Their safety lies primarily in the financial strength of the issuing bank. Marketability of negotiable CDs has improved over the years with the development of an active secondary market. They are unique among marketable securities in that interest is paid at maturity rather than through a discount.

Eurodollar Deposits: Eurodollars are dollar-denominated savings deposits and negotiable CDs on deposit at commercial banks outside of the United States. They can be found in such diverse places as London, Tokyo, and Frankfurt. Eurodollars can be obtained with very short-maturities, and, as far as the CDs are concerned, they are actively traded. Interest on these deposits is paid at maturity much as it is on domestic CDs. However, interest rates on Eurodollars are generally higher than their U.S. counterparts, which is partially explained by a somewhat greater risk associated with these deposits. Evidently many firms have decided that the higher returns more than compensate for this risk as these investments have grown dramatically in importance.

Repurchase agreements: Repurchase agreements or repos are novel arrangements designed to provide corporations with a flexible, safe, and convenient investment. Essentially, a repo is an agreement on the part of an owner of U.S. Government bonds to sell the bonds to an investor at a certain price and then buy them back at a later date for a higher price. The difference in price is the interest income to the buyer. In the meantime, the interest that accrues on the bonds remains in the possession of the original owner. Repurchase agreements normally involve commercial banks. One of their great advantages is the ease with which an investor can tailor the maturity. Backed as they are by government bonds, their quality is outstanding, and a good secondary market is available if the need arises.

Tax-Free Notes: More states and localities are selling short-term notes and bonds every year. While the dollar amounts of these securities is still relatively small, they may soon be a significant marketable security. The fact that interest on these securities escapes the high corporate federal income tax rate is not lost on many financial managers. They should be examined carefully, however, since there is considerable variation among them in terms of quality and secondary market activity.

Conclusion   As the preceding discussion indicates, it is not an easy task selecting marketable securities. The many alternatives exhibit differences in safety, maturity, flexibility, tax treatment, and trading activity. Moreover, the yields they pay are normally different, as table 6.3 indicates.

Table 6.3   Yields on Selected Marketable Securities on 2/4/85

Security	Maturity	Annual Yield
Commercial paper	3 months	8.55%
Certificates of deposit	3 months	8.55%
Bankers acceptances	3 months	8.40%
London Eurodollars	3 months	9.00%
Treasury bills	3 months	8.16%

Summary

Cash and marketable securities comprise the liquid assets of a business enterprise. Companies hold liquid assets for several reasons: 1) to cover the expected, transitory cash deficits resulting from the lack of synchronization in daily cash inflows and outflows (this is the transactions demand for liquidity); 2) unexpected cash disbursements are met by precautionary holdings of liquid assets; and 3) liquid assets can also serve as a temporary haven or store of value. There is an optimal quantity of liquid assets for every firm. Once this optimum is determined, the next task is to divide liquid assets between cash and marketable securities in a logical manner. Such an allocation is accomplished by comparing the interest earnings from marketable securities to the transactions costs incurred in trading securities. Only securities with certain characteristics qualify as true marketable securities. As a general rule, marketable securities should have the following characteristics: very short maturity (i.e., less than one year), practically no risk of default, and an active secondary trading market. By and large, the interest from these instruments is taxable income to a corporation. Among the more important marketable securities available to corporations are the following: U.S. Treasury Bills, commercial paper, negotiable certificates of deposit, banker's acceptances, repurchase agreements, and Eurodollar deposits.

The use of checks for most business transactions creates problems as well as opportunities for businesses, due to the existence of float. A firm attempts to reduce the negative float associated with incoming checks (cash receipts) and increase the positive float related to outgoing checks (cash disbursements). However, the further development of electronic funds transfer should significantly reduce the impact of float in the future. A summary of the key formulas from this chapter is presented in table 6.4 ■

Table 6.4   Summary of Key Formulas

Interest Income = Daily Interest Rate × Holding Period × Investment

$$\text{Daily Interest Rate} = \frac{\text{Annual Interest Rate}}{360}$$

After-Tax Yield = Yield (1 − Tax Rate)

$$\text{Yield} = \frac{\text{Par Value} - \text{Purchase Price}}{\text{Purchase Price}}$$

$$\text{Purchase Price} = \frac{\text{Par Value}}{(1 + \text{Yield})^1}$$

Key Terms/Concepts

Active resale market
Banker's acceptances
Checking accounts
Clearing float
Commercial paper
Compensating balance
Couriers
Dealer spread
Electronic Funds Transfer
  System (EFTS)
Eurodollar deposits
Federal Reserve
  Communications System
  (Fedwire)
Float

Liquidity
Mail float
Marketable securities
Maturity
Negative float
Negotiable certificates of
  deposit
Payment mechanism
Positive float
Precautionary demand
Processing float
Regional banking
Repurchase agreements

Safety from default
Short-term agency securities
Tax-free notes
Term structure of interest
  rates
Trading activity
Trading costs
Transactions demand
U.S. Treasury Bills
Wire transfers
Yields

Questions

1. Describe the difference between transactions and precautionary demands for liquidity.

2. Define float. What are the causes of float?

3. Why are long-term U.S. Government securities seldom used for liquid assets?

4. When comparing alternative marketable securities, why is it important to adjust their yields for income taxes?

5. What security is considered to be the most marketable and why?

6. A student at the University of Chicago has an opportunity to purchase a quality used car, if he can raise $5,000 within twenty-four hours. His parents have access to the cash, but they live in Seattle, Washington. How can this student obtain the money from his parents in the allotted time?

7. What is the major complicating factor involved in allocating liquid assets between cash and marketable securities?

8. Why is it so important that a company maintain an adequate level of liquidity?

9. Is it within the realm of possibilities that we will someday have a checkless society? Explain.

10. What is the central issue involved in managing cash receipts?

Problems

1. At a 15% interest rate, measure the interest earnings on $800,000 invested for the following numbers of days:
     A. 3 days.
     B. 5 days.
     C. 10 days.
     D. 30 days.
     E. 1½ days.

2. Firmlux Industries sells mattresses throughout the United States and Canada to several hundred retail distributors. Annual sales currently amount to $90,000,000. Right now, all customers pay by check sent directly to the Firmlux headquarters in Cincinnati. The company processes the checks, deposits them in a local bank and then waits for the checks to clear through the banking system. On average, it takes seven days from the time the checks are mailed until they are credited to Firmlux's checking account. A financial consultant has advised the firm to set up a regional collection and processing system that will consist of six banks strategically located around the country. Such a system should reduce float to three days, in contrast to the present seven days. The combined annual fees of the six banks will come to $95,000. Given that Firmlux can invest in marketable securities at 13.5%, should the company take the consultant's advice?

3. Sytex Corporation has been dealing with Fidelity National Bank for several years. In a typical year, the bank will clear and process some 500,000 checks for Sytex. For providing these services, Fidelity charges a fixed annual fee of $175,000. Sytex has just received a letter from the bank offering to change the way its fee is determined. Sytex is offered the following three alternatives: a) maintain a minimum compensating balance of $1,500,000 throughout the entire year; b) pay a service charge of $.40 per check handled; or c) stay with the current system. Sytex Corporation can presently earn 15% on short-term investments. Which is the lowest cost alternative under the current conditions? What are the key variables in this decision?

4. Would it be worthwhile to invest $12,000,000 for three days, at an interest rate of 16%, if the transactions costs are $30,000?

5. Cable Company must pay a Dallas based supplier $2,000,000 by the twentieth of the month. Under the conditions of sale, payment can be made by check and the bill is considered paid on the postmark date. Cable Company can write the check on either of its two banks. A check written on the Boston bank will provide positive float of approximately six days. On the other hand, a check written on Cable's Phoenix bank should produce positive float of three days. (a) On what day of the month should the check be written? (b) How much will Cable Company earn by using the Boston bank rather than the Phoenix bank? Assume the company can earn 18% on marketable securities.

6. Determine the annual interest rate or yield on $2,000,000 face amount of U.S. Treasury Bills that mature in sixty days. They can be purchased for $1,941,000.

7. The financial manager at Wilcox Enterprises has been studying the payroll check-cashing practices of the firm's employees. Wilcox meets its payroll every other Friday and management had always assumed that every one of the checks were cleared against the firm's checking account on Monday. The new financial manager has discovered otherwise. To be more specific, he has found that, on average, 50% of the payroll clears the bank on Monday, 30% on Tuesday and 20% on Wednesday. As a result, much of the money earmarked for payroll is sitting idle in a checking account. Based on a biweekly payroll of $3,000,000, what would Wilcox earn over a year, if it maintained just enough cash in its checking account to meet the average clearings? The company can earn 12% on marketable securities.

8. Fremont, Inc., is headquartered in Chicago. A London customer of the firm's is scheduled to write a check on June 15 for $9,000,000. If the check is sent by mail, it will take about eight days to arrive in Chicago. Given that Fremont, Inc., can earn 18% on short-term investments, would it be wise to fly an employee to London and return with the check on June 16. The plane fare is $2,000 round trip and an additional $500 will be needed for two nights lodging and meals. Are there any other factors that should be considered in this decision?

9. A security dealer is quoting a bid of 14% and an ask of 13⅞% on U.S. Treasury Bills that mature in 13 weeks. Based on a par value of $1,000,000 each, calculate the following, using equation 6.2:
    A. Bid price in dollars.
    B. Ask price in dollars.

10. The Jones Company of Houston has a relatively large number of customers located in the Pacific Northwest. As a matter of fact, the dollar volume from that area amounts to $22,500,000 a year. Portland Pacific Bank has offered to collect and process all checks from these customers, if the Jones Company agrees to maintain a compensating balance of $275,000 with the bank. In the opinion of the Jones Company, such an arrangement would reduce float from eight days to two days, thereby increasing the company's cash balance. At the time the offer was made, a 9% interest rate was available on temporary investments.
    Required:
    A. Determine the benefits and costs of accepting the bank's offer.
    B. What is the proper course of action?

11. Compute the annual yields on the following marketable securities:
    A. Commercial paper: $1,000,000 par value, matures in fifteen days, purchase price of $995,000.
    B. Banker's acceptance: $5,000,000 face value, matures in forty-five days, purchase price of $4,907,500.
    C. U.S. Treasury Bills: $100,000 par value, matures in ten days, purchase price of $99,650.

12. Dreyfus Corporation has $800,000 of excess cash on hand. The company plans to use this money to pay federal income taxes, which fall due in one week. In the meantime, it would like to invest the $800,000 in marketable securities, currently paying about 10.8%. On a transaction of this size, the commission will be $1,000. Should Dreyfus Corporation invest the $800,000 for one week?

13. Calculate after-tax yields on the following securities. Note: the federal income tax rate is 46%; the income from state and local government securities is exempt from federal income tax; and 85% of dividends paid to other corporations is excluded from federal income tax.
    A. Commercial paper yielding 13%.
    B. Municipal notes yielding 8%.
    C. Preferred Stock yielding 10%.
    D. Negotiable C.D.s yielding 14%.
    E. U.S. Treasury Bills yielding 12.5%.

14. Obtain a recent edition of the Wall Street Journal and locate the section titled "Treasury Issues/Bonds, Notes & Bills." Here you will find the current yields on U.S. Government securities, categorized by maturity. Using sample observations, construct a yield curve from this data.

15. Two bonds that are equal in all respects except maturity are described below.
    A. Short-term bond: $10,000 par value, 10% coupon rate, two-year maturity.
    B. Long-term bond: $10,000 par value, 10% coupon rate, fifteen-year maturity.
    Required:
    A. Compute the market price of each bond, given a market interest rate of 8%.
    B. Compute the market price of each bond, given a market interest rate of 12%.
    C. Discuss the findings.

16. Joyland Amusement Park's estimated daily cash receipts and disbursements for April, 1988 are presented below.

Day		Cash Receipts	Cash Expenditures
April	1	$10,000	$60,000
	2	15,000	55,500
	3	23,500	50,800
	4	33,800	46,000
	5	39,500	40,500
	6	11,600	34,800
	7	12,000	30,000
	8	17,500	31,500
	9	16,000	30,000
	10	22,000	32,000
	11	30,800	7,500
	12	34,500	7,500
	13	12,250	7,500
	14	16,000	7,500
	15	12,800	7,500
	16	13,000	7,500
	17	24,800	7,500
	18	26,500	7,500
	19	35,000	7,500
	20	17,500	7,500
	21	14,500	7,500
	22	15,000	7,500
	23	12,500	7,500
	24	20,000	7,500
	25	35,700	7,500
	26	48,000	7,500
	27	21,500	7,500
	28	17,000	7,500
	29	15,000	7,500
	30	18,500	7,500

Required:
  A. Compute the daily cash surpluses or deficits.
  B. Identify the days when liquid assets will be needed for transactions.
  C. Determine the maximum liquid asset holdings for transactions during the month.
  D. Find the overall cash surplus (deficit) for April.

17. Based on figures from the past ten years, the average daily cash transactions balance for a corporation is $80,000 in the month of July. Furthermore, the standard deviation is $60,000. Assuming the firm wishes to be 95% confident that it will be able to pay its bills on time, how much liquidity must it hold for precautionary reasons. Assume the daily cash flows are normally distributed.

Selected References

Beranek, William, *Working Capital Management*, Belmont, Calif.: Wadsworth, 1968.
Emery, Gary, "Some Empirical Evidence on the Properties of Daily Cash Flow," *Financial Management* (Spring 1981), pp. 21–28.
Gole, Bradley T., and Ben Branch, "Cash Flow Analysis: More Important Than Ever," *Harvard Business Review* (July–August 1981), pp. 131–36.
Mehta, Dileep, *Working Capital Management*, Englewood Cliffs, N.J.: Prentice-Hall, 1974.
Meiselman, David, *The Term Structure of Interest Rates*, Englewood Cliffs, N.J.: Prentice-Hall, 1962.
Miller, Merton H., and Daniel Orr, "A Model for the Demand for Money by Firms," *Quarterly Journal of Economics* (August 1966), pp. 413–35.
Smith, Keith V., *Guide to Working Capital Management*, New York: McGraw-Hill, 1979.
Stone, Bernell K., and Ned C. Hill, "Cash Transfer Scheduling for Efficient Cash Concentration," *Financial Management* (Autumn 1980), pp. 35–43.

▮ Finance in the News

Is controlled disbursement "a game companies play"? How much float can cash managers generate without raising the concern of the Federal Reserve Board? There is no question that float has the potential of generating substantial funds as shown in the following article.

The Race Is to the Slow Payer

Corporate cash managers, whose lives are devoted to squeezing pennies out of dollars and millions out of billions, have become enamored of an ingenious banking arrangement known as controlled disbursement. It lets them exploit the huge dollar potential in check-clearing float. It also enables them to avoid the idle checking account balances that so mortify cash managers.

Many large companies find controlled disbursement pleasantly profitable. On float alone—by the companies' own calculations—National Distillers earns $3 million a year, American Brands $5 million, and Foremost-McKesson $5.5 million.

Prior to 1979, what is now called controlled disbursement was generally called remote disbursement, the term referring to the distance—the greater the better—between the location of the bank on which a check is drawn and the location of the recipient of that check. If a New York company, say, paid a New York supplier by a check drawn on a Montana bank, the payer picked up an extra two or three days' float—free use of the money—before the check was debited to his account. At 10% interest, one day's float of $1 million throughout the year is worth $100,000; two days' float, $200,000.

In 1979, however, the Federal Reserve Board issued a statement strongly disapproving of remote disbursement on the grounds that it denied consumers and small businesses "prompt access to funds," in addition to undermining the efforts of the Fed staff to "improve the speed and efficiency of the check-clearing system." In a twinkling the term "remote disbursement" disappeared from the sales pitches of banks, to be replaced by "controlled disbursement."

The distinction, if there is one, largely has to do with intent. Does the customer primarily want to gain from float or to avoid idle balances? Perhaps both. As a banker recently put it, "Who knows the intent in the mind of a cash manager? We don't ask." All of which has led Lorin S. Meeder, the Fed's associate director of bank operations, to state flatly, "The line between controlled and remote disbursement is so fine as to be obscure."

Some corporate treasurers are candid about seeking float. When Herbert W. Eames Jr. became chief financial officer three years ago at J. Walter Thompson, the mammoth advertising agency head-quartered in New York, he discovered that the company was getting minimal float, issuing checks drawn on a New York bank. Paying for advertising time, it disbursed checks to the networks by hand. Messengers from the networks and some vendors would appear at the cashier's office on the eighth floor of the Graybar Building so that the checks could be deposited as soon as possible.

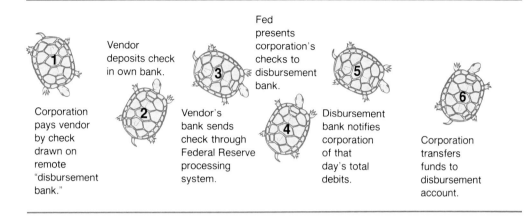

1 Corporation pays vendor by check drawn on remote "disbursement bank."

2 Vendor deposits check in own bank.

3 Vendor's bank sends check through Federal Reserve processing system.

4 Fed presents corporation's checks to disbursement bank.

5 Disbursement bank notifies corporation of that day's total debits.

6 Corporation transfers funds to disbursement account.

Eames soon set matters right. He opened a remote disbursement account (he candidly uses the term) at the Waukesha branch of the First Wisconsin National Bank. Thompson calculates that it now gets an average of 1½ days' additional float, even though some checks are still picked up by hand.

Whether it is called "remote" or "controlled," the phenomenon has grown enormously in the last few years. That is evident from a survey by Greenwich Research Associates, a financial consulting firm. Covering 1,217 large companies, including most of the FORTUNE 500, the survey showed that 59% maintained controlled disbursement accounts last year, up from 49% two years before. Also, 18% of the companies reported using remote disbursement, but the published data did not indicate how much overlap there was between the two groups.

A company wanting to make use of controlled disbursement has to find a bank that offers such accounts, but that's not much of a problem. They are now offered by over 130 banks around the country, including most of the leading banks in the East. As recently as 1978, perhaps three dozen banks offered controlled disbursement accounts. Among the pioneers in the early 1970s were the three largest banks in North Carolina—First Union National, North Carolina National, and Wachovia. "It took a long time for the idea to catch on," says James Hicks, head of the cash management department of First Union. "The service got legitimate when the New York banks recognized that their customers wanted it." Irving Trust was the first, followed by Citibank, Chase, Manufacturers Hanover, and Chemical.

All the banks provide essentially the same thing. A controlled disbursement account is a type that bankers call a "zero balance account"—it contains no cash at the end of the day after all checks have been paid, thus no funds are left idle. Sometime between 8:30 A.M. and 11 A.M. each day, Eastern Time, the bank informs the corporate customer how much money is needed to pay that day's checks. The customer provides the funds in one of several ways. He may use a wire transfer. Or he may draw from his "concentration" account—a major repository of funds—at a more central office of the same bank. Or he may invoke a standby line of credit.

To a cash manager, the great advantage of that morning telephone call is that he is told the precise sum he will need for disbursement purposes that day. If he has surplus money to invest, or if he has to borrow, he can operate in the money markets while they are most active. The markets begin to thin out after 11:30 A.M. The morning call and the zero balance at the end of the day constitute the control feature of the scheme. Without it, cash managers would have to fund their disbursement accounts in advance, trying to forecast the volume of checks that would arrive each day.

For the system to work, the controlled account normally cannot be located at a big-city bank, for such a bank cannot complete its tally for each customer early in the morning. A big-city bank receives two or three check deliveries from the nearest Federal Reserve processing center, the last at 11 A.M. It also receives checks from the local clearinghouse, as well as "direct sends"—checks that arrive by courier from distant banks throughout the morning and afternoon and are debited to the customers' accounts that day. So big-city banks cannot make that crucial early-morning call to the cash manager. Therefore, the large banks normally locate their controlled accounts at a branch in a small or medium-size city where there is only one check delivery from the Fed, early in the morning.

Thus all of Chase Manhattan's controlled disbursement accounts are at a branch in Syracuse, 240 miles from New York City but an hour from the Fed's processing center in Utica. The same with Chemical Bank. Morgan Guaranty Trust uses a sister bank in Wilmington, Delaware. Chicago's Harris Trust uses the Bank of Naperville, in the Chicago suburb. Besides getting only a single early-morning check delivery from the Fed, most of these banks decline to accept direct sends of checks from other banks for credit that day. If any such checks come in, the bookkeeping is done the following day.

Pittsburgh is a rare exception to the use of distant branches or affiliated banks for controlled disbursement accounts. A couple of years ago the Mellon Bank received an additional "transit routing number"—the bank identification code, magnetically imprinted one each check, that is essential in automatic check-sorting—and used it for controlled disbursement accounts at its main office. Mellon operates the system in the same fashion as if it were using a remote branch. A number of other city banks, usually smaller institutions, offer a less effective controlled service with a phone call in the early afternoon rather than in the morning.

The float advantage that comes from the geographic remoteness of the distant branches or affiliate banks is measurable. Twice a year, Phoenix-Hecht, a Chicago cash-management consulting firm, conducts a nationwide survey of check clearance times between cities. Its most recent figures show that the average time for a check drawn on a New York City bank and deposited in a New York City bank is 1.14 days. However, if that same check deposited in New York is drawn on Syracuse, the average clearance time is 1.92 days. The difference—0.78 of a day—is the additional float.

For checks drawn on Syracuse or on Wilmington and deposited all over the U.S., the average additional float time is a full day, as compared with drawing the check on a New York City bank. The most remote "drawee banks" in the Phoenix-Hecht studies are in Helena, Montana; Midland, Texas; and Grand Junction, Colorado. Their average clearance time to all points in the U.S. is around 3½ days.

Obviously, if the payer gains by remote disbursement, the payee loses. But the float loss to a corporation on the receiving end is unlikely to be more than two days beyond what a local check would entail. That is because the Fed normally does not make the payee's bank wait more than two days before it grants credit for an out-of-town check, even though three or more days may be required for the remote bank to pay the check. The difference in time between credit and payment constitutes "Fed float," which the Fed has been diligently seeking to reduce. (See "The Fed Goes into Business," FORTUNE, April 4.)

A bank credits corporate customers for a deposited check on the same day the bank itself receives credit from the Fed, or the day after. Not so, however, in the case of small businesses or consumers. These "retail customers," as the banks call them, have to wait much longer—often two weeks for the proceeds of out-of-town checks. Thus a disbursing company, which picks up a day or two in float, will inconvenience the small-fry payee for a disproportionately longer period. Usually a bank's justification for its treatment of retail customers is that it has to wait a long time for bounced checks to be returned. Cynics suggest that the banks' real interest is in profiting from the use of their customers' funds. After all, little more than 1% of all checks bounce, and even retail customers often make good on those that do.

Most corporations do not use controlled disbursement for payroll checks, and not many banks accept such accounts. A few years ago Seagram began to hear complaints from top executives in New York who found that their expense reimbursement checks were drawn on a bank in Arizona. The practice was stopped. Typically, controlled accounts are used to pay vendors. Many vendors, however, are small outfits, and corporations often make no effort to distinguish them from large vendors.

Not every company is candid with its vendors about its remote disbursement practices. Banks normally require customers to print the geographic location of the bank branch on checks, but many companies neglect to do so, merely printing the name of the bank. A sophisticated payee can ask his bank to look up the transit-routing code and tell him the paying bank's location. The unsophisticated, however, are likely to assume that Chemical Bank means a bank in New York City rather than one in Syracuse. The risk is that the recipient of a remotely disbursed check may prematurely issue checks of his own and then find that they bounce.

Companies vary in the ardor with which they pursue float. Some of the most ardent use of Troy printer, a computer-controlled machine that turns out checks bearing the names of various banks. These companies maintain several bank accounts in different parts of the country, and the printer dutifully produces a check drawn on the bank that is most remote from the payee's zip code.

Levi Strauss, the San Francisco blue jeans manufacturer, uses a Troy printer and four controlled disbursement accounts at banks around the country. Assistant Treasurer George F. Tucker explains, "We do periodic studies of how long it takes checks drawn on each bank to clear. We get tapes for each controlled disbursement bank once a month showing on what date the check cleared. We match that to our tape showing when each check was sent out." On the basis of this analysis, Tucker's staff periodically alters the zip code table that determines which vendor gets a check from what bank.

Foremost McKenson, the huge San Francisco-based wholesale distributor of health care products, foods, and spirits, goes further and uses nine banks. Assistant Treasurer Don Smith calculates that he gets a total of about six to seven days of float, including mail time—far more than if he disbursed out of San Francisco. Using an interest rate of 9%, he figures that the additional float is worth about $5.5 million a year.

It is not necessary, of course, to use a Troy printer to gain a float advantage. A few years ago several of the nation's leading brokerage houses helped themselves to a considerable amount of float by using a simple East–West crisscross. Merrill Lynch, for example, would mail checks drawn on West Coast banks to customers east of the Mississippi and checks on New York banks to customers west of the Mississippi. These were checks for the proceeds of securities sales. The Securities and Exchange Commission frowned sternly on the practice: Merrill Lynch was also hit by a class action suit, which it settled before trial.

The suit revealed some interesting figures. In 28 months, from September 1976 to the end of 1978, when the practice ended, Merrill Lynch disbursed around $1.23 billion in 365,000 checks, with an average daily float of $1,493,859, to New York State customers alone. Stephen P. Hoffman, the plaintiffs' principal lawyer, calculated that the company made $417,858 on the basis of 1½ days extra float and an average interest rate of 8%. Merrill Lynch claimed that the additional float time was one day and that its profit was $278,000. The profit on the entire nationwide operation was obviously much greater.

What was unusual about the case was that Merrill Lynch was playing the float game against customers, not vendors. The brokerage house now uses a simpler form of remote disbursement, sending out all interest and dividend checks from two West Coast banks, Wells Fargo and Security Pacific. Little float in California, but lots with addresses far from the West Coast.

The Fed has gradually been squeezing float since 1979 by speeding up its own internal operations and getting more reliable air-courier service. To expedite check clearing further, it recently began making its last check delivery to big-city banks at 11 A.M. instead of 10 A.M. and will go to noon "presentment," as it's called, on May 2. Under the new schedule, more checks can be cleared by a bank the day they arrive, and fewer will be delayed until the next day.

Starting in July, the Fed will extend the noon delivery time to certain banks elsewhere that have a very large check volume and are much used in controlled disbursement. Banks served by the Utica processing center are prime candidates. Bankers have a certain anxiety as to what noon presentment will mean for controlled disbursement because of the need for that early-morning telephone call. The bulk of checks—perhaps 80% to 85% of the dollar volume—will still arrive early in the morning. Some bankers believe their customers will be able to forecast volume for the remainder of the morning fairly accurately, and therefore go on operating as they now do. Other bankers are less certain. Another possibility is that the noon delivery of checks will delay money market participation to such an extent that the effective close of the markets will be pushed back into the early afternoon. Fed staffers make this argument, and some cash managers agree.

Meantime, companies continue to play the float game against each other. A useful device to *reduce* float when your company is the recipient of checks is the lock box—a post office drop serviced by your bank. Lock boxes speed up crediting because the banks pick up checks and quickly deposit them in the payee's account. Many companies that use controlled disbursement to gain float when they're payers also use lock boxes to reduce float when they're payees. But there are frustrations. "We no sooner set up a lock box," says one cash manager, "than a certain proportion of wise guys won't use it. They will send their checks to corporate headquarters, thereby adding a day or two of float time against us."

Levi Strauss's George Tucker arranged for a lock box in Minneapolis to foil one large customer who was remitting to the company's San Francisco headquarters checks drawn on a remote branch of a Texas bank. Tucker teamed up with some other frustrated suppliers of his Minneapolis customer and paid to have a courier fly the checks between Minnesota and Texas. The courier makes the trip to the bank counter by early afternoon, getting same-day use of the funds and cutting the float from three or four days to one. "Cash management," says Tucker, "is an art, a game of wits."

A company need not be of FORTUNE 500 size to benefit from controlled disbursement. Some bankers think it can be worthwhile for companies with annual volume of as little as $50 million. At that size, the gain from float alone might amount to only $20,000 to $30,000 a year, but the zero-balance feature would give the company the additional advantage of not having to keep funds idle in a checking account to cover its checks. Since the costs of controlled disbursement are moderate, it's the next best thing to something for nothing.

RESEARCH ASSOCIATE *Elizabeth S. Silverman*

7

Working Capital Management: Receivables and Inventory

Overview

In this chapter we will look into the various problems and decisions that are encountered in the management of accounts receivable and inventory. For those firms that have to deal with inventory and receivables in a significant way, these assets can have a large impact on profitability and risk and, thus, shareholder wealth. After studying the material in the present chapter, a student should have a sound understanding of how companies determine their holdings of receivables and inventory. Accounts receivable are part and parcel of a firm's credit program. We will closely examine the policies and procedures that make up a credit program. This examination will include the decision-making process that shapes the aforementioned policies and procedures. The policies and procedures associated with the management of inventory are examined in a similar manner ■

Objectives

By the end of the chapter the student should be able to:

1. Define credit management
2. List the benefits and costs of selling on credit
3. Explain the cost of carrying accounts receivable in terms of opportunity cost and risk
4. Explain the major policy issues involved in credit programs
5. Describe how credit policies are implemented and managed
6. List and describe sources of credit information
7. Explain the procedures for collecting unpaid bills
8. Describe how credit programs are evaluated
9. Explain how outside credit managers can be used in administering a credit program
10. Solve accounts receivable problems
11. Understand the terminology of inventory management
12. Calculate EOQ and explain the results
13. Explain the factors that affect optimal inventory balance under both ideal and imperfect conditions
14. Calculate and explain EOQ with quantity discounts
15. Explain the various demands of inventory control

Introduction _____

The management of accounts receivable and inventory is taken up in this chapter. Both of these current assets are very important to a business and should be managed in a manner befitting their significance. We will look into the management of accounts receivable first ■

Credit Management

Accounts receivable go hand in hand with credit sales. As we shall see later, accounts receivable are essentially a byproduct of a firm's credit program. For these reasons, management of accounts receivable would more appropriately be described as *credit management*.

Credit management consists of policies, procedures, and controls over all aspects of a credit program. A financial manger's obligation is to devise an optimal credit program for his or her firm and its owners. Before we consider the different aspects of a credit program, we will examine some necessary background information.

The Economics of Credit

Credit Sales   A significant proportion of business transactions takes place on a credit basis as opposed to a cash basis. Companies sell merchandise and services on credit for several reasons. Many firms feel that they must offer their customers credit if competitors are doing likewise. Used in this way, credit becomes a defensive maneuver. At other times, businesses may extend credit when regular lending institutions (e.g., banks and credit unions) are unable or unwilling to satisfy the demand. Finally, credit is often used as a marketing tool in much the same way that pricing and advertising are deployed. When used as a marketing tactic, credit becomes an offensive strategy.

Credit and Accounts Receivable   An indisputable result of credit selling is the buildup of accounts receivable. The relationship between credit sales and receivables is shown in table 7.1.

The situation revealed in table 7.1 can be stated as follows. On June 1, a firm changed from cash sales to credit sales. The collection period is fifteen days and daily credit sales amount to $5,000. No accounts receivable were outstanding prior to June 1. Each day thereafter, accounts receivable increased by the $5,000 daily credit sales through June 15, at which time it leveled out at $15 \times \$5,000 = \$75,000$. The receivables balance went no higher than $75,000 because the June 1 sales were collected on June 16 (15 days later), the June 2 sales were collected on June 17, and so on. Under these circumstances, old accounts will be replaced with new accounts every fifteen days and the accounts receivable balance will be a constant $75,000. Thus, the accounts receivable turnover is $360 \div 15 = 24$ times a year. This can also be found by dividing the annual sales ($1,800,000) by the receivables balance ($75,000).

Table 7.1   Relationship between Credit Sales and Receivables

Day	Credit Sales	Payment Received	Accounts Receivable
June 1	$5,000	$ 0	$ 5,000
2	5,000	0	10,000
3	5,000	0	15,000
4	5,000	0	20,000
5	5,000	0	25,000
6	5,000	0	30,000
7	5,000	0	35,000
8	5,000	0	40,000
9	5,000	0	45,000
10	5,000	0	50,000
11	5,000	0	55,000
12	5,000	0	60,000
13	5,000	0	65,000
14	5,000	0	70,000
15	5,000	0	75,000
16	5,000	5,000	75,000
17	5,000	5,000	75,000
18	5,000	5,000	75,000
19	5,000	5,000	75,000
20	5,000	5,000	75,000

Changes in either the collection period or daily credit sales can alter the receivables balance. For instance, a doubling of the collection period to 30 days would double the receivables balance to 30 × $5,000 = $150,000. By the same token, a threefold increase in the daily credit sales to $15,000 would triple the receivables balance to 15 × $15,000 = $225,000.

In actuality, of course, no firm would have a constant level of accounts receivable. To begin with, seldom are credit sales equal from day to day. Moreover, the collection period would not be identical for every customer. Consequently, receivables can be expected to vary over time. In an effort to surmount these problems, we shall focus on averages (i.e., average daily credit sales, average collection period, average receivables, and average turnover.)

Credit Benefits and Costs   There are benefits and costs associated with every credit program as well as risks. A brief description of each of these is provided below.

Benefits   The benefits derived from selling on credit are the profits contributed by additional sales. For this purpose, it is considered most appropriate to measure profit as the difference between revenue and variable cost. This particular profit is more formally known as the *contribution margin.*

Credit can lead to greater sales revenue for one or all of the following reasons: a) increased unit sales to current customers, b) sales to new customers, and c) higher selling prices.

Table 7.2   **Selecting Optimal Credit Standards**

Policy Credit Standards	1 Average Daily Credit Sales	2 Average Collection Period	3 Average Accounts Receivable Balance	4 Bad-Debt Ratio
A	$24,000	30	$ 720,000	1.5%
A and B	27,000	32	864,000	2.0%
A, B, and C	30,000	34	1,020,000	3.0%
A, B, C, and D	33,000	38	1,254,000	4.0%
A, B, C, D, and E	36,000	43	1,548,000	5.5%
A, B, C, D, E, and F	38,000	48	1,824,000	6.5%

Costs   A firm experiences several additional expenses when it sells on credit.

Administrative Costs: These costs can be broken down into credit application costs, maintenance costs, and collection costs. Application costs include all of the expenses associated with passing judgment on a credit application. Included among these are the fees paid for credit reports and the wages of credit analysts. Maintenance costs consist of record keeping and billing. Collection expenses range from the costs of writing dunning letters to legal fees.

Bad Debt Expense: With any credit program there will be some uncollectible accounts. Although they may only be a small proportion of sales their impact can be significant. A 3% bad debt ratio for a business with annual credit sales of $80,000,000 would generate $2,400,000 in bad debts.

Cost of Carrying Accounts Receivable: Accounts receivable are a direct result of credit selling, as we saw earlier. Like any asset, receivables must be financed (i.e., carried) at some interest rate cost. Stated differently, the money invested in accounts receivable could be invested in another alternative.[1] The foregone income from the alternative investment becomes an opportunity cost. We shall refer to these interest rates or opportunity costs as *required rates of return (RRR)*. If you recall from chapter four, the RRR consists of the risk-free interest rate (representing TVM) and a risk premium.

Risks   Selling on credit may not appear to be a risky venture, but it can be. Credit programs will vary in riskiness depending upon how they are managed. Bad debts are the major source of risk in a credit program. Not that a company expects to sustain zero bad debts. We saw just above that bad debts are a cost to be contended with. Instead, risk enters into the decision through the element of uncertainty, i.e., the uncertainty that bad debts could be much greater than estimated. This risk should be built into the RRR.

We are now ready to examine the principles of credit management.

---

[1]Technically, the investment in receivables should be at cost, the variable cost of labor, materials, etc. used in the production and sale of the product. In order to simplify matters, we shall consider the investment to be at selling price. This will tend to inflate the investment figure to some degree and therefore overstate interest costs.

Table 7.2   *Continued*

5 Daily Cost of Carrying Receivables	6 Daily Bad-Debt Cost	7 Daily Administrative Cost	8 Total Daily Credit Cost	9 Daily Contribution Margin	10 Benefits Minus Costs
$270	$ 360	$ 50	$ 680	$6,000	$5,320
324	540	75	939	6,750	5,811
383	900	100	1,383	7,500	6,117
470	1,320	150	1,940	8,250	6,310*
581	1,980	220	2,781	9,000	6,219
684	2,470	300	3,454	9,500	6,046

Credit Policies

Once a company has decided to sell on credit it then must determine credit policies. Sound credit policies are a prerequisite to an efficient and effective credit program. There are three major policy issues involved in every credit program: credit standards, credit terms, and collection effort. The success or failure of a credit program will be largely determined by these policies. *The optimal credit policies for a given business are selected essentially on the basis of benefit-cost analysis.*

Credit Standards   *Credit standards address the question: who will receive credit?* Potential customers can vary considerably in ability and desire to pay their bills in a timely manner. Standards should be used to differentiate credit applicants' credit worthiness. By setting very high credit standards the firm can minimize bad debts and late payments. However, such a policy would be at the expense of lost sales and foregone profits. Credit standards should be set with these considerations in mind as the following example shows.

Application: Beatrix, Inc. has decided to begin a credit sales program. The company's current daily sales are $20,000 and the contribution margin rate is 25%, or $5,000. As part of its credit plan, Beatrix must decide on a policy regarding credit standards. One standard would be to restrict credit to the very best credit risks only. At the other extreme, they could extend credit to anyone who asked for it. There are many standards in between these two extremes. The most acceptable credit standard will be the one that provides the best combination of benefits and costs.

Beatrix is able to categorize potential customers into six different credit qualities (A through F). An A rating goes to the highest quality group and a F rating to the lowest quality group. Given a predetermined set of policies for credit terms and collection effort the "estimated" daily benefits and costs associated with different credit standards are shown in table 7.2.

As lower-rated groups of customers are included in the credit program several things are evident. Sales increase (column 1) as the standards are lowered and more and more customers are brought into the fold. The contribution margins (25%) related to these sales are shown in column 9. Three expenses also develop as the credit standards are lowered. In the first place, the collection period rises (column 2), which, when multiplied by the higher daily sales, drives up the investment in accounts receivable (column 3). Assuming an annual RRR of 13.5% (.000375 per day), the daily cost of carrying the receivables increases in line with the larger receivables balance (column 5). The second thing expected to occur is a large increase in the bad-debt ratio (column 4). The bad-debt ratio is converted to a daily cost (column 6) when multiplied by daily sales. The final expense is attributed to a growing administrative burden (column 7). Column 8 reveals the total daily cost associated with each credit standard. The most acceptable credit standard is the one that provides the greatest difference between benefits (i.e. contribution margin) and costs. Column 10 contains the benefits minus costs (column 9 minus column 8) for each standard. There we can see that Beatrix would benefit most by extending credit to customers whose quality standards are classified A, B, C, and D. Beatrix would experience a reduction in net benefits should it sell on credit to customers in categories E and F. That is to say, the marginal benefits to be derived from these two groups of customers are less than their marginal costs. Accordingly, Beatrix, Inc., should have a credit standard policy that offers credit to customers falling in categories A, B, C, and D ■

Credit Terms   Credit terms are the arrangements under which credit will be extended. All credit programs must designate a *credit period*. The credit period is the number of days that customers are given to pay their bills. For example, customers might be given 60 days to pay from the date that goods are delivered. This credit period is summarized as net/60. *A distinction must be made at this time between the credit period and the average collection period. The credit period is the time in which bills should be paid whereas the average collection period measures the actual payment period. It is rare when these two time periods are identical, given the propensity of customers to pay early as well as late. Since it is to a customer's advantage to wait as long as possible to pay, it is normal for the collection period to exceed the credit period.* By extending the credit period, a firm hopes to generate additional sales. These added sales will be at the expense of, among other things, delayed payment and, thus, a larger cost to carry receivables. An example will help to show how a tradeoff is made between these benefits and costs.

Application: Alco Co. sells $25,000 worth of merchandise per day on a cash basis. The company's contribution margin is 25% and its relevant RRR is 13.5% per year (.000375 per day). By switching to a credit program, the company believes that a significant increase in sales and contribution margin will materialize. It has already settled on policies for credit standards and collection effort, but not credit period. Regardless of which credit period is selected, the average collection period is expected to be eight days longer. The "estimated" daily benefits and costs associated with different credit periods is shown in table 7.3. This table is designed exactly like the one used earlier to determine credit standards. The only difference is that credit periods replace credit standards.

Six credit periods are analyzed, from 30 to 105 days. While there is no requirement that only multiples of 15 days be considered, this is common practice. Furthermore, it is rare to find credit periods of less than 30 days. In the present situation, an extension of the credit period is expected

Table 7.3   Selecting Optimal Credit Period

Policy Credit Period	Average Daily Credit Sales	Average Collection Period	Average Accounts Receivable Balance	Bad-Debt Ratio
30	$33,000	38	$1,254,000	4.0%
45	36,000	53	1,908,000	4.5%
60	39,000	68	2,652,000	5.0%
75	42,000	83	3,486,000	5.5%
90	45,000	98	4,410,000	6.0%
105	48,000	113	5,424,000	6.5%

to generate sizable increases in sales and contribution margin. Not surprisingly, the collection period increases in line with the credit period, thereby leading to a dramatic increase in accounts receivable and interest charges. A less obvious result of relaxing the credit period is a rising bad debt ratio. It seems that some customers are more inclined to default when they are given a longer time to pay. While the reasons for such behavior are not clear, Alco has nevertheless incorporated it into its analysis. Administrative costs are also predicted to increase due to the higher level of credit sales and collection effort. Benefits minus costs are greatest for a credit period of 75 days. Based on this information, the optimal policy regarding the credit period will be 75 days ■

Cash discounts and *credit limits* are two other terms often found in credit programs. *Many firms offer credit customers price-cash discounts for paying earlier than the credit period.* For example, a 3% discount may be granted if payment is received in ten days with the full amount due in thirty days. In this case, the discount period is ten days and the credit period is thirty days. A customer that fails to pay by the tenth day will miss the discount, but gain twenty extra days of trade financing. Terms such as this are usually abbreviated as 3/10/n30. The first term is the discount, the second term is the discount period, and the last term is the credit period that is read as "net due in 30 days." The philosophy behind discounts is that many customers will be encouraged to pay earlier, thereby reducing the average collection period. In other words, the money tied-up in receivables will be reduced.

A credit limit sets the maximum dollar amount of credit that a customer may have outstanding at any given time. Such a limit is beneficial in that it restricts the firm's exposure to bad debts. On the other hand, a credit limit may also restrict credit sales. As a rule, greater limits are offered to those customers of superior credit quality, and, of course, businesses can obtain higher limits than individuals.

Many firms simply choose the predominant credit terms of their industry. While this approach is easy to apply, it will not necessarily generate the best terms for a particular business.

Collection Effort   Collection effort begins when a customer has failed to make payment by the end of the credit period. By making a determined and systematic effort to collect its past-due bills, a company can minimize bad debts and speed payments. An aggressive collection effort can be a very expensive process, however, and should therefore be carried out with due diligence. Specific collection practices and procedures are discussed below.

Finding the optimal collection effort can be approached in the same manner as that used to find optimal credit standards and credit terms.

Table 7.3   *Continued*

Daily Cost of Carrying Receivables	Daily Bad-Debt Cost	Daily Administrative Cost	Total Daily Credit Cost	Daily Contribution Margin	Benefits Minus Costs
$ 470	$1,320	$150	$1,940	$ 8,250	$6,310
716	1,620	160	2,496	9,000	6,504
995	1,950	175	3,120	9,750	6,630
1,307	2,310	200	3,817	10,500	6,683*
1,654	2,700	230	4,584	11,250	6,666
2,034	3,120	270	5,424	12,000	6,576

Table 7.4   Selecting Optimal Collection Effort

Policy Collection Effort	Average Daily Credit Sales	Average Collection Period	Average Accounts Receivable Balance	Bad-Debt Ratio	Daily Cost of Carrying Receivables
None	$35,000	44	$1,540,000	7.5%	$770
Weak	34,000	41	1,394,000	5.5%	697
Mild	33,000	38	1,254,000	4.0%	627
Determined	32,000	35	1,120,000	3.0%	560
Aggressive	31,000	33	1,023,000	2.5%	512

Application: Bayou Bros., Ltd., wishes to know the optimal degree of collection effort to pursue in their new credit program. Policies have already been set for credit standards and credit terms. The company presently has cash sales of $24,000 per day on which the contribution margin is 25%. Bayou's relevant RRR is 18% per year (.0005 per day). The company is able to differentiate five levels of collection effort (do nothing, weak, mild, determined, and aggressive). The "estimated" daily benefits and costs of these alternative policies are shown in table 7.4.

As the collection effort increases, average collection period and the bad-debt percentages are expected to decline. These are definitely beneficial since the carrying cost of receivables will fall along with bad debts expense. However, administrative costs rise dramatically as collection activity intensifies. In addition to this, sales will probably decline somewhat as the result of growing customer resentment to more aggressive collection procedures. The tradeoff between benefits and costs point to a mild collection effort as the most acceptable. Based on this analysis, Bayou Bros., Ltd., should follow a mild collection effort policy ∎

It is noteworthy that in all of the preceding examples the accounts receivable balance was a result or by-product of other decisions: *the search for the best credit policies led to a determination of the proper level of accounts receivable.*

Conclusion   The success of a credit program is to a large extent determined by well-designed credit policies. Selecting the most appropriate credit policy should be done with benefit-cost analysis. Table 7.5 summarizes the benefits and costs of the extremes for each policy. In the preceding examples, the best policy was the one that maximized the difference between benefits and cost. But these examples were purposely simplified to focus on benefit-cost analysis. Unfortunately, that simplicity obscured four elements that are critical to a thorough investigation of credit policies: risk, policy interrelationships, differential policies, and data gathering.

Risk: Alternative credit policies may differ not only in profitability, but also in risk. This is particularly true with regard to credit standards. The credit standard that maximizes profit may also subject the firm to a high level of risk. Although it might appear that risk is captured in the higher bad-debt ratio attributed to riskier customers, such is not the case. Bad debts can "turn out to be" much higher than what is expected of these customers. Management should thus account for the risk of a policy by altering the RRR.

Table 7.4   *Continued*

Daily Bad-Debt Cost	Daily Administrative Cost	Total Daily Credit Cost	Daily Contribution Margin	Benefits Minus Costs
$2,625	$ 40	$3,435	$8,750	$5,315
1,870	100	2,667	8,500	5,833
1,320	250	2,197	8,250	6,053*
960	500	2,020	8,000	5,980
775	750	2,037	7,750	5,713

Table 7.5   Ramifications of Major Credit Policies

Credit Standards

Rigorous Credit Standards	*Easy Credit Standards*
A. Low sales	A. High sales
B. Low bad debts	B. High bad debts
C. Short collection period	C. Long collection period
D. Low administrative costs	D. High administrative costs

Credit Terms

Rigorous Credit Terms	*Easy Credit Terms*
A. Low sales	A. High sales
B. Low bad debts	B. High bad debts
C. Short collection period	C. Long collection period
D. Low administrative costs	D. High administrative costs

Collection Effort

Rigorous Collection Effort	*Easy Collection Effort*
A. Low sales	A. High sales
B. Low bad debts	B. High bad debts
C. Short collection period	C. Long collection period
D. High administrative costs	D. Low administrative costs

Policy Interrelationships: It is not very realistic to expect that a good decision regarding one policy can be made in isolation of the other two policies. For instance, the optimal credit terms offered to low-risk customers may very well be different than the terms offered to high-risk customers. As another example, an optimal collection effort could very well be affected by the credit terms that are offered.

Because of the interrelationships among credit standards, credit terms, and collection effort, it is best to determine them simultaneously. A problem of this nature can be approached through a trial-and-error process, or, better yet, linear programming.

Differential Policies: In practice, a company may decide that multiple policies are preferable to a single policy. For example, rather than setting a flat credit limit for every credit customer, different credit limits may be offered, according to the customer's credit worthiness. Individualizing the credit decision in this way is nothing more than what a bank does when it tailors a loan to a specific borrower. Differential credit policies are expensive and time consuming to administer, however, and are therefore only practical for companies that make large credit sales. Most retailers would be excluded from this category.

Data Gathering: Credit policy decisions should be based on sound data. That means there must be reliable estimates of benefits (sales and contribution margins) and costs (interest rates, collection periods, and bad debts). Credit policies founded on poor information will invariably lead to a subpar credit program.

Control of the Credit Program

Having established sound credit policies, a firm must then devise procedures and practices to implement them. To be more specific, credit standards require some form of credit analysis, and, in addition, collection procedures must be established for a given collection effort. Finally, to assure that the credit program is being run in an efficient and effective manner, management must develop a performance appraisal system. These functions are normally housed in a credit department.

Credit Analysis   A policy on credit standards implies that it is possible to categorize potential customers according to their ability and desire to pay bills on time. *Credit analysis is the process of measuring a credit applicant's ability and desire to pay.* In other words, it is essentially an assessment of the probability that a potential customer will pay in full and on schedule. It is also necessary to review the credit worthiness of a firm's current customers from time to time. The intensity of credit analysis and the frequency with which it is performed depend in part on whether one is examining consumer credit or business credit, as well as the amount of money involved. With regard to the latter case, one would not perform an in-depth credit analysis on a customer who wants to buy only $250 worth of merchandise.

A standard framework for the conduct of credit analysis has developed over the years. It is popularly referred to as the *"four Cs of credit,"* which stands for capacity, capital, character, and conditions. A thorough analysis of these variables will go a long way toward measuring the payment ability and desire of a credit applicant.

Capacity: Capacity is a measure of the credit applicant's financial ability to pay debts under normal circumstances. Given that purchases on account are to be paid in a relatively short period of time (i.e., typically less than three months), the normal payment by a business customer would be derived from the forthcoming conversion of its inventory and accounts receivable into cash income.[2]

---

[2]Normal payment for an individual consumer should come from discretionary income, which is salary less living expenses and other debt payments.

Capital: The word capital, when used in the context of credit management, is defined as the difference between a credit applicant's assets and liabilities (i.e., equity or savings). What appears to be adequate capacity at the time credit is extended often ends up being something less. This is where capital comes in. *Adequate capital can provide a safety net should a customer's capacity turn out to be insufficient.* Debts that cannot be paid in the normal course of business might be collected through a sale of all or part of the delinquent customer's assets. Whether or not there exists adequate capital to play this role depends primarily upon the credit applicant's debt-to-asset ratio.

Generally speaking, it is inappropriate to give greater weight to capital than to capacity in a credit analysis. The reason for this is that businesses prefer to be paid in an ordinary manner so as to avoid the anguish and legal complications of an asset liquidation.

Character: It is not always sufficient for a credit applicant to possess a strong ability to pay. *A will to repay is also important.* This refers to a potential credit customer's character. The individual character of consumers and small businessmen is especially important in a credit analysis. A strong desire to meet one's responsibilities can overcome a weak capacity. By the same token, a financially strong applicant who also possesses a weak character may try to renege on his or her debts despite the fact that payment could easily be made. Character can be established by persons and organizations who are familiar with the applicant as well as the customer's prior debt-payment record.

Conditions: Companies neither like to turn away new business, nor do they care to cut off credit to an old and valued customer who has suddenly fallen on financially hard times. For these reasons, they may grant credit to a customer whose capacity and capital are below standard due to unusual conditions. To qualify as a "condition," the circumstance must have been beyond the credit applicant's control and there must be a good expectation that it will soon disappear, if it has not already. Some of the more common conditions are: recession-induced unemployment (for an individual) or sales decline (for a business); poor health and/or large medical expenses; and newly formed companies or young newlyweds whose prospects are bright.

Figure 7.1   Four Cs of credit analysis

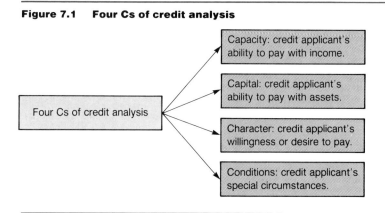

Sources of Credit Analysis Information   A credit analysis seeks to determine the capacity, capital, character, and conditions associated with each credit applicant. The financial analyst requires a considerable amount of information for this assignment. Several sources of credit information are described below.

Personal History: Prior credit experience with a customer can be helpful in the credit granting decision. Here is a first-hand source of one of the most relevant credit statistics available, i.e., *prior payment practice.* The analyst can ascertain quite readily whether or not these applicants have previously paid their bills to the company in full and on time.

Financial Statements: Probably the best source of information on capacity and capital is a customer's financial statements. Preferably, they should be audited and the more detailed the better. To obtain the most out of them one should perform financial statement analysis along the lines suggested in chapter 2. *The capacity to pay current debts can be substantially measured with liquidity analysis.* One should proceed by calculating current and quick ratios. From the seller's viewpoint, the higher these ratios are, the greater the likelihood of payment. A further step would be to evaluate these ratios by means of industry comparisons, time series, and decomposition analysis. *Capital protection can be discerned by means of solvency analysis.* In particular, the debt-to-assets or debt-to-equity ratios should be computed and evaluated. From the seller's standpoint, the lower these ratios are, the greater the protection that exists.

Suppliers and Bankers: Discussions with other firms that have done business with a credit applicant can be very informative. Not only can they report on the applicant's past payment record but they may also be able to advise on the applicant's character and near-term prospects. *A customer's present and former bankers are particularly good sources of information.* The difficulty one has with bankers, however, is getting them to discuss their client's current situation, history, and prospects. Although a bank often has in-depth knowledge of these matters, it may not feel free to pass this information on to another party. Frequently a firm can obtain this knowledge indirectly by going through its bank.

Personal Interview: An interview with the credit applicant can often elicit knowledge not obtainable elsewhere. After all, who is in a better position to evaluate payment capacity than the credit customer. In addition to capacity, a trained interviewer can often appraise the character of a potential customer in an interview. This is also the time to delve into any unusual conditions affecting the applicant. It goes without saying that a credit applicant's comments cannot always be taken at face value.

Credit Cooperatives: Many businesses belong to nonprofit organizations that gather credit information on consumers and businesses. These may be organized on a community-wide basis (credit bureaus), for a particular industry (in connection with trade associations), or nationally (credit interchange bureaus). Although there are differences in the way credit cooperatives are run, we can make some general observations. All of the members are required to pass along credit information on their customers as it becomes available. The co-op consolidates this data and summarizes it in a report for the members' use. A fee is normally charged each time a member calls for a credit report, with the money going to support the organization. Some credit cooperatives go so far as to provide an opinion on the credit worthiness of a customer.

Credit Reporting Companies: Businesses have been formed over the years to provide credit information and opinions. The largest and most well known of these companies is *Dun and Bradstreet.* An example copy of one of their credit reports is shown below in exhibit 7.1, along with a key to the credit ratings.

Conclusion: The cost of conducting a credit analysis will increase as more information is obtained and analyzed. Consequently, it should be conducted in a sequential manner wherein the additional cost of further analysis is compared with the potential benefits.

Exhibit 7.1

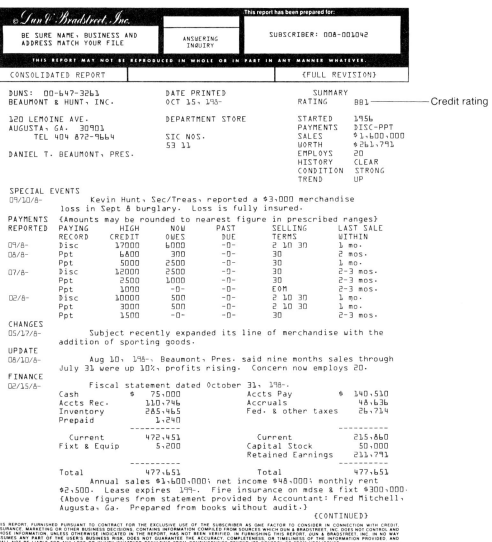

Source: *The D & B Rating* booklet published by Dun and Bradstreet Credit Services, 1985.

Exhibit 7.1   *Continued*

Dun & Bradstreet, Inc.		This report has been prepared for
BEAUMONT & HUNT, INC. AUGUSTA, GA.	OCT 15, 198-	PAGE 2 CONSOLIDATED REPORT

THIS REPORT MAY NOT BE REPRODUCED IN WHOLE OR IN PART IN ANY MANNER WHATEVER

```
                              --O--
                    On February 14, 198-  Kevin Hunt reported sales and profits
             in fiscal quarter ended Jan 31 as above those of prior year
             period because of an upsurge in local economy.  He expects full
             year sales to exceed 1.7 million.
PUBLIC FILINGS
03/25/8-            On Mar 17, 198-,, a suit in the amount of $250 was entered
             against subject by A. Henry Assoc. Augusta, Ga.  {Docket No
             27511}.  Cause of action goods sold & delivered.
05/28/8-            On May 21, 198-  a financing statement was filed naming
             subject as debtor and NCR Corp.  Dayton, Ohio as secured party.
             {Docket No 741170}.  Collateral: equipment.
08/10/8-            On Aug 10, 198-  K. Hunt reported action filed by A. Henry
             Associates was due to defective merchandise and had been settled.
             Court records reveal the suit was withdrawn.
BANKING
02/15/8-           Balances average moderate five figures.  Non-borrowing
             account.  Relations satisfactory.  Account opened June 1956.
HISTORY
02/15/8-     DANIEL T. BEAUMONT, PRES.           KEVIN J. HUNT, SEC & TREAS.
             DIRECTORS:  The Officers
                   Incorporated Georgia May 21, 1956.  Authorized capital
             stock of 200 shares, no par value common, fully issued.
                   DANIEL BEAUMONT, born 1926, married.  Graduate University
             of Pennsylvania.  1947-56 general manager Raymor Department Store,
             Atlanta, Ga.  1956 formed subject with K. Hunt.
                   KEVIN HUNT, born 1925, married.  Graduate Northwestern Uni-
             versity.  1946-1950 general manager United Dry Goods Inc.  1950-
             1956 merchandising manager, Raymor Department Store, Atlanta, Ga.
OPERATION
02/15/8-           Department store retailing dry goods, notions, household
             items, hardware, confections, toys, and sundry items.  Prices in
             low to moderate range.  Sales made to local trade on cash {40%}
             and revolving credit {60%} basis.
             EMPLOYEES:  Employs 18.
             LOCATION:   Rents 6000 square feet on ground floor and basement
             of multi story brick building in downtown area.  Premises neat.
             08-19 {400   /10  } 0754/0409632142               16 069 F
```

Key to Ratings

ESTIMATED FINANCIAL STRENGTH			COMPOSITE CREDIT APPRAISAL			
			HIGH	GOOD	FAIR	LIMITED
5A	$50,000,000	and over	1	2	3	4
4A	$10,000,000 to	49,999,999	1	2	3	4
3A	1,000,000 to	9,999,999	1	2	3	4
2A	750,000 to	999,999	1	2	3	4
1A	500,000 to	749,999	1	2	3	4
BA	300,000 to	499,999	1	2	3	4
BB	200,000 to	299,999	1	2	3	4
CB	125,000 to	199,999	1	2	3	4
CC	75,000 to	124,999	1	2	3	4
DC	50,000 to	74,999	1	2	3	4
DD	35,000 to	49,999	1	2	3	4
EE	20,000 to	34,999	1	2	3	4
FF	10,000 to	19,999	1	2	3	4
GG	5,000 to	9,999	1	2	3	4
HH	Up to	4,999	1	2	3	4

GENERAL CLASSIFICATION

ESTIMATED FINANCIAL STRENGTH			COMPOSITE CREDIT APPRAISAL		
			GOOD	FAIR	LIMITED
1R	$125,000	and over	2	3	4
2R	$50,000 to	$124,999	2	3	4

EXPLANATION

When the designation "1R" or "2R" appears, followed by a 2, 3 or 4, it is an indication that the Estimated Financial Strength, while not definitely classified, is presumed to be in the range of the ($) figures in the corresponding bracket, and while the Composite Credit Appraisal cannot be judged precisely, it is believed to fall in the general category indicated.

"INV." shown in place of a rating indicates that Dun & Bradstreet is currently conducting an investigation to gather information for a new report. It has no other significance.

"FB" (Foreign Branch) indicates that the headquarters of this company is located in a foreign country (including Canada). The written report contains the location of the headquarters.

ABSENCE OF A RATING--THE BLANK SYMBOL

A blank symbol (--) should not be interpreted as indicating that credit should be denied. It simply means that the information available to Dun & Bradstreet does not permit us to classify the company within our rating key and that further inquiry should be made before reaching a credit decision.

ABSENCE OF A LISTING

The absence of a listing in the Dun & Bradstreet Business Information File or in the Reference Book is not to be construed as meaning a concern is non-existent, has discontinued business, nor does it have any other meaning. The letters 'NQ' on any written report mean 'not listed in the Reference Book'. The letters 'FBN' on any written report also mean that the business is not listed in the Reference Book and that the headquarters is located in a foreign country.

EMPLOYEE RANGE DESIGNATIONS IN REPORTS ON NAMES NOT LISTED IN THE REFERENCE BOOK

Certain businesses do not lend themselves to a Dun & Bradstreet rating and are not listed in the Reference Book. Information on these names, however, continues to be stored and updated in the D&B Business Information File. Reports are available on these businesses but instead of a rating they carry an Employee Range Designation (ER) which is indicative of size in terms of number of employees. No other significance should be attached.

KEY TO EMPLOYEE RANGE DESIGNATIONS	
ER 1	1000 or more Employees
ER 2	500- 999 Employees
ER 3	100- 499 Employees
ER 4	50- 99 Employees
ER 5	20- 49 Employees
ER 6	10- 19 Employees
ER 7	5- 9 Employees
ER 8	1- 4 Employees
ER N	Not Available

Dun & Bradstreet Credit Services

a company of The Dun & Bradstreet Corporation

One Diamond Hill Road
Murray Hill, N.J. 07974-0027

Collection Practices   The collection effort begins when the credit period ends and a payment has not yet been received. As we saw earlier, collection efforts can vary considerably in degree. This is due to the fact that collection practices and procedures are so varied. A key element to consider in any collection program is the reaction of customers to the pressures and tactics that can be applied. In essence, hard feelings should not be unnecessarily provoked.

A company should normally begin the collection effort by using the least-expensive and least-abusive practice and progress from there until payment is received or the additional collection costs exceed the expected benefits, whichever comes first. Several collection practices are described below, listed in the order that they normally follow.

Written Communication: Collecting bills by mail can take many different forms. To start, a company may simply send out a second bill with the word "reminder" stamped on it. This is often sufficient because many times customers do overlook a bill. A "form" delinquent notice or letter may follow the reminder. Should this not be successful, personalized letters can be sent. The first of these might ask the customer if there is any problem, either with the bill or in paying it. Subsequent letters will take on a harsher tone and can even go so far as to threaten legal action. In sum, it is quite an art to determine the proper number, tone, and even the timing of collection correspondence. But once a set of procedures has been established, they can be administered by clerks.

Personal Contact: Many credit managers are of the opinion that personal communication is more effective than written communication. Telephone conversations and, better yet, face-to-face discussions certainly have a place in a collection program. Nevertheless, for several reasons they are normally used only after the written campaign has failed. For one thing, personal communication requires the time of higher-paid employees, since it must be handled carefully so as not to offend the customer. Extra care must be taken here when individual consumers are involved, because of the many new laws protecting them from high-pressure collection practices. When used judiciously, however, these procedures can be very effective in spurring collections.

Collection Agencies: A company that has failed to collect a bill by means of written and personal communication is left with three alternatives: they can write the bill off and forget about it; legal proceedings can be instituted; or the bill can be turned over to a collection service.

Collection agencies are independent businesses or law firms who collect bills for a fee. The fee is normally a percentage of the amount collected and can be as high as 50%. Since their fees are contingent on making collections, it may appear that a firm would have nothing to lose by hiring them. This would be a false assumption. Two costs may arise and both of them are difficult to measure. In the first instance, some of the customers that pay the collection agency may have paid the firm anyway. Secondly, collection agencies have been known to use heavy-handed tactics. Such tactics can come back to haunt the firm.

Legal Action: Suing a customer for payment is not an action to be taken lightly. Law suits are expensive and not always successful even when the firm has a legitimate case. Furthermore, a judgment in favor of the seller will not guarantee satisfaction if a customer has no means of payment. Despite these problems a company may see fit to take legal action if the sum involved is large or it wishes to make an example out of the case. And, of course, a law suit may bring a settlement without even going to trial.

Credit Program Evaluation

After a credit program is established, it should be evaluated on a regular basis to see if the policies and procedures are being carried out in an efficient and effective manner. In other words, is the credit department doing its job? An evaluation should go even further than this. Policies for credit standards, credit terms, and collection effort should be reviewed from time to time to determine if they are still optimal.

Program Performance Appraisal   The performance of a credit program can be measured, to some extent, by how well a company controls its collection period (or receivables turnover) and bad debt ratio. The collection period influences the investment in accounts receivable and, therefore, financing cost. Bad debts are influenced by the bad-debt ratio. Combined, these two costs loom large in the overall credit program. Without constant vigilance they can readily get out of hand. Consequently, management should frequently measure the collection period and bad-debt ratio and evaluate them.[3] In addition to the usual methods of ratio evaluation, one should compare them to what was expected in the original policy decisions.

Payment Patterns   It is quite often helpful to know the payment pattern of credit customers. A payment pattern shows the proportion of monthly credit sales that are typically collected in the month of sale and each month following. For example, a payment pattern of 10–50–30–10 means that, on average, 10% of a given month's credit sales are collected in the month of sale, 50% are obtained in the following month, 30% are received during the second month, and the remaining 10% are collected three months hence. Based on this particular payment pattern, a March credit sales of $500,000 would be collected, on average, as follows: $50,000 in March; $250,000 in April; $150,000 in May; and $50,000 in June.

Payment patterns can be readily obtained if a firm has maintained good collection records. Credit sales for each of several past months are traced through to the months of collection. Proportions are then calculated and averaged to obtain a payment pattern. A more sophisticated analysis would adjust the pattern for seasonal and cyclical factors.

Policy Review   Credit policies should be examined periodically to see if they can be improved. Changes in the economy or competition may call for different credit standards, for example. *Alteration of a credit policy should be based on a comparison of marginal benefits and costs.*

---

[3]When measuring the collection period and bad-debt ratios for an entire year, one can use the computational methods presented in chapter 2 (e.g., 360 days divided by the accounts receivable turnover and bad debts divided by annual credit sales, respectively). If, instead, they are measured more frequently, which they should be, different techniques will be required when a firm's sales are seasonal or otherwise unstable. The problem is that seasonal changes in credit sales can distort the meaning of these ratios.

Application: Jasonville Enterprises, a medium-size manufacturer, is in the process of reviewing its credit terms. The current terms are: credit period of 30 days, credit limit of $250,000, and no cash discount. These terms combined with the company's policies on credit standards and collection effort have produced the following situation:

Receivables turnover	= 9 Times
Annual credit sales	= $7,200,000
Average daily credit sales	= $7,200,000 ÷ 360 = $20,000
Average collection period	= 40 days
Bad-debt ratio	= 3.0%
Average receivables balance	= $20,000 × 40 = $800,000

By offering a 3% cash discount for payment in 5 days, Jasonville predicts that daily credit sales will rise to $21,000 ($7,560,000 annually), the average collection period should fall to 20 days and the bad-debt ratio will decline to 2.5%. Administrative costs are not expected to change. It also is expected that the cash discount will apply to 60% of sales. Given that Jasonville's contribution margin is 20% and its RRR is 18%, should it change its credit terms by initiating the cash discount? The benefit-cost analysis is shown below.

Expected Benefits

Annual sales will rise from $7,200,000 to $7,560,000, or $360,000. This will generate an *added* contribution margin of .20 × $360,000 = *$72,000.*
Accounts receivable will fall from $800,000 to $21,000 × 20 days = $420,000, or by $380,000. As a result, annual receivables carrying cost will *decline* by .18 × $380,000 = *$68,400.*
Bad debts will *decline* from .03 × $7,200,000 = $216,000 to .025 × $7,560,000 = $189,000, or *$27,000.*

Total Benefits = $72,000 + $68,400 + $27,000 = $167,400

Expected Costs

Lost annual revenue from cash discounts will be .03 × $7,560,000 × .60 = $136,080

Total Costs = $136,080

Since the annual marginal benefits of $167,400 exceed marginal costs of $136,080 the cash discount should be offered ▪

Additional Topics in Credit Management

Credit Information System   A credit program can be managed best when an information system is developed for it. If the information system is computerized, so much the better. Of utmost importance is a complete set of updated customer files in readily accessible form. This data combined with appropriate computer software will allow for, among other things, credit analysis, collections, and control.

Outside Credit Managers   The cost of administering a credit program (i.e., credit analyses, collections, and paperwork) can be very high. For a small business, these costs can be especially severe because it cannot benefit from any economies of scale. On a more practical level, there are certain fixed costs associated with running a credit program. Small businesses find it difficult to generate sufficient volume to cover these costs. At other times, businesses do not wish to deal with bad debts and the cost of carrying receivables. In situations such as these, a company may find it worthwhile to use an outside credit specialist to manage its program.

Credit Cards: General purpose credit cards (e.g., VISA and Mastercard) now allow small retailers the opportunity to sell on credit. The card sponsors will perform the credit analyses, handle collections, absorb bad debts, and provide immediate payment. For this service a retailer must pay 2% to 5% of the total billings, depending upon volume. The use of general purpose credit cards has another drawback: they restrict a credit program to the sponsor's credit policies and procedures.

Factors: Factors are companies that specialize in the credit programs of other businesses. In some instances, they limit their activity to merely "buying" receivables from a business and taking over collections. The factor pays less than the face value of the receivables (i.e., 70–80%) to account for expected bad debts and the fact that it must wait for payment. For an additional fee, factors will perform all credit analyses and take charge of the collection effort.

Credit Insurance   Bad debts are an inherent problem of extending credit. Some bad debts are to be expected in spite of a thorough credit analysis and determined collection effort. The fear of unusually large bad debts has led many firms to seek protection. This protection is provided by credit insurance on accounts receivable. If the consumer does not pay then the insurance company will. As tantalizing as this might sound there are some catches. Premium costs on these policies are high and they are highest for those companies most in need of protection. In addition to cost, there are normally several conditions attached to credit insurance policies: deductibles, coinsurance, and policy limits. These can best be explained by an example.

Application: Cyclops Corp. has a credit insurance policy on its credit customers. The policy has the following characteristics: one year of coverage; face value (i.e., limit) of $300,000; 80% coinsurance feature; and a $100,000 deductible. Under the terms of this policy, the insurance company would not cover the first $100,000 of bad debts, but will pay 80% of everything over that, up to $300,000. Should Cyclops experience $400,000 in bad debts, the insurance company would have to pay ($400,000 − $100,000) × .80 = $240,000 ∎

Inventory Management

We come now to the management of inventory. Inventory is critical to the profitability of a business and the well-being of its owners. It can be used in several ways: 1) materials can be stockpiled in anticipation of price increases; 2) inventory stocks can be used to offset late deliveries; 3) manufactured goods can be stockpiled to meet seasonal peaks in demand; 4) it may serve to reduce the need for frequent ordering; 5) a diverse inventory provides retail customers with the chance to shop; and 6) customers do not have to wait for merchandise or materials. For every firm, there is an inventory level that is optimal in terms of profit and risk. Management's job is to determine what this optimal amount of inventory is. Controls must also be applied to inventory to make sure that the optimal level is being maintained and adequately cared for. These issues will be discussed in this section.

A key to understanding inventory management is a knowledge of terminology. Some of the more important terms are defined below.

> *Order quantity (Q):* Number of units ordered.
> *Carrying cost (C):* Cost of carrying one unit of inventory for a year. It includes: interest expense (RRR), insurance, storage, spoilage, and property taxes.
> *Ordering cost (R):* Cost of placing one order. It includes: paperwork, freight charges (if they are not included in the purchase price), and handling.
> *Lead time (L):* Number of days it takes to place an order and have it delivered.
> *Order point (O):* The quantity of inventory that triggers an order for more.
> *Demand (D):* Number of units to be used or sold during a year.

As we shall see in the discussion to follow, carrying cost and ordering cost loom large in the inventory decision.

Optimal Inventory Balance Under Ideal Conditions

We shall confine the present discussion to finding the optimal inventory for a retailing business. By doing so, we can disregard the distinction between raw materials, work in process and finished goods. From a retailer's standpoint the only inventory is finished goods inventory. To further simplify the problem, we will assume that this retailer buys and resells only one product; the demand for this product is known with certainty and it is constant (i.e., the same every day); and the lead time is known with certainty. Under these ideal conditions, the inventory balance is determined solely by order size. This is true, because a firm that knows exactly how many units it needs and precisely how long it will take to receive a new order, will be in no danger of running short of merchandise. Therefore, a new order is received just as the previous order runs out. Consequently, the maximum inventory on hand is the order quantity. The inventory will then decline at a constant daily rate to zero. On average, the inventory balance is the order size divided by two. This is depicted in figure 7.2.

Figure 7.2   Relationship between order size and inventory balance

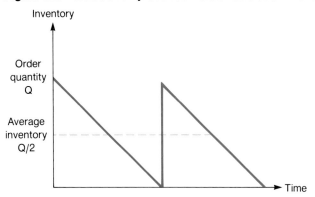

Order Size and Cost   At one extreme, a business could place a single order to last the entire year. Ordering costs would be minimized in this case, but the carrying costs associated with such a large inventory are exorbitant. At the other extreme, an order could be placed every day. It would arrive in the morning and be gone by closing time. Inventory is practically zero in this situation as well as carrying cost. However, ordering costs would be very high. These things should be evident at this point: the inventory balance is determined solely by the order size; order size affects carrying cost and ordering cost; and these two costs are diametrically opposed to each other (i.e., as one decreases, the other increases). *It follows that by finding the optimal order size we will simultaneously determine the optimal inventory.* The optimal order size, also called the *economic order quantity (EOQ)*, in turn depends upon the combined total of carrying cost and ordering cost. *The EOQ is the quantity associated with the lowest total cost.* More formally, total carrying cost is equal to carrying cost per unit multiplied by average inventory or $C\left(\dfrac{Q}{2}\right)$. Total ordering cost is equal to the cost of an order multiplied by the number of orders or $R\left(\dfrac{D}{Q}\right)$. Total cost (TC) is the sum of these two costs or:

Equation 7.1 $TC = C\left(\dfrac{Q}{2}\right) + R\left(\dfrac{D}{Q}\right)$

These relationships are depicted in figure 7.3. Cost is measured on the vertical axis and order quantity on the horizontal axis. Order quantity increases as we move to the right. For very small order quantities the total ordering cost is extremely high. As the order size increases (number of orders decreases) total ordering cost declines in a curvilinear fashion. Total carrying cost, on the other hand, is virtually nonexistent when the orders are small and frequent. However, it increases linearly as the order size and inventory rise. The net effect of these two costs is to cause total cost to decline over a certain range and then increase. The EOQ is the order quantity that coincides with the minimum total cost.

Figure 7.3   The economic order quantity (EOQ) is associated with the lowest total of carrying cost and ordering cost.

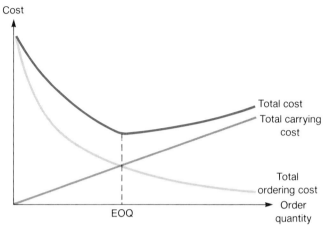

Cost

Total cost
Total carrying cost

Total ordering cost

Order quantity

EOQ

There are several ways to measure the EOQ including graphics, computer trial and error, and mathematics. We will proceed with the latter.

By means of calculus the economic order quantity is found from equation 7.1 to be:[4]

Equation 7.2 $EOQ = \sqrt{\dfrac{2RD}{C}}$

Example: Annual demand (D) equals 5,760 units (16 per day), ordering cost (R) is $540 per order, annual carrying cost (C) is $3 per unit, and lead time (L) amounts to 10 days. Assume a 360-day year.

The economic order quantity is found as follows:

$$EOQ = \sqrt{\frac{(2)(\$540)(5760)}{\$3}} = 1{,}440 \text{ units}$$

The total annual cost associated with this order size is:

$$TC = \$3\left(\frac{1{,}440}{2}\right) + \$540\left(\frac{5{,}760}{1{,}440}\right) = \$4{,}320$$

---

[4]The procedure is as follows:

$$TC = C\left(\frac{Q}{2}\right) + R\left(\frac{D}{Q}\right)$$

Taking the derivative of TC with respect to Q we obtain:

$$\frac{dTC}{dQ} = \frac{C}{2} - \frac{RD}{Q^2}$$

Setting $\dfrac{dTC}{dQ}$ equal to zero we obtain:

$$CQ^2 - 2RD = 0$$

Solving for Q:

$$Q = EOQ = \sqrt{\frac{2RD}{C}}$$

Figure 7.4   Inventory and ordering cycle for one year

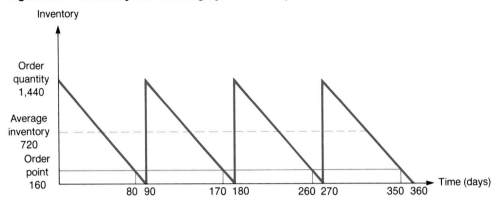

No other order size could achieve such a low cost. Order sizes of 200 and 3,600, for example, would generate annual costs of $15,852 and $6,264, respectively.

An order quantity of 1,440 would produce an optimal average inventory of 1,440 ÷ 2 = 720 units.[5] There will be 5,760 ÷ 1,440 = 4 orders placed each year, or every 90 days. Furthermore, a lead time of 10 days and daily demand of 16 require that an order should be placed when there are 10 × 16 = 160 units in inventory. In other words, an order should be placed 80 days after the last one is received. The 160 units, therefore, becomes the order point. These relationships are diagrammed for one year in figure 7.4 ■

Optimal Inventory Balance in an Imperfect World

The situation we have just described is somewhat unrealistic in that many simplifying assumptions were made. In practice, it is more difficult to determine the optimal inventory level as real world complications arise. Nevertheless, the basic analytical framework developed above can serve as a starting point to more complex solutions, not to mention the fact that it is also useful as a standard of reference. Four of the more serious and frequent complications are described here briefly.

Uncertain Demand   Seldom is the future demand for production materials or final products known with certainty. Business cycles, competition, and changing consumer tastes are just some of the factors that make it difficult to forecast demand. Basing inventory levels on normal or expected demand may prove costly should actual demand turn out to be greater than expected. A deficiency of materials can cause costly production shutdowns while a shortage of products can lead to missed sales opportunities and the profits thereon. Such costs and missed opportunities are more formally known as *stockout costs*. For these reasons, businesses typically hold inventory *safety stocks* to be used as a buffer against unanticipated increases in demand. Safety stocks are over and above the average inventory defined by EOQ

---

[5]The inventory balance in dollars would be found by multiplying average units by unit cost.

and do not necessarily affect the EOQ. Unfortunately, carrying costs will increase along with safety stocks. *Consequently, the proper quantity to hold in a safety stock should be based on a comparison of carrying costs incurred and stockout costs avoided.*

A very short lead time can also go a long way toward minimizing the problems associated with an uncertain demand.

Uncertain Lead Time   Lead times are also unpredictable. There are several reasons why this might occur: labor stoppages at suppliers, misplaced or erroneous paperwork, transportation tie-ups, and market shortages, to name a few. Unanticipated late deliveries will lead to stockout costs in much the same manner as unanticipated increases in demand. Correspondingly, safety stocks are used to mitigate these problems. It should be pointed out here that uncertain lead times can be troublesome even though demand is certain. When both of them are uncertain, safety stocks take on even greater significance.

Variable Demand   In addition to being uncertain, demand may vary systematically from day to day and month to month. Seasonal influences is a major factor involved here. The fundamental inventory analysis centered around EOQ assumed a constant demand. When demand is not constant every day some adjustments may be necessary to the basic EOQ model.

Quantity Discounts   Businesses frequently offer their customers purchase-price discounts when they order in large quantities. These discounts can complicate inventory decisions when they occur at quantities in excess of the EOQ. Now the optimal order size, and therefore inventory, will be determined not only by carrying and ordering costs, but also by purchase prices. A new total cost equation is needed:

Equation 7.3 $TC = C\left(\dfrac{Q}{2}\right) + R\left(\dfrac{D}{Q}\right) + P_i D$

Where P_i is the purchase price that applies to the i_{th} quantity. The optimal order quantity in the presence of quantity discounts is the one that minimizes this total cost equation.

Inventory Control

Given that a company knows what its optimal inventory should be, there remains the need to administer control over all inventory policies and practices. Some of the more common controls are listed below.

1. Improved forecasting of demand and lead times can minimize safety stocks
2. Monitor inventory practices to see if they are being carried out according to plan (e.g., are orders being placed on time, is insurance coverage adequate, etc.?)
3. Monitor carrying costs, stockout costs, and ordering costs, and be on the lookout for savings
4. Pay close attention to lead times and search for ways to shorten and/or stabilize them

5. Review policies on order size and safety stocks in the event that they can be improved on due to changing circumstances (i.e., changes in market interest rates)
6. Maintain a close surveillance on the amounts, locations, and condition of inventory items

A tremendous aid in inventory control is a computerized inventory information system.

Relationship of Inventory to Receivables

We are familiar with the normal relationship between inventory and receivables whereby inventory items become accounts receivable when they are sold on credit. Of less familiarity is the fact that receivables can often be used "in place of" inventory. For example, a manufacturer may try to entice distributors to hold the inventory it would normally carry by offering them an extended credit period. In essence, receivables are traded for inventory. Since both of these assets are carried at a cost, a decision such as this should be founded on a comparison of the two carrying costs.[6]

Summary

Accounts receivable and inventory are very important to most businesses and should be managed in a manner befitting their significance.

   Accounts receivable are essentially a byproduct of a corporation's overall credit program. As such, the process of managing accounts receivable is often referred to as credit management. Credit management consists of policies, practices, and controls relating to all aspects of a credit program. As with other asset related matters, the goal of credit management is to maximize shareholder wealth. Each credit program should have policy guidelines dealing with credit standards, credit terms, and collection effort. Furthermore, policies regarding credit standards and collection effort must be backed up with sound credit analysis procedures, in the first case, and thorough collection practices, in the second. No credit program is complete without some formalized process designed to measure its performance (i.e., efficiency and effectiveness). It is also wise to review credit policies and practices to determine if they can be improved.

   For every firm, there is an inventory level that is optimal, in that it maximizes the market price of common stock. Management's job is to determine, as closely as possible, what the optimal inventory level is, and then make sure that it is maintained and adequately cared for. The key variable in managing inventory is the order size. The order size, in turn, is primarily a function of ordering cost and carrying cost.

   The new formulas presented in this chapter are listed below.

Summary of Key Formulas

$$TC = C(Q/2) + R(D/Q)$$

$$EOQ = \sqrt{\frac{2RD}{C}}$$

TC with Quantity Discounts $= C(Q/2) + R(D/Q) + P_iD$ ∎

---

[6]For a further discussion of this topic see Michael Schiff, "Credit and Inventory Management—Separate or Together," *Financial Executive* (November 1972), pp. 28–33.

Key Terms/Concepts

Administrative costs
Bad-debt expense
Carrying cost
Cash discounts
Collection agency
Collection effort
Contribution margin
Cost of carrying accounts
  receivable
Credit analysis
Credit information sources
Credit information system
Credit limits
Credit management
Credit period

Credit policy
Credit program evaluation
Credit standards
Credit terms
Demand
Economic order quantity
  (EOQ)
Factor
Four Cs of credit analysis
  Capacity
  Capital
  Character
  Conditions

Inventory control
Lead time
Ordering cost
Order point
Order quantity
Outside credit manager
Quantity discounts
Required rate of return
Safety stock
Stockout costs

Questions

1. What is the difference between a credit period and a collection period?

2. Financial statement analysis can be very helpful with which aspect of credit management?

3. What is an inventory safety stock and why is it needed?

4. How would you respond to those who say that credit selling is a waste of time for a company, if its competitors do likewise?

5. It has been stated that the economic order quantity is the optimal order quantity. What, exactly, is being optimized?

6. How does credit insurance differ from the use of collection agencies?

7. How does the required rate of return enter into the financial management of inventory?

8. What is meant by the statement "the level of accounts receivable for a firm is a byproduct of many other decisions"?

9. What is the relationship between the following: a) order size and inventory level, b) lead time and order point, c) safety stock and order size, and d) carrying cost and frequency of ordering.

10. Someday, computer data banks will contain the credit histories of all individuals and businesses. What is your response to this statement?

11. Define the following terms: bad-debt expense, stockout costs, net/45, quantity discount, and cash discount.

Problems

1. A firm with annual credit sales of $72,000,000 and an average collection period of forty-five days, has an average investment in receivables of what amount?

2. Based on a bad-debt ratio of 2.5%, average daily credit sales of $2,400, and an accounts receivable turnover of 8 times, calculate the following:
   A. Average collection period.
   B. Average accounts receivable balance.
   C. Annual bad debts.

3. American Pesticides has average daily credit sales of $5,000, an average collection period of 36 days, and its contribution margin is 30%. Moreover, the firm must pay an interest rate of 16% to finance accounts receivable. From this information, determine the following:
   A. Average accounts receivable balance, at selling price.
   B. Average accounts receivable balance, at cost.
   C. Cost of carrying receivables, at selling price.
   D. Cost of carrying receivables, at cost.
   E. Accounts receivable turnover.

4. Historically, a business' credit customers have paid their bills in accordance with the following payment pattern: 0–50–30–20. Based on this payment pattern, how would you expect a July credit sales of $1,200,000 to be collected?

5. A company with annual credit sales of $36,000,000 and an average collection period of 40 days has an average investment in accounts receivable of what amount? What would the average receivables balance be if the collection period rose to 75 days?

6. The Houston Minerals Company sells on credit, with terms of net/30. Its accounts average 20-days overdue. Given annual credit sales of 1.8 million dollars, what is this company's average accounts receivable balance? Based on an RRR of 12%, find the annual cost of financing Houston Minerals' receivables.

7. Karg, Inc., is in the process of determining a policy for collection effort. The alternative policies and predicted consequences of each are shown in the table below. Given an RRR of 18% and a contribution margin of 33%, compare the daily benefits and costs of each alternative and select the one that is optimal.

Policy Collection Effort	Average Daily Credit Sales	Average Collection Period	Bad-Debt Ratio	Daily Administrative Cost
None	$40,000	66	8%	$ 75
Weak	40,000	64	7%	250
Mild	39,000	60	5%	500
Determined	37,000	56	3%	800
Aggressive	35,000	52	2%	1,150

8. For credit control purposes, Brass Brothers measures its accounts receivable turnover each month. This is done by dividing the credit sales of the previous twelve months by the month-ending accounts receivable balance. It just so happens that this ratio has declined in each of the last three months, causing management some concern. What might cause the receivables turnover to behave in this manner?

9. A large furniture wholesaler offers credit on terms of net/30 days. It is considering lengthening the credit period to 60 days, since this is the standard credit period used by their customers (furniture retailers). By increasing the credit period, the company believes it will experience a 20% sales increase on current annual sales of 18 million dollars. The contribution margin from the additional sales should be 25%. Credit customers are currently paying, on average, in 30 days, and it is assumed that they will pay in 60 days under the new policy. Three further pieces of information: bad debts, as a percentage of total sales, are expected to increase from 2% to 3% because of the new credit terms; the cost of administering the credit program will increase $35,000 per year; and an RRR of 18% shall be levied on any additional investment in accounts receivable. Is it wise to change the credit terms?

10. Anthrax Corporation offers credit terms of 1/10/n30. All sales are on credit and average $20,000 per day. Presently, 60% of sales receive the cash discount. Assuming that customers pay in either ten or thirty days, find Anthrax's average collection period.

11. The $3,000,000 in accounts receivable on Cordell Enterprise's books are shown below, broken down by credit quality.

Credit Quality Rating	Amount
A	$500,000
B	700,000
C	650,000
D	800,000
E	350,000

Concerned about the possibility of unusually large bad debts on these accounts, the firm has decided to acquire credit insurance. Protective Insurance Company is willing to insure all of the accounts rated D and above for a premium of $15,000. Terms of the policy are as follows: $800,000 face value, 80% coinsurance, and a $250,000 deductible. How much will Cordell collect from the insurance company if accounts rated A through D fail to pay; a) $200,000; b) $600,000; c) $1,300,000?

12. Northern Industries has been selling, on credit, to the same twelve companies for years. A new business recently contacted Northern about the possibility of buying $200,000 worth of merchandise, payable in 60 days. Northern's credit manager feels there is a 20% probability that this credit applicant will be unable to pay for the merchandise. The cost of producing a $200,000 order is $140,000. In addition, an RRR of 18% will be assessed on the investment in receivables (at cost). Are the odds and payoffs in favor of this transaction?

13. Despite a concerted effort, Williams Company has been unable to collect $20,000 from one of its larger customers. The account can be turned over to a collection agency. The agency charges a fixed fee of $2,500 plus one-half of the amount collected (in this case, $20,000). Based on past experience, there is a 40% chance that the agency will be successful. Does it make sense for Williams Company to employ the collection agency?

14. A large proportion of Cosco Company's sales are made on credit. However, the firm has a policy of offering credit only to customers with good to excellent credit ratings. It has been brought to management's attention that the firm may be passing up a golden opportunity by not extending credit to customers classified as average credit risks. The contention is that by offering these customers credit for sixty days, the firm will experience $1,080,000 in additional sales every year. The contribution margin on these sales should be 30%. Furthermore, it is unlikely that such a change in policy will affect the payment practices of current customers. There are some drawbacks, however. The average collection period and bad-debt ratio on the new accounts are expected to be 72 days and 5%, respectively. Cosco will also have to spend an extra $25,000 a year on its credit department. Last, but not least, an RRR of 15% will apply to any increase in Cosco's accounts receivable balance. Should the credit standards policy be changed?

15. A manufacturing concern had cost of goods sold equal to 7.2 million dollars and an inventory turnover of 4.8 times. Determine the following:
    A. Average daily production rate.
    B. Average inventory balance.
    C. Average holding period.

16. Heritage Corporation's inventory turnover is three times while the comparable industry figure is five times. What would cause such a discrepancy? Let us assume that the company's low inventory turnover is simply due to unusually large stocks of merchandise. Heritage, in deciding to reduce its inventory to the industry norm, should consider what factors?

17. Fantasy Stores sells 800,000 units of a particular item each year. The annual carrying cost for one of these items is $.30, whereas the cost of placing a single order is $8.00. Find the economic order quantity for this product. Calculate the total cost of carrying and ordering the EOQ for one year.

18. Durham Sporting Goods sells 8,000 pairs of golf shoes a year. The carrying cost and ordering cost associated with this product are derived below:

Per Unit Annual Carrying Costs		**Ordering Costs**	
Property taxes	$ .40	Freight	$300
Fire insurance	.50	Handling	125
Interest expense	1.50	Clerical	75
Obsolescence	.40		$500
Storage	1.20		
	$4.00		

Required:
A. Compute the EOQ.
B. Determine the total annual cost of carrying and ordering the EOQ.
C. What are the average number of golf shoes held in inventory?
D. How many orders are placed each year?

19. A chain of service stations is evaluating its inventory policy regarding automobile tires. The relevant information required for this evaluation is presented below.

Annual carrying cost per tire (C)	$ 2.40
Cost of placing one order (R)	$240.00
Annual demand for tires (D)	180,000 Units
Lead time (L)	6 Days

Based on this information, determine the following:
A. EOQ.
B. Average number of units in inventory.
C. Number of orders placed each year.
D. Total annual cost of carrying and ordering the EOQ.
E. Order point.
F. Length of time between orders.
G. Recompute B, D, and E, given that a safety stock of 1,000 tires is desired.
H. Effect on EOQ of an increase in the required rate of return.

20. Outdoor Living, Inc., manufactures lawn and garden equipment for sale to discount stores. Although the company's first production run is completed, the normal delivery time is not scheduled for two months. The firm's financial manager has determined that it will cost the company $260,000 per month to carry the inventory. Receivables, on the other hand, can be carried at a much lower cost (entirely made up of the RRR) of $150,000 per month. Will Outdoor Living come out ahead if it allows its customers three extra months of free credit in exchange for taking delivery now?

21. Steve's Steak House sells 6,000 T-bone steaks a year. Steve incurs a cost of $12 each time he places an order for T-bone steaks. On the other hand, it costs him $.75 a year to carry one of these items in inventory. In addition to these two expenses, Steve also considers quantity discounts when calculating an order size. The price-quantity schedule for T-bone steaks is presented below:

Order Size	Unit Purchase Price
0 to 249 units	$2.00
250 to 499 units	1.99
500 to 749 units	1.98
750 to 999 units	1.97
1,000 to 1,249 units	1.96
1,250 to 1,499 units	1.95
1,500 to 1,999 units	1.94
2,000 units and over	1.93

Based upon the information shown above, find the optimal T-bone steak order size. Note: begin by finding the EOQ.

Selected References

Beckman, Theodore N., and Ronald S. Foster, *Credits and Collections*, 8th ed., New York: McGraw-Hill, 1969.
Beranek, William, *Working Capital Management*, Belmont, Calif.: Wadsworth, 1968.
Carpenter, Michael D., and Jack E. Miller, "A Reliable Framework for Monitoring Accounts Receivable," *Financial Management* (Winter 1979), pp. 37–40.
Mehta, Dileep, "The Formulation of Credit Policy Models," *Management Science* (October 1968), pp. 30–50.
Nunlist, Robert A., Joseph C. Seibert, and Charles R. Turner, *Industrial and Consumer Credit Management*, Columbus, Ohio: Grid Publishing, 1983.
Lee, Sang M., *Introduction to Management Science*, Chicago: Dryden Press, 1983, pp. 432–82.
Smith, Keith V., *Guide to Working Capital Management*, New York: McGraw-Hill, 1979.
Snyder, Arthur, "Principles of Inventory Management," *Financial Executive* (April 1964), pp. 13–21.

■ Finance in the News

Inventory management is an important part of working capital management. Firms continually strive for that inventory level that is optimal in terms of profit and risk. Historically, this has meant having enough safety stock to handle unexpected changes in demand. Now, however, the emphasis is on caution with more manufacturers opting for too little inventory rather than too much.

Tightening Inventories: They Are Already Lean, But Business Wants Them Leaner

For the past two years business has kept inventories tight by historical standards. It's had plenty of incentive—high interest rates, low inflation, excess capacity, and shorter delivery times. Now it wants to tighten even more. "The word is caution," says a Chicago department store manager, speaking for most of the 200 executives responding to FORTUNE's spring survey of inventory plans.

For the first time since the recovery began, purchasing managers reported a sizable surplus. Final sales dropped at an annual rate of 6% last quarter, boosting nonfarm inventory accumulation at a worrisome $17.8-billion annual rate (see chart). The ratio of inventories to sales spiked upward, most notably in durable goods. Though the ratio is still about three percentage points below the average for 1978, a year considered normal in earlier times, business wants to trim it back by a hefty 2%. As an Alabama discounter put it, "We're afraid of getting stuck. We need money, not worthless stockpiles."

The FORTUNE survey, taken each quarter to gauge business attitudes toward this volatile sector of the economy, points up how pervasive the surpluses are. Manufacturers are stuck with the worst excesses, even though production has been almost level since last July.

Metals producers are in especially bad shape, reporting overhangs as high as 15%. With orders going nowhere, production cutbacks may be necessary to get inventories in line. Manufacturers of machinery—from low-tech car components to high-tech computers—are awash in stocks. Imports have been grabbing an ever larger share of their markets, and now the rise in capital spending is slowing. "Our customers show little evidence of having worked their excess inventories off in the past few months," says a distributor of electronic components. Food manufacturers have too much in their larders as well. The proportion of manufacturers who say they'd rather risk having too little inventory than too much has grown to 63%, from 43% a year ago.

Retailers confirm the extent of the glut: most of the winter pileup ended up on their shelves. Says a Chicago executive, "Retailers are trying to cut inventories with promotions and price cuts." Clothing merchants' racks are more crowded than ever. And department and furniture stores are scarcely better off. None of the other retailers want to increase stocks either, though stronger housing starts may thin out appliance dealers' showrooms this spring.

Car dealers are the single shining exception: sales are going strong at a 10.5 million annual rate, and dealers would like 25% more cars on their lots. "It would be a joy to have too many, so we could see how many more we could sell," says a California Chrysler dealer. The limits of demand for many cars aren't likely to be tested soon, though. Japanese models won't be as plentiful as was expected when the import quotas were lifted: the lion's share of the new allocations will go to so-called captive imports destined for GM and Chrysler. And domestic factories are running flat out. The August model changeovers will take place with almost no downtime, according to *Ward's Automotive Reports,* but inventories won't get ahead of recent levels before fall—if then.

Based on the outlook for final sales, **the pace of inventory accumulation should fall sharply this quarter and then decline steadily through mid-1986**. . . . FORTUNE estimates that final sales started to grow again this quarter and will increase 3% on average during the next year. That's less than half the 7.7% pace of last year. But combined with the 1.8% rise in inventories, it should suffice to bring the inventory-to-sales ratio down to the low levels executives desire by mid-1986.

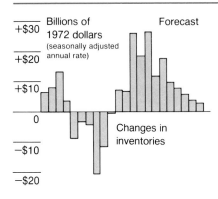

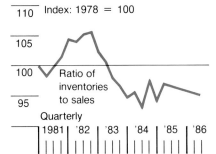

The only caveat is a possible overreaction to erratic final sales. Twice in the past year their growth swung wildly from 17% one quarter to an outright decline the next because of sudden shifts in the foreign trade balance. Business has maintained considerable aplomb so far on its roller-coaster ride, but nerves may be more severely tested by a future downtick, since sales will generally be growing more slowly.

Assuming business takes the vagaries in stride, the increasingly lower level of inventory building will still be a drag on GNP growth this year. **Industrial production is likely to slow to 3% during 1985.** That's well below the 6.1% of 1984, but good enough to keep the economy rolling through a solid third year of expansion.

FORTUNE, May 27, 1985.

Capital Budgeting: Cash Flow Analysis

Overview

The management of current assets was presented in the preceding three chapters. We shall now consider the management of capital assets. Capital assets, such as machinery, land, and buildings, are integral parts of most business organizations. Decisions are constantly being made about the acquisition, refurbishment, and sale or replacement of these assets. Such decisions fall within the jurisdiction of capital budgeting, the subject of the current chapter and the two chapters following.

There are six stages in capital budgeting. The present chapter focuses on what is arguably the most critical stage of capital budgeting, i.e., cash flow analysis. As we shall see in the forthcoming discussion, the cash flow consequences of a capital asset decision are determined, in most cases, only with considerable effort. First of all, the affected cash flows must be identified. In addition, some or all of the cash flows will have to be estimated. Finally, the impact of income taxes upon cash flows must be determined ■

Objectives

By the end of the chapter the student should be able to:

1. Explain why capital assets are covered separately from current assets
2. Describe the capital budgeting process
3. Apply the principles learned in chapter three (and added to in chapters four through seven) to cash flow analysis
4. Identify and estimate initial cash flows
5. Identify and estimate recurring cash flows
6. Identify and estimate terminal cash flows
7. Calculate net cash flows
8. Explain how the time value of money influences the choice of depreciation method
9. Explain how financial managers use tax considerations to judge capital asset proposals
10. Compute capital gains taxes for depreciable assets
11. Explain the process of cash flow analysis from identification through estimation through determining the impact of taxes
12. Derive net cash flow profiles

Introduction

Capital budgeting is concerned with the purchase, modification, and disposal of capital assets such as machinery, buildings, land, and equipment. Capital budgeting is a process that encompasses all aspects of these decisions, up to, but not including, the physical act. It is a crucial task because capital assets have a significant effect on a firm's profitability and risk. A capital budget, on the other hand, is a schedule of all capital asset proposals found to be acceptable. The ultimate objective of capital budgeting continues to be the maximization of stockholder wealth through an increase in the market price of common stock.

There are some very good reasons why capital assets are covered separately from current assets. In the first place, they last much longer than current assets. This feature tends to make them riskier. Secondly, the tax laws surrounding capital assets are important in their evaluation. Thirdly, current assets require more day-to-day attention than capital assets that are purchased, sold, and monitored much less frequently. Furthermore, individual capital assets involve much larger sums of money than distinct current assets ■

Capital Budgeting

Capital budgeting is composed of six stages, through which each capital asset proposal must pass. A listing of these stages and the normal order in which they occur is shown in table 8.1.

Table 8.1   Stages in the Capital Budgeting Process

---

1. Proposal
2. Cash flow analysis
3. Evaluate proposal
4. Evaluate capital budget
5. Implementation
6. Follow-up

The present chapter is devoted to a discussion of the second stage, or cash flow analysis. The remaining five stages are covered in the following two chapters. To avoid unnecessary confusion, our discussion will center on the acquisition of capital assets. This is because purchases are more numerous than other capital asset proposals, and they are somewhat easier to understand.

To obtain a better appreciation of capital budgeting one should understand the roles of the major participants. *There are three major parties involved in capital budgeting: sponsors, analysts, and decision makers.*

Sponsors submit proposals concerning capital assets, such as a request to buy a warehouse. These individuals are normally employees of the firm, but quite often include outsiders such as consultants and salespersons. It is helpful to keep in mind the unavoidable fact that sponsors are often overly optimistic about their proposals. However, experienced analysts and decision makers are constantly on the lookout for such bias.

Analysts examine all proposals in an effort to evaluate their profitability and risk. This information is then organized, hopefully in a clear manner, for presentation to decision makers. Performance of this task requires a great deal of information. This material may be provided by the sponsor, other employees, the analysts themselves, or outside organizations.

Decision makers do just that, they make the final decisions on proposals. They look at the sponsor's case, examine the risk and profit information provided by the analyst, take into account any other factors and then make their decisions. The exact manner in which these decisions are made will depend upon a firm's organizational structure and the kind of proposal under consideration.

In small firms these three tasks are often performed by the same person. This is rarely the case, however, in a medium-to-large corporation.

Cash Flow Analysis

Without question, the most important factor in a decision to purchase or not to purchase a capital asset are the cash receipts and expenditures that will result from that decision. In addition to the cash amounts, one must also consider "when" they occur because of the time value of money. We were introduced to cash flows in chapter 3, where we learned how they were involved with compound interest. The current chapter discusses cash flows in much more detail.

Cash flow analysis involves identifying the relevant cash flows associated with a capital asset proposal and then measuring them. Sometimes these are easy tasks. Typically, however, it is difficult to measure cash flows, and quite often there are problems in identification. Identification can be troublesome when there exists indirect cash flow repercussions. Cash flow measurement is difficult primarily for two reasons. To begin with, cash flows resulting from the purchase and use of capital assets primarily occur in the future. But the future is normally filled with uncertainty. Consequently, they must be estimated. Secondly, the profusion and complexity of corporate federal income tax laws make cash flow analysis much more difficult than otherwise.

Cash Flow Identification

How do we identify the cash flows produced by a capital asset that has not yet been purchased? We should start by asking the following question: *how will the asset change cash inflows and/or cash outflows for the overall business if it is acquired?* In other words, we are looking for incremental cash flows.

The identification process does not tell us the amounts of cash flows, but rather "what kind" they are (e.g., sales, advertising expense, trade-ins, etc.).

Sometimes it is relatively easy to identify the change in a firm's cash flows as a result of a capital asset acquisition. Thus, a plant expansion would ordinarily indicate an increased cash inflow from added sales. At other times it is not so obvious. For example, the acquisition of equipment for a new product could simultaneously generate sales (from the new product) and reduce sales of an existing product, if the products are substitutes for each other. In the second example we have an *indirect cash flow repercussion.* Another example of a repercussion would be the sale of an old machine made possible by the purchase of a new machine.

As a final example, what about the increased premium on an insurance policy resulting from the renovation of an office building. When trying to identify the cash flow impact of a capital asset, look at all possibilities. Practice and a fundamental understanding of economic principles are indispensible to cash flow identification. A good imagination is also very helpful. The identification stage is exceedingly important. If it is not done carefully, then all of the later work performed in the capital budgeting process may be useless.

As an aid in the identification and measurement process, it is helpful to divide cash flows into three categories: initial, recurring, and terminal.

Initial Cash Flows   Initial cash flows (ICF) are all of the cash expenditures and receipts that accompany the acquisition of a capital asset. As a general rule, they would occur within a short time of the decision to buy.[1] Consider, if you will, the acquisition of an automobile for personal use. In addition to the purchase price, other possible ICFs would be sales tax, rustproofing, excise tax, trade-in value of old car, and insurance premium.

The possibilities here are numerous but most of them would fall under one of the classifications shown in table 8.2.

Table 8.2   Initial Cash Flows

Purchase price
Construction costs
Delivery charges
Down time
Installation and preparation expense
Legal fees
Working capital changes
Trade-ins
Employee training expense
Income taxes

Do not be alarmed if some of the items in table 8.2 are unfamiliar to you. All of them will be addressed by example or otherwise in the remainder of the chapter. It is the rare capital asset that exhibits all of these cash flows. Nevertheless, table 8.2 provides a useful checklist for identifying ICFs.

There are several initial cash flows that often escape identification. Due to their frequency and importance, it is helpful to describe them briefly.

1. *Training and Hiring:* The purchase of replacement machinery and equipment often requires the retraining of current personnel. This is particularly true if the new capital assets are radically different from the old ones or they require a higher level of operator sophistication. The cost of training should be included in the initial cash flows.

    Expansion of operations will most likely entail the hiring of additional employees. While the cost of this activity is not normally as large as training expense, it should nevertheless be taken into account.

---

[1]The initial cash flows associated with some assets (e.g., new plant construction) can continue for several years before the asset is ready to use.

2. *Working Capital Changes:* Some capital asset proposals involve an increase in the size of operations. Due to the nature of business activity, it is inevitable for current assets (i.e., cash, receivables and inventory) to increase as the size of the business increases. By the same token, they can decrease as the level of operation falls. The relationship is not perfect, but it is rare when it does not occur. Increased production and sales will lead to larger inventory stocks of all kinds, greater accounts receivable and possibly additional cash balances. Cash outlays for these items should be considered in initial cash flows. It should be mentioned, however, that some current liabilities also increase automatically when sales grow (e.g., accrued wages and accounts payable). For this reason, the appropriate cash flow to consider is the difference between increased current assets and increased current liabilities.

A change in the size of operations is not the only capital asset decision that can affect working capital. The acquisition of a computer, for example, may allow for a reduction in inventory stocks.

3. *Down Time:* Installing a large machine and remodeling or enlarging a building are examples of capital asset proposals that can lead to down time. Down time is incurred when an operation or an entire business is forced to operate at less than capacity while installation and remodeling work is being done. Imagine the lost sales revenue suffered by a retailer during a four-month remodeling of its store. The foregone profit from these lost sales should be included in the initial cash flows attributable to the remodeling proposal.

4. *Opportunity Cost:* It is tempting to conclude that idle facilities are free to use as one pleases. For instance, an unused portion of a plant may be considered cost free for the addition of an employee cafeteria. However, this would be true only if the idle space has no other current or prospective use. If there is an alternative use, then the foregone cash benefits derived from that use should be considered in the cash flow analysis for the cafeteria. These foregone benefits represent an opportunity cost.

Recurring Cash Flows   Recurring cash flows (RCF) are the annual cash flows generated by the use of a capital asset. As with initial cash flows, RCFs can include both receipts and expenditures. Furthermore, the amounts do not have to be the same from period to period. Recurring cash flows associated with an automobile include maintenance, gasoline, insurance, repairs, and license fees.

A checklist of typical RCFs is shown in table 8.3. It is a useful identification checklist for most problems.

Table 8.3   Recurring Cash Flows

Sales revenue
Rental and interest income
Labor and materials expense
Selling and administration expense
Energy expense
Maintenance and repair
Income taxes

Each one of the items listed can be a cash inflow on some occasions and a cash outflow on others. For example, the acquisition of a certain piece of equipment could cause the firm's labor and materials expense to go up, whereas another type of equipment may cause these expenses to decline. And, *although recurring cash flows are typically spread out over a year, we will make the simplifying assumption that they all occur at the end of each year.*

Terminal Cash Flows   Terminal cash flows (TCF) are the final or concluding cash flows associated with capital assets. They take place at the time the asset is disposed of, which may or may not coincide with its useful life. TCFs are unique, one-time-only cash receipts and expenditures and should not be confused with recurring cash flows. Returning again to the automobile example, TCFs might consist of a selling price and fix-up costs (e.g., painting, new seat covers, etc.).

A checklist of common terminal cash flows is shown in table 8.4.

Table 8.4   Terminal Cash Flows

Sale of asset
Sales commissions
Presale fix-up costs
Removal expenses
Income taxes

This list of terminal cash flows is not meant to be all inclusive, and every capital asset would not give rise to all of the cash flows that are listed. As a matter of fact, there are no TCFs associated with some assets. Nevertheless, table 8.4 is a useful guide for the beginner in identifying the existence or nonexistence of these kinds of cash flows.

The three cash flow checklists just presented can be used for practically any kind of capital asset. You can get some idea of the variety from the following list: apartments, automobiles, computers, office buildings, forklift trucks, land, warehouses, bonds, machinery, and preferred stock. Take special note that all of the checklists include income taxes.

Net Cash Flows   *The ultimate objective of cash flow analysis is to determine the net cash flow (NCF) for each year that a capital asset is in the firm's possession.* This is accomplished by simply netting the cash receipts and expenditures for each year. Netting requires that receipts be given positive signs and expenditures negative signs. Therefore, a negative net cash flow indicates that it is an outflow and a positive net cash flow signifies that it is an inflow.

Following the classification scheme used above, we wish to know the *initial net cash flow (INCF), recurring net cash flows (RNCF)* and *terminal net cash flow (TNCF)* for each capital asset proposal. *The initial net cash flow is often referred to as the investment.*

Application: WXXY-TV feels that the acquisition of a Computer-Aided Photographic Analyzer (CAPA) will improve its screen images significantly. As a result, it will be able to charge more for advertisements. The company believes that a new CAPA will last for five years and would like to know its impact on cash flows.

The treasurer for WXXY has identified the following cash flow items: purchase price of the CAPA; installation charges; salvage value; increased advertising revenues; employee training expense; and income taxes.

The first thing to do is separate the cash flow items into initial, recurring, and terminal.

Initial Cash Flows (Today)	Recurring Cash Flows (Years 1–5)	Terminal Cash Flows (In 5 years)
Purchase price	Advertising revenues	Sale of asset
Installation	Income taxes	Income taxes
Training expense		
Income taxes		

After the types of cash flows have been identified they should be estimated. Following this, income taxes must be calculated. WXXY's treasurer is very fortunate in this regard. Not only does he know with certainty the magnitude of cash flows, but he has also found a tax specialist to perform this task. The cash flow measurements are shown in the cash flow statement below.

Initial Cash Flows (Today)		Recurring Cash Flows (Years 1–5)		Terminal Cash Flows (In 5 years)	
Purchase price	− $40,000	Advertising		Salvage value	+ $10,000
Installation		revenue	+ $20,000	Income taxes	0
expense	− 5,000	Income taxes	− 6,500		
Training					
expense	− 3,000				
Income taxes	+ 1,500				
INCF	− $46,500	RNCF	+ $13,500	INCF	+ $10,000

The cash outflows are given negative signs and the cash inflows positive signs. This is very important because we are striving for the net cash flows. Note that the income taxes under initial cash flows have a positive sign. This indicates a tax savings, which is not unusual, as we will discover later.

The final step in cash flow analysis is to draw up a *net cash flow profile*.

CAPA Net Cash Flow Profile

Year	0	1	2	3	4	5	5
Net cash flow	− $46,500	+ $13,500	+ $13,500	+ $13,500	+ $13,500	+ $13,500	+ $10,000

A net cash flow profile reveals the impact that a capital asset has on a firm's cash flows. In this example, the capital asset will lead to an immediate net cash outflow or investment of $46,500 followed by net cash receipts of $13,500 in years one through five and $10,000 in five years. Furthermore, these cash flows are known with certainty. Actually, the two cash flows in year five could be combined into a single amount of $23,500.

Notice that the recurring net cash flows are all positive (i.e., inflows). This is normally to be expected for a capital asset acquisition. However, there could be one or more periods when a RNCF is negative. Future outlays for remodeling a building or overhauling a machine may be large enough to bring about a negative RNCF ∎

Cash Flow Estimates

It is one thing to identify the types of cash flows associated with capital assets and quite another to measure them. Cash flow projections that can be relied upon with 100% assurance are rare in the business world. This is unfortunate because businesses could operate much more effectively. Nevertheless, the concept is valuable in and of itself as a standard of comparison.

Most cash flows pertaining to capital assets occur in the future, after the purchase decisions have been made. The future, as we all know, is full of surprises, and the future of a business is certainly no exception to the rule. It is very difficult to say precisely what a particular cash flow will be in the future, especially if the future is ten or twenty years away. Who can say for sure what future wages will be, or salvage values or even income tax rates? *The uncertainty of future cash flows is the major cause of business risk.*

Consider, for example, the uncertainty surrounding an airline's future cash revenues as the result of purchasing an additional airplane. The firm may be able to say with 100% confidence that sales revenue will go up. It is very doubtful, however, that the airline can be positive as to exactly how much it will rise. Sales revenue can be difficult to predict for many reasons: competition from old and new sources, business cycles, government actions, strikes, change in consumer tastes, and, of course, inflation, to mention just some of the imponderables.

Not all future cash flows from a capital asset are equally uncertain. There also exists varying degrees of cash flow uncertainty among different capital assets.

It is the role of management to try and estimate, as best it can, what future cash flows will be. *Generally speaking, cash flow estimates can be classified as to whether they are (a) objective estimates in the form of a probability distribution, or (b) subjective estimates.*

Objective Estimates   If it is not possible to know exactly what cash flows will be, the next best alternative is to know their probability distribution. A probability distribution of recurring fuel costs for a new truck fleet over the next three years might look like the example in table 8.5.

Table 8.5   Cash Flow Probability Distribution of Future Fuel Costs

Year	1	2	3	
Outcomes	RCF_1	RCF_2	RCF_3	Probability
A	$100,000	$150,000	$200,000	.20
B	$150,000	$150,000	$150,000	.30
C	$200,000	$200,000	$200,000	.30
D	$200,000	$300,000	$400,000	.20

There are four possible outcomes in this case. There is a 20% chance that outcome A will occur (i.e., $100,000 followed by $150,000 and $200,000), a 30% chance of B, and so on. While these figures are not as useful as they would be if they were certainties, they are nevertheless very valuable. Obviously, an objective probability assessment of future fuel costs is more useful than saying "I have no idea what fuel costs will be."

Subjective Estimates   Subjective estimates can vary significantly in degree of sophistication. Some of them are founded solely on simple "gut instinct." Others rely upon mathematical forecasting techniques and in-depth analysis of underlying economic factors. Subjective cash flow estimates are often referred to as *most likely cash flows.* A most likely cash flow estimate does not provide all of the possible outcomes as in a probability distribution, which is a disadvantage. Instead, it is a single best estimate. A typical most likely estimate might be stated as follows, "wages are predicted to be $40,000 annually for the next six years."

Estimation Techniques   You might be wondering where cash flow estimates come from? They must be developed, and there are a number of methods one can use to develop them. Some of the more popular methods are discussed below.

1. *Historical Data:* If the analyst can obtain valid historical data on a particular asset, this information can be used to approximate the future. With the aid of mathematical forecasting techniques, historical data can be especially useful. The most obvious problem with using historical data is that history is not always a reliable guide to the future. An additional problem concerns the exorbitant cost sometimes required to gather the data.
2. *Surveys:* Properly conducted surveys, such as those used to forecast consumer demand, can help in the prediction of future cash flows. Surveys are, of course, susceptible to bias and are not practical for many situations.
3. *Engineering Estimates:* Technological aspects of many assets can often be evaluated by experts prior to their purchase. Maintenance, useful life, and energy consumption are examples of things for which a technician could provide reasonable estimates.
4. *Subjective Probabilities:* The feelings of employees based on their experience, training, and intelligence can be very useful. For example, a marketing manager might be asked to provide a sales probability distribution for a new product, based upon his or her experience and feel for the market.

These techniques should not be considered substitutes for each other. Rather, all of them can be used to complement and verify one another.

Application: *National Inquisition,* a large weekly newspaper, would like to upgrade its printing press. An exciting new model has just come on the market. As part of their analysis they need to know the cash flow impact of the new press. Their current press was purchased and installed ten years ago for $5,000,000 and has been completely depreciated. However, it could last another six years with adequate maintenance. The new press is expected to last only six years due to the rapid pace of technological change. The firm plans to retain it for the full six years if it is acquired.

The financial manager for *National* has identified the following cash flows: purchase price of new press; installation and delivery charges; annual savings in labor costs, maintenance expense, and energy expense; acquisition of the new press will allow the sale of the old press; and income taxes should be affected. These items can be classified as follows:

Initial Cash Flows (Today)	Recurring Cash Flows (Years 1–6)	Terminal Cash Flows (In 6 Years)
Purchase of new press	Labor cost savings	None
Installation expense	Maintenance cost savings	
Sale of old press	Energy cost savings	
Income taxes	Income taxes	

Unlike the previous example, the cash flows associated with the printing press are anything but certain. Not one, but six cash flow sequences are predicted, and they are in the form of a probability distribution. The net cash flow profile in probability distribution form is shown below:

Net Cash Flow Profile Probability Distribution

Year	0	1	2	3	4	5	6	Probability
Event	*INCF*	$RNCF_1$	$RNCF_2$	$RNCF_3$	$RNCF_4$	$RNCF_5$	$RNCF_6$	
A	−$800,000	+ 56,846	+ 56,846	+ 56,846	+ 56,846	+ 56,846	+ 56,846	.05
B	−$800,000	+ 90,703	+ 90,703	+ 90,703	+ 90,703	+ 90,703	+ 90,703	.10
C	−$800,000	+133,333	+133,333	+133,333	+133,333	+133,333	+133,333	.10
D	−$800,000	+135,000	+167,000	+183,000	+200,000	+218,000	+230,000	.25
E	−$800,000	+271,095	+271,095	+271,095	+271,095	+271,095	+271,095	.30
F	−$800,000	+281,000	+310,000	+345,000	+395,000	+415,000	+425,000	.20

Note that the INCF is the same in each profile. This implies that it is known with certainty. While one cannot always be sure of the investment figure (e.g., nuclear power plant construction costs), quite often it is a certainty due to its current nature. On the other hand, the RNCFs have a wide range of possible values ■

Income Taxes

Corporations pay many types of taxes, but, without a doubt, the most significant is the corporate federal income tax. Not only is it the most onerous, it also has the distinction of being the most complex. Its importance is exemplified by the fact that each cash flow checklist in tables 8.2, 8.3, and 8.4 includes income taxes. Its complexity can be attested to by the thousands of intelligent, highly trained persons who devote the better part of their working days to struggling with this monster.

Federal income tax regulations are difficult even for professionals to understand and they are constantly changing. For these reasons, we will primarily confine ourselves to those income tax rules that are important to capital budgeting issues. The tax rules presented in this chapter are oversimplified in many instances, so as to avoid unnecessary confusion. However, even an elementary discussion should convince the reader that federal income tax laws can complicate financial decision making.

A financial manager wants to know how a capital asset will change the income taxes (a cash flow) of the business. The effect on income taxes will in turn influence the desirability of purchasing the capital asset. *In order to compute a change in income taxes, two pieces of information are necessary: income tax rates and changes in taxable income.*

While income tax rates are easily obtained, such is not normally the case with taxable income. *Taxable income is equal to gross income minus deductible expenses.* Although this may not appear to be a very difficult statement, the tax code has a way of mystifying it. Measuring taxable income is troublesome for three reasons. In the first place, accounting principles and tax laws are not in total agreement on the concepts of revenue and expenses. As a result, "accounting income statements" are often different from "tax income statements" (i.e., two sets of books). For the most part, we will ignore these disagreements and deal with fairly standard items. Secondly, income tax rules can be difficult to interpret. This can lead to errors or disputes that often end in court. The third problem arises because the government divides (some say arbitrarily) taxable income into two types: that generated through normal, everyday business activities (ordinary taxable income) and that obtained from the infrequent sale of capital assets such as land (capital gains).

We will conduct our study of income taxes by separating ordinary taxable income from capital gains. There are a number of distinct differences between them, not the least of which is that they are taxed at different rates.

Ordinary Income Tax

Ordinary Gross Income   Ordinary gross income includes not only sales revenue, but also other income such as rental receipts, royalties, and interest. The purchase of capital assets often leads to changes in a firm's ordinary gross income.

Cash Deductible Expenses   The law allows as a deduction from ordinary gross income those cash expenses incurred in generating that income. Included in this category are those items you would expect to find, such as cost of goods sold (wages, materials, utilities), selling expense, rent expense, and interest paid for borrowed funds.

Let us turn our attention to an important income tax principle. *Because of the existence of income taxes any business expense that can be deducted is partially paid for by the government.* Deductible expenses reduce taxable income, thereby reducing income taxes.[2] By the same token, a reduction in deductible expenses will cause taxes to rise. An illustration will help to clarify this principle.

Example: Shown in table 8.6 are two income tax statements for a corporation that pays an ordinary income tax rate of 40%. Statement A is without a selling expense and statement B includes a selling expense of $1,000,000. Otherwise, the gross incomes and deductions are identical for the two statements. Note that although statement B has $1,000,000 more in deductible expenses, it pays $400,000 less in income taxes. The government has paid $400,000 of the selling expense (40% of $1,000,000) in the sense that its tax receipts fall by $400,000.

---

[2]Technically, this statement is only true if the business is profitable.

Table 8.6   Ordinary Income Tax Statements

Statement A			Statement B		
Gross Income		$15,000,000	Gross Income		$15,000,000
Wages	$6,000,000		Wages	$ 6,000,000	
Selling expense	0		Selling expense	1,000,000	
Depreciation	3,000,000		Depreciation	3,000,000	
Interest expense	1,000,000		Interest expense	1,000,000	
Total deductible			Total deductible		
expenses	$10,000,000		expenses	$11,000,000	
Taxable income		$ 5,000,000	Taxable income		$ 4,000,000
Income taxes (.40)		$ 2,000,000	Income taxes (.40)		$ 1,600,000

Noncash Deductible Expenses (Depreciation)   Depreciation is important to capital budgeting primarily because it is a tax deductible expense. There are, of course, many tax deductible expenses, but depreciation deserves special attention for two reasons. First of all, *it is an expense that requires no cash outlay.* Secondly, special rules must be followed in order to compute depreciation for tax purposes. Prior to dealing with these issues, it would be helpful to point out the fact that depreciation means different things to different persons: economists, accountants, and tax authorities.

Economic Depreciation   Economists consider depreciation to be the decline in the market value of a capital asset from one time period to the next. Consequently, it is not possible to determine the precise amount of economic depreciation until after the time has elapsed. Thus, it is an after-the-fact depreciation. Computing economic depreciation also requires a market value appraisal every time a depreciation figure is desired. For example, the economic depreciation on an automobile for one year would be the difference between its resale value at the start of the year and the resale value at the end of the year.

Accounting Depreciation   Accountants are in general agreement with economists on how depreciation should be measured. However, they claim that such a procedure would be impractical because of the high cost of continual market value appraisals as well as the subjectivity of such appraisals. The ultimate purpose of accounting depreciation is to convey useful information to users of financial statements. In the preparation of financial statements, accountants prefer to estimate annual depreciation charges at the time the asset is acquired. Their estimates are based upon the asset's original cost, predicted useful life, estimated salvage value, and engineering projections of such things as wear and tear and obsolescence. Accountants believe that through following such a methodology, they can obtain a reasonably close approximation of economic depreciation.

Tax Depreciation   The government permits business a deduction for depreciation expense in the computation of ordinary taxable income. They allow estimates of depreciation to be based upon the original cost of the asset as do accountants. However, the government's rules on useful life, salvage value and wear and tear often differ from what accountants feel more accurately reflects the economics of an asset. For these reasons, the depreciation charges shown on an accounting income statement are often different from those on the income tax statement.

The tax authorities would be delighted if a business took depreciation tax deductions less than those allowed by law, as this would lead to more accelerated tax payments. From a business perspective, however, such a course would be foolish. *As a general rule, a firm should take all of the depreciation tax deductions it can, as early as it can.* Remember, the time value of money states that cash outflows should be delayed as long as possible, including taxes. There are legal limits, however, on depreciation deductions. They are limited by tax guidelines on useful life, salvage value, and wear-and-tear depreciation methods.

Thus, to compute the depreciation tax deduction we must have, in addition to the *original cost* of the asset, *tax life, tax salvage value,* and *tax depreciation method.* Tax depreciation methods have changed radically over the past few years, and it appears as if they could change again. To simplify matters, we shall make use of two traditional accounting depreciation methods, *straight-line (SL)* and *sum-of-the-years-digits (SYD),* to compute income tax depreciation.[3] SYD is often referred to as an accelerated depreciation method.

Measuring the Depreciation Tax Deduction   Now we are ready to compute the depreciation tax deduction. The procedure we will follow in every case is as follows:

A. *Original Cost:* Purchase price or construction costs plus charges for installation, delivery, etc., equal original cost.
B. *Depreciable Base:* Original cost less tax salvage value equals depreciable base.[4]
C. *Depreciation Fractions:* Depreciation method combined with tax life equals depreciation fractions.[5]
D. *Annual Depreciation:* Depreciable base multiplied by depreciation fractions equal annual depreciation.

Example: An asset can be purchased for $500,000 and installed for an additional $40,000. It has a "tax" life of 6 years and a "tax" salvage value of $120,000. What are the annual depreciation tax deductions under SL and SYD methods of depreciation? Use the information below and table 8.7.

Purchase price	$500,000
Installation	+ 40,000
Original cost	$540,000
Salvage value	− 120,000
Depreciable base	$420,000

---

[3]Many capital assets are depreciated under the terms of the accelerated cost recovery system (ACRS), which became law in 1982. SL and SYD are used for illustrative purposes only.

[4]In the event that an investment tax credit applies to a capital asset, one-half of the credit should be deducted from the asset's depreciable base. However, for sake of simplicity we will ignore this legal technicality.

[5]Straight-line fractions are found by dividing 1 by the tax life. Sum-of-the-years digits fractions are found by summing the years in the tax life and dividing this into the years in reverse order. For instance a tax life of 5 years would generate depreciation fractions of 5/15, 4/15, 3/15, 2/15, and 1/15.

Table 8.7   Depreciation Schedules

Sum-of-Years-Digits			Straight-Line		
Year	Depreciation Fraction	Depreciation Tax Deduction	Year	Depreciation Fraction	Depreciation Tax Deduction
1	6/21	$120,000	1	1/6	$70,000
2	5/21	100,000	2	1/6	70,000
3	4/21	80,000	3	1/6	70,000
4	3/21	60,000	4	1/6	70,000
5	2/21	40,000	5	1/6	70,000
6	1/21	20,000	6	1/6	70,000

As you can see, both methods generate total depreciation deductions of $420,000. However, they exhibit different amounts each year. SYD exhibits larger deductions than SL in the early years. This will cause ordinary taxable income and, therefore, taxes to be lower in the early years. Thus, from the standpoint of the time value of money, SYD is superior to SL and should be used if legally permissible. A lower salvage value and shorter tax life would also accelerate the depreciation deductions ■

Depreciation: A Noncash Expense   Depreciation is an expense on both accounting and income tax statements. Unlike other expenses though, there is no required cash outlay. The reason is so obvious, it is often overlooked. Long-lived assets are paid for, in cash, when they are first acquired. The expense (i.e., depreciation) is taken as the asset is used up.

Ordinary Taxable Income   Ordinary taxable income (loss) for a corporation is the difference between ordinary gross income and ordinary deductible expenses. Positive taxable income is multiplied by the tax rate to obtain income taxes due. If, on the other hand, taxable income is negative, the firm can benefit from a future reduction in taxes or tax refunds through what are called *carryover provisions*. Without going into all the details we shall simply say that if a firm incurs an ordinary taxable loss in a given year, that loss can be used as a tax deduction in prior and/or future profitable years. If it is carried over to prior years, the company files amended income tax returns to receive tax refunds.

We are mainly concerned with "changes" in a company's ordinary taxable income brought about by capital asset acquisitions.

Ordinary Income Tax Rates   For many years corporate ordinary taxable income has been taxed at more than one rate. As of this writing, the ordinary tax rate schedule is as shown in table 8.8.

Table 8.8   Corporate Federal Income Tax Rates

Bracket (Taxable Income)	Tax Rate
$ 0–$25,000	15%
$25,001–$50,000	18%
$50,001–$75,000	30%
$75,001–$100,000	40%
Over $100,000	46%

Memorize these rates if you wish, but we will use many different tax rates in this book. Applying the tax rate schedule above to a taxable income of $500,000 would generate an income tax of $209,750.

It is helpful to distinguish between average and marginal income tax rates. *Average tax rates* reveal the proportion of total taxable income paid in taxes. *Marginal income tax rates* apply to changes in taxable income. They are determined by a firm's current taxable income or "tax bracket." For example, given the current income tax rate schedule, a business with taxable income of $80,000 would face a marginal tax rate of 40% on any changes in taxable income. On the other hand, a company with taxable income of $200,000 would be in a marginal tax bracket of 46%. Since we are concerned about changes in taxable income, it stands to reason that we will be primarily interested in marginal income tax rates.

Capital Income Tax

Capital Gross Income   Capital gross income arises from the sale of a firm's capital assets. Capital transactions are, by definition, unusual. Included in this category would be the sale of office buildings, machinery, land, or common stocks held as investments.[6] The tax authorities look at the recurring nature of the transaction to decide if it is ordinary or capital. For instance, the sale of a used computer by a chemical company would be a capital transaction. On the other hand, the sale of computers by IBM would be classified as ordinary since computers are IBMs main business.

Classifying a transaction as ordinary or capital is by no means always as clear-cut as the previous examples would indicate. A court of law is often required to settle disputes over classification.

Capital Deductible Expenses   The government allows corporations to deduct certain expenses associated with the sale of capital assets. The two major tax deductions are selling expenses (i.e., brokerage commissions) and the original cost of the asset less the accumulated depreciation taken up to the time of sale.

Original cost is reduced by accumulated depreciation to account for the fact that an ordinary tax deduction was obtained on the previous depreciation charges. If this were not done, a business could get two deductions for the same expense. As we will see, this adjustment causes the computation of capital gains to be more involved. No such adjustment to original cost is necessary for those assets that are not depreciated, such as land and common stocks.

Capital Gains   Capital gain (loss) is the difference between sales proceeds and deductible expenses. Determining the income taxes on capital gains is somewhat involved because of the aforementioned adjustment for accumulated depreciation. The difficulty arises because prior depreciation deductions were used to reduce ordinary taxable income. If the asset did not actually decline in value as much as the accumulated depreciation then prior "ordinary" taxable income was understated and thus, income taxes were underpaid. When the asset is sold, these taxes will have to be paid. That is to say, the taxes will be *recaptured* by the government.

---

[6]To qualify as a capital transaction the asset must also have been held a minimum period of time, currently six months.

A procedure one can use to compute capital gains taxes for depreciable assets is as follows:

1. Compute the capital gain or loss
2. Divide a gain as follows:
    a) All capital gains up to the level of accumulated depreciation is taxable at the ordinary income tax rate, since it is a recapture of depreciation.
    b) All capital gains above the level of accumulated depreciation (if any exists) is taxable at the capital gains tax rate, since it represents appreciation in the assets value.
3. Should there be a capital loss, it would *save* taxes at the ordinary tax rate, since accumulated depreciation was understated.

An example will help to clarify this procedure.

Example: A company purchased a depreciable asset 4 years ago for $1,500,000 including installation charges. During that time it took total depreciation tax deductions of $800,000. The firm has an ordinary tax rate of 45% and a capital gains rate of 25%. Given that it would cost $30,000 to dispose of the asset today, compute the income taxes that will result from selling prices of $1,800,000, $1,200,000, and $600,000. The solution is shown in table 8.9.

Table 8.9   Capital Income Tax Statements

	$1,800,000	$1,200,000	$600,000
Sales proceeds	$1,800,000	$1,200,000	$600,000
Selling expenses	− 30,000	− 30,000	− 30,000
Cost less accumulated depreciation	− 700,000	− 700,000	− 700,000
Caital gain (loss)	$1,070,000	$ 470,000	($130,000)
Depreciation recapture	800,000	470,000	(130,000)
Asset appreciation	270,000	0	0
Tax on recapture (.45)	360,000	211,500	(58,500)
Tax on appreciation (.25)	67,500	0	0
Income tax due	$427,500	$211,500	($58,500)

The $1,800,000 selling price generated two kinds of income because the asset *appreciated* in value. On the other hand, the $600,000 selling price was $900,000 less than the original cost. It declined in value by more than the accumulated depreciation of $800,000. As a result, the company obtained insufficient depreciation deductions and thereby paid excessive ordinary income taxes. To correct for this, the government allows the company to deduct the $130,000 loss from its current ordinary gross income, thereby "saving" $58,500 in ordinary income taxes■

Note: *as of this writing, the corporate capital gains tax rate is 28%.* However, we will not confine ourselves to a 28% rate in this text since tax rates can and do change.

Tax Credits   Another tax regulation important to financial management is the tax credit. Tax credits are subtracted from income taxes rather than gross income. Accordingly, they are better than tax deductions because the corporation gets a dollar-for-dollar reduction in taxes from them.

Only one tax credit will concern us in this text and it is called the *investment tax credit*. The investment tax credit was designed to stimulate capital formation. Whether it has been successful at encouraging capital formation is difficult to say, but it can certainly reduce the cost of some fixed capital assets. Although the rules and regulations of this credit change repeatedly, there are certain basic characteristics that have been maintained. In general: it applies only to certain qualified capital assets; it is a percentage of an asset's purchase price plus installation charges; the percentage increases with the useful life of the asset up to a maximum amount (currently 10%); and the tax credit can be taken only once, at the time the asset is purchased. We will not venture beyond these guidelines. The text will indicate whether or not a capital asset qualifies for this credit and the applicable percentage. Tax credits are subtracted from the firm's income taxes that are due on the next tax payment date. However, we will make the simplifying assumption that credits can be taken immediately. Note: tax credits used in this text may deviate from currently permissible tax credit percentages.[7]

Example: Big Al Roofing Company wants to acquire a new tarring machine. The purchase price is $30,000 and another $3,000 will be needed to adapt it with other equipment. An examination of the tax regulations indicates this machine is eligible for a 7% investment tax credit. What is the amount of the credit? It is .07 × $33,000 = $2,310. Furthermore, it can be taken only once. This tax savings, in effect, reduces the initial investment cost from $33,000 to $30,690 ▪

Conclusion   Capital asset decisions are heavily influenced by federal income taxes. Income tax laws are complex and not something to be taken lightly. Expert tax advice should be obtained, and it should be obtained before a purchase decision is made, not after. Although income tax laws make capital budgeting more difficult, that is no excuse for ignoring them. Income taxes are cash flows and ignoring them can lead to serious mistakes.

Application: Kim Lee, the principal owner and operator of the Lusk Theater, is so pleased with his current movie theater that he is contemplating the construction of another one. He expects to own the new movie house only five years and then sell it. At that time he plans to enter the emerging theater-pizza parlor business. Mr. Lee requires cash flow data to make his movie decision.

Mr. Lee has identified the following cash flows in connection with the new theater: ticket sales; concession business; employee wages; cost of film rentals; maintenance and utilities expense; construction costs; expenditures for furnishings and fixtures; sale of the theater in five years that will be partially offset by a real estate sales commission; and income taxes. Furthermore, cash flows have been estimated subjectively. A classification of these cash flows and their most likely estimated values are shown below.

Initial Cash Flows (Today)		Recurring Cash Flows (Years 1–5)		Terminal Cash Flows (In 5 Years)	
Construction costs	−$250,000	Ticket revenue	+$260,000	Sale of theater	+$250,000
Furnish and fixtures	− 120,000	Concession revenue	+ 100,000	Sales commission	− 20,000
Income taxes	?	Maintenance expense	− 6,000	Income taxes	?
		Utilities expense	− 28,000		
		Wage expense	− 54,000		
		Cost of concessions	− 82,000		
		Film rental	− 30,000		
		Income taxes	?		

---

[7]Currently the investment tax credit is 6% for assets being depreciated over a three-year period and 10% for assets being depreciated over a five-year period.

Mr. Lee's company pays a tax rate of 40% on ordinary income and 20% on capital gains. The theater has a tax life of seven years; a tax salvage value of $160,000; and the tax method is sum-of-years digits. Furthermore, an investment tax credit of 8% can be taken on the construction costs plus furnishings and fixtures.

The firm's taxable income is not initially affected by the purchase of the theater since there is no immediate change in gross income or deductions. However, income taxes will fall at the outset due to the tax credit. The credit is .08 × $370,000 = $29,600. Deductions for furnishings, fixtures, and construction costs will come later in the form of depreciation.

More than likely, there will be changes in Lusk Theater's ordinary taxable income and thus income taxes over the next five years. Two sources of ordinary gross income are evident and six separate deductions, including depreciation. How much taxable income changes will depend on depreciation deductions.

Construction costs	$250,000
Furnishings and fixtures	+ 120,000
Original cost	$370,000
Salvage value	− 160,000
Depreciable base	$210,000

Depreciation Schedule

Year	Depreciation Fractions	Depreciation Deductions
1	7/28	$ 52,500
2	6/28	45,000
3	5/28	37,500
4	4/28	30,000
5	3/28	22,500
Accumulated depreciation		$187,500

Depreciation deductions were not calculated for years 6 and 7 since Mr. Lee is going to sell the theater after 5 years. Here we have a situation where the tax life of an asset exceeds the *holding period* of the business. This happens quite often. It is also evident, given the large selling price, that the useful life of the theater is greater than the other two time periods.

Recurring Income Tax Statements

Year	1	2	3	4	5
Gross income*	$360,000	$360,000	$360,000	$360,000	$360,000
Cash deductions**	− 200,000	− 200,000	− 200,000	− 200,000	− 200,000
Depreciation	− 52,500	− 45,000	− 37,500	− 30,000	− 22,500
Taxable income	107,500	115,000	122,500	130,000	137,500
Income taxes (.40)	$ 43,000	$ 46,000	$ 49,000	$ 52,000	$ 55,000

* Gross income consists of ticket sales and concession revenues.
** Deductions include wages, film rentals, utilities, maintenance, and cost of concessions.

The sale of the theater at termination is a capital transaction. As such, income taxes may be affected.

Terminal Income Tax Statement

Sales proceeds	$250,000
Sales commissions	− 20,000
Cost less accumulated depreciation	− 182,500
Capital gain	$ 47,500
Depreciation recapture	$ 47,500
Asset appreciation	0
Tax on recapture (.40)	$ 19,000
Tax on appreciation (.20)	0
Total income tax	$ 19,000

Lusk Theater must pay $19,000 in income taxes on the sale of the theater. All of the tax is a result of taking excessive depreciation.

All of the cash flows, along with their appropriate signs, are brought together below in the cash flow statement.

Cash Flow Statement

Initial Cash Flows (Today)		Terminal Cash Flows (In 5 Years)	
Construction costs	−$250,000	Sale of theater	+$250,000
Furnishings and fixtures	− 120,000	Sales commission	− 20,000
Income tax credit	+ 29,600	Income taxes	− 19,000
INCF	−$340,400	TNCF	+$211,000

Recurring Cash Flows (Years 1–5)

Ticket revenue	+$260,000	+$260,000	+$260,000	+$260,000	+$260,000
Concession revenue	+ 100,000	+ 100,000	+ 100,000	+ 100,000	+ 100,000
Maintenance expense	− 6,000	− 6,000	− 6,000	− 6,000	− 6,000
Utilities expense	− 28,000	− 28,000	− 28,000	− 28,000	− 28,000
Wage expense	− 54,000	− 54,000	− 54,000	− 54,000	− 54,000
Cost of concessions	− 82,000	− 82,000	− 82,000	− 82,000	− 82,000
Film rental	− 30,000	− 30,000	− 30,000	− 30,000	− 30,000
Income taxes	− 43,000	− 46,000	− 49,000	− 52,000	− 55,000
RNCF	+$117,000	+$114,000	+$111,000	+$108,000	+$105,000

From the cash flow statement we can generate a most likely net cash flow profile.

Movie Theater Net Cash Flow Profile

Year	0	1	2	3	4	5	5
Net cash flow	−$340,400	+$117,000	+$114,000	+$111,000	+$108,000	+$105,000	+$211,000

Here we have a capital asset that requires an investment outlay of $340,400 followed by a stream of net cash inflows. Because so many capital assets produce cash flow profiles such as this, it is often referred to as a *standard cash flow profile* ■

Summary

Three business applications of cash flow analysis have been presented, all of them dealing with capital asset purchases. These applications represent the three different types of recurring cash flows that can occur: the kind that increase revenue (CAPA); those that lower expenses (printing press); and those that have an impact on revenues *and* expenses (theater). Cash flows had to be identified for each proposal. Estimates of these cash flows were then provided. The first estimate was a certainty, the second conformed to a probability distribution, and the third was a subjective assessment. For the final example, income taxes were explicitly considered. Each cash flow analysis ended with a net cash flow profile.

A businessperson cannot make an intelligent decision regarding assets, liabilities, or equity without considering their cash flow consequences on the business. Problems of cash flow identification, estimation, and income taxes can make a financial manager's job difficult, but they are, nevertheless, necessary. A cash flow analysis should be performed on every capital asset proposal. The goal in each case is to determine a net cash flow profile. We shall make great use of net cash flow profiles in the following chapter.

The process of cash flow analysis is summarized in figure 8.1 ■

Figure 8.1   Stages of cash flow analysis

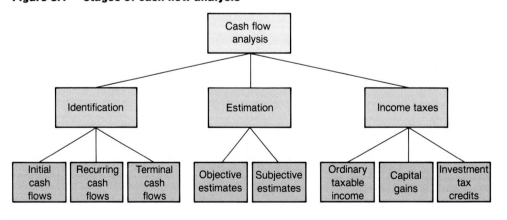

Key Terms/Concepts

Analysts
Annual depreciation
Capital budgeting
Capital gains
Carryover provisions
Cash flow analysis
Cash flow identification
Cash flow profiles
Decision maker
Deductible expenses
Depreciable base
Depreciation
    Accounting depreciation
    Economic depreciation
    Tax depreciation

Depreciation fraction
Forecasting techniques
Holding period
Indirect cash flow
  repercussion
Initial cash flows
Net cash flows
Objective estimates
Ordinary gross income
Ordinary income tax rates
    Average tax rates
    Marginal tax rates
Ordinary taxable income

Original cost
Recurring cash flows
Sponsors
Straight line depreciation
Subjective estimates
Sum-of-the-years-digits
  depreciation
Tax life
Tax salvage value
Terminal cash flows
Useful life

Questions

1. Briefly describe the three phases of cash flow analysis.

2. How are tax credits different from tax deductions?

3. Under what set of circumstances will the capital gains tax rate apply to capital assets?

4. Capital assets are said to be quite different from current assets. List the factors that lead one to this conclusion.

5. Conceive of a situation in which a capital asset proposal has implications for working capital.

6. Why would a firm normally prefer to use an accelerated depreciation method (e.g., sum-of-the-years digits) for tax purposes?

7. Generally speaking, which types of cash flows are the most difficult to estimate?

8. What is capital budgeting? How is capital budgeting different from a capital budget?

9. Briefly define the following terms: economic depreciation, initial cash flows, depreciable base, ordinary income, and sponsor.

Problems

1. Based upon your current knowledge of business and economics, identify the major cash flow consequences of the following capital asset proposals:
   A. Adding on a restaurant to a motel.
   B. Replacing a centralized computer system with personal computers.
   C. Converting a single-screen movie theater into a double-screen theater.
   D. Discontinuing the service department of an automobile dealer.

2. Based upon your current knowledge of business and economics, describe the uncertainties surrounding the cash flow estimation required of the following capital asset proposals:
   A. Moving Pizza Hut's headquarters from Wichita, Kansas to Dallas, Texas.
   B. Avon's purchase of Tiffany's.
   C. Introducing robots on General Motor's assembly line.
   D. Pillsbury's entry into the breakfast cereal market.

3. Describe the net cash flow profile shown below:

Outcome	INCF	RNCF$_1$	RNCF$_2$	RNCF$_3$	RNCF$_4$	RNCF$_5$	RNCF$_6$	TNCF	Probability
a)	$60,000	$ 7,500	$ 7,500	$ 7,500	$ 7,500	$ 7,500	$ 7,500	$15,000	.10
b)	$60,000	$ 7,000	$ 8,000	$ 9,000	$10,000	$11,000	$12,000	$15,000	.15
c)	$60,000	$ 8,000	$ 8,000	$ 8,000	$12,000	$12,000	$12,000	$20,000	.25
d)	$60,000	$14,000	$14,000	$14,000	$14,000	$14,000	$14,000	$10,000	.25
e)	$60,000	$20,000	$18,000	$16,000	$14,000	$12,000	$10,000	$10,000	.15
f)	$60,000	$16,000	$16,000	$16,000	$16,000	$16,000	$16,000	$20,000	.10

4. Mirro Company purchased some equipment five years ago for $800,000. For tax purposes it has been depreciating the equipment over eight years to a zero salvage value, by the sum-of-the-years-digits method. The company would now like to sell this asset. Given an ordinary income tax rate of 40% and a capital gains rate of 25%, compute the income tax payments or savings associated with the following selling prices:
   A. $150,000.
   B. $1,150,000.
   C. $600,000.

5. A capital asset is purchased for $1,500,000 and installed for a further $300,000. Derive the depreciation schedules for this asset under the following conditions:
   A. Straight line, six-year life, $150,000 salvage value.
   B. Sum-of-the-years digits, five-year life, no salvage value.
   C. Straight line, four-year life, $600,000 salvage value and an investment tax credit of 10%.

6. IBC Corporation had ordinary gross income last year of $5,000,000 and deductible expenses of $2,800,000. The company pays 28% on all income up to $200,000 and 50% on everything over that figure. What is its income tax liability?

7. A corporation faces an ordinary income tax rate of 45%. Assuming that this firm is currently profitable, figure the tax effect of the following changes to its income tax statement:
   A. Revenue increases $800,000.
   B. Labor costs decline $220,000.
   C. Depreciation deductions rise by $200,000.
   D. Revenue falls by $150,000.
   E. Cost of goods sold go up $450,000.
   F. Combined effect of A and E.
   G. Combined effect of B and D.
   H. Combined effect of A and B.
   I. Inclusion of a $120,000 investment tax credit.

8. A piece of construction machinery can be purchased for $250,000. Delivery and assembly costs will add on a further $15,000. Although the asset is expected to last for eight years, the buyer plans to dispose of it in five years for an estimated $100,000. Not only is the machinery eligible for an 8% investment tax credit, it can also be depreciated for income taxes. The tax life is four years, the tax salvage value is zero, and the tax method straight line. What is the INCF associated with this capital asset? Derive the tax depreciation schedule.

9. The Z-Bar Corporation acquired a garage ten years ago for $75,000 and renovated it for an additional $25,000. It is being depreciated for tax purposes over fifteen years to a salvage value of $10,000. The depreciation method being employed is straight line. The firm now wishes to sell the garage and purchase a new one. Z-Bar's ordinary income tax rate is 48% and its capital gains rate is 30%. Regardless of what the garage is sold for, a real estate commission of $5,000 will be assessed against the seller. Determine the tax payments or savings that will result from the following selling prices: a) $45,000, b) $65,000, c) $25,000, and d) $115,000.

10. Ralph Johnson Enterprises bought 10,000 shares of Berkley, Inc., common stock four years ago for $75 per share plus $8,000 in brokerage commissions. The company recently sold the stock for $105 per share. Brokerage commissions on the sale amounted to $10,000. Ralph Johnson's capital gains tax rate is the only one that applies in this problem since intangible capital assets are not depreciated. Given a capital gains tax rate of 25%, determine the effect that this transaction will have on Ralph Johnson's income taxes?

11. A $400,000 machine has the potential of lowering a firm's labor costs by $180,000 per year, for five years. At the end of five years, it is estimated that the asset can be sold for approximately $50,000. If acquired, the machine would be depreciated on a straight-line basis to a zero salvage value, over five years. A 10% investment tax credit is allowed and the firm's income tax rates are 46% on ordinary income and 30% on capital gains. Determine the net cash flow profile for this proposal.

12. Bob's Brooms, Inc., sells some 2 million high quality brooms each year and could sell more, but is limited by plant capacity. A proposed plant expansion will cost an estimated $12 million. It is believed that the expansion will permit a 50% increase in output for the next 20 years. The residual value at the end of the holding period will probably amount to very little.

   The brooms will be sold for $9 apiece, of which $4 shall be applied to direct labor and materials expense. General, administrative, and selling expenses are expected to rise by $800,000 annually due to the expansion. Although the plant expansion is not eligible for an investment tax credit, the full cost can be depreciated over 20 years to a zero salvage value, using straight-line depreciation. Bob's income tax rates are 40% for ordinary income and 20% for capital gains. Derive the net cash flow profile for this investment proposal.

13. Ellis Shoe Corporation is considering the acquisition of a piece of land located close to its manufacturing facilities. There is no intention of expanding the shoe company's manufacturing operations. Rather, the plan is to hold the land for five years and sell it at a higher price. It can be purchased today for $500,000. Land is not eligible for investment tax credit or depreciation tax deductions. However, local property taxes of $15,000 (a deductible expense) will be assessed on the property every year. Having considered recent trends in land values within the area and other factors, Ellis Shoe's financial manager has derived the following selling price probability distribution:

Selling Price	Probability
$ 350,000	.20
$ 550,000	.30
$1,000,000	.30
$1,800,000	.20

Ellis Shoe's income tax rates are 40% on ordinary income and 28% on capital gains. Furthermore, the company will be required to pay a 6% real estate commission on the selling price. Using the expected value of selling price, derive the land proposal's net cash flow profile.

14. The marketing vice-president at Krelor Potato Chip Company feels that the market is ready for a yogurt flavored chip. Machinery and equipment to produce this product will cost $190,000 plus an additional $20,000 to install it. It is the marketing executive's belief that this product will have a life cycle of eight years. His revenue estimates are as follows:

Year	1	2	3	4	5	6	7	8
Sales ($)	80,000	95,000	120,000	135,000	135,000	115,000	90,000	60,000

According to the plant manager, the costs of producing the new product will be about 50% of sales. He also believes that the machinery and equipment can be disposed of in eight years for $25,000. For tax purposes, these assets will be depreciated over six years to a salvage value of $30,000, by the straight-line method. They are not eligible for the investment tax credit. Krelor is in a 40% ordinary income tax bracket and a 20% capital gains bracket. Derive the net cash flow profile for this proposal.

15. Wabash Valley Advertising Corp. is currently paying an outside firm $60,000 annually to do its printing. An up-to-date printing press can be acquired and installed for $100,000. Paper and supplies for the press are estimated at $10,000 per year and a full-time master printer would be paid an annual wage of $25,000. It is likely that the press would be used for seven years, at which time it could be sold for $35,000. The tax life of the machine is eight years, tax salvage value is zero, tax depreciation method is straight line, and an investment tax credit of 8% is allowed. Wabash Valley's ordinary tax rate is 45% and its capital gains rate is 25%. Derive the net cash flow profile for the printing press.

16. Zebloc Corp. is considering the purchase of an old warehouse on Chicago's west side near the airport. The seller is asking $2,200,000 for this property, as is. A further $1,400,000 will be required to modify and restore the property. For tax purposes, the property will be depreciated over fifteen years using straight-line depreciation, to a $300,000 salvage value. The entire expenditure would be eligible for an 8% investment tax credit.

    Zebloc plans to use the warehouse for ten years, at which time they expect to sell it for about $3,000,000. The facility allows Zebloc to cease annual rental payments of $475,000 on a Milwaukee warehouse, and should provide $225,000 of additional revenue each year due to improved customer service. The company's ordinary income tax rate is 50% and its capital gains rate is 20%. Construct the net cash flow profile for the warehouse proposal.

17. A relatively new apartment building is available on the market for $500,000. Mary Roberts, a real estate high roller, is very interested in this piece of property, not only as a source of rental income, but also capital gain. She predicts that the building's 18 units can be rented for a combined total of $72,000 per year. There are only three operating expenses associated with the property: insurance, property taxes, and maintenance. These expenses will amount to approximately $22,000 per year. If she buys the apartment, Ms. Roberts would hold it for ten years and sell it for a projected price of $800,000. The apartment is not eligible for an investment tax credit, but the allowable depreciation deductions are very generous. The government will allow the property to be written off over ten years to a zero salvage value, using sum-of-the-years-digits method. Mary's ordinary tax rate is 40% and her capital gains rate is 20%. Determine the apartment's net cash flow profile.

18. Sunnyvale Nursing Homes is looking into the prospects of building and operating its eighteenth nursing home. The particulars of this proposal are shown below.

Initial Cash Flow Information

Cost of land	$ 35,000
Building construction and improvements	$840,000
Equipment and furnishings (replaced every ten years)	$225,000

Recurring Cash Flow Information

Annual Revenues

Room rental	$456,000
Sale of pharmaceuticals	$ 30,000
Donations	$ 24,000

Annual Operating Expenses

Utilities	$10,000
Nurses	$64,000
Nurses aids	$60,000
Doctor (part time)	$30,000
Manager	$30,000
Supplies	$68,000
Maintenance	$15,000
Other	$15,000

Terminal Cash Flow Information

Sale of building and improvements in thirty years	$100,000
Sale of equipment and furnishings in 10, 20, and 30 years	$ 30,000
Sale of land in thirty years	$ 75,000
Real estate commission	($ 15,000)

Tax Information

Investment Tax Credits

A 10% credit is allowed on the equipment and furnishings.

Depreciation

Building and improvements will be written off over thirty years to a zero salvage value, on a straight-line basis.

Equipment and furnishings will be written off over five years to a zero salvage value, on a straight-line basis.

Tax Rates

Ordinary income tax rate equals 50%.
Capital gains tax rate equals 30%.

Assuming that Sunnyvale retains the nursing home for thirty years, construct the net cash flow profile.

19. The Jayhawk Company grocery chain acquired a truck and semitrailer five years ago for $150,000. Although it has been completely depreciated for tax purposes, Jayhawk's financial manager believes that it could be used for another four years. However, the maintenance and repair costs would be rather large. As an alternative, the company could replace the old truck with a new model that sells for $200,000. There are several advantages to buying a new truck: better gas mileage (a savings of $12,000 per year); lower repairs and maintenance (a savings of $18,000 per year); a tax credit of 7% is available on new trucks; and depreciation

tax deductions can be taken on the new truck. Furthermore, a freight company has offered to buy the old truck for $50,000. The new truck will last for at least four years and reasonably can be expected to have a residual value of $60,000. It shall be depreciated on a straight-line basis to a $25,000 salvage value, over four years. Jayhawk's ordinary tax rate is 40% and its capital gains rate is 30%. What is the net cash flow profile associated with the truck replacement?

20. A restaurant chain is considering the purchase of a $420,000 computer to be used for inventory and bookkeeping purposes. If acquired, the company plans to use it for fifteen years, at which time it shall be sold for a predicted $75,000. The computer is expected to benefit the restaurant in a number of ways: 1) reduce food spoilage by $25,000 per year; 2) allow the layoff of four employees who together earn $65,000 annually; 3) provide $12,000 per year of additional revenue by being leased to other businesses over the weekends; and 4) permit the firm immediately to reduce its inventory stock by $100,000. There is a negative side to the computer, however. A computer programmer and technical assistant must be employed at a cost of $36,000 per year. Annual maintenance and utility expenses will increase $6,000 as well. The computer will be depreciated as follows: straight line, no salvage, and a fifteen-year life. The restaurant's tax rates are 40% for ordinary income and 25% for capital gains. Prepare a net cash flow profile.

21. The financial manager for International Airlines thinks that his company should acquire a stake in Mountain Airlines, a young, regional airline that has great potential. According to the financial manager, 100,000 shares of Mountain Airlines common stock can be purchased on the market for $30 per share plus a brokerage commission of ¼ of 1%. He projects that Mountain Airlines will pay a $2.50 per share dividend in each of the next four years. More importantly, however, the financial manager is confident that the stock will double in value over that period. He advises his superiors to buy 100,000 shares of the stock, hold it for four years and then sell it on the market. Construct the net cash flow profile for this proposal based upon the financial manager's projections. International Airlines tax rates are 50% on ordinary income and 20% on capital gains.

22. Kipler Aluminum Corporation is in the process of reappraising its physical plant. In particular, Kipler management is wondering whether or not to replace the smelter. The smelter was purchased ten years ago for $20 million and, although it has been depreciated down to $8 million, Kipler can sell it today for only $4 million. However, with adequate maintenance it could last another ten years and then be sold for approximately $2 million. New smelters on the market are more automated than older models and less labor intensive. They are also more energy efficient and easier to maintain. A replacement would not, however, increase plant capacity. The best available new smelter sells for $30 million, has an estimated useful life of ten years, and an estimated residual value of $5 million. It is also eligible for a 10% investment tax credit. The old smelter is being depreciated on a straight-line basis over fifteen years, to a $2 million salvage value. The new smelter will be depreciated on the same basis. An operating cost comparison of each smelter is shown below.

	Estimated Operating Costs	
	Old Smelter	New Smelter
Annual energy expense	$5,650,000	$2,500,000
Annual labor expense	$3,000,000	$2,000,000
Annual maintenance expense	$1,500,000	$1,000,000

Kipler Aluminum's ordinary income tax rate is 40%, and its capital gains tax rate is 30%.
Based upon the preceding information, derive the net cash flow profile associated with the replacement proposal.

Selected References _____

Bierman, Harold, Jr., and Seymour Smidt, *The Capital Budgeting Decision,* 6th ed., New York: Macmillan, 1984.

Gordon, Laurence A., and George E. Pinches, *Improving Capital Budgeting: A Decision Support System Approach,* Reading, Mass.: Addison-Wesley, 1984.

Hertz, David B., "Risk Analysis in Capital Investment," *Harvard Business Review* (January–February 1964), pp. 95–106.

Hilber, Frederick S., "The Derivation of Probabilistic Information for the Evaluation of Risky Investments," *Management Science* (April 1963), pp. 443–457.

Levy, Haim, and Marshall Sarnat, *Capital Investment and Financial Decisions,* 2nd ed. Englewood Cliffs, N.J.: Prentice-Hall, 1982.

Petty, J. William, David F. Scott, Jr., and Monroe F. Bird, "The Capital Expenditure Decision-Making Process of Large Corporations," *Engineering Economist* (Spring 1975), pp. 159–72.

Pinches, George E., "Myopia, Capital Budgeting and Decision Making," *Financial Management* (Autumn 1982), pp. 6–19.

Van Horne, James C., "A Note on Biases in Capital Budgeting Introduced by Inflation," *Journal of Financial and Quantitative Analysis* (January 1971), pp. 653–58.

■ Finance in the News

Cash flow analysis is important for both large and small firms as well as in personal financial management. For example, what are the initial, recurring, and terminal cash flows resulting from your college education? How can you and/or your parents best budget funds for it? The following article presents some possible answers—at least with respect to housing expenses.

How to Beat the High Cost of College Housing _____

It's plain that the cost of a college education keeps climbing toward the stratosphere. But while you can't bargain down those tuition charges, you may be able to cut your costs by buying your student offspring a place to live, instead of merely paying rent to a dormitory or rooming house. Some pioneering parents are finding that this is not the extravagance it may seem at first glance. Besides, it could well provide your son or daughter a better quality of life during the college years.

The key to the savings is a little-known provision of a tax law enacted in 1981. Aiming primarily to benefit coal miners who had fallen victim to black-lung disease, Congress liberalized the deductions that can be taken when someone rents out a home to a relative. So, instead of forking out cash for rental quarters, you buy a small home or condo near campus and rent it to your youngster. During the school years this permits you to take deductions for mortgage interest, real estate taxes, maintenance, and other expenses, as well as depreciation. And with luck, you should be able to sell the property for a profit—taxed at the capital-gains rate—after the graduation ceremony.

'It Might not Work in Cleveland'

"It might not work in a place like Cleveland," says Ralph Van Sky, president of Van Sky/Leverich Investments in Castle Rock, Colo., "but it seems feasible in a college town where the inflation rate is climbing and good housing is scarce." A real estate speculator himself ("mostly in raw land"), Van Sky already has purchased two condo units in Colorado Springs for his sons, 18 and 21, who plan to start school there next fall as business majors. "If you can offset your costs with tax benefits and an inflationary increase in the property values, you're way ahead," he figures.

In laying out the advantages of such a plan to clients, Stanley H. Breitbard, national director of executive financial services at accountants Price Waterhouse, notes that the cost of residential property in different college towns can vary widely. But assume, he suggests, that a condo near campus can be had for $80,000, with $20,000 down and a 30-year mortgage at 13% for the rest.

If you settle on $600 a month as a fair-market rent, your son or daughter pays you $7,200 a year. It's taxable income to you, but you get deductions for nearly $8,000 in interest expense, $1,500 worth of property taxes and insurance fees, and almost $8,000 worth of depreciation. So you wind up with a tax loss of about $9,600—a savings of nearly $5,000 if you are in the top income-tax bracket. Since depreciation deductions do not require you to lay out any cash, Breitbard says, they give an extra boost to your cash flow. He calculates that you should end the first year with a positive cash flow of about $2,600. And over four years, you save about $18,000 in taxes and are ahead about $8,000 in cash.

Can Your Child Handle It?

A major question when you discuss the possibilities with your accountant: Where does your child come up with $600 a month—or other "fair-market" rent in his or her college town—to provide the income that lets you merit the deductions? A part-time job will help the youngster cover some of the rent, and a roommate can provide the balance. (If you contemplate giving your offspring additional funds to return to you as "rent," you must build up his or her bank account well in advance: "Substantial gifts made . . . at or about the time of the lease or periodically during the year" could produce a challenge to your deductions, says the Joint Taxation Committee of Congress.) A roommate can even justifiably be charged more than half the monthly total, notes Breitbard, with your own offspring entitled to a reduction because he or she has maintenance responsibilities on the property: keeping it clean, making minor repairs, and screening roommates and replacement tenants during vacation periods.

Before you nail down any such arrangement, get a clear idea in you own mind of how much responsibility your son or daughter is prepared to handle. "Some kids are equipped for it at 18," says Van Sky, "and others won't be ready at 50." During a student's first year, particularly, it might be best to let him or her live in a traditional dorm and learn the campus routine. A condo, of course, will involve fewer maintenance chores than a house. And if you doubt your youngster's ability to handle them, outsiders will take them on for a small percentage (perhaps 5%, which would be deductible to you) of the rent.

Get a Fix on the Resale Market

Another consideration: Since you will have to tap your savings or skip other investments for the downpayment, calculate what kind of return you'll be missing while the funds are tied up in real estate. Talk, too, to realtors in the college town to get a fix on the chances for the house or condo to appreciate. "Even if the market stays flat like it's been for the last few years, the kind of properties we're talking about—the ones more parents are taking on—are easy to resell because they're close to campus," says Bill Scott, owner of Boardwalk Realty in Fort Collins, Colo., home to Colorado State University. In a case where a profit looks unlikely, you may be content simply to break even—if you think your offspring will get better grades in a place of his or her own than in a crowded and noisy dorm or rooming house.

EDITED BY DONALD H. DUNN

Reprinted from the April 4, 1985 issue of *Business Week* by special permission. © 1985 by McGraw-Hill, Inc.

Capital Budgeting: Proposal Evaluation

Overview

The previous chapter introduced the subject of capital budgeting and the intricacies of cash flow analysis. This chapter continues our discussion of capital budgeting by taking up the matter of capital asset proposal evaluation. The evaluation of a capital asset determines whether or not the asset is acceptable or unacceptable. As we shall see, capital asset proposals should be evaluated on the basis of an asset's profitability and risk, as well as the time value of money. It will become apparent that the two most important ingredients in a proposal evaluation are the net cash flow profile described in chapter 8 and the required rate of return presented in chapter 4.

In addition to examining the evaluation process for a single capital asset proposal, we will also explore the evaluation procedures associated with mutually exclusive capital asset alternatives ■

Objectives

By the end of the chapter the student should be able to:

1. Explain how capital asset decisions are related to the goal of improving stock prices via the stock valuation model
2. Discuss the evaluation methods and criteria used to make decisions regarding the acquisition, modification, and sale of capital assets
3. Calculate and interpret the net present value of a capital asset purchase
4. Calculate and interpret profitability indexes
5. Calculate and interpret internal rates of return
6. Compare discounted cash flow models for a given situation
7. Select from mutually exclusive assets
8. Appreciate the importance of the RRR to capital budgeting
9. Understand the importance of cash flow analysis to capital budgeting

Introduction

Decisions regarding the proposed purchase, modification, or sale of capital assets are extremely important to a firm. These investment decisions should be made with one over-riding objective in mind: how will they affect stockholder wealth in terms of the market price of common stock. We will not purchase, modify, or sell a capital asset if such an action is expected to reduce stock prices. Furthermore, when there are alternative choices, all of which are worthwhile, we should select the one that is expected to increase stock prices the most.

It is very difficult conceptually to connect an asset decision directly with the market price of a firm's common stock. What we need is a practical intermediate objective. To aid us in this matter, we can call upon the stock valuation model of chapter 4. There it was stated that stock prices are a function of future corporate profits (i.e., dividends), time value of money, and the degree of risk facing a firm. Profitability and risk are, in turn, primarily a function of a firm's assets, and capital assets in particular. This link between capital assets and stock prices will serve as our operational decision criteria: *decisions regarding capital assets shall be based upon the evaluation of an asset's contribution to a firm's profit and risk, with due regard for the time value of money* (figure 9.1).

Figure 9.1   Evaluating capital asset proposals

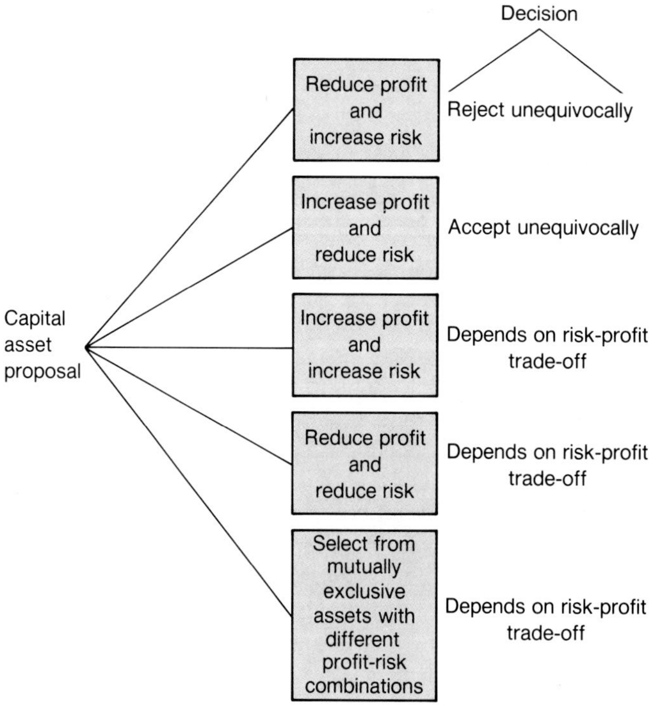

It is imperative that management evaluate both the profit and risk consequences of a capital asset decision. A manager, for instance, might forego a particular asset proposal that holds great profit potential for his or her firm, if the asset also exposes the business and its investors to an inordinate amount of risk. This is due to the fact that most investors (i.e., stockholders) have an aversion to risk and demand to be compensated for incurring it. They do so by requiring a greater rate of return from their investments when risk is present. The greater the degree of risk, the higher the *required rate of return (RRR)*. Should investors earn less than the RRR, they will be dissatisfied. Just how much additional return is necessary for a given amount of risk depends upon investors' risk-return trade-offs. These are the same issues that were discussed at length in chapter 4. They are repeated here because they are particularly relevant to the subject of capital budgeting.

The objective of the present chapter is to describe the evaluation methods and criteria that should be used to make optimal decisions regarding the acquisition, modification, and sale of capital assets. All of the evaluation methods incorporate profit, risk, and the time value of money. To simplify matters, the presentation will concentrate on proposals to purchase capital assets. Proposals to enlarge a production plant, replace an old machine, build an additional warehouse, and select a computer from among several alternative models, are all examples of capital asset acquisitions.

The decisions to be evaluated are: *whether to accept or reject proposals to acquire capital assets.* An acceptable capital asset proposal being that which is expected to increase the market price of a company's common stock ■

Evaluating the Acceptability of Capital Asset Proposals

In the final example of the preceding chapter, Lusk Theater's management was presented with a proposal to purchase an additional movie theater. A cash flow analysis was conducted to identify and subjectively estimate the impact that the new theater will have on cash flows, including income taxes. The results of that analysis were summarized in a net cash flow profile, which is duplicated below.

Movie Theater Net Cash Flow Profile

Year	0	1	2	3	4	5	5
	INCF	$RNCF_1$	$RNCF_2$	$RNCF_3$	$RNCF_4$	$RNCF_5$	TNCF
Net cash flow	−340,400	+117,000	+114,000	+111,000	+108,000	+105,000	+211,000

According to this cash flow profile, an estimated net cash flow of $340,400 is to be invested today, followed by an estimated series of net cash flows that are to be received over the next five years (assume that the cash receipts are at year end). If this proposal is accepted, the $340,400 will be supplied by investors. In other words, the proposed theater must be financed.

Is the proposed theater expected to be profitable? Yes, because the *aggregate net cash flow* associated with the asset is positive. The aggregate net cash flow is simply the sum of all of the net cash flows (both positive and negative) in the cash flow profile. In general, the projected profit from a capital asset proposal can be found as follows:

$$\text{Cash Profit} = \Sigma \text{ Net Cash Flows} = \Sigma \text{ Net Cash Inflows} - \Sigma \text{ Net Cash Outflows}$$

If the total inflows exceed the total outflows, then the proposal is profitable.[1]

Total net cash inflows for the theater equal $766,000 while the total net cash outflows are $340,400. Consequently, the proposal is projected to show a profit of $766,000 − $340,400 = $426,000. However, it would be wrong to make an accept or reject decision based solely on profit expectations. By focusing solely on profit, one would be ignoring the time value of money and risk. These two factors have the ability to convert a potentially profitable investment into a bad investment.

Consider the time value of money in relation to the movie theater proposal. The $426,000 profit is not concentrated in a short period of time. On the contrary, the $340,400 cash investment takes place immediately, while the $766,000 in cash receipts are spread over the next five years. Due to the time value of money, these net cash flows are not directly comparable as they now stand. In particular, the cash receipts are overvalued relative to the initial investment. To correct for the time factor, we must adjust all of the net cash flows by the interest rate that gives rise to the time value of money. As you will recall from chapter 4, the time value of money is measured by the risk-free rate of interest. The preferred method of adjustment is to bring all of the cash receipts back to the present (i.e., when the decision is being made) by discounting with the TVM. In so doing, cash receipts are reduced by the risk-free interest rate. The later ones reduced more than the earlier ones. By converting all of the cash receipts into present values, the element of time is no longer clouding the picture. We can then proceed by comparing the adjusted cash receipts to the initial cash investment.[2] What we are really accounting for here is the fact that investors in Lusk Theater could earn at least the risk-free interest rate on their $340,400 investment. In other words, the TVM is an opportunity cost.

When a proposal involves some degree of risk, as the theater certainly does, this should be incorporated into the decision-making process.[3] The addition of a risk premium to the TVM is the generally accepted way to incorporate risk. Together, the interest rates representing TVM and risk constitute the RRR. Now, by discounting all future cash receipts by the RRR, we are effectively removing from them the risk-free interest income that investors can earn elsewhere plus a compensation for risk bearing. We shall assume that investors in Lusk Theater can earn a risk-free interest rate of 10%, and they also demand a risk premium of 5% on the proposed new theater. Accordingly, the RRR for this problem is 15%.

Based on the preceding discussion, should management accept or reject the proposal? There are three approaches that we can take to measure the acceptability of a capital asset proposal. All of them incorporate *discounted cash flow*. They are net present value (NPV),

---

[1]Readers may be wondering why the profit computation presented here does not resemble what they learned in accounting. Accounting is basically concerned with measuring the profit of an entire business over a prior, arbitrary period of time. We are interested in knowing the profit of an individual asset over its future useful life. The differences between the two are substantial.

[2]Another way of adjusting for the TVM is to compound all net cash flows forward to a common date, at the risk-free rate of interest. In so doing, the earlier cash flows will generate interest for a longer time than the later cash flows. Once this is accomplished, the future value of cash receipts can be compared to the future value of the cash investment.

[3]A discussion of capital asset risk measurement is provided in the appendix to this chapter.

profitability index (PI), and internal rate of return (IRR). Although basically they say the same things, there are situations when the NPV method is superior to the others. In addition, many businessmen have a personal preference for a particular measure. We will discuss the basics of each of these three measures in turn.

Discounted Cash Flow Acceptance Measures

Net Present Value   Net present value (NPV) is a method used to measure the acceptability of capital asset purchases. It does this by combining the net cash flow profile of the asset with the required rate of return. The future cash receipts (i.e., the recurring and terminal net cash flows) are discounted back to the present (i.e., PV) and then compared to the investment (i.e., INCF). This comparison is made by subtracting the INCF, thus the name "net" present value. The investment is subtracted because the RNCFs and TNCFs from asset acquisitions are, as a group, positive, while INCFs are negative.

In general terms, the NPV model looks as follows:

Equation 9.1

$$NPV = \frac{RNCF_1}{(1+RRR)^{t_1}} + \frac{RNCF_2}{(1+RRR)^{t_2}} + \ldots + \frac{RNCF_n + TNCF}{(1+RRR)^{t_n}} - INCF$$

Where:

NPV = Net present value
$RNCF_j$ = Recurring net cash flows
$TNCF$ = Terminal net cash flow
$INCF$ = Initial net cash flow
RRR = Required rate of return
n = Total number of recurring net cash flows
t_j = Number of time periods interest is applied to a cash flow
Decision Rule: NPV > 0 Accept
NPV < 0 Reject

This formula is almost identical to the discounting model, equation 3.6. We simply replaced the Cs with NCFs and i with RRR. There is one important difference, however. A present cash flow (INCF) has been included that, as stated earlier, causes PV to become NPV.

A worthwhile capital asset is one with a positive NPV and an unacceptable capital asset has a negative NPV. A positive NPV indicates that the present value of all future cash receipts exceeds the current net cash investment to acquire these receipts.[4] In other words, the cash receipts are more than large enough to cover all cash outlays, the TVM, and a compensation for risk. This excess value belongs to the owners.

---

[4]NPV can also be used to measure the acceptability of an asset sale. In this case, an asset would be sold if its INCF exceeded the PV of lost benefits.

Application: Applying the NPV model to the movie theater purchase appears as follows:

$$NPV = \frac{\$117{,}000}{(1.15)^1} + \frac{\$114{,}000}{(1.15)^2} + \frac{\$111{,}000}{(1.15)^3} + \frac{\$108{,}000}{(1.15)^4} + \frac{\$316{,}000}{(1.15)^5} - \$340{,}400$$

In operational form:

$$NPV = \$117{,}000DF_{.15/1} + \$114{,}000DF_{.15/2} + \$111{,}000DF_{.15/3} + \$108{,}000DF_{.15/4}$$
$$+ \$316{,}000DF_{.15/5} - \$340{,}400$$

Thus:

$$NPV = \$117{,}000(.8696) + \$114{,}000(.7561) + \$111{,}000(.6575) + \$108{,}000(.5718)$$
$$+ \$316{,}000(.4972) - \$340{,}400$$

Therefore:

$$NPV = \$479{,}790 - \$340{,}400 = \$139{,}390$$

The NPV of the theater purchase is a positive $139,390. The theater is acceptable. The firm and its owners will get $139,390 more in present value of benefits than the present cost of acquiring these benefits. Keep in mind, however, that the above NPV is not a sure thing. It is a most likely estimate at best.

Notice the great disparity between the earlier cash profit of $426,000 and the NPV. The former was greatly inflated due to a total disregard for the time value of money and risk (i.e., RRR).

NPV is very sensitive to the size of RRR. An examination of the general NPV model indicates that there exists an inverse relationship between NPV and RRR. For instance, an RRR of 20% would lower the theater's NPV to $79,582. This principle is shown in figure 9.2 ■

Profitability Index   The profitability index (PI) is simply a different way of comparing the present value of RNCFs and TNCF to the INCF. Rather than netting the investment figure, we divide by it. The resulting figure is a ratio. Many persons refer to it as the *benefit-cost ratio*. If the PI is greater than one, the asset is acceptable.

In general terms the profitability index would appear as follows:

Equation 9.2 $$PI = \frac{\dfrac{RNCF_1}{(1+RRR)^{t_1}} + \dfrac{RNCF_2}{(1+RRR)^{t_2}} + \ldots + \dfrac{RNCF_n + TNCF}{(1+RRR)^{t_n}}}{INCF}$$

Decision Rule: PI > 1 Accept
PI < 1 Reject

Application: Application of the PI model to the theater purchase looks as follows:

$$PI = \frac{\dfrac{\$117{,}000}{(1.15)^1} + \dfrac{\$114{,}000}{(1.15)^2} + \dfrac{\$111{,}000}{(1.15)^3} + \dfrac{\$108{,}000}{(1.15)^4} + \dfrac{\$316{,}000}{(1.15)^5}}{\$340{,}000}$$

In operational form:

$$PI = \frac{\$117{,}000DF_{.15/1} + \$114{,}000DF_{.15/2} + \$111{,}000DF_{.15/3} + \$108{,}000DF_{.15/4} + \$316{,}000DF_{.15/5}}{\$340{,}000}$$

Therefore:

$$PI = \frac{\$486{,}790}{\$340{,}000} = 1.43$$

Figure 9.2   Relationship between the net present value (NPV) of a capital asset and the required rate of return (RRR)

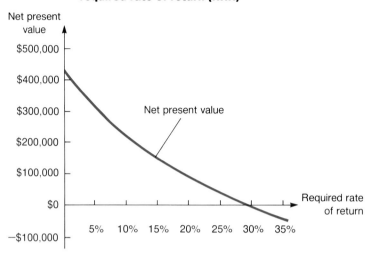

As you can see, we are dealing with the same numbers that were used for NPV, but in a different perspective. As you might expect, the answer is the same. A PI of 1.41 indicates that the theater is very promising.

Since the PI provides information identical to NPV, you may be wondering why both are presented. The answer is twofold: in the first place, many businesspersons prefer working with ratios as opposed to an esoteric dollar figure like NPV; second, PIs are somewhat more conducive to computer problem solving. Admittedly, these are not earthshaking reasons, but they are reasons. As we see later on, however, NPV is superior to PI for making certain kinds of investment decisions.

Internal Rate of Return   Internal rate of return (IRR) is a further discounted cash flow technique that can be used to determine the acceptability of capital asset proposals. It is common knowledge that there are many persons in business who prefer to work with "rates" of return, or rates of profitability when dealing with capital assets, rather than NPV or PI. Therefore, the net cash flow profile can be converted into a rate of return (i.e., interest rate) on the initial investment.

The rate of return computed with the compound interest discounting model is specifically referred to as the internal rate of return. *IRR is the compound annual interest rate earned on capital assets.* It can be found from the discounting model (equation 3.6) by substituting the INCF for PV, inserting the appropriate cash flows and time periods and then solving for IRR in place of i.

In general terms, it can be found as follows:

Equation 9.3

$$INCF = \frac{RNCF_1}{(1 + IRR)^{t_1}} + \frac{RNCF_2}{(1 + IRR)^{t_2}} + \ldots + \frac{RNCF_n + TNCF}{(1 + IRR)^{t_n}}$$

Decision rule: IRR > RRR   Accept
IRR < RRR   Reject

It is evident that the IRR model uses the same information as the NPV and PI models. That is, they all use the same cash flows and time periods and, in addition, they all involve discounting. Unlike the other two, however, IRR is not conveniently isolated for ready solution. Instead, it is buried in the formula. *IRR can be found, but it is normally going to involve a trial-and-error process.* To be more specific, we are looking for that interest rate (IRR) that will make the future cash flows (RNCF and TNCF) equal to the PV (INCF). Several problems like this were encountered in chapter 3. It might be a good idea to review some of those before going on.

Computation of the IRR does not end our work. We must still determine if it is high or low. To answer that question, we need to have a standard of comparison. What could be a better benchmark than the required rate of return? If the IRR on a prospective capital asset is 9% and the investors require instead a 12% rate of return, one could hardly recommend such an investment to them. The rate of return from an asset should be sufficient to compensate for the TVM and risk. Our decision criteria thus becomes: a capital asset is acceptable if the IRR exceeds the RRR.

Application: The IRR model applied to the theater purchase looks as follows:

$$\$340{,}400 = \frac{\$117{,}000}{(1 + IRR)^1} + \frac{\$114{,}000}{(1 + IRR)^2} + \frac{\$111{,}000}{(1 + IRR)^3} + \frac{\$108{,}000}{(1 + IRR)^4} + \frac{\$316{,}000}{(1 + IRR)^5}$$

In operational form:

$$\$340{,}400 = \$117{,}000 DF_{IRR/1} + \$114{,}000 DF_{IRR/2} + \$111{,}000 DF_{IRR/3} + \$108{,}000 DF_{IRR/4} + \$316{,}000 DF_{IRR/5}$$

After trial and error:

IRR is just over 28%.

Since the IRR of 28% is greater than the RRR of 15%, it is clearly apparent that the theater has the potential to be very rewarding. However, we should not lose sight of the fact that this IRR is only a prediction and, as such, should be used with caution ■

Multiple IRRs   There is a peculiar phenomenon that occurs once in a while with the computation of IRR. It just so happens that under extreme conditions an asset can generate more than one IRR. For this to happen, there must be reversals in recurring cash flows from positive to negative or vice versa, and they must involve relatively large sums of money. Consider the following illustration: INCF = $-\$5{,}000$, $RNCF_1 = +\$20{,}000$, $RNCF_2 = -\$16{,}800$, $t_1 = 1$ and $t_2 = 2$. Compute IRR.

$$\$5{,}000 = +\frac{\$20{,}000}{(1 + IRR)^1} - \frac{\$16{,}800}{(1 + IRR)^2}$$

Through trial and error two IRRs are found: $IRR_1 = 20\%$ and $IRR_2 = 180\%$. If the $-\$16,800$ cash flow were followed by a large positive cash flow, say $18,000, we *could* very well obtain a third IRR. It is possible to get an additional IRR for every cash flow reversal. Fortunately the existence of multiple IRRs is rare. While there are techniques available to deal with multiple IRRs, they are not entirely satisfactory and are outside the scope of this text. Nevertheless, one should be on the lookout for situations that may give rise to them.

Due to the difficulties often encountered in computing the IRR, it would be useful on occasion to have a simple approximation method. The average rate of return (ARR) is such a method.

Average Rate of Return   The average rate of return provides only an approximation of the IRR, but it is much easier to compute. It is useful in those situations where one only needs an approximate rate of return (e.g., business-lunch discussions). An ARR may also prove helpful as a starting point in a trial-and-error search for IRR. Generally speaking, the more uniform the recurring net cash flows, the more closely ARR approaches IRR. The equation for ARR is as follows:

Equation 9.4 $$ARR = \dfrac{\dfrac{\Sigma\, NCF/N}{}}{\dfrac{INCF + TNCF}{2}}$$

The numerator in this equation is the sum of all the net cash flows associated with the purchase and use of an asset (defined earlier as cash profit) divided by the number of years the asset is owned (N). In other words, it is an annual average cash profit. The denominator, $(INCF + TNCF) \div 2$, is a simple average of the cash invested in an asset over its life. Dividing one by the other will produce an annual average rate of return.

Application: An ARR calculated for the theater would be done as shown below:

$$ARR = \dfrac{\dfrac{\$426{,}400}{5}}{\dfrac{\$340{,}400 + \$316{,}000}{2}} = \dfrac{\$85{,}200}{\$328{,}200} = 26\%$$

Recall that the theater generated an IRR of just over 28%. The ARR was found to be 26%. While the two answers are not identical in this particular example, one would have to agree that the ARR can be helpful ■

Measuring Acceptability Given Objective Cash Flow Estimates   Discounted cash flow computations are handled a little differently when a net cash flow profile is in the form of an objective probability distribution.

Application: A cash flow analysis was performed on a new printing press in chapter 8. The result of that analysis was a net cash flow profile in the form of a probability distribution. That profile is repeated below.

Net Cash Flow Profile Probability Distribution

Year	0	1	2	3	4	5	6	
Event	*INCF*	$RNCF_1$	$RNCF_2$	$RNCF_3$	$RNCF_4$	$RNCF_5$	$RNCF_6$	*Probability*
A	−$800,000	+ 56,846	+ 56,846	+ 56,846	+ 56,846	+ 56,846	+ 56,846	.05
B	−$800,000	+ 90,703	+ 90,703	+ 90,703	+ 90,703	+ 90,703	+ 90,703	.10
C	−$800,000	+133,333	+133,333	+133,333	+133,333	+133,333	+133,333	.10
D	−$800,000	+135,000	+167,000	+183,000	+200,000	+218,000	+230,000	.25
E	−$800,000	+271,095	+271,095	+271,095	+271,095	+271,095	+271,095	.30
F	−$800,000	+281,000	+310,000	+345,000	+395,000	+415,000	+425,000	.20

With this profile and an RRR, it is possible to measure the acceptability of buying the printing press. The necessary RRR is presumed to be 8%.

NPV, PI, and IRR are calculated for each possible net cash flow profile following the same procedures used earlier for most likely net cash flows. For outcome E these three measures would be, respectively:

$$NPV = \frac{\$271,095}{(1.08)^1} + \frac{\$271,095}{(1.08)^2} + \frac{\$271,095}{(1.08)^3} + \frac{\$271,095}{(1.08)^4} + \frac{\$271,095}{(1.08)^5} + \frac{\$271,095}{(1.08)^6} - \$800,000$$

$$NPV = \$453,272$$

$$PI = \frac{\frac{\$271,095}{(1.08)^1} + \frac{\$271,095}{(1.08)^2} + \frac{\$271,095}{(1.08)^3} + \frac{\$271,095}{(1.08)^4} + \frac{\$271,095}{(1.08)^5} + \frac{\$271,095}{(1.08)^6}}{\$800,000}$$

$$PI = 1.567$$

$$\$800,000 = \frac{\$271,095}{(1 + IRR)^1} + \frac{\$271,095}{(1 + IRR)^2} + \frac{\$271,095}{(1 + IRR)^3} + \frac{\$271,095}{(1 + IRR)^4} + \frac{\$271,095}{(1 + IRR)^5} + \frac{\$271,095}{(1 + IRR)^6}$$

$$IRR = 25\%$$

Following suit, these computations are repeated for the other five outcomes. The NPV, IRR, and PI for all six possibilities along with their probabilities of occurrence are summarized below in a probability distribution.

Probability Distribution of Acceptance Measures

Outcome	NPV	PI	IRR	Probability
A	−$537,201	0.329	−20%	.05
B	− 380,680	0.524	−10%	.10
C	− 183,602	0.771	0%	.10
D	+ 53,789	1.067	+10%	.25
E	+ 453,272	1.567	+25%	.30
F	+ 840,496	2.051	+35%	.20

With this information in hand it is possible to compute an average (i.e., mean) for each of the measures. When discussing the future, statisticians prefer the term *expected value* to average and abbreviate it with the symbol E(X) as opposed to $\overline{X}$. Expected value is a weighted average, where probabilities are the weights.

The general equation for expected value is:

Equation 9.5 $E(X) = P_1(X_1) + P_2(X_2) + \ldots + P_n(X_n)$

Where:

P_i = The probability of the i_{th} outcome
X_i = The value of the i_{th} outcome
n = The total number of outcomes
$E(X)$ = The expected value

The expected NPV of the printing press is:

$$E(NPV) = (.05)(-\$537,201) + (.10)(-\$380,680) + (.10)(-\$183,602) + (.25)(\$53,789)$$
$$+ (.30)(\$453,272) + (.20)(\$840,496) = +\$234,240$$

The expected PI is:

$$E(PI) = (.05)(.329) + (.10)(.524) + (.10)(.771) + (.25)(1.067) + (.30)(1.567)$$
$$+ (.20)(2.051) = 1.293$$

The expected IRR is:

$$E(IRR) = (.05)(-20\%) + (.10)(-10\%) + (.10)(0\%) + (.25)(+10\%) + (.30)(+25\%)$$
$$+ (.20)(+35\%) = 15\%$$

All three acceptability measures indicate that the printing press is potentially worthwhile. That is, E(NPV) is positive, E(PI) is greater than one, and E(IRR) exceeds RRR of 8% ■

Comparison of Discounted Cash Flow Models   All three discounted cash flow measures of acceptability indicated that the movie theater would be a worthwhile venture. That is, NPV was positive, PI was greater than one, and IRR exceeded the RRR. This was also true of the printing press proposal. Given the fact that they use the same information and employ the same mathematical framework, this should come as no surprise. *They will always point in the same direction when applied to a single asset.* Under those circumstances, we can use any of the three to measure the acceptability of capital asset purchases, according to personal preference. Capital assets that are shown to be unacceptable by these measures are normally rejected. However, when trying to select from among alternative capital assets NPV, PI, and IRR may not give the same directions, as we shall see.

Selecting from Alternative Capital Assets

Numerous times during its life a business is faced with the problem of choosing among alternative capital assets. They are alternatives in the sense that only one will be selected. Situations like this arise so often they have been given a name, *mutually exclusive assets.* Mutually exclusive is a term borrowed from statistics meaning that the occurrence of a particular event automatically precludes the occurrence of any other event. Mutually exclusive assets are those that can perform essentially the same service or do the same work. An example is different brands or styles of computers for a data processing system. Another example is a variety of sizes and qualities of trucks for use in a delivery service. The selection of an IBM computer system would preclude the purchase of a Control Data computer system if only one is needed. Along the same lines, an acquisition of vans would eliminate bigger trucks from the picture for a delivery service that desires only one size. When the firm is faced with alternative assets, its accept/reject analysis expands from "would the purchase of a computer be acceptable?" to "which computer would be the most acceptable?" Here we have a high-level case of comparison shopping. It is assumed in each of the forthcoming examples that the alternatives are equal in terms of risk (i.e., the RRRs are the same) and that their cash flows have been estimated subjectively (i.e., most likely estimates).

Ranking Alternatives   *Optimal selection from mutually exclusive assets is accomplished by appropriately measuring the acceptability of each alternative investment and then choosing the one that is most acceptable.*

Example: A company is trying to decide among three mutually exclusive assets (A, B, and C). The corporation's RRR is 10% for each of the alternatives. The net cash flow profiles and acceptability measures of each alternative are shown in the table below.

Year	0	1	2	3	4	4	Acceptance Measures		
NCF	INCF	RNCF$_1$	RNCF$_2$	RNCF$_3$	RNCF$_4$	TNCF	NPV	PI	IRR
A	−$50,000	+$14,000	+$14,000	+$14,000	+$14,000	+$17,535	+$ 6,356	1.13	15%
B	−$50,000	+$16,812	+$16,812	+$16,812	+$16,812	0	+$ 3,294	1.07	13%
C	−$50,000	+$ 7,000	+$14,000	+$21,000	+$28,000	+$13,140	+$11,809	1.24	18%

An examination of the various measures reveals that all three alternatives are worthwhile. *C clearly ranks as the best of the choices because it has the highest NPV, PI, and IRR.* Alternative A ranks second, and B ranks third ▪

Conflict in Ranking   In the previous example, all three measures of acceptability ranked alternative C as the best. Occasionally, however, they can give conflicting signals. For instance, one alternative could have the greater NPV while another alternative has a superior IRR. *Conflicts in ranking can arise when the alternatives exhibit radically different net cash flow profiles.*

Example A: A decision must be made between two mutually exclusive assets, X and Y. The applicable required rate of return is equal to 10%. Net cash flow profiles and acceptability measures of each alternative are shown in the table below.

Year	0	1	2	3	3	Acceptance Measures		
NCF	INCF	RNCF$_1$	RNCF$_2$	RNCF$_3$	TNCF	NPV	PI	IRR
X	−$80,000	0	0	+$120,000	0	$10,156	1.13	14%
Y	−$80,000	+$60,000	+$32,000	+$ 8,500	0	$ 7,377	1.09	17%

Here we have a situation where one of the alternatives has a superior IRR, but the other ranks higher in terms of PI and NPV. In situations such as this it is best to rely upon NPV for ranking. This can be explained as follows: if only presented with the choice of earning 17% or 14% profit, investors would surely choose the former. However, if told the 17% alternative would add $7,377 to their wealth, but the 14% option would contribute $10,156, most would select the latter. Dollars, not percentages, are the bottom line. *When conflicts in ranking occur, select the alternative with the greatest NPV* ■

A more typical instance of radically different net cash flow profile is a situation where the alternatives require significantly different investment outlays.

Example B: Two types of equipment with differing capacities are available to produce a certain product. A small capacity operation can be acquired and installed for $150,000. The large capacity equipment can be purchased and installed for $900,000. Both operations will last for five years and the applicable RRR is 12%. The net cash flow profiles and acceptability measures of these two pieces of equipment are shown in the table below.

Year NCF	0 INCF	1 $RNCF_1$	2 $RNCF_2$	3 $RNCF_3$	4 $RNCF_4$	5 $RNCF_5$	5 TNCF
Small	−$150,000	+$ 50,150	+$ 50,150	+$ 50,150	+$ 50,150	+$ 50,150	$ 0
Large	−$900,000	+$238,840	+$238,840	+$238,840	+$238,840	+$238,840	+$200,000

	Acceptance Measures		
	NPV	PI	IRR
Small	$30,781	1.21	20%
Large	$74,450	1.08	15%

The small capacity equipment generates a higher IRR and PI than the large capacity equipment. However, the latter has the highest NPV. In situations such as this we should be guided as before, by NPV. Accordingly, we would choose the large capacity equipment ■

Conflicts in ranking can readily occur when there are large differences in asset size. NPV is the appropriate decision measure under these circumstances because IRR and PI, by their very nature, are independent of size. This is a characteristic of all percentages and ratios. To state the case briefly, what would you rather have: a 30% rate of return on an investment of $100 or a 20% rate of return on an investment of $10,000?

If you study the previous examples regarding mutually exclusive assets, you will notice that the alternatives have equal lives. Obviously, not all mutually exclusive assets can be expected to have equal lives. When they do not, it may be necessary to make some adjustments before measuring their acceptability.

Alternatives of Unequal Life   Quite often, mutually exclusive assets exhibit different useful lives. Some buildings retain their value longer than others, bonds have different maturities, and machinery can vary in the rate of obsolescence. In some cases, the difference can be substantial, say 3 to 1. With some exceptions the difference in lives should be neutralized before profit is measured.[5] A good, but by no means the only, way to accomplish this objective is to arrange the alternatives so that they cover the same time span.[6] If this is not done, it is possible for all of the three acceptance measures to rank them incorrectly.

Application: A plant nursery must choose one of two vegetations to plant on a fallow piece of land. Trees can be purchased and planted for an INCF of $17,500. They will be harvested in six years, at which time it is estimated that they can be sold for a TNCF of $50,000. Alternatively, shrubs can be acquired and planted for an INCF of $15,000. They will be harvested in only two years and sold for a predicted TNCF of $25,000. To avoid unnecessary confusion, we will assume that the cost of maintaining both vegetations (i.e., RNCFs) will be insignificant. The nursery's relevant RRR is 12% for each proposal.

If these alternatives were ranked on the basis of NPV without any adjustment for their unequal lives, we would have the following result:

$$NPV_{Trees} = \frac{\$50,000}{(1.12)^6} - \$17,500 = +\$7,830$$

$$NPV_{Shrubs} = \frac{\$25,000}{(1.12)^2} - \$15,000 = +\$4,930$$

From this analysis, the trees would be the best choice. But what about the intervening four years, from the time the shrubs are harvested until the trees are sold? Surely something can be done with the land for those four years. Several options may be available, but a reasonable choice would be to plant shrubs two more times. By doing this, we place the alternatives on an equal footing. The net cash flows associated with three shrub plantings would be $-\$15,000$ today, $+\$25,000 - \$15,000$ $= +\$10,000$ in two years, $+\$25,000 - \$15,000 = +\$10,000$ in four years and finally, $+\$25,000$ at the end of six years. The NPV generated by these cash flows is:

$$NPV_{Shrubs} = \frac{\$10,000}{(1.12)^2} + \frac{\$10,000}{(1.12)^4} + \frac{\$25,000}{(1.12)^6} - \$15,000 = +\$11,992$$

As it turns out, three sequential shrub plantings have a NPV of $11,992, which is substantially greater than that of the trees. Therefore, the shrubs would be the optimal choice.

Placing these alternatives on the same time span has reversed their NPV rankings. Rankings by IRR and PI can also be reversed in these situations. However, one should not expect to see a reversal in rankings every time a situation like this arises ∎

Net Present Value

Although many businesspersons prefer, for personal reasons, to use IRR, the fact remains that *NPV is generally a superior measure of acceptability*. It allows for a more optimal selection from mutually exclusive assets when a conflict in ranking exists. Furthermore, whereas it is sometimes possible to get multiple IRRs from a given set of figures, there can only be one NPV. The PI is also inferior to NPV, although to a lesser extent. It does no harm to compute all three, as long as NPV is accorded top status.

Given that NPV is so important, it would be worthwhile to explore in more detail exactly what it means from an economic standpoint. Actually, it is profit after an adjustment has

---

[5]For an excellent discussion of when to adjust for unequal lives see "Some Guidelines for Evaluating Capital Investment Alternatives with Unequal Lives," *Financial Management*, Spring 82, by Gary W. Emery.
[6]Another method is to assume the longer-lived alternative is sold at the same time that the shorter-lived asset ceases to exist.

been made for the required rate of return; it is the present value of profit that translates into an addition to stockholder wealth. But let us go from the abstract to the "bottom line." What exactly does it mean to the owners of the business? The answer to that question can be given in a couple of ways, and we can use the movie theater example to present them.

Application: The theater is expected to generate a NPV of $139,390 given a RRR equal to 15%. This means that if Lusk Theater "borrowed" the NPV from a bank at 15% compound annual interest, it could immediately distribute the $139,390 to the owners to spend anyway they wish. This is possible because excess net cash inflows from the theater will be sufficient to pay off the loan plus interest. By getting money "up front" this way rather than having to wait for cash dividends, the owners' wealth increase is more identifiable.

NPV can also be explained in the context of its influence on stock prices. Let us assume that Lusk Theater has 100,000 shares of common stock outstanding prior to the theater purchase. Furthermore, let us assume that the stock is selling on the stock market at that time for $40 per share. The $340,400 investment necessary to construct and equip the theater is provided by retained earnings. As the stock market comes to recognize that the theater will increase Lusk Theater's future net cash inflows, it will bid up the price of the stock by the present value of those cash inflows, or $479,790. That is an increase per share of $479,790 ÷ 100,000 shares = $4.80. The new price is, thus, $44.80. This increase in market value exceeds the owner's per share equity investment of $340,400 ÷ 100,000 shares = $3.40 by $1.40, thereby making them that much richer. The $1.40 is also the NPV per share of common stock.

In both examples, the stockholders' wealth was increased by $139,390. This is the significance of NPV ■

Payback Period

A discussion of asset acceptability would not be complete without some mention of the payback period. *The payback period is the length of time (in years) it takes to recover the original investment.* It is that period of time in which RNCFs are equal to the INCF. It can be measured by simply summing the RNCFs until they equal the investment. The number of years needed to generate this sum of money is the payback period.

The theater being considered by Lusk Theater will generate RNCFs of $117,000, $114,000, $111,000, $108,000, and $105,000 over the next five years. At that rate, it will take almost three years to recover the $340,400 investment. Therefore, the theater's payback period is three years.

There are two problems associated with the payback period. In the first place, the payback period does not measure profit, but instead measures the period of time to break-even (i.e., cash inflows = cash outflows). This results from the fact that it does not consider any RNCFs, or a TNCF for that matter, beyond the payback period. Secondly, payback does not consider the required rate of return. For these reasons, it is not a suitable acceptance measure.

Given the problems inherent in payback period as a measure of acceptability, one has to wonder why it is used. The reason is very clear, businesspersons like it. They like it because it is straightforward, easy to compute, and understandable. Many businesspersons who are familiar with the weaknesses of payback period and knowledgeable in discounted cash flow techniques will nevertheless place a great deal of weight on payback. Quite simply, custom and convenience are difficult to overcome.

The payback period is actually of more benefit in risk measurement as demonstrated in the appendix to this chapter.

Summary

Decisions regarding the proposed purchase, modification, or sale of capital assets are extremely important to a firm. These investment decisions should be made with one overriding objective in mind: how will they affect stockholder wealth in terms of the market price of common stock? In an operational sense, this means that decisions regarding capital assets shall be based upon an evaluation of an asset's contribution to the firm's profitability and risk, with due regard for the time value of money.

A capital asset's profitability is incorporated in its net cash flow profile, while risk and the time value of money are accounted for in the required rate of return. There are three fundamentally sound procedures that can be used to measure the acceptability of a capital asset proposal. All of them make use of discounted cash flow. They are net present value, profitability index, and internal rate of return. When applied to independent capital asset proposals, all three of these models will provide the same accept-reject signals. Consequently, the choice of which to use is a matter of personal preference. However, when choosing among mutually exclusive investment alternatives the models often send conflicting signals. In these instances, one is better off relying exclusively on net present value. A less effective measure of an asset's worth is the payback period. Nevertheless, this technique remains popular with many businesspersons.

In evaluating various capital assets, the following formulas are useful.

Summary of Key Formulas

$$\text{Cash Profit} = \Sigma \text{ Net Cash Flows} = \Sigma \text{ Net Cash Inflows} - \Sigma \text{ Net Cash Outflows}$$

$$NPV = \frac{RNCF_1}{(1 + RRR)^{t_1}} + \frac{RNCF_2}{(1 + RRR)^{t_2}} + \ldots + \frac{RNCF_n + TNCF}{(1 + RRR)^{t_n}} - INCF$$

Decision rule: NPV > 0 Accept
NPV < 0 Reject

$$PI = \frac{\dfrac{RNCF_1}{(1 + RRR)^{t_1}} + \dfrac{RNCF_2}{(1 + RRR)^{t_2}} + \ldots + \dfrac{RNCF_n + TNCF}{(1 + RRR)^{t_n}}}{INCF}$$

Decision rule: PI > 1 Accept
PI < 1 Reject

$$INCF = \frac{RNCF_1}{(1 + IRR)^{t_1}} + \frac{RNCF_2}{(1 + IRR)^{t_2}} + \ldots + \frac{RNCF_n + TNCF}{(1 + IRR)^{t_n}}$$

Decision rule: IRR $>$ RRR   Accept
IRR $<$ RRR   Reject

$$ARR = \frac{\Sigma \, NCF/N}{(INCF + TNCF)/2}$$

Appendix: Capital Asset Risk Measurement

Capital asset risk exposure arises from the fact that most cash flows cannot be predicted with 100% accuracy. Construction costs, tax rates, wages, selling prices, sales volume, material costs, uncollectible accounts, and salvage values are just some of the cash flows or determinants of cash flows that are difficult to predict. The reasons for cash flow uncertainty are as varied as the following list indicates: weather (construction costs); politics (tax rates); labor union activities (wages); competition (selling prices); consumer attitudes (sales volume); wars (material costs); mismanagement (uncollectable accounts); and technological change (salvage values). A discussion of business risk would not be complete without also mentioning business cycles, which can significantly influence an array of cash flow items.

There are a number of ways to measure the amount of risk associated with an asset. The particular method employed will depend upon the definition of risk, the sophistication of the analyst and the type of cash flow estimates one is working with. It is useful to categorize capital asset risk measurement techniques according to whether or not cash flow estimates are subjective or objective. Mathematical statistics can be used with the latter, but not the former.

Risk: Objective Cash Flow Estimates

When estimated net cash flow profiles are in the form of a probability distribution, one may use the statistical techniques developed in chapter 4 to measure the riskiness of capital asset proposals. Specifically, equations 4.1 through 4.8. But first, each net cash flow outcome in the probability distribution should be converted into an IRR by means of equation 9.3.

If you recall from the discussion in chapter 4, there are three statistical approaches to measuring asset risk. They are briefly summarized below:

Risk of an Asset in Isolation: Variance of IRR

$$\text{Var(IRR)} = \sum_{i=1}^{n} P_i[\text{IRR}_i - E(\text{IRR})]^2$$

$$\text{SD(IRR)} = \sqrt{\text{Var(IRR)}}$$

Risk of Asset in a Firm Context: Variance of Portfolio IRR

$$\text{Var(IRR}_p) = W_a^2\text{Var(IRR}_a) + W_f^2\text{Var(IRR}_f) + W_aW_f\, 2\, \text{Cov(IRR}_a, \text{IRR}_f)$$

$$\text{SD(IRR}_p) = \sqrt{\text{Var(IRR}_p)}$$

Risk of Asset in a Market Context: Systematic Risk (Beta)

$$\beta = \frac{\text{Cov(IRR}_a, \text{IRR}_m)}{\text{Var(IRR}_m)}$$

Risk: Subjective Cash Flow Estimates

When an analyst only possesses a single, most likely estimate of cash flows, it is not possible for him or her to compute standard deviations or Beta. Therefore, alternative methods are required. The inability to use statistical techniques or a general distrust of them also encourages many financial analysts to seek alternative measures of risk.

Listed below are a number of capital asset characteristics that can aid in the evaluation of risk. They are logically related to the cause of risk (i.e., cash flow uncertainty) and do not require the existence of probability distributions or statistical training.

1. *Useful life:* As a general rule, assets that are planned for long term use are somewhat more risky than others. The reason being, that it is more difficult to forecast twenty or thirty years into the future, than three or four.
2. *Abandonment:* Readily marketable business property exhibits less risk. A high resale value can place a floor under losses when an acquisition proves to be unprofitable. The speed with which the asset can be disposed of is also important.
3. *Experience:* Assets with which the firm is familiar (either through their own or others' experience) can be approached with less trepidation than totally new ventures.
4. *Size:* Investments that are large relative to the size of the business making them, are, all other things the same, more risky than small investments. Sheer size courts danger due to the fact that substantial losses on an expensive asset can force a firm out of business.
5. *Contractual Cash Flows:* The greater the confidence one has in future cash flows, the less risk exposure associated with those cash flows. Therefore, assets that possess a large contractual element in their cash flows are, all other things equal, less risky. For example, an outside maintenance contract to care for a fleet of trucks is a recurring cash flow expense item that management can have a great deal of confidence in.
6. *Credibility of Sponsor:* Capital asset proposals typically have sponsors behind them. These sponsors may have a track record. If so, one can look at the results of their past recommendations for clues as to the reliability of their current proposals.
7. *Payback Period:* A good case can be made for the proposition that assets with short payback periods are safer than those with long paybacks. The reasoning runs as follows: it is important to recoup the investment quickly before tax laws change, competition increases or obsolescence occurs. Although payback is considered by many financial experts as naive, it remains very popular with the business community.
8. *Sensitivity Analysis:* Another practical means of evaluating risk is to play *"what-if" games.* What-if games are more commonly known as sensitivity analysis. With regard to capital asset risk assessment, we wish to know the sensitivity of IRR and NPV to net cash flow outcomes different from the most likely estimates. Since the main objective is to assess risk, only net cash flow outcomes detrimental to the firm should be examined. For example, what if recurring cash inflows are 25% below most likely estimates; what if recurring cash outflows are 10% above estimates; or what if recurring cash inflows last only for 5 years rather than 7 years?

Application of sensitivity analysis to the movie theater example should help to clarify the technique. The most likely net cash flow profile, if you recall, was given as:

Time	0	1	2	3	4	5	5
NCF	−$340,400	+$117,000	+$114,000	+$111,000	+$108,000	+$105,000	+$211,000

This net cash flow profile generated an IRR of 28%. What if the TNCF turns out to be only $12,000 due to a low selling price for the theater. What impact would this have on IRR? First we adjust the cash flow profile as follows:

Time Period	0	1	2	3	4	5	5
NCF	−$340,400	+$117,000	+$114,000	+$111,000	+$108,000	+$105,000	+$12,000

The adjusted net cash flow profile is then inserted into the IRR equation thereby producing an IRR of 20%. The IRR still exceeds the RRR of 15% in spite of a tremendous fall in the theater's value. Other "what if" adverse possibilities can be tried and all of the results tabulated. Sensitivity analysis is especially conducive to computer interaction whereby the analyst can obtain immediate feedback. Sensitivity analysis is not only an excellent method of deducing risk, it is also useful for answering the inevitable "what if" questions posed by superiors and customers.

Screening for Risk

An attempt should be made to identify assets with unmanageable risk. Risk that no amount of profit can overcome. Screening for risk presents somewhat of a problem, however, because it is not as well understood as profitability. A particular management may reject assets out of hand for the following reasons:

1. The payback period is longer than what management feels is a prudent time period. Determination of this prudent time period (sometimes called a cutoff point) is admittedly not a very scientific process. It can vary from one asset to another as well as from one management to another.
2. A statistically determined probability of loss exceeds the level management feels it can live with. The exact level of this critical probability (e.g., 5, 10, or 20%) is determined to a large extent by management's attitude toward risk.
3. Some very conservative firms refuse to invest in almost every asset with which they lack experience.
4. Assets requiring relatively large investments are often eliminated from consideration in the early stages of analysis due to the severe impact they might have on profit, not to mention the firm's very existence. One must keep in mind, however, that, in and of itself, great size does not always imply excessive risk.
5. Severe problems identified with sensitivity analysis (i.e., numerous "what ifs" that lead to losses) could nullify an asset right at the start.
6. A relatively large standard deviation or Beta may eliminate an asset from further consideration.

Key Terms/Concepts

Average rate of return
Benefit-cost ratio
Discounted cash flow

Expected value
Internal rate of return
Mutually exclusive assets

Net present value
Payback period
Profitability index

Questions

1. What are mutually exclusive investment proposals?
2. Describe the relationship between net present value and stockholder wealth maximization.
3. Why is profit an unsatisfactory means to evaluate the acceptability of a capital asset proposal?
4. Generally speaking, when should one refrain from evaluating capital assets by means of the internal rate of return?
5. What purpose is served by computing the average rate of return?
6. Despite its many shortcomings, the payback period remains a popular acceptance criteria of businesspersons. Why is this so?
7. The RRR, as applied to capital budgeting, is sometimes referred to as a "hurdle rate." What is the connotation of the term "hurdle rate"?
8. Briefly define the following terms: profitability index, sensitivity analysis, E(NPV), and discounted cash flow.

Problems

1. Compute the NPV, IRR, and PI for a capital asset proposal that is represented by the following net cash flow profile:

	INCF	RNCF$_1$	RNCF$_2$	RNCF$_3$	RNCF$_4$	RNCF$_5$	TNCF
Year	0	1	2	3	4	5	5
NCF	($800)	$225	$225	$225	$225	$225	$150

The RRR is assumed to be 13%.

2. Ajax Sulfur Company is investigating a capital asset proposal that calls for an INCF investment of $200,000. The asset is expected to provide Ajax with annual RNCFs of $35,398 for ten years. Determine the NPV for this investment assuming the RRR is: a) 8%, b) 10%, c) 12%, d) 14%, and e) 16%.

3. Given an RRR of 12%, calculate NPV, IRR, PI, and payback period for the following net cash flow profile:

Year	0	1	2	3	4
NCF	−$900,000	+$200,000	+$300,000	+$400,000	+$500,000

Is this proposal acceptable?

4. A salesman has just introduced XYZ Corporation's management to an automated mamiliograph that he says will contribute $50,000 of revenue annually, for up to five years. Furthermore, he claims that the mamiliograph can be sold for $12,000 in five years. The machine sells for $100,000 and will require $20,000 of expenses each year to operate it. Ignoring the impact of income taxes, address the following questions:
   A. Derive a net cash flow profile for the mamiliograph based upon the salesman's claims.
   B. Compute the IRR and NPV. The applicable RRR is 20%.
   C. Is the mamiliograph an acceptable acquisition based on these findings?
   D. Holding other factors constant, what would the RNCFs have to be in order to generate an IRR on this investment of 24%?

5. Find the NPV and PI of the net cash flow profile displayed below. The relevant required rate of return is 15%.

	INCF	$RNCF_1$	$RNCF_2$	$RNCF_3$	$RNCF_4$	$RNCF_5$
Year	0	1	2	3	4	5
NCF	($200,000)	$125,000	$125,000	($150,000)	$125,000	$125,000

6. Indicate what effect (increase, decrease, or no change) the following circumstances would have on a positive NPV.
   A. Required rate of return increases.
   B. An investment tax credit is granted.
   C. Sum-of-the-years-digits depreciation is substituted for straight-line depreciation.
   D. The useful life of the asset is extended by three years.
   E. Estimate of TNCF is raised.
   F. Income tax rates rise.

7. Shown below are the net cash flow profiles of two mutually exclusive investment proposals, X and Y.

Year	0	1	2	3	3
NCF_X	($80,000)	$25,000	$25,000	$25,000	$47,500
NCF_Y	($80,000)	$35,040	$35,040	$35,040	0

Required:
   A. Given an RRR for both proposals of 12%, calculate their NPVs.
   B. Compute the IRR for each alternative.
   C. Which alternative is the most acceptable (or least unacceptable)?

8. Shown below are the net cash flow profiles for two mutually exclusive investment proposals, A and B. The RRR for both proposals is 10%.

Year	0	1	2	3	4
NCF$_A$	−$ 5,000	+$ 2,117	+$ 2,117	+$ 2,117	+$ 2,117
NCF$_B$	−$40,000	+$14,011	+$14,011	+$14,011	+$14,011

Required:
- A. Find the NPV and IRR for alternative A.
- B. Find the NPV and IRR for alternative B.
- C. Which alternative is the most acceptable?

9. Holiday Winds Motel owns a large vacant lot next to the motel complex that is due to be sold in five years. The new motel manager would like to convert the property into a public recreation area in the meantime. Three alternatives are available: a tried and true miniature golf course; a currently faddish water slide; or a dirt-bike track, which is in the early stages of popularity. The risk of each proposal is different, thus necessitating different RRRs. The net cash flow profiles and RRRs of these mutually exclusive alternatives are presented below.
Required:
- A. Derive the IRR and NPV for each alternative.
- B. Calculate the payback period for each alternative.
- C. Which is the best proposal?

Year	Dirt-Bike Track	Water Slide	Miniature Golf Course
0	−$185,000	−$185,000	−$185,000
1	+$ 45,000	+$ 75,000	+$ 56,500
2	+$ 55,000	+$ 70,000	+$ 56,500
3	+$ 65,000	+$ 60,000	+$ 56,500
4	+$ 75,000	+$ 45,000	+$ 56,500
5	+$ 85,000	+$ 25,000	+$ 56,500
RRR	14%	12%	10%

10. The maintenance manager for Anderson and Sons, Inc., is recommending a new air conditioning unit for the company's office building. It seems the current unit is extremely energy inefficient compared to the newer models on the market. Information concerning two of the new air conditioning models follows: Model Z6 sells for $10,000 and it should lower the firm's utility bills by about $8,000 per year—it is expected to last for only two years; Model A24 costs $10,000 and will reduce utility bills by approximately $4,000 per year—this model will probably function for six years. Neither unit is expected to have any residual value. Ignoring income tax considerations and assuming that the company will need air conditioning for at least six years, which model is most acceptable? The RRR for both is 10%.

11. Return to problem 17 in chapter 8. If you have not already done so, construct the net cash flow profile called for in that problem.

   Required:

   A. Using the net cash flow profile and an RRR of 10%, solve for the NPV associated with the apartment.

   B. Recompute the NPV assuming that the terminal selling price of the apartment is $500,000 instead of $800,000.

12. A Memphis Tennessee petrochemical firm has been told by the Environmental Protection Agency to reduce pollutant emissions by at least 60%. Two devices are available to perform the task, an Atomizer and a Durofilter. Other than the tax deductions they will provide, neither of these pieces of equipment will benefit the firm. Consequently, the company should select the one with the lowest after-tax cost (in present value terms). Relevant information concerning the Atomizer and Durofilter are displayed below. Carefully note that the Atomizer has a shorter lifespan than the Durofilter. The Atomizer is also less risky, as exemplified by its lower RRR. The company's ordinary tax rate is 40% and its capital gains tax rate is 25%.

	Atomizer	**Durofilter**
Purchase price	$10,000,000	$17,500,000
Estimated installation charges	$ 1,000,000	$ 1,200,000
Estimated residual values	0	0
Estimated yearly maintenance	$ 325,000	$ 400,000
Estimated useful life	5 years	10 years
Investment tax credit	.07	.10
Depreciation method	Straight line	Straight line
Depreciation life	5 years	10 years
Depreciation salvage value	0	0
Required rate of return	11%	13%

   Required:

   A. Derive the net cash flow profile for each alternative.

   B. Which pollution control device has the lowest present value of cost?

13. Joel Ridgeway is examining the possibility of buying a residential home, having it restored, and then renting it. The home under consideration can be purchased for $40,000 with an additional $12,000 needed for restoration. Mr. Ridgeway's intentions are to rent the residence for six years and then sell it for an expected $75,000. However, he will need to spend about $2,000 in preparing the home for sale, not to mention a 7% real estate commission. (In real estate, only sellers pay the commission). The home can be rented for $400 per month, which we will treat as $4,800 received at the end of each year. Property taxes and insurance are the only recurring expenses, and they will total $600 per year. Mr. Ridgeway's income tax rates are 30% on ordinary income and 15% on capital gains. He can depreciate the house over twenty years using the straight-line method, to a zero salvage value. However, there is no investment tax credit available. Mr. Ridgeway's RRR is 7%. Derive the net cash flow profile for this investment and from it compute the NPV and IRR. Is this an acceptable capital asset purchase?

14. Develop various "what if" situations for the rental home of the preceding problem and measure their impact. For example, what if the house goes unrented for two of the six years?

15. The net cash flow profile of a capital asset proposal is shown below. The RRR for this asset is 12%. What is its net *future* value?

	INCF	RNCF$_1$	RNCF$_2$	RNCF$_3$	RNCF$_4$	RNCF$_5$
Year	0	1	2	3	4	5
NCF	($50,000)	$16,000	$16,000	$16,000	$16,000	$16,000

16. George Smith wishes to know if he can justify replacing his personal automobile on economic grounds. The new car he is considering will be less costly to maintain and much more fuel efficient. Consequently, a replacement may very well be financially desirable. Since we are dealing with personal assets here, income tax considerations can safely be ignored.

Mr. Smith sees his alternatives as: (1) restoring the old car and keeping it for five more years or (2) buying a new car and holding it for five years. The cash flow information for each alternative is displayed below:

Renovation of old car if it is kept	$ 750
Trade-in value of old car today	$2,000
Trade-in value of old car in five years	$ 300
Price of new car	$8,000
Preparation cost of new car (i.e., rust proofing)	$ 400
Trade-in value of new car in five years	$2,500
Annual operating costs of old car	$2,650
Annual operating costs of new car	$1,000

Rather than treating these as separate proposals, they can be combined into one package: the purchase of a new car will automatically dictate the sale of the old car. Construct the net cash flow profile for the combined proposal. Assuming that Mr. Smith's RRR is 10%, calculate an NPV. Would replacing the old car be an acceptable decision?

17. Louise's Motor Homes purchased a business jet four years ago for $1,200,000. The capital budgeting analysis at that time indicated the plane would be a worthwhile venture for the company. Not only was it expected to reduce commercial airline costs significantly, but also improve the efficiency of top executives. Three important developments occurred shortly after the jet was purchased: deregulation of commercial airlines led to significant fare reductions; Louise's sold two distant plants, thereby reducing the need for travel; and airport landing fees for private aircraft doubled, primarily as a result of an air controllers strike. As a result of these changes, Louise's financial manager has expressed reservations about keeping the plane. The jet should last another six years, at which time it will be worth an expected $200,000. However, if sold now the plane would bring $720,000.

If retained, the plane will save an estimated $160,000 annually in commercial airline fares plus executive time valued at $90,000 per year. Annual operating costs associated with the airplane amount to $80,000 (including the pilot's salary and landing fees). The plane is being depreciated on a straight-line basis to a zero salvage value, over eight years. Thus, four years of depreciation remain. Louise's income tax rates are 45% on ordinary income and 20% on capital gains. The RRR in this instance is 9%. Should the airplane be retained?

18. John Slade, a recent graduate of the Harvard Business School, wishes to celebrate by purchasing a quality sports car. At the present time he does not own an automobile. Having had extensive training in financial management, Mr. Slade is going to select a sports car on the basis of capital budgeting. Specifically, he will select the car having the lowest present value of costs. In line with this, he has determined his RRR to be 8%. Information on three cars that are particularly attractive to him is assembled below.

	Pontiac TransAm	Datsun 280Z	Mercedes-Benz	
Purchase price	$13,500	$20,000	$36,500	
Preparation	$ 600	$ 300	0	
Annual operating costs	$ 2,400	$ 2,000	$ 1,700	
Overhaul	0	0	$ 3,000	(in 8 yrs)
Trade-in value	$ 4,000	$ 7,000	$15,000	
Holding period	4 yrs.	8 yrs.	16 yrs.	

Income tax guidelines are notably absent from the information gathered above. That is because we are dealing with personal rather than business assets.
Required:
   A. Construct a net cash flow profile for each car.
   B. Determine which of these three automobiles has the lowest present value of costs.

Selected References

Bacon, Peter W., "The Evaluation of Mutually Exclusive Investments," *Financial Management* (Summer 1977), pp. 55–58.

Bierman, Harold, Jr., and Seymour Smidt, *The Capital Budgeting Decision,* 6th ed. New York: Macmillan, 1984.

Brick, Ivan E., and Daniel G. Weaver, "A Comparison of Capital Budgeting Techniques in Identifying Profitable Investments," *Financial Management* (Winter 1984), pp. 29–39.

Dorfiner, Robert, "The Meaning of the Internal Rate of Return," *Journal of Finance* (December 1981), pp. 1010–23.

Ezzell, John R., and William A. Kelly, Jr., "An APV Analysis of Capital Budgeting under Inflation," *Financial Management* (Autumn 1984), pp. 49–54.

Hertz, David B., "Risk Analysis in Capital Budgeting," *Harvard Business Review* (January–February 1964), pp. 95–106.

Levy, Haim, and Marshall Sarnot, *Capital Investment and Financial Decisions,* 2nd ed. Englewood Cliffs, N.J.: Prentice-Hall, 1982.

Nelsen, Charles R., "Inflation and Capital Budgeting," *Journal of Finance* (June 1976), pp. 923–31.

Porterfield, James T. S., *Investment Decisions and Capital Costs,* Englewood Cliffs, N.J.: Prentice-Hall, 1965.

Schall, Lawrence D., and Gary L. Sundem, "Capital Budgeting Methods and Risk: A Further Analysis," *Financial Management* (Spring 1980), pp. 7–11.

Finance in the News

How well are discounted cash flow models used in industry? The answer is not clear-cut. Companies realize the importance of discounting cash flows to current dollars, but they also realize that there are other variables to consider. The following article highlights considerations that must be made in evaluating major capital expenditures.

The Misuse of a Sound Investment Tool

Discounted cash flow has been getting a bad name. Critics charge that the technique has contributed to America's competitive decline and that managers using DCF have systematically rejected investments critical to the livelihood of many U.S. industries.

But the problem isn't DCF itself. The problem is its frequent misapplication.

DCF is a sound conceptual model for valuing the firm. It properly focuses on cash, rather than accounting profits. High reported earnings don't help you if you get less cash out of a business than you put in. DCF also properly emphasizes the opportunity cost of the money you invest. It recognizes that the cash you get out should be greater than the cash you put in *plus* the interest you could have earned by investing the money elsewhere. So the DCF approach discounts future cash flows to current dollars, recognizing the alternative return the company could realize if it had the cash now rather than in the future.

All this is economic common sense. A firm will maximize its value by maximizing the discounted cash flows of its investments. An investment with a higher DCF is superior to one with a lower DCF.

The problem is that what works well in theory doesn't always work well in practice. It is exceedingly difficult to apply DCF correctly in evaluating single capital investments. If your company is using DCF calculations, don't be lulled by the reams of figures: Be sure to test the assumptions behind the numbers. This is especially important in large organizations, where the sensitivities in the calculation are often clouded as the investment proposal climbs through the hierarchy.

The difficulties in applying DCF correctly fall into two categories.

The first is in identifying the relevant cash flows. Far from being an exact science, this requires imprecise assumptions about market growth, price levels and, perhaps above all, the likely actions of competitors.

In evaluating a major capacity addition, for example, most companies would consider the additional profit resulting from the incremental capacity as the relevant cash flow. But a more meaningful measure might be the difference between a project's cash flows and the cash flows associated with not investing. Giving up market share to a competitor may allow it to undercut your position in the products and volume that remain. Your cost position may deteriorate relative to that of other competitors who may invest even though you do not. Your cash flows may erode.

Too often, managers neglect to ask, "What will happen if we *don't* make this investment?" GM declined to invest in response to Toyota's challenge because small cars looked less profitable than its then-current mix. As a result, Toyota was able to expand and eventually challenge GM's base business. Many American companies that thought global expansion would be too risky, today find their world-wide competitive positions eroding. They didn't evaluate carefully enough the results of *not* building a strong world-wide position.

It is impossible to quantify with any precision the impact of competitive scenarios that may or may not occur. The best that can be done is to attach a probability to each scenario—a "qualitative" and subjective judgment.

Similarly, while many companies devote considerable effort to projecting market growth, they typically assume that prices move and market shares will behave as they have in the past. But price levels may be depressed either by too much capacity addition, or by low-cost capacity additions that displace the very high-cost facilities. Most DCF analyses do not address these possibilities. It is assumed that an individual competitor's actions do not affect market price mechanisms or other competitors' behavior.

Many incremental projects such as product line or plant additions are analyzed by DCF. Yet few companies are able to accurately predict the increases in overhead and logistics cost resulting from these investments, which increase plant complexity.

DCF is more easily applied to calculate the gains from simple cost-reducing investment, e.g., the acquisition of labor-saving equipment. Yet other companies are making cost-saving investments as well. Thus, if prices reflect the changing cost structure of a competitive industry, actual earnings may be lower than anticipated. This may explain why most companies' returns fall far short of their hurdle rates for investment.

The second difficulty is the choice of discount rate. This requires a reasonable assessment of what the company can actually earn on its money if it doesn't make the investment. Many companies use a discount rate which is higher than that at which they can actually reinvest the funds. This can result in gradually liquidating a business which doesn't earn these unrealistically high returns.

This problem gains added complexity in an era of fluctuating inflation and interest rates. Reasoning that risky investments should yield more than riskless government notes, many companies have raised their discount rates in recent years. But anyone analyzing an investment proposal should ask whether the high returns that have recently been available from government securities will last over the lifetime of the proposed investment. If not, then it may be profitable to make long-term investments that yield less in the short term than prevailing interest rates. Maximizing short-term gain does not necessarily result in long-term gain, if you lose your opportunity to continue reinvesting at the high hurdle rate.

As a result of such difficulties, many well-managed companies have moved away from reliance on discounted cash flow, or similar models such as the internal rate of return. Such companies still aim for high DCF, but they recognize that they can't reach that aim by applying DCF analysis to every specific project. Instead they focus on competitive quality levels, competitive cost position, share quality levels or share of market as more reliable proxies for the longer-term value of the firm.

Even more important, many well-managed companies insist that investment projects should flow from a sound strategic plan for the business, and should be analyzed within that framework. The essence of a strategic plan is that it explicitly considers the competition and charts a course to build and maintain competitive advantage. It highlights key assumptions and their sensitivities.

A Preferable Loss

Line managers, financial staff and planners who propose and review investments should explicitly question the rigid use of DCF in company capital budgeting systems. The weight of a capital proposal and the yards of figures presented as backup are unfortunately no guarantee that the assumptions used are correct. Alternative competitive assumptions may seem "qualitative" in contrast to lots of numbers. They may strain an organization's tolerance for ambiguity. And it may be uncomfortable to move away from that single number that sums it all up, the internal rate of return. But the loss of methodological tidiness is preferable to surrendering competitive position today, and tomorrow perhaps even losing your core business.

THE WALL STREET JOURNAL, MONDAY, NOVEMBER 1, 1982

Manager's Journal
by Eileen M. Rudden

Capital Budgeting: Further Topics

Overview

The present chapter concludes our discussion of capital budgeting. Chapters 8 and 9 contained the first three stages of capital budgeting: proposal, cash flow analysis, and proposal evaluation. We will now study the final three stages of capital budgeting: evaluate the capital budget, implementation, and follow-up. Although the final stages of capital budgeting are generally not as analytically involved as the earlier stages, they are very important tasks. The chapter opens with a further look into the proposal stage of capital budgeting and concludes with a comprehensive example, which takes us through all six stages of capital budgeting ■

Objectives

By the end of the chapter the student should be able to:

1. Describe the various types of capital asset proposals
2. Explain the concept of capital rationing
3. Discuss the financial and nonfinancial considerations of capital budgeting
4. Explain the entire capital budgeting process
5. Work through and discuss a capital budgeting case problem

Introduction

In the previous two chapters we examined the most critical elements of the capital budgeting process. To reiterate, a proposal is made and is followed by a cash flow analysis (identification, estimation, and taxes) of the proposal. Profitability and risk are then evaluated by bringing the RRR to bear on the proposal's net cash flow profile.

This chapter will present another look at proposals, as well as the additional stages: evaluation of the capital budget, implementation, and follow-up. This discussion of capital budgeting will conclude with a comprehensive example problem ■

Capital Asset Proposals

Capital budgeting begins with a proposal to take some action with regard to capital assets. The action could be one of the following: acquire an additional asset, sell or alter an existing asset, or possibly replace an existing asset with a different one. In line with the previous chapters, our discussion will center on the acquisition of capital assets.

Proposals can be as informal as a simple one-paragraph memorandum or as formal as a detailed one-hundred page typed report complete with data and legal documentation. As a general rule, each proposal has a sponsor. It was stated earlier that sponsors can often be overzealous in their recommendations. This is particularly true when they stand to benefit personally. Nevertheless, they are indispensable to the capital budgeting process and thus the prosperity of a business and its owners. Good proposals are not always easy to find. When a machine breaks down or a plant is operating beyond capacity, it does not require a genius to recommend a machine replacement or a plant expansion. Many of the best capital asset proposals, however, come from ideas generated through hard investigative work and creative thinking. Since these elements are in relatively short supply, it behooves management to encourage them. Developing a proper environment for creativity and provision of adequate rewards for hard work are just two of the things management can do to stimulate ideas. Even the obvious proposals, like those mentioned just above, may not get on the drawing board if the organizational and reward mechanisms in a business are poorly structured.

Not every proposal will be given the go-ahead for analysis and rightly so. A screening procedure must be established to eliminate those recommendations that have not been well thought-out in advance, not to mention those that are totally without substance. Others may be clearly illegal and, thus, unacceptable. One would also hesitate spending much time examining an inexpensive asset. Many businesses require that all proposals must pass a feasibility study before submitting them to the formal capital budgeting process.

A discussion follows of the various kinds of capital asset proposals that are made. A brief description will be given of each type, followed by an example.

Types of Capital Asset Proposals

Change in Capacity   Change in capacity refers to an increase or decrease in the size of a firm's current operations. Capacity decisions normally affect a wide assortment of long-term assets such as: acquisition of land, plant construction, and machinery and equipment purchases. The useful life for an expansion can be 30 years or more.

Example: A consulting firm hired by Ryco Industries has made the following recommendation to Ryco's management: the firm should increase production capacity by 20% in preparation for a significant increase in demand that should materialize within the next two years ■

Replacement   Replacements are among the most frequent capital asset proposals. Machinery, equipment, office furnishings, fixtures, and entire buildings are replaced from time to time. The reasons for so many replacements range from the basic problem of wear and tear to changes in consumer tastes or the fact that something better comes along. An interesting question related to whether or not an asset should be replaced is: when should it be replaced?

Example: The industrial engineering division of the production department at a large Midwest steel manufacturer is proposing the following: replacement of all blast furnaces with one of two new models (i.e., mutually exclusive) that require 50–70% less energy and 20–30% less labor ■

Remodeling   Although somewhat related to replacement, remodeling deserves a place of its own. It covers overhauling, retooling, face-liftings, and changeovers. Proposals in this area have become more common with the growth of service industries.

Example: Julian Valero, the manager of a Boggs supermarket in Los Angeles, has made the following request to corporate headquarters: although the store's facilities are still in good condition, they are drab and should be upgraded to fit the tastes of a more affluent clientele moving into the area. Carpeting, fancier lighting, plants, and a new layout would do the trick ■

Government Mandated   Government regulatory agencies have become more frequent sponsors of capital asset proposals. In most cases their proposals are mandatory. They might require investment expenditures for safety, pollution control, alterations for the handicapped, or beautification. When these "requests" are mandatory and if there is only one way to do them, a business does not really face a decision. However, there are often two or more acceptable types of equipment or alterations that can get the job done. These alternatives become mutually exclusive proposals and management will want to pick the best one. Due to the nature of the assets, they will seldom provide positive benefits to the firm (society is the beneficiary). Therefore, the "best one" will be that alternative with the lowest cost (i.e., minimize losses).

Example: Tapco Enterprises has been told the following by the Environmental Protection Agency: they must install pollution control equipment to reduce air pollutants from their main factory. There are two models on the market capable of meeting the EPA's guidelines. One is significantly cheaper than the other, but would probably last only half as long ■

New Product   Within limits, it is possible for a retailer to add new products without affecting fixed assets. Manufacturers do not ordinarily have this luxury even when they are operating below capacity. For them to produce and sell new products could require new plants, more land, different machinery and equipment, and even additional distribution facilities. All of these capital assets should be proposed as a single package and evaluated accordingly.

Example: The vice-president in charge of marketing for Nathan's Apparel, Inc., has made the following proposal to top management: Nathan's should look into the manufacture and sale of children's clothing. The marketing executive bases her proposal on research that indicates a higher birth rate and an increased concern for children's attire on the part of parents ■

Inventions and Innovations   Inventions and innovations consist of totally new ideas, products, and processes. In the main, they allow a firm to use its present resources more efficiently or serve its customers more effectively. Computers, copying machines, manufacturer's outlets, and corporate jets are examples of capital assets falling into this category.

Example: A sales representative for Compu Corp. has approached the management of Landis Department Stores with the following proposal: if Landis would install a computer (preferably Compu Corp.'s) they could improve inventory control, reduce bookkeeping costs, and improve customer service ■

Financial Assets   Many manufacturing and commercial firms buy stocks and bonds with the intention of holding them for a number of years. The reasons for the purchase of these "nonproductive" assets are varied. Companies often buy common stock and bonds of their major suppliers or customers. Stock may also be purchased as a prelude to a possible merger or to take advantage of tax incentives.

Example: The financial manager for an aircraft manufacturer made the following recommendation to the board of directors: a significant common stock purchase should be made in the manufacturer's major steel supplier. Not only is it a good investment, it would also pull the two firms closer together ■

Divestiture   Companies do sell capital assets from time to time. While many of these sales are of the trade-in variety, a substantial number are outright dispositions based on their own merits. Machinery, stores, factories, and entire product lines are sold everyday by businesses. Some are disposed of to make room for replacement assets, others are abandoned because they have become losers, and still others are sold because they do not fit with the firm's plans.

Example: Performance reports at G. C. Taylor Drug Co. have highlighted the following situation: the forty Taylor pilot drug stores have exhibited deteriorating performance results since their opening five years ago. They were an attempt to bring the manufacturer into the retailing end of the business, but it appears to have been a mistake. A sale may therefore be indicated ■

Make vs. Buy   Businesses often find it preferable to manufacture a part or product that they are currently purchasing from an outside supplier. This is the "make vs. buy" decision. Since it quite often involves capital assets, it is necessary to consider it as a capital budgeting decision.

Example: It has come to the attention of Zykof Corp. that a purchased part they are presently using in the manufacture of swing sets could be made internally at a lower cost ■

The various types of capital asset proposals are listed in table 10.1.

Table 10.1   Types of Capital Asset Proposals

Change in plant capacity
Replacement
Remodeling
Government mandated
New product
Inventions and innovations
Financial assets
Divestitures
Make vs. buy

Evaluate the Capital Budget

Once a proposal has been received and thoroughly evaluated in terms of risk and profitability, it is time to decide if it should be accepted or rejected. The person or group making these decisions will have to accept the responsibility for them. Consequently, they will want to examine the analysts' work very carefully, for this is the major input into their decision. Having assured themselves that the analysis has been performed in a responsible manner, they must determine acceptability.

The general rule is: *accept capital asset proposals that generate profits that more than compensate for risk and the time value of money and reject the rest.* That is to say, if the proposals have positive NPVs, a PI greater than one, or an IRR greater than RRR they should be accepted. As we shall see, however, *acceptance of a proposal does not guarantee that it will be implemented. What acceptance does guarantee, is a place in the capital budget.*

The capital budget will contain those proposals that have overcome all preceding hurdles. It is from this list that management will make its final selections. A summary capital budget form for an amusement park appears in exhibit 10.1. Companies also use specially designed worksheets for cash flow analysis and proposal evaluation. Documents such as these are quite useful, in that they formalize and expedite the capital budgeting process. Once entered in the capital budget a proposal can still be rejected if capital rationing is necessary. Furthermore, only one from each set of mutually exclusive capital assets will be selected.

Capital Rationing   A great deal of discussion has been devoted to the purchase of capital assets and more will follow. We must never forget, however, that funds must be raised before capital assets can be purchased. Fund raising, or financing, is covered extensively in the third section of this text. Generally speaking, assets and liabilities can be discussed separately. There is one major exception to this rule and that is the situation where funds are limited. *Limited financing gives rise to what is popularly known as capital rationing.* The word capital meaning, in this case, money. When funds are limited, investment decisions also become fund-raising or financing decisions. There are two reasons for this: (1) capital assets compete with each other for financing when funds are in short supply and (2) capital assets can generate future funding on their own. The latter instance works this way: capital assets are purchased, they then proceed to generate positive future net cash flows and, consequently, these future cash inflows become available to finance the purchase of additional assets. As long as funds are plentiful in the future, there is no problem. However, when there is an expected shortage of funds, the forthcoming net cash inflows from capital assets purchased today, can influence future purchases.

Exhibit 10.1   Summary capital budget form

Proposal	Sponsor	Investment	Payback	RRR	NPV	PI	IRR	Comments
Replace Ferris wheel	Maintenance department	$190,000	5 yrs.	14%	$100,000	1.53	24%	Cannot be postponed
Purchase water slide	Sales representative	$175,000	3 yrs.	18%	$120,000	1.69	25%	All competing parks have one
Restore roller coaster	Maintenance department	$260,000	7 yrs.	13%	$125,000	1.48	18%	
Enlarge parking lot	Grounds-keeper	$115,000	6 yrs.	12%	$ 35,000	1.30	18%	
Install gourmet restaurant	Marketing manager	$350,000	8 yrs.	18%	$150,000	1.20	22%	This will add prestige to the park
Convert dance pavillion into haunted house	Park general manager	$ 90,000	4 yrs.	20%	$ 10,000	1.11	22%	
Replace parachute jump with a moon walk	Park general manager	$ 75,000	5 yrs.	16%	$ 60,000	1.80	33%	
Replace parachute jump with a pirate ship	Marketing manager	$140,000	8 yrs.	18%	$ 90,000	1.64	24%	

A current shortage of funds can affect the way assets are selected. Before we examine that issue, a definition of limited funds is required. *Funds are limited when the total investment needed to purchase all acceptable capital assets exceeds the available funds from internal cash flow and/or the external sale of securities.* The funds that are available, must be allocated among the competing assets; that is, there must be capital rationing.

Capital assets should be selected on the basis of NPV when capital rationing exists, but the objective and methodology are changed somewhat from before.[1] *The objective in capital rationing is to select from among all acceptable capital asset proposals, that group which provides the greatest total net present value.* This can be an exacting procedure for at least three reasons: (1) the existence of mutually exclusive assets; (2) capital assets are normally indivisible (i.e., all or nothing); and (3) the effects of size differences.

---

[1]The profitability index is also a good technique to ration capital. The IRR, however, can be very misleading when used for this purpose.

Example: Consider the list of proposed asset acquisitions shown in table 10.2.

Table 10.2   Hypothetical Capital Budget

Proposal	Investment (INCF)	NPV
C	$2,100,000	$1,200,000
A	900,000	800,000
J	2,700,000	650,000
G*	2,200,000	600,000
B	1,000,000	550,000
F*	2,200,000	400,000
H**	1,500,000	200,000
I	1,300,000	150,000
D**	500,000	100,000
E	2,000,000	(150,000)

There are ten proposals, ranked in descending order of NPV. F and G are mutually exclusive alternatives as are D and H. Proposal E has a negative NPV and, following our accept-reject rule, would not normally be included in the capital budget. However, there are instances in which this rule is broken, as we shall see.

If funds are plentiful, the selection process is very easy. Simply pick the mutually exclusive alternatives with the highest NPVs (G and H) and all others with positive NPVs (C, A, J, B, and I) for a total investment of $11,700,000. Let us assume, however, that only $8,000,000 of capital is currently available for investment. This requires capital rationing with the objective of maximizing total NPV.

Capital rationing should be performed according to the following steps:

1. Select a group of assets whose total INCF is equal to or less than the capital constraint; be sure to include only one from each set of mutually exclusive assets
2. Sum the NPVs of the asset group
3. Repeat steps #1 and #2 until all possible combinations have been accounted for
4. Choose the asset group with the greatest total NPV

A trial-and-error procedure such as this is made to order for a computer.[2] The group that maximizes NPV includes A, B, C, D, G, and I, with a combined NPV of $3,400,000. While this group requires a total investment of exactly $8,000,000, this need not be the case. Asset indivisibility can lead to an optimal total investment that is less than the capital constraint. Asset E was eliminated from consideration at the outset because it has a negative NPV. Interestingly, alternative D was selected over H even though D has a lower NPV. This is due to D's much smaller investment. Asset J was also excluded, mainly because of its large investment relative to NPV ▮

Another, more difficult, problem exists with capital rationing when future funding is limited. The interest rate used to compute NPV is no longer the RRR, but rather the internal rates of return on future capital asset proposals. Those assets, that is, that can only be financed with the future net cash inflows generated by today's acquisitions. This particular

---

[2]It is a linear programming problem where we are attempting to maximize total
NPV subject to a capital constraint.

interest rate is often referred to as the *reinvestment rate*. Obtaining these future reinvestment rates can be very difficult, if not impossible, because of the tremendous amount of forecasting required. Nevertheless, if one wishes to perform capital rationing with perfection, they must be obtained.[3]

Capital rationing is brought about by a shortage of funds relative to worthwhile investment opportunities. The question can be raised as to why a shortage of funds would exist to begin with. There are two primary reasons for a money shortage. In the first place, there may be provisions in a firm's existing loan contracts that specifically limit the amount of additional debt financing. Secondly, management often places self-imposed limits on the total capital assets purchased in a given period of time. This last one, although actually a spending constraint, has the same effect as a funding constraint.

Nonfinancial Considerations   The preceding accept-reject and selection rules are basically valid for those proposals that are clearly beneficial or detrimental. In a business environment where decisions are always based on strict financial considerations, unfettered by politics, emotions, etc., these rules would be universally applicable. However, we do not live in such a world, and, as a result, rules based on economic logic are often influenced by nonfinancial considerations, especially when proposals are marginal.

Nonfinancial considerations include those intangible factors often surrounding capital asset decisions. For example, there are some capital expenditures that add a sense of prestige to the firm and its employees. Although these assets primarily serve other functions, the fact that they are prestigious can be a significant factor. Their effect on employee morale, productivity, and recruiting is difficult to put into dollars and cents but can be real nonetheless. New office buildings and the latest in advanced equipment are two examples of assets with prestigious side effects.

The goodwill of the local community and concern for society in general, can influence capital asset decisions. Safety, antipollution, beautification, and conservation are issues on the minds of corporate management everywhere.

Businesses must also be careful to consider the impact of change on their employees. Many capital assets can bring about radical change in working conditions and job requirements. Should these changes cause anxiety or fear in employees, then turnover and productivity can be adversely affected. The acquisition may have to be introduced gradually or even forfeited in extreme cases.

Conflicts of interest often arise between management and owners. Management makes the final decision on what to buy or sell, and as long as they act the way owners would act, if they were running the company, there are no problems. At times, however, management will act in its own interest rather than the owners'. For example, management may reject a very good proposal—to replace some inefficient equipment—because it would be admitting they had made a mistake on the original purchase.

Internal company politics can also play havoc with rational decision making. Favoritism, infighting, and jealousy are present to a degree in every organization. Sound projects are often sabotaged by jealous colleagues while weak proposals are allowed to pass as a favor. Unfortunately, situations such as this occur more often than we would care to admit.

---

[3]See Martin H. Weingartner, ''Capital Rationing: n Authors in Search of a Plot,''
Journal of Finance, (December 1977), p. 1403–31.

Another consideration that crops up more than it should is emotion. Emotions cause persons to do things they would not do otherwise, and bad investment decisions are no exception. Fear, pride, and greed are but some of the emotions that, by coloring normal thought processes, can lead managers and owners astray.

After studying financial and nonfinancial factors a decision must be made as to whether or not a proposal should enter the capital budget. Typically, financial factors are paramount in identifying clear-cut winners and losers. It is very difficult to justify the acceptance of a sure loser or rejection of an obvious winner on the basis of intangible considerations, no matter how meritorious or influential they are.

Decisions concerning *marginal* proposals, on the other hand, can easily be swayed by nonfinancial considerations. For example, the choice between two alternatives that have comparable NPVs may be made on the basis of political or managerial needs. Even some projects whose NPV differences are more than "marginal" can be influenced by factors that are not financially related. In the capital rationing example presented earlier, proposal E could have been included in the capital budget with a negative NPV, because of nonfinancial considerations.

Implementation

Implementation covers all of the arrangements that should be taken care of from the time a proposal has been selected until it is actually acquired and in use. Some of the more common arrangements are discussed below.

Many capital asset proposals (e.g., expansions) require additional employees. Such an increase in the labor force will necessitate recruitment, interviews, and hiring so the asset can be ready to use as soon as it is in place. Considerable paperwork and legal documentation are required when many capital assets change hands. This should not be taken lightly. It would be a shame to waste a lot of hard work and money at this stage just because someone overlooked the fine print in a contract. In some cases it is also beneficial to notify interested parties: current and prospective customers; employees who will be directly involved; and, when significant capital assets are involved, the financial press may be entitled to know. Although the financial manager may not be directly involved in these details, they are an integral part of the capital budgeting process.

There remains one extremely important activity to implement. It is so important in fact that an entire section of this text is devoted to it. This activity is financing. Sales of capital assets, of course, do not require financing, but purchases cannot be consummated without it. Funds must be acquired before a capital asset is purchased or constructed. Financing is a complex subject, as we will discover later. For that reason, there is little that can be said about it at this stage except to emphasize the fact that funds must be obtained.

Follow-Up

A follow-up is an examination conducted after a capital asset has been purchased. It would be foolish to devote a lot of time to evaluating a proposal, spend $5,000,000 on it, and then forget about it. There are several valid reasons for wanting to follow-up on acquisitions.

In the first place, a follow-up can provide information that may prove useful in future capital budgeting analyses. Learning from one's mistakes and identifying biases is a useful exercise in any endeavor.

Figure 10.1   Capital budgeting process

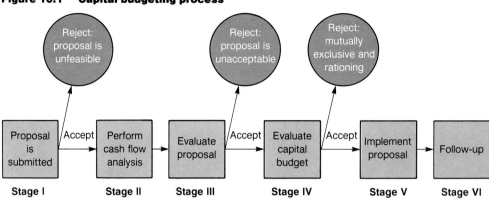

A second reason for conducting a review is to assess the performance of the three major parties involved in capital budgeting. Specifically: (1) was the sponsor's idea good; (2) did the analysts carry out their duties satisfactorily; and (3) did the decision makers make the right decisions?

Third, an examination may point up areas that require attention. For example, an asset might be being used inefficiently or incorrectly. This way, problems can be attended to at an early stage.

Finally, a follow-up may reveal a situation whereby the firm would benefit more by disposing of an asset prematurely (abandonment) than holding onto it as long as originally planned. In some instances, an acquisition should be abandoned if it is not working out well (i.e., minimize losses). At other times, a premature sale is called for when an asset has increased significantly in value.

A diagram of the complete capital budgeting process is shown in figure 10.1. Each square represents a particular stage in the process. The circles show the points where rejection may occur. As you can see, a capital asset proposal can be rejected at three different stages in the course of evaluation.

An example of the complete capital budgeting process is presented below.

Comprehensive Example

Proposal   Dianne and Linda's Auto Salvage Yard has been prospering since Dianne Wilson and Linda Frederick purchased it four years earlier. As well as being the sole owners of the company they also co-manage it. Two days ago, a sales representative for Cleveland Tool Co. approached them about an automobile compacter his company is running a special on. The salvage yard buys wrecked automobiles for $25 and resells them to Midwest Steel Company for recycling. The junkers bring an average selling price of $70. Midwest Steel is located in Springfield, Ohio, some thirty miles from Dianne and Linda's company.

According to the sales rep, if the junkers could be sold in compact form, they would bring an average price of $150 each. He bases the significant price differential on the value of the compacting process and a wider potential market. Furthermore, current freight charges of $12 per unit would be cut in half if the cars are shipped in compact form. For the next two weeks the compacter can be purchased for $142,000 plus installation charges of $8,000. The sales rep claims that only two semiskilled laborers will be needed to run the machine (current semiskilled laborers working at the yard are paid $12,000 a year.) He also says the machine is practically maintenance free and it is eligible for a 10% investment tax credit.

Dianne and Linda would like to evaluate quickly this proposal before the sale expires. Through a few well-placed phone calls, including one to a compacter owner in Cincinnati, they have verified the salesman's claims. They also discovered two additional expenses. Their annual electricity bill will rise $2,500 and insurance premiums will increase $500 a year. If they purchase the compacter they plan to keep it for six years and then sell it for an estimated $30,000. They recognize that all of these figures are estimates and, accordingly, are susceptible to change in the future.

The key element in the success of this venture is the junker volume over the next six years. Based on the average of the last four years, the "most likely" annual volume should be 700 units.

For tax purposes the compacter and associated installation charge are depreciated on a straight-line basis over 6 years (coincidentally equal to the holding period) to a zero salvage value. Dianne and Linda's Auto Salvage Yard has a 35% ordinary tax rate and a 15% capital gains tax rate.

Cash Flow Analysis   An identification of the relevant cash flows and their estimated values are shown below.

Initial Cash Flows (Today)		Recurring Cash Flows (Years 1–6)		Terminal Cash Flows (Year 6)	
Purchase price	−$142,000	Salvage revenue	+$56,000	Sale of compacter	+$30,000
Installation charges	− 8,000	Shipping expense	+ 4,200	Income taxes	?
Income taxes	?	Insurance expense	− 500		
		Utilities expense	− 2,500		
		Wage expense	− 24,000		
		Income taxes	?		

The salvage revenue is the difference between the new selling price of $150 and the old selling price of $70 multiplied by a volume of 700 units. The reason for using the price differential is that the company is only concerned with the cash flows attributable solely to the compacter. In other words, it only wants the changes that will occur. It would be wrong to give the compacter credit for the full $150 because $70 can be obtained for the junkers whether the compacter is purchased or not. The annual shipping expense will fall, therefore it is shown as a cash inflow. Note the absence of the salvage yard's costs for the junkers. These costs are irrelevant because they will exist with or without the compacter.

Neither ordinary taxable income nor capital gains are immediately affected by the initial cash flow expenditures. They will, however, become depreciation deductions later. A tax credit is immediately available and it is .10 × $150,000 = $15,000.

There are several ordinary business transactions under the recurring cash flow category. It is quite likely that ordinary taxable income and, hence, ordinary income taxes will change. Taxes are determined from the income tax statements for each year and they, in turn, require depreciation deductions.

Purchase price	$142,000
Installation	+ 8,000
Original cost	$150,000
Salvage value	− 0
Depreciable base	$150,000

Depreciation Schedule

Year	Depreciation Fraction	Depreciation Deduction
1	1/6	$ 25,000
2	1/6	25,000
3	1/6	25,000
4	1/6	25,000
5	1/6	25,000
6	1/6	25,000
Accumulated depreciation		$150,000

Since the recurring cash flows, depreciation deductions, and ordinary tax rate are identical in each of the six years, it is only necessary to construct one income tax statement.

Recurring Income Tax Statements (Years 1–6)

Gross income	$56,000
Cash deductions*	− 22,800
Depreciation	− 25,000
Taxable income	$ 8,200
Income taxes (.35)	$ 2,870

*Deductions are comprised of $27,000 in additional insurance, wages, and utilities *less* a reduction in shipping expense of $4,200.

Finally, it is necessary to calculate the income taxes associated with terminal cash flows. The sale of the compacter is a capital transaction and should be treated as such.

Terminal Income Tax Statement

Sales proceeds	$30,000
Selling expense	− 0
Cost less accumulated depreciation	− 0
Capital gain	$30,000
Depreciation recapture	$30,000
Asset appreciation	0
Tax on recapture (.35)	$10,500

The compacter's net cash flows are determined in the cash flow statement shown below.

Cash Flow Statement

Initial Cash Flows (Today)		Recurring Cash Flows (Years 1–6)		Terminal Cash Flows (In 6 Years)	
Purchase price	−$142,000	Salvage revenue	+$56,000	Sale of compacter	+$30,000
Installation charges	− 8,000	Shipping expense	+ 4,200	Income taxes	− 10,500
Tax credit	+ 15,000	Insurance expense	− 500	TNCF	+$19,500
INCF	−$135,000	Utility expense	− 2,500		
		Wage expense	− 24,000		
		Income taxes	− 2,870		
		RNCF	+$30,330		

Compacter Net Cash Flow Profile

Year	0	1	2	3	4	5	6	6
NCF	−$135,000	+$30,330	+$30,330	+$30,330	+$30,330	+$30,330	+$30,330	+$19,500

Proposal Evaluation   Acceptability of the compacter is determined by whether or not NPV is positive, PI is greater than one, and IRR is greater than RRR. Dianne and Linda consider the interest rate on six year U.S. Government bonds to be fairly representative of time value of money. It is currently 7%.

Dianne and Linda do not have the benefit of a cash flow probability distribution to aid them in assessing the element of risk. Like most investors, though, they do not like risk, they make an attempt to measure it, and they wish to be compensated for it. Uncertainty as to what actual cash flows will be is the crux of the problem. The INCF is almost rock solid.

Later cash flows, particularly the more distant ones, are much less assured. Based on a subjective six-year forecast of factors underlying the cash flows (e.g., prices, wages, volume, etc.), Dianne and Linda believe that a definite element of risk exists. Furthermore, the payback period of over four years is somewhat unsettling. However, the asset is not large enough to threaten the firm's existence and it has very good abandonment potential. Although the evaluation does not provide a quantitative measure of risk, such as standard deviation, they believe they possess a subjective measure of the risk involved and feel they should be compensated accordingly.

Given that there is some risk associated with the compacter, the owners wish to be compensated for it and they will do so by including a risk premium in the RRR. After some deliberation, Dianne and Linda decide on a risk premium of 4%. Accordingly, the risk-adjusted RRR will be 7% + 4% = 11%.

The compacter's NPV is found as follows:

$$NPV = \frac{\$30,330}{(1.11)^1} + \frac{\$30,330}{(1.11)^2} + \ldots + \frac{\$30,330 + \$19,500}{(1.11)^6} - \$135,000$$

$$NPV = +\$3,736$$

The corresponding PI is found as follows:

$$PI = \frac{\frac{\$30,330}{(1.11)^1} + \frac{\$30,330}{(1.11)^2} + \ldots + \frac{\$30,330 + \$19,500}{(1.11)^6}}{\$135,000}$$

$$PI = 1.028$$

The IRR is found as follows:

$$\$135,000 = \frac{\$30,330}{(1 + IRR)^1} + \frac{\$30,330}{(1 + IRR)^2} + \ldots + \frac{\$30,330 + \$19,500}{(1 + IRR)^6}$$

$$IRR = 12\%$$

Capital Budget Evaluation   All three of the acceptance measures indicate that the compacter should be purchased. NPV is positive, PI is over one, and IRR is greater than RRR. However, it is just marginally acceptable. As a result, there may be some nonfinancial considerations that would make the asset unacceptable. On the other hand, there may be some intangible benefits to bolster it.

Dianne and Linda cannot envision any nonfinancial drawbacks from the purchase. There are two intangible benefits, however. Salvage yards are not the most glamorous businesses to be in. A compacter machine might be just the thing to add some lustre to their company. In addition, personal satisfaction would be derived from not having to cater to Midwest Steel any longer. It seems that the steel firm is a very demanding customer.

All things considered, the compacter is acceptable. It's profit potential is more than sufficient to cover the time value of money and risk. Furthermore, the nonfinancial factors are all in its favor.

Ordinarily, this would only qualify the asset to become part of the capital budget, from which it might be eliminated in capital rationing. But because this is the only capital asset under consideration by the firm and since capital is not limited, it is not only acceptable, it should be purchased.

Implementation   The automobile compacter has been analyzed in detail and a purchase is indicated. However, several things still need to be done before the machine is purchased and put into operation.

Semiskilled workers must be interviewed for the two positions that will come open. This will be followed by the hiring and any necessary indoctrination. A decision needs to be made on exactly where to locate the machine. The owners feel that potential customers for the compacter's output should be contacted and orders obtained *before* the machine begins production, due to the short start-up and delivery time. All relevant paperwork required to place the order must be taken care of including any legal details. The actual cash expense associated with the aforementioned details is insignificant and therefore not included in the cash flow analysis.

One very important item remains, the acquisition of funds that will be used to purchase the compacter. Dianne and Linda's Auto Salvage Yard must raise $135,000. There are several avenues open to them including loans from banks, insurance companies, possibly the government, and, of course, equity financing. The funding could also be a combination of these. The sale of common stock is considered to be their best financing option and the one they will employ. Therefore, the owners will draw on their personal savings and purchase more stock in the company.

Follow-Up   This particular capital asset is similar to most in that it is not necessary to develop a follow-up or feedback system prior to the acquisition. However, one should eventually be determined by Dianne and Linda, and the sooner the better. The follow-up plan they finally settle on is rather simplified, as you might expect of a small company. It requires an annual comparison of actual cash flows with those that were estimated as well as a reappraisal of the compacter's remaining useful life and salvage value.

In a larger organization, the analysis of an investment such as this would normally be performed by someone other than the persons who will make the decision to accept or reject it. That is not the case here, however, since the analysts and decision makers are the same individuals.

This concludes our capital budgeting example. A useful exercise for the student would be to go back over the problem and see if you can think of any reasonable cash flows, implementations, intangible factors, risk elements, etc. that could have been included.

Summary

Capital assets are vital to a business. As such, they should be evaluated in a logical and systematic manner. An evaluation process has been presented in this and the previous two chapters that is intended to meet these requirements. The process can be summarized as follows: a recommendation to buy, sell, or modify a capital asset is proposed; if the proposal merits attention, a cash flow analysis is performed in three parts (identification, estimation, and income taxes) with the object of obtaining a net cash flow profile; acceptability is measured by one or all of the discounted cash flow techniques (i.e., NPV, IRR, or PI), which incorporate the net cash flow profile and the required rate of return; proposals that are accepted into the capital budget may be eliminated due to capital rationing or because there is a more attractive alternative; a proposal that has overcome all of the preceding hurdles must be implemented; the process ends with a follow-up plan.

By following this process, one will make capital asset decisions strictly on the basis of financial factors. On occasion, however, nonfinancial considerations can intervene to such an extent that a different decision results ■

Key Terms/Concepts

Capital budget	Follow-up	Reinvestment rate
Capital budgeting	Implementation	Screening procedure
Capital rationing		

Questions

1. Briefly describe the acceptance criteria for independent capital asset proposals.

2. It is best to rank mutually exclusive investment alternatives by which of the following measures: IRR, PI, or NPV?

3. Selecting from among a set of mutually exclusive investment alternatives can depend upon the existence of capital rationing as well as the alternatives relative rankings. Explain.

4. Give an example of a technological proposal.

5. Define the term "capital rationing."

6. Why is it important that a company follow up on its capital asset acquisitions? Would it be of any value to conduct a follow-up in connection with capital asset divestitures? Explain.

7. What is a government-mandated capital asset proposal? Give an example of one of these proposals.

8. What is the most important facet in the implementation stage of capital budgeting?

Problems

1. Develop an example for each type of proposal described in the first section of this chapter.

2. Identify nonfinancial considerations that might be associated with the following capital asset proposals:
    A. Lights are installed in Wrigley Field, Chicago.
    B. A department store is moved from its original downtown location to a suburban shopping mall.
    C. An employee physical fitness center is constructed on the company premises.

3. The 1986 capital budget for SCN Corporation is presented below. Nine acceptable proposals are included in the capital budget along with their INCFs. The proposals are ranked in descending order of NPV, and those that are mutually exclusive are earmarked as such. That is, A and D are mutually exclusive alternatives as are G and F. Given that SCN Corporation has access to only $6 million of financing, how should it be allocated among the nine proposals?

Proposal	INCF (Investment)	NPV
*A	$1,300,000	$650,000
*D	800,000	550,000
E	600,000	400,000
B	2,000,000	350,000
@G	800,000	250,000
C	1,500,000	200,000
H	1,200,000	100,000
@F	600,000	100,000
I	300,000	50,000

4. Nucor, Inc., is a large supermarket chain operating in the South. The corporation is in the process of evaluating its 1987 capital budget. Thirteen proposals are entered in the budget (see below) including two mutually exclusive computer models and two alternative delivery vehicles. The computer software proposal is conditioned upon what happens with regard to the computer proposals. That is, the software must be purchased if a computer is acquired, whereas none will be needed in the event that neither of the computers are purchased. With regard to the employee cafeteria, a decision has already been made to acquire it despite its negative NPV. Nucor's management has decided not to spend over $7,500,000 on capital assets in 1987. Ration the $7,500,000 in the most optimal manner possible under the circumstances.

Proposal	Investment	NPV
*Computer model A	$1,600,000	$1,100,000
Additional forklift trucks	1,150,000	850,000
Install delicatessans	1,200,000	775,000
Replace airconditioning system	650,000	600,000
*Computer Model B	1,250,000	600,000
@Delivery vans	1,100,000	500,000
@Delivery trucks	800,000	375,000
Expand warehouse	1,300,000	350,000
Replace cash registers	650,000	250,000
Build additional store	1,500,000	200,000
Remodel two stores	500,000	175,000
Computer software	300,000	-----
Headquarter's employee cafeteria	500,000	(225,000)

Selected References

Bierman, Harold, Jr., and Seymour Smidt, *The Capital Budgeting Decision,* 6th ed. New York: Macmillan, 1984.

Gordon, Lawrence A. and George E. Pinches, *Improving Capital Budgeting: A Decision Support System Approach,* Reading, Mass: Addison-Wesley, 1984.

Kim, Suk H., and Edward J. Farragher, "Current Capital Budgeting Practices," *Management Accounting* (June 1981), pp. 26–30.

Schall, Lawrence D., Gary L. Sundem, and William R. Geijsbeels, Jr., "Survey and Analysis of Capital Budgeting Methods," *Journal of Finance* (March 1978), pp. 281–87.

Schnell, James S., and Roy S. Nicolosi, "Capital Expenditure Feedback: Project Reappraisal," *Engineering Economist* (Summer 1974), pp. 253–61.

Weaver, James B., "Organizing and Maintaining a Capital Expenditure Program," *Engineering Economist* (Fall 1974), pp. 1–36.

Weingartner, H. Martin, "Capital Rationing: n Authors in Search of a Plot," *Journal of Finance* (December 1977), pp. 1403–31.

▪ Finance in the News

When evaluating capital asset expenditures, both qualitative and quantitative considerations must be made. The following article about Borg Warner Corp.'s Borg & Beck Division illustrates a variety of production-related benefits that can arise from a "financial" decision.

Buying Now Avoids 'Paying' Later

Maintaining production on today's machining and assembly lines is considered sacrosanct by most manufacturers. Yet, all too often, outdated equipment prevents this goal from being realized. One solution for sustaining production levels is an ongoing modernization program that can take a company's manufacturing capability from where it is today to where it wants to be tomorrow.

Recent turning machine acquisitions at Borg-Warner Corp.'s Borg & Beck Div., Sterling Heights, MI, provide an example of the many benefits of such a policy. They are used in the annual production of 80,000 11 and 12-in. torque converters for off-the-road equipment manufacturers such as Deere & Co., J I Case Co., Clark Equipment Co., Caterpillar Tractor Co., and Ford Tractor Operations. In all, six 219-VNP turning machines, purchased from Motch Manufacturing Div. of Oerlikon Motch Corp., Cleveland, replaced previous-generation Motch & Merryweather equipment. The new 2-spindle, vertical, numerically programmed chuckers perform boring, turning, facing, chamfering, trepanning and grooving operations.

Ease of Tool Change

The greatest benefits of the new equipment are ease of tool change, flexibility and a reduced scrap rate, according to John Svendor, manufacturing engineering manager at Borg & Beck. "We chose our cutting tools so that they will easily adapt to a different part family and our toolholders are designed so that they can run several parts without a major tooling change. This allows us to react quickly to a change in the model mix. Consequently, simple tooling changes involve replacing an insert or holder and require a maximum of one hour," he says.

Changeover on the previous cam and hydraulic machines from one converter hub diameter to another required two days of extensive tool block changes, adjustments to limit switches and hydraulic stops, cam replacements and fine tuning. Some extensive model changes took a week before the machine was debugged and running.

Scrap rate with the new machines is reduced to 1½ percent. With the previous equipment, scrap rate was 8–10 percent.

97 Percent Uptime

In addition to maximizing output by virtue of producing 120 ''good'' parts per hour, the 12-in. converter line is achieving uptime of 97 percent compared to 60–70 percent previously.

This improvement is partially due to the diagnostics in the General Electric (Charlottesville, VA) Mark Century 1050 HV controls that give in-house technicians the capability to troubleshoot and solve 20 percent of downtime problems. The controls and NC servo drive system replace limit switches, dogs and the extensive maintenance required on the old equipment to provide Borg & Beck with higher accuracy and repeatability than was previously possible. While the old machines could not hold ±.001-in. accuracy, the new $190,000 Oerlikon Motch machine tools can, and Svendor is confident that value can be split to ±.0005 in. for a subsequent bearingizing operation. ''That accuracy reflects in the part's appearance—it looks like a high precision part,'' he says.

Leadtimes also have improved. Converter orders received in the morning can be in assembly that afternoon and shipped the next day.

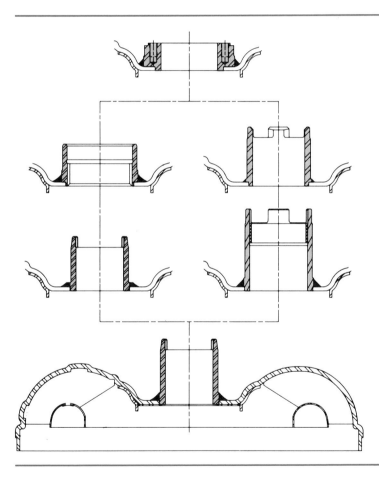

Flexibility

In addition, the new equipment can be used on other products if a significant change in product mix occurs.

"One of the first questions on every justification is 'What happens to the machinery if that job is no longer here?' Our corporation has taken the stand that new machinery purchases must be flexible. The one-piece-of-machinery-for-one-product is old thinking," Svendor adds.

Although other machinery manufacturers of similar equipment were considered, Borg & Beck selected Oerlikon Motch because of satisfaction with its previous equipment, a good service record and a good working relationship with that company. The first two machines, programmed and debugged at Oerlikon Motch, and incorporating tooling designed by Werth Engineering Inc., Bridgeport, MI, worked extremely well. Borg & Beck then chose to do the tooling and debugging in-house on the following four machines to save over $100,000. While this saving was nice, Svendor admits, "If I could do it again, we would have left the tooling design completely to Oerlikon Motch. To debug tooling and make programming changes in a production environment is very difficult—especially for families of parts. It's well worth $100,000 in saved time, energy and frustration to bring in equipment that is proven."

Future purchases he points out, may lean toward equipment manufacturers that also provide complete in-house tooling design. Svendor believes a machine builder's in-house design provides a better marriage of tooling to machinery than occurs when a builder contracts out the tooling. He mentions such possibilities as Olofsson Corp. (Lansing, MI) or Saginaw Machine Systems Inc. (Troy, MI).

Each of the six Oerlikon Motch machines perform the same basic function. After facing the 1010 steel converter stamping, an OD is turned, followed by a chamfer of the OD and ID. Next, a thrust surface is faced and a hub is bored. The only difference in the five part families is the internal hub. Made from 1137 steel and heat treated to 35 HRC, hubs are from 1 to 2 in. in diameter and vary from 2 to 3 in. in length; some have splines or undercuts while others have bearing diameters that have to be bored.

The modernization program is fulfilling its purpose of improving productivity and enabling Borg & Beck to address the market of low-volume orders they formerly couldn't. Through periodic capital expenditures they are moving continuously from today's manufacturing capabilities into tomorrow's. They have found that you pay, in one way or another, for both old and new equipment. The latter, however, gives you a future.

Michael J. Wilson
Associate Editor

Reprinted by permission from "Buying Now Avoids Paying Later," in the January, 1985 issue of *Production Magazine*.

Liability and Equity Management

We have just spent a considerable amount of time exploring the ins and outs of asset management. Businesses must have both current assets and capital assets. Assets, in turn, give rise to liabilities (i.e., debt) and equity, since financing is necessary for the purchase of assets. At first glance, financing appears to be a rather straightforward issue, whereby a company looks for investors who are willing and able to acquire its liabilities and equity, in return for compensation. Looks, however, can be deceiving. Debt and equity come in many forms. As we shall see, the costs of different forms of financing can vary widely, due to differing degrees of risk. The picture is further clouded by legal complexities (e.g., income taxes) and the myriad institutions and traditions that make up the financial markets.

Liability and equity management embraces principles, practices, and procedures that are necessary to deal with the complexities of financing decisions. We shall encounter several important financing decisions in the next six chapters. In the process, we will be exposed to a great deal of related and valuable information. Liabilities and equity should be managed in accordance with the objective of shareholder wealth maximization. This means that financial decisions will be analyzed and evaluated in terms of their impact on stockholder profits and risk exposure. The latter being invoked within the required rate of return ■

11

Financial Forecasting and Financial Structure

Overview

Assets give rise to a need for financing (i.e., liabilities and equity). Before a firm engages in financing, it should have answers to three basic questions: (1) What are its funding requirements? That is, how much funding is needed, when is it needed, and how long is it needed? (2) What will be the proportionate shares of debt and equity financing? (3) If debt financing is employed, will it be short-term debt, long-term debt, or some combination of the two? The objective to strive for when addressing these issues is the maximization of stockholder wealth. These topics are dealt with in this chapter under the following respective headings: financial forecasting, financial leverage, and debt maturity composition. The strategic issues addressed in the current chapter are critical to an understanding of specific liability and equity management issues that will arise in subsequent chapters ■

Objectives

By the end of the chapter the student should be able to:

1. Differentiate among temporary and permanent assets and relate them to temporary and permanent financial requirements
2. Compare and contrast the methods used for forecasting temporary financial needs versus permanent financial needs
3. Explain the concept of financial structure, including the aspects of debt versus equity and the maturity composition of debt financing
4. Discuss the benefits and risks of financial leverage
5. Compare and contrast the three major theories of financial leverage
6. Discuss the qualitative factors that affect a firm's level of debt
7. Explain the relationship between the lives of a firm's assets and the maturities of its financial obligations

Introduction

In this chapter we shall examine the broader aspects of liability and equity management. As the first topic, we discuss financial forecasting—why it is useful and how it is accomplished. Financial structure is encompassed within the second and third topics of the chapter. The first financial structure topic is composed of the issues surrounding the use of debt as opposed to equity financing. The final topic focuses on another financial structure question: what is the appropriate maturity composition for liabilities? ■

Financial Forecasting

A forecast of future financial requirements can be extremely useful to a business. Knowing ahead of time the amount of funds that will be needed, when they will be needed, and for how long, allows for planning. In essence, a financial forecast provides a financial manager with the information and the time to design and implement a superior financial strategy. The information can help in deciding such matters as: whether debt or equity financing should be used, and would the funds best be obtained on a short-term or a long-term basis. A financial manager can use the time to contact various lenders and financial advisors, negotiate terms, and prepare any necessary legal and accounting documents.

Most businesses are faced with two principal types of financial requirements. *Temporary financing* is required to fund seasonal and transitory increases in working capital, primarily accounts receivable, and inventory. *Permanent financing* is necessary to fund capital asset acquisitions and the greater working capital required of a growing business. This situation is revealed in figure 11.1.

Figure 11.1   Asset requirements of a growing and seasonal firm

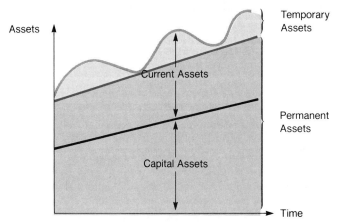

Here we see that, over time, a growing business will need a permanent increase in both current and capital assets as well as temporary additions to current assets. This asset growth can only be met with financing.

Financial forecasting is an attempt to estimate a firm's temporary and permanent financing requirements. Since the forecasting methods are somewhat different for each of these, we will discuss them separately. Before doing so, we should mention a third financial requirement, *replacement financing.* These are funds that are used to replace maturing debt obligations such as bank loans and bonds.

Forecasting Temporary Financial Needs   Temporary or seasonal financial requirements can be estimated quite well by means of *cash budgets. A cash budget is a forecast of the forthcoming year's cash inflows and cash outflows broken down by months or, better yet, weeks.*[1] It is a good practice to update and, if necessary, revise the cash budget each month. *Seasonal funding is needed for those months when cash deficits exist.* A cash deficit arises whenever cash outflows exceed cash inflows and a firm lacks adequate excess cash reserves to meet the shortfall. For instance, a company begins the month of March with $850,000 in cash balances, of which $500,000 is its desired minimum (i.e., precautionary) cash reserves.[2] Cash inflows during the month are $2 million while cash outflows amount to $3 million. The March cash deficit equals the $1 million shortfall less the available excess cash reserves of $350,000, or $650,000. Temporary financing can be repaid during those months when cash surpluses exist. A *cash surplus* arises whenever the cash inflows for a given month exceed the cash outflows. Temporary financial requirements can be more readily identified with a cash budget than by trying to predict seasonal variations in working capital directly. The problem with the latter method is that it does not provide sufficient accuracy.[3] Cash budgets are only as good as the numbers that go into them. Therefore, one should devote an adequate amount of time and effort to making the cash flow predictions.

Construction of a cash budget normally begins with a month-by-month sales forecast for the coming year. The sales forecast is both the most important and most difficult part of the cash budget. For that portion of sales made on credit, one must also know the monthly payment pattern. With this information in hand, it is relatively easy to calculate cash receipts for each month. Monthly cash expenditures are somewhat easier to predict than receipts. For one thing, a firm has more control over its expenditures. Furthermore, some expenditures are contractual, including such items as rent and interest payments. Nevertheless, there is a large element of uncertainty surrounding expenditures, particularly those that are directly related to sales. Wages, materials (manufacturing) and merchandise (retailing) would fall in this category. When forecasting monthly cash outflows, one must remember to account for payments in the month they are made, not incurred, which can be different due to accruals. Finally, under no circumstances should depreciation, a noncash expense, be included in a cash budget.

---

[1] We are referring to cash "flows" here and not cash "balances" a firm may have on hand.

[2] The term cash is used in the broad sense here to include both checking deposits and marketable securities.

[3] It might be helpful to review the discussion of cash conversion cycles in chapter 5, pages 130–31.

Figure 11.2   Cash flow process of a manufacturing firm captured by a cash budget

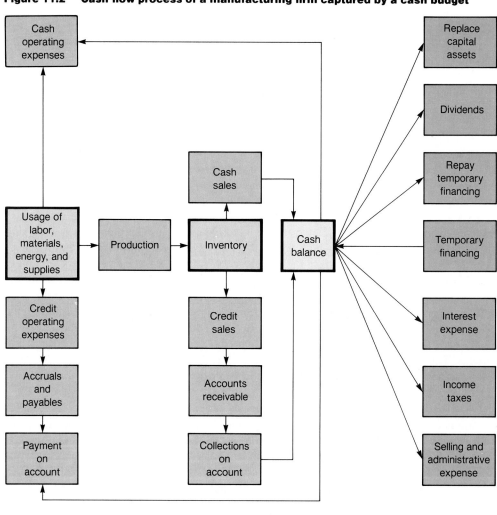

Application: In early December, 1984, Regis Boat Company is preparing a monthly cash budget for 1985. Regis manufactures small boats for the leisure market, and, as one would expect, its sales are highly seasonal. However, due to a small production facility and other factors, its manufacturing schedule is constant each month. All sales are on credit and the historical payment pattern reveals that 60% are normally collected in the following month, 30% in two months, and the remaining 10% in three months. Bad debts are minimal. Wages are paid in the month that work is performed. Orders are placed every month for materials and supplies, but they are not paid for until the following month. Since labor and materials are used at a uniform rate, the cash payments for them will be constant from month to month. In addition to these expenditures, regular monthly outlays will be made for utilities, maintenance, sales promotion, and general and administrative expenses. Concerning sales promotion, cash outlays are much higher during the spring and summer selling season. There are three other items that will require the expenditure of cash during the year: dividends are to be paid quarterly in March, June, September, and December; taxes are paid semiannually in March and September; and a piece of equipment is due to be replaced in December.

The sales forecast for 1985 is $32,000,000. It is broken down by month in table 11.1.

Table 11.1   Monthly Sales Forecast

Month	Sales Estimate
January	$ 0
February	800,000
March	2,000,000
April	4,000,000
May	7,000,000
June	6,000,000
July	6,000,000
August	4,000,000
September	1,000,000
October	600,000
November	400,000
December	200,000

Note how the sales are concentrated in the spring and summer months, from April through August. On the other hand, cash collections from these sales will be concentrated in the months from June through October. For instance, May sales of $7 million will be collected according to the following pattern: $4,200,000 (60%) in June, $2,100,000 (30%) in July, and $700,000 (10%) in August. There will also be cash collections early in the year from credit sales made during the last three months of 1984, which were, respectively: October $600,000, November $400,000, and December $200,000. Regis begins 1985 with a cash balance of $600,000. However, the firm desires a minimum cash reserve of only $450,000 throughout the year. Thus, excess cash reserves currently amount to $150,000. In order to simplify matters, we shall assume that funding is obtained at the outset of a deficit month and repayments occur at the end of a surplus month. The 1985 cash budget for Regis Boat Company is shown in table 11.2.

Table 11.2   Regis Boat Co. 1985 Cash Budget

	January	February	March	April	May
Collections:					
3 months past	$ 60,000	$ 40,000	$ 20,000	$ 0	$ 80,000
2 months past	120,000	60,000	0	240,000	600,000
1 month past	120,000	0	480,000	1,200,000	2,400,000
1. Cash inflows	$ 300,000	$ 100,000	$ 500,000	$1,440,000	$3,080,000
Payments:					
Wages	$1,200,000	$1,200,000	$1,200,000	$1,200,000	$1,200,000
Materials	400,000	400,000	400,000	400,000	400,000
Utilities	80,000	70,000	60,000	30,000	30,000
Supplies	200,000	200,000	200,000	200,000	200,000
General	350,000	350,000	350,000	350,000	350,000
Promotion	10,000	10,000	30,000	50,000	60,000
Maintenance	80,000	80,000	80,000	80,000	80,000
Other:					
Dividends			400,000		
Taxes			750,000		
Equipment					
2. Cash outflows	$2,320,000	$2,310,000	$3,470,000	$2,310,000	$2,320,000
3. Net cash flow (1)−(2)	($2,020,000)	($2,210,000)	($2,970,000)	($ 870,000)	$ 760,000
4. Beginning cash balance	$ 600,000	$ 450,000	$ 450,000	$ 450,000	$ 450,000
5. Minimum cash balance	$ 450,000	$ 450,000	$ 450,000	$ 450,000	$ 450,000
6. Cash surplus (Deficit) (3)+(4)−(5)	($1,870,000)	($2,210,000)	($2,970,000)	($ 870,000)	$ 760,000
7. Deficit financing	$1,870,000	$2,210,000	$2,970,000	$ 870,000	0
8. Surplus repayment	0	0	0	0	$ 760,000
9. Cumulative financing	$1,870,000	$4,080,000	$7,050,000	$7,920,000	$7,160,000
10. Ending cash balance (5)+(6)+(7)−(8)	$ 450,000	$ 450,000	$ 450,000	$ 450,000	$ 450,000
11. Excess cash balance (10)−(5)	0	0	0	0	0

The cash budget displayed in table 11.2 provides much useful information.[4] In the early months of the year cash inflows (line 1) are insufficient to cover estimated cash outflows (line 2), resulting in cash shortages (line 3). Moreover, since excess cash reserves are inadequate at the outset, cash deficits are expected in each of these months (line 6). During this time interval, products are being produced, but seldom sold. When sales finally start to materialize in March and April there is a lag in cash inflows, as the company awaits collections. In other words, the boat inventory is being built up early in the year followed by an increase in accounts receivable. Finally, in May cash receipts start to exceed expenditures and cash surpluses result (also line 6). Surpluses remain in the late summer and early fall despite a fall in sales, because collections from the heavy sales months are still coming in. In essence, the earlier situation is reversed, as inventory and then receivables fall. A new cash flow cycle begins toward the end of the year with cash expenditures surpassing receipts. However, cash surpluses are still in evidence, thanks to the excess cash reserves at the end of October (line 11) that can be used to cover the cash flow shortfalls in November and December (line 3).

Temporary financing (line 7) is needed to cover the cash deficits that occur in the first four months of the year. To be more specific, funds totaling $1,870,000 are required for January, if Regis is to meet its financial obligations for that month. A further $2,210,000 must be raised in connection

---

[4]Interest charges on temporary financing are excluded from this cash budget so as to keep the problem manageable. For that same reason, interest income from marketable securities is also excluded.

Table 11.2 *Continued*

June	July	August	September	October	November	December
$ 200,000	$ 400,000	$ 700,000	$ 600,000	$ 600,000	$ 400,000	$ 100,000
1,200,000	2,100,000	1,800,000	1,800,000	1,200,000	300,000	180,000
4,200,000	3,600,000	3,600,000	2,400,000	600,000	360,000	240,000
$5,600,000	$6,100,000	$6,100,000	$4,800,000	$2,400,000	$1,060,000	$ 520,000
$1,200,000	$1,200,000	$1,200,000	$1,200,000	$1,200,000	$1,200,000	$1,200,000
400,000	400,000	400,000	400,000	400,000	400,000	400,000
50,000	60,000	60,000	40,000	30,000	50,000	60,000
200,000	200,000	200,000	200,000	200,000	200,000	200,000
350,000	350,000	350,000	350,000	350,000	350,000	350,000
60,000	60,000	50,000	40,000	30,000	10,000	10,000
80,000	80,000	80,000	80,000	80,000	80,000	80,000
400,000			400,000			400,000
			750,000			
						1,000,000
$2,740,000	$2,350,000	$2,340,000	$3,460,000	$2,290,000	$2,290,000	$3,700,000
$2,860,000	$3,750,000	$3,760,000	$1,340,000	$ 110,000	($1,230,000)	($3,180,000)
$ 450,000	$ 450,000	$ 450,000	$3,660,000	$5,000,000	$5,110,000	$3,180,000
$ 450,000	$ 450,000	$ 450,000	$ 450,000	$ 450,000	$ 450,000	$ 450,000
$2,860,000	$3,750,000	$3,760,000	$4,550,000	$4,660,000	$3,430,000	$ 250,000
0	0	0	0	0	0	0
$2,860,000	$3,750,000	$ 550,000	0	0	0	0
$4,300,000	$ 550,000	0	0	0	0	0
$ 450,000	$ 450,000	$3,660,000	$5,000,000	$5,110,000	$3,880,000	$ 700,000
0	0	$3,210,000	$4,550,000	$4,660,000	$3,430,000	$ 250,000

with February's deficit, followed by financing requirements of $2,970,000 for March and $870,000 for April. Cumulative peak funding requirements for the year 1985 will therefore amount to $1,870,000 + $2,210,000 + $2,970,000 + $870,000 = $7,920,000 (line 9). This financing is temporary in the sense that cash surpluses will be available from May through October to repay investors. Repayments begin in May when $760,000 is used to retire a portion of the financing (line 8). Repayments continue until the financing is wiped out, which occurs at the end of August (line 8). Note that the company has accounted for a minimum cash balance throughout the year (line 5) ■

Cash budgets can provide a business with very specific information concerning its seasonal financing needs, such as: when it will begin, how long it will last, and the amounts required. It is another matter to determine the exact form, terms, and source of temporary financing, since there are many alternatives available. These and other financing issues will be addressed in the remainder of this chapter and the five chapters following it. Before we leave this discussion on cash budgets, it should be reemphasized that the figures in a cash budget are, for the most part, estimates. To be more specific, they are most likely estimates, such as those discussed in chapter 4.[5] Actual cash flows will differ from budgeted figures to some degree. Consequently, one should use cash budgets only as guides for financial planning.

---

[5]Probabilistic cash budgets can also be constructed.

Forecasting Permanent Financial Needs   Future permanent funding requirements normally do not have to be estimated with as much accuracy as temporary needs. However, they should be forecasted further into the future (five years ahead is not uncommon). The problem is basically one of predicting the annual increases in permanent assets (both capital and current) for which additional funds will be required. These permanent funds will be partially provided by the automatic increase in current liabilities (e.g., accrued wages and accounts payable) that come with a larger business.[6] The task facing the financial manager, then, is to forecast the year-by-year increases in permanent assets and *automatic liabilities*.

There are numerous techniques available for long-run forecasting and they vary considerably in complexity. We will confine our discussion to one of the more basic methods. The forecasting technique we shall employ here is based on the assumption that assets and automatic liabilities are closely related to sales. Therefore, if one knows what these relationships are, it is possible to predict future increases in these two items given a sales forecast. Admittedly these are some big assumptions and ifs. Nevertheless, this method can provide broad estimates that are useful for planning.

Relationships between sales and assets and sales and automatic liabilities can be obtained from historical patterns. Once these relationships are found, they can be combined with the sales forecast to achieve our objective.

Application: In early 1985, Zyco Corp. is in the process of forecasting its permanent financial needs for 1985, 1986, and 1987. Zyco Corp.'s sales, total assets, and automatic liabilities for the last ten years are shown in table 11.3.

Table 11.3   Ten Years of Historical Data on Sales, Total Assets, and Automatic Liabilities

Year	Sales	Total Assets	Automatic Liabilities
1975	$ 6,100,000	$4,250,000	$ 580,000
1976	7,200,000	4,700,000	650,000
1977	8,250,000	4,100,000	625,000
1978	9,250,000	5,400,000	700,000
1979	9,800,000	4,800,000	680,000
1980	12,500,000	6,900,000	920,000
1981	11,800,000	6,300,000	850,000
1982	11,250,000	5,500,000	755,000
1983	14,150,000	6,200,000	950,000
1984	14,900,000	7,225,000	1,050,000

[6]As a company's sales and production grow, it will spontaneously employ more workers, use more energy, and purchase more materials and supplies. Since payment for most of these resources can usually be delayed for a period of time (e.g., a supplier grants credit for sixty days, workers are paid biweekly, or a public utility bills its customers monthly), financing is obtained automatically.

Figure 11.3   Regression forecast of total asset requirements for a business

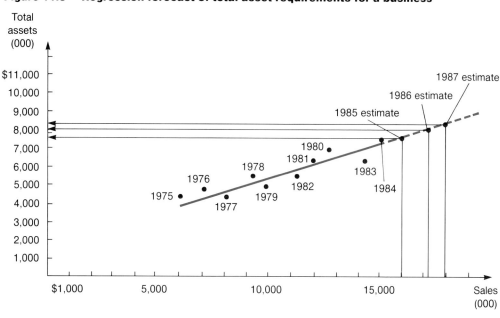

The sales figures are for an entire year while the assets and liabilities represent annual lows. This is necessary to eliminate any seasonal asset and/or liability increases related to temporary financing. Reasonably good relationships between two variables (i.e., sales and assets) can be found by plotting their paired historical values on a scatter diagram and visually fitting a curve to them.[7] This curve (more formally known as a regression line) will describe the relationship between the two variables, and with it, one can forecast.

The yearly total assets and sales of Zyco are plotted in figure 11.3, with assets on the vertical axis and sales on the horizontal axis. The solid curve fitted to the points shows a definite positive relationship between sales and assets. By extending the curve on out (the dashed portion) we can

---

[7]A much better method for fitting curves to historical data is the *method of least squares.* Briefly stated, the method of least squares is a mathematical procedure that can be used to generate an equation from historical data on two or more variables.

For example, a linear equation in two variables (X and Y) of the form $Y = a + bX$ is conducive to least squares. Y is the dependent variable (i.e., assets) and X the independent variable (i.e., sales). Through the application of the least squares method, parameters a and b can be found with the following equations:

$$a = \frac{\Sigma X_i^2 \Sigma Y_i \; \Sigma X_i \Sigma X_i Y_i}{n \Sigma X_i^2 - (\Sigma X)^2} \qquad b = \frac{n \Sigma X_i Y_i - \Sigma X_i \Sigma Y_i}{n \Sigma X_i^2 - (\Sigma X_i)^2}$$

where: X_i = Values of the variable X
Y_i = Values of the variable Y
n = sample size

Once the parameters of this equation are found, the formula can be used for forecasting Y for a given X.

Figure 11.4   Regression forecast of automatic liability sources of financing

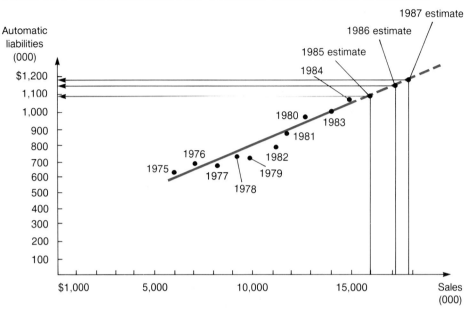

forecast assets for given sales estimates. Assuming the sales estimates are (1985) $16,000,000, (1986) $17,300,000, and (1987) $17,800,000, we can see on the vertical axis that total assets will be about $7,500,000, $8,200,000, and $8,600,000, respectively. This process is repeated in figure 11.4 for sales and automatic liabilities. For the same sales estimates, automatic liabilities are forecasted to be $1,080,000, $1,145,000, and $1,190,000, respectively.

The permanent financing requirements for each year are equal to the predicted annual increase in total assets less the predicted annual increase in automatic liabilities. As of the end of 1984, total assets were equal to $7,225,000, and automatic liabilities amounted to $1,050,000. The projected annual increases in these levels and the corresponding financial requirements are as follows:

	Projected Increase in Total Assets	Projected Increase in Automatic Liabilities	Projected Increase in Permanent Financing
1985	$275,000	$30,000	$245,000
1986	700,000	65,000	635,000
1987	400,000	45,000	355,000

Zyco Corp. can now plan for permanent financing with the knowledge that it will need approximately $245,000 in 1985, $635,000 in 1986, and $355,000 in 1987.

We must not lose sight of the fact that this financial forecast is rather crude. In particular, a great deal of weight is given to the relationship between sales and assets. Assets do not move in lockstep with sales as the scatter diagrams above reveal. Also, we are dealing with uncertain sales estimates. Greater accuracy, however, can be achieved only with more intensive analysis. For one thing, the permanent levels of current assets can change for any one of a number of reasons besides sales (i.e., interest rate movements). Specific capital asset acquisitions, on the other hand, are determined in capital budgeting ■

Financial Structure

The financial structure of a business has two aspects. The first aspect concerns the relative proportions of debt and equity financing that are most appropriate. That is, should a firm obtain 80% of its funds from equity and 20% through debt or some other percentages, say 60% and 40%. Determining the maturity composition of debt financing is the second aspect of financial structure. Liabilities can be incurred for as short a period of time as a few weeks or as long as many years. It is important that a good deal of thought go into the selection of debt maturities. Financial structure is examined in more detail below, beginning with the issue of debt vs. equity.

Financial Structure: Debt vs. Equity

One of the most important issues encountered in financing a business is deciding what proportion of total funds will be in the form of debt financing. Every firm needs equity capital, but not every firm must use debt capital.[8] Equity can be obtained from the sale of common stock and retained earnings.[9] Debt, on the other hand, comes in numerous forms: bank loans, public sale of bonds, accrued wages, trade credit, and leases. Why would a business, one that could obtain all of its funding requirements with equity, borrow money? There are two basic reasons.

In the first instance, debt can be obtained at a lower cost than equity. This results partly from the fact that creditors are willing to accept less than stockholders due to their much safer relative position (i.e., prior claim on earnings and assets). Another major factor holding down the cost of debt is the tax deductibility of interest charges. Dividends paid to stockholders, on the other hand, are not deductible for tax purposes. In essence, the government subsidizes debt financing and thereby creates an artificial bias away from equity financing. The second reason why borrowing may be attractive also has to do with its cost. *As a rule, the cost of debt financing is fixed over its life, regardless of how successful the borrower may be at investing the funds.*[10] A company that borrows money from a bank at 10% and reinvests it in physical assets yielding 25% is only required to pay the bank a 10% interest rate. All of the excess (i.e., 15%) accrues to the owners. Companies attempt to use these low, fixed-cost debt funds as a lever to generate higher earnings per share and returns on equity for the owners, thus giving rise to the term *financial leverage.* Financial leverage is not to be confused with operating leverage. *Operating leverage* is concerned with the trade-off between fixed and variable operating costs (see the appendix to this chapter).

The aforementioned beneficial aspects of debt must be kept in perspective. Interest charges must be met before the owners receive anything, and, unlike dividends, they are mandatory in both good times and bad. The principal on debt must also be repaid on predetermined dates, while there is no such requirement for equity.[11] A business and its owners can experience severe hardships from these requirements. For one thing, net income and dividends

---

[8]Small businesses are usually limited in their ability to raise equity capital. Consequently, they may have no choice with regard to borrowing funds.

[9]To simplify matters, we will ignore preferred stock in the present discussion.

[10]In recent years, a number of business loans and bonds have been issued with variable interest rates and profit-sharing clauses. However, these forms of business debt are still in a minority.

[11]Failure to meet interest or principal payments on debt is legally termed a *default.*

are potentially more volatile from year to year. For another, creditors often place restrictions on a borrower's actions. The ultimate hardship, *bankruptcy,* is certainly made more likely when debt exists. These disadvantages and others have led some firms to avoid borrowing almost completely. In reality, then, debt financing adds an element of risk as well as opportunity.[12] Management will attempt to balance these opposing forces so as to further the interests of their employers, the stockholders. Since all businesses use some degree of debt financing, the problem is one of deciding how much to use (i.e., in relation to equity). Before addressing this topic, we will examine in more detail the risks and rewards of financial leverage.

Financial Leverage   The intent of the present section is to reveal the way in which debt financing affects stockholders' earnings per share and return on equity. For this purpose, we will find it necessary to use only that portion of the income statement of direct concern to creditors and stockholders: *earnings before interest and taxes (EBIT)* through *net income (NI)*. The degree of leverage will be dictated by the *debt-to-assets ratio (D/A)* that, if you recall from chapter 2, is total liabilities divided by total assets. Thus, if D/A is .20 then 20% of all financing is in the form of debt and 80% is represented by equity. We shall make use of three additional financial relationships here: *return on equity (ROE)* = NI ÷ stockholders' equity; *return on assets (ROA)* = EBIT ÷ total assets and *earnings per share (EPS)*.

Application: The Stritch Company requires $40,000,000 in total assets. These assets can be financed in varying proportions of debt and equity. Equity capital will be obtained through the sale of common stock at $40 a share, while debt funds can be acquired with bonds paying 10% annual interest. To finance the entire $40 million in assets with equity would thus require the issuance of one million shares of common stock. Furthermore, this firm is in a 40% ordinary income tax bracket. The results of five different degrees of leverage are displayed in table 11.4 under the assumption that the ROA is 20% (i.e., EBIT is $8 million).

Table 11.4   **The Impact of Varying Degrees of Financial Leverage on Return on Equity and Earnings per Share**

Debt-to-assets ratio	0	.20	.40	.60	.80
Debt	$0	$ 8,000,000	$16,000,000	$24,000,000	$32,000,000
Equity	40,000,000	32,000,000	24,000,000	16,000,000	8,000,000
Shares of stock	1,000,000	800,000	600,000	400,000	200,000
EBIT	$ 8,000,000	$ 8,000,000	$ 8,000,000	$ 8,000,000	$ 8,000,000
Interest (10%)	−0	− 800,000	− 1,600,000	− 2,400,000	− 3,200,000
EBT	$ 8,000,000	$ 7,200,000	$ 6,400,000	$ 5,600,000	$ 4,800,000
Taxes (40%)	− 3,200,000	− 2,880,000	− 2,560,000	− 2,240,000	− 1,920,000
Net income	$ 4,800,000	$ 4,320,000	$ 3,840,000	$ 3,360,000	$ 2,880,000
Return on equity	12%	13.5%	16%	21%	36%
EPS	$4.80	$5.40	$6.40	$8.40	$14.40

[12]It is often called *financial risk* in order to distinguish it from asset risk.

Table 11.5   The Relationship between Financial Leverage, Return on Assets, and Stockholder Returns

D/A = 0%

Return on assets	−10%	0%	10%	20%	30%
EBIT	($4,000,000)	$0	$4,000,000	$8,000,000	$12,000,000
Interest (10%)	−0	−0	−0	−0	−0
EBT	($4,000,000)	$0	$4,000,000	$8,000,000	$12,000,000
Taxes (40%)	−(1,600,000)	−0	− 1,600,000	− 3,200,000	− 4,800,000
Net income	($2,400,000)	$0	$2,400,000	$4,800,000	$7,200,000
Return on equity	(6%)	0%	6%	12%	18%
EPS (1,000,000 shares)	($2.40)	$0	$2.40	$4.80	$7.20

D/A = 60%

Return on assets	−10%	0%	10%	20%	30%
EBIT	($4,000,000)	$0	$4,000,000	$8,000,000	$12,000,000
Interest (10%)	− 2,400,000	− 2,400,000	− 2,400,000	− 2,400,000	− 2,400,000
EBT	($6,400,000)	($2,400,000)	$1,600,000	$5,600,000	$9,600,000
Taxes (40%)	− (2,560,000)	− (960,000)	− 640,000	− 2,240,000	− 3,840,000
Net income	($3,840,000)	($1,440,000)	$ 960,000	$3,360,000	$ 5,760,000
Return on equity	(24%)	(9%)	6%	21%	36%
EPS (400,000 shares)	($9.60)	($3.60)	$2.40	$8.40	$14.40

Under the all-equity situation, ROE is 12% and EPS equals $4.80. Exchanging $8 million of debt for equity leads to an increase in both ROE and EPS despite the fact that EBIT remains unchanged. As more and more debt is used in place of equity the shareholders experience ever-increasing rewards. At the highest leverage position, ROE and EPS have increased two hundred percent, from 12% to 36% and $4.80 to $14.40, respectively.

This extremely favorable example of financial leverage is purposely misleading, however. The outcome here is heavily influenced by the given ROA and resulting EBIT. We would observe a much different outcome should the ROA fall appreciably below 20%. This can be seen by comparing the all-equity financial structure with one of the leveraged alternatives (e.g., D/A = 60%) for different ROAs.

In table 11.5, ROA takes on values from −10% to a positive 30%. It is evident that the impact of a varying ROA and EBIT on stockholders is quite different for the two financial structures. *The potential ROE and EPS under the leveraged situation are much higher than the all-equity alternative. On the other hand, stockholders can suffer to a greater extent with the leveraged financial structure*■

Earnings variability is certainly more likely in the presence of financial leverage. Net income can be high one year, and low or negative the next. As we saw in chapter 4, uncertainty of this kind is translated into risk in the minds of most investors. Furthermore, an extended period of negative earnings will lead to financial insolvency and, with it, bankruptcy. Bankruptcy is the ultimate risk facing investors. With financial leverage, then, one must be prepared to take the good with the bad. Furthermore, the extremes between good and bad increase as the proportion of debt rises.[13]

---

[13]Interest rates can also be expected to rise as a firm increases the level of debt.

Figure 11.5   Financial leverage in a probability distribution context

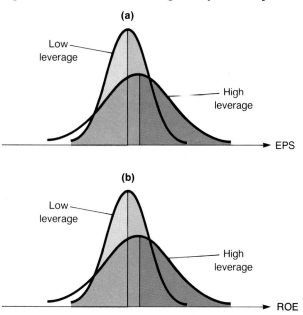

If it is possible to describe a company's EPS and ROE as normally distributed random variables, then we can display the effects of leverage as shown in figure 11.5. Note that expected EPS and ROE are superior for the high leverage situation but they are also much more variable and thus riskier.

A Further Look at Financial Leverage   A graphical representation of the relationship between EBIT, EPS, and leverage is shown in figure 11.6. Figure 11.6 was derived from the information in table 11.4. Several things can be gleaned from this diagram: (1) The 60% D/A financial structure requires an EBIT of $2,400,000 (the interest charges) before EPS becomes positive; (2) EPS are equal for the two alternatives when EBIT amounts to $4,000,000. This is referred to as the *indifference EBIT;* (3) Beyond the indifference EBIT there is an advantage to debt financing. EBITs lower than $4 million, however, favor all-equity financing; and (4) The sensitivity of EPS to leverage is revealed by the slope of the curve. The greater the degree of leverage, the greater the slope.

A graphical representation of the relationship among ROA, ROE, and leverage is also illuminating. Again using the information in table 11.4, figure 11.7 was constructed. As in figure 11.6, the curve representing a 60% D/A financial structure has a much greater slope than the all-equity curve. This signifies that a given change in ROA will have a greater impact (both positive and negative) on ROE under the leveraged situation. When there is

Figure 11.6   Graphical depiction of the relationship between EPS, EBIT, and leverage

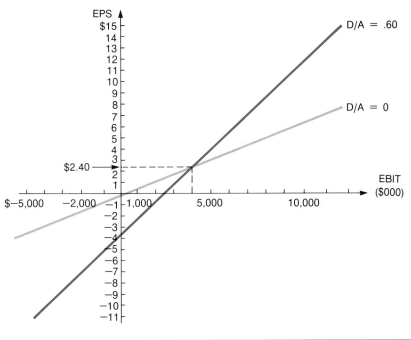

no debt in existence, the stockholders can obtain some return on their investment even though the assets are returning very little. With leverage, however, ROA must be at a certain level before the owners reap any rewards (in this case 6%). At an ROA of 10%, the two alternative financial structures provide the same ROE (i.e., 6%). This is the *indifference ROA* that corresponds to the indifference EBIT in figure 11.6. Beyond the indifference ROA, there is an advantage to debt financing. Below this point, however, the advantage lies with an all-equity financial structure.

Although it is not evident from figure 11.7, the indifference ROA of 10% is identical to the 10% cost of borrowed funds used in this example. This observation brings us to an important financial principle: *businesses can use financial leverage to achieve greater returns on their stockholders' investments and higher earnings per share whenever ROA exceeds the interest rate paid on borrowed funds.* A firm that can borrow money at one rate and turn around and invest it in assets at a higher rate will generate greater profit for its owners. Were it possible to predict ROA with certainty, then it would be a relatively easy matter to determine the appropriate degree of financial leverage: all or none. Since this is seldom possible, a business is left with a difficult decision to make. What level of debt is optimal from the standpoint of potential rewards and possible risks? We will approach this question from a theoretical standpoint first and then a practical perspective.

Figure 11.7   Graphical depiction of the relationship between ROA, ROE, and leverage

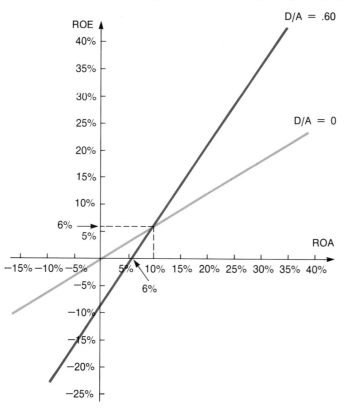

Optimal Degree of Financial Leverage: Theory

An excellent way to approach the financial leverage issue is by examining the financing costs of a corporation. Debt and equity funds are obtained in the financial markets at a cost. These costs are the required rates of return demanded by investors and they contain risk premiums to compensate for the dangers of financial leverage just as they contain premiums to compensate for asset risk. *The objective of the firm is to find the combination of debt and equity that produces the lowest weighted average cost of financing.* By doing so, stockholder wealth will be maximized.

In the discussion to follow we will assume that there is only one form of equity capital (common stock) and a single type of debt (bonds). These assumptions are made merely to simplify the presentation. They in no way alter the general conclusions to be reached. The percentage cost of equity will be represented by the symbol K_e and the percentage cost of debt (i.e., interest rate) by the symbol K_d. The weighted average cost of financing is K and it is found with equation 11.1.

Figure 11.8   Traditional theory of financial leverage

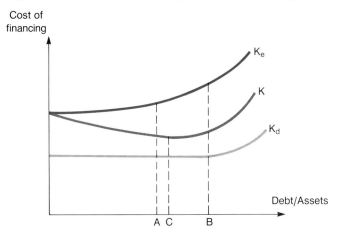

Equation 11.1 $K = W_dK_d + W_eK_e$

Where:

W_d = The weight ascribed to debt financing and it is calculated with the debt-to-asset ratio

W_e = The weight ascribed to equity financing and it is calculated with the equity-to-asset ratio, or $1 -$ debt-to-asset ratio

For example, given $K_e = 18\%$, $K_d = 12\%$, and a debt-to-asset ratio of .40, the weighted average cost of financing would be $K = (.40)(12\%) + (.60)(18\%) = 15.6\%$.

There are three major theories regarding financial leverage: traditional, Modigliani–Miller, and contemporary. As we shall see, the two major elements in each of these theories are their assumptions regarding investor attitudes toward the risks of debt financing, and the way legal complications (e.g., taxes and bankruptcy) are incorporated.

Traditional Theory   The traditional theory of financial leverage holds that an optimal amount of debt financing exists for each business. In other words, by using lower cost debt in place of equity, the weighted average cost of financing (K) for a business will decline up to a point and then increase as more debt is used. The main reason given for this outcome is that investors in bonds and stocks are little concerned about the risks of borrowing when leverage is relatively low, but make an about-face as leverage becomes excessive. This increased concern about debt leads both groups of investors to require greater compensation for the added risk. This is shown in figure 11.8.

Figure 11.8 is constructed so that leverage (as measured by the debt-to-asset ratio) increases from left to right. At the extreme left there is no debt and, therefore, K is equal to K_e. When debt is first exchanged for equity, K_e rises gradually as stockholders demand only minor compensation for the additional risk. K_d remains constant. The increasing K_e is outweighed by the lower K_d causing K to decline. Once leverage has grown to a critical level

Figure 11.9   M–M theory of financial leverage

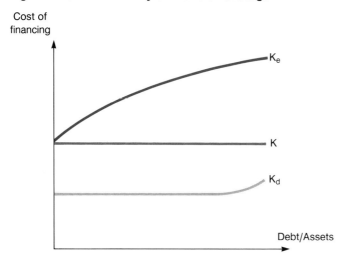

(point A), K_e begins to rise at a much faster rate and eventually overwhelms K_d, thus leading to a reversal in K. The weighted average cost of financing then begins to rise dramatically at the point (B) that creditors become nervous and demand higher interest rates on their bonds. A minimum K is achieved at debt-to-asset ratio C. This point dictates the optimal degree of financial leverage. Furthermore, it is reasonable to expect the optimal leverage to vary from one company and industry to another.

Modigliani–Miller Theory   In a classic article, *Franco Modigliani and Merton Miller (M–M)* countered the long-held traditional theory of financial leverage.[14] A brief summary of their argument is presented here.

M–M essentially said that in a perfect financial environment, unfettered by laws, taxes, transactions costs, and investor ignorance, it is not possible to reduce a firm's average financing cost by the use of debt. They base their position on the premise that stockholders and creditors will respond sooner and more firmly to debt financing than the traditional theory indicates. This response will affect the costs of debt and equity such that their weighted average will not change. The M–M theory is presented in figure 11.9.

The cost curves in figure 11.9 are drawn based on the reasonable assumption that stockholders are much more sensitive to the risks of leverage than creditors. However, as leverage becomes very high, creditors begin to lose most of the protection afforded by their preferred position and substantially raise their interest rates in response.

At zero leverage, K is equal to K_e. As debt enters into the financial structure of a company the risk to owners increases, leading them to require higher and higher returns on their investment. More importantly, however, the owners will respond much sooner and more forcefully than in the traditional theory.

---

[14]Franco Modigliani and Merton H. Miller, "The Cost of Capital, Corporation Finance, and the Theory of Investment," *The American Economic Review*, Vol. XLVIII, No. 3 (June 1958), pp. 261–97.

According to M–M, at all levels of debt K_e is exactly sufficient to offset the lower K_d and, thus, hold K constant. The benefits of lower cost debt are offset by the additional risks. Consequently, there is no value in using financial leverage and, thus, there exists no optimal degree of leverage. And why should there be? After all, a business' real resources (i.e., products, labor force, assets, and management) and earnings (EBIT) are unaffected by how the firm is financed. Leverage simply affects the way EBIT is divided.

M–M go on to state that even if debt could be used to lower a firm's average cost of financing, there is no need for the corporation to do the borrowing. The stockholders could borrow on their own (homemade leverage) to partially finance the purchase of stock.

Contemporary Theory   The contemporary theory of financial leverage contends that M–M are correct given their assumptions and the traditional view is correct, but for the wrong reasons. According to the contemporary theory, some of M–M's assumptions are not realistic. More importantly, however, relaxing these assumptions will have an uneven influence on debt and equity financing. *There are two factors in particular that can lead to an optimal degree of financial leverage for a given firm: the tax deductibility of interest expense and bankruptcy costs.*[15]

Interest payments to creditors are tax deductible expenses for a corporation. For example, 50% ordinary income tax rate means that a 16% interest rate actually costs the firm 8% after taxes. The government is paying the other 8%, in effect, by allowing this firm to reduce its taxable income and, thus, income taxes. No such tax deduction is allowed on the dividend payments to stockholders. Here we have a government supported bias in favor of debt financing, and it is substantial. In the example above, creditors require 16%, but the company must pay only 8%. Because of this "tax effect," a company can substantially lower its weighted average cost of financing with the use of debt.[16] According to the contemporary theory, bankruptcy, another legal complication, is the overriding factor in keeping financial leverage from being extremely high. The time, legal expense, and uncertainty associated with bankruptcy proceedings increase the risks for stockholders and creditors. As a result, they will raise their required rates of return to account for these greater risks. The effects of taxes and bankruptcy on the costs of financing are shown in figure 11.10.

There are two costs of debt shown in figure 11.10. The dashed curve (K_d) is the cost of debt without consideration of tax deductibility while K_d^* is the cost of debt after taxes (i.e., K_d multiplied by one minus the tax rate). As debt is added to the financial structure, the average cost of financing (K) declines due to K_d^* being lower than K_d. After a point, bankruptcy costs start to outweigh the tax benefits of debt and K rises. Thus, an optimal degree of leverage exists.

---

[15]Another factor that seems to be gaining recognition is the influence of corporate stockholder limited liability on debt. According to this argument, stockholders may be willing to go more deeply into debt than otherwise, because they are protected on the downside by limited liability. The benefits of financial leverage are unlimited, but the costs are not. This idea comes under the subject of "agency relationships."

[16]As a matter of fact, M–M recognized the importance of taxes in their original article.

Figure 11.10   Contemporary theory of financial leverage

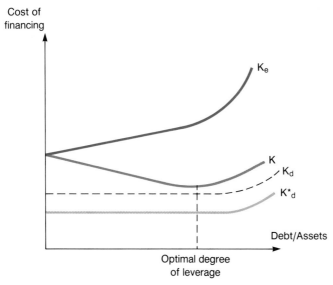

Source: Taken from the *1984 Historical Chartbook*, Board of Governors of the Federal Reserve System, Washington, D.C., p. 96.

Conclusion   *Both traditional and contemporary theories specify an optimal degree of financial leverage, but their reasons are different.* The traditional theory attributes the falling and then rising average cost of financing to changing investor attitudes toward risk. The contemporary theory claims that K declines because of the favorable tax treatment accorded debt and then rises at relatively high degrees of leverage, due to the high costs associated with bankruptcy proceedings.

Most finance professionals in business and the academic community endorse either the contemporary or traditional theories or some combination of the two. That is, they believe that debt financing can be of value to a business by lowering its weighted average cost of financing.

Having considered the various theories surrounding financial leverage, we are prepared to discuss the practical side of this subject.

Optimal Degree of Financial Leverage: Practice

There is general agreement that financial leverage can be beneficial to most businesses. A consensus also believes there is a unique optimal degree of leverage for each of those companies. The trouble is, how does a business determine approximately what its optimal debt-to-asset ratio is? Several procedures incorporating statistics have been developed to deal with this problem. References to many of these are included in the reading list at the end of this chapter. The objectives of the present discussion are simply to frame the problem and point out some important considerations.

The Ideal Situation   The optimal degree of financial leverage is the one that provides the lowest weighted average cost of financing. Under ideal conditions, management would be able to predict the costs of equity and debt for various degrees of financial leverage. That is, the risk premiums for each class of investor can be foretold. Selecting the optimal debt-to-asset ratio would then be a simple matter, as the following example illustrates.

Example: A company can have any one of nine degrees of financial leverage, ranging from zero to .80. The projected cost of equity and after-tax cost debt for each alternative and the corresponding weighted average (calculated with equation 11.1) are shown in table 11.6.

Table 11.6   Determining the Minimum Average Cost of Financing

D/A	0	.10	.20	.30	.40	.50	.60	.70	.80
$K_d^{\cdot}$	5%	5%	5%	5.5%	5.5%	6.0%	6.5%	7.5%	9%
K_e	12%	12.5%	13%	13.5%	14%	14.5%	15.5%	17%	19%
K	12%	11.75%	11.4%	11.1%	10.6%	10.25%	10.1%	10.35%	11%

It is evident that the financial structure with 60% debt is optimal. By selecting this alternative, the average cost of financing can be reduced from 12% to 10.1%, not an inconsiderable sum. Unfortunately, financial managers do not have the luxury of such perfect foresight and must look elsewhere for a solution ∎

Important Considerations   Some of the more important considerations for management regarding the appropriate level of debt are briefly described below.

1. *Sales Stability:* As a general rule, companies with stable year-to-year sales revenues can carry more debt in their financial structures. Stable sales implying, not always correctly, that there will be stable EBIT.
2. *Collateral:* Considering the fact that many loans must be backed by collateral, a firm with many collaterable assets is in a better position to borrow money. A collaterable asset is one that can be sold at a predictable price and without undue effort.
3. *Control:* Controlling stockholders in a corporation may find it necessary to use debt financing in order to maintain control of the business. This situation could arise if, for some reason, the only available source of equity is the sale of stock to other investors. By bringing in other stockholders, control of the business would be diluted. However, this would not occur if the funds are raised through the sale of bonds or bank loans.
4. *Interest Rates:* The same interest rate is not charged to all businesses, and interest rates do not remain unchanged. As the cost of debt approaches the cost of equity, financial leverage becomes less attractive.
5. *Tax Rate:* All other things the same, the higher a firm's tax rate the greater the advantage to borrowing money. This of course refers to the tax deductibility feature of interest payments.
6. *Stockholder Attitudes:* A survey of owner attitudes regarding the appropriate degree of financial leverage can be helpful.

Table 11.7   Selected Industry Debt-to-Equity Ratios

Industry	Debt/Equity
Airlines	2.3
Clothing	1.2
Coal mining	1.1
Auto manufacturing	2.0
Dairy production	0.9
Furniture manufacturing	0.8
Newspaper publishing	0.7
Farm machinery	1.9
Computer manufacturing	1.2
Household appliances	1.1
Railroad transportation	1.4
Radio & TV broadcasting	1.2
Grocery stores	1.8
Restaurants and bars	2.6

From the book *Almanac of Business and Industrial Financial Ratios,* 1984 edition, by Leo Troy. Copyright © 1984 by Prentice-Hall, Inc. Published by Prentice-Hall, Inc., Englewood Cliffs, N.J. 07632.

7. *Management Attitudes:* While it is true that management's main concern should be the owners, as a practical matter it is difficult for them not to interject their personal feelings. Consequently, the amount of a debt a company employs will be affected by management's attitudes toward this element of risk.

8. *Expected Inflation:* There is an old saying in economics that debtors gain during inflationary times because they can repay interest and principal in deflated dollars. This statement is only true, however, when the interest rate includes an inflation premium less than the actual future inflation. A management that goes into debt merely to benefit from future inflation is betting that its inflation forecast is superior to the lender's inflation forecast.

9. *Industry Averages:* The average debt-to-asset ratio for the industry in which a company operates can serve as a reference point. A degree of financial leverage significantly different from that of the industry generally requires considerable explanation. Financial leverage is heavily influenced by the characteristics of an industry as revealed in table 11.7. There we see that debt-to-equity ratios range from a high of 2.6 to a low of 0.7.

10. *Free Financing:* Finally, a company should take advantage of all the free debt financing it can get. This could include accrued wages, taxes payable, and accounts payable.

Conclusion   A business should attempt to identify its optimal degree of financial leverage. Once having done so, the company should see to it that the optimal debt-to-asset ratio is achieved. Preferably, this debt-to-asset ratio will be maintained at all times unless and until underlying factors change, thereby leading to a new optimum. However, given the volatility of financial markets and tax laws, these changes can occur frequently.

Financial Structure: Debt Maturity

Subsequent to determining the optimal amount of debt to use in its financial structure, a business must select the appropriate maturity composition for that debt. Maturity composition is the proportional amount of liabilities with various maturities, such as: 20% due in three months, 25% due in three months to a year, 15% due in one year to five years, 10% due in five years to fifteen years, and 30% due in more than fifteen years. Due to the fact that common stock and retained earnings have no fixed due date, the maturity decision is relegated to liabilities. Debt maturity can have a profound effect on the profitability and risk of a company as the following discussion will reveal.

A business can borrow money for practically any length of time. What, if any, considerations should be given to the selection of debt maturities? A good starting point for this presentation is to restate the reason for financing. Recall that funds are obtained via equity and liabilities solely for the purpose of acquiring the use of assets. The returns (ROA) generated by these assets should be sufficient to cover the costs of the financing (i.e., interest and dividends). *It stands to reason therefore, that the lives of a firm's assets would have some bearing on the maturities of its financial obligations, specifically liabilities.* And so they will. When debt maturities are shorter than asset lives the debt must be refinanced. Conversely, when debt maturities exceed asset lives a reinvestment in new assets is required. *Refinancing* and *reinvestment* can have a large influence on a company's profitability and risk, as the following application will reveal.

Application: The relationship among asset life, debt maturity, profitability, and risk can be best understood with an example. In this example, Carter Company, Inc., wishes to buy a single asset, a semitrailer truck, and the optimal degree of financial leverage calls for 50% debt and 50% equity. The truck is expected to last for five years and it will cost $100,000. One half of the cost, or $50,000, will be obtained with common stock, and the remaining $50,000 can be acquired through a bank loan. The loan can be obtained for one year, five years, or fifteen years according to the firm's wishes. Regardless of which maturity is selected, the interest rate will be 12% over the life of the loan. Assuming a 30% income tax rate and an ROA of 16% in each year of the truck's life, this business would have first-year results as shown below:

EBIT	$16,000
Interest at 12%	6,000
EBT	$10,000
Taxes at 30%	3,000
NI	$ 7,000
ROE	14%

Stockholders can achieve an ROE of 14% the first year of the truck's life regardless of whether the firm borrows for one, five, or fifteen years. However, if the loan is for only one year, then it must be *refinanced* at the end of the first year in order to continue carrying the asset. Refinancing can be harmful if interest rates have risen during the year. Let us assume that the initial loan was for one year and interest rates have risen from 12% to 15%. With a new 15% loan on the books, the results for the second year would be as follows:

EBIT	$16,000
Interest at 15%	7,500
EBT	$ 8,500
Taxes at 30%	2,550
NI	$ 5,950
ROE	11.9%

Net income and ROE fall as a result of having to refinance at a higher interest rate.[17] On the other hand, profitability would not have changed had the loan been for five or fifteen years since a 12% interest rate would remain in effect. Each time a refinancing takes place there exists a risk of paying higher interest rates. On the other hand, refinancing can raise NI and ROE if loan interest rates fall.

There is no need to refinance the five-year and fifteen-year loans during the life of the truck. A fifteen-year loan, however, creates a new set of problems. After five years, the asset will no longer exist, but the loan has ten years left to run at 12% interest. The problem now becomes one of *reinvestment* in a new asset. A new truck can be purchased in five years, but the ROA may not be as high as on the original asset. A business recession may be underway, and, as a result, a new truck will only generate an ROA of, say, 7%. An investment in this asset would produce the following results for the sixth through tenth years.

EBIT	$7,000
Interest at 12%	− 6,000
EBT	$1,000
Taxes at 30%	300
NI	$ 700
ROE	1.4%

The NI and ROE are very low in this case. But the firm is in a bind; it must earn something to pay the ongoing interest charges.[18] Had the loan been for one or five years, the business could simply decide not to reinvest in such a low yielding asset, or maybe a new loan can be acquired at a reduced cost because interest rates have fallen along with the ROA. For example, a new loan at 4% interest could make an asset returning only 7% very attractive. The fifteen-year loan does not provide for this kind of flexibility.

Each time a reinvestment is required, there exists the risk of earning a lower return on the new asset. It is also true, however, that the fifteen-year loan could turn out to be a superior alternative if the return on the replacement asset is higher ∎

The objective of the preceding example was to expose those risks and rewards that occur when a business does not equate the maturity of its liabilities with the lives of its assets. *The conservative approach to debt maturity is a matching strategy whereby debt maturity equals asset life.* (A five-year truck is funded with a five-year loan.) It is more or less neutral in its effects. To select one of the other two alternatives is to inflict the firm with additional risk for which there should be a real possibility of additional profit. As indicated in the application above, refinancing and reinvestment can be rewarding only if interest rates fall or ROA rises, respectively. Unfortunately, predicting which way either of these will go is very difficult. Nevertheless, many businesses frequently conclude that the potential rewards of reinvestment or refinancing outweigh the risks.

The matching strategy does not require that a business finance every asset with a loan of equal duration. A reasonable solution can be obtained by equating the average asset life to the average debt maturity.

---

[17]Another option would be to sell the truck and use the proceeds to get out of debt. The trouble with this alternative is that the truck may not bring a satisfactory price.

[18]It may be possible to terminate the loan before maturity. However, this usually requires the payment of a sizable penalty.

Table 11.8   Debt Maturity Considerations

1. Asset Life > Debt Maturity: refinancing is required in this situation. The risk in such a strategy is that interest rates may rise in the future. Profits can be increased if interest rates fall in the future.
2. Asset Life < Debt Maturity: reinvestment is required in this situation. The risk in this strategy is that asset rates of return may fall in the future. Profits can be enhanced if ROAs rise in the future.
3. Asset Life = Debt Maturity: neither reinvestment nor refinancing is required in this case. Consequently, there is no risk associated with this strategy. On the other hand, there is no opportunity to take advantage of beneficial changes in interest rates or ROAs.

There are two additional factors that can influence the choice of debt maturities: the term structure of interest rates and flotation costs. The first topic was covered briefly in chapter 6. The *term structure of interest rates* acknowledges the fact that loans and bonds of varying maturities typically have different interest rates. Furthermore, it is normal for rates to increase with maturity (i.e., the longer the maturity the higher the interest rate) as figure 11.11 reveals.

As indicated in figure 11.11, in times past it has often been less expensive to borrow short-term, sometimes significantly so. Such differences in the relative costs of short-term and long-term debt may induce a company to move away from a matching strategy. For example, a business might finance a ten-year asset with a two-year loan simply because two-year interest rates are currently lower than ten-year rates. However, this in no way reduces the risk of having to refinance at higher rates in the future.

Figure 11.11   Long-term and short-term interest rates

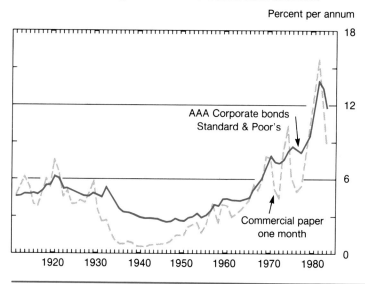

While the term structure of interest rates tends to favor debt that is shorter term than assets, flotation costs do just the opposite. *Flotation costs* consist of the various fixed expenses that are encountered in fund raising: legal fees, paperwork, commissions, etc. The frequent refinancings that are required when debt maturities are less than asset lives subject a firm to high-flotation costs. In some cases, flotation costs are so prohibitive that they favor the use of a debt maturity longer than asset life.

Summary

Financial forecasting, or, as some refer to it, financial planning, is intended to provide a financial manager with information on the size, timing, and duration of funding requirements. This information is useful in planning and preparing for financing. Regression analysis is a helpful technique for measuring permanent funding requirements (related to permanent assets). Cash budgets, on the other hand, are quite useful in measuring temporary funding needs (related to temporary assets).

Financial leverage and the maturity composition of debt combine to determine a company's financial structure. Financial leverage refers to the relationship between debt and equity, as measured by the debt-to-asset ratio. The maturity composition of debt is concerned with the maturities or lives of a firm's liabilities.

Decisions regarding financial leverage are especially crucial to a firm and its owners. Therefore, careful attention should be directed toward the profit and risk consequences of varying degrees of financial leverage. The maturity composition of debt is also important to a company. The safest maturity composition strategy is to match the lives of a firm's liabilities to the lives of its assets. By following this prescription, a business can avoid the risks associated with reinvestment and refinancing ■

Appendix: Operating Leverage

Most businesses have some discretion over the relative proportions of capital assets and labor that are utilized in the production process. A *labor-intensive* firm is one that uses a relatively large work force to produce a given level of output. A clothing manufacturer is an example of such an enterprise. A *capital-intensive* firm, on the other hand, utilizes substantial numbers of capital assets, such as equipment, tools, buildings, and machinery. Electric utilities are good examples of capital-intensive companies.

Labor is considered to be a variable input, since it can usually be altered to fit a firm's sales and production volume. Thus, an increase in volume can be met by adding more workers and/or working the existing labor force longer hours. Conversely, a reduction in volume can be accompanied by, for example, worker layoffs. It is precisely because of this flexibility that labor usage is thought to be a *variable operating cost* (i.e., wages and employee benefits). Other variable costs also exist, for such things as materials usage and sales commissions.

Most capital assets are fixed inputs in the sense that they are impractical and uneconomical to add to or subtract from as volume changes.[19] Nevertheless, a fixed stock of capital can normally be used in the production of a wide range of volume. Because of these characteristics, capital asset usage is considered a fixed operating cost (i.e., depreciation and rent). In addition to capital assets, fixed costs are incurred for things like executive salaries, advertising, and certain types of research and development.[20]

---

[19]We are referring here to temporary variations in volume. More permanent changes in a company's output can be met with additions to or subtractions from the stock of capital, if so desired.

[20]A third category of costs are semi-variable costs. A semi-variable cost is one that contains both a fixed portion and a variable portion.

As we saw in our earlier discussion of capital budgeting, capital assets can often be substituted for labor with desirable consequences. However, an important consideration in such a decision is the impact that fixed operating costs can have on earnings. The presence of fixed operating costs can magnify changes in a firm's earnings whenever sales rise and fall. This phenomenon is termed *operating leverage.* Furthermore, earnings changes are magnified more so as fixed operating costs (capital assets) increase in proportion to variable operating costs (labor), that is, as the degree of operating leverage rises. The impact on operating leverage on earnings can be observed most clearly if we focus on earnings before interest and taxes (EBIT) rather than net income.

Two measures are particularly helpful in analyzing operating leverage: contribution margin and break even. The *contribution margin* tells the percentage of a firm's revenue that can be applied to fixed cost and profit. It is found as follows:

Equation 11.2   Contribution Margin $= 1 -$ Variable Cost Percentage of Sales

Break even is the sales volume at which total revenue equals total cost and earnings are zero. When sales are above the break-even level earnings are positive. At sales levels below break even, earnings become negative. Break even can be found as follows:

Equation 11.3 $\text{Break even} = \dfrac{\text{Fixed Cost}}{\text{Contribution Margin}}$

Application: Kermit, Inc., can manufacture and sell its products in either of two ways:

Alternative A (Low Operating Leverage): Fixed costs are $5,000,000 per year and variable costs amount to 70% of sales. Accordingly, the contribution margin is $1 - .70 = 30\%$.

Alternative B (High Operating Leverage): Fixed costs are $12,000,000 per year and variable costs amount to 40% of sales. Accordingly, the contribution margin is $1 - .40 = 60\%$.

Both sets of cost figures apply only over a *relevant annual sales range* of $15,000,000 to $35,000,000. The firm's expected annual sales are $25,000,000. Table 11.9 describes the effects on EBIT under each alternative for given levels of sales.

Table 11.9   The Impact of Varying Degrees of Operating Leverage on Earnings before Interest and Taxes

	Alternative A *Low Operating Leverage*		
Sales	$15,000,000	$25,000,000	$35,000,000
Fixed cost	− 5,000,000	− 5,000,000	− 5,000,000
Variable cost (.70)	− 10,500,000	− 17,500,000	− 24,500,000
EBIT	($500,000)	$ 2,500,000	$ 5,500,000

	Alternative B *High Operating Leverage*		
Sales	$15,000,000	$25,000,000	$35,000,000
Fixed cost	− 12,000,000	− 12,000,000	− 12,000,000
Variable cost (.40)	− 6,000,000	− 10,000,000	− 14,000,000
EBIT	($3,000,000)	$ 3,000,000	$ 9,000,000

Figure 11.12a   Low operating leverage

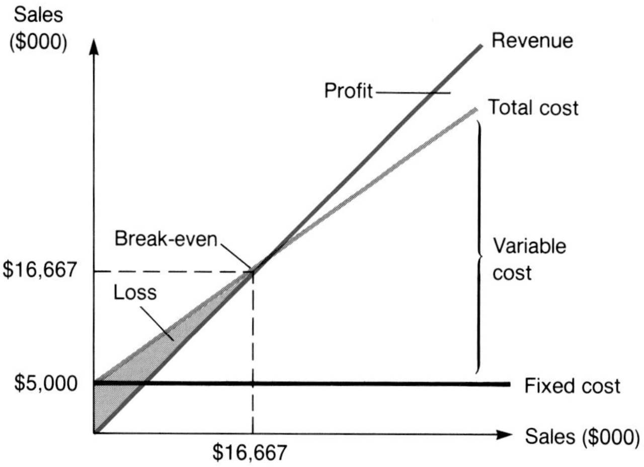

Alternative A's break-even sales volume is:

$$\text{Break Even} = \frac{\text{Fixed Costs}}{\text{Contribution Margin}} = \frac{\$5,000,000}{.30} = \$16,666,666$$

Alternative B's break-even sales volume is:

$$\text{Break Even} = \frac{\text{Fixed Costs}}{\text{Contribution Margin}} = \frac{\$12,000,000}{.60} = \$20,000,000$$

It is evident that earnings can take on a much wider range of values under the high operating leverage alternative. For instance, if sales are $35,000,000, B will produce an EBIT of $9,000,000, whereas A's profit would amount to only $5,500,000. At the other extreme, a sales of $15 million will generate a negative EBIT for alternative B of $3 million, whereas alternative A would suffer a loss of only $500,000. Alternative B's much greater potential loss can be attributed to a higher level of fixed costs that must be met regardless of what revenues happen to be. On the other hand, B has superior earnings potential due to a much larger contribution margin (60% for B versus 30% for A). Alternative A has both a lower profit potential and less exposure to losses. Furthermore, A's break-even level is significantly lower than B's ($16,666,666 versus $20 million). To B's credit, its earnings are superior to A's at the expected sales level of $25 million. From the standpoint of Kermit, Inc. and its investors the high operating leverage alternative (B) is both riskier and potentially more rewarding than the low operating leverage alternative (A). It is within this context that a decision between these alternatives should be made.

Before leaving this topic, it will be helpful to examine Kermit, Inc.'s operating leverage predicament diagramatically. This is accomplished in figures 11.12a and 11.12b, which are constructed from the information in table 11.9 ■

Figure 11.12b   High operating leverage

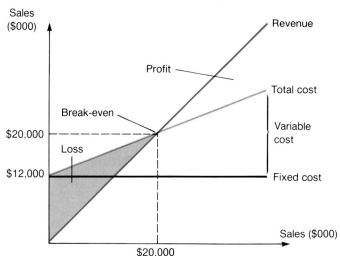

Questions

1. What is measured with cash budgets?

2. Two facets of debt financing create the opportunity for exceptional stockholder profits. What are they?

3. Does it seem reasonable that firms in the same industry would have similar debt-to-asset ratios? Explain.

4. Preferred stock can be used to obtain financial leverage, but not with the same consequences as debt (e.g., loans and bonds). Why are the consequences not the same?

5. Why are creditors willing to accept a lower RRR than equity investors?

6. Discuss the following statement: "while the explicit cost of debt may be lower than the cost of equity, one must also take into account the implicit cost of debt when comparing the two types of financing."

7. The contemporary theory of financial leverage reaches a conclusion that more closely resembles which of the other two theories?

8. Explain how the risks and rewards of financial leverage are captured in the weighted average cost of financing.

9. Briefly define the following: permanent assets, automatic liabilities, and maturity matching.

10. What is the danger or risk associated with refinancing?

Key Terms/Concepts

Automatic liabilities	Financial structure	Refinancing
Cash budget	Flotation costs	Reinvestment
Contribution margin	Maturity matching	Replacement financing
Debt maturity	Operating leverage	Temporary financing
Financial forecasting	Optimal level of debt	Weighted average cost of
Financial leverage	Permanent financing	financing

Problems

1. Derive the ROE from the following information: debt-to-asset ratio equals .40; interest rate on debt equals 12%; total assets are $500,000; tax rate is 30%; and ROA equals 20%.

2. A business has 20,000 shares of common stock outstanding and the current earnings per share are $1.25. What would EPS be if this firm borrowed $1 million at a 12% interest rate and invested the money in assets that earned 16%? Ignore income taxes.

3. Given a debt-to-asset ratio of .50, an ROA of 20%, a zero tax rate, and cost of debt equal to 15%, what is the ROE?

4. A debt-to-equity ratio of .40 corresponds to a debt-to-asset ratio of what?

5. An individual acquires an asset for $500,000 by borrowing $300,000 at an interest rate of 10% and financing the remainder with equity. What will be the ROE, if the asset earns a return of 20%, 10%, 5%? Ignore income taxes.

6. Given: common stock can be sold for $25 a share; the cost of debt is 8%; income tax rate equals 50%; total assets are $15 million; and a 15% ROA will produce an EBIT of $2,250,000. Required:
   A. Find the ROE and EPS for debt-to-asset ratios of 0, .25, .50, and .75.
   B. Repeat A by allowing the cost of debt to rise as financial leverage increases. The applicable interest rates will be 8% for the .25 Debt-to-Asset ratio, 10% for the .50 D/A ratio, and 13% for the .75 D/A ratio.

7. Compute the after-tax cost of debt (K_d') for the following problems:
   A. Interest rate is 16% and tax rate is 30%.
   B. Interest rate is 8% and tax rate is 40%.
   C. Interest rate is 12% and tax rate is 50%.
   D. Interest rate is 11% and tax rate is 42%.

8. The total asset requirements of a new business are $20 million. The company will be financially structured in one of two ways: (1) all equity—funds will be raised by selling 400,000 shares of common stock at $50 per share; (2) half equity and half debt—funds will be raised by selling 200,000 shares of stock at $50 per share and borrowing $10 million at a cost of 15%. The new firm's income tax rate is 35%. The assets of this company will generate one of five ROAs: −25%, −10%, 5%, 20%, or 35%. Show the impact of these ROAs and related EBITs on ROE and EPS under each of the two financial structures: (1) numerically and (2) graphically.

9. Referring to the preceding problem, let us assume that the probabilities of the five ROAs are as follows:

Return on Assets	Probability
-25%	.10
-10%	.15
5%	.30
20%	.25
35%	.20

Required:
   A. Find the expected value and standard deviation of EPS for the all-equity alternative.
   B. Find the expected value and standard deviation of EPS for the half-equity and half-debt alternative.
   C. Describe the findings in A and B.

10. Johnson, Inc., has debt of $4 million and equity of $6 million. The firm can borrow money at a cost of 12%. Stockholders, however, require a rate of return equal to 18%. Given an income tax rate of 25%, compute Johnson's after-tax weighted average cost of financing.

11. The total asset requirements of a new business are $75 million. This firm will be funded with one of three degrees of financial leverage: (1) raise $75 million in equity with 300,000 shares of common stock; (2) raise $50 million in equity with 200,000 shares of common stock and borrow $25 million at a cost of 12%; (3) raise $25 million in equity with 100,000 shares of common stock and borrow $50 million at a cost of 12%. The new firm will pay an income tax rate of 40%.
Required:

   A. Determine the EPS under each alternative for EBITs of -$10 million, $5 million, and $20 million.
   B. Graphically illustrate, on the same diagram, the EBIT-EPS relationship for each of the three degrees of financial leverage.
   C. What EBIT will produce the same EPS (indifference point) for all three alternative financial structures?
   D. Assuming that an EBIT of $15 million is assured, which degree of financial leverage is preferable?
   E. Why do these alternative financial structures have the same indifference point? Will this always be the case?

12. A company can be financed entirely by equity, in which case there will be 200,000 shares of stock. An alternative would be to use debt for half of the financing. By following this course of action, there will only be 100,000 shares of stock outstanding. The cost of the debt is $400,000 per year. Given a tax rate of 40%, what EBIT will produce the same EPS (indifference point) for the financing alternatives?

13. Displayed below are the costs of debt and equity that will be experienced by a business, according to the degree of financial leverage it chooses. Determine the debt-to-asset ratio that minimizes this company's weighted average cost of financing.

D/A Ratio	0	.10	.20	.30	.40	.50	.60	.70	.80	.90
K_d^*	8%	8%	8%	9%	10%	11%	13%	15%	18%	22%
K_e	13%	13%	14%	15%	17%	19%	22%	25%	28%	32%

14. Gytex, Inc. has been in business for six years. According to its most recent balance sheet, Gytex has $2 million in assets, no debt financing and 100,000 shares of common stock outstanding. The company needs to raise an additional $1 million for an expansion project. Gytex can borrow the entire amount at a cost of 12% or it can issue 50,000 shares of common stock for $20 per share. The company's income tax rate is 45%.
Required:
   A. For ROAs of 0%, 10%, 20%, 30%, and 40%, calculate the EPS and ROE associated with each financial structure.
   B. Graphically illustrate the EPS-EBIT and ROE-ROA relationships for each financing arrangement.
   C. Determine the indifference ROA and corresponding EBIT.

15. Carmel Enterprises' sales, total assets, and automatic liabilities for the last ten years are presented in the table below. Sales estimates for the next five years are as follows: (1985) $90,000,000; (1986) $92,500,000; (1987) $94,750,000; (1988) $96,000,000; and (1989) $99,600,000.
Required:
   A. Develop relationships between sales and assets and sales and automatic liabilities for forecasting purposes.
   B. Forecast Carmel Enterprises' financial requirements for each of the next five years.

Year	Sales	Total assets	Automatic liabilities
1975	$40,500,000	$20,100,000	$3,020,000
1976	46,225,000	22,190,000	3,325,000
1977	50,450,000	23,710,000	3,500,000
1978	65,500,000	29,475,000	4,420,000
1979	70,275,000	30,920,000	4,635,000
1980	60,350,000	29,450,000	4,415,000
1981	65,000,000	30,750,000	4,610,000
1982	72,500,000	31,500,000	4,725,000
1983	80,750,000	33,675,000	5,950,000
1984	85,400,000	36,020,000	5,380,000

16. It is late 1986 and the Walter Reagan Company is preparing its cash budget for 1987. Walter Reagan's sales are very seasonal, as shown in the accompanying table. Included in this table are sales for the last two months of 1986 and estimated monthly sales for 1987. In addition to being seasonal, all sales are made on credit. The historical payment pattern indicates that one-half of a given month's sales are collected the same month, while the balance is collected the following month.

	Month	Sales
1986	November	$650,000
	December	485,000
1987	January	405,000
	February	350,000
	March	280,000
	April	265,000
	May	220,000
	June	205,000
	July	190,000
	August	325,000
	September	380,000
	October	515,000
	November	890,000
	December	710,000

Each month, Walter Reagan manufactures goods that are to be sold in the following month. Manufacturing costs (i.e., wages, maintenance, and materials) are approximately 60% of sales and they are paid for in the month they are incurred. Selling and administrative expenses amount to 15% of sales each month. Lease payments of $25,000 and income taxes of $30,000 will be paid in March, June, September, and December. A $40,000 interest payment is due in March and another is due in September. Lastly, a machine must be replaced in August at a cost of $725,000. Construct the 1987 cash budget. Identify the months during which the company will require temporary financing. The company begins 1987 with a cash balance of $75,000, which also happens to be its minimum cash balance.

17. Canadian Sunset, Ltd., is an elite vacation resort located in northern British Columbia. It provides luxury accommodations, gourmet food, and first rate facilities for golf, tennis, horseback riding, and other forms of entertainment. Due to the inclement weather of the region, the resort is only open for business from June through September, August being its biggest month. It is now December, 1987, and the company is gathering data for the 1988 cash budget.

Projected billings for the coming summer are as follows: (June) $2,300,000; (July) $3,200,000; (August) $4,500,000; and (September) $2,000,000. By and large, guests pay their bills in the month following their stay. The monthly expense to run the resort during this time is expected to be $450,000 plus 30% of billings. There are a number of expenditures during the year in addition to these: insurance premiums in the amount of $75,000 and interest payments equal to $500,000 are to be paid in April and October; a $200,000 property tax payment is due in November; dividends equal to $450,000 and income taxes amounting to $400,000 shall be paid in February, May, August, and November; a lawsuit will be settled for $250,000 in January. During the eight months that the resort is closed, a considerable amount of activity and expense continues. For example, repairs and maintenance, care for the horses, taking reservations and record keeping. These off-season expenses should be about $200,000 per month.

Prepare the 1988 cash budget for Canadian Sunset, Ltd. Will the resort need temporary funding? When is it needed? For how long shall the funding be necessary? What level of financing is required? You may assume that Canadian Sunset, Ltd., starts 1988 with a cash balance of $400,000, although its desired minimum cash reserve is only $200,000.

18. A shipping company is going to acquire a new $500,000 tugboat that is expected to last for six years. The boat will be financed with debt and there are two maturities available: (1) a six-year loan can be obtained at an interest rate of 15%, or (2) three consecutive two-year loans can be arranged, the cost of the first one being 13%. Given an income tax rate of 40% and assuming that the tugboat's ROA will be 20% in each of its six years, do the following:
    A. Calculate the annual net income generated by the tugboat, assuming that it is financed with the six-year loan.
    B. Calculate the annual net income generated by the tugboat, assuming that it is financed with three of the two-year loans and interest rates rise. The second loan will be obtained at a cost of 16%, while the third loan (i.e., second refinancing) shall incur an interest rate of 18%.
    C. Repeat B, this time under the premise that interest rates decline. The first refinancing will cost 11%, while the second refinancing shall cost 8%.

19. Given an asset that should last four years and is to be financed with debt, answer the following questions:
    A. Explain how a debt with an eight-year maturity could be superior to a debt with a four-year maturity.
    B. Explain how a debt with an eight-year maturity could be inferior to a debt with a four-year maturity.

20. Ted Carson is a normally conservative fellow when it comes to money matters. However, an acquaintance of his has thoroughly convinced him that CBC Computer, Inc., would be a terrific company to invest in. According to this acquaintance, CBC's stock should double in one year (a 100% rate of return). Mr. Carson has savings of $20,000 to put into the stock, but would prefer to invest twice that amount in order to reap a much larger profit. His broker will loan him the extra $20,000 at an interest rate of 16%. He decides to borrow the money and buy $40,000 of CBC stock. Ignoring income taxes and brokerage commissions, determine Mr. Carson's net income and ROE, if, after one year, the stock has: (1) gone up 100%; (2) gone up 30%; (3) stayed the same; or (4) gone down 60%.

Selected References

Barnea, Amir, Robert A. Haugen, and Lemma W. Senbet, "Market Imperfections, Agency Problems, and Capital Structure: A Review," *Financial Management* (Summer 1981), pp. 7–22.

Baxter, Nevins D., "Leverage, Risk of Ruin, and the Cost of Capital," *Journal of Finance* (September 1967), pp. 395–404.

Brennon, M. J., and E. S. Schwartz, "Corporate Income Taxes, Valuation, and the Problem of Optimal Capital Structure," *Journal of Business* (January 1978), pp. 103–15.

Chen, Andrew H., and E. Han Kim, "Theories of Corporate Debt Policy: A Synthesis," *Journal of Finance* (May 1979), pp. 371–84.

Donaldson, Gordon, "New Framework for Corporate Debt Capacity," *Harvard Business Review* (March–April 1962), pp. 117–31.

Ferri, Michael G., and Wesley H. Jones, "Determinants of Financial Structure: A New Methodological Approach," *Journal of Finance* (June 1979), pp. 631–44.

Gordon, Myron J., and Clarence C. Y. Kwan, "Debt Maturity, Default Risk, and Capital Structure," *Journal of Banking and Finance* (December 1979), pp. 313–29.

Lee, Wayne Y., and Henry H. Barker, "Bankruptcy Costs and the Firm's Optimal Debt Capacity," *Southern Economic Journal* (April 1977), pp. 1453–65.

Morris, James R., "On Corporate Debt Maturity Strategies," *Journal of Finance* (March 1976), pp. 29–37.

Schneller, Meir I., "Taxes and the Optimal Capital Structure of the Firm," *Journal of Finance* (March 1980), pp. 119–27.

Scott, David, Jr., and John D. Martin, "Industry Influence on Financial Structure," *Financial Management* (Spring 1975), pp. 67–73.

Van Horne, James C., *Financial Management and Policy,* 6th ed. Englewood Cliffs, N.J.: Prentice-Hall, 1983, chapters 9 and 10.

Finance in the News

Corporate treasurers have recently relied heavily on short-term debt. However, disinflation, lower interest rates, and a strong equity market have caused stocks to rally. What effect will this have on the financial structure of corporations? It is yet too early to tell, and as indicated in the following article, treasurers are still "sitting on the fence."

Corporate Treasurers Are Still Sitting on the Fence

For year after year of frightening inflation, corporate treasurers were forced to live dangerously by relying on volatile short-term debt. Now they sense a sea change: the welcome prospect of disinflation, accompanied by lower interest rates and a strong equity market. Yet treasurers are not rushing to escape from their precarious dependence on short-term debt, and for good reason. Stocks have rallied, but many are waiting for evidence that the spurt will last. Interest rates have fallen, but not by nearly as much as the inflation rate. "With 3% inflation, people are anticipating lower long-term rates," says John Crosby, managing director at Merrill Lynch Capital Markets. "If you're the chief financial officer and you think rates are going to come down, why do anything?"

So most companies are simply staying short. At Allied Corp., Treasurer William F. Loftus notes that a current spread of about 4 percentage points between short-term rates and long-term fixed rates "makes it awful attractive" to borrow short. That's a strategy that makes eminent sense to those treasurers who feel that the long-term direction of long-term interest rates is down.

For the moment, companies that have decided to go long anyway are still looking for flexible debt instruments—such as bonds that can be redeemed early or "called" if and when rates fall. Many companies continue to go to the Euromarkets, where the cost of capital remains well below domestic costs. So far this year, companies have sold only $8.6 billion of straight-debt securities on the domestic markets—well below the $11 billion worth in the first two months of 1984, notes analyst Michael Dahood at Smith Barney, Harris Upham & Co.

Many treasurers can afford to do some fence-sitting just now. The recovery has brought improved earnings and cash flow to most companies, and that means external financing requirements are lower than they have been in some time. Two exceptions: companies in the capital-starved high-tech sector and companies that have been playing the merger game. Chevron, which is busy refinancing short debt taken on to fund its acquisition of Gulf Corp., recently sold $500 million of long-term debt—1985's largest straight-debt issue so far.

'Blended' Rate

A few treasurers are taking advantage of a receptive long-term market. Frederick W. Zuckerman, Chrysler's treasurer, says he is happy with the "blended" rate of just under 13% on two recent long issues that raised $650 million. Given the size of the U.S. budget deficit, he believes rates will rise. But if he is wrong, Zuckerman figures that "our business will be good, and the higher price for money will be relatively insignificant."

At Salomon Bros., where economist Henry Kaufman is the resident Cassandra on the subject of corporate leverage, the forecasters say that both corporate profits and internal cash generation will run out of gas in the second half of the year as capital investment needs grow. They project that companies will need to raise $124.7 billion in 1985, a big increase over the $72.9 billion last year.

But even Dr. Doom believes that the economy is changing in a way that could reduce the pressure on balance sheets that are loaded with short-term debt. If stocks continue gaining, Salomon projects that companies will issue $31 billion in new stock this year, compared with $248 billion last year. More important, rising stock prices are likely to mean fewer corporate takeovers—something that in 1984 cost corporate America a net $89.1 billion in lost equity. For 1985, Salomon still predicts more equity retirements than new issues, but for a far more modest net loss of $26.8 billion.

Just as caution reigns on the debt side, very few corporations are jumping right into equities. "CFOs had been saying they need 10% above book value to issue new stock. When they get that, they want 20%. They're waiting," says one bank lending officer.

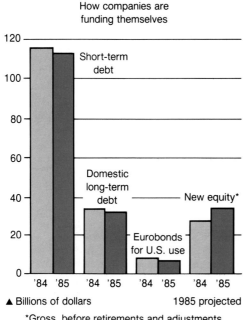

How companies are funding themselves

▲ Billions of dollars   1985 projected

*Gross, before retirements and adjustments

Date: federal reserve board, Salomon Bros.

But bankers, who are the prime source of short-term corporate funds, face growing competition from the stock market as well as from bonds. Some bellwether initial public offerings are selling well. And while a number of companies are pushing ahead with stock buyback plans, others are beginning to experiment with more convertible debt—subordinated debentures that convert to common stock at a specified market price—on the growing chance that the stock market will stay hot.

Last month, Automatic Data Processing Inc. raised $100 million with convertible debt that yields 7.5% and would convert to stock at a premium of 25%. Underwriters recently registered a dozen similar offerings. "In this cycle of the market, people like to receive some current income but still have a play on what is now perceived as a positive equity market," says Merrill's Crosby. He says issuers get lower effective rates than they can with commercial paper or bank loans—as well as the chance to add equity capital to their balance sheets later.

A number of analysts believe that subordinated debt of various kinds will continue to be popular. But Richard West, dean of New York University's business school, also foresees a lot more creativity coming on the equity side, with new classes of stock emerging: "There is no reason that the equity part of the balance sheet must have only one type and the debt side have 48 kinds."

Exotic Hybrid

In fact, money market preferred stock, a recent innovation that sets dividend rates in an auction every 49 days, has "totally taken off," says Robbin Boehmer, an analyst at Securities Data Co., who notes that this version has accounted for 48% of all new preferred stock issued this year. Since the first auction last October, nearly $1 billion worth has been put in play, says Ronald L. Gallatin at Shearson Lehman Brothers Inc., which developed the product and has issued four such preferred series itself. U.S. Steel Corp. has issued three, including the largest to date.

But if some exotic hybrids are still being nurtured, the continuing strength of the stock market has given force to new garden-variety equities, as well. Several large initial public offerings have surfaced this year. The biggest is ICM Property Investors Inc., a real estate trust, which raised $115 million in a Jan. 25 offering at $20 per share. The IPO outlook is cheering venture capitalists. While investors are still wary about new high-tech stocks, a recent IPO by D. H. Blair & Co. raised $4 million at $5 per unit (composed of four shares and four warrants) for Investment Technologies Inc. on Jan. 30. By Feb. 28 those units were trading at 13⅝, says James Davis of IDD Information Services Inc. Davis says that "86% of IPOs this year have outperformed the [over-the-counter] market. It's a sign that IPOs are going to be good this year and that there will be a lot more to come."

Few observers expect to see big blue-chip companies out issuing quantities of common stock anytime soon. Still, Public Service Electricity & Gas Co. raised $182 million in a new issue in January. And at Dean Witter Reynolds Inc., which cultivates medium-size corporate clients, Director M. William Benedetto says, "We're out there telling companies, 'If you have any intention of tapping the equity market in 1985, get ready now.' " With a little more assurance, both long-term debt and new equity markets could be much more lively in months to come.

By Elizabeth Ehrlich in New York

Financial Markets and Institutions

Overview

Growing companies, as well as firms with seasonal operations, are usually unable to generate internally all of their funds requirements. Consequently, these firms will seek outside financing in the financial marketplace through the sale of securities and the acquisition of loans. Financial markets are comprised of numerous institutions and individuals who contribute in various ways to the financing of business, government, and consumers. Besides investors, financial markets are also home to advisors, exchanges, publishers, brokers, banks, security dealers, and government regulators, to name a few. We will become acquainted with most of these market participants in this chapter. More importantly, we shall study the role that financial markets and their participants play in corporate fund raising. It will become quickly apparent in the discussion to follow that the financial marketplace is laden with jargon and a multitude of classifications, such as: primary market vs. secondary market, money market vs. capital market, public vs. private market, and formal vs. informal market ■

Objectives

By the end of the chapter the student should be able to:

1. List and explain the alternative methods by which a firm can obtain financing
2. Distinguish among the various subdivisions of financial markets
3. Discuss the role of the SEC in the public sale of securities
4. Discuss the procedures related to and the process of selling securities
5. Distinguish between public fund raising and private fund raising
6. Describe the various secondary markets including the New York Stock Exchange and the over-the-counter (OTC) market
7. Differentiate between security brokers and dealers

Introduction _____

In the preceding chapter we saw how financial needs were measured and forecasted, addressed the decision concerning debt vs. equity, and discussed the question of debt maturity. Having dealt with these general issues a company is then faced with two additional considerations: (1) selecting the specific type and terms of its financial obligations, and (2) determining the most appropriate method and time to raise funds. The first of these topics is dealt with at length in the next several chapters. We will discuss the second topic in the present chapter.

The primary goal of this chapter is to examine some of the alternative methods by which a business corporation can obtain financing. In this regard, the student will become acquainted with many aspects of the financial markets. A minor objective concerns the importance of timing to a financial strategy.

Corporations, as a group, obtain some of their funding needs "internally" by means of earnings retention. Retained earnings are, after all, nothing more than business savings. In an average year, retained earnings will comprise a significant proportion of new corporate financing. While normally the largest single source of corporate financing, retained earnings do tend to fluctuate considerably from year to year because of business cycles. This is shown in figure 12.1.

Figure 12.1   Annual corporate retained earnings, 1974–1984

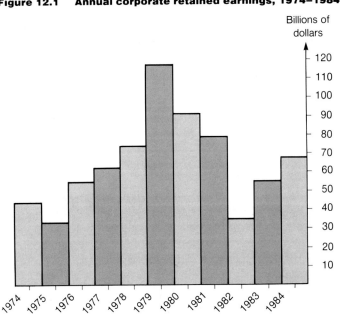

Source: Various issues of the *Federal Reserve Bulletin*, Board of Governors of the Federal Reserve System, Washington, D.C.

Accruals are another important means of financing. Included within this category are the automatic liabilities that arise spontaneously in the course of doing business (e.g., accrued wages and accounts payable). They are automatic in the sense that management does not normally need to take overt action to obtain these funds.[1] However, despite the existence of retained earnings and accruals, many businesses find it desirable and/or necessary to look elsewhere for financing. When they do so, they become participants in the financial marketplace—the current focus of our attention ■

Institutional Investors

Corporations obtain outside financing from many sources. Individual investors, particularly wealthy individuals, provide large sums of money directly to corporations by purchasing securities. More often than not, however, individuals invest indirectly through financial intermediaries or, as we shall refer to them, institutional investors.

Commercial Banks: Commercial banks are the major players in financing business. They accept deposits from individuals, businesses, and other organizations and then loan much of the money to corporations.

Trust Funds: College endowment funds, charitable organizations, and research foundations receive donations from individuals and businesses for the support of their activities. These funds are heavily invested in corporate stocks and bonds. The dividends and interest from these investments are used for such things as faculty salaries, acquisition of paintings, and research grants.

Insurance Companies: Insurance companies collect premiums from policyholders in exchange for protecting their lives, autos, homes, etc. Since premiums are received well in advance of claims payments, the money can be invested in, among other things, corporate securities and loans. This is particularly true for life insurance companies. As a result, insurance companies currently hold well over $400 billion in corporate securities.

Finance Companies: Finance companies specialize in financing the credit sales of wholesalers and retailers. They do so in one of two ways: (1) by loaning money to a business secured by its accounts receivable, or (2) through an outright purchase of a firm's accounts receivable. Finance companies acquire their funds principally by borrowing from banks and selling commercial paper.

Investment Companies: Investment companies pool the money of individual investors who are seeking professional management and diversification. In turn, investment companies place most of these funds in corporate securities. Mutual funds are the largest group of investment companies.

Pension Funds: Billions of dollars are contributed to employee pension funds each year. Given the lag of many years between contributions and benefits, there is ample opportunity to earn something on contributions. Consequently, pension fund managers are hired with the responsibility of investing these funds. Not surprisingly, corporate securities are major outlets for pension money.

---

[1] Even here, however, management has some discretion, as we shall see in the following chapter.

Financial Markets

The financial marketplace is a general term used to group all of the varied financial transactions that take place in an economy. Financial transactions are strictly intangible or paper transactions, whereby money is exchanged for loans, securities, and deposits. Individuals, businesses, government, and institutional investors from all over the United States and around the world participate to one degree or another in financial markets. It is here that loans are arranged and securities are bought and sold. Occasionally, financial transactions take place without any money changing hands, through, for example, trades of stocks for bonds. Our main concern is how businesses and particularly corporations acquire funds in the marketplace.

Among the many divisions and subdivisions in the financial market, two are especially important. The *primary financial market* is the name used to describe the original sale of securities and extension of loans. A sale by General Motors of its own common stock is a primary market transaction. These securities are being issued for the first time and General Motors is the recipient of the money. A *secondary financial market* involves transactions in existing loans and securities. It is essentially a resale market that provides liquidity to investors who, for one reason or another, often decide they no longer wish to hold a particular investment. None of the money received from the sale of loans and securities in the secondary market will go to the companies that stand behind them.

Primary and secondary markets are further subdivided into short-term financial arrangements (one year or less) and long-term financial arrangements (five years and more). The former is commonly referred to as the *money market* and the latter as a *capital market*.[2] These divisions will be used to frame the discussion that follows.

Primary Capital Market

Corporations obtain long-term funding in the primary capital market principally by selling stocks and bonds. The relative importance of these securities is shown in figure 12.2.

Two things are very evident from figure 12.2. First of all, bond issues are, and have been for some time, a more important source of financing than stock.[3] Secondly, preferred stock is extremely insignificant in the aggregate, often less than 3% of the other two combined. However, it is an important source of funds for certain businesses. In addition to stocks and bonds, there are two other long-term financing instruments that are gaining in importance, term loans and leases. All of these financial instruments will be thoroughly described and analyzed in later chapters. Of major concern to us now are the procedures used to sell securities and place loans.

---

[2]Businesses seldom arrange financing to last between one and five years. When they do, it is referred to as *intermediate-term financing*.

[3]Most equity financing comes from retained earnings. Bonds, on the other hand, are not quite as important as Figure 12.1 indicates. A significant portion of gross bond issues are used to retire old issues that have matured.

Figure 12.2   Annual gross proceeds of long-term corporate security offerings, 1968–1984

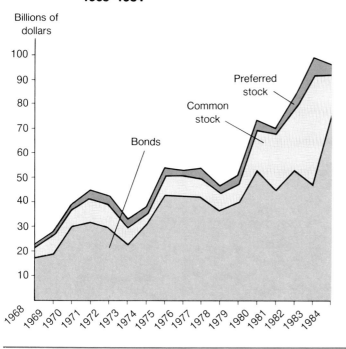

Source: Various issues of the *Securities and Exchange Commission Statistical Bulletin*, U.S. Securities and Exchange Commission, Washington, D.C.

Public Fund Raising   Stocks and bonds can be sold to investors in the open or public market. *A useful definition of a public market is a market in which all investors have an opportunity to purchase a firm's securities.* A public offering provides the greatest exposure and competition for a company's securities, thereby insuring a fair price. There are two major participants in the public sale of stocks and bonds, The Securities and Exchange Commission and investment bankers.

Investment Banking   Investment banking firms, such as Goldman Sachs and Salomon Bros., are specialists in the public sale of securities. Most businesses sell stocks and bonds infrequently, seldom more than once a year. As a result, they are not able to develop the expertise and connections that are necessary to a successful security offering. This reality, coupled with the fact that a great deal of money is usually involved in a stock or bond sale, leads most corporations to hire the services of an investment banker. A corporation will usually choose as its investment banker a firm with which it has previously done business. It is not unusual, however, for a business to select an investment banker through *competitive bidding.* Investment bankers provide three basic services, any one or all of which can be acquired: advice, guaranteed prices, and marketing.

Figure 12.3a   Common stock prices of selected companies, February 13–March 2, 1984

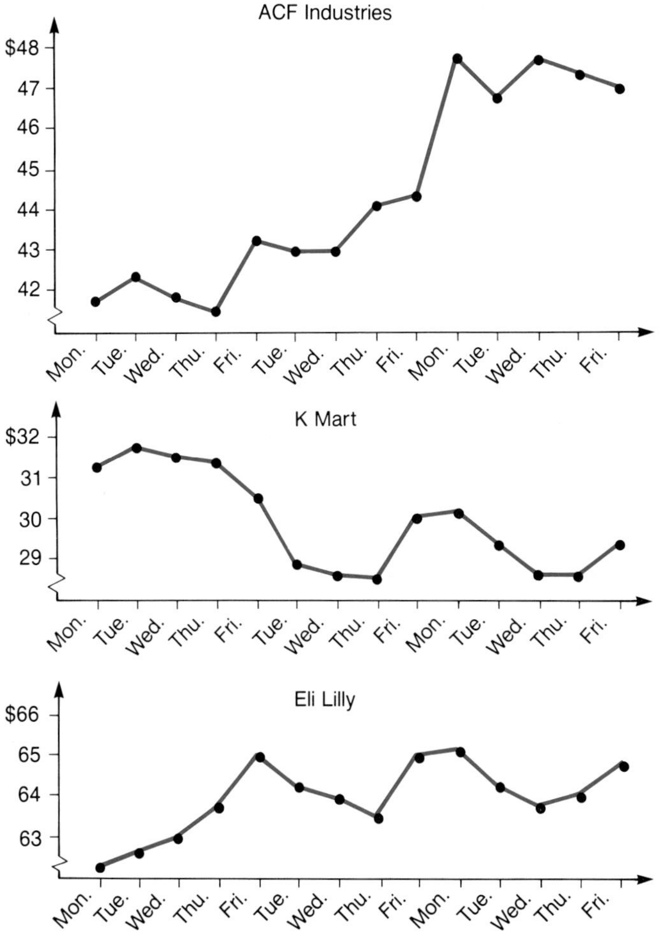

ACF Industries

K Mart

Eli Lilly

Advisory Capacity   Investment bankers are in a good position to provide much valuable advice. Since they closely monitor the financial markets, they are familiar with what investors currently desire in a given bond issue: interest rates, collateral, maturity, etc. Through their expertise in forecasting future market developments, investment bankers may be able to select the most opportune time to sell securities. Based on their advice, for example, a company might be able to delay a bond issue for a few months when market interest rates are expected to be lower. As another example, they might recommend acceleration of a stock issue by a few weeks to avoid a predicted stock market slump. Investment bankers can also help with the administrative burden surrounding security issues. Stock and bond certificates must be printed, buyers' names need to be recorded, legal documentation is required, and bond rating agencies may be consulted. Their advice is particularly valuable in dealing with securities law and government agencies, especially the U.S. Securities and Exchange Commission. It goes without saying that companies are charged for this valuable advice.

Figure 12.3b Average corporate bond yields, February 13–March 2, 1984

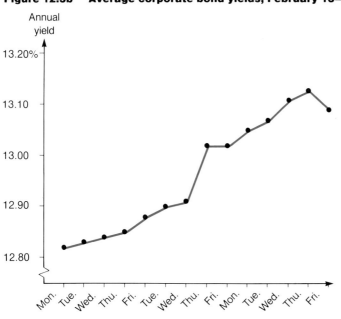

Source: Moody's Yield Averages, *Moody's Bond Survey,* Moody's Investor Service, New York, N.Y.

Price Guarantee   Investment bankers will, for a fee, guarantee the interest rate on a bond issue or the price of a common stock issue. Considering that: (1) interest rate quotes are readily available on similar bond issues, and (2) current stock prices can be easily obtained from the secondary stock market, one may question the necessity of a guarantee. The fact of the matter is, one can never be sure what interest rates or stock prices will be, even in the very near future. They can change suddenly, as figures 12.3a and 12.3b reveal. A company desiring to sell securities is faced with the prospect that market interest rates will be higher, or the stock market lower, on the date of sale. Add to this the uncertainty of how the market will receive a particular company's securities, and the desirability of a guarantee becomes clearer. Based on current market increase rates, for example, an investment banker might guarantee a firm an interest rate of 14% on its bonds. If this rate proves to be insufficient to investors, then the banker has to pay the difference. The same is true with regard to common stock. For example, a guaranteed price of $30 per share must be paid by the investment banker even though the stock is sold for only $27 a share. *To minimize the risk to the investment banker, prices and rates are normally set as close to the offering date as possible.*

These firms are willing to bear such risk because they are very good at predicting stock prices and interest rates. Moreover, their fees for this service are substantial and they increase with the degree of risk. In addition, the investment banker who originates the sale will usually bring in other bankers to share the risk. This group is called a *syndicate.* The originating firm is referred to as the *manager* of the syndicate, which can be composed of ten or more firms.[4]

[4]Financial futures markets have developed in recent years. Companies or their investment bankers can use these markets to hedge (guarantee) against adverse market movements.

Figure 12.4   Investment banking syndicate and dealer network

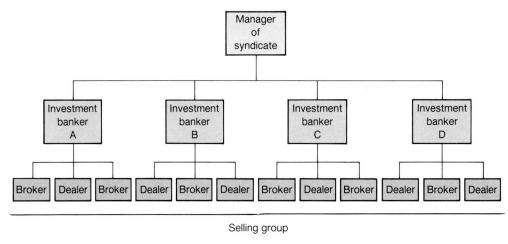

Selling group

There are times, however, when investment bankers are reluctant to guarantee a security offering. This could occur because financial markets are exceptionally unstable. At other times, the firm wishing to sell securities may be a new business or one that has never raised funds in the public market. It is especially difficult to price a common stock issue for a business whose shares are not traded on the secondary stock market. For their part, some corporations do not wish to pay the guarantee fees that could amount to as much as $4 million on a $100 million offering. These companies would normally be large, well-known, and financially sound corporations who feel that their stature will minimize the risks of entering the public financial markets. When an investment banker is hired to sell securities in the absence of a price guarantee, they do so on a *best-efforts basis*. This simply means that they will try to get the best interest rate or stock price possible.

Regardless of whether securities are sold on a guaranteed or best-efforts basis, adverse market conditions can lead to a reduction in the size of an issue or, in the extreme, a temporary cancellation of the entire issue.

Marketing   The actual sale of securities to the public is handled in the marketing function. The originating investment banker (manager) allocates a prearranged number of securities to each member of the syndicate. Syndicate members then parcel out most of their shares to security brokers and dealers across the country and even around the world (figure 12.4). This *selling group* will then attempt to sell the securities on instructions from the syndicate as to price and time. Each member of the selling group is compensated by the syndicate, which in turn will charge the issuing corporation.

The idea behind forming a selling group, which can involve a hundred or more firms and offices spread worldwide, is that a large and widespread sales force is less apt to disrupt the market for a company's securities. Quite often the entire issue is sold in one day. The customer list might include pension funds, insurance companies, individual investors, investment companies, foreign commercial banks, and college endowment funds to name a few.

Figure 12.5   Services provided by an investment banker

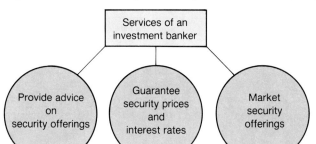

At one time, the insurance term "underwriting" was used to describe the price guarantee role of an investment banker. Now that term is commonly used to describe all three activities and the investment banker is often called an *underwriter.*

Investment Banking Fees   Underwriters obtain compensation for their services from the gross sales proceeds of a security issue. They subtract out their compensation and pay the remainder to the corporation that issued the securities.[5] A sale of common stock can serve to explain this procedure.

Example: A firm wishes to raise $80 million from the sale of common stock. Based on current stock market conditions and other factors the company and underwriting syndicate agree that the stock is worth $25 a share on the market. This will then become the offering price for $80,000,000 ÷ $25 = 3,200,000 shares. The *offering price* of a security issue is critical to an *investment banking relationship* because it determines so many other things. The investment bankers and corporation then negotiate a lower guaranteed price of, say, $24 per share or 3,200,000 × $24 = $76,800,000 (the size of the discount depending on the risk). Accordingly, the investment bankers will receive a risk-bearing fee of $1 per share or $3,200,000. Furthermore, a sales commission of 1% of the sales proceeds (i.e., $800,000) will be deducted from the guaranteed price in addition to an advising fee amounting to $450,000. Out of the $80 million stock issue therefore, the company will obtain $75,550,000. The difference of $4,450,000 belongs to the investment banking syndicate for services rendered and is called the *underwriters' spread.* In percentage terms, the underwriters' spread is 5.56% of the offering price. Whether or not the investment bankers really earn the full fee will depend upon the actual selling price of the stock. If it sells for less than $25, then, of course, their earnings will be correspondingly less. In any event, the corporation will receive $75,550,000 ■

Securities Law

The Law   Federal legislation was passed in the 1930s to deal with what many informed persons felt were irresponsible and unethical business practices of the time. Corporations provided their investors and the public with very little information, financial or otherwise, about their performance and activities. And what was provided was not always correct. Security prices were often manipulated by investment firms and many investors made huge

---

[5]A corporation can arrange to receive its funds prior to the actual sale of securities.

profits by trading on inside information. It was not uncommon for stock to be purchased with 10% equity and 90% debt, resulting in widespread speculation and defaults. These practices were then, and are now, considered to be harmful to small, uninformed investors and a hindrance to the functioning of the economy. The *Securities Act of 1933* was designed primarily to increase the quantity and quality of information provided by publicly owned corporations, so that investors could make informed judgments about stocks and bonds. The *Securities Exchange Act of 1934* placed controls on trading practices in securities and also created the *Securities and Exchange Commission (SEC)* to administer both of these acts. Additional legislation has been passed since then with the primary intent of strengthening the original securities laws.

Registration   Our immediate concern is with the portion of securities law that relates to the public sale of securities. According to the law, a corporation that wants to sell securities across state lines or through the mail, must provide "full disclosure" of all material facts relating to the securities. This information is to be contained in a *registration statement* that must be approved by the Securities and Exchange Commission before the securities can be sold. To meet the requirements of full disclosure a registration statement should include such information as: several past years of complete and audited financial statements; relevant information about top management and the board of directors; the planned use for the funds to be acquired; any legal proceedings involving the company; future plans for the business; and a detailed explanation of outstanding debts. Investment bankers are extremely helpful in the preparation of this document.

After the registration statement has been drafted, it is filed with SEC headquarters in Washington, D.C., where it is reviewed for completeness and accuracy. If the SEC is not satisfied with the document, it will be returned to the company for correction and/or comment. This process will continue until the statement is approved. *Once approved by the SEC, the registration statement becomes effective and the securities can be sold.* If all goes well and the SEC is not overburdened, the review process can take as little as 20 days. However, the *waiting period* is normally longer than this. In the meantime, an underwriter can begin contacting potential investors, but it must do so very carefully because there is no assurance that the registration will become effective. An investment banker cannot make any overt offers to potential customers, only noncommittal announcements that a sale is pending.

A potential investor can obtain a copy of the registration statement from the SEC. However, many investors are content to receive from the company a free condensed version of the registration statement called a *prospectus.* The prospectus must be prepared along with the registration statement and every potential investor is entitled to receive one.

The registration process is time-consuming and expensive. It takes from one to three months to prepare a statement and up to several weeks for the SEC approval. During this time, market conditions can change considerably. In addition to being time-consuming, there are legal costs, accounting fees, and various other expenses required for the preparation of a registration statement. These expenses are generally higher for a common stock issue because more information is needed. Large, publicly owned corporations will usually have on hand most of the information needed for the registration statement. Consequently, their costs and preparation time are much less than other businesses.

Exemptions   Under certain conditions, a corporation is not required to register its securities: (1) the issue is for less than $500,000; (2) there are less than 35 investors and they are knowledgeable investors (i.e., life insurance companies and bank trust departments) who have the ability to protect themselves; (3) securities are sold only intrastate, thereby coming under state securities laws; (4) the maturity is less than 9 months. A security offering must meet only one of these criteria to avoid SEC registration.

Security issues are often designed specifically to avoid registration with the SEC. However, one disadvantage of this is that the securities purchased in an unregistered offering cannot be resold on the secondary market.

Shelf Registration   Securities law was changed recently to allow corporations more latitude in selling securities. By means of a *shelf registration* a company can obtain a security registration that is good for two years. At any time during this period, a firm's investment banker can sell its securities to the public without delay. Not only will this allow for better market timing, it will also cut down on the number of registrations that are required.

Flotation Costs   Flotation costs are the initial expenses incurred when selling securities in the public market. *They are comprised of two segments, underwriters' spread and administrative expense.* The underwriters' spread was defined earlier as the difference between the gross proceeds of a security sale and the amount that the company actually receives. Investment bankers retain the difference as their fee for advising, marketing and risk bearing. *Administrative fees include the costs of preparing a registration statement and incidental expenses such as printing the stock or bond certificates and recording the names of investors.*

Table 12.1 contains some interesting statistics concerning the flotation costs of several common stock and bond issues. Each of these issues was sold using the full services of an investment banker. To allow for a more meaningful evaluation, the costs are shown as a percentage of gross proceeds.

Table 12.1   Flotation Costs (Expressed As a Percentage of Gross Proceeds)

Size of Issue (Millions of Dollars)	Bonds			Common Stocks		
	Underwriters' Spread (%)	Administrative Expenses (%)	Total Cost (%)	Underwriters' Spread (%)	Administrative Expenses (%)	Total Cost (%)
Under 0.5 ⎫				13.3	10.4	23.7
0.5–0.9 ⎬	9.9*	3.4*	13.3*	12.6	8.3	20.9
1.0–1.9 ⎭				11.0	5.9	16.9
2.0–4.9	4.0	2.2	6.2	8.6	3.8	12.4
5.0–9.9	2.4	0.8	3.2	6.3	1.9	8.1
10.0–19.9	1.2	0.7	1.9	5.1	0.9	5.9
20.0–49.9	1.0	0.4	1.4	4.1	0.5	4.6
50.0 and Over	0.9	0.2	1.1	3.3	0.2	3.5

Source: U.S. Securities and Exchange Commission, Cost of Flotation of Registered Equity Issues, 1971–1972 (U.S. Government Printing Office, 1974).

*Due to an inadequate number of small bond issues, all of the categories under $2 million were averaged together.

Two things stand out in table 12.1. In the first place, *flotation costs are higher for common stock issues than bond issues.* The reason for this is that stock is considered to be risker than bonds, both from the standpoint of investment bankers and the SEC. Accordingly, underwriters demand a larger fee for guaranteeing prices, and the SEC requires a more comprehensive registration statement. The second conclusion to be drawn from the data is *the much greater relative cost associated with small issues.* This can be attributed principally to the fixed costs associated with any offering. In particular, administrative expenses and underwriter advising fees are not materially affected by the size of an offering. As a result, large security issues allow these fixed costs to be spread over a larger quantity of funds, thus reducing their impact.

Private Fund Raising   Corporations can obtain long-term funds by selling their securities and placing their loans privately as opposed to publicly. *A private financing involves only one or a few chosen investors in direct negotiation with the corporation.* Since they are small in number, private investors must have access to large sums of money, which excludes almost everyone but institutional investors.

All term loans and leases are arranged privately with institutional investors. A significant proportion of bond issues are also placed privately. In a typical year, about 20% of all corporate bond issues are sold in this manner. But there are years when the proportion is much higher. For example, as recently as 1978, 46% of all corporate bond issues were privately placed.[6] Common stock is seldom sold in this manner. The primary reason seems to be a reluctance on the part of investors to purchase unregistered common stock that cannot be resold.

Common stock financing aside, private long-term fund raising is extremely important to corporations and a real alternative to the public markets. At this point, a few hypothetical examples are in order.

Example A: IT&G Corp. has decided to borrow privately $200 million with a 10-year term loan. Due to the size of the loan, IT&G must make arrangements with a dozen different commercial banks to provide the funds. Although there are several participating banks, there is really only one loan outstanding. One of the twelve banks will be selected to serve as manager of the group and handle most of the details ■

Example B: Nixon Motor Co. has come to the conclusion that it would be in its best interests to lease a $12 million machine rather than borrowing the funds to purchase it. Forthright Insurance Co. has agreed to purchase the asset and lease it to Nixon under terms negotiated by the two parties ■

Example C: The treasurer for SBC Records has been authorized by the board of directors to sell, in the most efficient way, $25 million in bonds. In an effort to accomplish this task, the treasurer contacts the vice-president in charge of corporate bond investments for Velcro Pension Fund. Within a matter of three days, the pension fund has decided to acquire the entire bond issue on terms favorable to SBC Records ■

---

[6]Statistical Bulletin, Securities and Exchange Commission, Washington, D.C.

Advantages of Private Placements   The advantages of private over public fund raising are numerous, as the following list shows:

1. As stated earlier on page 322, securities and loans offered to fewer than 35 sophisticated investors are exempt from SEC registration. This can be important to a company that wishes to raise funds in a hurry. Furthermore, the expenses of preparing a registration statement can be avoided.
2. Many companies find the privacy of a private placement to their liking. For one reason or another, they do not wish to open up their books and business practices to competitors, labor unions, or the government.
3. Securities sold to the public should normally be fairly standardized products without a lot of special features or creative provisions. A private offering, on the other hand, is much more suitable for such things. In other words, it will allow more opportunity for a company to tailor terms and provisions to its specific needs.
4. Because only one or a few investors are involved, it is much easier to work out a solution to any problems that may arise in the future (e.g., temporary cash flow difficulties that hinder the payment of interest). Imagine the communication and coordination problems one would face in trying to work out a problem with 2,000 bond investors spread over the globe.
5. Investment bankers' services are not necessary in private fund raising. However, their advice can prove very helpful even in these situations. Furthermore, their many contacts permit them to identify potential institutional investors. When employed in this manner, underwriters are not nearly as expensive.

Disadvantages of Private Placements   Given all of the advantages for private financing, one may wonder why any firm would go into the public market. However, there are several drawbacks associated with private financing:

1. An investor who is approached by a firm seeking private long-term funding knows quite well what this firm is trying to avoid in the public market. As a result, the investor will attempt to share in these benefits of avoidance by charging the firm a higher interest rate than the public market would require. Whether and to what extent this tactic will succeed, depends to a large extent upon the number of alternative investors available to a company (i.e., its bargaining position).
2. There are times when institutional investors simply do not have any funds to invest.
3. One of the advantages given for private funding was the ease with which future problems are solved. At times this benefit can turn into a detriment. For example, a single lender, knowing it holds all the cards, may be able to force some concessions from a company that is anxious to change the terms of a loan.

4. For many large, well-known corporations, some of the drawbacks of public
   financing are irrelevant. To begin with, these companies are already producing
   much of the information that goes into a registration statement. Their
   financial records and business practices are, for the most part, public
   knowledge. Furthermore, they are often in a position to sell their securities on
   a "best efforts" basis and thereby eliminate the investment banker's biggest
   fee. For such corporations, a private placement is by no means an obvious
   choice.
5. Legal restrictions on institutional investors may prohibit them from making
   certain investments.

Rights Offerings   A corporation has an alternative to a public or private sale of common
stock. It can offer present stockholders the right to buy new shares at a given price. Since
the current owners are familiar with the business, the SEC registration requirements are
much less than on a public issue. Moreover, an underwriter's services are not nearly as important here. The explanation for the latter being that legal arrangements are more simplified and a customer base is already at hand. For these reasons, a corporation may select this
avenue for a common stock issue.[7] This procedure is more formally known as a *rights offering* and it is discussed in detail in chapter 15.

Primary Money Market

Corporations obtain short-term funding in the primary money market. In line with the
matching principle discussed in the preceding chapter, most short-term financing is used to
fund short-term assets such as receivables and inventory. The two principal categories of this
funding are *commercial paper* and short-term bank loans. Short-term bank loans are commonly referred to as *bank commercial loans*. The relative importance of these two financial
arrangements is shown in figure 12.6.

Bank commercial loan extensions have varied considerably over time, particularly since
1970. They were negative during 1953 and 1975 as a result of repayments exceeding extensions. At the other extreme, bank loans totaled some $55 billion in 1982. There is no question
that bank loans are more important than commercial paper. The latter, however, are growing
very rapidly and reached a sales high of $19 billion in 1981. In addition to bank loans and
commercial paper, firms in certain industries borrow substantial sums from business finance
companies.

Bank loans are all privately arranged between a corporate borrower and one or more
commercial banks. When several banks join together to make a large loan, the arrangement
is called a *loan participation*. It is difficult to overemphasize the importance of bank short-
term lending to businesses. The figures shown in figure 12.6 really do not tell the whole story,
since banks make substantial indirect loans to business through third parties. They also buy
a considerable amount of commercial paper. A more complete discussion of bank lending is
contained in chapter 13.

---

[7]A few states have laws that require all new common stock issues to be offered
first to existing owners so as not to dilute their interest in the firm.

Figure 12.6   Short-term borrowing in the private domestic nonfinancial sector

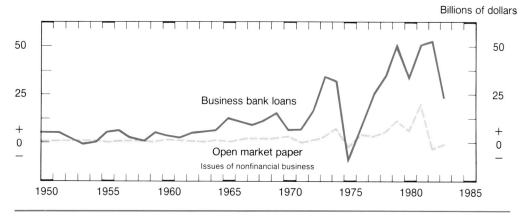

Source: Taken from the *Federal Reserve System 1984 Historical Chartbook*, Board of Governors of the Federal Reserve System, Washington, D.C.

Finance companies also make their loans through private one-on-one negotiations.

Commercial paper (corporate I.O.U.s) is becoming a very popular means to raise short-term money. It is practically the only mechanism by which corporations can publicly obtain short-term funds. *Roughly 25% of all commercial paper is sold publicly through commercial paper dealers on both a guaranteed and best-efforts basis.* The remainder is privately placed. A public sale of commercial paper is exempt from SEC registration requirements as long as its maturity is under nine months, which is usually the case. Commercial paper dealers (who may also be investment bankers) charge fees based on sales effort and degree of risk. These expenses will, in effect, reduce the funds actually received by a company from a commercial paper sale.

Despite the relative ease with which commercial paper is publicly issued, compared to long-term securities, most of it is privately placed with institutional investors. For one thing, a private arrangement allows a company to tailor the terms of its paper to its own particular needs rather than those of the general market. For another, the commercial paper dealer can be avoided by going private. All factors considered, corporations usually choose the private route for their commercial paper. It is worth noting here, that many nonfinancial corporations invest in commercial paper (see the discussion on marketable securities in chapter 6). Sears, for example, might purchase the commercial paper issued by Boeing and hold it as a marketable security.

Regardless of how commercial paper is issued, the nature of this market at the present time dictates that the issuers should be large, well-known and financially strong corporations.

Secondary Financial Markets

Trading in outstanding corporate securities takes place in the secondary financial markets. It is here that individuals and institutional investors exchange registered corporate stocks and bonds for money. Government securities and residential mortgages are also traded in secondary markets. *When persons speak of the market value of a security they are usually referring to its price on the secondary market.* Secondary markets are strictly resale markets; they are not used for corporate fund raising. However, despite the fact that companies do not acquire funds from these markets, they are nevertheless indirectly very important to corporate finance. Thus, a brief description of secondary financial markets is provided here.

Importance of Secondary Markets to Corporate Finance A corporation can benefit from secondary market trading in its securities in at least two ways. In the first place, most investors appreciate the opportunity to sell their security holdings on short notice. The ability to do so provides them with *liquidity* in case they require cash for, say, an emergency, or simply because a better investment has come along. Imagine, if you will, the prospect of having to wait some 20 or 25 years for a bond to mature. Common stock, on the other hand, has no maturity date, and the issuing corporation is under no obligation to buy it back. There is no question that investors value the liquidity offered by secondary markets, particularly for common stock. As a consequence, corporations are able to sell their stock at a somewhat higher price and their bonds with a lower rate of interest.

A second major benefit of secondary markets is the information that they provide to corporate management. *The most important piece of information provided by these markets is an up-to-the-minute price for each common stock that is traded.* These market prices are readily available to all interested parties. By checking the secondary market, corporate management can determine what the "market" thinks about their company. The feelings of the market are expressed in the price of the corporation's common stock. Management can also quickly observe the market's reaction to their decisions. A favorable market reaction is signified by a rising stock price, whereas an unfavorable reaction is shown by a declining stock price. In a sense, secondary stock markets are like continuous public opinion polls, where opinions are expressed by an expenditure of money. Primary common stock issues, on the other hand, are too seldom to be of much use for this purpose.

Several stock market averages or indices have been developed by private organizations to keep investors and corporate managers abreast of overall secondary stock market movements. Included among these indices are the *Dow Jones Averages, Standard & Poor's 500 Stock Index, New York Stock Exchange Index,* and the *National Association of Security Dealers Index.*

Not all corporate stocks and bonds are traded in the secondary market. Securities must be registered with the SEC before they can be sold or resold to the public. For reasons mentioned earlier, many companies often choose to avoid registration and acquire some or all of their funds privately. Small companies would not normally have secondary market activity in their securities simply because they have a very small group of stockholders and/or they are not well known to the investment community.

Types of Secondary Financial Markets   There are two basic types of secondary markets for corporate securities, formal and informal. In the description of these two markets to follow, the reader should be aware of the fact that they are becoming more alike all the time.

Formal Secondary Market   A formal secondary market (also called an *exchange*) for corporate securities is characterized by: (1) a central trading facility where traders gather to buy and sell securities; (2) detailed trading rules governing such things as short selling, limit orders, margin requirements, payment procedures, and record keeping; (3) trading is conducted by means of an open auction in which verbal bid and offer prices are made publicly; (4) a company must be listed before its securities can be traded. To be *listed* on an exchange, a corporation must pay an annual fee and have a minimum level of sales, profits, assets, and stockholders. The requirements vary from one exchange to another.

The most prominent secondary financial market is the *New York Stock Exchange.* Although some corporate bonds are traded there, the NYSE is principally involved in the exchange of common stock of large corporations. Other prominent exchanges specializing in common stocks are American Stock Exchange (New York), Pacific Stock Exchange (San Francisco), Midwest Stock Exchange (Chicago), and Philadelphia Stock Exchange.

Each day of activity in New York Stock Exchange listed stocks is summarized the following day in the financial pages of major newspapers. Exhibit 12.1 is a portion of such a financial page taken from the May 4, 1984, *Wall Street Journal.* Reading from left to right, an investor who is interested in Ball Corporation common stock (the fourth stock down) can determine the following: in the previous fifty-two weeks Ball stock reached a high of $36.38 and a low price of $28.50; dividends of $1.16 a share were paid during the last year for a yield of 3.6%; the market price divided by the most recent earnings per share is 9; eight thousand shares were exchanged on May 3 at prices ranging from $32.12 to $32.50 and closed the day at $32.12; the closing price was unchanged from the previous day. A symbol pf to the right of a company name indicates that this is a preferred stock.

A discussion of formal secondary markets would not be complete without mentioning the important role played by *brokers.* An investor who wishes to buy or sell a security on an exchange must go through a broker. Furthermore, that broker must be a member of the exchange. A *brokerage commission* is paid on each trade, and it varies with the size of the transaction. This normally is not a problem because most investors would prefer to have a professional trader handle their transactions on an exchange. This is especially true if the exchange is 2,000 miles away. There are, however, a number of large, sophisticated investors who would like to use an exchange without paying for a broker. Although some security brokers are independent traders, the majority are associated with brokerage firms such as Merrill Lynch and E. F. Hutton. These brokerage firms purchase memberships (in stock market parlance they are called seats) on the various exchanges.

Exhibit 12.1 Stock quotations, May 3, 1984

52 Weeks High	Low	Stock	Div.	Yld %	P-E Ratio	Sales 100s	High	Low	Close	Net Chg.
26⅜	16½	Bkrinti	.92	4.1	..	1437	23¼	22¼	22¼ –	¾
27⅞	20	Baldor	.32	1.4	18	77	22¾	22½	22¾ +	¼
13⅞	1⅛	viBaldU		..	..	338	1⅜	1¼	1⅜ +	⅛
36⅜	28½	BallCp	1.16	3.6	9	80	32½	32⅛	32⅛	
28⅛	14⅝	BallyMf	.20	1.1	145	761	18⅞	18¾	18⅞ +	⅛
26⅞	9⅝	BallyPk		..	14	40	13¾	13¼	13½ +	½
34¼	27¾	BaltGE	3	9.4	6	120	32	31¾	31¾	....
31⅛	20¾	BnOne	n.96b	4.0	9	461	24¼	23⅝	24⅛ +	¼
49⅛	29⅜	BanCal	1.20	2.4	9	44	49⅛	49⅛	49⅛	....
7⅝	4¾	BanTex	.20	4.0	..	35	5	4⅞	5	....
59¾	38	Bandag	1.10	2.5	11	28	44	43½	43½ –	¾
46¼	34½	BkBos	2.32	6.4	5	554	36⅜	36	36 –	¼
53⅛	51¾	BkBos	pf1.13e	2	2.2	67	52½	52¼	52½ +	¼
34¼	27¼	BkNY	s 1.84	6.2	5	273	30¼	29¾	29⅞ +	⅛
38	27⅛	BkofVa	1.52	4.3	7	59	36	35⅝	35¾ –	¼
25⅛	18⅜	BnkAm	1.52	7.6	10	714	20	19¾	20 +	¼
53¾	48¼	BkAm	pf4.81e	9	.3..	359	51⅝	51½	51½ +	½
86½	73½	BkAm	pf7.61e	9	.0..	100	85	85	85	....
21¼	15½	BkAm	pf2.88	..	..	179	16¾	16½	16¾	....
28	21¾	BkARty	1.92	7.5	9	43	26	25¾	25¾ –	¼
50½	38¼	BankTr	2.45	5.6	5	773	43⅝	43¼	43½ –	⅛
24½	21⅛	BkTr	pf2.50	11.	..	5	21¾	21⅝	21¾ –	⅛
41	35½	BkTr	pf4.22	11.	..	1	38	38	38 –	½
12¾	8½	Banner	.03e	.3	44	7	9¾	9¾	9¾	....
46¾	26⅛	Bard	.40	1.5	12	235	27⅝	26⅝	27¼ –	⅜
26⅛	19	BarnGp	.80	3.9	13	23	21¼	20¾	20¾ –	⅝
42½	32¼	Barnet	1.36	3.5	8	58	39⅛	38¾	38⅞ –	⅛
45¼	37	Barni	pf2.38	5.9	..	20	40½	40¼	40¼ –	¼
33	22⅛	BaryWr	.48	1.8	16	37	27½	27	27¼	....
14½	8⅝	BASIX	.10b	1.0	11	49	9¾	9½	9⅝ +	⅛
30⅝	19¼	Bausch	s.76	3.8	12	463	21¼	20½	20¾ –	¼
31¼	15⅛	BaxfTr	s.33	1.8	12	7974	18⅜	17¾	18 –	½
21¾	12	BayFin	.10e	.5	6	366	21½	20	21½ +	1¾
23⅜	19¾	BayStG	2.48	11.	7	22	22⅞	22¼	22¼ –	¼
41	28⅜	Bearing	1	3.1	14	8	32¼	32	32¼	....
36	25	BeatFd	1.70	5.6	7	4504	30½	29⅞	30⅛ –	⅜
65½	47	Beat	pf3.38	6.0	..	92	56¼	56⅛	56⅛ –	½
53½	33⅝	BectnD	1.15	3.3	26	167	35½	34¾	34¾ –	¾
12¼	8⅛	Beker		..	29	385	9	8⅝	8⅝ –	¼
21⅛	12¼	BeldnH	.40	2.6	8	35	15¼	15	15⅛ –	⅜
29¼	19⅛	BelHw	s .50	2.0	8	664	25¼	24⅞	25¼ +	¼
29¼	19½	BelHw	pf.60	2.4	..	12	25⅛	24¾	25 +	¼
75⅛	65	BellAt	n6.40	9.0	7	2188	71¼	70⅝	70⅞ +	¼
27⅛	20⅞	BelCd	g2.18	..	..	1231	24⅜	24⅛	24⅜ +	⅜
39⅛	24⅛	Bellind	.32	1.2	12	160	26¼	25¾	26¼ +	⅛
98¼	83⅞	BellSo	n7.80	8.5	8	1336	92⅜	91¾	92 –	⅛
32¾	27⅞	BelSo	wi	..	..	118	31	30⅞	31	....
42	35¾	Belo	n .72	1.7	13	98	42	41¾	42	....
22⅜	17½	Bemis	s	..	13	2	22	22	22 +	¼
86¾	74½	Bndx	pf4.04	4.9	..	7	83	82½	82¾ +	¼

Informal Secondary Market Informal secondary markets for corporate securities are comprised of a rather loosely knit group of *dealers* who communicate via telephone, telex, and computer. They are not housed in a centralized trading facility, their trading rules are minimal, listing is not required, and bid and offer prices are made on the telephone or a computer screen rather than by open auction. The name *over-the-counter (OTC)* is used to describe these markets. Practically all corporate bonds are traded in the OTC as well as the common stocks of most small- and medium-size corporations. Common stocks that are currently listed on an exchange are also frequently traded in the OTC.

Security dealers dominate the OTC.[8] *Whereas brokers are hired to find buyers for sellers and vice versa, dealers actually buy and sell on their own account.* They do not charge commissions, but rather hope to profit by buying securities at one price and quickly reselling them at a higher price. As a practical matter, no security dealer would be willing or able to trade all the bonds and stocks on the OTC. Consequently, dealers usually specialize by type of security, industry, and region of the country. In the extreme, a security dealer located in the city of Houston might only deal in Texas oil industry stocks. However, an investor is not forced to look for a needle in a haystack when trading in the OTC, because dealers regularly communicate and trade with one another. When queried about a security, a dealer in that security will respond with a *bid-ask quote.* For instance, when asked about the price of a given common stock a dealer might reply, 28 bid—29 ⅛ ask. This means that he or she is willing to buy the stock for $28 a share or sell it for $29.12 a share. The difference of $1.12 is the dealer spread (i.e., markup). These spreads can vary considerably from one security to the next and even from one dealer to the next. An investor is wise to shop around for the best deal.

As the preceding discussion indicated, investors can buy and sell outstanding corporate securities on exchanges and in the OTC. In the process they will use either brokers or dealers. While these markets are used for the vast majority of secondary trading, this need not be the case. For example, there is nothing to prohibit two neighbors from exchanging registered bonds and stocks, as long as they are careful to fill out the proper forms. Individuals occasionally advertise stocks and bonds for sale in local newspapers much as they would a used car. Institutional investors often trade large blocks of securities among themselves without the benefit of brokers or dealers. Such transactions are often said to constitute the *third market.*

Regulation of Secondary Markets   The U.S. Securities and Exchange Commission (SEC) has responsibility not only for registering publicly issued securities, but also policing trading practices in the secondary markets. SEC regulation of the secondary markets is designed to protect small investors and promote market efficiency. In line with these objectives the SEC: (1) monitors *insider trading;* (2) guards against security *price manipulation* intended to deceive the markets; (3) passes judgment on the operating practices of brokers, dealers, and the various exchanges; (4) controls, along with the Federal Reserve, the amount of debt that can be used to purchase securities—this is accomplished by means of *margin requirements,* currently set at a minimum of 50%; (5) requires up-to-date financial statements from all corporations whose securities are traded in the secondary market. These reports are in addition to the registration statement, which is only required for new issues of stock and bonds. The most important of these updated statements is the *Form 10-K annual report.*

---

[8]Many firms that provide brokerage services will also act as dealers.

Timing

When to acquire funds can be just as important as the form in which the funding comes or the method used to obtain it. This is especially true for long-term financing, which can commit a firm for many years. The price of every company's common stock changes over time, some more so than others. In like manner, interest rates on borrowed funds move up and down. For periods as short as a year, the changes can be significant. Holiday Inns, for example, could have sold common stock in 1982 for as little as $23.75 and as much as $38.75. Pacific Telephone and Telegraph Co. on the other hand, paid 12.35% on a bond issue on July 16, 1980 and then paid 15.12% on a similar bond issue only 104 days later. These are not isolated examples by any means.[9]

The timing of a stock issue is of more than passing interest. Clearly, the present owners of a company would not be happy with a management that sold stock for $25 a share when a price of $30 could have been obtained two months later. When to borrow is also important. A postponement of a $50 million bond issue to achieve a one percent reduction in interest rates would save $500,000 per year.

The major difficulty one faces in trying to correctly time an acquisition of funds is predicting the future. Timing is a relatively easy exercise when done with hindsight. Not so when dealing with the future. Will stock prices and interest rates go up or down, by how much and when? More than one bond issue has been delayed with the expectation of declining interest rates only to see them rise. An in-depth analysis of the timing issue is beyond the scope of this text. The present discussion was designed merely to introduce this important, but complicated, subject.

Summary

Without financial markets, businesses would find it extremely costly and inconvenient to obtain outside financing. The financial system in the United States is the largest and most highly developed in the world. Nowhere else are funds invested or acquired in as an efficient and effective manner. Moreover, the multitude of financial transactions are carried out with a minimum of dishonesty and malfeasence. The important elements of this chapter are summarized in figure 12.7 ■

Key Terms/Concepts

Bank commercial loans
Best-efforts basis
Bid-ask quote
Capital market
Commercial paper
Flotation costs
Insider trading
Institutional investor
Investment banking
Margin requirement
Money market

New York Stock Exchange
OTC
Price guarantee
Primary financial markets
Private placement
Prospectus
Public market
Registration of securities
Rights offering
Secondary financial markets

Securities & Exchange Commission
Security dealer
Shelf registration
Stock broker
Stock exchange
Third market
Timing
Underwriters' spread
Underwriting

[9]See William C. Freund, "The Dynamic Financial Markets," *Financial Executive*, May, 1965, pp. 11–26, 57–58.

Figure 12.7   Important elements of the business financial market

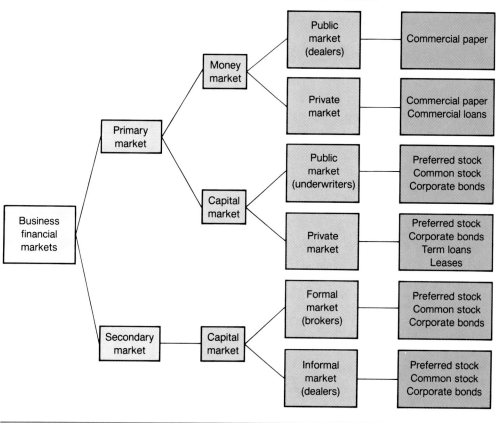

Questions

1. How would you distinguish between the money market and the capital market? How would you distinguish between the primary market and the secondary market?

2. List the corporate securities that are typically found in the capital market.

3. Briefly describe the functions of an investment banker.

4. What advantages are there in forming a syndicate and dealer network?

5. When is a registration statement required? What purpose or purposes is this document supposed to serve?

6. What is meant by the term "timing" as used in this chapter?

7. Flotation costs consist of what elements?

8. How do corporations benefit by the existence of secondary security markets?

9. Does the Federal Reserve System play a role in corporate financing? Explain.

10. Corporations obtain the bulk of their short-term funds from two sources. Name these two sources and tell what proportion of each is raised privately.

11. Practically all common stock issues are sold publicly. What is the reason for this?

12. List five institutional investors.

Problems

1. An investment banker has agreed to underwrite and sell Bludhorn Corporation's common stock issue. The issue is comprised of 1,500,000 shares. Bludhorn will be charged an advisory fee of $250,000 in addition to a sales commission of $1 million. Having agreed on an offering price of $37, the parties then concur that the firm should be guaranteed a price of $35.75, but in no event will it receive more than this amount. SEC registration costs and other expenses will amount to $575,000, and they are the responsibility of Bludhorn.
   A. Determine the underwriter spread associated with this offering.
   B. Calculate the underwriter spread as a percentage of the offering price.
   C. Determine the total flotation costs associated with this security offering.
   D. How would the investment banker fare if the stock is sold for only $33.

2. On January 1, 1986, Carol Wayne bought 300 shares of ABC, Inc., common stock on the New York Stock Exchange. She paid a price of 19¼ for the shares and, in addition, was charged a brokerage commission of $108. She sold the shares for 23½ on December 31, 1986. Her broker assessed a commission of $112 on the sale. Calculate the annual rate of return Ms. Wayne earned on this investment. Be sure to include the brokerage commissions in your computations.

3. Given total flotation costs of $6.5 million, how many $1,000 par value bonds must be sold in order to net the issuing company $85 million. You may assume the bonds are sold for their par value.

4. Using figure 12.2, find the approximate compound annual percentage growth rate of corporate bond issues from 1974 through 1984.

5. Bob Stevens recently contacted a security dealer about Turbin Watson Corporation common stock. The dealer quoted him a bid of 33½ and an ask of 35¼. If Mr. Stevens purchased 200 shares of the stock, what total amount of money did he pay?

6. You are given the following NYSE Composite Transactions Report, taken from the Wall Street Journal on May 6, 1986.

52 Weeks				Yield	P/E	Sales				Net
High	Low	Stock	Div.	(%)	Ratio	(100s)	High	Low	Close	Change
46½	34	Coger	2.20	6.2	10	235	35	35¼	35	+⅜

   A. How many shares of Coger stock were traded on May 5, 1986?
   B. What was the price of Coger stock at the close of trading on May 4, 1986?
   C. What was the highest price at which this stock traded during the last year?
   D. Coger common stock pays an annual dividend of what amount?

Selected References

Black, Ernest, "Pricing a Corporate Bond Issue: A Look behind the Scenes," *Essays in Money and Credit,* New York: Federal Reserve Bank of New York, 1964, pp. 72–76.

Cooper, Kerry S., and Donald R. Fraser, *The Financial Marketplace,* Reading, Mass.: Addison-Wesley, 1982.

Eiteman, Wilford J., Charles A. Dice, and David K. Eiteman, *The Stock Market,* 4th ed., New York: McGraw-Hill, 1969.

Hayes, Samuel L., III, "The Transformation of Investment Banking," *Harvard Business Review* (January–February 1979), pp. 153–70.

Kaufman, Herbert M., *Financial Institutions, Financial Markets, and Money*, New York: Harcourt Brace Jovanovich, 1983.

Logue, Dennis E., and Richard J. Rogalski, "Does It Pay to Shop for Your Bond Underwriter?" *Harvard Business Review* (July–August 1979), pp. 111–17.

Skousen, K. Fred, *An Introduction to the SEC*, 2nd ed., Cincinnati: South-Western Publishing, 1980.

Smith, Clifford W., Jr., "Alternative Methods for Raising Capital," *Journal of Financial Economics* (November 1977), pp. 273–307.

▮ Finance in the News

As was indicated in the chapter, corporations obtain long-term funding in the primary capital market principally by selling stocks and bonds. Where can investors obtain information about general trends in interest rates and the related impact on stocks and bonds? Obviously there are a variety of private financial advisors, but in addition the Wall Street Journal provides a wealth of data. Following is the widely read "Credit Markets" column that is run in every issue of the *Wall Street Journal*.

Short-Term Rates Continue to Decline Amid Perception of Easier Fed Stance ____

Short-term interest rates continued to fall amid what many analysts say are signs that the Federal Reserve System is easing its credit hold in an effort to bolster the economy.

Rates plunged at yesterday's auction of Treasury bills to their lowest levels in more than two years. The average rate on new 13-week bills tumbled to 7.62% from 8.04% at last week's sale and was the lowest since a 7.619% rate set Jan. 17, 1983. The rate on new 26-week bills averaged 7.87%, down from 8.27% last week and was the lowest since a 7.728% average also set Jan. 17, 1983.

Also falling sharply was the interest rate on federal funds, or reserves that banks lend one another. For much of the day the funds rate hovered between 6½% and 7½%. The funds rate has been averaging less than 8% in the past few days, down sharply from an average of about 8½% in recent weeks.

Lower Prime Rate Seen

Recent declines in the banking industry's borrowing costs could pave the way for a cut in the prime lending rate to 10¼%, or even 10%, from the current 10½%. If the weakness in the federal funds rate persists, "We should see a prime-rate cut late this week or early next," said Samuel Kahan, a vice president of Heinold Commodities Inc., Chicago. The prime, or base, rate on corporate loans has been 10½% since mid-January.

The Fed "has decided to ease its credit policy," Mr. Kahan said. Fed officials are concerned about the "fragility of the financial system," and want to "pre-empt a further weakening of the economy," he added. The government last week estimated that the economy grew at only a 1.3% annual rate in the first quarter, after adjusting for inflation, down from a 4.3% pace in last year's fourth quarter.

Still, many analysts contend that it isn't clear whether the Fed has changed its credit policy. "We need more data before we can better interpret the Fed's intentions," said William V. Sullivan Jr., a senior vice president at Dean Witter Reynolds Inc. He noted that the federal funds rate, which is watched closely for clues to Fed policy, often fluctuates widely around the April 15 federal income tax date.

Even those who say the Fed has eased contend that yesterday's funds rate was much lower than Fed officials would like to see. They noted that the central bank moved to drain reserves yesterday through the temporary sale of U.S. government securities. When the Fed sells securities, it absorbs reserves because dealers draw on their bank accounts to pay for their purchases.

A Mild Action

Nonetheless, analysts generally viewed yesterday's Fed maneuver as being a relatively mild action, especially in comparison with the Fed's extremely large injections of reserves in the past two weeks. These analysts say that Fed policy appears to be consistent with a funds rate of about 8% to 8¼%.

Mr. Kahan of Heinold Commodities said the Fed appears to be "setting the stage for a possible lowering" of the discount rate. But he said that a discount-rate cut would depend on how the economy performs this month. The discount rate, which has been at 8% since late last December, is the fee the Fed charges on loans to banks and savings institutions.

Many economists say the Fed will leave its discount rate unchanged. They argue that the economy will pick up steam this quarter and that the Fed doesn't need to provide additional stimulus. Bernard Schoenfeld, a vice president at Irving Trust Co., predicts that the economy will expand at about a 4½%–to–5% annual rate this quarter.

Durables Report Today

The government today is expected to report that new orders for durable goods rose last month. A survey of 37 analysts by Money Market Services Inc., Belmont, Calif., shows a median estimate of a 0.5% increase, which would compare with a 1.2% decline in February. Individual estimates ranged from a drop of 1.5% to a gain of 2.5%.

In the credit markets yesterday, the Treasury's 11¼% bonds due 2015 closed at 100¼, up from 99 29/32 Friday. That cut the yield to 11.22% from 11.26%. The government's 11¼% notes due 1995 rose to 100 26/32 from 100 21/32, trimming the yield to 11.11% from 11.13%.

On the corporate front, a $75 million issue of Staley Continental Inc. sinking-fund debentures was offered to investors through Merrill Lynch Capital Markets. The 12⅜% debentures, due May 1, 2015, were priced at 99.026 to yield 12.5%. The issue is non-refundable for 10 years. It is rated Baa-2 by Moody's Investors Service Inc. and single-A-minus by Standard & Poor's Corp.

Prices of Recent Issues

Current quotations are indicated below for recent issues of corporate senior securities that aren't listed on a principal exchange.

Issue			Moody's Rating	Bid	Asked	Chg.		Yield %
UTILITIES								
DukePwr	12⅝s	'15	Aa2	102⅞	103⅛	....		12.23
MtnStsT&T	12¼s	'25	A1	99¾	100	....		12.25
NY Tel	12¼s	'24	A2	99¾	100	....		12.25
PacTel	12¾s	'25	A1	102⅝	102⅞	....		12.39
SoCalEd	13s	'15	Aa2	104¾	105	....		12.36
INDUSTRIALS								
E Kodak	12¼s	'15	Aaa	102¾	103¼	....		11.85
K mart	12¾s	'15	A1	102⅝	103⅛	+	⅛	12.35
Texaco	13⅝s	'94	A1	108¾	109⅛	....		11.96
FOREIGN								
Ontario	12½s	'94	Aaa	106⅜	107¼	....		11.19
PrvQueb	12¾s	'94	A1	106½	107	−	⅞	11.50
QuebHydro	11¾s	'12	A1	97⅛	97⅝	....		12.04

Source: PaineWebber Inc. (Quotes are for round lots)

Wall Street Journal, April 23, 1985

By Edward P. Foldessy and Tom Herman

Short-Term Debt Financing

Overview

In chapter 11 we saw how a firm can determine its preferred debt level, as well as the maturity composition of its liabilities. Chapter 12 described the general procedures that are followed in raising equity capital and debt funds (both short- and long-term). This chapter will examine in detail the more significant types of business short-term debt. Short-term debt includes those liabilities that are payable within one year or less, such as accounts payable, accrued wages, commercial loans, and commercial paper. The following chapters, chapters 14 through 16, are concerned with corporate long-term financing.

The present chapter will explain the important features of each short-term debt alternative. Included in the discussion will be the measurement of interest rates, an analysis of terms and provisions, and a description of the procedures to follow in acquiring short-term funds. All of this information is essential to making intelligent decisions in this area ■

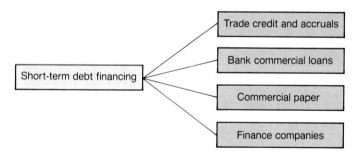

Objectives

By the end of the chapter the student should be able to:

1. List and describe the various sources of short-term debt financing
2. List and discuss the features of trade credit
3. Calculate the annual cost of trade discounts
4. Explain the significance of and difference between special purpose loans and lines of credit
5. Discuss several common provisions of commercial loans
6. Discuss the use of collateral (or security) in the acquisition of loans
7. Describe how the cost of bank commercial loans is determined
8. Calculate the effective annual interest rates on several types of commercial loans
9. Explain the considerations involved in applying for bank loans
10. List and describe the common characteristics of commercial paper
11. Calculate the cost of commercial paper
12. Differentiate among consumer finance companies, sales finance companies, and commercial finance companies
13. Describe the process of factoring

Introduction

Many assets are acquired with short-term debt financing. Short-term debt consists of all those liabilities that must be paid within one year. Included in this classification are trade credit, accruals, bank commercial loans, commercial paper, and finance company loans. Trade credit and accruals are used as financing largely because they occur spontaneously in the course of business and they are free. In line with the matching principle, other forms of short-term debt provide funding for temporary or seasonal increases in working capital, as estimated by cash budgets. We will explore in detail each of these methods of financing in the present chapter ■

Trade Credit and Accruals

Trade credit is generated when a company acquires supplies, merchandise, or materials and does not pay for them immediately. These transactions typically show up on the buyer's balance sheet as accounts payable and the seller's balance sheet as accounts receivable. Trade credit can result in a considerable amount of financing when the payment period is long. For instance, credit purchases of $2 million a week would accumulate to $12 million in accounts payable, given a payment period of six weeks. *When combined, trade credit represents the largest source of short-term financing for a typical company.*

Accruals represent services that have been provided to a business, but have not yet been paid for. Wages are normally paid on a delayed basis, giving rise to accrued wages. Other frequent accruals found on corporate balance sheets are for rent and taxes. Accrued wages can be an especially important source of funding. A company with $3,000 in daily labor costs can generate up to $14 \times \$3,000 = \$42,000$ in financing by paying its employees every fourteen days. By switching to a monthly payroll, this firm could increase accrued wages up to a maximum of $30 \times \$3,000 = \$90,000$.

Trade credit and accruals are very tempting for two reasons. In the first instance, there is little effort needed to acquire them. Trade credit is readily offered by suppliers in many industries, wages are traditionally paid on a delayed basis and taxes can be paid quarterly. In addition to being easy to obtain, they also occur automatically when the need arises. As business picks up and more labor and materials are used, trade credit and accruals will rise spontaneously to assist in the financing of these assets. The second reason for their attractiveness has to do with their extremely low cost. There is no explicit interest rate charged for this financing, although it may be hidden in the wage rate or purchase price.

There are several special features associated with trade credit that require elaboration.

Acquiring Trade Credit   Trade credit is not available just for the asking. Suppliers will perform a credit analysis on new customers to see if they are worthy to receive credit. The credit quality of current customers is also reexamined regularly. The specifics of credit analysis were presented in chapter 7. Companies that fail to meet a supplier's credit standard either will not receive credit or will do so only under very restrictive terms. However, a rejection by one supplier is no guarantee that its competitors will do likewise. As we saw in chapter 7, credit standards are a complex decision for a business. Consequently, one should not be surprised to find varying standards being applied by different suppliers, even in the same industry. A buyer is therefore advised to shop around.

Once credit has been established, a business can purchase goods on *open account,* which is very similar to an individual's charge account at a department store. Buying on open account is a very easy and informal process when compared to, say, borrowing from a bank. Nevertheless, open account purchases are debts and, as such, are legally enforceable financial obligations.

In an effort to make a credit purchase more formal, a supplier will occasionally ask the customer to sign a *promissory note.* This is frequently done for delinquent accounts.

Trade Credit Terms   Credit terms were discussed in chapter 7 from the perspective of the credit seller. We shall now examine credit terms from the standpoint of the credit customer.

Maximum Credit Limit   Companies usually limit the maximum amount of credit a customer can have outstanding at any time. For instance, a furniture manufacturer has been granted a credit limit of $800,000 by a lumber company. Under these terms, the furniture manufacturer cannot allow its accounts payable with the lumber company to exceed $800,000. Credit limits may vary based on, among other things, a customer's credit worthiness and the volume of business it does with a given supplier.

Credit Period   To repeat what was said in chapter 7, a credit period is the number of days that a credit customer has in which to make payment. Although normally in multiples of 15 days, a credit period can be for any length of time and, as far as the buyer is concerned, the longer the credit period the better.

Cash Discount   In certain lines of business it is common practice to allow price discounts to credit customers who pay early (i.e., before the end of the credit period). To qualify for the discount, payment must be made within a specified number of days, known as the *discount period.* When a cash discount is offered, it is common practice to summarize the credit period and discount in the following manner: 4/15/n60. The first number is always the discount, the second number is the discount period, and the last number is the credit period. In words, the previous terms state that a 4% discount can be obtained if payment is made within 15 days (discount period), whereas the net or full amount is due in 60 days (credit period). Take note that the credit period is not in addition to the discount period, but instead overlaps it, as shown in figure 13.1.

Starting Date   Credit periods and discount periods require starting dates. A supplier who requires payment in 45 days must also specify when the 45 day period begins. It could begin on the day the goods are purchased, the date they are received by the customer, or some other time. *The starting date is of more than passing interest considering that it can significantly lengthen the time that a customer has to make payment.*

Starting dates are surprisingly quite varied. The determining factor seems to be the nature of a supplier's business. A few examples would serve to illustrate this. For companies that must ship their goods a long distance, the favored practice is to set the starting date as of the *receipt of goods (ROG).* Under terms of 3/20/n50/ROG, goods received on April 10 must be paid for by April 30 to receive the cash discount. Otherwise, full payment is due by May 30th.

Figure 13.1   Credit period of sixty days combined with a cash discount period of fifteen days

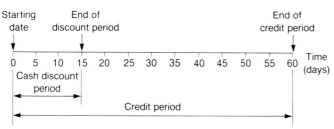

Suppliers who make numerous sales to the same customers, often allow them to start the credit and discount periods at the *end-of-the-month (EOM)* in which the goods are received. That is, the starting date for goods received on June 6, June 17, and June 28 would be June 30. Under terms of 4/10/n45/EOM, goods received on August 12 should be paid for by September 10 in order to be eligible for the 4% discount. The credit period ends on October 15. This procedure facilitates record keeping for both the customer and supplier. It also extends the time for payment.

Seasonal dating is used by manufacturers that have a strong seasonal pattern to their sales. Under this system, a starting date is set far into the future, generally in the midst of the big season. Toy manufacturers are a good example. They begin delivering toys to retailers in September in anticipation of the Christmas season. However, the credit and discount periods begin much later. Terms might be: 3/10/n60/December 1. Under these terms, the toy retailers will have until December 10 to take advantage of the cash discount, whereas the full amount of the bill is due by January 30 of the following year. Manufacturers are willing to offer such lenient credit terms primarily because they can shift the burden of carrying inventory to wholesalers and retailers.

Payment Period   We have just discussed the credit period, discount period, and starting date. Of utmost importance to the credit customer is a further time category, the *payment period: this is the time interval between receipt of the goods (i.e., when they become an asset) and payment for them.* The time period, in other words, when the customer receives financing.

Payment periods are not necessarily the same as the discount and credit periods. They could be different for two reasons. The most likely reason is that the starting date is later than the delivery date. For instance, the payment periods for goods delivered on August 8 under terms of 3/15/n60/EOM would be: 38 days to receive the discount and 83 days to meet the final due date. Of course, only one of these payment periods will apply, depending on whether or not the discount is taken. Under no circumstances would the payment periods in this example be shorter than 38 days and 83 days.[1] However, the payment period associated with the final due date can be lengthened by making a late payment. In the preceding

---

[1] According to the time value of money, payments should be delayed as long as possible.

example, the payment period can be increased to 95 days by delaying payment 12 days beyond the credit period. This practice is referred to as *stretching the payables.* By stretching its accounts payable, a credit customer is receiving additional free trade credit from its suppliers. Sometimes a supplier will voluntarily grant an extension for good cause. However, there are risks associated with paying late. For one thing, there is a high probability that a firm's credit rating will be damaged.

Cost of Trade Credit   It is convenient to describe trade credit as a free source of debt financing, in as much as there is no explicit interest charge. However, there are at least two situations when this is not true.

Missed Cash Discounts   Missing a cash discount may not appear to be a financing decision, but it clearly is. In some quarters, it is considered bad business to miss a cash discount. But this may not be the case at all. By foregoing a discount, a business is literally "buying time." The cost is the discount and the time is the interval from the end of the discount period to the end of the credit period. A company can obtain extra days of trade credit, but at the cost of missing a cash discount. Let us say, for instance, that a firm has purchased $400,000 in goods under terms of 5/15/n75. By foregoing a discount of $20,000 (i.e. $400,000 × .05) the company can acquire 60 additional days of financing. This trade credit is clearly not free. Nevertheless, acquiring funds in this manner is often less expensive than other short-term sources such as bank commercial loans and commercial paper.

An annual interest rate can be derived from a missed cash discount and the resulting additional payment time. By so doing, one can more easily make a cost comparison with alternative sources of funds. Equation 13.1 provides such an interest rate.

Equation 13.1 $$\text{Interest Rate} = \underbrace{\frac{\text{Discount}}{1 - \text{Discount}}}_{\text{Percentage Cost}} \times \underbrace{\frac{360 \text{ days}}{\text{Credit Period} - \text{Discount Period}}}_{\text{Number of Periods in a Year}}$$

Example A: The annual interest rate implied by payment terms of 4/15/n45 is found as follows:

$$\text{Interest rate} = \frac{.04}{1 - .04} \times \frac{360}{45 - 15} = .04167 \times 12 = 50\%$$

Clearly, this is a very high interest rate and one that most firms could improve on ∎

Example B: A missed cash discount under terms of 2/10/n110, would imply an annual interest rate of:

$$\text{Interest Rate} = \frac{.02}{1 - .02} \times \frac{360}{110 - 10} = .02041 \times 3.6 = 7.35\%$$

Here we have a situation where, by missing a cash discount, a firm can acquire short-term financing at a relatively low interest rate ∎

Hidden Cost   As we saw in chapter 7, extending credit can be a rather costly undertaking for a supplier. Most firms try to recover this cost by including it in the price of their merchandise. Cash discounts are evidence of this. But it is often difficult for a customer to know the size of this added charge, especially if all competing suppliers offer the same terms. *If it were possible to separate the cost of extending credit from the price of the goods, a company would know what it is paying for trade credit.*

Bank Commercial Loans

Next to trade credit, bank commercial loans are the single most important means of raising short-term corporate financing. Banks have been making seasonal and temporary loans to business for centuries. Up until the late nineteenth century, banks confined their activities almost exclusively to short-term business lending; financing merchant ships' cargo and crop loans to farmers were principle activities. Although their loans are much more varied today, commercial loans remain a very significant part of bank lending. We will examine several features of these loans in this section.

Types of Commercial Loans   Banks make two basic types of commercial loans: special purpose loans and lines of credit. These lending arrangements are usually evidenced by the signing of a note (exhibit 13.1).

Special Purpose Loans   A special purpose commercial loan is granted for a specific purpose and fixed period of time. The funds are usually received all at once and repaid in like manner. While the maturity of these loans is normally less than one year, they may extend for as long as two or three years. Special purpose loans are particularly well suited for construction financing. For instance, a firm might borrow $10 million from a bank for one year to finance the construction of an office building. Once the construction is completed, a more permanent form of financing (i.e., a bond issue) can be obtained, with the proceeds used to pay off the special purpose loan.

Lines of Credit   *A line of credit is a prearranged loan commitment under which a bank (or group of banks) agrees, in writing, to lend up to a given amount of funds for one year.* Companies can draw on all or part of these funds any time during the year. These loans can be repaid at any time during the year and in any amount. Since they are arranged in advance, little more than a phone call is needed to access a line of credit. Interest is charged on only those funds that are actually borrowed, even though the line of credit may be much higher. *Such flexibility in a line of credit makes it an excellent vehicle for funding seasonal financial requirements.* A line of credit is essentially determined by the borrower's projected cash budget for the coming year.

Exhibit 13.1   Lending note

	TERRE HAUTE FIRST NATIONAL BANK TERRE HAUTE, IN 47808	Loan Number _____ Date _____ , 19 ____ Maturity Date _____ , 19 ____ Loan Amount $ _____ Renewal Of
BORROWER'S NAME AND ADDRESS "I" includes each borrower above, jointly and severally	**LENDER'S NAME AND ADDRESS** "You" means the lender, its successors and assigns.	

I promise to pay to you, or your order, at your address listed above the

PRINCIPAL sum of _____ Dollars $ _____

☐ **Single Advance:** I have received all of this principal sum. No additional advances are contemplated under this note.

☐ **Multiple Advance:** The principal sum shown above is the maximum amount of principal I can borrow under this note. As of today I have received

the amount of $ _____ and future principal advances are contemplated.

    Conditions: The conditions for future advances are _____

_____

☐ **Open End Credit:** You and I agree that I may borrow up to the maximum amount of principal more than one time. This feature is subject to all other

    conditions and expires no later than _____ 19 _____.

☐ **Closed End Credit:** You and I agree that I may borrow up to the maximum only one time (and subject to all other conditions).

PURPOSE: The purpose of this loan is _____

INTEREST: I agree to pay interest on the principal balance(s) owing from time to time as stated in this section.

☐ **Fixed Rate:** I agree to pay interest at the fixed, simple rate of _____ % per year.

☐ **Variable Rate:** I agree to pay interest at the initial simple rate of _____ % per year. This rate may change as stated below.

    ☐ **Index Rate:** The future rate will be _____ the following index rate _____

_____

    ☐ **No Index:** The future rate will not be subject to any internal or external index. It will be entirely in your control.

    ☐ **Frequency and Timing:** The rate on this note may increase as often as _____

        An increase in the index will take effect _____

    ☐ **Limitations:** The rate on this note will not at any time (and no matter what happens to any index rate used) go above or below these limits

        ☐ **Maximum Rate:** The rate will not go above _____

        ☐ **Minimum Rate:** The rate will not go below _____

Post Maturity Rate: I agree to pay interest on the principal owing after maturity, and until paid in full, as stated below.

    ☐ on the same fixed or variable rate basis in effect before maturity (as indicated above).

    ☐ at a rate equal to _____

☐ **ADDITIONAL CHARGES:** In addition to interest, I ☐ have paid ☐ agree to pay   the following additional charges _____

PAYMENTS: I agree to pay this note as follows

☐ **Interest:** I agree to pay accrued interest _____

☐ **Principal:** I agree to pay the principal _____

☐ **Installments:** I agree to pay this note in _____ payments. The first payment will be in the amount of $ _____

    and will be due _____ , 19 ____ A payment of $ _____ will be due on the _____ day of

    each _____ thereafter. The final payment of the entire unpaid balance of

    principal and interest will be due _____ , 19 ____.

☐ **Effect of Variable Rate:** An increase in the interest rate will have the following effect on the payments:

    ☐ The amount of each scheduled payment will be increased.

    ☐ The amount of the final payment will be increased.

    ☐ _____

ADDITIONAL TERMS:

☐ **SECURITY:** This note is secured by : _____

_____

_____

_____

☐ If checked, no agreement was signed today securing this note.

(This section is for your internal use. It may not include every agreement or item of collateral securing this note. You will not lose any security by omitting it from this section.)

© 1984 BANKERS SYSTEMS, INC. ST. CLOUD, MN   FORM UN-IN   7/17/84

SIGNATURES: I AGREE TO THE TERMS OF THIS NOTE (INCLUDING THOSE ON THE OTHER SIDE). I have received a copy on today's date.

_____

_____

Source: Terre Haute First National Bank, Terre Haute, IN.

Exhibit 13.1 *Continued*

ADDITIONAL TERMS

APPLICABLE LAW: The law of the state in which you are located will govern this note. Any term of this note which is contrary to applicable law will not be effective, unless the law permits you and me to agree to such a variation.

PAYMENTS: Each payment I make on this note will first reduce the amount I owe you for charges which are neither interest nor principal. The remainder of each payment will then reduce unpaid earned interest, and then unpaid principal. If you and I agree to a different application of payments, we will describe our agreement on this form.

INTEREST: If I receive the principal in more than one advance, each advance will start to earn interest only when I receive the advance. The interest rate in effect on this note at any given time will apply to the entire principal advanced at that time. If the interest rate on this note is variable, decreases in the interest rate will have the corresponding opposite effect on my payment that increases will have (as shown on the front of this form). No matter how the interest rate is computed, it will never be higher than the highest rate allowed by law.

INDEX RATES: If you and I have agreed that the interest rate on this note will be variable and will be related to an index rate, then the index we select will function only as a tool for setting the rate on this note. You do not guarantee, by selecting any index, that the rate on this note will have a particular relationship to the rate you charge on any other loans or any type or class of loans with your other customers.

SINGLE ADVANCE LOANS: If this is a single advance loan, you and I expect that you will make only one advance of principal. However, you may add other amounts to the principal if you make any payments described in the "PAYMENTS BY LENDER" paragraph below.

MULTIPLE ADVANCE LOANS: If this is a multiple advance loan, you and I expect that you will make more than one advance of principal.

If this is closed end credit, then repaying a part of the principal will not entitle me to additional credit.

If this is open end credit, then repaying a part of the principal will entitle me to additional credit, unless the open end feature has expired. You will not ordinarily make an advance if it would cause the unpaid principal amount to become greater than the maximum principal amount, or if the unpaid principal amount is already greater than the maximum principal amount. You will never be obligated to make such an advance, even if you occasionally do so.

PAYMENTS BY LENDER: If you are authorized to pay, on my behalf, charges I am obligated to pay (such as property insurance premiums), then you may treat those payments as advances and add them to the unpaid principal under this note.

POST MATURITY RATE: For purposes of deciding when the "Post Maturity Rate" applies, the term "maturity" means the date of the last scheduled payment of principal and, where repayment is on demand, the date you make your demand. If repayment is on demand with an alternate maturity date(s), then "maturity" is either the date you make your demand or the final alternate maturity date, whichever is earlier.

SET-OFF: You have the right to set off any amount I owe you under this note against any right I have to receive money from you. If my right to receive money from you is owned by someone else not paying this note, your set-off can only reach funds I could have reached with my own request or endorsement. Your right of set-off does not extend to accounts where my rights are only as a fiduciary. It also does not extend to my IRA or other tax-deferred retirement account.

Your right of set off applies without your first telling me you are going to use it. It applies no matter what sort or value of collateral is on this loan. It also applies no matter who else has agreed to pay this note.

You will not be liable for wrongful dishonor of a check where such dishonor occurs because you set-off this debt against my account.

DEFAULT: I will be in default if any one or more of the following occur:
(1) I fail to make a payment on time or in the amount due.
(2) I fail to keep the collateral insured, if required.
(3) I fail to keep any other promise I have made in connection with this loan.
(4) I fail to pay, or keep any other promise, on any other loan or agreement I have with you.
(5) Any other creditor of mine attempts to collect the debt I owe him through court proceedings.
(6) I die.
(7) I go into bankruptcy, whether by my own choice or not.
(8) I do or fail to do something which causes you to believe that you will have difficulty collecting the amount I owe you.
(9) Anything else happens which causes you to believe that you will have difficulty collecting the amount I owe you.

REMEDIES: If I am in default on this note, you have the following remedies:
(1) You may demand immediate payment of all I owe you under this note.
(2) You may set off this debt against any right I have to the payment of money from you.
(3) You may demand more security or new parties obligated to pay this note in return for not using any other remedy.
(4) You may make use of any remedy you have under state or federal law.
(5) You may make use of any remedy given to you in any agreement securing this note.
(6) If this is a multiple advance loan, either open end or closed end, you may refuse to make advances to me while I am in default.

By selecting any one or more of these remedies you do not give up your right to later use any other remedy. By deciding not to use any remedy should I default, you do not waive your right to later consider the event a default if it happens again.

WAIVER: I give up my rights to require you to do certain things. I will not require you to:
(1) demand payment of amounts due (presentment),
(2) obtain official certification of nonpayment (protest),
(3) give notice that amounts due have not been paid (notice of dishonor).

I also give up all rights under valuation and appraisement laws.

ATTORNEYS' FEES: If you must hire a lawyer to collect this note, I must pay his or her fee, plus court costs (except when prohibited by law).

SECURITY: The portion of this form identifying agreements securing this note is for your internal reference only. The fact that you do not list an agreement in that portion of the form does not mean that the agreement does not secure this note.

ADDITIONAL PARTIES AND SECURITY: I understand that I must pay this note even if someone else has signed it. You may sue me, or anyone else, or any of us together, to collect this note. You do not have to tell me this note has not been paid. You may release any cosigner and I will still be obligated to pay the note. If you give up any of your rights it will not affect my duty to pay this note. Extending new credit or renewing this note will not affect my duty to pay this note.

GUARANTEE: By signing below, I unconditionally guarantee the payment of any amounts owed under this note. I also agree that all the other terms of the note will apply to me.

X _____

X _____

DATE OF TRANSACTION	PRINCIPAL ADVANCE	BORROWER'S INITIALS (not required)	PRINCIPAL PAYMENTS	PRINCIPAL BALANCE	INTEREST RATE	INTEREST PAYMENTS	INTEREST PAID THROUGH
	$		$	$		$	
	$		$	$		$	
	$		$	$		$	
	$		$	$		$	
	$		$	$		$	
	$		$	$		$	
	$		$	$		$	
	$		$	$		$	
	$		$	$		$	
	$		$	$		$	
	$		$	$		$	
	$		$	$		$	

FORM UN-IN BACKSIDE REVISION DATE 7/17/84

Table 13.1   Regis Boat Co. 1985 Cash Budget

	January	February	March	April	May
Collections:					
3 months past	$ 60,000	$ 40,000	$ 20,000	$ 0	$ 80,000
2 months past	120,000	60,000	0	240,000	600,000
1 month past	120,000	0	480,000	1,200,000	2,400,000
1. Cash inflows	$ 300,000	$ 100,000	$ 500,000	$1,440,000	$3,080,000
Payments:					
Wages	$1,200,000	$1,200,000	$1,200,000	$1,200,000	$1,200,000
Materials	400,000	400,000	400,000	400,000	400,000
Utilities	80,000	70,000	60,000	30,000	30,000
Supplies	200,000	200,000	200,000	200,000	200,000
General	350,000	350,000	350,000	350,000	350,000
Promotion	10,000	10,000	30,000	50,000	60,000
Maintenance	80,000	80,000	80,000	80,000	80,000
Other:					
Dividends			400,000		
Taxes			750,000		
Equipment					
2. Cash outflows	$2,320,000	$2,310,000	$3,470,000	$2,310,000	$2,320,000
3. Net cash flow (1)−(2)	($2,020,000)	($2,210,000)	($2,970,000)	($ 870,000)	$ 760,000
4. Beginning cash balance	$ 600,000	$ 450,000	$ 450,000	$ 450,000	$ 450,000
5. Minimum cash balance	$ 450,000	$ 450,000	$ 450,000	$ 450,000	$ 450,000
6. Cash surplus (Deficit) (3)+(4)−(5)	($1,870,000)	($2,210,000)	($2,970,000)	($ 870,000)	$ 760,000
7. Deficit financing	$1,870,000	$2,210,000	$2,970,000	$ 870,000	0
8. Surplus repayment	0	0	0	0	$ 760,000
9. Cumulative financing	$1,870,000	$4,080,000	$7,050,000	$7,920,000	$7,160,000
10. Ending cash balance (5)+(6)+(7)−(8)	$ 450,000	$ 450,000	$ 450,000	$ 450,000	$ 450,000
11. Excess cash balance (10)−(5)	0	0	0	0	0

Example: The Regis Boat Co. cash budget that was developed in chapter 11 is duplicated in table 13.1. From an examination of this cash budget, the management of Regis Boat Co. can foresee cash deficits occurring in each of the first four months of 1985, as shown on line 6. The cumulative deficit is expected to reach a peak of $7,920,000 in April (line 9). The firm's line of credit should be at least as large as the biggest cumulative deficit, with something to spare for any contingencies that may arise. Therefore, a line of credit in the neighborhood of, say, $10 million should be arranged for 1985. About the first of January, the line will be drawn on, followed by additional loans in the next three months. The loans can then be repaid from the cash surpluses that begin to materialize in May ■

A line of credit can be formal or informal. *Under an informal arrangement, a bank states that it will do its best to have funds available when the borrower calls for them.* Under most circumstances, this will suffice. However, there is no contractual guarantee that a loan will be forthcoming. Should a company be concerned about this, a *formal guarantee* can often be obtained from a bank. Banks will grant these if the borrower agrees to pay a *commitment fee* (usually less than 1%) on the portion of the line that is not being used.

Table 13.1   *Continued*

June	July	August	September	October	November	December
$ 200,000	$ 400,000	$ 700,000	$ 600,000	$ 600,000	$ 400,000	$ 100,000
1,200,000	2,100,000	1,800,000	1,800,000	1,200,000	300,000	180,000
4,200,000	3,600,000	3,600,000	2,400,000	600,000	360,000	240,000
$5,600,000	$6,100,000	$6,100,000	$4,800,000	$2,400,000	$1,060,000	$ 520,000
$1,200,000	$1,200,000	$1,200,000	$1,200,000	$1,200,000	$1,200,000	$1,200,000
400,000	400,000	400,000	400,000	400,000	400,000	400,000
50,000	60,000	60,000	40,000	30,000	50,000	60,000
200,000	200,000	200,000	200,000	200,000	200,000	200,000
350,000	350,000	350,000	350,000	350,000	350,000	350,000
60,000	60,000	50,000	40,000	30,000	10,000	10,000
80,000	80,000	80,000	80,000	80,000	80,000	80,000
400,000			400,000			400,000
			750,000			
						1,000,000
$2,740,000	$2,350,000	$2,340,000	$3,460,000	$2,290,000	$2,290,000	$3,700,000
$2,860,000	$3,750,000	$3,760,000	$1,340,000	$ 110,000	($1,230,000)	($3,180,000)
$ 450,000	$ 450,000	$ 450,000	$3,660,000	$5,000,000	$5,110,000	$3,180,000
$ 450,000	$ 450,000	$ 450,000	$ 450,000	$ 450,000	$ 450,000	$ 450,000
$2,860,000	$3,750,000	$3,760,000	$4,550,000	$4,660,000	$3,430,000	$ 250,000
0	0	0	0	0	0	0
$2,860,000	$3,750,000	$ 550,000	0	0	0	0
$4,300,000	$ 550,000	0	0	0	0	0
$ 450,000	$ 450,000	$3,660,000	$5,000,000	$5,110,000	$3,880,000	$ 700,000
0	0	$3,210,000	$4,550,000	$4,660,000	$3,430,000	$ 250,000

A requirement with most lines of credit is a *cleanup period*. A cleanup period says that a company must be out of debt to the bank for some continuous period of time (30 to 90 days) during the year. This is to insure that the funds are only being used for temporary financing.

Although a line of credit is usually good for only one year, they are occasionally written for longer periods of time. Renewals are not automatic. The bank will reevaluate a borrower's credit worthiness before it decides whether or not to renew the line of credit.

Commercial Loan Provisions   In the discussion to follow, we will examine three provisions found in many bank commercial loans: compensating balances, protective covenants, and collateral.

Compensating Balances   When a bank makes a loan to a business customer, it will often require that the borrower maintain a certain percentage of the loan in a noninterest bearing checking account. These deposits will remain frozen in the account until the loan is paid off. This provision is commonly referred to as *compensating balances*. It works this way: a bank grants a commercial loan of $2 million; a provision of this loan is a compensating balance requirement of 15%. As a result, the customer will receive a $2 million loan and simultaneously deposit $300,000 of it in a checking account. The $300,000 compensating balance will remain in the borrower's checking account, only to be used to repay the loan. In the meantime, the borrower is assessed interest on the full $2 million even though it has the net use of only $1,700,000. As we shall see later on, compensating balances can distort the interest rate on a loan.

A major objective in requiring compensating balances is to encourage business borrowers to become regular depositors at the lending bank. For those firms who are already checking account customers, a compensating balance provision may be irrelevant.

Protective Covenants   Banks attempt to include various provisions in their business loans, both commercial and otherwise, which serve to reduce the chances of default. We will refer to these as protective covenants. Some of the more common protective covenants are described here.

Dividend Restriction   The company is limited in paying dividends during the life of the loan. This is intended to maintain asset levels or, stated differently, to conserve cash. For example, a loan provision stipulates that the borrower cannot pay dividends in excess of 40% of earnings.

Minimum Liquidity Ratios   The importance of liquidity ratios to creditors, particularly short-term creditors, has been mentioned on several occasions. It is not surprising, therefore, that bankers would try to force their business customers into maintaining minimum levels for these ratios. A loan provision might state, for example, that the company's current ratio cannot go below 2.5, and the quick ratio cannot fall below 1.5, during the life of the loan.

Key-Man Insurance   Businesses that rely heavily upon the services of one or two individuals, would suffer great hardship if one of these persons died. Banks recognize the inherent risks in loaning money to one of these companies. Therefore, as a precondition, they usually require life insurance coverage on these individuals with the bank as beneficiary.

Debt Limits   A bank, or any creditor for that matter, would ideally like to see its loan as the only liability on the borrower's books. As a practical matter, however, this is not likely to happen. What banks can do, is attempt to control the amount of a firm's indebtedness. This can be done by including a debt limit provision in the loan contract. Such a provision can be written in several ways. It might state, for example, that the borrower's debt-to-equity ratio cannot exceed a certain level. In other cases, it might require prior approval of the bank before any additional debt can be incurred.[2]

Protective covenants, such as those presented above, are designed for the benefit of the lender. From the borrower's perspective, they represent an infringement upon management's freedom to make decisions. As such, they should be granted only reluctantly, if at all. Trade-offs might be possible here. For instance, a lower interest rate may be granted in exchange for dividend restrictions. Another possibility would be to trade the protection afforded by collateral in exchange for having no prescribed limit on debt.

---

[2]Restrictions can also be placed on other types of contractual obligations, such as leases.

Collateral   It is a fact of life in business that some companies will experience severe financial problems. Sometimes these problems are so severe that the firm is bankrupt and must cease operations. When this happens, the creditors and owners are left with a company that is producing no revenue and, more importantly, no profit with which to pay interest and dividends. Their only hope for salvation rests in the value of the firm's assets. By liquidating the assets, they may be able to recover their investments. Such an outcome would be highly unlikely, however, for several reasons: (1) the assets may be severely depleted as the result of several years of losses; (2) assets of bankrupt companies normally are not in great demand; (3) legal fees and court costs are usually involved in business liquidations; and (4) feuding often occurs among the claimants, which can tie up a liquidation for several years.

Creditors are certainly in a better position than owners because of their preferred status, but even they cannot be assured of recouping all of their investment. A creditor can improve the odds by obtaining a pledge of collateral from the borrower at the time that the loan is extended. *Collateral is specified property (assets) in which a designated creditor has preference over other creditors.* Such a creditor is said to be in a more *secured* position. Creditors who lack collateral are known as *unsecured creditors* and their loans are called *unsecured loans.* Those that have collateral are referred to as *secured creditors* and their loans are called *secured loans.* Preferably, the collateral should be worth more than the principal amount of the loan.

A legal distinction exists concerning the types of assets that serve as collateral. *Personal property* includes those assets that are relatively easy to move or transport (e.g., automobiles, business inventories, equipment, and common stock). *Real property* is more permanent in nature (e.g., land, buildings, and fixtures). The law requires that collateral for a loan must be carefully documented and recorded. To this end, personal property is pledged by means of a *security agreement,* a sample of which is shown in the appendix to this chapter. Real property is pledged by means of a *mortgage.* There are many other legal aspects surrounding secured loans, but these are sufficient for our purposes.

Many bank commercial loans are secured by personal property, particularly in the case of loans to riskier businesses. Accounts receivable and inventory are the two most common forms of collateral for these loans. And rightly so, since commercial loans are primarily used to finance these same assets.[3]

Pledging Accounts Receivable   Accounts receivable serve as collateral for many bank commercial loans and a majority of finance company loans. Depending on the quality of the receivables, these loans will vary from 70% to 90% of the receivables value. A creditor whose loan is secured by a firm's accounts receivable, has the sole right to seize them in the event that the borrower defaults. Essentially, this means that the bank is entitled to receive all collections from the receivables until the loan and accrued interest are satisfied.

Many creditors are not willing to wait for a default to occur before they exercise control over the receivables. For example, the loan agreement may require a company to pay off its loan with the money collected from the pledged receivables. In other cases, accounts are

---

[3]Financial assets (e.g., stocks and bonds) make very good collateral, not only for bank commercial loans, but all types of indebtedness.

notified that they are to make payment directly to the bank, thus bypassing the firm. Arrangements such as these, while strengthening collateral, require constant vigilance on the part of a lender and are a definite administrative burden for the borrower.

Pledging Inventory   Inventory is a popular form of collateral in the agribusiness and automotive retailing industries. *Creditors are particularly fond of inventoried goods with the following characteristics: not subject to obsolescence, easily liquidated (i.e., marketable), and nonperishable.* Goods possessing these characteristics include raw materials, new automobiles, and farm commodities. If a company defaults on a loan secured by inventory, the secured creditor has the sole legal right to seize the property and sell it to retire the debt and any accrued interest.

Creditors encounter several difficulties when inventory serves as collateral: (1) goods may spoil, deteriorate, or even be stolen while in storage; (2) damage can occur to the property from fire, rain, etc.; and, most importantly, (3) the property might be disposed of fraudulently, leaving the lender unprotected. Some of these difficulties can be managed by requiring the borrower to maintain insurance on the inventory. As for the rest, several special arrangements have been devised to deal with them.

Public Warehousing: Public warehouses are licensed storage facilities (e.g., grain elevators and chemical tanks) operated by bonded managers. Activities of these organizations are regularly inspected by a state or federal government agency. Banks have found public warehouses an excellent place to keep certain kinds of inventory collateral. Not only will the property be cared for, but it also remains out from under the borrower's control. Commodities such as wheat, corn, vegetable oil, and cotton are particularly well suited for public warehouses. A business is simply instructed to deliver pledged inventory to one of these facilities as a condition of the loan. Ownership of the goods is evidenced by a *negotiable warehouse receipt,* which is usually endorsed over to the creditor for the life of the loan. The bank can use this receipt to seize the property should the borrower default on the debt. A business can retain its property by settling the loan. A negotiable warehouse receipt for the ownership of grain is shown in exhibit 13.2.

Ordinarily, a bank can rest assured knowing that its collateral is in the care of a public warehouse manager who is licensed, bonded, and regulated. Unfortunately, managers of these facilities have occasionally abused the public trust by attempting to enrich themselves through the unauthorized sale of property left in their care.

Field Warehousing: There are many situations in which a public warehouse is not suitable as a guardian of inventory collateral. Raw material, such as sheet metal and timber, which are needed daily in production, do not lend themselves to this arrangement. It is most convenient for these goods to remain on company grounds. A system known as field warehousing has been developed to deal with this problem.

Private field warehousing firms are employed to keep watch over collateral located at production sites. For example, one of these companies might be hired to keep track of timber used at a paper mill. To this end, the field warehousing firm might construct a temporary fence on company grounds to hold the timber. An employee of this firm is stationed at the gate during the day, clipboard in hand, to make sure that the timber is only used in the production of paper. At night, the gate is locked and, in extreme cases, guard dogs are placed inside. Field warehousing is a costly and cumbersome method to monitor inventory. For these reasons, companies should carefully consider secured loans when field warehousing is involved.

Exhibit 13.2 Sample warehouse receipt

LICENSE NUMBER 3-7964

PILLSBURY ELEVATOR
DUBUQUE, IOWA
THE PILLSBURY COMPANY, PROPRIETOR
INCORPORATED UNDER THE LAWS OF DELAWARE

RECEIPT No 1025

CCC WHSE. CODE NO. 9-2786
The Undersigned Warehouseman Claims A Lien On Said Grain For Charges And Liabilities As Follows:

LICENSED AND BONDED UNDER THE UNITED STATES WAREHOUSE ACT
COPY—NOT NEGOTIABLE WAREHOUSE RECEIPT FOR GRAIN

VOID

SOYBEANS ______¢ PER BUSHEL FOR THE FIRST 90 DAYS OR FRACTION THEREOF, THEN ______¢ PER BUSHEL PER DAY. ALL OTHER GRAINS ______¢ PER BUSHEL FOR THE FIRST 90 DAYS OR FRACTION THEREOF, THEN ______¢ PER BUSHEL PER DAY.

RECEIVED FROM: ______ OF ______

For storage in the above-named warehouse in the course of Interstate or Foreign Commerce, grain of the quantity, kind, and grade described herein for which this receipt is issued subject to the United States Warehouse Act, the regulations thereunder for grain warehousemen, and the terms of this contract. Grade, according to U. S. official standards, and weight are as determined by an inspector and weigher licensed under said act. Said grain is Fully Insured by the undersigned warehouseman against loss or damage by fire, lightning, inherent explosion, tornado, cyclone, and windstorm unless otherwise stated hereon. Said grain is accepted upon condition that the depositor or holder of this receipt shall demand delivery not later than one year from the date of this receipt. The undersigned warehouseman is not the owner of said grain either solely, jointly, or in common with others unless otherwise stated hereon. Upon return of this receipt properly indorsed and payment of the warehouseman's lien claimed hereon, said grain or grain of the same or better grade will be delivered to the above named depositor or his ORDER.

Date Issued	Kind of Grain	Grade & Sub Class	Dock.%	Lbs. of Gr. incl. Dock.	Gross Bushels	Net Pounds	Net Bushels

Elevation Chgs. Prepaid Per Bu.		Date Storage Pd. Through		
In @ ¢	Out @ ¢	Mo.	Day	Yr.

ISSUED AT DUBUQUE, IOWA
THE PILLSBURY COMPANY LICENSED WAREHOUSEMAN
BY ______

Handling and other accrued charges according to the tariff of the company. Full amount of charges furnished on request.

The Issuance Of A Fraudulent Receipt, Or Illegal Conversion Or Removal Of The Products Represented By This Receipt Is Punishable By A $10,000 Fine Or Imprisonment For 10 Years Or Both.

SUPPLEMENTAL INFORMATION *For purposes of the Uniform Grain Storage Agreement only (Not part of Warehouse Receipt)*										Date Received			Received By			FOR CCC USE ONLY			
Test Wt. Lbs.	Moisture %	Protein % Splits or Sounds	TD %	HD %	FM %	Shr. Brok. %	Tot. Def. %	Other Quality Factors	Car Initial and No.	Mo.	Day	Yr.	Trk.	Brg.	Rail	Chgs.	Type Stg.	Area	Loan/Purchase No.

Courtesy of the Pillsbury Company, Grain Merchandising Division.

Floor Planning: Most short-term loans to automobile and farm implement dealers are secured by the inventories of these businesses. Sales of these items would be rather difficult if they were stored in a public warehouse or kept under surveillance by a field warehousing firm. Given this constraint, creditors use what is called a *floor plan* to maintain control of their collateral. Under a floor plan, all pledged vehicles are left in the possession of the dealer, but the creditor retains all titles. Individual loans are made on each unit. As the vehicles are sold, the proceeds are forwarded immediately to the lender, who then releases the titles. The creditor's main protection comes from holding the titles. It is nearly impossible to sell a car to an honest consumer without the official title. The lender can also make unannounced on-site inspections to determine whether or not all pledged vehicles are accounted for. An actual floor plan agreement is shown in exhibit 13.3.

Cost of Bank Commercial Loans One thing that will be apparent in our discussion of interest rates on bank commercial loans is the omission of compound interest. Technically speaking, compound interest could apply to short-term loans, but seldom is it done so in practice. There are two possible reasons for this. In the first place, many of these loans contain aspects that are not easy to incorporate into compound interest formulas. Secondly, for short-term loans, especially those under one year, little accuracy is lost by ignoring compounding.

A key interest rate for any commercial bank is the *prime rate.* This is the rate charged on short-term loans to a bank's most credit-worthy business customers. Firms of lower credit standing are usually assessed an interest rate that is tied to the prime rate (e.g., prime rate plus three percent).[4] Normally, there is close uniformity of prime rates from one bank to the next. As a result, it is common for businessmen and bankers to speak of "the" prime rate.

[4]Although generally accepted for many years, this definition of the prime rate has come under attack recently. It seems a number of bank commercial loans have been extended at rates lower than the quoted prime rates. Therefore, the prime rate is a standard or base rate of interest that is charged on loans of a predetermined level of risk. Loans with a greater than standard risk wil be charged rates above the prime and vice versa.

Exhibit 13.3   Sample floor plan, wholesale agreement

Wholesale Agreement

This acknowledgment is made this _____ day of _____, 19___ between Terre Haute First National Bank, hereinafter called Bank, and _____
_____, hereinafter called Dealer. This acknowledgment is set forth to familiarize dealers with Terre Haute First National Bank's wholesale finance plan, hereinafter called Plan, policies and procedures.

Floor plan rate is defined in Schedule "A". Schedule "A" may be amended from time to time at the sole discretion of the Bank and any such amendment shall become effective upon delivery of written notice to Dealer.

Interest charges are accrued based on the daily outstanding and will be billed monthly. Said charges are due five (5) working days from date statement is received.

All new units which are financed under the Plan shall be secured by a trust receipt in an amount equal to and not to exceed _____% of manufacturer's invoice. Manufacturer's invoice is defined as dealer cost at point of manufacture, exclusive of any and all freight or transportation charges and excepting discounts, bonuses and refunds and rebates. Dealer shall provide manufacturer's invoice to be attached to each security agreement to be processed. Used units are to be financed at _____% of _____ Book value. Titles and or proof of ownership shall be inspected at time security agreement is to be processed. Bank at its discretion shall retain titles and/or proof of ownership with security agreement. Unit shall be at Dealer's place of business at time security is executed.

Curtailments will be required in instances where manufacturers make such requirements a condition of their respective repurchase agreements or unit reaches maturity and Dealer, with Bank's approval, wishes to extend maturity.

Units financed under the plan will mature in full _____ days from date of security agreement.

Dealer shall pay sold units financed under the Plan in full five (5) working days from date of delivery or date of sale whichever occurs first. Sale shall be constituted by payment.

Dealer shall provide proof of insurance to include comprehensive coverage in sufficient amounts to cover inventory financed under Plan; and manufacturer's Certificate of Origin and/or Titles whichever is applicable.

Bank shall physically inspect units, and manufacturer's Certificate of Origin and/or Titles whichever is applicable, financed under the Plan on a periodic basis. Inspector will in certain instances verify date of sale or delivery and purchaser of units sold and not paid at time of audit. All units sold and not paid at the time of audit should be paid to Inspector or within a reasonable time thereafter.

Dealer will allow Bank personnel to inspect records in order to ascertain Dealer's financial condition to include inspection of financial statements, on a periodic basis. Bank will request Dealer to furnish a copy of an independent audit report on an annual basis.

Dealer will obtain prior approval for additions of new lines of merchandise that are to be financed under the Plan. Dealer will be required to submit a current financial statement, product information from prospective manufacturer. Lines of credit will be reviewed to ascertain whether present line is adequate to accommodate new product line.

Bank will annually review lines of credit in order to conform with policy which requires that lines of credit be re-established on an annual basis.

Any failure to comply or cooperate with provisions of this acknowledgment may result in termination of the wholesale accommodation.

Source: Terre Haute First National Bank, Terre Haute, IN.

Prime rates can and do change in response to market conditions, although not as frequently as other interest rates. As a matter of fact, *many bank loans are written so that the interest rates vary with changes in the prime rate.*

Example: Antok Enterprises borrowed $500,000 from Mid States Bank for the period April 1 through September 30, 1986. The interest rate was 2% plus whatever the bank's prime rate happened to be. The prime rate at the time the loan was taken out was 13%. It rose to 14% on May 15 and then declined to 13½% on July 31. As a result, Antok paid 15% from April 1 to May 15, 16% from May 16 to July 31, and 15½% from August 1 to September 30 ▪

Interest rates on bank loans, as well as most other interest rates, are quoted on an annual basis. Thus, a rate of 14% is understood to be an annual rate, unless stated otherwise. For loans that are for less than a year, a simple pro rata adjustment is made in the quoted annual rate. For example, a two-month loan made at a rate of 12% would have one-sixth of that rate, or 2%, assessed upon it. This issue was addressed in chapter 3.

Our discussion of bank loan interest rates would be ended here, were it not for the fact that these rates are not always what they seem. *There are two banking practices that can cause the quoted rate to be different from the true or effective rate. These practices are discounted loans and the aforementioned compensating balances.*

In a normal situation, a loan of $50,000 for one year at 12% interest would and should mean the following: the borrower receives the use of $50,000 for one year, at which time he repays the $50,000 plus $6,000 (i.e., 12% of $50,000) in interest, or $56,000. Now interject a 10% compensating balance into this example. Under this situation, the borrower must deposit $5,000 in a checking account until the loan is paid off, thereby reducing the useable funds to $45,000. However, the 12% interest rate still applies to the full $50,000. An interest expense of $6,000 for the use of $45,000 is not truly a 12% interest rate. A further complication arises when the loan is discounted.[5] In banking parlance, this means that the interest is taken out in advance. In other words, the $6,000 in interest would be subtracted from the $50,000, not added onto it. The borrower receives the use of $44,000 and repays $50,000 one year later. Here again, an interest cost of $6,000 for the use of $44,000 is effectively not a 12% interest rate. Effective annual interest rates on bank commercial loans can be found with equation 13.2.

Equation 13.2 $\text{Interest rate} = \dfrac{\text{Interest Expense}}{\text{Usable Funds}} \times \dfrac{360 \text{ days}}{\text{Loan Maturity}}$

We will now use this formula to calculate the effective annual interest rates on several types of bank commercial loans.

----

[5]This is not to be confused with discounting as used in compound interest.

Example A: Interest Added On, No Compensating Balance

Maturity = 45 days   Quoted Interest Rate = 14% or 1.75% for 45 days
Interest Expense = $14,000   Compensating Balance = 0
Loan = $800,000   Usable Funds = $800,000

$$\text{Effective Rate} = \frac{\$14,000}{\$800,000} \times \frac{360}{45} = 14\%$$

Example B: Interest Added On, A 20% Compensating Balance

Maturity = 30 days   Quoted Interest Rate = 12% or 1% for 30 days
Interest Expense = $8,000   Compensating Balance = $160,000
Loan = $800,000   Usable Funds = $800,000 − $160,000 = $640,000

$$\text{Effective Rate} = \frac{\$8,000}{\$640,000} \times \frac{360}{30} = 15\%$$

Example C: Interest Discounted, No Compensating Balance

Maturity = 60 days   Quoted Interest Rate = 15% or 2.5% for 60 days
Interest Expense = $20,000   Compensating Balance = 0
Loan = $800,000   Usable Funds = $800,000 − $20,000 = $780,000

$$\text{Effective Rate} = \frac{\$20,000}{\$780,000} \times \frac{360}{60} = 15.38\%$$

Example D: Interest Discounted, A 15% Compensating Balance

Maturity = 90 days   Quoted Interest Rate = 16% or 4% for 90 days
Interest Expense = $32,000   Compensating Balance = $120,000
Loan = $800,000   Usable Funds = $800,000 − $32,000 − $120,000 = $648,000

$$\text{Effective Rate} = \frac{\$32,000}{\$648,000} \times \frac{360}{90} = 19.75\%$$

Note the discrepancies between quoted interest rates and effective interest rates in examples B, C, and D. *Furthermore, all of these interest rates are on a before-tax basis.* The effective rate of 19.75% in example D, for instance, would be only 11.85% after taxes for a firm in a 40% tax bracket ∎

Computing effective interest rates is a necessary task if we wish to make a valid comparison among alternative loans. Six banks may have six different ways of administering their loans. Consequently, a comparison of their quoted rates may be very misleading.

One further point needs to be made regarding discounted loans and compensating balances. Refer again to example D. Here, a firm borrowed $800,000, but was able to use only $648,000 because of a compensating balance requirement and discounted interest. If the firm really needs $800,000, it will have to borrow a larger sum. To determine this larger loan, one should first combine the applicable interest rate (4%) and compensating balance (15%). This percentage (19%) represents the proportion of the loan that the company will not receive. It will, however, be able to use one minus that amount, or 81%. By the use of algebra, we can solve for the new loan as follows: $800,000 = .81 Loan, or Loan = $987,654.

Loan Preparation   Often, too little attention is given to the application for bank credit by the borrower. As a result of this, time is wasted and much misunderstanding can result between the two parties to the negotiation. This can lead to three undesirable consequences: (1) the loan may not be consummated; (2) the provisions of the loan are not appropriate for the company; and (3) the borrower is placed at a serious disadvantage relative to the lender who is more experienced and better equipped to negotiate a loan.

It is essential that the credit seeker be equipped to efficiently and intelligently negotiate the loan if he wishes to avoid any of the aforementioned problems. This is where loan preparation comes in. The preparations for acquiring a loan can be broken down into two areas: (1) what the lender wants to know and (2) what the borrower needs to know.

The bank loan officer is interested in estimating whether the loan will be repaid, with interest, and with a minimum of trouble. It is important that the borrower's representative place himself or herself in the loan officer's position and try to identify the information that will help the banker to deal with these issues. Typically, a loan officer will wish to examine historical and projected financial statements, reasons for the loan, projected cash budgets, credit history of the firm, quality and availability of collateral, caliber of management, and company prospects. This information should be prepared in advance by the borrower and in such a way that it is authoritative and easy to comprehend. Furthermore, the borrower should be ready to answer any questions that might arise, particularly with regard to any of the above information that places the firm in a poor light. A well-rehearsed and researched loan preparation, in and of itself, can make a good impression on those who are making the credit decision.

Not only must the borrower be concerned with the creditor's problems when preparing for the loan request, he or she must also consider the specific characteristics of the loan from the firm's viewpoint. Characteristics such as protective covenants, compensating balances, flexibility to draw down funds (all the funds may not be needed at once), repayment schedule, which assets are to be used for collateral, and the method of computing the interest rate are normally important provisions in a loan contract. Some consideration should be given to each of these, as to how they would best fit with the firm's financial situation. Furthermore, any possible trade-offs among these provisions or between a provision and the interest rate should be explored. It is important to recognize the fact that the creditor does not necessarily have the sole discretion to determine these factors, and, in fact, the bank may be indifferent as to how certain terms are written. The credit seeker should therefore be prepared to argue for specific terms (e.g., which assets can serve as collateral and which cannot) that are important to the company. Without having given consideration to loan characteristics beforehand, the borrower will be in a poor position to negotiate them.

In summary, the financial manager in charge of financing for a firm should see to it that the application for bank credit goes smoothly and takes into consideration the needs of his or her firm as well as those of the lender. By doing so, the financial manager can increase the chances of a successful loan application and with terms beneficial to the firm. This can be achieved through careful loan preparation.

Banking Relationships   Many financial authorities feel that it is important for a business to maintain a close working relationship with its bank or banks. There are several potential advantages in having a close business (or even personal) relationship with one's banker. Bankers are valuable sources of financial information and worthwhile advice. These services are often free of charge to close customers. All other things being equal, it is more difficult for a banker to deny credit to a close, long-time acquaintance. These customers will usually be given the benefit of the doubt. It is also easier to arrange loans or work out difficulties with current loans when a banker has an intimate understanding of a borrower's business.

On the other hand, there is a price to be paid for having a close banking relationship. These arrangements are two-way streets. Bankers will be loyal only if their customers are loyal. Being a loyal customer will mean, among other things, occasionally having to bypass lower interest rates offered by competing banks. It also means that the borrower will be divulging more information on its operations and practices, whether it likes it or not.

Comparison Shopping   *It can pay to shop around when looking for a bank loan,* as the following two scenarios show: a business is turned down by one bank, but receives royal treatment from the next; three separate banks charge the same borrower effective interest rates that range from 14% to 16%. Such diverse behavior is not uncommon in banking because, contrary to popular opinion, bankers are not all alike. Among other things, they often possess different lending philosophies. Banks also vary in such matters as organizational structure, size of operation and available funds. All of these factors can lead to dissimilar behavior on the part of banks. Thus, comparison shopping can be rewarding in this area.

Commercial Paper

Commercial paper is a short-term debt security issued by corporations. While traditionally an important alternative to bank loans, it has become increasingly popular in recent years. As we saw in the preceding chapter, most commercial paper is sold directly to other corporations and institutional investors in private transactions. A significant amount, though, is issued in the open market by commercial paper dealers. *By and large, commercial paper has been sold only by large, well-known, financially strong corporations (e.g., General Electric, DuPont, and Ford).* This is no longer the case, however, as more and more new and medium-size firms are becoming involved.

Many companies are willing to pay to have their commercial paper rated for quality by an independent investment advisory firm, in the belief that this will make the paper more attractive to investors. Moody's Investors Services, Inc. and Standard and Poors, Corp. are two such firms. Moody's *commercial paper rating* guidelines are shown in exhibit 13.4.

Common Characteristics   There are four characteristics common to most commercial paper:

1. *Nonsecured:* Investors receive no specific collateral to support their investment. It is primarily for this reason, that only companies with excellent credit ratings are able to sell commercial paper.
2. *Large denomination:* Due to the fact that commercial paper is sold only to large investors, it normally comes in denominations of $100,000 or more.

Exhibit 13.4   Moody's commercial paper ratings

Moody's Commercial Paper Ratings

The term "commercial paper" as used by Moody's means promissory obligations not having an original maturity in excess of nine months. Moody's makes no representation as in whether such commercial paper is by any other definition "commercial paper" or is exempt from registration under the Securities Act of 1933, as amended.

Moody's Commercial Paper ratings are opinions of the ability of issuers to repay punctually promissory obligations not having an original maturity in excess of nine months. Moody's makes no representation that such obligations are exempt from registration under the Securities Act of 1933, nor does it represent that any specific note is a valid obligation of a rated issuer or issued in conformity with any applicable law. Moody's employs the following three designations, all judged to be investment grade, to indicate the relative repayment capacity of rate issuers:

Issuers rated Prime-1 (or related supporting institutions) have a superior capacity for repayment of short-term promissory obligations. Prime-1 repayment capacity will normally be evidenced by the following characteristics:

— Leading market positions in well established industries.
— High rates of return on funds employed.
— Conservative capitalization structures with moderate reliance on debt and ample asset protection.
— Broad margins in earnings coverage of fixed financial charges and high internal cash generation.
— Well established access to a range of financial markets and assured sources of alternate liquidity.

Issuers rated Prime-2 (or related supporting institutions) have a strong capacity for repayment of short-term promissory obligations. This will normally be evidenced by many of the characteristics cited above but to a lesser degree. Earnings trends and coverage ratios, while sound, will be more subject to variation. Capitalization characteristics, while still appropriate, may be more affected by external conditions. Ample alternate liquidity is maintained.

Issuers rated Prime-3 (or related supporting institutions) have an acceptable capacity for repayment of short-term promissory obligations. The effect of industry characteristics and market composition may be more pronounced. Variability in earnings and profitability may result in changes in the level of debt protection measurements and the requirement for relatively high financial leverage. Adequate alternate liquidity is maintained.

Issuers rated Not Prime do not fall within any of the Prime rating categories.

If an issuer represents to Moody's that its Commercial Paper obligations are supported by the credit of another entity or entities, then the name or names of such supporting entity or entities are listed within parentheses beneath the name of the issuer, or there is a footnote referring the reader to another page for the name or names of the supporting entity or entities. In assigning ratings to such issuers, Moody's evaluates the financial strength of the indicated affiliated corporations, commercial banks, insurance companies, foreign governments or other entities, but only as one factor in the total rating assessment. Moody's makes no representation and gives no opinion on the legal validity or enforceability of any support arrangement. You are cautioned to review with your counsel any questions regarding particular support arrangements.

Source: *Moody's Bond Record*, Moody's Investor Service, New York, N.Y.

3. *Short Maturity:* Commercial paper can escape SEC registration requirements if it has a maturity under nine months. In actuality, most of it falls due within two months.
4. *Discounted:* Commercial paper is sold at a discount from par value. The difference between these two amounts is the interest expense for the issuing corporation. There is no stated interest rate on these securities, as such. Furthermore, the par value is paid all at one time, on the maturity date.
5. *Form of a Check:* A commercial paper certificate is much the same as a personal check written on the issuing corporation. The primary difference between the two is that a commercial paper certificate is made out for payment on a future date.

Alternative to Bank Commercial Loans   Commercial paper is, for the most part, an alternative to bank loans. For reasons that are not entirely clear, *interest rates on commercial paper are often lower than bank loan rates,* depending, of course, on the borrower and the bank. This can be seen in figure 13.2, where one-month maturity commercial paper rates are compared to bank prime rates over the last 50 years. Furthermore, there are no compensating balances, collateral, or protective covenants associated with commercial paper. These factors combine to make commercial paper a very attractive means of raising money, at least for those firms that can take advantage of it. Publicly placed commercial paper has at least one other claimed advantage over bank loans, and that is the notoriety that comes from public exposure.

Cost of Commercial Paper   Unlike most loans, there is no contractual interest rate associated with commercial paper. That is, the borrower is not required to pay a specified percentage, say 8%, on a certain date or dates. However, an interest expense certainly exists. It results from the fact that commercial paper is sold at a discount from par or face value. The borrowing firm receives one amount of money and repays a higher amount on some future date. The difference between these two amounts is the interest cost.

Example: There is a $30,000,000 par value issue of paper that matures in 90 days. Given a selling price of $28,800,000, the interest expense would be $1,200,000 for the use of $28,800,000 for 90 days. These figures can be easily converted into an annual interest rate for comparative purposes. We proceed as follows: calculate the 90-day rate by dividing the usable funds into the interest expense, or $1,200,000 ÷ $28,800,000 = .0417. Convert the 90-day rate to an annual rate by multiplying it by the number of 90-day periods in a year, or .0417 × 4 = 16.67%. Of course, on an after-tax basis the cost would be much lower ■

A general expression for calculating the cost of commercial paper is provided by equation 13.3.

Equation 13.3 $$\text{Interest Rate} = \frac{\text{Par Value} - \text{Sales Proceeds}}{\text{Sales Proceeds}} \times \frac{360 \text{ days}}{\text{Days to Maturity}}$$

Figure 13.2   Short-term interest rates in business borrowing: prime rate, effective date of change; commercial paper, quarterly averages

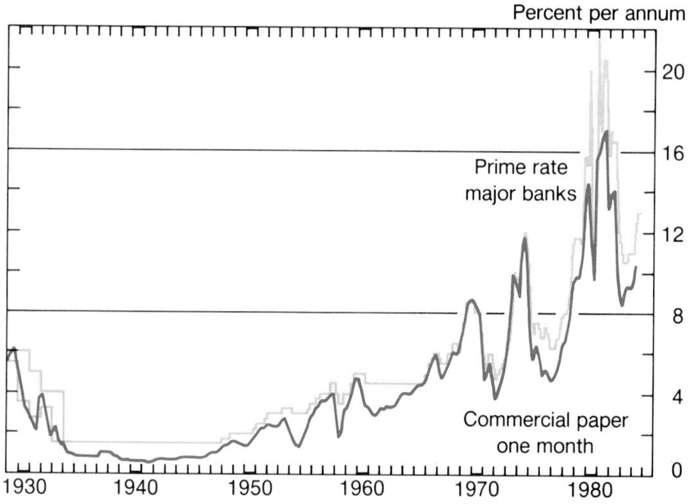

Source: Taken from the *1984 Historical Chartbook*, Board of Governors of the Federal Reserve System, Washington, D.C., p. 99.

Equation 13.3 is an approximation of a compound interest formula. But, as stated earlier, strict adherence to compounding can be safely ignored for short-term loans. One cannot, however, ignore flotation costs when the services of a commercial paper dealer are used to market paper. In this instance, *sales proceeds should be reduced by the amount of the flotation costs. The effect of this adjustment will be to raise the interest rate.*

A financial manager can easily determine the approximate interest rate that will have to be paid on a forthcoming issue of commercial paper. This is possible because interest rates on recent issues of similar companies are quoted daily in the financial press.

Finance Companies

Finance companies are generally of three types: consumer finance companies, sales finance companies, and commercial finance companies.

Consumer finance companies, like Household Finance, make secured loans to individual consumers for the purchase of boats, cars, vacations, etc. As such, they are not directly involved in business lending. *Sales finance companies* specialize in financing the inventories and customers of certain retail businesses (e.g., auto and appliance dealers). All of their loans are secured. These finance companies are distinguished by the close working relationships they have with their clients, many of whom they deal with regularly over a number of years. *Commercial finance companies* function more nearly like commercial banks than the other two. All of their loans are made to businesses. Furthermore, the loans are usually short-term. In most cases, these loans are used to finance temporary buildups of accounts receivable and inventory, which are, in turn, used to secure the loans.

Commercial finance companies are heavily engaged in *factoring* accounts receivable, an activity that has been practiced for years in the textile trade. Many commercial and manufacturing businesses factor, that is sell, their accounts receivable to these financial institutions. Finance companies specializing in this activity are referred to as *factors*. By turning their receivables immediately into cash in this manner, companies can shorten their cash flow cycles and thus reduce funding requirements. In this sense, factoring is a financing arrangement. The essentials of factoring can be described thusly. A factor ordinarily has an ongoing relationship with its client firms. At the end of each business day a client delivers all of its new accounts receivable to the factor's office. Those accounts found to be acceptable by the factor are purchased for between 75% and 90% of the accounts' face value. The size of the discount will depend upon: credit quality of the accounts, expected collection period, level of market interest rates, and other services rendered by the factor (e.g., credit analysis and bookkeeping). The factor accepts all responsibility for bad debts if the accounts are purchased on a nonrecourse basis. Credit customers may or may not be notified that their accounts have been sold to a finance company. In the event that they are not notified, the client will receive all customer payments, which it must then immediately transfer to the factor. In addition to providing up-front cash, factors can take over a client firm's entire credit operation, as we saw in chapter 7.

As a general rule, interest rates charged by finance companies are higher than one would pay on bank loans and commercial paper. This is explained, in part, by the fact that their clientele is, on average, a higher risk group.[6]

In the aggregate, sales and commercial finance companies are not as important to short-term business financing as trade credit, bank loans, or commercial paper. Nevertheless, they loom very large in certain industries, particularly auto retailing.

Specialized Forms of Short-Term Financing

Small firms often have great difficulty raising funds, both short-term and long-term. However, there are a number of possibilities outside normal lending channels. A firm may be able to obtain short-term financing from a large, well-healed customer or supplier who is not only familiar with the firm's operations, but has a vested interest in seeing the firm prosper and survive. If they do not already have all of their funds tied up in the business, officers may be able to provide funding. Some small companies avail themselves of the Small Business Administration (SBA). An agency of the United States Government, the SBA guarantees bank loans to eligible small businesses.

---

[6]For a more complete discussion on finance companies, see William A. MacPhee, *Short-Term Business Borrowing: Sources, Terms, and Techniques.* Homewood, Ill.: Dow Jones-Irwin, 1984.

Summary

We have just scrutinized the major kinds of business short-term debt. Each of them has unique features, positive aspects and limitations. By and large, trade credit and accruals are the preferred source of short-term debt, because of their very low cost and flexibility. Unfortunately, accruals and trade credit are limited in amount. Bank commercial loans and commercial paper, on the other hand, are close substitutes for one another. Commercial loans can provide a borrower with more convenience and flexibility than commercial paper, whereas commercial paper is usually less expensive. However, for many companies commercial paper is not a viable alternative. These firms must turn to commercial banks or finance companies for the bulk of their short-term funding.

The importance of bank commercial loans to the typical business cannot be overemphasized. It is attested to by the very close relationships that many companies develop with their bankers over the years. There are several things one should understand about banks and bank loans: management should thoroughly prepare for a loan request; although there are real advantages in a close banking relationship, one should not ignore the possible benefits from "shopping around"; the terms and provisions of commercial loans may be as important as the interest rate; and finally, interest rates on commercial loans can be very deceiving, due to the existence of compensating balances and the practice of discounting.

Finance companies are another source of short-term business financing. Their presence is very large in certain lines of business, notably automobile retailing. In addition to making loans, finance companies are dominant in accounts receivable factoring.

Table 13.2 summarizes much of the material in this chapter ∎

Table 13.2   A Summary of Short-Term Financing Methods

Method	Major Sources	General Characteristics
Accruals	Employees and government	Generated automatically and there is no cost associated with them.
Trade credit	Suppliers	Generated automatically and features several key credit terms (cash discount, credit period, maximum limit).
Special purpose loan	Commercial banks and finance companies	Protective covenants, secured or nonsecured, compensating balance, and the interest rate is tied to the prime rate.
Line of credit	Commercial banks	In addition to those for special purpose loans, they are prearranged, renewable, and may require loan committment fees.
Commercial paper	Corporations, banks, and the public money market	Nonsecured, issued at a discount, and used primarily by large, well-established corporations.
Factoring	Finance companies	Sale of accounts receivable.
Floor plan	Commercial banks and finance companies	Secured loans used to finance retail inventories of motor vehicles. A separate loan is made on each vehicle. Other features are similar to a bank line of credit.
Other loans	Officers, suppliers, and customers	The one fairly common trait of these loans is their nonsecured status.

Appendix: Security Agreement

ILA-1025-09/79

SECURITY AGREEMENT
(Equipment)

_____("Borrower")

of _____County, Indiana, grants to the Terre Haute First
National Bank, Terre Haute, Indiana ("Bank"), a security interest in the following described property:

_____

_____

_____

_____

together with all tools, accessories, parts, equipment and accessions now in, attached to or which
may hereafter at any time be placed in or added to the above-described property; and also any
replacements of such property (all of which is referred to herein as "Collateral") to secure the
payment of that certain indebtedness evidenced by a promissory note or notes executed by the
Borrower in favor of the Bank in the principal sum of ($_____)

_____Dollars of even
date herewith and any extensions or renewals thereof and all other liabilities of the Borrower
in favor of the Bank, direct or indirect, absolute or contingent, now existing or hereafter arising,
all of which the Borrower agrees to pay without relief from valuation or appraisement laws and
with attorneys' fees; and the payment of any and all future advances that may be made by the
Bank to the Borrower during the term of this Agreement shall likewise be secured by the Collateral, equally with and to the same extent as monies originally advanced under this Agreement.

Borrower hereby warrants to and agrees with the Bank that:

1. The Collateral is being acquired for business use, and the Collateral ☐ will ☐ will not
be acquired with the proceeds of the loan of this date. (In the event the Collateral will be acquired with the proceeds of the loan, the Bank may disburse such proceeds to the seller of the
Collateral.)

2. The Collateral will be kept at the address of the Borrower set out below, which in the case of a business is the address of the principal office of such business within this state. Borrower will not remove the Collateral from the state without the prior written consent of the Bank. If the Collateral is being acquired for farming use and the Borrower is not a resident of Indiana, the Collateral will be kept at the address set forth in the description of the Collateral. Borrower will immediately give written notice to the Bank of any change of address and in the case of a business, any change in its principal place of business and if the Collateral consists of equipment normally used in more than one state, and of any use of the Collateral in any jurisdiction other than a state in which the Borrower shall have previously advised the Bank such Collateral will be used.

3. In the event the Collateral will be attached to real estate, the description of such real estate and the known owner of record of such real estate are set forth in the description of the Collateral. If the Collateral is attached to such real estate prior to the perfection of the security interest granted herein, the Borrower will, on demand, furnish the Bank with a disclaimer or disclaimers, executed by persons having an interest in such real estate.

4. Borrower has, or will acquire, full and clear title to the Collateral, and, except for the security interest granted herein, will at all times keep the Collateral free from any adverse lien, security interest or encumbrance.

5. No financing statement covering all or any portion of the Collateral is on file in any public office.

6. Borrower authorizes the Bank at the expense of the Borrower to execute and file a financing statement or statements on its behalf in those public offices deemed necessary by the Bank to protect its security interest. In addition, Borrower will deliver or cause to be delivered such other documents as the Bank may request to secure the loan referred to herein including, without limiting, any certificate or certificates of title to the Collateral with the security interest of the Bank noted thereon.

7. Borrower will not sell or offer to sell or otherwise transfer the Collateral or any interest therein without the prior written consent of the Bank.

8. Borrower will at all times keep the Collateral insured against loss, damage, theft and other risks in such amounts under such policies and with companies as shall be satisfactory to the Bank, which policies shall provide that loss thereunder shall be payable to the Bank as its interest may appear and the Bank may apply the proceeds of such insurance against the outstanding indebtedness of the Borrower, regardless of whether all or any portion of such indebetedness is due and owing. All policies of insurance so required shall be placed in the possession of the Bank.

Upon failure of the Borrower to procure such insurance or to remove any encumbrance upon the Collateral or if such insurance is cancelled, the indebtedness secured hereby shall become immediately due and payable at the option of the Bank without notice or demand or the Bank may procure such insurance or remove any encumbrance on the Collateral and the amount so paid by the Bank shall be immediately repayable and shall be added to and become a part of the indebtedness secured hereby and shall bear interest at the rate of three percent (3%) per annum above the Bank's prime rate.

9. Borrower will keep the Collateral in good order and repair and will not waste or destroy the Collateral or any portion thereof. Borrower will not use the Collateral in violation of any statute or ordinance or any policy of insurance thereon and the Bank may examine and inspect such Collateral at any reasonable time or times wherever located.

10. Borrower will pay promptly when due all taxes and assessments upon the Collateral or for its use or operation.

11. The occurrence of any one of the following events shall constitute an event of default under this Agreement: (a) nonpayment when due of any installment of the indebtedness hereby secured or failure to perform any agreement contained herein; (b) any statement, representation, or warranty at any time furnished the Bank is untrue in any material respect as of the date made; (c) Borrower becomes insolvent or unable to pay debts as they mature or makes an assignment for the benefit of creditors or any proceeding is instituted by or against the Borrower alleging that such Borrower is insolvent or unable to pay debts as they mature; (d) entry of a judgment against the Borrower; (e) loss, theft, substantial damage, destruction, sale or encumbrance to or of all or any portion of the Collateral, or the making of any levy, seizure or attachment thereof or thereon; (f) death of the Borrower if the Borrower is a natural person or of any partner of the Borrower if the Borrower is a partnership; (g) dissolution, merger or consolidation or transfer of a substantial portion of the property of the Borrower if the Borrower is a corporation or a partnership; or (h) the Bank deems itself insecure for any other reason whatsoever. When an event of default shall occur and be existing, the note or notes and any other liabilities of the Borrower to the Bank may at the option of the Bank and without notice or demand be declared and thereupon immediately shall become due and payable and the Bank may exercise from time to time any rights and remedies of a secured party under the Uniform Commercial Code or any other applicable law. Borrower agrees in the event of default to make the Collateral available to the Bank at a place acceptable to the Bank which is convenient to the Borrower.

If any notification of disposition of all or any portion of the Collateral is required by law, such notification shall be deemed reasonably and properly given if mailed at least ten (10) days prior to such disposition, postage prepaid to the Borrower at its latest address appearing on the records of the Bank. Any proceeds of any disposition of the Collateral may be applied by the Bank to the payment of the expenses of retaking, holding, repairing, preparing for sale and selling, and shall include reasonable attorneys' fees and legal expenses and any balance of such proceeds shall be applied by the Bank toward the payment of the indebtedness owing the Bank.

No delay on the part of the Bank in the exercise of any right or remedy shall operate as a waiver thereof, and no single or partial exercise by the Bank of any right or remedy shall preclude other or further exercise thereof or the exercise of any other right or remedy. If more than one party shall execute this Agreement, the term "Borrower" shall mean all parties signing this Agreement and each of them, and all such parties shall be jointly and severally obligated hereunder. The neuter pronoun, when used herein, shall include the masculine and the feminine and also the plural. If this Agreement is not dated when executed by the Borrower, the Bank is authorized, without notice to the Borrower, to date this Agreement.

This Agreement has been delivered at Terre Haute, Indiana, and shall be construed in accordance with the laws of the State of Indiana. Wherever possible each provision of this Agreement shall be interpreted in such manner as to be effective and valid under applicable law, but if any provision of this Agreement shall be prohibited by or invalid under applicable law, such provision shall be ineffective to the extent of such prohibition of invalidity, without invalidating the remainder of such provision or the remaining provisions of this Agreement.

This Agreement shall be binding upon the heirs, administrators and executors of the Borrower and the rights and privileges of the Bank hereunder shall inure to the benefit of its successors and assigns.

IN WITNESS WHEREOF, this Agreement has been duly executed on this _____ day of _____, 19_____ .

_____

Address _____   _____

_____

Source: Terre Haute First National Bank, Terre Haute, IN.

Key Terms/Concepts

Accruals
Bank commercial loans
Cleanup period
Collateral
Commercial finance
  companies
Commitment fee
Compensating balance
Consumer finance companies
Debt limits
Dividend restrictions
End-of-month (EOM)
Factoring

Field warehousing
Floor plan
Key-man insurance
Line of credit
Minimum liquidity ratios
Mortgage
Negotiable warehouse receipt
Open account
Payment period
Personal property
Pledging accounts receivable
Pledging inventory
Prime rate

Promissory note
Protective covenants
Real property
Receipt of goods (ROG)
Sales finance companies
Seasonal dating
Secured loans/creditors
Security agreement
Small Business Administration
  (SBA)
"Stretching the payables"
Trade credit
Trade credit terms
Unsecured loans/creditors

Questions

1. What is the "prime rate"?

2. Inventory that serves as collateral for bank and finance company loans should possess certain desirable characteristics. What are these characteristics?

3. Why are compound interest formulas seldom used to compute the costs of short-term credit?

4. Is there any justification for the following statement, "nothing is free, including trade credit?"

5. Lines of credit are used with which type of short-term debt? What are the advantages to using a line of credit, from the borrower's viewpoint?

6. What would cause the payment period on trade credit to exceed the credit period?

7. Besides cost, what should one consider when choosing among alternative bank commercial loans?

8. What types of assets are normally financed with short-term debt? How are these funding requirements measured?

9. Briefly define the following: compensating balances, protective covenants, and EOM.

Problems

1. A firm that purchases $96 million of goods each year on credit, has an average accounts payable balance of $12 million. What is this firm's accounts payable turnover?

2. Fission Industries purchases about $25,000 per day of a certain raw material on credit. Its supplier offers credit terms of net 60/ROG, and Fission always waits until the last day to make payment. What is the average level of this account payable? Determine the additional trade credit that Fission could obtain if it "stretched" payments an extra 30 days?

3. An auto company buys tires on the basis of the following credit terms: 2/30/n40/EOM. Required:
   A. Specify the credit period.
   B. Specify the discount period.
   C. Determine the amount of discount that could be obtained on a $300,000 purchase.
   D. Convert a foregone discount into an annual rate of interest. You may assume that payment will be made at the end of the credit period.
   E. What is the starting date for both the discount and credit periods?

4. Crusade Company is considering the issue of $25,000,000 of commercial paper to finance an inventory buildup. The paper will mature in 75 days and can be sold for $24,150,000. Compute the annual interest rate that Crusade Company will be paying for these funds. Recompute the interest rate, assuming that $150,000 of the sales proceeds are paid to a commercial paper dealer.

5. A company buys $72 million worth of merchandise on credit during a typical year. Accounts payable presently show a balance of $12,400,000. Based solely on this information, derive the average payment period.

6. Compute the annual rates of interest that would be incurred by missing cash discounts under the following credit terms:
    A. 1/10/n90.
    B. 3/30/n75.
    C. 2/10/n30.

7. XYZ Company's suppliers sell on terms of net 40/ROG. XYZ buys, on average, $120,000 worth of merchandise from these suppliers each day of the year. Determine the maximum amount of trade credit that XYZ can obtain under these circumstances.

8. Calculate the annual *after-tax* cost or interest rate in connection with a $10 million face amount of commercial paper that is sold for $9,600,000. The commercial paper matures in three months and the borrower's tax rate is 40%.

9. A $250,000 bank commercial loan is scheduled to mature in 75 days. The quoted annual interest rate on this loan is 14¼%. Find the effective annual interest rate under each of the following conditions:
    A. Interest is added onto the loan and there exists a 25% compensating balance.
    B. Interest is discounted from the loan and there is no compensating balance.
    C. Interest is discounted from the loan and there exists a 25% compensating balance.
    D. Which set of terms provides the lowest cost?

10. A company must have the use of $20 million for six months. The firm's bank has agreed to provide the funds, but only under the following conditions: a compensating balance of 10% is required, and the interest will be discounted at an annual rate of 16%. How much must this company borrow in order to net $20 million?

11. A firm that pays wages each week could acquire how much additional employee financing by switching the payroll to once every four weeks?

12. Given credit terms of 2/15/n45/EOM, specify the payment periods for a customer who receives delivery of goods on September 8.

13. Beatrice Corporation wishes to issue commercial paper with a total par value of $50 million. The paper will mature in 120 days, and the company's financial manager estimates that the annual cost should be 18%. Solve for the sales proceeds from the commercial paper issue.

14. Fox Enterprises received $2 million worth of supplies on August 1. The terms of sale are net 45/September 30. What is the payment period?

15. A bank commercial loan of $2 million has been executed. The loan is discounted at an annual interest rate of 18%, and it is to be repaid in six months. The borrower's income tax rate is 35%. Determine the effective annual interest rate on this loan, before-taxes and after-taxes.

16. Find the effective annual cost of a bank commercial loan that possesses the following characteristics: 15% quoted annual interest rate; $100,000 in loan proceeds; twelve-month maturity; and 20% compensating balance.

17. Referring to the preceding question, what must the loan proceeds be in order for a borrower to have the use of $100,000?

18. Given credit terms of 3/30/n90, calculate the annual interest rate that would result from foregoing the cash discount. Recompute the interest rate, assuming that payment is 20 days late.

19. The effective annual interest rate on a bank commercial loan is 15%. Given an income tax rate of 45%, compute the after-tax cost.

20. Trelor, Inc., orders raw materials once every three months, with the typical order amounting to $6 million. Suppliers require payment thirty days after delivery. Assuming that Trelor pays its bills on time, what is the company's average accounts payable balance?

21. Compute the effective annual interest rate on a $5 million bank loan that matures in four months. The quoted annual interest rate on the loan is 15% and interest will be discounted from the loan proceeds. Furthermore, the bank requires a 15% compensating balance.

22. Green Publishing Company currently has a $5 million line of credit with Chase Manhattan Bank. Under the conditions of the loan, Green can borrow any amount, up to $5 million, for as long as one year. An annual interest rate of 3% plus the prime will be assessed on the outstanding loan balance. The company has drawn on its line of credit only once. One hundred and thirty-five days ago, Green borrowed $3 million, and it has paid nothing on the loan (principal or interest) in the meantime. At that time, the prime rate was 13½%. Thirty days later, the prime rose to 15%. It remained at that level for sixty days and then declined to its present level of 14¼%. Green wishes to repay the loan and accrued interest today. What will the company have to pay?

23. According to its cash budget, Duval Sporting Goods will require about $350,000 of financing for an upcoming three-month period. The company is faced with three alternatives. Bank X has agreed to lend $450,000 for three months at an annual interest rate of 15½%. The loan requires a 20% compensating balance. Bank Y has also approved Duval's credit application. It has agreed to lend the firm up to $500,000 for as long as one year. The interest rate on this loan is 20% per annum, and it will be discounted. However, there is no compensating balance. Lastly, Duval could make use of trade credit in this situation. By passing up a cash discount of 5%, the firm can wait an additional 90 days to pay its accounts payable of $375,000.
    A. Evaluate the three loans in terms of cost.
    B. What other factors should Duval consider in making this decision?

Selected References _____

Conover, C. Todd, "The Case of the Costly Credit Agreement," *Financial Executive* (September 1971), pp. 40–48.

Fisher, D. J., "Factoring—An Industry on the Move," *The Conference Board Record* (April 1972), pp. 42–45.

Glasgo, P. W., W. Landes, and A. F. Thompson, "Bank Discount, Coupon Equivalent and Compound Yields," *Financial Management* (Autumn 1982), pp. 80–84.

Gupta, Manok C., "Optimal Financing Policy for a Firm with Uncertain Fund Requirements," *Journal of Financial and Quantitative Analysis* (December 1973), pp. 831–47.

Hurley, E. M., "Commercial Paper Market," *Federal Reserve Bulletin* (June 1977), pp. 525–36.

Mansfield, Charles F., Jr., "The Function of Credit Analysis in a U.S. Commercial Bank," *Journal of Commercial Bank Lending* (September 1979), pp. 21–34.

Quill, G. D., J. C. Cruci, and B. D. Shuter, "Some Considerations about Secured Lending," *Journal of Commercial Bank Lending* (April 1977), pp. 41–56.

Schwartz, Robert A., "An Economic Analysis of Trade Credit," *Journal of Financial and Quantitative Analysis* (September 1974), pp. 643–58.

Smith, Keith V., *Guide to Working Capital Management,* New York: McGraw-Hill, 1979.

■ Finance in the News

While many companies either pledge or factor their accounts receivable to financial institutions, that is not the only way that receivables are useful from a financing viewpoint. Companies are beginning to issue more *bonds* and *commercial paper* with receivables as security; and treasurers are realizing that they can use these current assets to reduce financing costs. "Turning Assets into Cash" explains how this has worked for several well-known companies.

Turning Assets into Cash _____

A promising new financing vehicle deploys high-quality receivables to reduce borrowing costs. Comdisco Inc., a Chicago-based computer leasing company with a royal blue-chip clientele but only a humble BB+/Ba2 rating for its outstanding debt, recently found a way to parlay the high caliber of its customer base into a triple-A bond issue. After putting some leases with solid investment-grade companies in a special-purpose subsidiary, it privately placed $35 million in 4½-year bonds backed by these receivables. This innovative structure enabled Moody's Investors Service to look directly at the credit quality of the leases themselves and to grant the cachet of its highest ratings based on the estimable credit history of Comdisco's customers.

The charm of this financing lies in its lowered borrowing costs. The receivables-backed bonds that Comdisco debuted saved the company an estimated three-eighths of one percentage point over its traditional bank financings, according to Assistant Treasurer Thomas P. Sullivan.

The computer leasing company deal could usher in a multibillion-dollar market in receivables-backed financings, say investment bankers who are working on similar proposals. Moody's is studying proposals for financings involving automobile, farm-equipment, mobile home and airline ticket receivables, reports Vice President M. Douglas Watson, adding that there has been a "geometric progression" of interest in the concept over the last few months.

Receivables-backed financing is applicable to virtually any noncancelable consumer or corporate installment debt, asserts Stephen J. Powers, senior vice president of Bankers Trust Co., which helped structure the Comdisco deal. Receivables-backed financings could easily surpass $1 billion this year, he forecasts, with credit card receivables as the biggest potential source of assets backing these bonds. In time, receivables-backed financing may even rival the mortgage-backed securities market in size, predicts one investment banker.

As novel as the idea is of using the payments owed by a company's customers as the collateral for a bond, it has forebears—as do most new financial brainchildren. In this case, the parent of the 4½-year bond was receivables-backed commercial paper offering, which saw the light of day last spring. In March, Gelco Corp., which leases auto and trucks to companies, established a $100 million commercial paper program, after it garnered an A-1 rating from Standard & Poor's for the offering. Like Comdisco, Gelco Corp.'s long-term debt is not quite investment grade (it is rated BB- by Standard & Poor's), but the lessees of its vehicle fleets are household-name companies.

The Gelco deal, like the bond arrangement, involves a legal rigmarole. Some of the high-quality lease receivables are pledged to a special-purpose corporation whose sole activity is making loans to Gelco, with which it is not affiliated. In short, a dummy corporation with high-class assets earns the high-class rating, not the parent. More importantly, Gelco gets the cash.

The mechanism also translated into substantial savings for Gelco. The auto and truck lessor previously had to resort to banks, which typically charged three-eighths-to-five-eighths of a percentage point above the London interbank rate (LIBOR), recently 9.6%, according to Gelco's Assistant Treasurer James Geiser. By contrast, Gelco's commercial paper was trading recently at 8.75%—about a tenth of a point above the Federal Reserve AA composite rate. A big differential even when start-up and maintenance costs for the commercial paper facility are added in, says Geiser.

Even higher-rated companies could find this technique cost-effective, says Bankers Trust's Powers. He is currently working on proposals for two "single-A or better-rated industrial companies." Merrill Lynch Money Markets Inc., which structured the Gelco deal, is preparing a medium-term issue backed by retail installment debt for an "investment grade" company, reports Gordon B. Pattee, managing director.

Firestone Tire & Rubber Co., which enjoys a A/Bbb long-term debt rating, concurs. It chose to finance its burgeoning portfolio of auto service receivables by setting up two commercial paper programs that use separate special purpose corporations to buy the receivables and issue the paper. "This was a more efficient way to finance these receivables," explains Assistant Treasurer Peter W. Chehayl. "It's making those assets work harder." He estimated that the program saves Firestone about three-quarters of a percentage point over financing these receivables through their sale to banks.

Like mortgage-backed securities, receivables-backed financings must provide protection against possible defaults or delinquencies. In the Comdisco offering, Bankers Trust used a layer of insurance covering about 13.5% of the pool to "build it up to a triple-A rating," explains Comdisco's Sullivan. Merrill Lynch, on the other hand, plans to overcollateralize the issue—that is, make the receivables pool larger than would be strictly necessary to make principal and interest payments, in order to protect against possible defaults.

Merrill Lynch argues that overcollateralization is preferable to insurance, saying that the additional cost of insurance runs contrary to the whole concept of receivables-backing. Says Pattee: "We want to rely totally on the creditworthiness of the receivables." But Bankers Trust's Powers maintains that, in the long run, his approach is more cost-effective since fewer of the company's assets are put to work raising the same amount of funds. Besides, he argues, the third-party credit enhancement adds to the credibility and marketability of the issue.

The more esoteric structure favored by Merrill Lynch has already made for a more arduous progression through the rating agencies. The deal has been in front of Standard & Poor's for more than six months now.

Pattee accepts these delays with philosophical forbearance. The agencies' struggle is reminiscent of the one that attended the birth of the mortgage-backed securities market in the mid-Seventies. "There's a learning curve that the agencies had to go down," Pattee said. "It's exactly the same thing now."

Unlike mortgage-backed securities, a "cookie cutter" approach to receivables-backed financings is impossible, cautions Vice President Miles Federman of Standard & Poor's. Instead of the comparatively homogenous assets behind mortgage-backed securities, receivables-backed financings draw on a diverse range of potential receivables pools, each with different behavioral patterns. Standard & Poor's has already compiled extensive generic data on loss rates, delinquencies, payment rates and demography for oil company, department store, farm equipment and other receivables pools.

The serious attention creditworthy companies are paying to receivables-backed financing suggests that collateralized financing has shrugged of the stigma that was once attached to it. This, too, is a legacy of the mortgage-backed securities market, investment bankers observe. In the past, "collateralizing debt was frowned upon," notes Firestone's Chehayl, "It was considered a second-class form of financing." But more recently, asset-based financing has earned a new respectability, he says, as "treasurers have realized that this is an efficient way of financing a company." Indeed, today "a company is regarded as a tad more adept" if it can use its assets to lower financing costs, says Bankers Trust's Powers.

by Elizabeth Kaplan

14

Long-Term Debt and Preferred Stock

Overview

As we saw in chapter 13, all of the short-term financing methods are liabilities. This chapter begins our discussion of business long-term financing, or what is more commonly referred to as capital. Here we will analyze two categories of capital: long-term debt and preferred stock. In chapter 15 another important category of capital is considered, common stockholder equity. Chapter 16 ends our discussion of long-term financing with a description of the techniques used to measure the costs of the various forms of capital.

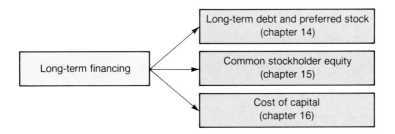

We shall examine the three most common forms of long-term debt in the current chapter: bonds, term loans, and leasing. Preferred stock is also covered in this chapter, because it shares many characteristics with long-term debt ■

Objectives

By the end of the chapter the student should be able to:

1. List the common sources of long-term debt financing
2. Understand the terminology of bond mathematics
3. Calculate the market value of bonds
4. Understand the various corporate bond provisions
5. Discuss the reasons for and process of refunding a bond issue
6. Understand the reasons a corporation might have its bonds rated prior to issuing them
7. Explain the relationships among bond rating, risk level, and interest rates
8. Work with term loan mathematics problems
9. Construct loan amortization schedules
10. Calculate and interpret term loan refunding problems
11. Understand the various term loan provisions
12. Understand the terminology of leasing
13. Understand the various leasing provisions
14. Work with leasing mathematics
15. Explain the lease versus buy decision and its implications
16. Compare and contrast the various types of long-term debt
17. Understand the terminology of preferred stock

Introduction

In this chapter we will study the major categories of long-term corporate debt. The examination will take a close-up look at important characteristics, intricacies, and ramifications associated with each long-term debt instrument. However, we will not delve into the calculation of interest rates at this time since that is the subject of chapter 16. Due to its close association with long-term debt, preferred stock is included in the present chapter.

Most long-term corporate debt falls into one of three categories: term loans, bonds, and leases. For the most part, the maturities of these instruments range from five to thirty years. And, in line with the matching principle discussed in chapter 11, they are principally used to fund long-term capital assets. It is appropriate that we separate the discussions of short-term debt and long-term debt, due to their numerous distinct features ■

Corporate Bonds

As we saw in chapter 12, bond certificates are issued by corporations to raise long-term funds. They are also the major financing instrument of the federal, state, and local governments. A corporate bond is a contractual promise made by the issuing corporation to pay specified amounts of interest and principal on predetermined dates. Interest payments are to be made semiannually while the principal is normally repaid at maturity. A failure on the part of a corporation to make the promised payments constitutes a default (i.e., breach of contract), with legal remedies available to investors. The discussion to follow is an in-depth examination of several important factors relating to corporate bonds.

Bond Mathematics   When the mathematics of compound interest are applied to bonds, the results are very interesting.[1] But before we proceed into this subject, some background material is in order.

A bond investor can expect to receive (and the issuing company is required to pay) interest and a par value. *Par value* is the principal or face amount of a bond that is due and payable on the *maturity date*. A par value can be any amount, but is usually in round numbers such as $1,000 or $25,000 per bond. However, for the sake of clarity, a $1,000 par value will be used in all of the illustrations. Bond interest payments, commonly referred to as *coupons,* are paid semiannually and they are based on a bond's *coupon rate* and par value. Coupon rates are found on the face of a bond certificate along with the maturity date and par value (exhibit 14.1).

The annual coupon on a bond is derived through multiplying the coupon rate by the par value. For instance, a 12¼% coupon rate and $1,000 par value would indicate an annual coupon interest payment of .1225 × $1,000 = $122.50. The semiannual coupon is one-half of this amount, or $61.25 every six months. The final semiannual coupon is paid at maturity along with the par value.

---

[1]The present discussion of bond mathematics applies not only to corporate bonds, but to most other types as well.

Exhibit 14.1   Sample corporate bond certificate

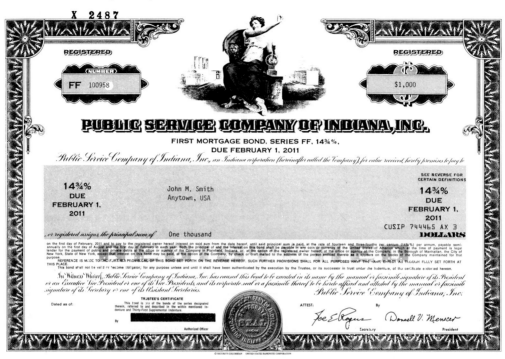

Courtesy of *Public Service Indiana.*

The par value, coupon rate, and maturity date of a bond are contractual and, thus, not subject to change. When combined with a market determined required rate of return, these four factors generate the market value of a bond. *The market price of a given bond is equal to the present value of the bond's future coupon payments and par value (cash flows), discounted at the market-determined RRR.*[2] One must be careful, however, to halve the market interest rate since the cash flows are semiannual. The discounting model, equation 3.6 can be converted into a bond valuation formula simply by using bond terminology in place of the general notation, as shown below:

Equation 14.1

$$\text{Bond Value} = \frac{\text{Coupon}/2}{(1+\text{RRR})^1} + \frac{\text{Coupon}/2}{(1+\text{RRR})^2} + \cdots + \frac{\text{Coupon}/2}{(1+\text{RRR})^{2n}} + \frac{\text{Par Value}}{(1+\text{RRR})^{2n}}$$

Where:

$$\begin{aligned}
\text{Bond Value} &= \text{Market value or market price of bond} \\
n &= \text{Number of years to maturity} \\
\text{Par Value} &= \text{Face value of the bond} \\
\text{Coupon}/2 &= \text{Semiannual coupon payment, and there are } 2 \times n \text{ of them.} \\
\text{RRR} &= \text{Market-determined semiannual required rate of return}
\end{aligned}$$

---

[2]The RRR will vary from bond to bond based on the degree of risk.

Only when the coupon rate is equal to the RRR will a bond sell in the market at par value. This is shown in the following example:

Application: Zytex Corporation issued $25 million par value of bonds in 1980 that are due to mature in the year 2000. Each bond has a par value of $1,000 and a coupon rate of 14%. Accordingly, the semiannual coupon is ($1,000 $\times$ .14) $\div$ 2 = $70. It is now five years later, in 1985, and the market still requires a 14% rate of return on these bonds. Based on this information, Zytex's bonds will each have a market value of:

$$\text{Bond Value} = \frac{\$70}{(1.07)^1} + \frac{\$70}{(1.07)^2} + \ldots + \frac{\$70}{(1.07)^{30}} + \frac{\$1,000}{(1.07)^{30}}$$

Since the coupons are an annuity, we can use annuity discount factors here. Thus,

$$\text{Bond Value} = \$70 \text{ ADF}_{.07/30} + \$1,000 \text{ DF}_{.07/30}$$

$$\text{Bond Value} = \$70(12.4090) + \$1,000(.1314) = \$1,000$$

Market interest rates change constantly. As a consequence, it is rare when a particular bond's fixed coupon rate is exactly what the market demands. *If the required rate of return on a bond exceeds the fixed coupon rate, the bond's market price must be below the par value.* In this way, the bond will yield what the market wants. *On the other hand, the market value of a bond will be above par value when the required rate of return is less than the coupon rate.* Referring to the preceding example, market required rates of return of 16% and 12% would generate two vastly different prices for a Zytex bond.

$$\text{Bond Value} = \frac{\$70}{(1.08)^1} + \frac{\$70}{(1.08)^2} + \ldots + \frac{\$70}{(1.08)^{30}} + \frac{\$1,000}{(1.08)^{30}} = \$887.45$$

$$\text{Bond Value} = \frac{\$70}{(1.06)^1} + \frac{\$70}{(1.06)^2} + \ldots + \frac{\$70}{(1.06)^{30}} + \frac{\$1,000}{(1.06)^{30}} = \$1,137.64$$

In the first case, the bond is said to be selling at a *discount* from par value equal to $1,000 − $887.45 = $112.55. In the second scenario, the bond is selling at a *premium* above par value equal to $1,137.64 − $1,000 = $137.64. The financial press would say that these bonds are selling at 88¾% and 113¾% of par, respectively.[3]

It is even somewhat unusual for bonds to be issued at par value. As a case in point, a firm and its investment banker might believe that investors will want an interest rate of 13¾% on the firm's new $50 million par value, twenty year bond issue. The par value of each bond is $1,000 and there are 50,000 of them. Accordingly, they issue the bonds with a 13¾% coupon. If it turns out that the market is not receptive to 13¾%, but instead wants a higher rate of return, say 14%, then the bonds must each be sold at a discounted price of:

$$\text{Bond Value} = \frac{\$68.75}{(1.07)^1} + \frac{\$68.75}{(1.07)^2} + \ldots + \frac{\$68.75}{(1.07)^{40}} + \frac{\$1,000}{(1.07)^{40}} = \$983.35$$

The price of the entire issue would be 50,000 $\times$ $983.35 = $49,167,500.

To generalize even further, we can state that market interest rates and bond market prices are inversely related. As interest rates rise, bond prices fall and vice versa. *And, as we saw in chapter 6, the impact of fluctuating market interest rates on bond prices is greater for long-term bonds than short-term bonds.*

---

[3]Corporations occasionally issue bonds without coupons. These "zero coupon" bonds are sold at deep discounts.

Figure 14.1   **The market value of a discounted bond approaches par value as the maturity date draws closer.**

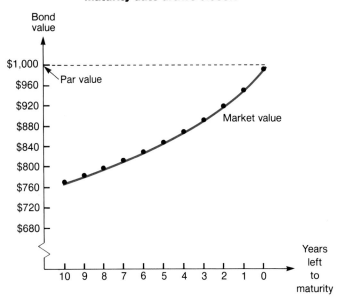

One final observation is in order here. *A bond that is not currently priced at par value will none-theless move systematically in that direction as the maturity date approaches.*[4] Consider, for instance, a $1,000 par value, 8% coupon bond that is due to mature in ten years. A market required rate of return of 12% will cause this bond to sell for $770.60. Holding everything else the same, one year later this same bond would sell for $783.40, or an increase of $12.80.[5] The price will continue to increase as the maturity date draws closer, as diagrammed in figure 14.1 ■

Corporate Bond Provisions   In addition to par value, maturity date, and coupon, there are many other provisions associated with corporate bonds. While the former terms are shown on the bond certificate, the latter are to be found in the bond *indenture. With one exception, bond provisions are designed primarily to benefit bondholders.* As such, they may be detrimental to the business. Some of the more common provisions are described below.

Trustee   Publicly issued bonds can involve hundreds or thousands of widely dispersed investors. In the interest of convenience and orderliness, a trustee is usually appointed to represent these numerous creditors in future dealings with the corporation. A trustee's job can be very easy when the corporation pays on time and strictly adheres to the provisions of the indenture. At the other extreme, a trustee can be thrust into the middle of a complex

---

[4]This assumes that the market required rate of return on the bond does not change in the meantime.

[5]An investor in this bond will receive $80 in coupons during the year in addition to the $12.80 capital gain, or a total income of $92.80. It is worth noting that this $92.80 income provides a rate of return of 12% on the $770.60 initial bond value.

lawsuit. To adequately carry out its duties, a trustee should be an independent, third party. Large commercial banks are often selected as trustees, and, of course, they are paid for their services.

Sinking Fund   Rather than having the corporation retire (i.e., repay) the entire bond issue par value at maturity, many bond investors prefer a gradual repayment. Such a repayment scheme is known as a sinking fund. The specific characteristics of sinking funds vary from one bond issue to another, so it is difficult to generalize. A couple of simplified examples would be instructive, however.

Example A: A $40 million par value, twenty year bond issue is to be repaid by means of a sinking fund. The sinking fund requires that $2 million par value of bonds (one-twentieth) are to be retired annually at par. The bonds that are to be retired each year are chosen by lottery ■

Example B: A $100 million, twenty-five year bond issue is to be gradually retired by means of a sinking fund. The sinking fund requires that one-twentififth of the bonds are to be purchased annually in the open market, at market prices ■

Conversion Privilege   A few corporate bonds will grant investors the right to exchange them for a predetermined number of shares of common stock. This right is known as a conversion privilege and bonds that grant it are commonly referred to as convertible bonds.

A conversion privilege can be extremely desirable to some investors when there is a high probability that a company's stock will increase in value on the market. From a financing standpoint, a firm may be able to capitalize on such investor behavior. Given the relationship of equity to convertible bonds, however, we will examine the financial implications surrounding them more thoroughly in the equity financing chapter that follows this one.

Acceleration Clause   An acceleration clause allows bondholders to demand immediate and full repayment of par value whenever a serious default occurs (e.g., an interest payment is missed). This simple clause vastly improves a creditor's legal claim and is a must in all long-term loans. Although the acceleration clause is not called upon in most instances, it can serve to place bondholders in a much better bargaining position.

Collateral   We discussed the importance of collateral to creditors in connection with bank commercial loans in chapter 13. Collateral is also used to secure many corporate bond issues. Due to the extended maturities of bonds, the most logical collateral for them would be real property such as buildings and land. However, it is not unusual when certain types of personal property are used as security for bonds (e.g., commercial aircraft and machinery). Typically, the assets that are purchased with the bond issue proceeds will also serve as collateral.

Real property collateral is evidenced by means of a *mortgage*. Correspondingly, bond issues backed by collateral are called *mortgage bonds*. In the event that the same property serves as collateral for two bond issues, the issue with a prior claim is designated a *first mortgage* bond while the other is called a *second mortgage* bond. Second mortgage bond-holders will receive nothing from the collateral until and if the first mortgage bondholders are completely reimbursed. Corporate bonds that have no collateral backing are often referred to as *debentures*.

Without specific collateral backing, a bond issue will automatically grant to investors only the rights of general creditors. Some bonds are issued to investors with a provision that they do not have the rights of a general creditor. This right has been assigned to some other creditor. Such bonds are said to be *subordinated*. Nevertheless, these bonds will still have a claim on earnings and assets ahead of preferred and common stock. It is worth noting here, that a company could have several bond issues outstanding all at one time, some with mortgages, some without mortgages, and others that are subordinated. All other things the same, we could expect different interest rates on these bonds because they expose investors to different degrees of risk.

Protective Covenants   Protective covenants are safety features that creditors like to see included in loans and bond indentures. We looked at several of them in the previous chapter in connection with bank commercial loans. To that list we could add, at this time, the following covenants: restrictions are placed on executive salaries; audited financial statements must be drawn up on a regular basis; and the amount of lease payments that can be contracted for is fixed.

Call Provisions   Unlike the previous provisions, a call provision is exclusively for the benefit of the corporation.[6] *A call provision allows a company to retire (i.e., call) a bond issue prior to maturity.* Corporations often find it advantageous to retire a bond issue prior to maturity. One reason they might wish to do so is to be rid of some provision or provisions in an indenture. A new bond issue with more appropriate provisions is used to retire (and replace) the old issue. Another reason for early retirement would be simply to reduce indebtedness. That is, a firm may wish to move to a more optimal degree of financial leverage by using equity to pay off a bond issue. A third and probably more common reason for early retirement is to take advantage of lower interest rates. Proceeds from the sale of lower rate bonds are used to retire higher rate bonds. A firm may be able to sell bonds with a lower interest rate because its financial condition has improved. Bond investors, in recognizing the firm's improved credit worthiness, should be willing to lower their risk premiums and, thus, the RRR. A more probable cause of lower interest rates would be that market rates in general have fallen. Calling bonds to take advantage of lower interest rates is a rather complicated decision process termed *refunding,* to which we will return below.

As the discussion above clearly indicates, a call provision can be a valuable addition to a bond indenture. Unfortunately, it does not come free. By and large, bondholders will be the losers if a corporation sees fit to retire its bonds, much like a zero-sum game. In an effort to lure prospective investors into accepting a call provision in a new bond issue, a company will have to do one or all of three things: (1) pay a higher rate of interest on the bonds than otherwise; (2) agree not to call the bonds for some period of time, say five years; and (3) agree

---

[6]A bond issue can be retired early without a call provision, but to do so would require the voluntary approval of investors.

to pay a *call premium* (i.e., penalty) if the bonds are actually called. A call premium is typically equal to a bond's coupon rate, and it usually declines as the bond approaches maturity and early retirement becomes less likely.[7] The call premium plus 100% (of the par value) is termed the *call price.*

Example: A $75 million par value, 12% coupon, twenty-five year bond issue has the following call provisions: the bonds cannot be called for the first five years; thereafter, the bonds can be called at any time; the call prices are 112% of par for years 6–10, 108% of par for years 11–15, 104% of par for years 16–20, and 100% of par for years 21–25. Therefore, if the bonds are retired after twelve years the company would have to pay 1.08 × $75,000,000 = $81,000,000, of which 8% or $6,000,000 is the call premium. ■

Refunding a Bond Issue   Whether to retire an old bond issue with the proceeds of a new bond issue, in order to capitalize on lower interest rates, is a refunding decision. *The decision to refund is essentially a benefit-cost analysis.* Benefits of refunding are the cash savings in coupon interest payments over the remaining life of the old bonds. The cash costs of refunding include the call premium on the old bonds and any flotation costs to be incurred in selling the new bond issue. However, these costs and benefits cannot be compared directly to one another because the benefits are in the future while the costs are in the present. What we must do then, is to discount all of the benefits (RNCFs) back to the present at the RRR and compare this to the cost of refunding (INCF). In other words, we must calculate a net present value.

Before we proceed with an example, several things should be clarified. *The new or replacement bond issue should be equal in value to the old bond issue.*[8] This is necessary to avoid altering a firm's degree of financial leverage or debt-to-equity ratio. *Moreover, the new bond issue should have a maturity equal to the remaining life of the old bonds.* This requirement is necessary to maintain the debt maturity of a firm. By means of these two requirements we are, in essence, holding the financial structure of the firm constant so that we can concentrate solely on the merits of refunding. The RRR to be used in the refunding analysis is subject to some controversy. However, most experts feel that it is quite reasonable to use the interest rate on the new bond issue.[9] Another thing to consider here is the impact of income taxes. Call premiums, flotation costs, and interest payments all influence taxable income, and in ways that could affect a refunding decision. However, we will ignore taxes for the present since they are rather complicated to deal with in this situation. The impact of income taxes on the refunding decision is demonstrated in an appendix at the end of this chapter.

---

[7]As the maturity date draws closer, there is simply less time in which to benefit from early retirement. For example, a 2% reduction in interest rates would be much more tantalizing if it could be obtained for ten years, rather than three years.

[8]For an alternative view on this matter see Kenneth E. Riener, "Financial Structure Effects of Bond Refunding," *Financial Management* (Summer 1980), pp. 18–23.

[9]See Thomas H. Mayor and Kenneth G. McCoin, "The Rate of Discount in Bond Refunding," *Financial Management,* 3 (Autumn 1974), pp. 54–58.

Application: Rayco Department Stores has a bond issue outstanding with the following terms: par value of $40 million; coupon rate of 14%; matures in 2005; and the current call price equals 110% of par value. It is now 1985 and Rayco can sell bonds with an interest rate of 12%. The new bonds will be sold publicly, thus requiring the services of an investment banker and an SEC registration. Flotation costs should amount to approximately $1,600,000. Would a refunding be a wise decision?[10]

Cash Cost (Today)

Call Premium of .10 × $40,000,000 = $4,000,000 *plus* Flotation Costs of $1,600,000 *equals* a Current Cash Cost of $5,600,000.

Cash Benefits (Years 1–20)

Coupon Interest on Old Bonds of (.14 × $40,000,000) ÷ 2 = $2,800,000 *less* Coupon Interest on New Bonds of (.12 × $40,000,000) ÷ 2 = $2,400,000 *equals* Semiannual Cash Benefits of $400,000.

Net Present Value of Refunding

$$NPV = \frac{\$400,000}{(1.06)^1} + \frac{\$400,000}{(1.06)^2} + \ldots + \frac{\$400,000}{(1.06)^{40}} - \$5,600,000$$

$$NPV = \$400,000 \; ADF_{.06/40} - \$5,600,000 = \$6,018,520 - \$5,600,000 = \$418,520$$

Since the NPV is positive, refunding should take place[11] ◼

Bond Ratings   *Corporations usually find it worthwhile to have their bonds rated for investment quality prior to issuing them.* This is particularly true for bonds that are sold in a public offering and need the exposure of a standardized rating. Another reason for rating bonds before their issuance is to determine whether they should be brought to market at all. A low rating can increase the interest rate on a bond considerably. If a bond receives a very low rating (below Baa), the issuing company may decide to cancel the offering, or at least postpone it until the firm's financial condition warrants an improved rating. Moody's Investors Service and Standard & Poor's Corporation are the major bond rating firms. For a fee, these firms will thoroughly examine the credit-worthiness of a company and the provisions of its new bond issue. Based on that investigation, an investment quality or risk rating will be assigned to the prospective new bond issue. The ratings made by Moody's Investor's Service and an accompanying description of each are provided in exhibit 14.2.

As exhibit 14.2 indicates, higher rated bonds are considered less risky than lower rated bonds. This should carry over into interest rates, and it clearly does as indicated in figure 14.2. There we see that companies selling Baa bonds, for example, must pay higher interest rates than firms selling A-rated bonds. Obviously, bond ratings do matter.

---

[10]It is assumed that both bond issues are sold at par.

[11]Sinking funds can pose somewhat of a problem in bond refunding analysis. See, for example, John D. Finnerty, "Evaluating the Economics of Refunding High-Coupon Sinking-Fund Debt," *Financial Management* (Spring 1983), pp. 5–10.

Exhibit 14.2   Moody's bond ratings

MOODY'S BOND RATINGS

Purpose: The system of rating securities was originated by John Moody in 1909.

The purpose of Moody's Ratings is to provide the investors with a simple system of gradation by which the relative investment qualities of bonds may be noted.

Rating Symbols: Gradations of investment quality are indicated by rating symbols, each symbol representing a group in which the quality characteristics are broadly the same. There are nine symbols as shown below, from that used to designate least investment risk (i.e., highest investment quality) to that denoting greatest investment risk (i.e., lowest investment quality):

Aaa Aa A   Baa Ba B   Caa Ca C

For explanation of municipal rating symbols, in particular the **A 1** and **Baa 1** groups see page 191.

Absence of Rating: Where no rating has been assigned or where a rating has been suspended or withdrawn, it may be for reasons unrelated to the quality of the issue.

Should no rating be assigned, the reason may be one of the following:
1. An application for rating was not received or accepted.
2. The issue or issuer belongs to a group of securities or companies that are not rated as a matter of policy.
3. There is a lack of essential data pertaining to the issue or issuer.
4. The issue was privately placed, in which case the rating is not published in Moody's publications.

Suspension or withdrawal may occur if new and material circumstances arise, the effects of which preclude satisfactory analysis; if there is no longer available reasonable up-to-date data to permit a judgment to be formed; if a bond is called for redemption; or for other reasons.

Changes in Rating: The quality of most bonds is not fixed and steady over a period of time, but tends to undergo change. For this reason changes in ratings occur so as to reflect these variations in the intrinsic position of individual bonds.

A change in rating may thus occur at any time in the case of an individual issue. Such rating change should serve notice that Moody's observes some alteration in the investment risks of the bond or that the previous rating did not fully reflect the quality of the bond as now seen. While because of their very nature, changes are to be expected more frequently among bonds of lower ratings than among bonds of higher ratings, nevertheless the user of bond ratings should keep close and constant check on all ratings-both high and low ratings-thereby to be able to note promptly any signs of change in investment status which may occur.

Limitations to Uses of Ratings: Bonds carrying the same rating are not claimed to be of absolutely equal quality. In a broad sense they are alike in position, but since there are a limited number of rating classes used in grading thousands of bonds, the symbols cannot reflect the fine shadings of risks which actually exist. Therefore, it should be evident to the user of ratings that two bonds identically rated are unlikely to be precisely the same in investment quality.

As ratings are designed exclusively for the purpose of grading bonds according to their investment qualities, they should not be used alone as a basis for investment operations. For example, they have no value in forecasting the direction of future trends of market price. Market price movements in bonds are influenced not only by the quality of individual issues but also by changes in money rates and general economic trends, as well as by the length of maturity, etc. During its life even the best quality bond may have wide price movements, while its high investment status remains unchanged.

The matter of market price has no bearing whatsoever on the determination of ratings which are not to be construed as recommendations with respect to "attractiveness." The attractiveness of a given bond may depend on its yield, its maturity date or other factors for which the investor may search, as well as on its investment quality, the only characteristic to which the rating refers.

Since ratings involve judgments about the future, on the one hand, and since they are used by investors as a means of protection, on the other, the effort is made when assigning ratings to look at "worst" potentialities in the "visible" future, rather than solely at the past record and the status of the present. Therefore, investors using the rating should not expect to find in them a reflection of statistical factors alone, since they are an appraisal of long term risks, including the recognition of many non-statistical factors.

Though ratings may be used by the banking authorities to classify bonds in their bank examination procedure, Moody's Ratings are not made with these bank regulations in view. Moody's Investors Service's own judgment as to desirability or non-desirability of a bond for bank investment purposes is not indicated by Moody's Ratings.

Moody's Ratings represent the mature opinion of Moody's Investors Service, Inc. as to the relative investment classification of bonds. As such, they should be used in conjunction with the description and statistics appearing in Moody's Manuals. Reference should be made to these statements for information regarding the issuer. Moody's Ratings are not commercial credit ratings. In no case is default or receivership to be imputed unless expressly so stated in the Manual.

KEY TO MOODY'S CORPORATE RATINGS

Aaa

Bonds which are rated **Aaa** are judged to be of the best quality. They carry the smallest degree of investment risk and are generally referred to as "gilt edge." Interest payments are protected by a large or by an exceptionally stable margin and principal is secure. While the various protective elements are likely to change, such changes as can be visualized are most unlikely to impair the fundamentally strong position of such issues.

Aa

Bonds which are rated **Aa** are judged to be of high quality by all standards. Together with the **Aaa** group they comprise what are generally known as high grade bonds. They are rated lower than the best bonds because margins of protection may not be as large as in **Aaa** securities or fluctuation of protective elements may be of greater amplitude or there may be other elements present which make the long term risks appear somewhat larger than in **Aaa** securities.

A

Bonds which are rated **A** possess many favorable investment attributes and are to be considered as upper medium grade obligations. Factors giving security to principal and interest are considered adequate but elements may be present which suggest a susceptibility to impairment sometime in the future.

Baa

Bonds which are rated **Baa** are considered as medium grade obligations, i.e., they are neither highly protected nor poorly secured. Interest payments and principal security appear adequate for the present but certain protective elements may be lacking or may be characteristically unreliable over any great length of time. Such bonds lack outstanding investment characteristics and in fact have speculative characteristics as well.

Ba

Bonds which are rated **Ba** are judged to have speculative elements; their future cannot be considered as well assured. Often the protection of interest and principal payments may be very moderate and thereby not well safeguarded during both good and bad times over the future. Uncertainty of position characterizes bonds in this class.

B

Bonds which are rated **B** generally lack characteristics of the desirable investment. Assurance of interest and principal payments or of maintenance of other terms of the contract over any long period of time may be small.

Caa

Bonds which are rated **Caa** are of poor standing. Such issues may be in default or there may be present elements of danger with respect to principal or interest.

Ca

Bonds which are rated **Ca** represent obligations which are speculative in a high degree. Such issues are often in default or have other marked shortcomings.

C

Bonds which are rated **C** are the lowest rated class of bonds and issues so rated can be regarded as having extremely poor prospects of ever attaining any real investment standing.

Note: Moody's applies numerical modifiers, **1**, **2** and **3** in each generic rating classification from **Aa** through **B** in its corporate bond rating system. The modifier **1** indicates that the security ranks in the higher end of its generic rating category; the modifier **2** indicates a mid-range ranking; and the modifier **3** indicates that the issue ranks in the lower end of its generic rating category.

Source: *Moody's Bond Record*, Moody's Investor Service, New York, N.Y.

Figure 14.2   Moody's bond yields by rating category, 1982–1984

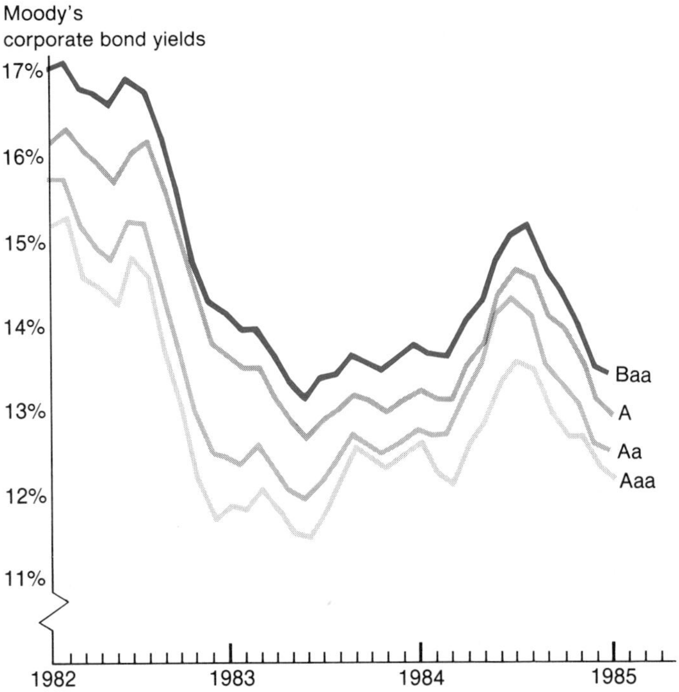

Moody's
corporate bond yields

Source: *Moody's Bond Record*, Moody's Investor Service, New York, N.Y.

Term Loans

Term loans are long-term (i.e., maturities in excess of five years) installment loans used to acquire debt funds. They are evidenced by means of *promissory notes* signed by the borrower, who agrees to repay the loan principal together with interest charges in equal installments. Interest is figured on the unpaid loan balance, in accordance with compound interest. An example promissory note is shown in exhibit 14.3.

Corporations obtain term loans directly from institutional investors in private negotiations. Principal investors are commercial banks and life insurance companies. Interest rates on these loans can either be fixed for the life of the loan or allowed to vary according to a predetermined arrangement. We will examine some of the important features of term loans in this section.

Exhibit 14.3   Sample installment note

N R
B C D   Officer

$ _____

_____	

INSTALLMENT NOTE (INTEREST FOLLOWING)

No. _____   Due _____

TERRE HAUTE, INDIANA _____ , 19 _____

The undersigned, jointly and severally, promise(s) to pay to the order of

TERRE HAUTE FIRST NATIONAL BANK

at its Main or any Branch Office in the City of Terre Haute, Indiana

_____ /100 Dollars

in the following installments: $ _____ on the _____ day of each

calendar month, commencing _____ , 19 _____ and continuing until

_____ of such installments shall have been paid, and _____

on _____ , 19 _____ , together with interest upon successive unpaid balances

at the rate of _____
percent per annum payable with each installment so long as there exists no default in the payment of any installment of principal or interest, all without relief from valuation or appraisement laws and with attorneys' fees.

  If any one of the said installments is not paid when due or if for any reason the holder deems itself insecure, the entire unpaid amount of this Note shall, at the option of the holder hereof, immediately become due and payable without notice or demand. The makers and indorsers severally waive presentment for payment, protest, notice of protest, and notice of nonpayment of this Note.

ADDRESS _____   _____

F. 1025 3-64

Source: Terre Haute First National Bank, Terre Haute, IN.

Term Loan Mathematics   The four principal components of a term loan are: *loan face value, annual installment payments, interest rate* (i.e., the lender's RRR), and *number of years to maturity*. Given that term loan installment payments are an annuity, these four variables can and should be related by means of the annuity discounting equation (3.14).[12] This equation is replicated below along with its operational counterpart.

$$PV = C\left[\frac{1 - \frac{1}{(1+i)^n}}{i}\right] \quad \text{or} \quad PV = C(ADF_{i/n})$$

---

[12]The annuity compounding formula could also be used in this situation, but not as easily.

If we substitute loan face value for PV, RRR for i, installment payment for C, and allow n to stand for years to maturity, we can generate the following term loan equation:

Equation 14.2   Loan Face Value $=$ Installment $(ADF_{RRR/n})$

Term loans are often designed with other than annual installment payments. Therefore, when using equation 14.2 with monthly, quarterly, or semiannual loan payments, one must be careful to adjust RRR and n accordingly. Knowledge in the use of this formula can be of great benefit not only to financial managers but consumers as well, whose auto and home loans are treated identically. Given any three of the four variables in equation 14.2, we can solve for the unknown.

Example A: What are the annual installment payments on a $1,200,000 term loan that matures five years given an RRR of 15%. Substituting into equation 14.2 we obtain the following solution:

$1,200,000 $=$ Installment $(ADF_{.15/5})$

$$Installment = \frac{\$1,200,000}{ADF_{.15/5}} = \frac{\$1,200,000}{3.3522} = \$357,974$$

Each payment of $357,974, it should be emphasized, includes both principal and interest ∎

Example B: How many quarterly payments of $100,000 each would be necessary to pay off a $1,525,000 term loan at 16% interest? The solution is:

$1,525,000 $=$ $100,000 $ADF_{.04/n}$

$$ADF_{.04/n} = \frac{\$1,525,000}{\$100,000} = 15.250$$

From the annuity discount factor table we can see that n is equal to 24 quarterly payments ∎

The information in table 14.1 should increase our understanding of equation 14.2 and the relationships of the four variables contained therein.

Table 14.1   Annual Installment Payments on a $2 million Term Loan for Selected Interest Rates and Maturities

	8%	10%	12%	14%	16%
5 years	$500,914	$527,593	$554,816	$582,564	$610,818
10 years	$298,058	$325,489	$353,970	$383,428	$413,805
15 years	$233,658	$262,947	$293,647	$325,616	$358,712
20 years	$203,705	$234,918	$267,759	$301,973	$337,336
25 years	$187,357	$220,337	$255,001	$290,998	$328,025

Here we have a $2 million loan that is repaid, with interest, in equal annual installments. Listed in the main body of the table are payments that would be required on this loan for selected interest rates and maturities. As we move from left to right across the table, we observe the relationship between payments and interest rate. Although not perfect, the association is positive and, for the most part, linear. Moving down the table exposes the relationship between payments and maturity. Here the association is negative, but definitely not linear. Payments fall rapidly at first, but then much more gradually, eventually leveling out. One might wonder here what the exact relationship is between the loan and loan payments. It is positive, linear, and proportional. For example, a doubling of the loan will exactly double the payment, regardless of the interest rate or maturity. For a $1 million loan, we could simply divide all of the payments in table 14.1 exactly in half.

Remaining Loan Balance   There are many occasions when we need to know the *remaining balance* on an installment loan after several payments have been made. Remaining balances are needed for financial statements and in refunding analyses. Although this may sound like a difficult problem, all that we are really asking for is the present value of the remaining payments. Equation 14.2 can be used here, if we replace loan face value with remaining balance and redefine n as the remaining time to maturity.

Example: The original maturity of a $75,000 loan was twenty years. The RRR on the loan is 12% and it is being paid off in monthly installments of $825.80. What is the remaining balance on the loan after five years? In other words, what is the balance after sixty payments have been made? The solution is:

Remaining Balance = $825.80 $ADF_{.01/180}$ = $825.80 (83.3217) = $68,807

This loan has been reduced by $6,193 over the last five years ∎

Variable Rate Loans   Many term loans are extended today with *variable interest rates*. This is in response to the difficulties encountered by many lenders with volatile interest rates over the last decade. While there are differences in the way variable rate loans are handled, it is possible to generalize on the subject. The interest rate varies with market interest rates, usually in accordance with a predetermined formula such as: 4% plus the current average rate on five-year government bonds. Rate changes can take place only on appointed dates (e.g., anniversary date of the loan) and they can be lowered as well as increased.[13] New rates are to be applied on the remaining balance of a loan at the time the rate is changed. The remaining installment payments are adjusted to fit the new interest rate, as the following example demonstrates.[14]

---

[13]Frequently, a limit is placed on the amount by which an interest rate can change.

[14]An alternative to altering the remaining payments is to adjust the remaining years to maturity.

Example: An $800,000 variable rate, term loan is obtained in 1985. It has a fifteen-year maturity and an initial RRR of 12%. Annual installment payments begin at $117,459 and they will remain at that level as long as the interest rate does not change. Calculate the final ten payments on this loan assuming that the interest rate is raised to 15% in 1990.

First, we must find the remaining balance, as follows:

$$\text{Remaining Balance} = \$117{,}459 \text{ADF}_{.12/10} = \$117{,}459 \, (5.6502) = \$663{,}667$$

The remaining balance, in essence, will become a new loan with a 15% interest rate and ten year maturity. The new payments will therefore be:

$$\$663{,}667 = \text{Installment} \, (\text{ADF}_{.15/10})$$

$$\text{Installment} = \frac{\$663{,}667}{\text{ADF}_{.15/10}} = \frac{\$663{,}667}{5.0188} = \$132{,}236 \ \blacksquare$$

Loan Amortization Schedule   Term loan installment payments must be large enough to repay the loan principal plus the interest charges. Each payment, therefore, contains a portion that is interest charge and a portion that is principal repayment. Consequently, the loan balance will decline with each payment thus leading to a remaining balance. We must be able to separate these two portions occasionally, in preparing income tax returns, for example. How do we go about this, considering that the portions are different for every payment? We first calculate the interest portion of each payment by multiplying the remaining or unpaid loan balance by the interest rate. The interest portion is then subtracted from the payment to determine the principal portion. For this task it is helpful to construct a *loan amortization schedule.*

Example: Table 14.2 contains a loan amortization schedule for a $2 million, ten-year, 12% term loan that requires annual installment payments of $353,970.

Table 14.2   Loan Amortization Schedule

Time Period (Year)	Remaining Loan Balance	Installment Payment	Interest Portion	Principal Portion
0	$2,000,000	$0	$0	$0
1	1,886,030	353,970	240,000	113,970
2	1,758,384	353,970	226,324	127,646
3	1,615,420	353,970	211,006	142,964
4	1,455,300	353,970	193,850	160,120
5	1,275,966	353,970	174,636	179,334
6	1,075,112	353,970	153,116	200,854
7	850,155	353,970	129,013	224,957
8	598,204	353,970	102,019	251,951
9	316,018	353,970	71,784	282,186
10	(30)	353,970	37,922	316,048

Figure 14.3   **Allocation of term loan installments to principle and interest (loan has face value of $2 million, ten-year maturity, 12% interest rate, and payments of $353,970 per year)**

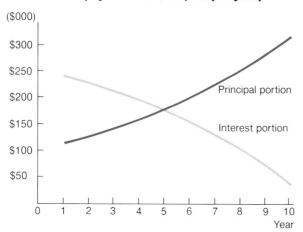

We shall begin our discussion of table 14.2 by focusing on the second row or year one. A payment of $353,970 is made, out of which .12 × $2,000,000 = $240,000 is interest expense. By subtracting the interest charge from the loan payment we obtain the principal portion, or $353,970 − $240,000 = $113,970. The principal repayment will reduce the loan balance for the second year to $1,886,030. Continuing on, the $353,970 payment in two years will consist of .12 × $1,886,030 = $226,324 in interest and $353,970 − $226,324 = $127,646 in principal. This principal repayment, in turn, will reduce the loan balance further, to $1,758,384. This process is repeated over and over again until all payments are accounted for. As you might guess, loan amortization schedules are very conducive to computer solution.

There are two further observations we can make about loan amortization schedules such as the one in table 14.2. With the exception of a small error due to rounding, the principal portion of the final payment is just sufficient to retire the loan. This is as it should be. Also note how the interest charges decline each year while the principal repayments rise (figure 14.3). This is due to the fact that the interest rate is being applied to the gradually declining loan balance, in accordance with compound interest ■

Term Loan Provisions   *Term loans have most of the same provisions as corporate bonds, although not with the same frequency or specifics.* One provision term loans will not have is a trustee, since most of them are privately arranged. Acceleration clauses are common features and many of these loans are backed by collateral. Term loans can also contain a variety of protective covenants. However, one notable exception is a sinking fund, which are irrelevant for installment loans. On rare occasions, these loans are convertible into shares of common stock, similar to convertible bonds. An increasingly common feature allows term loan investors the opportunity to participate in a company's net income, much like participatory preferred stock. Term loans usually have a provision to allow for early retirement and for essentially the same reasons that bonds do. Rather than calling it a call provision, however, it goes by such names as *prepayment clause* and instead of call premium one is more likely to see an expression such as *prepayment penalty*. Refunding of term loans is discussed below.

Refunding a Term Loan   The decision to refund a term loan is analyzed in much the same manner as a bond refunding. There are a couple of important differences, however. Whereas the benefits of a bond refunding equaled the difference in coupons between the old and new issues, term loan benefits are equal to the difference in installment payments between old and new loans. Furthermore, since term loans are all privately placed, flotation costs are usually a minor consideration.[15] As with bonds, a term loan refunding decision is complicated by income tax considerations. These tax implications will not be considered in this text.

Application: Four years ago, Superior Cement Company negotiated a $5 million term loan with Bankcorp National. The loan's original maturity was for twelve years at a fixed interest rate of 13%. It is being repaid in equal annual installments of $844,937. A prepayment clause exists in the loan agreement. It allows Superior to retire the debt at any time with the understanding that a penalty can be assessed. The penalty is 12% of the remaining loan balance at the time of refunding. Flotation costs are minimal. Superior is currently in a position where it can arrange a 10% term loan. A new term loan would be equal to the remaining balance on the old loan, which is presently $4,054,684. Furthermore, the new loan shall have a maturity of eight years (the remaining maturity of the old loan). The annual payments on such a loan would be $760,030. Should refunding take place?

Cash Cost (Today)

Prepayment penalty of .12 $\times$ $4,054,684 = $486,562

Cash Benefits (Years 1–8)

Payment on old term loan of $844,937 *less* payment on new term loan of $760,030 *equals* annual cash benefits of $84,907.

Net Present Value of Refunding

$$NPV = \frac{\$84,907}{(1.10)^1} + \frac{\$84,907}{(1.10)^2} + \ldots + \frac{\$84,907}{(1.10)^8} - \$486,562$$
$$NPV = \$84,907\ ADF_{.10/8} - \$486,562 = \$452,970 - \$486,562 = (\$33,592)$$

Since the NPV is negative, we would have to say that a refunding should not take place ■

---

[15]There may be some loan origination fees that could be important in the decision to refund small loans.

Leasing

A lease is a contract under which the owner of a capital asset (lessor) agrees to let a business (lessee) use (i.e. rent) the asset for a stated period of time. The lessee, in turn, agrees to pay rent to the lessor for a stated period of time.

Our primary concern is with the lessee, who sees a lease as a means to acquire the use of an asset.[16] The use of an asset is normally all that a business really wants anyway. Ownership, per se, does not bestow many economic benefits.[17] Moreover, lessees have most of the rights that an owner would have. The point here is that leasing is an alternative to financing. That is, *leasing the use of an asset is a reasonable alternative to financing the purchase of that asset.*

There are two basic types of leases, financial and operating. The major difference between them is *cancellability:* an *operating lease* can be canceled with relative ease whereas a *financial lease* cannot. Operating leases (sometimes called service leases) are generally short-term agreements on assets that have a useful life longer than the term of the lease. For example, computer systems, which may become obsolete if leased for a long period of time, frequently have operating leases. Financial leases are longer term than operating leases. They are commonly used for leasing fixed assets such as land and buildings. We will devote our attention to financial leases since they have more implications for financial management.

The noncancellability feature of financial leases holds great significance for a lessee. Basically, the lessee is locked into a series of rental payments that must be paid in good times and bad. A failure to do so can lead to serious financial problems such as: a damaged credit rating; an end to the use of the asset; and, in the extreme, bankruptcy. *In many respects, financial leases and rental payments are very similar to term loans and installment payments.* It is no wonder that most financial experts equate leasing with debt financing and so shall we. Therefore, *when we speak of leasing as an alternative to financing we will be referring specifically to debt financing.*

A discussion of leasing is well worth our time. The importance of leasing is evidenced by the tremendous growth in this financing method since the mid-1960s. In addition to the greater volume of these transactions, leasing is also more widespread, applying to a variety of assets, such as: railroad cars, computers, automobiles, airplanes, buildings, and land. The variety of entities who act as lessors has also risen to include: leasing companies, banks, insurance companies, wealthy individuals, mutual funds, and even other corporations.

Lease Provisions   Leases involving businesses are often written for twenty years or longer and involve substantial sums of money. Furthermore, the asset that is being leased may be critical to the lessee's business. For these reasons, it is wise for the lessor and lessee to draw up a written lease agreement in consultation with their attorneys. A lease agreement should contain detailed provisions that explain the rights and responsibilities of the two parties. We shall briefly examine, from the viewpoint of the lessee, those lease provisions that are most important to the subject of financial management.

---

[16]Some leases arise out of the sale of a capital asset that is then leased back to the seller. The popular name for this arrangement is "sale and leaseback".

[17]This statement is elaborated upon more fully in a later section.

Term of a Lease   Along with rental payments, the term of a lease is probably the most important provision in a lease agreement. *The term of a lease is the life of the lease, or that interval of time during which all rights and obligations of the lessor and lessee are in force.* At the end of the lease term, the lease expires and all rental payments and use of the asset cease. Although they can be for any length of time, lease periods are normally set to match the asset's expected useful life.

Cancellability   As we stated earlier, a financial lease is noncancellable. This means that neither party can cancel the lease agreement as long as the other party is fulfilling its obligations. Such a provision will be clearly stated in the lease agreement. A noncancellability provision presents no problem as long as both parties are satisfied. For many reasons though, a renter may wish to get out from under a lease before the end of the lease term: the asset has become obsolete, a useful service is no longer provided by the asset, rental payments are out of line with the market, or the lessee is having financial problems, to mention a few. A noncancellability provision can be tempered with various kinds of *escape clauses*. A lessee, for example, may be allowed to terminate a lease if a substantial penalty is paid to the lessor. Of course, a lease, like all contracts, can be cancelled at any time and under any conditions if both parties give their consent.

Renewal Options   Lessees often find it desirable to be able to renew a lease when it has expired. This right is granted by a renewal option and it is particularly important for leases with short lives. A renewal option is especially advantageous to a renter if the terms and provisions of the renewal are spelled out in the lease agreement. In this way, the risk of renewal is placed on the lessor's shoulders, who must accept the lessee's decision. Consider, for instance, a lease for a fleet of trucks that can be renewed in five years, at the option of the lessee. The renewal rental is $40,000 per year. When the renewal date arrives, comparable trucks are renting for $75,000 on the market. Obviously, the lessee has struck an excellent bargain, even though it may not have been predicted when the lease was drawn up five years earlier. On the other hand, the lessor has suffered an opportunity loss.

Purchase Option   Circumstances can change for a lessee so that what once was a smart decision to rent, afterwards becomes prudent to buy. A lessee can reserve this opportunity by requesting a purchase option, which is nothing more than a right to buy the property from the lessor in the future. This can be a very valuable right under certain circumstances. Care must be taken in designing these provisions so that the tax authorities do not construe the lease to be an installment sale.

Property Maintenance   Most capital assets must be cared for and protected. In the first place, repairs are needed from time to time in order to keep the asset in working order and maintain resale value. Secondly, valuable property should be insured against fire, water damage, vandalism, etc. Lastly, some classes of capital assets (buildings in particular) are assessed property taxes by local governments. Property taxes must be paid or the asset will revert to the government. Many lessors prefer to take care of these property maintenance expenses themselves, thereby relieving the renter of this obligation. What is and is not to be taken care of by the lessor should be spelled out clearly in the lease agreement.

Improvements to Property   Renters of all kinds, not just businesses, like to make changes to their leased property. Some changes, the addition of carpeting and electricity, add to the property's value. These are classified as improvements. Other alterations, a change of wall color or the installation of a neon sign, may not add to a property's value. Unless stated otherwise, any improvements made and paid for by the lessee will revert to the lessor at the expiration of the lease. A provision can be written into the lease to compensate the renter, in whole or in part, for any improvements that are made. Such a provision would be very important to a lessee who planned to make considerable improvements to the property.

Rent   The provision for rental payments is central to any lease agreement. Here the lessee should bargain for the lowest rental payments possible while at the same time negotiate for the most desirable payment specifics. With regard to the latter suggestion, reference is being made to the frequency of payments and whether or not they are fixed for the life of the lease or variable. If, for example, it is more suitable for a lessee to pay rent monthly or quarterly rather than annually, then that scheme should be sought. Although rental payments are typically the same each period, they can also vary over time, due to, say inflation.

Mathematics of Leasing   Businesses are better informed lessees when they understand the methodology used by lessors to determine rental payments. Lessors are investors in capital assets. Like any investor, they wish to recoup their initial investment outlay (i.e., cost of the asset) and earn at least the applicable required rate of return. Lessors also expect to be reimbursed for any recurring property maintenance expenses that they agree to incur, such as, insurance, property taxes, and repairs. Other than the possibility of a salvage value for the asset when the term of the lease is over, a lessor must rely solely upon rent to meet the previously stated objectives.

A lessor should also consider income taxes in the rent payment computation simply because they can make a significant difference. Rent is considered to be ordinary gross income for tax purposes, and thus taxable. Property maintenance expense is a deduction for tax purposes, while the salvage value of the property may lead to capital gains or losses. As owner of the asset, the lessor is entitled to a depreciation deduction, as well as any allowable investment tax credits.

Rent, maintenance expense, salvage value, and income taxes are cash flows, and the investment is a present value. Accordingly, a lessor can solve for rental payments with the discounting model of compound interest in the form shown below:

Equation 14.3

$$V - ITC = \frac{[R - M - D][1 - T] + D}{(1 + RRR)^1} + \cdots$$
$$+ \frac{[R - M - D][1 - T] + D}{(1 + RRR)^n} + \frac{SVAT}{(1 + RRR)^n}$$

Where:

$$V = \text{Value of leased asset (e.g., cost of asset, investment outlay)}$$
$$ITC = \text{Investment tax credit}$$
$$R = \text{Rental payments received by lessor}$$
$$M = \text{Property maintenance expense paid by lessor}$$
$$D = \text{Depreciation tax deduction}$$
$$T = \text{Ordinary income tax rate}$$
$$n = \text{Term of a lease}$$
$$SVAT = \text{Salvage value of asset adjusted for taxes}$$
$$RRR = \text{Required rate of return}$$

The recurring term: $[R - M - D] [1 - T] + D$, requires some explanation. It is an abbreviated method to compute income taxes and net the cash inflows and outflows. In other words, it provides us with a shortcut to finding rental revenue minus maintenance expense and income taxes. Taxes are calculated and deducted in one step by multiplying taxable income $[R - M - D]$ by one minus the tax rate. To borrow from our earlier discussion on capital budgeting, we have simply combined the cash flow and income tax statements. The result is a recurring net cash flow received by the lessor.

The rental payments derived from equation 14.3 are the minimum that a lessor would accept. The actual rent may be higher than this depending upon many factors, the most important being the prevailing degree of competition faced by the lessor. Furthermore, this equation assumes that all of the rental payments occur at the end of each period (i.e., not paid in advance). And, lest we forget, in the event that rental payments are other than annual, we must adjust RRR and n accordingly.

Application: Security Life Insurance Company has been asked by a national hotel chain if it would purchase the Capistrano Hotel and lease it to the chain for 20 years. The hotel is located in downtown Jacksonville, Florida, and can be purchased today for $3,600,000. However, an investment tax credit of 10% is allowed that will reduce the net investment by $360,000. Security Life does not foresee a salvage value for the hotel of any importance. Should the insurance company decide to buy and lease the property, it would prefer to pay the $75,000 annual maintenance expense itself. For tax purposes, the hotel has a life of twenty years, no salvage value, and it must be depreciated on a straight-line basis. Therefore, the annual depreciation deduction will be $180,000. Given that Security Life's ordinary tax rate is 40% and its RRR is 12%, what is the minimum annual rental payment? We shall proceed by substituting the above information into equation 14.3.

$$\$3,600,000 - \$360,000 = \frac{(R - \$75,000 - \$180,000)\,(1 - .40) + \$180,000}{(1.12)^1} + \ldots$$
$$+ \frac{(R - \$75,000 - \$180,000)\,(1 - .40) + \$180,000}{(1.12)^{20}}$$

Since the numerators on the right side of the equation are identical, we can use an annuity discount factor to simplify the computations:

$$\$3,240,000 = [(R - \$75,000 - \$180,000)\,(1 - .40) + \$180,000]\,ADF_{12/20}$$

Simplifying we obtain:

$$\$3,240,000 = [.60R + \$27,000]\,ADF_{12/20}$$

Solving for R:

$$.60R = \frac{\$3,240,000}{ADF_{12/20}} - \$27,000 = \frac{\$3,240,000}{7.4694} - \$27,000 = \$406,770$$

Therefore:

$$R = \frac{\$406,770}{.60} = \$677,950$$

An annual rental payment of $677,950 will be sufficient to return the insurance company's investment, cover property maintenance, pay income taxes, and generate a compound annual rate of return equal to 12%.

A salvage value should logically reduce the rental payment. For instance, a salvage value adjusted for taxes of $1 million would lower the rent from $677,950 to $654,810. Should the lessor demand a higher RRR because of an increase in risk, the rental payment would rise. Given an RRR of 15%, for instance, Security Life's minimum rental would rise from $677,950 to $817,716. By the same token, a lower RRR would produce a smaller rent.

Solving for the minimum rental payment is quite easy in the absence of salvage values, property maintenance expenses, and, particularly, income taxes. We can simply apply equation 14.4 when rental payments occur at the end of each period, or equation 14.5 if rental payments are received at the beginning of each peroid.

Equation 14.4 $$C = \frac{R}{(1 + RRR)^1} + \frac{R}{(1 + RRR)^2} + \ldots + \frac{R}{(1 + RRR)^n}$$

Equation 14.5 $$C = \frac{R}{(1 + RRR)^0} + \frac{R}{(1 + RRR)^1} + \ldots + \frac{R}{(1 + RRR)^{n-1}} \blacksquare$$

Lease vs. Borrow and Buy   To this point in the discussion, we have been indoctrinated on the definition of leasing, examined the important provisions of lease agreements and gone behind the scenes to look at the determination of rental payments. The issue before us now is whether to lease a capital asset or acquire financing with which to purchase it.

The leasing decision is a financing decision, not an asset decision. The decision to acquire the services of a capital asset is made in capital budgeting, based on acceptance criteria such as NPV. Here we are concerned with *how* to acquire an acceptable capital asset. Should it be leased or should it be purchased with debt financing.[18] *This is the lease versus borrow and buy decision.* There are several factors to be considered when making this decision, some more important than others.

Arguments in Favor of Leasing

Leasing Is Less Harmful to a Firm's Financial Statement   Generally accepted accounting practices require all borrowing to be listed in the balance sheet as liabilities, but only certain leases must be so recorded.[19] By leasing an asset, a firm can restrict its liabilities and, therefore, improve the debt-to-equity and debt-to-assets ratios calculated by investors. Whether or not such subterfuge works is very debatable. For one thing, the accounting profession is

[18]The contractual nature of rental payments causes leasing to be much more like debt than equity.

[19]Accounting treatment of leases is thoroughly covered in *Intermediate Accounting*, 4th ed., by Donald E. Kieso and Jerry J. Weygandt, John Wiley and Sons, NY (1983), pp. 95–1007.

expanding the number of leases that should be shown on the balance sheet. Furthermore, those lease agreements that are not recorded in the balance sheet must be explained in a footnote. Finally, professional investors and loan officers are not so naive as to ignore sizable leases just because they are unrecorded.

Leases Are Not Burdened with Restrictive Loan Provisions   As a rule, leases do not contain provisions that interfere with a business's general operations, as in the case of a bond issue or term loan. On the other hand, most leases will restrict somewhat the use of the leased asset. One must decide which of the two is the lessor evil.

Leasing Is a More Efficient Source of Financing   According to this argument, leasing is superior to debt financing for two reasons: (1) borrowing is more time consuming than leasing, because the latter is arranged privately, and (2) leasing can provide for 100% financing, whereas seldom can one borrow to purchase a capital asset without putting up some equity. The first claim is questionable when we consider that term loans and bond issues can also be arranged privately. As for the second assertion, companies seldom raise funds solely to purchase a single asset, unless that asset is extremely large in relation to the size of the firm. In that case, some equity funds would not only be required by creditors, but also necessary to maintain the firm's optimal degree of financial leverage. Moreover, it is doubtful that a lessor could be found who is willing to completely finance and lease such an asset.

Leasing Allows the Renter to Shift the Risk of Obsolescence to the Lessor   Capital assets certainly do become obsolete, but whether and in what degree this risk can be shifted to the owner is open to question. About the only hope that a lessee has of shifting this risk is the ability to terminate the lease prior to the end of the asset's useful life. In order for this to exist, the lease term must be shorter than the useful life of the asset, or an escape clause is included in the noncancellability provision of the lease agreement. Unfortunately for the renter, when these conditions are present the rental payments are likely to be much higher.

Arguments in Favor of Buying

A Buyer Will Benefit from Any Salvage Value, A Renter Will Not   Salvage or residual values can be substantial. In the case of buildings and land, residual values can be exceptionally large, often in excess of the original purchase price. It is also true that owners will receive the money from the sale of these assets. But lessors are owners too, and, in a competitive environment at least, they should consider expected salvage values in the determination of rental payments. Earlier, we saw an example of how a salvage value caused the rental payments to decline. The question of who benefits from salvage values really revolves around the additional question of whether or not lessors pass expected salvage values on to renters in the form of lower rents.

Buyers Will Benefit from the Value Added by Improvements   Assuming there are no lease provisions to the contrary, this argument has some validity. But, as we saw earlier, arrangements can be made to compensate a lessee for actual, identifiable property improvements. There are several ways to accomplish this: (1) rent payments can be lowered, (2) the lessor can pay for part or all of the improvements, and (3) a renter can claim a portion of the salvage value when the asset is sold. Without such arrangements, there is no question that, all other factors equal, a firm would be better off to borrow the money and buy the asset.

Buyers Have Certain Tax Advantages that Are not Available to Renters   Three principle income tax benefits are available to the owner of a capital asset that has been purchased with borrowed funds: Interest deductions, depreciation deductions, and investment tax credit. The potential tax savings from these three items can be substantial. At first glance, it may seem foolish that a business would even think of renting given the harmful income tax consequences. However, it might not be so foolish after all. Although a renter must give up the tax benefits of ownership, it is now entitled to a tax deduction for rental payments. Whether one set of tax benefits is superior to the other is not that important. *The central question is: what effect will these various deductions and credits have?* In other words, deductions, credits, and, for that matter, income will not affect everyone's income taxes in the same way. This should not be suprising given the complexity of federal income tax regulations. Capital gains are treated differently than ordinary income; ordinary losses are treated unlike ordinary income; some organizations are taxed while others are not; and the list could go on and on.

With the purchase of most debt-financed capital assets comes depreciation and interest deductions and an investment tax credit. Is it not conceivable, given what was just said, that one party might derive a greater reduction in taxes from these items than another party? Certainly it is. Consider, for instance, two businesses, A is in a 25% tax bracket, and B is in a 50% tax bracket. B will get twice the tax savings from a deduction as A. Were B to buy a capital asset that A needs and lease it to A, both firms might benefit simply because they are treated differently for tax purposes.

Unlike all of the other arguments for and against leasing, *tax law complications are very difficult to argue with or ignore.* It is probably safe to say that the decision to lease or borrow and buy is made on the basis of income taxes more than anything else. The impact of taxes will show up in the costs of leasing and borrowing that are to be covered in chapter 16.

Preferred Stock

Preferred stock is a long-term form of equity financing. In the aggregate, it is not a significant source of funds (refer back to figure 12.2). On an individual basis, however, it can be important. Preferred stock is quite popular for certain situations and within certain industries. *Although it is legally classified as equity, preferred stock is really a hybrid of debt and common stock equity, since it contains important elements of each.*

Preferred stock dividends are paid on a quarterly basis. The dividends are usually determined by a preferred stock issue's dividend rate and par value (typically $100 per share).

Example: The dividend rate on a $20 million issue of preferred stock is 12%, and each share has a par value of $100. Per share dividends are equal to $100 $\times$ .12 = $12 per year, or $3 each quarter. Dividends for the entire issue would be $20,000,000 $\times$ .12 = $2,400,000 annually or $600,000 quarterly ■

Preferred stock dividends can be paid only after a firm has met all of its interest charges on debt. *Unlike debt, there is no legal obligation to pay preferred dividends, with the exception that they must be paid before any dividends can be distributed to common stockholders.* Furthermore, a company's credit rating can be damaged if it fails to pay preferred dividends. Consequently, businesses are very reluctant to discontinue dividend payments on their preferred stock.

In rare instances, preferred stock dividends can be *cumulative* (dividends that are missed in one quarter become part of the next quarter's obligation), or *participating* (tied to net income). Seldom will a preferred stock issue have a maturity date. As a rule, preferred shareholders are not allowed to vote for the board of directors. Many preferred stock issues contain call provisions to allow for their early retirement, and a few are convertible into common stock. Last, preferred stock issues may contain protective covenants similar to those found with bond issues.

Preferred stock ranks between debt and common stock in terms of its claim on earnings and assets. It would seem to be a reasonable alternative to either of these, but the fact of the matter is, it is seldom used. One reason seems to be that corporate managers have difficulty equating preferred stock with equity financing. It follows, therefore, that financial managers consider it to be an alternative to long-term debt. In such a matchup, debt has a tremendous advantage simply because interest charges on debt are tax deductible, whereas preferred stock dividends are not. Despite these handicaps, preferred stock is quite popular in three instances: (1) public utilities in many states are limited in the amount of debt they can carry, and utilities with a preference for more debt than the law allows often turn to preferred stock to make up the difference; (2) it is frequently used in bankruptcy reorganizations; and (3) preferred stock also has certain tax advantages when used in corporate mergers and acquisitions.

Preferred Stock Mathematics   Preferred stock, like bonds, is frequently issued in the public financial market. Many preferred shares are also traded in the secondary market. Consequently, preferred stock can have a market value or market price. The market price of a preferred stock will often diverge from par value, because the dividend rate and par value are contractual and thus not subject to change. As market interest rates rise, the market value of a preferred stock will fall. On the other hand, a decline in market interest rates will lead to a rise in the market price of preferred stock. At the new price, investors are able to earn the market RRR. This is precisely what happens with bonds, as we saw earlier.

The market value of a share of preferred stock is equal to the present value of the stock's future dividend payments (cash flows), discounted at the market-determined RRR. Preferred stock does not normally have a maturity date. Thus, the dividends continue indefinitely, and there is no payment of par value. Furthermore, the RRR must be a quarterly rate, since the dividend payments are quarterly. The preferred stock valuation model is presented below:

Equation 14.6

$$\text{Preferred Stock Value} = \frac{\text{Dividend}/4}{(1 + \text{RRR})^1} + \frac{\text{Dividend}/4}{(1 + \text{RRR})^2} + \cdots + \frac{\text{Dividend}/4}{(1 + \text{RRR})^\infty}$$

Where:

Preferred Stock Value = Market value or market price of a share of preferred stock

Dividend/4 = Quarterly dividend payments lasting to infinity

RRR = Market-determined, quarterly required rate of return

Preferred stock dividends are a perfect illustration of a perpetuity.[20] As such, equation 14.6 can be greatly simplified, as follows:

Equation 14.7   Preferred Stock Value = $\dfrac{\text{Dividend}/4}{\text{RRR}}$

Application: Three years ago Relco Enterprises issued 350,000 shares of $100 par value preferred stock. The dividend rate on these shares is 8%. Per share dividends are $100 × .08 = $8 per year, or $2 each quarter. At the present time, the market requires a rate of return on these shares amounting to 12%. Therefore, the market price of a Relco preferred share is:

Preferred Stock Value = $\dfrac{\$2.00}{.03}$ = $66.67

The market value of the entire Relco issue is 350,000 × $66.67 = $23,334,500. Should the market RRR decline to 6% at a later date, then a share of Relco preferred stock will sell on the market for:

Preferred Stock Value = $\dfrac{\$2.00}{.015}$ = $133.33 ■

Summary

The three most common forms of long-term debt financing for a business enterprise are bonds, term loans, and leasing. Because they are liabilities of a company, the payments on these forms of capital are legally enforceable obligations. Although technically classified as equity capital, preferred stock possesses many of the same characteristics as long-term debt, particularly bonds. However, there are two important distinctions between bonds and preferred stock. For one thing, the payment of preferred stock dividends is not mandatory, and they are not deductible for income tax purposes. Corporate bonds and preferred stock are sold publicly and in private transactions. Term loans and leases, on the other hand, are strictly private funding arrangements. A number of important provisions can apply to each of these forms of capital. A financial manager is advised to consider these provisions carefully before agreeing to them, since they all, except refunding, are detrimental to the firm's interests. The mathematical (i.e., compound interest) properties of bonds, term loans, leases, and preferred stock are not only relevant to financial management, but quite interesting in their own right. In particular, there are the market values associated with bonds and preferred stock, as well as term loan installment payments and lease rental payments. A further look at the mathematical properties of these forms of long-term financing will come in chapter 16, when we consider the cost of capital ■

Appendix: Bond Refunding Decision with Taxes

In this appendix we will study the bond refunding decision within an environment of income taxes. The decision criteria remains the same as before: a bond issue should be refunded if the present value of future benefits (RNCFs) exceeds the cost to carry out the refunding (INCF). However, when taxes enter the picture, the analysis becomes more involved.

---

[20]Refer to the explanation of perpetuities in chapter 3.

There are several tax features to consider in a bond refunding. Bond coupon interest expense is a tax deduction in each and every year it occurs. Thus, interest payments on a new bond issue will produce tax savings each year, whereas the interest charges on a retired bond issue will no longer be around to provide tax savings. Call premiums are also deductible for tax purposes, and they can be written off immediately. Flotation costs, too, are tax deductible expenses; but, unlike the previous two items, flotation costs are not deductible at the time they are incurred. Instead, a firm must *amortize* these costs annually over the life of a bond issue, on a straight-line basis. For instance, flotation costs of $1,500,000 and an original bond maturity of thirty years would combine for an amortization tax deduction equal to $1,500,000 ÷ 30 years = $50,000. In the event a bond issue is retired prior to maturity, a company can write off the unamortized portion of the flotation cost. Returning to the preceding illustration, if this bond issue is retired after ten years, the unamortized flotation cost of $1 million (i.e., 2/3 of the total) would be immediately deducted for tax purposes.

Application: Ten years ago, Argus Enterprises issued bonds with a $50,000,000 par value, twenty-five year maturity, and 12% coupon. The firm incurred flotation costs totaling $2,500,000 on this issue. The flotation cost tax amortization is thus $100,000 per year. If the bonds were called for refunding today, Argus would have to pay a call premium of 8%. The company's credit standing has improved over the years, to the point where it can now sell bonds at the lower interest rate of 10%. A new, $50,000,000, fifteen year, 10% coupon bond issue can be sold in the public market at a cost of $2,700,000. The flotation cost tax amortization would be $180,000 per year in this case. Argus Enterprises' income tax rate is 45%. Given an RRR of 10% (the interest rate on the new bonds), would a refuding be desirable in this situation? In order to simplify matters, we will assume that the coupon payments on both bond issues are annual rather than semiannual. Such an assumption will have little effect on the final answer. The solution is provided in table 14.3 ■

Key Terms/Concepts

Acceleration clause
Bond indenture
Bond ratings
Call premium
Call price
Call provisions
Conversion privilege
Coupon rate
Cumulative preferred stock
Debentures
Escape clause

Financial lease
Lessee
Loan amortization
Loan face value
Maturity date
Mortgage bonds
Operating lease
Participating preferred stock
Par value
Prepayment clause
Prepayment penalty

Purchase option
Refunding
Remaining loan balance
Renewal option
Sinking fund
Subordinated bonds
Term loans
Term of the lease
Trustee
Variable interest rates

Questions

1. Describe the assets that are normally financed with long-term corporate debt.

2. Bonds are seldom traded in the secondary market at par value. Explain why this is true.

3. Provide the names of the two major bond rating agencies. What other corporate debt securities are rated by these firms?

4. The desirability of refunding a corporate bond issue declines as the issue approaches maturity. What is the reason for this?

5. Briefly define the following corporate bond terms: sinking fund, subordination, and trustee.

6. How would you respond to a layman who asked the question, "Are corporate bonds and term loans essentially the same?"

Table 14.3   Bond Refunding Analysis with Income Taxes

Initial Cash Flows

Cash Outflows

Call premium paid on old bonds (.08 × $50,000,000)	$4,000,000
Flotation costs paid on new bonds	2,700,000
Total cash outflows	$6,700,000

Cash Inflows

Tax savings from call premium on old bonds (.45 × $4,000,000)	$1,800,000
Tax savings from unamortized flotation costs on old bonds (.45 × $1,500,000)	675,000
Total cash inflows	$2,475,000

Net Cash Flow

Initial Net Cash Flow	($4,225,000)

Annual Recurring Cash Flows

Cash Inflows

Interest payments on old bonds (.12 × $50,000,000)	$6,000,000
Tax savings from interest payments on new bonds (.45 × $5,000,000)	2,250,000
Tax savings from amortized flotation costs on new bonds (.45 × $180,000)	81,000
Total cash inflows	$8,331,000

Cash Outflows

Interest payments on new bonds (.10 × $50,000,000)	$5,000,000
Lost tax savings from interest payments on old bonds (.45 × $6,000,000)	2,700,000
Lost tax savings from amortized flotation costs on old bonds (.45 × $100,000)	45,000
Total cash outflows	$7,745,000

Net Cash Flow

Recurring Net Cash Flow	$ 586,000

Net Present Value

$$NPV = \frac{\$586,000}{(1.10)^1} + \frac{\$586,000}{(1.10)^2} + \ldots + \frac{\$586,000}{(1.10)^{15}} - \$4,225,000$$

$NPV = \$586,000 ADF_{.10/15} - \$4,225,000 = \$232,175$

Since the NPV is positive, the refunding should be given the go-ahead.

---

7. Why do term loans not provide for sinking fund provisions? Are these loans ever backed by collateral?

8. Why is it more appropriate to include leasing in a discussion of long-term debt financing, rather than covering the topic in capital budgeting?

9. List the factors that go into determining rental payments.

10. From a lessee's point of view, what circumstances would favor leasing a given asset, as opposed to borrowing money to purchase the asset?

Problems _____

1. Find the market value of a bond that possesses the following characteristics: $20,000 par value, ten years remaining to maturity, and a 14% coupon. The market-determined RRR is 10%.

2. Relco Company is setting up a sinking fund to retire a $30 million par value bond issue in fifteen years. If the fund earns 6% interest, find the equal annual contributions to the fund, such that $30 million will be available in fifteen years. There will be fifteen contributions and they begin in one year.

3. An 8% coupon, $1,000 par value, twenty-year bond is selling for $700 on the market. At this price, the bond is yielding 12%. If market interest rates do not change, what should the bond sell for in: (a) five years, (b) ten years, (c) fifteen years?

4. What would *you* be willing to pay for a $1,000 par value bond that pays $70 in coupon interest semiannually? The bond matures in ten years, and *your* RRR is 18%.

5. A $25 million bond issue was sold on the open market recently. Investment bankers recommended a 9½% coupon and a twenty year maturity for these securities, and that is how they were marketed. However, the market demanded a 10% interest rate, causing the bonds to be discounted. Determine the proceeds from this bond issue.

6. A $50 million issue of zero coupon bonds is scheduled to be sold in one week. Each of the bonds has a $10,000 par value and twenty-five year maturity. Given a market required rate of return of 9%, determine the proceeds from one of these bonds.

7. Two bonds that are equal in all respects, except maturity, are described below:
   A. Short-term bond: $20,000 par value, 8% coupon, three-year maturity.
   B. Long-term bond: $20,000 par value, 8% coupon, thirty-year maturity.

   Required:
   A. Determine the market price of each bond, given an RRR of 4%.
   B. Determine the market price of each bond, given an RRR of 12%.
   C. What are the implications of your findings?

8. Smith & Company has a $30 million bond issue outstanding on which it pays a 15% coupon. The bonds were sold five years ago and, as of now, they have fifteen years left to maturity. Interest rates have fallen recently, thereby allowing Smith & Company the opportunity to sell a new bond issue for the much lower interest rate of 12%. The old bond issue can be retired early, but in order to do so, Smith & Company must pay a call premium of 13.5%. Furthermore, the costs of floating a new bond issue will amount to $750,000. Would this company be wise to refund its bonds? Ignore income taxes.

9. Determine the NPV outcome of replacing a $10 million, 10%, twenty-year bond issue, with a $10 million, 8%, twenty-year bond issue. The call premium on the old bond issue is 10%, while the flotation costs of the new bond issue are $900,000. Ignore income taxes.

10. The state of Indiana has a particular bond issue outstanding in the amount of $150 million. The issue pays a coupon rate of 9½% and is scheduled to mature in eighteen years. Unlike most bonds, the coupons on this issue are paid only once a year. According to the indenture, the bonds can be called for refunding at any time. However, in order to refund the issue, the state must pay a call premium to investors. Originally 12½%, the call premium was set to decline by ½% per year during the life of the bond issue. The premium is currently 9%. The state is presently in a position to borrow funds at 8%, primarily because its bond ratings have been upgraded by Moody's and Standard & Poor's. Indiana's State Treasurer is examining the merits of replacing the old 9½% bond issue with a new and identical 8% bond issue. Two things are troubling him, however, the cost of a refunding operation and the possibility that interest rates might soon fall even further. There would be various fees and expenses

associated with a new bond issue (i.e., hiring an investment banker). These expenses would amount to about $2.5 million. And, of course, there is the matter of the call premium. With regard to the future of interest rates, a majority of experts believe that rates will decline by 1% in three years. a) Ignoring, for the moment, the outlook for interest rates, would it be worthwhile to refund the old bond issue today? b) Would it be better to wait three years and refund, assuming the state can borrow then at 7%?

11. Sonny Corporation is negotiating a $1.5 million term loan with William Penn Insurance Company. Sonny has agreed to pay off the loan over ten years at a cost of 14%.
    Required:
    A. What is the annual payment on this loan?
    B. What is the total amount of interest that will be paid over the life of this loan?
    C. Determine the loan balance after three payments have been made.

12. How many years would it take to retire a $2,280,000 installment loan, if the payments are $500,000 and the interest rate is: (a) 12%, (b) 16%, (c) 8%?

13. A $5 million term loan requires twenty-five annual payments of $727,500 each. Given that the interest rate on the loan is 14%, derive the remaining loan balance after ten payments have been made.

14. A $12,000 automobile loan is to be repaid, with interest, in monthly installments over five years. The interest rate on the loan is 12%. Solve for these installment payments.

15. Determine the final "balloon" payment on a $50,000 loan that matures in six years. Each of the first five annual payments are $5,000, and the applicable interest rate is 15%.

16. The payments required on a loan are $500,000 every three months for five years. If the required rate of return on the loan is 16%, find the face amount of the loan.

17. Commerce Bank made a $1 million term loan to Babcock Enterprises five years ago at an interest rate of 12%. The loan has ten years remaining to maturity, and each installment payment is $146,823. Commerce Bank now wishes to sell this loan to First City Bank. First City has agreed to purchase the loan, but only if it is priced at a level that allows the bank to earn a return of 15%. What is the remaining balance of this loan on the books of Commerce Bank? Determine the maximum price that First City Bank is willing to pay.

18. Given: installment loan = $200,000; maturity = 4 years; interest cost = 10%.
    Required:
    A. Solve for the annual payment.
    B. Produce the loan amortization schedule.

19. Morton Industries has recently taken out a $750,000 term loan. The loan is to be repaid in ten equal annual installments of $143,785.60. Morton Industries is being charged an interest rate of 14% on this loan. The firm would like to know how much interest it will be paying each year for tax purposes and therefore, has asked you to construct a loan amortization schedule.

20. Ohio Cement Company needs to borrow $5 million. The company's financial manager feels that the best financial arrangement would be a ten year, single payment loan. Although it considers this to be a rather unusual payment scheme, an insurance company has agreed to the request. Given that an interest rate of 13% is assessed on the loan, calculate the value of the single payment.

21. A variable rate term loan of $45,000 is to be repaid in annual installments over thirty years.
    Required:
    A. Given an initial interest rate of 10%, how large is each payment?
    B. What will each of the remaining payments be if, after five years, the interest rate on this loan has risen to 12%?

22. A supermarket owner-manager is reviewing the term loan on his store to determine if it would be beneficial to refund the loan at current low interest rates. The loan carries an interest rate of 12%, has a remaining balance of $410,817 and will mature in twenty years. A prepayment penalty of 4% of the remaining balance must be paid, if the loan is retired early. A new loan can be obtained at a cost of 10%. The origination fees on a new loan would amount to $8,500. Payments on both loans are to be made annually. Ignoring the effects of income taxes, answer the following questions:
    A. What is the annual payment on the current loan?
    B. What is the annual payment on the replacement loan?
    C. Determine the annual savings from refunding.
    D. Determine the initial cost of refunding.
    E. What is the NPV of refunding?
    F. Should refunding take place?

23. Sarah Michaels borrowed $65,000 five years ago to finance the purchase of her home. The loan was written for thirty years, at an interest rate of 15%. Her monthly installment payments on this loan are $821.90. Market interest rates have fallen significantly over the past few months, in some cases by 4%. Sarah has contacted the Savings and Loan Association holding her loan about the possibility of a refunding. According to the loan officer she talked to, Sarah can take out a new loan with an interest rate of 12%. However, the origination fees on this loan will amount to $1,300. In addition, she must pay a penalty of $3,200 for the privilege of retiring the old loan. What would you do if you were in Sarah's place?

24. A wealthy individual has agreed to buy an asset for $2 million and lease it to a tenant for ten years. This individual does not expect the asset to have any significant salvage value. What annual rental payment is necessary to recoup the cost of the leased asset and produce an RRR of 15%? The rental payments begin in one year, and the lessor's income tax rate is zero.

25. A $1.2 million office building is to be leased for five years and then sold by the lessor for $400,000. The lessee is responsible for all upkeep of the building. It is the lessor's intention to earn a rate of return of at least 18% on this investment. Ignoring the effects of income taxes, find the minimum annual rental payment that would be acceptable to the lessor. The rental payments begin *immediately*.

26. A lessor is trying to determine the annual rental payment that will be sufficient to recover the $1.8 million cost of an asset, while at the same time producing an interest rate of 5%. Furthermore, the lessor wishes to be reimbursed for agreeing to take care of all maintenance work, estimated at $20,000 per year. The lease will run for thirty years, and the first rental payment is due in one year. The property is not expected to have a residual value. For income tax purposes, the asset is to be depreciated over thirty years to a zero salvage value, using the straight-line method. The lessor's ordinary income tax rates are 50% on ordinary income and 25% on capital gains. Find the rental payment that the lessor is looking for.

27. Referring to the preceding question, work the following problems:
    A. What would the rental payment be, if the residual value is changed from zero to $2.8 million?
    B. What would the rental payment be, if the income tax rate is lowered from 50% to 30%?
    C. What would the rental payment be, if the interest rate is raised from 5% to 10%?

28. Foreman, Inc., recently obtained $15 million from a preferred stock offering. The issue is comprised of 30,000 shares of $500 par value stock. Given a dividend rate of 13.5%, find the following:
    A. Quarterly dividends per share.
    B. Quarterly dividends for the entire issue.

29. Determine the market value of a preferred stock that has a par value of $100 and a dividend rate of 9%. The market's RRR is: (a) 3%, (b) 9%, (c) 15%.

30. Quaker Automotive, Inc., sold $80 million in bonds five years ago when market interest rates were very high. Rates are much lower today. The bonds carry a coupon rate of 16% and will not mature for another twenty years (an original maturity of twenty-five years). Flotation costs on this issue were $4 million. If so desired, the firm can retire the bond issue today at a call price of 116. A new $80 million bond issue wold require an interest rate of only 12%. Flotation costs on such an offering will amount to $4 million. Quaker Automotive's income tax rate is 40%. Taking into account income tax ramifications, should Quaker Automotive refund the old bond issue? You may assume that coupon interest payments on both bond issues are made annually.

Selected References

Bierman, Harold, Jr., *The Lease versus Buy Decision*, Englewood Cliffs, N.J.: Prentice-Hall, 1982.

Bower, R. S., "Issues in Lease Financing," *Financial Management* (Winter 1973), pp. 25–33.

Gill, Richard C., "Term Loan Agreements," *Journal of Commercial Bank Lending* (February 1980), pp. 22–27.

Jin, F. C., and J. E. Wert, "The Effects of Call Risk on Corporate Bond Yields," *Journal of Finance* (December 1967), pp. 637–52.

Kalotay, A., "Sinking Funds and the Realized Cost of Debt," *Financial Management* (Spring 1982), pp. 43–54.

Laber, G., "Implications of Discount Rates and Financing Assumptions for Bond Refunding Decisions," *Financial Management* (Spring 1979), pp. 7–12.

Marks, Kenneth, and Warren Law, "Hedging Against Inflation with Floating Rate Notes," *Harvard Business Review* (March–April 1980), pp. 106–12.

Ofer, Aharon R., and Robert A. Taggart, Jr., "Bond Refunding: A Clarifying Analysis," *Journal of Finance* (March 1977), pp. 21–30.

Paller, Phillip R., John E. Stewart, and Benjamin S. Newhousen, "The 1981 Tax Act: Accounting for Leases," *Financial Executive* (January 1982), pp. 16–26.

Smith, Clifford W., Jr., and Jerold B. Warner, "On Financial Contracting: An Analysis of Bond Covenants," *Journal of Financial Economics* (June 1980), pp. 117–61.

Van Horne, James C., "A Linear-Programming Approach to Evaluating Restrictions under a Bond Indenture or Loan Agreement," *Journal of Financial and Quantitative Analysis* (June 1966), pp. 68–83.

Common Stockholder Equity

Overview

Debt financing was covered in the preceding two chapters. In that discussion we learned about the many varied types of liabilities and examined their major characteristics. Despite all of the attention devoted to debt, a company does not live by this source of funding alone. Equity capital, common stockholder equity to be exact, is the most basic of all forms of business financing. Without some equity, a firm would find it impossible to raise funds with any type of liability. We will study the subject of common stockholder equity in the present chapter. A number of equity issues will be addressed: the causes of equity dilution; retained earnings as an alternative to the sale of common stock; dividend relevancy; stockholder rights; dividend policies and procedures; convertible bonds; and common stock warrants. The discussion on liability and equity management is concluded in chapter 16, when we take up the matter of cost of capital ■

Objectives

By the end of the chapter the student should be able to:

1. Explain the stock valuation model
2. Explain the effect of equity dilution on current stockholders, including calculations where appropriate
3. Discuss the factors a firm must consider when making equity financing decisions
4. Discuss the trade-offs between paying dividends and retaining earnings
5. Discuss the factors that influence dividend payout rates
6. Explain the terminology and procedures of dividend payments
7. List and describe the common dividend practices of corporations
8. Explain the various rights of common stockholders
9. Define ''warrant'' and explain its terminology and value
10. Define ''convertible securities'' and explain their terminology and value

Introduction

Equity represents the ownership of a business. It is the fundamental source of financing for business enterprise and the alternative to debt financing. To most persons, the word "equity" when used in connection with a corporation, means common stockholder equity. *Common stockholder equity is comprised of funds derived from the sale of common stock (external equity) and profits that are retained in the firm (internal equity).*

In this chapter we will examine various aspects of equity financing. The discussion begins with a review of the stock valuation model and, following this, the signal concept of equity dilution is presented. These two topics will help to prepare us for the material that follows. From there, the presentation will move on to an analysis of common stockholder equity financing. The important issues surrounding dividend policy and practice will be the next topic of discussion, followed by a brief description of stockholder rights. The chapter ends with a look at two of the more uncommon forms of equity, convertible bonds and warrants ■

Stock Valuation Model

The stock valuation model from chapter 4 is duplicated below:

Equation 15.1

$$\text{Stock Value} = \frac{\tilde{\text{DPS}}_1}{(1 + \text{RRR})^1} + \frac{\tilde{\text{DPS}}_2}{(1 + \text{RRR})^2} + \cdots + \frac{\tilde{\text{DPS}}_n}{(1 + \text{RRR})^n}$$

Where: DPS stands for dividends per share and n is the life of the corporation. In words, the stock valuation model says that the market price or market value of a share of common stock is equal to the present value of estimated dividends per share ($\tilde{\text{DPS}}_i$), discounted by the required rate of return (RRR). The importance of this model lies in the fact that the objective of financial management is to maximize the market price of a firm's common stock. Let us, therefore, examine equation 15.1 more closely.

According to the stock valuation model, the value of a share of common stock is a function of future estimated DPS and an RRR, whereby RRR is negatively related to stock value and DPS positively related. Dividends are derived from net income. DPS are equal to *earnings per share (EPS)* multiplied by the *dividend payout rate (DPR)*. EPS, in turn, is equal to *net income (NI)* divided by the number of *common shares outstanding (Shares)*. These relationships are displayed below:

$$\text{DPS} = \text{EPS} \times \text{DPR} = \text{NI/Shares} \times \text{DPR}$$

The required rate of return is a function of the time value of money and risk. The former is measured by the risk-free interest rate and the latter is accounted for by a risk premium. Therefore:

$$\text{RRR} = \text{Risk-free Interest Rate} + \text{Risk Premium}$$

The stock valuation model, in conjunction with the relationships developed above, will be of assistance to us many times throughout this chapter.

Equity Dilution

Equity dilution refers to the impact on current common stockholders from an increase in the number of common shares outstanding. *While there are several kinds of equity dilution, the most important one, and the one we are primarily concerned with, is a reduction in the market price of common stock.* Not all dilution is bad, nor will an increase in outstanding shares always cause stock prices to decline. The determining factors are: who acquires the stock, current shareholders or new shareholders; what price the new shares are sold for; and how many new shares are sold. Three possibilities exist here.

Case I: New shares issued to current owners at less than the prevailing market price will result in dilution. However, current shareholders will not be harmed in this instance, because their overall position does not change.

Example: Tyco Corporation has decided to "split" its common stock, two shares for one. In other words, the company will "give" every owner two shares of new common stock in exchange for each share they now own. On the day before the split takes place, Tyco's stock is selling for $50 a share on the stock market. After the split, the market price will be as indicated by equation 15.1. With twice as many shares outstanding and no additional funds provided to increase assets and earnings, DPS must be halved. Accordingly, the stock price should decline by 50%, to $25 per share.[1] Tyco shareholders are in the same financial position after the split that they were in before. That is, 2 new shares $\times$ $25 = 1 old share $\times$ $50. Here we have an instance of harmless dilution ■

Case II: Additional shares issued to new stockholders at less than the prevailing market price will result in dilution that is damaging to current shareholders.

Example: Seagraf's, Inc., wishes to sell 250,000 shares of common stock in a private placement. The company currently has 500,000 shares outstanding. The stock is currently selling on the market for $60 a share, for a total value of 500,000 $\times$ $60 = $30 million. Assuming that the new stock is sold for $48 a share, we can find the diluted price as follows: Seagraf's obtains 250,000 $\times$ $48 = $12 million in additional equity financing, which is an increase of $12 million ÷ $30 million = 40%. Given a corresponding 40% increase in earnings and dividends, equation 15.1 indicates a new market price of 1.40 $\times$ $60 = $84. The larger earnings and dividends will be more than offset, however, by the 250,000 ÷ 500,000 = 50% increase in outstanding shares. Thus, the diluted price will be $84 ÷ 1.50 = $56. As a consequence, the current owners shall lose $4 per share to the new stockholders ■

Case III: New shares issued at the prevailing market price will not bring about dilution regardless of who the buyers are.

---

[1]Common stock splits are normally used to reduce the market price of a stock that has risen considerably in value. The main goal of this exercise is to keep the stock price in a more "normal" price range. For further information on the economic ramifications of stock splits, see J. A. Millar and B. D. Fielitz, "Stock Split and Stock Dividend Decisions," *Financial Management* (Winter 1973), pp. 35–45.

Diluted market prices can be determined without having to go through complex maneuvers such as those outlined in the preceding examples. One simply has to use equation 15.2, shown below:

Equation 15.2 $DMP = W_c P_c + W_n P_n$

Where:

DMP = Diluted market price of common stock

P_c = Market price of current shares

P_n = Issuing price of new shares

W_c = Relative number of current shares = $\dfrac{\text{Current Shares}}{\text{Current Shares + New Shares}}$

W_n = Relative number of new shares = $\dfrac{\text{New Shares}}{\text{Current Shares + New Shares}}$

Equation 15.2 essentially states that *the diluted market value of a share of common stock is a weighted average of the current price and the new price.* Applying this equation to the example for Case II, we would obtain the following:

$$DMP = \frac{500,000}{750,000} \times \$60 + \frac{250,000}{750,000} \times \$48 = \$56$$

Common Stockholder Equity Financing

Common stockholder equity is comprised of common stock and retained earnings. Corporate ownership is signified by common stock share certificates, an example of which is shown in exhibit 15.1.

Although seemingly quite different, common stock and retained earnings are very similar in that these funds are provided by the same group of investors, i.e., common stockholders. Why do we say that common stockholders are the source of retained earnings? Simply because the net income of a corporation belongs to the common shareholders, whether it is paid out to them in the form of dividends or retained in the company. The similarity between these two types of equity would be much more evident, if corporations issued shares of stock in exchange for retained earnings. Which, by the way, they often do.

In the eyes of management, stockholders, and creditors, therefore, one dollar of retained earnings is much the same as one dollar in common stock. Nevertheless, there are acknowledged differences between them that should be taken into consideration. For, the fact remains, on most occasions retained earnings and common stock are alternative forms of equity financing.[2] As such, one of them may be superior to the other. Before we examine the pros and cons of financing with retained earnings or common stock, it would be worth our while to look into the matter of how one measures the need for equity financing in general.

In any given year, a firm's equity funding requirement is based on two factors: (1) total asset additions during the year, as specified, for example, by the capital budget; and (2) the optimal degree of financial leverage (i.e., debt-to-asset ratio). An example will help to demonstrate this point.

---

[2]Very small corporations find it almost impossible to sell more shares of stock unless current owners purchase it.

Exhibit 15.1   Sample common stock certificate

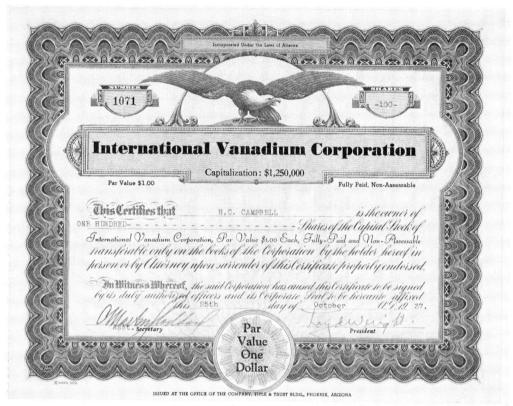

NUMBER
1071

SHARES
-100-

International Vanadium Corporation

Capitalization: $1,250,000

Par Value $1.00

Fully Paid, Non-Assessable

This Certifies that   H.C. CAMPBELL   is the owner of

ONE HUNDRED- -Shares of the Capital Stock of International Vanadium Corporation, Par Value $1.00 Each, Fully-Paid and Non-Assessable transferable only on the books of the Corporation by the holder hereof in person or by Attorney upon surrender of this Certificate properly endorsed.

In Witness Whereof, the said Corporation has caused this Certificate to be signed by its duly authorized officers and its Corporate Seal to be hereunto affixed this 25th day of October A.D. 19 37.

ASST. Secretary

President

Par
Value
One
Dollar

ISSUED AT THE OFFICE OF THE COMPANY, TITLE & TRUST BLDG., PHOENIX, ARIZONA

Application: Wyatt Enterprises plans to add $15 million in assets during 1988. Furthermore, the company's optimal debt-to-asset ratio is thought to be .35. Consequently, assets worth .35 × $15,000,000 = $5,250,000 shall be financed with debt, leaving $9,750,000 to be funded with equity ◼

In the above example, Wyatt Enterprises needs 1988 equity financing of $9,750,000. Should these funds be provided by retained earnings, a sale of common stock, or some combination of the two? The answer depends to a large extent upon Wyatt's 1988 net income. If the net income is zero or negative, then earnings retention can be excluded as an alternative. If, instead, Wyatt's earnings are $11 million, the picture changes considerably. In this case, the firm's management has the luxury of being able to choose retained earnings for the entire equity requirement, part of it, or none of it. Unless, of course, dividends consume a significant portion of the earnings.

Retained earnings, common stock, or some of each, is a question facing Wyatt Enterprises and hundreds of actual corporations every day. It is a very difficult question, and one we shall examine below and in the next section.

The sale of common stock would appear to be less appealing than earnings retention for a number of reasons:

1. Almost all common stock is sold publicly with the help of investment bankers and following SEC guidelines. As we saw in chapter 12, the cost (i.e., *flotation costs*) and time required of such an undertaking can be substantial. Retained earnings, on the other hand, are already available.
2. Many companies wish to avoid the *publicity* associated with a public stock offering. This is particularly true for firms that do not wish to divulge sensitive business matters.
3. *Stockholder approval* is sometimes required before additional stock can be sold. While this is not usually a major obstacle, it can be an irritant.
4. There are many corporations, even today, in which one or a few shareholders have a controlling interest. In an effort to maintain *control,* these owners may elect to retain earnings rather than sell common stock to outsiders.

Whether or not retained earnings have an edge over common stock in all situations is far from clear. What is clear is that *earnings retention is much greater than the sale of common stock in the aggregate,* and it has been for a number of years (figure 15.1). What is not revealed by figure 15.1 is the fact that many times firms meet their equity financing requirements with a combination of retained earnings and common stock. A major factor in the retained earnings–common stock decision, and something that has only been alluded to up until now, is the decision a corporation must make with regard to retained earnings and dividends. Dividends and retained earnings are opposite sides of the same coin. Profits that are not retained in the business must, by definition, be paid out to owners as dividends and vice versa. To state the matter differently, each dollar of net income paid out as dividends will reduce retained earnings by one dollar. Likewise, an extra dollar of retained earnings will reduce dividends by one dollar. As a consequence, a firm's decision concerning dividends necessarily affects its decision concerning retained earnings, which in turn affects its decision regarding the sale of common stock. We shall now turn our attention to dividends.

Dividends

The overriding objective of financial management is to satisfy common stockholders, and nothing pleases them more than an increase in the market value of their shares. By the same token, owners are most distressed when the value of their stock holdings decline. According to the stock valuation model, stock prices are heavily influenced by dividends per share. It should come as no surprise then, that the subject of financial management provides coverage of dividends.

Net income is the source of dividends. Net income is also the source of retained earnings. Given the importance of DPS to stock prices, it may seem paradoxical to assert that dividends would ever be reduced to make way for additional retained earnings. If one considers

Figure 15.1   Equity financing of U.S. corporations, 1974–1984

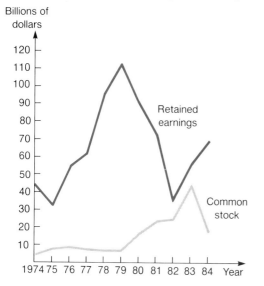

Billions of dollars

120
110
100
90
80
70
60
50
40
30
20
10

Retained earnings

Common stock

1974 75 76 77 78 79 80 81 82 83 84   Year

Source: Various issues of the *Federal Reserve Bulletin*, Board of Governors of the Federal Reserve System, Washington, D.C.

what retained earnings can be used for, however, the paradox disappears. For one thing, retained earnings can be used to invest in additional assets. If these assets are sufficiently profitable, future EPS, and thus DPS, will be larger than they would have been otherwise. These higher future dividends per share will cause the market price of common stock to rise, possibly by more than the initial reduction in DPS.[3] Retained earnings might also be used to reduce a company's debt, in an effort to lower the degree of financial leverage toward a more optimal level. This too would benefit shareholders.

It is a mistake, then, to believe stockholders are hurt when a firm allocates all or a portion of profit to retained earnings at the expense of dividends. They may, in fact, be better off. Pay dividends or retain earnings is the issue before us. Since the dividend payout rate (DPR) simultaneously captures both dividends and retained earnings (i.e., the earnings retention rate is one minus the DPR), we will use the term often in the ensuing discussion. As a point of reference, figure 15.2 shows the average dividend payout rate of U.S. corporations for each year since 1970. The rate has fluctuated between 30% and 65% over this period with a mean of about 45%. However, the DPR varies considerably from one firm to the next.

Is there an optimal dividend payout rate for a given firm, and, if so, how does one go about determining it? These questions are addressed below.

---

[3]The extent of the price increase depends upon the rate of return earned on assets that are acquired, as well as the RRR.

Figure 15.2   Dividend payout rate of U.S. corporations, 1970–1984

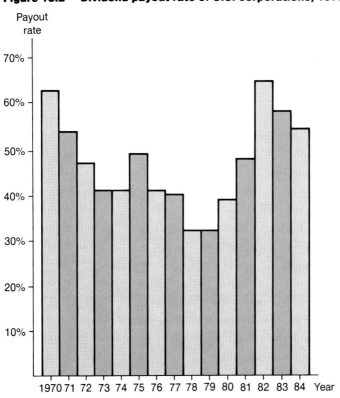

Source: Various issues of the *Federal Reserve Bulletin*, Board of Governors of the Federal Reserve System, Washington, D.C.

The Dividend-Retained Earnings Debate   There are essentially two schools of thought concerning the appropriate dividend payout rate for a corporation. One school claims that the proportion of earnings paid out in dividends is irrelevant. The other school believes just the opposite. According to this school, the dividend payout rate is relevant, in the sense that it can affect the market price of a company's common stock.

Dividend Irrelevancy   The irrelevance of dividends, and therefore retained earnings, has been advocated most strongly and eloquently by *Franco Modigliani and Merton Miller (M—M)*. Their case was presented in a 1961 article that has generated a considerable amount of controversy over the years.[4] The essentials of M—M's argument run as follows: corporations and their stockholders are indifferent as to whether profits are retained in the business or distributed as dividends, with one exception. The lone exception relates to those instances when a business has no worthwhile use for retained earnings. In this case, the rule to follow

---

[4]M. H. Miller and F. Modigliani, "Dividend Policy, Growth, and Valuation of Shares," *Journal of Business*, 34 (October 1961), pp. 411–33.

is: profits should never be retained by a company if the shareholders can earn a greater return on these funds than the firm can. The situation is entirely different for companies with acceptable investment opportunities. *According to M—M and their followers, it makes absolutely no difference whether these firms retain their earnings or pay dividends.* This argument is based on the following three major assumptions:

1. Common stock is a perfect substitute for retained earnings. Consequently, a firm needing equity financing can either retain earnings, if it has them, or it can pay dividends and replace the net income with a sale of common stock.
2. Stockholders are indifferent between receiving a dollar of dividends or accruing a dollar of capital gains (i.e., increased stock price) as the result of earnings retention.
3. Owners can adjust their individual stockholdings to fit their own particular desires for consumption and savings independent of a company's dividend payout ratio. For example, XYZ Corporation could pay a stockholder, Mr. A, $500 in dividends. If the firm does pay the dividend and Mr. A has no current need for it, he can simply use the money to buy more XYZ stock. In this way, Mr. A's investment is identical in amount to what it would have been, had the company retained the $500. If, on the other hand, XYZ Corporation does not pay a dividend and Mr. A needs the cash for consumption, he can sell $500 worth of his higher priced XYZ stock.

Dividend Relevancy   Those who believe the size of dividend payout rates are relevant can point to a number of factors in support of their position. These factors are described below, and, as will become apparent, most of them take issue with M—M's assumptions.

Costs of Selling Stock and Paying Dividends   Clearly, the sale of common stock is not a perfect substitute for retained earnings. We discussed this issue earlier. Flotation costs, in particular, are a definite discouragement to issuing common stock. There is also a considerable expense associated with the payment of dividends, such as record keeping and postage. These two cost factors tend to encourage a low dividend payout rate.

Dividend Restrictions Imposed by Creditors and Statute   Many loan contracts and bond indentures contain provisions that restrict the payment of dividends to a certain percentage of earnings. These provisions are designed to protect or strengthen creditors' interests. Creditors are also protected in a number of states by statutory limits on dividend payments. One of the more popular laws prohibits dividend payments in excess of a company's net income. As a result of this law, a corporation cannot pay dividends from stockholders' equity, the effect of which would be to raise the debt-to-asset ratio. Although many firms have legitimate reasons for paying dividends when profits are negative, there are always a few that might try to defraud creditors.

Liquidity Problems   A profitable company may find it difficult to pay dividends on a certain date simply because it is temporarily short of cash. However, businesses can and do obtain short-term loans for this purpose. Nevertheless, liquidity problems will occasionally bring about a lower dividend payout rate than otherwise would be the case.

Dividend Uncertainty   A strong case is made that stockholders consider future dividends to be more uncertain (i.e., riskier) than current dividends.[5] The greater uncertainty of future dividends shows up in the valuation of common stock, as investors require higher rates of return from the more distant dividends per share. For example, stockholders might discount fifth year DPS by an RRR of 13%, sixth year DPS by an RRR of 13½%, seventh year dividends by an RRR of 14%, and so on. Under these circumstances, earnings retention might be inadvisable, despite the fact that future DPS would be larger. Consequently, dividend uncertainty favors a high dividend payout rate.

Transactions Costs   While it is generally true that investors can adjust their individual stockholdings to achieve a certain level of consumption or savings, there are transactions costs associated with this practice. For one thing, buying and selling stock on a regular basis is inconvenient and time consuming for investors.[6] More importantly, brokerage fees are required on most security transactions.[7] Small investors are especially disadvantaged by frequent security trading, when compared to institutional investors.

Whether and to what extent transactions costs should influence dividend payout rates is problematical since transactions may be called for when payout rates are high and low. That is, some stockholders want to receive dividends, while others do not. We shall return to this matter shortly.

Income Tax Considerations   Federal income tax law treats ordinary income (dividends) and capital gains (increase in stock prices) differently. In particular, ordinary income tax rates are much higher than capital gains tax rates. Stated differently, a two dollar capital gain can provide a stockholder with more after-tax income than a two dollar dividend. A case could therefore be made that capital gains and retained earnings are preferable to dividends and ordinary income.[8] Certainly there are a number of investors who feel this way. But not all of them do. Many institutional investors are exempt from all income taxes, including such organizations as museums, universities, and churches. Furthermore, a variety of tax shelters are available to large numbers of tax paying shareholders. A major effect of these shelters is to reduce the tax differential between ordinary income and capital gains.[9]

As with transactions costs, it is difficult to say what overall impact taxes have had or should have on dividend payout rates. The most interesting theory holds that like-minded groups of investors seek out corporations with dividend payout rates to their liking. Thus, tax-exempt organizations and investors in need of cash income will invest in companies with consistently high dividend payout rates. Stockholders seeking to minimize their taxes or who are in no need of cash income for consumption will prefer to invest in firms that have consistently low payout rates. This theory is referred to as the *clientele effect*.[10]

---

[5]See, for example, M. J. Gordon, "Dividends, Earnings and Stock Prices," *Review of Economics and Statistics*, 41 (May 1959), pp. 99–105.

[6]Owners of stocks that are not traded in the secondary market will find it almost impossible to alter their holdings frequently.

[7]A brokerage fee is not required for stock purchased directly from the issuing corporation.

[8]See M. J. Brennan, "Taxes, Market Valuation, and Financial Policy," *National Tax Journal*, 22 (December 1970), pp. 417–27.

[9]See M. H. Miller and M. S. Scholes, "Dividends and Taxes," *Journal of Financial Economics*, 6 (December 1978), pp. 333–64.

[10]See F. Black and M. S. Scholes, "The Effects of Dividend Yield and Dividend Policy on Common Stock Prices and Returns," *Journal of Financial Economics*, 1 (May 1974), pp. 1–22.

Informational Content   The informational content theory can be summarized as follows: *A change in dividend payment might convey information to investors about a company's future risk and/or profitability.* That is, the market believes management is trying to tell it something whenever dividend changes take place. As a result, stock prices can be affected merely by the stock market's interpretation as to the meaning of a higher or lower dividend payment. A positive interpretation will lead to a higher stock price, and a negative interpretation will result in a lower stock price. In fact, however, management may not be making a statement about the future prospects of the firm at all. It simply feels that a change in dividends is called for by present circumstances. After some time, the market will realize it has erred, and the stock price will move back to where it was. Such unnecessary fluctuation in the market price of a stock is troubling to stockholders.

There is some evidence to support this theory.[11] By and large, the effects of informational content are short-run, as events unfold to reveal the true meaning of a dividend change. But short-run or not, informational content is a further consideration in the dividends-retained earnings decision.

Dividend Stability   A stable dividend per share is valued for three reasons. First of all, there is less chance to convey erroneous informational content. Secondly, shareholders who use dividends for current consumption appreciate the predictability afforded by a stable dividend per share. Finally, some institutional investors are limited, by law, to the purchase of stock in corporations that pay a consistent dividend.[12]

Conclusion   Having examined the major issues surrounding the dividend-retained earnings controversy, several conclusions can be reached.

1. Selecting the appropriate dividend payout rate for a corporation can be a truly complex and confusing undertaking.[13]
2. At any given point in time, there are many businesses that retain a larger portion of their profits than they would otherwise because of concern for control of the company, liquidity problems, or restrictions imposed by creditors and state statutes.
3. Transactions costs and the tax differential between ordinary income and capital gains are important considerations for many individual investors. In line with the clientele effect, a firm may want to align itself with a certain class of stockholders to avoid having to deal with these two complications.
4. Selecting the optimal dividend payout rate is difficult for almost every company because of two opposing forces. While flotation costs of common stock tend to favor retained earnings, the greater uncertainty associated with future dividends would seem to favor a high payout rate. Unfortunately, there is no solid evidence at the present time to indicate which of these two factors is stronger.

---

[11]See R. R. Pettit, "Dividend Announcements, Security Performance, and Capital Market Efficiency," *Journal of Finance*, 27 (December 1972), pp. 993–1007.

[12]See John Lintner, "Distribution of Income of Corporations among Dividends, Retained Earnings, and Taxes," *American Economic Review*, 46 (May 1956), pp. 97–113.

[13]See Fischer Black, "The Dividend Puzzle," *Journal of Portfolio Management*, 2 (Winter 1976).

Another difficult, and, as yet, unresolved issue is the way in which management should deal with the informational content coming from a change in dividends. As we shall see below, corporations have devised a number of policies and practices to cope with the complexities of the dividend-retained earnings decision. But first of all, we should look into dividend payment procedures.

Dividend Payment Procedures   Common stock dividends are normally paid quarterly, if they are paid at all. With each payment there are four critical dates: *announcement date, payment date, holder-of-record date,* and *ex-dividend date.* These are best described by means of an example. Kayto, Inc., announces in the financial press on July 10 that it is going to pay a $1.25 per share dividend. Payment is to be made on August 31 to all stockholders of record as of August 15. The ex-dividend date is August 9. An explanation of the ex-dividend date follows.

A problem arises when shares of stock are traded on the stock market shortly before the holder-of-record date. Since several days can elapse before a corporation is notified of an exchange of shares, the parties to the trade will be unsure as to who shall receive the dividends. In other words, will the old owner receive the dividends or the new owner? The stock exchanges have alleviated this problem with a ruling that dividends will automatically go to whoever owns the stock five business days prior to the holder of record date. *Four business days prior to the holder-of-record date the stock trades ex-dividend, meaning that anyone who buys it on or after that date is not entitled to the dividend.*

Returning to the Kayto, Inc., example, let us assume August 15, the holder-of-record date, falls on a Wednesday. The ex-dividend date is four business days prior to this, or Thursday, August 9. Therefore, whoever owns Kayto common stock on August 8 shall receive the dividend. It is interesting to note here, that stock prices drop by the amount of the dividend on the ex-dividend date.

In addition to regular quarterly dividends, a number of corporations pay *extra dividends* from time to time. To emphasize the fact that these dividends are "extra," some firms go to the trouble of making out separate checks to cover them.

As a rule, dividends are paid in cash. Occasionally, however, some firms give their owners additional shares of stock in lieu of cash dividends. For example, a company that grants a *stock dividend* of 10%, will issue one new share of stock for each ten shares outstanding. Accordingly, a shareholder who owned 5,000 shares of stock before the stock dividend, owns 5,500 afterwards. In reality, stockholders gain little or nothing from stock dividends. In fact, they are much like watered-down stock splits. Nonetheless, they occur rather frequently, apparently on the theory that something is better than nothing.

A relatively new and increasingly popular dividend scheme is the *dividend reinvestment plan.* Cut to the essentials, these plans give shareholders the opportunity to have their cash dividends automatically reinvested in newly issued shares at the going market price. Consider, for example, Mrs. Domino, an owner of 200 shares of ABC Corporation stock. ABC has just announced a $1.50 per share dividend. Ordinarily, Mrs. Domino would receive a check for $1.50 × 200 = $300. But, having no current need for the money, she has enrolled in the firm's dividend reinvestment plan. Her $300 is retained in the firm and she acquires $300 worth of new stock, less a small handling fee. Many investors like these plans because they can reinvest their dividends without incurring transactions costs.

Dividend Policies and Practices   Corporations have devised several policies and practices to cope with the complexities surrounding the determination of an optimal dividend payout rate. As one might expect, *the dividend practices and policies of a given business are heavily influenced by its environment and individual characteristics.* Included among these conditions are the following:

1. Company size: large corporations can issue common stock at a lower cost and with less trouble than small- and medium-size firms. In addition, large firms have many more stockholders to contend with.
2. Tradition: a firm's past dividend policies and practices appear to influence what it does currently.[14] This would seem to tie in with the informational content theory of dividends.
3. Stockholder profile: a knowledge of the present owners' income tax situations and consumption-savings preferences is very helpful.
4. Growth rate: simply put, growing businesses can find more uses for retained earnings than firms that are mature or declining.
5. Earnings stability: firms with a stable net income (i.e., little fluctuation from year to year) would appear to have more leeway in selecting a dividend payout rate.

In the light of all that has been said so far, we shall now scrutinize the more popular dividend policies and practices of American corporations.

One Hundred Percent Payout Rate   A very high dividend payout rate is found with businesses whose stockholder clientele have a strong desire for current consumption and are indifferent toward taxes. In addition, these firms are usually typified by stable earnings and infrequent, but sizable, financing requirements. High payout rates are often accompanied by dividend reinvestment plans.

Firms in dying industries frequently have high dividend payout rates. As a matter of fact, such firms are known to pay *liquidating dividends.* That is, dividends in excess of net income.

Zero Payout Rate   Rapidly growing companies usually retain all or a large portion of profits. The same is true of businesses whose shareholder clientele have a preference for capital gains. Corporations such as these (which may be one in the same) often go years without paying a cash dividend, although stock dividends are sometimes provided.[15] Of course, when they do begin to pay dividends, the dividend will, in all probability, be extremely large. Corporations with zero dividend payout rate policies are rarely lacking in good investment outlets for retained profits, even if it means buying other businesses. When investment opportunities are lacking, however, rather than paying dividends, it is not uncommon for profits to be used in buying back shares of stock. If handled properly, such *stock repurchases* are a way to distribute profits to stockholders at the more favorable capital gains tax rates.

---

[14]See John Lintner, ''Distribution of Income of Corporations among Dividends, Retained Earnings, and Taxes,'' *American Economic Review,* 46 (May 1956), pp. 97–113.

[15]A nominal dividend is sometimes paid in order to qualify a firm's stock for purchase by some regulated institutional investors.

The dividend policies of most corporations lie somewhere between the one hundred percent and zero payout rate extremes. We shall briefly examine three of them here.

Residual Dividend Policy   In an effort to minimize the flotation costs associated with the sale of common stock, a company can treat dividends as a residual. Dividends will be whatever is left over from net income after all equity financing requirements are met. A drawback to this policy is that it disregards the issue of dividend uncertainty. Furthermore, a residual dividend policy can result in a very unstable pattern of dividends, although a few companies feel this problem can be offset somewhat with stock dividends.

Fixed Payout Rate Policy   A fixed payout rate policy is just that. A business decides on the appropriate percentage of profits to be paid out as dividends, normally between 30% and 70%, and a determined effort is made to maintain it. Such a policy is easy to administer, reduces the chances of erroneous informational content (as long as the rate does not change), appeals to a wide range of investors, and contains some of the flexibility provided by a residual dividend policy. Nevertheless, a fixed dividend payout rate will lead to large fluctuations in DPS, if a company's net income is unstable. But perhaps the greatest drawback with this policy is the initial step of selecting the appropriate payout ratio. Dividend reinvestment plans and extra dividends can add flexibility to a fixed payout rate policy.

Managed Dividend Policy   A managed dividend policy can take on many forms, but the underlying theme is continuity and stability of dividends per share. To achieve continuity and stability, dividends are usually continued during periods of negative earnings, and they are raised only when a company is confident that the higher dividend can be maintained. Regarding the latter practice, dividend changes will normally lag behind earnings changes by a year or two. Firms that follow a managed dividend policy also frequently make use of extra dividends and stock repurchases. These are employed when profits are exceptionally large and/or worthwhile investment opportunities are scarce, with the hope that stockholders will not consider such unorthodox earnings disbursements as permanent.

A managed dividend policy is difficult to administer and necessarily results in a dividend payout rate that fluctuates widely around a predetermined target rate. And, for better or worse, this policy treats retained earnings as a residual.

Residual, managed, and fixed payout rate policies can produce radically different patterns of DPS. Figure 15.3 displays a variety of dividend payment plans that could be followed in association with a given hypothetical earnings pattern. One thing that clearly stands out in this figure is the extreme variability of dividends per share under a residual policy in contrast to the stability of a managed policy. Note, too, the close relationship between DPS and EPS under a fixed payout rate policy.

Rights of Common Stockholders

Certain legal rights are conferred upon common stockholders as the owners of a corporation.

Common stockholders have the right to examine a corporation's books. However, this right is not as comprehensive as it may seem. As a practical matter, owners are limited to published financial statements. A lawsuit is usually required to obtain further information

Figure 15.3   **Dividends per share are a function of earnings per share and dividend policy.**

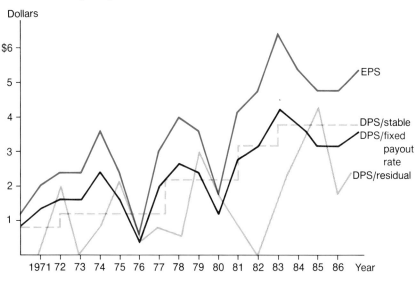

since corporate management is loathe to part with sensitive material that may find its way into the hands of a competitor.

Common stockholders have the right to expect management to run the company in their interest.

Common stockholders have the right to know about important current events affecting the corporation. Included here are the following: new products, stock repurchases, large lawsuits, top management changes, and important investments. Moreover, fairness dictates that important events should be publicized as soon as possible, and all shareholders must have equal access to the information.

Common stockholders are the residual claimants to corporate profits.

Common stockholders have the right to vote for the board of directors. This is an extremely important right, since the board of directors selects a corporation's top managers. Ordinarily, a shareholder is entitled to one vote for each share of stock owned, and he or she must vote for every board seat that is open. For instance, an owner of 2,000 shares would be able to cast 2,000 votes for each board of directors seat that is up for election. The election of directors takes place at the annual stockholders' meeting. For those owners who are unable to attend, and there are usually many, an arrangement has been devised whereby they can assign their votes to anyone who does attend. The arrangement referrred to is voting by *proxy,* and the process is regulated by the Securities and Exchange Commission. In a typical situation, management sends proxy materials to each stockholder prior to the annual meeting. Included along with the ballot, will be managements' recommended slate of directors. Most owners are content to go along with these recommendations and simply sign the ballot and return it to management. Occasionally, however, a proxy fight develops, with the opposing parties competing for stockholder votes to elect their candidates.

Common stockholders have the right to maintain their proportional ownership in a corporation. In other words, a shareholder who owns 12% of a firm's outstanding shares must be given the opportunity to purchase 12% of any new shares that are issued. Legally, this is known as a *preemptive right.* Most states have passed laws to void this right for owners of companies headquartered within their boundaries. However, such laws can be superceded by including the preemptive right in a corporation's charter. Preemptive right or not, a firm may want to give the current owners the first opportunity to purchase new shares of common stock, simply because the flotation costs are much lower than on a public offering (see chapter 12).

The sale of new common stock to existing stockholders is formally known as a *rights offering.* Rather than saying the stock is purchased, it is common practice to say the shares have been subscribed to. The *subscription price* is the price at which the new shares will be sold. *By setting the subscription price below the stock's market price, a firm increases the chances that all of the new shares will be sold.* In order to insure that proportional ownership is maintained, each stockholder receives one right per share of stock owned. These rights are then used to subscribe to the new shares. The mechanics of a rights offering can best be demonstrated by an example.

Application: Dana, Inc., wishes to raise $40,000,000 by means of a rights offering. The company presently has 10,000,000 common shares outstanding, thus 10,000,000 rights must be issued. Dana common stock is currently selling on the stock market for $68 per share. A subscription price of $20 per share has been chosen for the new shares. The number of new shares to be issued is found as follows:

$$\text{Number of New Shares} = \frac{\text{Funds to be Raised}}{\text{Subscription Price}} = \frac{\$40,000,000}{\$20} = 2,000,000 \text{ shares}$$

To determine the number of rights needed to buy one share of the new stock, we proceed as follows:

$$\begin{array}{l}\text{Number of Rights} \\ \text{Needed to Buy} \\ \text{One New Share}\end{array} = \frac{\text{Number of Rights Issued}}{\text{Number of New Shares}} = \frac{10,000,000}{2,000,000} = 5 \text{ Rights}$$

Under the terms of Dana's rights offering, one new share of stock can be acquired (i.e., subscribed to) for five rights plus $20. Thus, an owner of 150,000 shares of Dana stock would receive 150,000 rights. These rights will entitle him to buy $150,000 \div 5 = 30,000$ new shares for $20 \times 30,000 = \$600,000$. Before the rights offering, this investor owns $150,000 \div 10,000,000 = 1.5\%$ of Dana, Inc. Should he use the rights and subscribe to the new shares, his proportional ownership after the offering will be $180,000 \div 12,000,000 = 1.5\%$, which is exactly the same ■

There are five important dates associated with a rights offering: *announcement date*—the date on which a rights offering is publicized; *holder-of-record date*—the date a corporation examines its shareholder records to identify who shall receive the rights; *ex-rights date*—four business days before the holder-of-record date (stock purchased on or after this date will not be entitled to any rights; it serves the same purpose as the ex-dividend date described earlier); *distribution date*—rights are mailed on this date; *expiration date*—the date that the rights offering ends. If rights are not used prior to this date, they will become worthless to the holder. The dates for Dana, Inc.'s hypothetical rights offering are shown below:

Announcement date	March 10
Ex-rights date	April 6
Holder-of-record date	April 10
Distribution date	April 25
Expiration date	May 31

The fact that the subscription price in a rights offering is lower than the market price should lead to dilution, and it does.

Example: Equation 15.2 can be used to compute the diluted market price (DMP) of Dana, Inc.'s common stock, as shown below:

$$DMP = W_cP_c + W_nP_n = \frac{10,000,000}{12,000,000} \times \$68 + \frac{2,000,000}{12,000,000} \times \$20 = \$60$$

As indicated above, the market price of Dana stock will be reduced from $68 to $60 due to the rights offering. This is not harmful dilution, however, since the additional shares are acquired by existing stockholders. Each of them should be as well off after the rights offering, as they were before it. Consider, for instance, a Dana shareholder who owned five shares prior to the rights offering. Her five shares were then worth 5 × $68 = $340. If she subscribes to one share of the new stock with five rights and $20, the total value of her investment after the offering will be 6 × $60 = $360. The $20 stock gain is exactly offset by the $20 expenditure ■

For one reason or another, many stockholders would rather not subscribe to additional shares. Two alternatives are available to these investors. They can sell their rights or they can ignore them. Rights have value, and they are assignable. Thus, they can be sold just like shares of stock. The *value of a right* is attributable to the fact that it allows the holder to buy common stock for under the market price. The value of a right can be found with the following formula:

Equation 15.3   Value of a Right = $\dfrac{\begin{array}{c}\text{Diluted Market Price}\\ \text{of Stock}\end{array} - \begin{array}{c}\text{Subscription Price}\\ \text{of Stock}\end{array}}{\begin{array}{c}\text{Number of Rights Needed to Purchase}\\ \text{One Share}\end{array}}$

Example: Using equation 15.3, the value of a Dana, Inc., right would be:

$$\text{Value of a Right} = \frac{\$60 - \$20}{5 \text{ Rights}} = \$8 ■$$

The money received from the sale of rights will do no more than nullify a stockholder's losses stemming from dilution.

Although shareholders cannot gain from a rights offering, they will suffer a loss if they fail to either exercise their rights or sell them. These are the only two ways that a stockholder can keep from being harmed by the inevitable dilution. *A stockholder who throws his or her rights away or allows them to expire will soon witness a decline in the market price of the stock with nothing to show in return.*

Special Forms of Equity Financing

In this section we shall examine two specialized forms of equity financing, common stock warrants and convertible securities. Each contains unique characteristics that make them suitable for specific financing situations.

Warrants   Warrants are issued by corporations in conjunction with other financial instruments, seldom on their own. They might, for example, be included with a preferred stock issue, whereby an investor receives two warrants with each share of preferred stock purchased.

A warrant is an option to buy a specified number of shares of common stock in a given firm at a stated price for a predetermined period of time. The word *option* means that an owner of warrants has a right to buy the specified stock, under the terms of the warrant, if so desired. The corporate issuer, on the other hand, must abide by the warrant holder's decision. An actual example of warrants are those issued some time ago by International Harvester, the Chicago-based manufacturer of farm machinery and trucks. Each of these warrants entitles the owner to purchase one share of International Harvester common stock for $5 until December 15, 1993.

Terms of a Warrant   Every warrant must have an exchange ratio, exercise price, and expiration date. The *exchange ratio* specifies the number of shares of common stock that can be acquired with one warrant. Although exchange ratios of one and ten are fairly popular, there are no hard and fast rules here. The *exercise price* is the price an investor must pay for each share of stock acquired with warrants. A company must carefully select the exercise price to include in its warrants, because the success of a warrant issue is heavily dependent on it. *It is customary for the exercise price to be set considerably higher than the concurrent market price of the underlying common stock.* Lastly, the *expiration date* specifies when the warrant is terminated. The company's obligation and the investor's option expire on this date. Expiration dates are usually set at a considerable distance in the future, say five years, from the day the warrants are issued. The exchange ratio, exercise price, and expiration date for the International Harvester warrants are respectively: 1, $5, and December 15, 1993.

Value of Warrants to Investors   Warrants have value, otherwise investors would have no interest in obtaining them. In theory, a *warrant's value* is a function of the following: market value of the underlying stock, exchange ratio, and exercise price. These factors are brought together in the equation displayed below:

Equation 15.4

$$\text{Theoretical Value of a Warrant} = \left[\text{Market Price of Stock} - \text{Exercise Price} \right] \times \text{Exchange Ratio}$$

Application: Let us apply this equation to an example. Avco Enterprises recently issued 20,000 warrants. Each of these warrants allows the holder to purchase ten shares of Avco stock for $50 per share at any time during the next ten years. The current market price of Avco common stock is $30. Therefore, the theoretical value of an Avco warrant is:

$$\text{Theoretical Value of a Warrant} = (\$30 - \$50) \times 10 = -\$200$$

According to our computations, Avco's warrants have a negative value. In other words, the company would apparently have to pay investors to take them. But such an outcome is ludicrous. What we are really saying is that the theoretical value is zero (i.e., worthless). But this should not be too surprising, given that the warrant permits the purchase of stock at a price above the market price. Why, you may ask, would a firm even bother to issue a security that is worthless? But are Avco's warrants really worthless? They will, after all, be good for ten years. Conceivably, the price of Avco's stock could rise to the exercise price of $50 and beyond in such a long span of time. Let us assume the stock price rises to $90 in one year. An individual who owns an Avco warrant will have the right to purchase ten shares of Avco stock for $50 × 10 = $500, at a time when the ten shares are worth $90 × 10 = $900 on the market. This is a profit of $900 − $500 = $400. The opportunity for such a profit is surely worth something to somebody. Let us assume investors are willing to pay $25 for an Avco warrant and the chance to earn a large profit. Under these circumstances, the market value of a warrant would exceed its theoretical value (i.e., $25 > $0). Likely paying customers for Avco warrants are investors who are interested in the firm's common stock. Some of them will prefer the warrants over the stock, because of the greater profit potential. This is exemplified below:

Bill Meyers has $300 to invest. He can purchase ten shares ($300 ÷ $30) of Avco stock on the secondary market or twelve new warrants ($300 ÷ $25) from the company. Bill is convinced that Avco stock will go to $60 in one year. If he buys shares of stock, his predicted profit should be: ($60 × 10 shares) − ($300 investment) = $300, or a rate of return equal to $300 ÷ $300 = 100%.[16] Should he instead buy ten warrants good for 120 shares of stock, his predicted profit shall be: ($60 × 120 shares) − ($50 × 120 shares) − ($300 investment) = $7,200 − $6,000 − $300 = $900, or a rate of return equal to $900 ÷ $300 = 300%.[17] The much higher potential profit associated with the warrants may entice Bill to pay $25 (or more) for one of them, even though it is theoretically of no value. In the event that the stock price goes higher than $60, the warrants will fare even better. A $90 price, for example, would mean a $600 profit for the stock investment and a $4,500 profit on the warrants.

Warrants can magnify the profit from an increase in a stock's price. With warrants an investor has control over many more shares of stock for a given amount of money. It is much like the leverage a business hopes for when it borrows funds to acquire assets. There, we called it financial leverage, here we shall refer to it as *option leverage*.

---

[16]As a stockholder, he would be entitled to any dividends paid during the year.

[17]A warrant investor does not need to purchase stock from the firm to realize his profit. He can simply sell the warrants, which trade in the secondary markets just like shares of stock.

Just as financial leverage has its risks so too does option leverage. In order for Avco's warrants to outperform the stock, the market price of the stock must rise well above $50. That would be a considerable and highly unlikely increase from its current price of $30. On the other hand, one could make a very nice profit on the stock if the price rose to only $35 or $40. Moreover, if the market concludes after a time that Avco stock is not going to increase substantially in value before the warrants expire, in all probability the warrant market value of $25 will disappear very quickly. Were this to occur, a warrant investor would lose everthing.

The most interesting feature of warrants is the fact that investors are willing to pay a premium for them (i.e., market value > theoretical value). We have attributed this to an attraction on the part of some investors for the enormous profit potential of option leverage. *But option leverage and the attractiveness of it are dependent upon the relation between a warrant's exercise price and the market price of the underlying stock.* This is revealed below in figure 15.4 in connection with the warrants of Avco Enterprises. Here we see that investors are unwilling to pay anything for Avco warrants when the price of Avco stock is significantly below the exercise price (point A). While option leverage is exceptionally high at this point, the market is indifferent to it simply because there is so little chance that the stock price will ever exceed the exercise price. The situation changes as the stock price approaches the exercise price (point B). There is now a much better chance for the price of Avco's stock to surpass the warrant exercise price and the market price of the warrants turns positive, even while the theoretical value is zero. The market price of the warrants continues to rise along with the price of the underlying stock. Once the stock price overtakes the exercise price we see that the theoretical value of the warrants becomes positive and pulls the market value higher. But, with the warrants now so much more expensive, option leverage opportunities are considerably less. Therefore, the market value premium over the theoretical value also diminishes. At very high stock prices (point C) the warrants are almost as costly as the stock, and leverage opportunities are practically nonexistent. Under these circumstances, the market value of the warrants equals their theoretical value.

The expiration date has no effect on a warrant's theoretical value, but it can influence the market value. *In principle, the market value of a warrant is directly related to the number of years it will be in existence.* In other words, a warrant that expires in one year will have a lower market value than one maturing in five years, all other things being equal. Simply put, a longer time period increases the probability that the market price of the underlying stock will rise above the exercise price ■

Figure 15.4   Comparing the market value of a warrant with its theoretical value

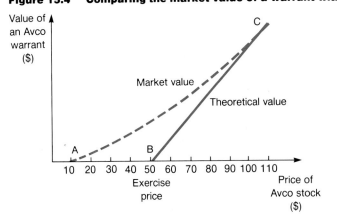

Value of Warrants to Corporations   So much for how investors benefit from warrants. How can an issuing corporation and its shareholders benefit? In the case of Avco Enterprises, the company is able to issue securities for $25 apiece; securities that require no interest or dividend payments. This does not mean warrants are a free form of financing, however, for the possibility exists that Avco's stock price will rise above the exercise price. If this happens, warrant holders can purchase new common shares from the company at a bargain price. The end result is dilution and, unlike a rights offering, it is harmful dilution, since warrant holders are seldom the current owners of the company. But, then again, the dilution may be acceptable if it is relatively minor, or if it does not occur for a long time.

As mentioned at the outset of this section, *warrants are seldom used to raise funds directly.* A firm normally issues them in conjunction with more common forms of financing in hopes that they will hold down the cost of the latter. For instance, a firm that normally would be required to pay an interest rate of 15% on its bonds, instead obtains a reduced rate of 12% by donating warrants to the bond investors. Warrants are also used occasionally to compensate investment bankers for underwriting services rendered. Given the growing popularity of stock options in general, we may well see firms making greater and more varied use of warrants.

Warrants are not a suitable form of financing for every firm. In particular, investors must believe there is a reasonable chance that a company's stock price will advance substantially. Otherwise, they are unlikely to place any value on a firm's warrants.

Convertible Securities   Corporate bonds and preferred stock are often issued with convertability provisions. Due to the significance of this provision, it is regularly used as part of the security name. Thus we have convertible bonds and convertible preferred stock. *Convertible bonds and preferred stock are unique in that they can be exchanged, at the option of the investor, for shares of common stock in the issuing corporation.* We shall confine our discussion to convertible bonds, since they are more numerous than convertible preferred stock and possess many of the same characteristics.

Convertible Bond Terms   Convertible bonds have standard bond features including the following: coupon interest rate (one-half paid semiannually), maturity date, and par value. They must also have a *conversion ratio.* The conversion ratio is the number of shares of common stock that can be exchanged (i.e., converted) for each convertible bond in an issue.

A conversion ratio of twenty-five means an owner of one of these convertible bonds can, if so desired, exchange it for twenty-five shares of common stock in the firm that issued the bonds. Assuming there are 20,000 of these bonds in the entire issue, the potential total exchange is $20,000 \times 25 = 500,000$ shares of stock. Conversion ratios should be designed to adjust automatically for stock splits and stock dividends. Referring to the example above, a three for one stock split by the firm that issued the convertible bonds should cause the conversion ratio to triple to seventy-five. In some instances, conversion ratios are programmed to decline over the life of the bond issue.

Related to the conversion ratio is the *conversion price*. This is the price a convertible bondholder effectively pays for each share of common stock if the bond or bonds are converted. The conversion price is found with the following formula:

Equation 15.5 $\text{Conversion Price} = \dfrac{\text{Par Value of Convertible Bond}}{\text{Conversion Ratio}}$

For instance, a $5,000 par value convertible bond with a conversion ratio of forty would dictate a conversion price of:

$$\text{Conversion Price} = \frac{\$5,000}{40} = \$125$$

Conversion ratios are set so that the conversion price is initially higher than the market price of the common stock.

Value of Convertible Bonds to Investors   Certain investors are attracted to convertible securities. Before inquiring why this is so, we should first realize there are at least two different ways to value convertible bonds. On the one hand, what are they worth as regular corporate bonds, disregarding the convertability provision? Alternatively, what is the value of the convertability provision, ignoring the fact that it is associated with a bond? In other words, what is the value of the stock into which the bond is convertible? We shall refer to the former as *bond value* and the latter as *conversion value.*

A convertible bond's bond value can be found with equation 14.1, the bond valuation formula of chapter 14, which is duplicated below:

$$\text{Bond Value} = \frac{\text{Coupon}/2}{(1 + \text{RRR})^1} + \frac{\text{Coupon}/2}{(1 + \text{RRR})^2} + \ldots + \frac{\text{Coupon}/2}{(1 + \text{RRR})^{2n}}$$
$$+ \frac{\text{Par Value}}{(1 + \text{RRR})^{2n}}$$

A convertible bond's conversion value is found as follows:

Equation 15.6

$$\text{Conversion Value} = \text{Conversion Ratio} \times \text{Market Price of Common Stock}$$

Application: Dapo, Inc., has a $40 million issue of convertible bonds outstanding. Each bond has a $1,000 par value, 9% coupon, fifteen years remaining to maturity, and a conversion ratio of fifty. At the moment, Dapo's stock is selling on the market for $19. An RRR of 12% (6% semiannual) applies to Dapo's regular bonds. The bond and conversion values are solved for below:

$$\text{Bond Value} = \frac{\$45}{(1.06)^1} + \frac{\$45}{(1.06)^2} + \ldots + \frac{\$45}{(1.06)^{30}} + \frac{\$1,000}{(1.06)^{30}} = \$793$$

$$\text{Conversion Value} = 50 \times \$19 = \$950 \ \blacksquare$$

The key feature of a convertible bond is that its market price will never be worth less than the greater of these two values. The convertible bonds in the preceding example will therefore have a market value of at least $950. Market forces assure such an outcome.

Figure 15.5   A convertible bond will sell at the greater of its conversion value or bond value.

Value of a
Dapo, Inc.
convertible
bond ($)

$793

$15.86

Conversion value

Bond value

Market price of
Dapo stock ($)

The very fact that a convertible bond sells on the market at the higher of its conversion value or bond value is the major attraction of these securities to investors. A typical convertible bond investor sees them as a way to invest in common stock, while retaining much of the safety provided by bonds.[18] This is possible because the bond value places a floor below which a convertible bond's market price will not fall. No matter what happens to the conversion value, one can be reasonably confident that the bond value will hold up.[19] Refer back to the Dapo, Inc., example. The bond value and conversion value of Dapo's convertible bonds were found to be $793 and $950, respectively. The conversion value is based on a current stock price of $19. If this price falls to, say, $9.75, then the conversion value will decline to $50 \times \$9.75 = \$487.50$. However, the market value of the convertible bond will not go below the bond value of $793. Although a loss is sustained, it is much less than if one is holding shares of stock outright. On the other hand, an increase in the price of Dapo's stock brings about a corresponding increase in the conversion value. Let us say that the stock price rises from $19 to $26. The conversion value becomes $50 \times \$26 = \$1,300$ and lifts the market value of the convertible bond up with it. Thus, a convertible bond investor can match a stock investor on the upside. Figure 15.5 illustrates these points in relation to Dapo's convertible bonds.

The asymmetrical nature of convertible bonds, the safety of a bond and the appreciation potential of common stock, is so attractive to some investors that they are willing to pay a premium above the bond value or conversion value, whichever is greater. This is illustrated in figure 15.6. Here we see how the market price of a convertible bond (solid curve) is likely to exceed both its bond and conversion values throughout a certain range of stock prices (A to B). There is little or no *premium* when the stock price causes the conversion value to be substantially below the bond value, to the left of point A. Investors are purely showing a

---

[18]As a rule, convertible bonds have only a subordinated claim on assets.
[19]Bond values are susceptible to changes in market interest rates. For a discussion of this subject turn to chapter 14.

Figure 15.6   **The market value of a convertible bond can exceed both its conversion value and its bond value.**

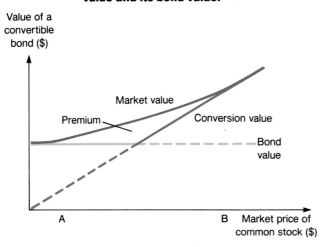

lack of interest in a convertible bond with little or no prospect of ever being worth anything as common stock. The premium also disappears at relatively high stock prices and conversion values, to the right of point B. This occurs because the bond value safety floor is too low to be of value to investors.

Value of Convertible Bonds to Corporations   Due to the fact that convertible bonds can be sold at a premium over their bond and common stock conversion values, a company may at times find them to be a more suitable financing mechanism than regular bonds or common stock.

The willingness of investors to pay a premium over bond value allows convertible bonds to be sold at lower interest rates than regular bonds. The interest rates can be as much as one-third lower, depending on the size of the premium.[20] When used in this manner, a firm does not want or expect its bonds to be converted, at least not for a long time.

Convertible bonds are often used in place of common stock when the stock price is thought to be temporarily depressed on the market. Rather than issuing stock at an abnormally low price, a firm can instead issue convertible bonds with a conversion price higher than the current stock price. If and when the price of the stock rises above the conversion price, investors will convert the bonds into shares of stock. Such an undertaking is less expensive than financing with regular bonds while the stock price is low and refunding the bond issue with common stock after its price has risen. Flotation costs are required twice with the latter operation, but only once if convertible bonds are used. But, there is no guarantee that convertible bond investors will elect to convert once the stock price does rise above the conversion price. Many of them may be contented to hold onto the bonds. To prevent this from happening, a company should have the ability to call the bonds, thereby forcing conversion.

---

[20]Interest rates and bond prices are inversely related.

The major drawback to financing with convertible bonds is the dilution that will result if they are converted. Dilution will occur because the conversion price has to be lower than the stock price for conversion to take place. Dilution becomes more serious as the market price of the stock rises further above the conversion price. A company can limit the magnitude of dilution by including a call provision in the convertible bond issue.

Summary

Since it represents the ownership of a corporation, common stockholder equity is the most basic of all forms of corporate financing. It follows, therefore, that common stockholders are the most important class of corporate investors. The two principle sources of common stockholder equity are the sale of common stock and retained earnings. In addition to these, there are common stock warrants as well as preferred stock and bond issues that are convertible into common shares. As has been stated on several occasions in this book, the primary goal of financial management is the maximization of stockholder wealth. This is accomplished by maximizing the market price of common stock. A firm's decisions with regard to common stockholder equity and common stock dividends may have a significant effect on the market price of its stock. One such decision is whether to use retained earnings, sell common stock, or combine them in an equity financing. This decision is complicated by the controversy surrounding the dividend-retained earnings decision. Pricing an issue of common stock (e.g., offering price or conversion price) is another equity decision with which a firm must contend. The complicating factor in this instance is market price dilution.

Common stockholders are entitled to certain rights or privileges as the owners of a corporation. Of these privileges, the two most important are the right to all excess income of the business (i.e., revenues minus all expenses including taxes and interest) and the right to vote for members to the board of directors ■

Key Terms/Concepts

Announcement date	Expiration date	Residual dividend policy
Bond value	Ex-rights date	Rights of common
Common stockholder equity	Extra dividends	stockholders
Conversion price	Fixed payout rate policy	Rights offering
Conversion ratio	Holder-of-record date	Stock dividends
Conversion value	Liquidating dividends	Stock repurchases
Convertible securities	Managed dividend policy	Stock splits
Diluted market value	Modigliani and Miller model	Stock valuation model
Distribution date	One hundred percent payout	Stock valuation model
Dividend reinvestment plan	rate policy	Subscription price
Dividend relevancy	Option	Treasury stock
Equity dilution	Option leverage	Value of a right
Exchange ratio	Payment date	Value of warrants
Ex-dividend date	Preemptive right	Warrant
Exercise price	Proxy	Zero payout rate policy

Questions

1. Under what circumstances will the market price of a company's common stock become diluted?

2. If stockholders are truly indifferent between dividends and earnings retention, it follows that retained earnings are always preferable to the sale of common stock. Explain.

3. Why should earnings retention lead to higher common stock prices?

4. The ex-dividend date is how many business days prior to the holder-of-record date?

5. In what way are personal income taxes involved in the dividend controversy?

6. What is the "preemptive right?"

7. Convertible bonds and warrants expose the stockholders of the issuing firm to the same type of risk. Briefly describe the nature of this risk.

8. If you had to make a choice, would you say that preferred stock is more like bonds or common stock?

9. Why is preferred stock used so little in relation to common stock and bonds?

Problems

1. Dareby Mining Company plans its financing around two ratios. It trys to maintain a debt-to-assets ratio of .40 and a dividend payout rate of .30. Dareby's net income for the current year is $36 million, which is an EPS of $4 based on 9 million outstanding common shares. Given that the company requires $75 million in additional financing, answer the following questions:
    A. What is the total equity financing requirement?
    B. How much of the equity requirement can be met with retained earnings?
    C. Calculate the current dividends per share.

2. Seetomas Corporation must raise $30 million, 40% of which will come from debt financing. Although the firm has earned $20 million this year, one-half of it is earmarked for dividends. How much money must Seetomas raise through the sale of common stock?

3. Terrance, Inc., has six million shares of common stock outstanding. The company wants to raise $18 million by means of a rights offering. Given a subscription price of $36, determine: A. the number of common shares to be issued under the rights offering, B. the number of rights needed to buy one share of the new stock.

4. Garrett Corporation had 1986 EBIT of $8,650,000. Interest expense totaled $2,400,000 and income taxes came to $2,800,000. In addition, preferred stock dividends of $600,000 were paid during the year. Calculate the dividends per share of common stock, assuming there are 2 million shares outstanding and the dividend payout rate is 65%.

5. A firm has 450,000 shares of common stock outstanding. How many shares will there be if the following happen:
    A. Stock dividends of 20% are distributed to shareholders.
    B. The stock is split four for one.
    C. A reverse stock split of two for five is instituted.

6. The common stock of National General Corporation is expected by the stock market to pay dividends per share of $3.25 in each of the next thirty years. Moreover, an 18% required rate of return is assessed on these dividends. Work the following problems:
    A. Compute the market value of National General's common stock.
    B. Compute the market value of National General's common stock, assuming that the market raises its dividend estimate by 25%.
    C. Compute the market value of National General's common stock, assuming that the RRR is raised to 24%.

7. Kerr-Barnett Industries paid a third quarter DPS of $.75 on 2,500,000 shares. Net income for the quarter was $4,687,500. Calculate the dividend payout rate.

8. All other things being equal, what would you prefer, a $40 per share dividend in twenty years, or a $4 per share dividend today? Your required rate of return is 10%.

9. Coral Caskets Inc. warrants entitle the holder to purchase 7.5 shares of Coral Caskets common stock. The warrants have an exercise price of $15 and expire on June 30, 1992. Find the theoretical value of a Coral Caskets warrant if the firm's stock price is: $8, $17, $30, and $80.

10. In 1980, Richard's Cafeterias issued convertible bonds with a total par value of $25 million that mature in 2005. The conversion ratio, par value, and coupon rate of each bond are twenty, $1,000, and 8%, respectively. At the time the bonds were issued Richard's common stock was selling for $38 on the stock market, and investors were demanding an interest rate of 10% on the firm's regular bonds. Based upon this information, determine the following:
    A. Conversion price.
    B. Number of new common shares if all bonds are converted.
    C. Bond value of the convertible bond at time of issue.
    D. Conversion value of the convertible bond at time of issue.

11. Bemis Manufacturing must raise $80 million to cover the cost of various asset acquisitions. Bemis's optimal debt-to-asset ratio is .60, and the firm follows a residual dividend policy. The company's net income for the current year is at an all time high of $40 million. What will Bemis pay in dividends, both in dollars and payout rate? You may assume that dividends are paid only once a year.

12. A company has 500,000 shares of common stock outstanding. The stock is currently selling on the market for $45. Calculate the diluted market price under each of the scenarios presented below:
    A. 500,000 shares are sold for $30.
    B. 500,000 shares are sold for $5.
    C. 100,000 shares are sold for $20.
    D. 100,000 shares are sold for $5.

13. Stock repurchases refer to a company buying its own stock. Repurchased shares are technically referred to as treasury stock. Show the balance sheet changes that would occur if a firm repurchased 20,000 shares of common stock for cash, assuming the shares are bought for $28.

14. The outstanding common shares of Topco, Inc., amount to 2,500,000. Karen Wilson, an owner of 200,000 shares, is planning to attend the upcoming annual stockholders' meeting at which five directors are to be elected. What is Karen's proportional ownership of Topco, Inc.? How many votes can she cast at the meeting for each board seat that is up for election?

15. Northwest Industries has 4.5 million shares of common stock outstanding. The firm wishes to raise $24 million by means of a rights offering. A $16 subscription price has been set for the new common shares. At the present time, Northwest's stock is trading on the market for $40.
    A. Derive the number of new common shares to be issued under the rights offering.
    B. How many rights will it take to purchase one share of the new stock?
    C. Find the diluted market price of Northwest's stock resulting from the rights offering.
    D. Calculate the value of a right.

16. Warrants were issued two years ago by Metro Corporation in connection with a bond offering. The exchange ratio, exercise price and expiration date are five, $8, and 1990, respectively. It is now 1986, and the warrants can be purchased on the secondary market for $12. Metro common stock, on the other hand, is selling for $6. Calculate the dollar profit and rate of return an investor would earn under the following circumstances:
    A. Invest $600 in warrants and the stock price rises to $9 in one year.
    B. Invest $600 in stock and the stock price rises to $9 in one year.
    C. Invest $600 in warrants and the stock price rises to $15 in one year.
    D. Invest $600 in stock and the stock price rises to $15 in one year.

17. Velcro Corporation has a $30 million issue of convertible bonds outstanding. The issue carries a coupon rate of 10% and has twelve years remaining to maturity. Each of the $5,000 par value bonds is convertible into two hundred shares of Velcro common stock. Velcro can retire the bonds at any time by paying a call price of 125 (125% of par value). The present market price of Velcro stock is $30. Furthermore, the RRR on the firm's regular bonds is 14%.
    A. Find the conversion price.
    B. Determine the bond value of a Velcro convertible bond.
    C. Determine the conversion value of a Velcro convertible bond.
    D. In order to force conversion, the company should call the bonds only when the stock price has risen above what level?

18. The financial manager of Garnett Enterprises has decided that the firm's upcoming common stock sale should be made through a rights offering. The subscription price has been set at $10, which is substantially below the stock's current market price of $52. Garnett Enterprises presently has 800,000 common shares outstanding. Assuming that the firm requires $4 million from the stock offering, answer the following questions:
    A. How many new common shares will be sold under the rights offering?
    B. How many rights are needed to purchase one share of the new stock?
    C. The market price of Garnett's stock should decline to what, as a result of the rights offering?
    D. What is the value of one right?

19. A firm received $1 million from the sale of 20,000 warrants several years ago. The warrants have an exercise price of $25 and an exchange ratio of ten. None of the warrants have been exercised to this date. In the absence of the warrants, the market price of this company's stock would now be $50. However, the warrants do exist, and the market anticipates that all of them will soon be exercised. Consequently, the inevitable dilution is already incorporated in the market price of the stock. Compute the diluted market price of the stock, assuming that this company has 500,000 common shares outstanding at the present time.

20. Jatro Bros., Inc., a profitable and closely held company, has the ability to grow, but for three obstacles: (1) under no circumstances will the firm borrow funds and expose itself to the risk associated with debt; (2) for fear of losing control, the owners refuse to sell more common stock; (3) the owners would prefer a 100% dividend payout rate. As a consequence, the earnings and dividends per share are expected to be $5 per year for the next ten years, which is exactly what they are today. Recompute the EPS and DPS that would exist today and in each of the next ten years, if Jatro immediately began a 50% dividend payout rate policy, and retained earnings could be invested to earn a 20% rate of return.

Selected References

Bacon, P. W., "The Subscription Price in Rights Offerings," *Financial Management* (Summer 1972), pp. 59–64.

Black, Fischer, "The Dividend Puzzle," *Journal of Portfolio Management* (Winter 1976).

Brennan, M. J., and E. S. Schwartz, "Convertible Bonds: Valuation and Optimal Strategies for Call and Conversion," *Journal of Finance* (December 1977), pp. 1699–1715.

Donaldson, Gordon, "In Defense of Preferred Stock," *Harvard Business Review* (July–August 1962), pp. 123–36.

Eiseman, Peter C., and Edward A. Moses, "Stock Dividends: Management's View," *Financial Analysts Journal* (July–August 1978), pp. 77–80.

Hayes, Samuel L., III, and Henry B. Reiling, "Sophisticated Financing Tool: The Warrant," *Harvard Business Review* (January–February 1969), pp. 137–50.

Hubbard, P. M., Jr., "The Many Aspects of Dilution," *Financial Analysts Journal* (May–June 1963), pp. 33, 36–40.

Melicher, Ronald W., and J. Ronald Hoffmeister, "Issuing Convertible Bonds," *Financial Executive* (June 1980), pp. 20–23.

Soter, Dennis S., "The Dividend Controversy—What It Means for Corporate Policy," *Financial Executive* (May 1979), pp. 38–43.

Stewart, S. S., "Should A Corporation Repurchase Its Own Shares?" *Journal of Finance* (June 1976), pp. 911–26.

Finance in the News

The Finance in the News feature in chapter 11 alluded to the question of whether a firm should utilize short-term financing versus long-term debt/equity financing. This feature suggests a compromise, convertible bonds. Note how convertible bonds provide some of the bond features discussed in chapter 14 as well as some of the equity features discussed in chapter 15.

Convertible Bonds Are Looking Good

The market rally in August made stocks look enticing, but some market strategists worry that high interest rates will stifle further gains. That puts investors in a quandary: should they take a chance that the rally will keep going, or should they lock in the bond market's plump yields and forget about stocks? There's a way to straddle the fence. With convertible bonds, investors can pocket high yields while keeping a hand in the stock market too.

In a bulletin following the rally, Smith Barney advised clients that the convertible market looked "extremely attractive" because stock prices had gone up faster than convertible prices. A convertible bond can be traded for a predetermined number of shares of the issuing company's stock at any time during the bond's life. The value of those shares, called the conversion value, is usually less than the bond price, since investors are paying a premium to get the higher yield of the bond. As stock prices rise, the difference between the bond's price and its conversion value—known as the conversion premium—narrows.

The trick is to find convertibles with modest conversion premiums and a high yield, such as those in the sampler below. One example is the **GTE 10.5% bond of 2007**, recommended by Jack Levande, a convertible bond strategist at E. F. Hutton. The bond outyields GTE's common stock by a good margin, but at the beginning of August, the convertible's price was more than 30% above the value of the underlying stock. And as Levande explains, "When the conversion premium gets much above 20% you don't get much play on the stock." When the stock market rallied, the value of the GTE convertible's underlying shares shot up while the convertible's price just meandered. Now the conversion premium stands at a mouth-watering 16%.

The **Alco Standard 9% bond of 2007**, is a favorite at Goldman Sachs. The bond sells at an equally tempting conversion premium, 16%, and yields 5.6 percentage points more than the underlying stock. Smith Barney is recommending a list of convertibles including the **McKesson 9.75% bond of 2007** and the **Olin Corp. 8.75% bond of 2008**.

If stock prices should decline, as they did in the first half of this year, convertibles will too, but probably not by as much. Smith Barney strategists tracked the performance of 30 actively traded convertibles over the first seven months of this year, a rough time for stocks. Investors who owned the underlying stocks during those trying months had a negative total return on their investment (change in market value plus dividends) of 13%. Convertible owners also lost money, but only about half as much as stockholders.

Convertible Bond	Recent Price	Market Value of Underlying Stock	Yield on Bond	Yield on Stock
Alco Standard 9%, due 2007	$960	$824.42	9.38%	3.8%
GTE 10.5%, due 2007	$1,040	$894.06	10.1%	7.3%
McKesson 9.75%, due 2006	$1,000	$825.82	9.75%	6.6%
Olin 8.75%, due 2008	$967.50	$828.85	8.96%	4.4%

Fortune September 17, 1984

16

Cost of Capital

Overview

Chapters 14 and 15 described in considerable detail the various types of long-term financing. In addition to retained earnings and the sale of common stock, a firm can acquire capital by issuing bonds and preferred stock, or arranging term loans and leases. Convertible bonds and common stock warrants are also used occasionally to obtain long-term funds.

In the previous discussion concerning these financing instruments little attention was devoted to the measurement of their costs (i.e., interest rates), either individually or collectively because the subject of the cost of capital is worthy of a separate chapter. We will study the procedures that can be used to measure the costs of six kinds of long-term financing: retained earnings, common stock, bonds, preferred stock, term loans, and leases.

The chapter concludes with a description of how to obtain an overall cost of capital for a business ■

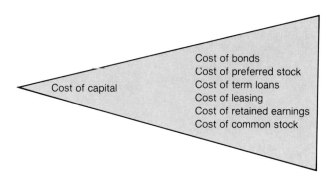

Cost of capital

Cost of bonds
Cost of preferred stock
Cost of term loans
Cost of leasing
Cost of retained earnings
Cost of common stock

Objectives

By the end of the chapter the student should be able to:

1. Calculate the costs of various types of long-term financing
2. Appreciate the difficulty encountered when trying to measure the cost of common stockholder equity
3. Combine the costs of various forms of capital into a weighted average or overall cost of capital
4. Define what is meant by the cost of capital
5. Understand how a business can use the cost of capital
6. Understand the important role of income taxes in cost of capital measurement

Introduction

In the previous two chapters, we talked at great length about the major forms of long-term corporate financing (i.e., capital). During that discussion we examined the important terms, provisions, and properties associated with each of these financing forms. We also looked into some of the important issues surrounding their use. The only long-term financing subject that has not been thoroughly explored up to this point is cost measurement. That is, measuring the cost of capital.

The cost of capital is the interest rate or interest rates that a business agrees to pay, explicitly or implicitly, to investors in its bonds, stocks, and other forms of long-term financing. The cost of capital is the compensation demanded by long-term investors for having to tie up their money (time value of money) and exposing themselves to risk (risk premium). The cost of capital is also the required rate of return (RRR). We thus have three terms to describe the same thing:

$$\text{Interest Rate} = \text{Required Rate of Return} = \text{Cost of Capital}$$

The purpose of this chapter is not to describe the economic factors that underlie a cost of capital, since this was covered in chapters 4 and 11. We will not dwell on the many ways in which the cost of long-term financing can or should be employed in financial management, for we have already done so on numerous occasions under the guise of RRR (e.g., capital budgeting). *The objective of the current chapter is instead, to explain how a business can measure its cost or costs of capital.* There are several forms of long-term financing, and their costs can vary widely due to different degrees of risk, income tax laws, and, to a lesser extent, flotation costs. To accommodate these numerous interest rates, the letter K will be used to represent the cost of capital in general. Subscripts are then used with K to classify each of the individual costs, thereby making it easier for us to differentiate them in the discussion to follow. Thus:

K_b = Cost of Bonds
K_p = Cost of Preferred Stock
K_r = Cost of Retained Earnings
K_c = Cost of Common Stock
K_t = Cost of Term Loans
K_l = Cost of Leasing

Costs of capital are measured for two primary reasons. In the first place, one could hardly choose from among the various forms of long-term financing, unless their costs are known. In the second place, the cost of capital is the required rate of return used in capital budgeting, about which more will be said later in the chapter.

Furthermore, *we are only going to be concerned with the cost of new or additional capital:* that financing, in other words, which will be used to acquire additional assets. Before proceeding, one further introductory comment is in order. Unlike the cost of short-term financing presented in chapter 13, compound interest equations should definitely be used to determine the cost of long-term financing.

Cost of Long-Term Financing

Cost of Bonds   Corporate bonds usually carry a coupon interest rate. However, the coupon rate will be equal to the cost of bonds (K_b) only if a borrower receives precisely par value from the sale of a bond issue. This is entirely possible in a private placement, where flotation costs are minimal and interest rates are negotiated on a face-to-face basis. In a public offering, however, the receipts from a bond issue are seldom equal to par value. In the first place, flotation costs are present in a public offering. Secondly, there is great difficulty in selecting a coupon rate that exactly matches the market's RRR, as we saw in chapter 14. This causes the bonds to sell at a premium or discount from par value. Consider, for example, a $30,000,000 par value bond issue that is sold in a public offering for $31,115,000 (a premium of $1,115,000). Given flotation costs of $2,500,000, the borrower will receive the "net" use of $31,115,000 − $2,500,000 = $28,615,000. We shall refer to the net cash receipts from a bond issue or any other public security offering as the *net proceeds*. The net proceeds from a public security offering can be found as follows:

$$\text{Net Proceeds} = \text{Sales Proceeds} - \text{Flotation Costs}$$

The cost of bonds (K_b) should be figured on the net proceeds. K_b *is the compound interest rate that equates the future semiannual coupon payments and par value (cash flows) to the net proceeds (present value) of a bond issue.* We can measure K_b with equation 16.1, shown below:

Equation 16.1

$$\text{Net Proceeds} = \frac{\text{Coupon}/2}{(1 + K_b)^1} + \frac{\text{Coupon}/2}{(1 + K_b)^2} + \ldots + \frac{\text{Coupon}/2}{(1 + K_b)^{2n}} + \frac{\text{Par Value}}{(1 + K_b)^{2n}}$$

Where:

Coupon/2 = Semiannual coupon payments on an entire bond issue or a single bond, and there are 2 × n of them

Net proceeds = Net cash receipts from an entire bond issue or a single bond

Par Value = Face value of an entire bond issue or a single bond

K_b = Semiannual cost of an entire bond issue or a single bond

n = Number of years to maturity

Note that equation 16.1 can be used with an entire bond issue or a single bond of an issue. Regardless of which is used, the answer will be the same.

Example: Kolfax Industry's new $50 million par value bond issue was offered on the public capital market by an investment banking syndicate. The issue was sold for $47 million (a discount of $3 million), and flotation costs amounted to $1,912,000. The bonds carry a coupon rate of 14% and mature in ten years. The cost of this bond issue is found as follows:

Net Proceeds = $47,000,000 − $1,912,000 = $45,088,000

Semiannual Coupon Payment = ($50,000,000 × .14) ÷ 2 = $3,500,000

Therefore:

$$\$45,088,000 = \frac{\$3,500,000}{(1 + K_b)^1} + \frac{\$3,500,000}{(1 + K_b)^2} + \ldots + \frac{\$3,500,000}{(1 + K_b)^{20}} + \frac{\$50,000,000}{(1 + K_b)^{20}}$$

Arranging in operational form:

$$\$45,088,000 = \$3,500,000DF_{K_b/1} + \$3,500,000DF_{K_b/2} + \ldots + \$3,500,000DF_{K_b/20}$$
$$+ \$50,000,000DF_{K_b/20}$$

Trial and error procedures must be used to solve for interest rates when there are unequal cash flows, as there are in this problem. Thus, through trial and error K_b is found to be 8%. The semiannual cost of Kolfax Industry's bonds is 8%. However, this should be converted to a *standard annual rate of interest.* Accordingly, the cost of Kolfax Industry's bond issue is 8% × 2 = 16%.[1] Could you have predicted in advance that K_b would be higher than the coupon rate (16% vs. 14%) in this example? ∎

Interest payments on bonds are a tax deductible expense for a business. As a consequence, the actual cost of bonds is lower than would otherwise be the case.[2] This can be satisfactorily dealt with by making the following adjustment:[3]

Equation 16.2 $K_b^* = K_b(1 - \text{Tax Rate})$

Where:

K_b^* is the *after-tax cost of bonds.*

In the above example, we determined the cost of Kolfax Industry's bonds to be 16%. Assuming that Kolfax's income tax rate is 45%, the after-tax cost of its bonds would be:

$$K_b^* = 16\%(1 - .45) = 8.8\%$$

It would be inappropriate to leave this section without mentioning *zero-coupon bonds,* which have become an increasingly popular form of long-term financing. Since there are no interest payments associated with these securities, they will sell at very deep discounts from par value. Cost to the company is strictly based on the difference between par value and net proceeds (which could be less than sales proceeds, if flotation costs are present). *The cost of zero coupon bonds is the compound interest rate that equates the par value (cash flow) to the net proceeds (present value),* and it can be determined as follows:

Equation 16.3 $\text{Net Proceeds} = \dfrac{\text{Par Value}}{(1 + K_b)^n}$

Note carefully, that the K_b found with equation 16.3 will automatically become an annual interest rate since the time period (n) is in years.

---

[1]Technically speaking, the sophisticated equivalent annual interest rate is the appropriate measure, and it is found as follows:

   Equivalent Annual Rate = $(1.08)^2 - 1 = 16.64\%$

[2]This assumes the business has taxable income.

[3]The best method is to treat tax savings as cash flows and include them as they occur.

Example: A $40 million zero coupon bond issue is sold to net the issuing corporation $9,576,000. The bonds mature in fifteen years. The cost of this bond issue is found as follows:

$$\$9,576,000 = \frac{\$40,000,000}{(1 + K_b)^{15}}$$

In operational form:

$$\$9,576,000 = \$40,000,000DF_{K_b/15}$$

Solving for the Discount Factor:

$$DF_{K_b/15} = \frac{\$9,576,000}{\$40,000,000} = .239$$

Therefore, from the discount factor table we see that a 15 period DF of .239 corresponds to an interest rate of 10%. Thus, the before-tax annual cost of this bond issue is $K_b = 10\%$ ■

Cost of Preferred Stock   A corporation pays quarterly dividends on its preferred stock based upon the dividend rate and par value. In as much as these securities have no maturity date, the dividends will continue indefinitely, and thus the payment of par value can be disregarded. The dividend rate on preferred stock is much like a bond coupon rate. The cost of preferred stock (K_p) will equal the dividend rate only if a company receives exactly par value from the sale of a preferred stock issue. But this seldom happens. As in the case of bonds, preferred stock is often sold at a discount or premium from par value. Moreover, flotation costs are incurred in public offerings. Consequently, the net proceeds of a preferred stock issue are usually unequal to par value. And, more often than not, they are less than par value.

Net proceeds of a preferred stock issue are the relevant base upon which K_p should be calculated. *The cost of preferred stock is the compound interest rate that equates a perpetual stream of future dividend payments (cash flows) to the net proceeds (present value) of an issue.* We can measure K_p with equation 16.4, shown below:

Equation 16.4

$$\text{Net Proceeds} = \frac{\text{Dividend}/4}{(1 + K_p)^1} + \frac{\text{Dividend}/4}{(1 + K_p)^2} + \ldots + \frac{\text{Dividend}/4}{(1 + K_p)^\infty}$$

Where:

Net Proceeds = Net cash receipts of an entire preferred stock issue or a single
share

Dividend/4 = Quarterly dividend payments on an entire stock issue or a single
share, and there are an infinite number of them

K_p = Quarterly cost of preferred stock

Preferred stock dividends are a perfect illustration of a perpetuity (see chapter 4). As such, equation 16.4 can be greatly simplified, as follows:

$$\text{Net Proceeds} = \frac{\text{Dividend}/4}{K_p}$$

Rearranging, we obtain:

Equation 16.5 $K_p = \dfrac{\text{Dividend}/4}{\text{Net Proceeds}}$

Example: Preferred stock with a par value of $15 million is due to be sold in a public offering. The dividend rate on these shares is 10%. Assume the issue is sold for $14,825,000 and flotation costs are $936,100. The cost of this preferred stock issue is measured as follows:

Net Proceeds = $14,825,000 − $936,100 = $13,888,900

Quarterly Dividend Payment = ($15,000,000 × .10) ÷ 4 = $375,000

Therefore:

$K_p = \dfrac{\$375,000}{\$13,888,900} = 2.7\%$

The cost of the above preferred stock is 2.7% per quarter. However, an annual cost is more meaningful. On an annual basis, K_p thus becomes 2.7% × 4 = 10.8%[4] ∎

Unlike interest payments on bonds, preferred stock dividends are not a tax deductible expense. *Accordingly, there is no need to adjust the cost of preferred stock downward for income taxes.* ∎

Cost of Term Loans   Almost all term loans are privately arranged through direct negotiations involving the borrower and one or a few lenders. With the exception of some minor legal and accounting fees, flotation costs are practically nonexistent in these financing arrangements and can therefore be ignored in most cases.[5] Furthermore, because the interest rate can be tailored to the specifications of investors, the proceeds from a term loan will equal its face value (i.e., no discount or premium). There is usually no need, therefore, to calculate net proceeds in order to measure the cost of term loans (K_t).

As we saw in chapter 14, term loan interest charges and principal repayments are usually combined in regular, equal installment payments. Installment payments can be monthly, quarterly or annually. *The cost of term loans is the compound interest rate that equates the future installment payments (cash flows) to the loan face value (present value).* We can measure K_t with equation 16.6, shown below:

Equation 16.6

$$\text{Loan Face Value} = \frac{\text{Installment}}{(1 + K_t)^1} + \frac{\text{Installment}}{(1 + K_t)^2} + \cdots + \frac{\text{Installment}}{(1 + K_t)^n}$$

In this case, n is the total number of installments, as determined by the frequency of payments (monthly, etc.) and maturity of the loan. Since we are dealing with an annuity, equation 16.6 can be arranged in a more simplified operational form, as follows:

$$\text{Loan Face Value} = \text{Installment}(\text{ADF}_{K_t/n})$$

---

[4] The sophisticated equivalent annual rate is $(1.027)^4 - 1 = 11.25\%$.
[5] For small loans, such as consumer loans, these fees may be relatively large. In these situations, it is appropriate to compute the net proceeds of a loan prior to solving for the interest rate.

Rearranging, we obtain:

Equation 16.7 $ADF_{K_t/n} = \dfrac{\text{Loan Face Value}}{\text{Installment}}$

Equation 16.7 can be used to find K_t directly from the annuity discount factor tables.

Example: Kansas Meat Packing Company has been offered a term loan of $3 million by Wichita National Bank. The company would be required to make annual payments of $603,900 for eight years, if it accepts the loan. The cost of this installment loan is found as follows:

$$\$3,000,000 = \frac{\$603,900}{(1 + K_t)^1} + \frac{\$603,900}{(1 + K_t)^2} + \cdots + \frac{\$603,900}{(1 + K_t)^8}$$

Arranging in operational form:

$$\$3,000,000 = \$603,900 ADF_{K_t/8}$$

Rearranging, and solving for ADF:

$$ADF_{K_t/8} = \frac{\$3,000,000}{\$603,900} = 4.9677$$

From the annuity discount factor table we see that an eight period ADF of 4.9677 corresponds very closely to an interest rate of 12%. Thus, the cost of this term loan (K_t) is 12%. Conversion to an annual rate is unnecessary in this problem, since we are dealing with annual payments ∎

Taking into consideration the fact that interest payments on term loans are a tax deductible expense, the actual cost of these loans is much lower than indicated by equations 16.6 or 16.7. An adjustment, such as the one used earlier in connection with bonds, is called for. Therefore:

Equation 16.8 $K_t^* = K_t(1 - \text{Tax Rate})$

Where:

K_t^* is the *after-tax cost of term loans.*

In the preceding example, we found the cost of a term loan to be 12%. Given that the borrower's income tax rate is 48%, the after-tax cost of the loan would be:

$$K_t^* = 12\%(1 - .48) = 6.24\%$$

Term loans are occasionally designed with irregular payments.

Example: A $456,375 loan requires the following annual payments: $50,000 in one year; $100,000 in two years; $150,000 in three years; $200,000 in four years; and $250,000 in five years. To solve for the interest rate on this loan, we first set up the problem, as follows:

$$\$456,375 = \frac{50,000}{(1 + K_t)^1} + \frac{\$100,000}{(1 + K_t)^2} + \frac{\$150,000}{(1 + K_t)^3} + \frac{\$200,000}{(1 + K_t)^4} + \frac{\$250,000}{(1 + K_t)^5}$$

Trial and error procedures are then required to derive K_t from this equation. Accordingly, the cost of the loan is 15%. After taxes, of course, the cost would be much lower than 15% ∎

Cost of Lease Financing   It was argued in chapter 14 that leasing is a financing mechanism or, to be more specific, a debt financing mechanism.[6] As a reasonable first approximation, the cost of leasing (K_l) can be determined much like the cost of term loans, with equation 16.6. One needs only to substitute the value of a leased asset for loan face value and rent for installment payment. However, rental payments normally occur at the beginning rather than the end of a period (i.e., paid in advance). These points are demonstrated below in equation 16.9.

Equation 16.9

$$\text{Value of Leased Asset} = \frac{\text{Rent}}{(1 + K_l)^0} + \frac{\text{Rent}}{(1 + K_l)^1} + \cdots + \frac{\text{Rent}}{(1 + K_l)^{n-1}}$$

In this case, n is the total number of rental payments, as determined by the frequency of payments (e.g., monthly, annually, etc.) and term of the lease. Note that the first rental is paid immediately ($t = 0$) and the final rental is paid with one period remaining in the lease term ($t = n - 1$). However, the calculations become more difficult than indicated by equation 16.9 once we introduce a number of complications, in particular the foregone benefits of asset ownership.[7] The effect of these complications on the cost of leasing is presented in an appendix to this chapter.

Despite its simplicity, equation 16.9 can usually provide us with a reasonable approximation to the true cost of leasing. *The cost of leasing is the compound interest rate that equates the future rental payments (cash flows) to the value of the leased asset (present value).*

Example: Rosco Corporation's treasurer is in the process of determining the cost of a proposed lease. The firm can rent a parking garage located adjacent to its downtown headquarters for a period of ten years. The rent will be $672,000 per year, payable at the first of each year. Were it to buy this garage, or one similar to it, Rosco would have to spend $4 million. The cost of this lease can be found with equation 16.9, as follows:

$$\$4,000,000 = \frac{\$672,000}{(1 + K_l)^0} + \frac{\$672,000}{(1 + K_l)^1} + \cdots + \frac{\$672,000}{(1 + K_l)^9}$$

Trial-and-error procedures could be used to solve for K_l in the problem, but there is an easier method. Recognizing that the first rental is already a present value, and the remaining rentals are an ordinary annuity, we can reformulate the problem, as follows:

$$\$4,000,000 = \$672,000 + \$672,000 \, \text{ADF}_{K_l/9}$$

---

[6]A lease most closely resembles a term loan.

[7]There are three complications. First and foremost, a firm that acquires the use of capital assets by leasing them, may forego important privileges of ownership, such as: depreciation tax deductions, investment tax credits and salvage values. All of these benefits are retained by the lessor, as the owner of the property. Secondly, rental payments often include property maintenance charges that have nothing to do with the cost of financing (e.g., janitorial service). Finally, rental payments may not be constant over the term of a lease.

Solving for the ADF:

$$ADF_{K_l/9} = \frac{\$4,000,000 - \$672,000}{\$672,000} = \frac{\$3,328,000}{\$672,000} = 4.9524$$

From the annuity discount factor table we see that a nine period ADF of 4.9524 corresponds to an interest rate of 14%. Thus, the cost of leasing (K_l) is 14% per annum[8] ∎

Taking into consideration the fact that rent is a tax deductible expense, the actual cost of leasing is considerably lower than indicated by equation 16.9. Moreover, the methodology used to determine the *after-tax cost of leasing (K_l^*)* is the same as that used to find the after-tax costs of bonds and term loans. Therefore:

Equation 16.10 $K_l^* = K_l(1 - \text{Tax Rate})$

We can apply equation 16.10 to the preceding example. Assuming Rosco Corporation's income tax rate is 30%, the firm's after-tax cost of leasing the garage can be determined as follows:

$$K_l^* = 14\%(1 - .30) = .098$$

Accordingly, the Rosco Corporation would be paying 9.8% after taxes to lease the garage. But it is only a rough approximation of the true cost, as stated earlier. A more realistic and therefore more reliable approach is provided in the appendix to this chapter. Regardless of which technique is used to measure the cost of leasing, however, the entire subject is under considerable contention at the moment.

Cost of Common Stockholder Equity

In general, the cost of common stockholder equity is the RRR of those investors who are willing and able to be the owners of a corporation. A given RRR is comprised of the risk-free interest rate and a risk premium. The risk premium, in turn, compensates investors for the risks they will face as stockholders. To wit: assets may prove to be unprofitable and there are dangers that accompany the use of debt financing. Although dividend payments to common stockholders are not mandatory, in the legal sense, investors expect them and are very disappointed when they earn a rate of return that is less than the RRR. This disappointment can manifest itself in at least two ways. The market price of common stock will fall and, in some instances, corporate management is replaced.

Measuring the cost of common equity capital is much more difficult than measuring the costs of bonds, term loans, preferred stock, or leases. In each of these situations a corporation is dealing with financial obligations on which future payments are contractual. This makes the payments both mandatory, and thus predictable, and easy to identify.[9] For example, mandatory rental payments are found in a lease agreement, and required bond coupon payments are dictated by the coupon rate and par value shown on the face of a bond certificate. Accordingly, there is little guesswork involved in measuring the costs of leasing, bonds, term

---

[8]Had the rentals been more frequent than once a year, an annual conversion would be necessary.
[9]Although they are not legally required, most firms treat preferred stock dividends as if they were mandatory.

loans, and preferred stock. As we saw earlier in the chapter, the procedures are, for the most part, purely mechanical. Contractual amounts are inserted in various equations, which are then solved mathematically. Dividend payments to common stockholders, on the other hand, are seldom easy for a firm to estimate. For one thing, they are not contractual. For another, common dividends are tied to corporate profits, which are unpredictable. To make matters even worse, if the financial manager in a firm is able to estimate dividend payments with a high degree of confidence, there is no assurance that common stock investors have the same expectations. And, after all, corporate managements' major objective is to satisfy common stockholders, not management.

There are two sources of common stockholder equity: retained earnings and the sale of common stock. Consequently, there are two costs that a firm's management must measure: cost of retained earnings (K_r) and cost of common stock (K_c). Given the similarities between retained earnings and common stock, it should come as no great surprise to learn that their costs are very similar.

As stated earlier in the chapter, our interest is centered on what it will cost a company to raise new or additional common equity.

Cost of Retained Earnings   One thing should be made very clear at the outset of the forthcoming discussion: *retained earnings are not a free form of financing.* The net income of a corporation belongs to the common stockholders, all of whom will have to forego alternative uses for these earnings if they are retained in the business rather than paid out in dividends. In other words, *there is an opportunity cost associated with retained earnings.* A failure on the part of management to compensate their stockholders for these lost opportunities would have dire consequences. To state the matter somewhat differently, corporate owners require a rate of return (RRR) from any profits that are retained in a business just as they would from the purchase of common stock. In both instances, stockholders are tying up their money in a risky investment. And, while it is true that dividends are not paid on retained earnings directly, owners expect their compensation to come indirectly in the form of additional dividends on their shares of stock.

Measuring the cost of retained earnings or common stock presents real problems for most corporations. A firm knows that its owners wish to be compensated for having to leave their profits in the business. Furthermore, a company knows that dividends are the accepted means of compensation. But there exists no contractual agreement between a firm and its stockholders stating precisely what and when the dividends will be. As a result, dividend payments must be estimated by both management and common stock investors. In essence, this means that K_r must also be estimated. One might ask why management simply does not ask the owners what rate of return they are demanding and be done with it. While such an effort might well succeed in a company with few stockholders, it is not practical for large corporations whose shareholders number in the thousands or even millions. Several techniques have been devised to assist the management of large, widely held companies in measuring the costs of retained earnings and common stock. In order to use these techniques, it is mandatory that a firm's stock be traded on the secondary stock market, since the market price of common stock is central to each of them. These measurement techniques, or models, are presented below in the following order: stock valuation model, capital asset pricing model, and price-earnings ratio.

Using the Stock Valuation Model to Measure K_r The *stock valuation model* (equation 4.10) can be of assistance in measuring the costs of retained earnings and common stock. This model states that the market value (i.e., market price) of a share of common stock is equal to the present value of estimated annual dividends per share (DPS). The interest rate that equates estimated dividends to market price is the RRR that investors expect to earn on a given stock. Equation 4.10 is duplicated below:

$$\text{Stock Value} = \frac{\tilde{DPS}_1}{(1 + RRR)^1} + \frac{\tilde{DPS}_2}{(1 + RRR)^2} + \ldots + \frac{\tilde{DPS}_n}{(1 + RRR)^n}$$

In this case, n is the expected life of the corporation.

The RRR on common stock should also apply to retained earnings. After all, both forms of equity capital will expose investors to the same opportunities and risks. From a company's standpoint, the RRR of common stock investors becomes the cost of common stockholder equity or, in this instance, the cost of retained earnings (K_r). The stock valuation model is rewritten below with K_r substituted for RRR.

Equation 16.11

$$\text{Stock Value} = \frac{\tilde{DPS}_1}{(1 + K_r)^1} + \frac{\tilde{DPS}_2}{(1 + K_r)^2} + \ldots + \frac{\tilde{DPS}_n}{(1 + K_r)^n}$$

Given the market price of common stock, it is possible to derive K_r from equation 16.11, if one can determine the dividend estimates of investors. Before we encounter this issue, it would be worth our while to return to a statement that was made about RRRs in chapter 4. A required rate of return is the minimum that an investor will accept. It is reasonable to assume that any rational investor would gladly take a higher rate of return if it is offered. Therefore, *K_r represents the minimum cost of retained earnings.* Common stockholders, more so than other investors, hope that they will earn an even higher rate of return. Nevertheless, these same investors shall be satisfied earning only K_r. It is also worth noting that a K_r derived from the stock valuation model will include the stock market's desired risk premium.

The financial manager of a firm whose stock is traded on the stock market can use equation 16.11 to find K_r, *if the manager can determine the dividend estimates of investors.* Forecasting common stock dividends is a very difficult task in its own right. Deciphering the dividend forecasts of others is doubly difficult. Basically, a manager must pretend to be an average common stockholder and look at the firm through the eyes of this pseudo-investor. A financial manager wants to estimate the company's future dividend payments in roughly the same way that a typical investor would. An entire field of study is devoted to common stock valuation and the estimation of earnings and dividends. Obviously, therefore, the subject matter is quite complex. Nevertheless, some simplified examples would be instructive at this point.

Example A: The management of Tamby Corporation has decided to retain $10 million out of the current year's net income of $15 million. The firm's dividends have grown at an average annual compound rate of 8% over the last ten years. This growth is expected to continue for the foreseeable future. Tamby's stock price is presently $48 and DPS for the current year are $2.40. Therefore DPS_1 = $2.40(1.08)^1$, DPS_2 = $2.40(1.08)^2$, etc., and n approaches infinity (∞). Based upon this information, calculate Tamby Corporation's cost to retain these earnings. Inserting the relevant figures into equation 16.11 will produce the following:

$$\$48 = \frac{\$2.40(1.08)^1}{(1 + K_r)^1} + \frac{\$2.40(1.08)^2}{(1 + K_r)^2} + \ldots + \frac{\$2.40(1.08)^\infty}{(1 + K_r)^\infty}$$

Solving the above equation for K_r is not as ominous as it appears. Because it contains a cash flow dividend stream with many of the same properties as a perpetuity, the formula can be substantially reduced, as shown below:[10]

$$\$48 = \frac{\$2.40(1.08)}{K_r - .08}$$

Solving for K_r, we obtain:

$$K_r = \frac{\$2.40(1.08)}{\$48} + .08 = .134$$

Therefore, Tamby Corporation's cost of retained earnings is 13.4%. Of course, investors would be more than happy to receive over 13.4% ◼

Example B: The dividends of a large Southern company have fluctuated within a rather narrow range during the last few years. On average, the annual DPS were $2.95. Since there are no major changes forecasted for this firm or its industry, it is presumed that a $2.95 DPS will continue for the life of the business, estimated at thirty years. This business' common stock is currently selling on the market for $23 a share. The firm would like to know what cost should be assigned to any forthcoming retained earnings. By applying equation 16.11 to the information in this problem, K_r can be found as follows:

$$\$23 = \frac{\$2.95}{(1 + K_r)^1} + \frac{\$2.95}{(1 + K_r)^2} + \ldots + \frac{\$2.95}{(1 + K_r)^{30}}$$

Since the dividends are an annuity, annuity discount factors can be applied here, thus:

$$\$23 = \$2.95 ADF_{K_r/30}$$

Solving for the ADF:

$$ADF_{K_r/30} = \frac{\$23}{\$2.95} = 7.797$$

From the annuity discount factor tables K_r is determined to be between 12% and 13% ◼

---

[10]Formally, this is known as the perpetual dividend growth valuation model. In general terminology, the model appears as follows:

$$P = \frac{D_0(1 + g)}{K_r - g}$$

Where: D_0 = Current annual DPS
      P = Market price of common stock
      g = Annual growth rate of dividends
      K_r = Cost of retained earnings

One must not be fooled by the apparent precision with which the cost of retained earnings can be found by means of this model or the two that follow. *No matter how sophisticated the analysis or mathematics, we will always end up with estimates or approximations of the true K_r.* Furthermore, this K_r will apply to new or additional retained earnings only if the following conditions hold: funds are used to acquire assets equal in risk to a firm's current assets; there can be no significant alteration in the firm's degree of financial leverage.

Many financial experts are of the opinion that the capital asset pricing model (CAPM) will generate K_rs that are both truer and more versatile than those found with the stock valuation model.[11]

Using the Capital Asset Pricing Model to Measure K_r   The *capital asset pricing model* was examined briefly in chapter 4 and can be summarized as follows: investors expect a rate of return from securities (e.g., stocks and bonds) in relation to the risk-free interest rate and a security's systematic (i.e., nondiversifiable) risk. Since investors expect to earn this return, it becomes a required rate of return. *Systematic risk* is measured with the statistic *Beta (β),* and the risk-free interest rate is approximated by the interest rate on U.S. Government bonds.[12] The CAPM is formally represented by equation 4.9, which is repeated below:

$$E(R_j) = R_f + \beta[E(R_m) - R_f]$$

Where:

$E(R_j)$ = Expected rate of return on security j.
R_f = Risk-free interest rate.
$E(R_m)$ = Expected rate of return on the market portfolio.

$$\beta = \frac{Cov(IRR_j, IRR_m)}{Var(IRR_m)}$$

Where:

$Var(IRR_m)$ = Variance of market portfolio rate of return.
$Cov(IRR_j, IRR_m)$ = Covariance of security j rate of return and market portfolio rate of return.

The cost of retained earnings can be derived from the CAPM, but we must first restate the model in terms of K_r, thus:

Equation 16.12 $K_r = R_f + \beta[E(R_m) - R_f]$

[11]For further information on the use of the CAPM to measure the cost of common stockholder equity, refer to Mark E. Richardson, "A Mean-Variance Synthesis of Corporate Financial Theory," *Journal of Finance,* 28 (March 1973), pp. 167–81, and Thomas E. Copeland and J. Fred Weston, *Financial Theory and Corporate Policy,* Addison-Wesley Publishing Company, Reading, Mass., 2d ed., (1979), pp. 272–98.
[12]Due to their extremely short maturity, U.S. Government Treasury Bill yields are believed to be the closest approximation to the risk-free interest rate.

Figure 16.1   A corporation's cost of retained earnings is positively related to the Beta of its common stock plus the risk-free interest rate.

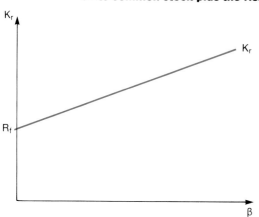

In this case, Beta is the systematic risk of a firm's common stock. And, as pointed out in chapter 4, a broad stock market index, such as the Standard & Poor's 500, usually serves as a proxy for the market portfolio of all capital assets. According to equation 16.12, the cost of retained earnings for a given firm is directly related to the Beta (i.e., degree of risk) of its common stock. This is demonstrated in figure 16.1.

Example: Given a risk-free rate of 6% and an expected market return of 13%, compute the cost of retained earnings for Airmont Airlines. The β of Airmont's common stock is estimated to be 1.65. Accordingly, K_r is found in the following manner:

$$K_r = .06 + 1.65(.13 - .06) = .06 + 1.65(.07) = 17.55\%$$

Now, let us assume that investors in another airline are faced with the same risk-free rate and market prospects as Airmont's stockholders. However, the common stock of the other airline has an estimated β of 2.2. The cost of retained earnings for this firm would be:[13]

$$K_r - .06 + 2.2(.13 - .06) - .06 + 2.2(.07) = 21.4\%$$

There are two significant drawbacks with the CAPM as a technique to measure K_r. In the first place, a financial manager must assess investors' feelings on the future of the stock market. Furthermore, he will have to estimate the Beta for his company's common stock. These are both very difficult exercises.

Using the Price-Earnings Ratio to Measure K_r   Although it is a rather simplistic technique, the *price-earnings ratio (P/E)* is favored by many corporations to measure the costs of retained earnings and common stock. In general, the price-earnings ratio is found by dividing current earnings per share into the current market price of common stock. Cut to its

---

[13]The capital asset pricing model can also be used to find the costs of bonds, term loans, leases, and preferred stock. However, we have no need for it in those situations.

essentials, the P/E describes what the stock market is willing and able to pay for $1 of a particular firm's earnings. For example, a P/E of eight implies that investors are willing to pay a multiple of eight times current earnings per share.

By taking the inverse of the price-earnings ratio, one obtains the *earnings-price ratio (E/P)*. Thus, a P/E of eight converts to an E/P of .125 or 12.5%. It is the E/P that serves as the cost of retained earnings. That is, K_r equals E/P. The computational formula for the earnings-price ratio is shown below.

$$\textbf{Equation 16.13}\quad K_r = E/P = \frac{\text{Earnings per Share}}{\text{Market Price of Common Stock}}$$

Example: Roberts, Inc., had earnings per share for the last twelve months of $.80, and the firm's common stock is currently priced at $5.00. Roberts, Inc., relies upon its earnings-price ratio to measure the cost of retained earnings. The K_r is determined as follows:

$$K_r = E/P = \frac{\$.80}{\$5.00} = 16\% \blacksquare$$

There are several advantages with using P/E to measure K_r. In the first place, it is based on readily available information (i.e., reported earnings and market prices), thereby eliminating the need for any estimation. Secondly, the P/E is a very simple computation to make. Thirdly, the P/E is relatively easy to comprehend. Last, rightly or wrongly, investors pay a great deal of attention to price-earnings ratios when making decisions to buy or sell common stock. For these reasons, this model is quite popular as a measure of the cost of retained earnings.

Despite the aforementioned advantages, there is very little economic logic to support the use of P/E to measure K_r. For one thing, investors buy future, not current, dividends. Furthermore, dividends will equal earnings only if a company has a 100% payout rate. From a practical standpoint, this technique is unsuitable for a corporation that is operating at a loss. To do so would generate a negative cost of retained earnings. Such an outcome is not only absurd, but also points up the logical inconsistencies in the P/E model.

Cost of Common Stock   *The cost of common stock (K_c) would equal the cost of retained earings except for the fact that flotation costs are associated with the sale of common stock.* Accordingly, common stock is somewhat more expensive than retained earnings. The relationship among K_c, K_r, and flotation costs is approximated quite nicely with equation 16.14:

$$\textbf{Equation 16.14}\quad K_c = \frac{K_r}{1 - F}$$

Where F is the *flotation cost percentage,* which is found as follows:

$$\textbf{Equation 16.15}\quad F = \frac{\text{Flotation Costs}}{\text{Sales Proceeds}}$$

Figure 16.2   Two-tier cost of common stockholder equity

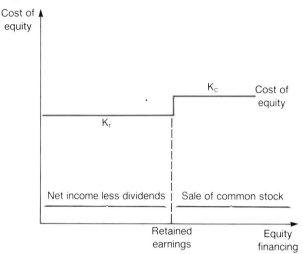

Example: Dominiques of Dallas can sell one million shares of common stock for $32 per share. Flotation costs of the issue will amount to $1,920,000. Given that Dominiques' cost of retained earnings is 20%, what is its cost of common stock? First, we determine the flotation cost percentage.

$$F = \frac{\text{Flotation Costs}}{\text{Sales Proceeds}} = \frac{\$1,920,000}{\$32,000,000} = 6\%$$

Dominiques' cost of common stock is found, as follows:

$$K_c = \frac{K_r}{1 - F} = \frac{.20}{1 - .06} = 21.28\%$$

As you can see in this example, K_c is slightly larger than K_r (21.28% vs. 20%) ■

In an effort to capitalize on the lower cost of retained earnings relative to common stock, many firms issue common shares only as a last resort. Equity requirements are met as fully as possible with retained earnings. Common shares are issued only when net income is insufficient to meet dividend and equity funding needs. One such practice was described in chapter 15, under the heading of residual dividend policy. Companies that follow this practice are faced with a stairstep cost of equity capital, such as the one shown in figure 16.2.

One other significant point needs to be made before we leave the cost of common stockholder equity. *Since dividends are not a tax-deductible expense, there will be no after-tax adjustments made to K_r or K_c.*

Weighted Average Cost of Capital

Long-term financing is normally used to fund the purchase of capital assets. Capital assets, in turn, are evaluated in capital budgeting. As we saw in chapters 9 and 10, capital asset proposals are considered to be acceptable if they meet the following criteria: positive net present value (NPV), profitability index (PI) greater than one, and internal rate of return (IRR) exceeds the RRR. A key factor in each of these decision criteria is the required rate of return. Throughout the earlier discussion of capital budgeting and carrying over into the ensuing problems we were always "given" an RRR to work with. It is now time to measure this particular RRR. For starters, *the RRR used in capital budgeting is a company's cost of long-term financing (i.e., cost of capital)*. But which cost of capital? Most corporations have at their disposal at least six different forms of long-term financing. Although some firms make use of only common stockholder equity, many more partake of one or more of the debt alternatives (e.g., leasing, bonds, and term loans), and a few issue preferred stock. A company that obtains capital in a variety of forms with varying costs should use an average cost of capital as its RRR. However, a simple average will not suffice. It is imperative that a weighted average be employed in this situation. Accordingly, we are interested in knowing the *weighted average cost of capital (WACC)*. In general, the WACC can be determined with equation 16.16, shown below:

Equation 16.16

$$\text{WACC} = W_b K_b^* + W_p K_p + W_t K_t^* + W_l K_l^* + W_r K_r + W_c K_c$$

Where:

Ws are the percentage weights assigned to each cost of capital.

Note that the costs of bonds, leases, and term loans are all included on an after-tax basis. This is not merely a recommendation. It is an important requirement, if one wishes to measure a firm's true cost of financing.[14] Moreover, each of the costs relates to new fund-raising. We are not concerned with, say, the interest rate on an outstanding bond issue that was sold some years earlier. The reason being, such a cost is a sunk cost and essentially irrelevant for current decision making.

Equation 16.16 is generalized to include all six major forms of long-term financing. For a business that employs only common stock and bonds, for example, the relevant formula would be:

$$\text{WACC} = W_c K_c + W_b K_b^*$$

On the other hand, equation 16.16 must be expanded whenever convertible bonds or warrants are in the picture.[15]

---

[14]Recall from chapter 8 that the net cash flow profiles associated with capital asset proposals are on an after-tax basis. Consistency requires us to treat the RRR in a similar fashion, since the two are combined to form NPV.

[15]Two WACC formulas are required for those firms who prefer lower cost retained earnings to the sale of common stock. One equation shall contain K_r, while the other includes only K_c. The latter formula will come into play only when stockholder equity requirements exceed earnings, thereby dictating the sale of common stock.

Determining the Weights   Two sets of figures are necessary to calculate the WACC: capital costs (Ks) and their respective weights (Ws). We have already examined the procedures for measuring costs of capital and will now take up the determination of capital weights.

An average cost of capital should be a weighted average, because a business normally employs unequal amounts of long-term financing. *The most commonly used weighting scheme has the cost of each capital weighted by a capital's proportional book value.*[16] For example, a firm employs three forms of capital: common stock, retained earnings, and term loans. The outstanding book values of each are as follows: $20 million of common stock, $45 million in retained earnings and $35 million of term loans, for a total of $100 million. The proportional book values are derived below.

$$\text{Common Stock Proportion} = \frac{\$20,000,000}{\$100,000,000} = .20$$

$$\text{Retained Earnings Proportoin} = \frac{\$45,000,000}{\$100,000,000} = .45$$

$$\text{Term Loan Proportion} = \frac{\$35,000,000}{\$100,000,000} = .35$$

These proportions will serve as the capital cost weights for this firm (i.e., $W_c = .20$, $W_r = .45$, and $W_t = .35$).

A weighted average cost of capital based on book value weights assumes that additional long-term funds will be raised in the same proportions as in the past. Such an assumption is derived from the fact that most companies have preferred debt-to-asset ratios and dividend payout rates, which they strive to maintain.[17] For instance, a particular corporation's optimal capital structure calls for 15% preferred stock, 35% bonds, and 50% common stock. To maintain these proportions, a $20 million financing should consist of $3 million in preferred stock, $7 million in bonds, and $10 million of common stock.[18]

It would be instructive at this point to see how a WACC is calculated.

---

[16]A weighting system that utilizes proportional market value is theoretically superior. See, for example, Timothy J. Nantell and C. Robert Carlson, "The Cost of Capital As a Weighted Average," *Journal of Finance*, 30 (December 1975), pp. 1343–55.

[17]Costs of capital are affected by a firm's financial leverage. In particular, the cost of common stockholder equity rises as the debt-to-asset ratio increases and falls as the degree of financial leverage declines.

[18]As a practical matter, corporations frequently raise long-term funds in proportions other than those indicated by book value weights. A company might, for example, meet all of its capital requirements for a given year by issuing bonds, even though it has several other forms of long-term financing on the books. The following year, the same firm might rely solely on retained earnings. Changing financial market conditions can lead to such behavior, as well as a desire to minimize flotation costs. Although these are temporary divergences that tend to balance out over time, they can complicate the measurement of WACC.

Example: The capital portion of Colorado Aluminum Corporation's balance sheet is shown below:

Term loans	$ 9,000,000
Bonds	22,500,000
Preferred stock	9,000,000
Common stock	27,000,000
Retained earnings	22,500,000
Total long-term debt and stockholder equity	$90,000,000

If the company were to raise additional long-term funds today, it would incur the following capital costs:

$$K_t^* = 8\%$$
$$K_b^* = 6\%$$
$$K_p = 9\%$$
$$K_c = 13\%$$
$$K_r = 12\%$$

Assuming Colorado Aluminum Corporation obtains new capital in book value proportions, determine the firm's WACC. To begin with, the capital cost weights must be calculated, thus:

$$W_t = \frac{\$9,000,000}{\$90,000,000} = .10$$

$$W_b = \frac{\$22,500,000}{\$90,000,000} = .25$$

$$W_p = \frac{\$9,000,000}{\$90,000,000} = .10$$

$$W_c = \frac{\$27,000,000}{\$90,000,000} = .30$$

$$W_r = \frac{\$22,500,000}{\$90,000,000} = .25$$

The next step is to incorporate the costs and weights into equation 16.16, as follows:

$$WACC = .10(8\%) + .25(6\%) + .10(9\%) + .30(13\%) + .25(12\%)$$

Solving for WACC, we obtain:

$$WACC = .008 + .015 + .009 + .039 + .03 = .101$$

Therefore, Colorado Aluminum's weighted average cost of capital is 10.1%.

Figure 16.3   Risk-adjusted WACC

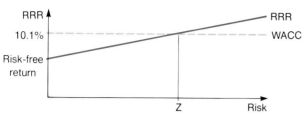

Risk-Adjusted WACC   We said at the outset of this section that the WACC should serve as the RRR in capital budgeting. The required rate of return is extremely important to capital budgeting. It is used both in the computation of NPV and compared to IRR. But because capital assets possess different degrees of risk, they must be evaluated with different RRRs.[19]

Technically speaking, therefore, a WACC is a suitable RRR only for those capital asset proposals that typify a firm's overall or average risk. The WACC must be risk-adjusted downward for assets that are less risky than the firm and upward for assets which are more risky than the firm. This is depicted in figure 16.3 in connection with the earlier Colorado Aluminum example.

As indicated in figure 16.3, capital asset proposals that are equal in risk to Colorado Aluminum's current mix of assets (point Z) will be assessed an RRR equal to the firm's WACC, or 10.1%. Assets that are lower in risk (to the left of point Z) shall be assessed lower RRRs, while assets that are riskier than the company (to the right of point Z) must overcome RRRs that are in excess of the WACC.[20]

Summary

The cost of capital is the compound annual rate of interest required by investors in a long-term security or loan. The costs of debt, term loans, leasing, and preferred stock can be measured quite satisfactorily by means of compound interest formulas. However, even here one must take into account the presence of flotation costs, intrayear cash flows, and income tax deductions. The costs of retained earnings and common stock are much more difficult to derive, simply because dividend payments are not contractual and, thus, not predictable. Nevertheless, a number of procedures are employed to deal with this problem, such as the stock valuation and capital asset pricing models. Once a firm has measured the costs for each of its capital sources, it should then combine them into a weighted average cost of capital. The weighted average cost of capital, in turn, is the applicable RRR in capital budgeting. All of the key cost of capital formulas are brought together in table 16.1 ■

---

[19]This matter is discussed at length in chapters 4 and 9.

[20]For a more in-depth look at the weighted average cost of capital see: Fred D. Arditti, "The Weighted Average Cost of Capital: Some Questions on Its Definition, Interpretation, and Use," *Journal of Finance,* 28 (September 1973), pp. 1001–8; Michael J. Brennan, "A New Look at the Weighted Average Cost of Capital, *Journal Of Business Finance,* 5, No. 1 (1973) pp. 24–30; G. V. Henderson, Jr., "In Defense of the Weighted Average Cost of Capital," *Financial Management* (Autumn 1979), pp. 57–61.

Table 16.1 Cost of Capital Equations

Corporate Bonds

Equation 16.1 $\text{Net Proceeds} = \dfrac{\text{Coupon}/2}{(1 + K_b)^1} + \dfrac{\text{Coupon}/2}{(1 + K_b)^2} + \ldots + \dfrac{\text{Coupon}/2}{(1 + K_b)^{2n}} + \dfrac{\text{Par Value}}{(1 + K_b)^{2n}}$

Equation 16.2 $K_b{}^{\cdot} = K_b(1 - \text{Tax Rate})$

Equation 16.3 $\text{Net Proceeds} = \dfrac{\text{Par Value}}{(1 + K_b)^n}$

Preferred Stock

Equation 16.4 $\text{Net Proceeds} = \dfrac{\text{Dividend}/4}{(1 + K_p)^1} + \dfrac{\text{Dividend}/4}{(1 + K_p)^2} + \ldots + \dfrac{\text{Dividend}/4}{(1 + K_p)^\infty}$

Equation 16.5 $K_p = \dfrac{\text{Dividend}/4}{\text{Net Proceeds}}$

Term Loans

Equation 16.6 $\text{Loan Face Value} = \dfrac{\text{Installment}}{(1 + K_t)^1} + \dfrac{\text{Installment}}{(1 + K_t)^2} + \ldots + \dfrac{\text{Installment}}{(1 + K_t)^n}$

Equation 16.7 $\text{ADF}_{K_t/n} = \dfrac{\text{Loan Face Value}}{\text{Installment}}$

Equation 16.8 $K_t{}^{\cdot} = K_t(1 - \text{Tax Rate})$

Leasing

Equation 16.9 $\text{Value of Leased Asset} = \dfrac{\text{Rent}}{(1 + K_l)^0} + \dfrac{\text{Rent}}{(1 + K_l)^1} + \ldots + \dfrac{\text{Rent}}{(1 + K_l)^{n-1}}$

Equation 16.10 $K_l{}^{\cdot} = K_l(1 - \text{Tax Rate})$

Common Stockholder Equity

Equation 16.11 $\text{Common Stock Value} = \dfrac{\tilde{\text{DPS}}_1}{(1 + K_r)^1} + \dfrac{\tilde{\text{DPS}}_2}{(1 + K_r)^2} + \ldots + \dfrac{\tilde{\text{DPS}}_n}{(1 + K_r)^n}$

Equation 16.12 $K_r = R_f + \beta[E(R_m) - R_f]$

Equation 16.13 $K_r = E/P = \dfrac{\text{Earnings Per Share}}{\text{Market Price of Common Stock}}$

Equation 16.14 $K_c = \dfrac{K_r}{1 - F}$ Where: $F = \dfrac{\text{Flotation Costs}}{\text{Sales Proceeds}}$

Weighted Average Cost of Capital

Equation 16.16 $\text{WACC} = W_b K_b{}^{\cdot} + W_p K_p + W_t K_t{}^{\cdot} + W_l K_l{}^{\cdot} + W_r K_r + W_c K_c$

Appendix: More on the Cost of Lease Financing

Measuring the after-tax cost of leasing (K_l) is more complicated than was indicated earlier in the chapter. There are two major reasons for this. First and foremost, a company that acquires the use of capital assets by leasing them, may forego important privileges of ownership, such as: depreciation tax deductions, investment tax credits, and salvage values. All of these benefits are retained by the lessor, as the owner of the property. Secondly, rental payments often include property maintenance charges that have nothing to do with the cost of financing (e.g., janitorial service).

Once we introduce the aforementioned complications plus the fact that rent is a tax deductible expense, the calculations become more difficult. We must turn to equation 16.17, shown below, to find the *after-tax cost of leasing* (K_l).

Equation 16.17
$$V = ITC + \frac{(R - M)(1 - T) + DT}{(1 + K_l)^0} + \frac{(R - M)(1 - T) + DT}{(1 + K_l)^1}$$
$$+ \ldots + \frac{(R - M)(1 - T) + DT}{(1 + K_l)^{n-1}} + \frac{SVAT}{(1 + K_l)^n}$$

Where:

V = Value of leased asset
ITC = Investment tax credit
R = Rental payment
D = Depreciation tax deduction
T = Ordinary income tax rate
M = Property maintenance expenses
$SVAT$ = Salvage value adjusted for taxes
n = Total number of rental payments
K_l = After-tax cost of leasing

According to equation 16.17, the cost of leasing is influenced in the following way: a lost investment tax credit (ITC) causes K_l to be higher; rent (R) is positively related to K_l, with higher rental payments leading to a higher cost of leasing, all other things the same; if property maintenance services are provided by the lessor, then the cost of these services (M) should be subtracted from the rental payments, thereby lowering K_l; the tax deductibility of rent is accounted for by multiplying it by one minus the tax rate $(1 - T)$. This adjustment can significantly reduce K_l; foregone tax savings attributable to depreciation tax deductions are represented by the recurring term (DT), which is depreciation multiplied by the tax rate.[21] These foregone tax savings result in a higher K_l; a foregone salvage value (SVAT) will also lead to a higher K_l. However, salvage values can have income tax implications (see chapter 8). Equation 16.17 is also designed so that rental payments occur at the beginning of each period.

---

[21]Depreciation tax deductions may not be allowed immediately (time period 0).

Example: The Packwood Coal Company wishes to acquire the services of a giant steam shovel. The shovel will either be purchased with borrowed funds or leased. It sells for $1,500,000 (including installation and freight charges), and it has an estimated useful life of six years. As the owner of this asset, Packwood would be the beneficiary of the following: depreciation tax deductions, a 10% investment tax credit, and a $405,000 salvage value at the end of the shovel's useful life. For tax purposes, this asset can be depreciated on a straight-line basis, over six years, to a $300,000 salvage value. An equipment leasing company has agreed to purchase the steam shovel and lease it to Packwood for $395,000 a year. The term of the lease would be six years (identical, in this case, to the useful life and tax life), and the rent is due at the beginning of each year. Moreover, the $395,000 rental payment includes reimbursement for property maintenance services valued at $40,000 per year. Assuming that Packwood Coal Company's income tax rate is 45%, find K_i^*. Note, we are not analyzing whether to puchase the steam shovel, for that has already been decided. We only wish to know the cost of financing this asset by leasing. The figures to be inserted into equation 16.17 are as follows:

V = $1,500,000	ITC = $150,000
R = $395,000	M = $40,000
D = $200,000	T = 45%
n = 6	SVAT = $357,750[22]

Therefore:

$$\$1,500,000 = \$150,000 + \frac{(\$395,000 - \$40,000)(1 - .45) + (\$200,000)(.45)}{(1 + K_i^*)^0} + \ldots$$

$$+ \frac{(\$395,000 - \$40,000)(1 - .45) + (\$200,000)(.45)}{(1 + K_i^*)^5} + \frac{\$357,750}{(1 + K_i^*)^6}$$

Combining terms and simplifying, we obtain:

$$\$1,500,000 = \$150,000 + \frac{\$285,250}{(1 + K_i^*)^0} + \frac{\$285,250}{(1 + K_i^*)^1} + \ldots + \frac{\$285,250}{(1 + K_i^*)^5} + \frac{\$357,750}{(1 + K_i^*)^6}$$

Solving by trial and error, K_i^* is determined to be slightly above 16%. The 16% interest rate is an after-tax cost, and it is an annual cost■

The after-tax cost of leasing should be compared to the after-tax cost of other forms of long-term debt, principally bonds and term loans. For instance, the K_i^* of 16% in the above example would make leasing preferable to, say, a term loan with a K_i^* of 18%, all other things being equal.

We have just examined a method for measuring the cost of leasing. It is not the only method that is available, and it is not always the best approach to follow.[23] Nevertheless, it is a sound procedure and one that is applicable to most situations. It is also versatile enough to handle irregular rental payments or accelerated depreciation methods if the need arises.■

[22]There is a capital gain on the sale of the steam shovel equal to $105,000. The entire gain is taxed at the ordinary rate of 45%, for a tax of $47,250. Thus, the SVAT amounts to $405,000 − $47,250 = $357,750. Capital gains and losses are discussed in chapter 8.
[23]Alternative methods to measure the cost of leasing are discussed in Robert W. Johnson and Wilbur G. Lewellen, "Analysis of the Lease-or-Buy Decision," *Journal of Finance,* 27 (September 1972), pp. 815–24; A. Ofer, "The Evaluation of the Lease versus Purchase Alternatives," *Financial Management* (Summer 1976), pp. 67–74; and Haim Levy and Marshall Sarnat, "Leasing, Borrowing, and Financial Risk," *Financial Management* (Winter 1979), pp. 47–54. For information regarding corporate practices in this area see Paul F. Anderson and John D. Martin, "Lease vs. Purchase Decision: A Survey of Current Practice," *Financial Management* (Spring 1977), pp. 33–40.

Key Terms/Concepts

After-tax cost of capital
Beta
Book value weights
Capital asset pricing model
Cost of bonds
Cost of capital
Cost of common stock

Cost of leasing
Cost of preferred stock
Cost of retained earnings
Cost of term loans
Flotation costs
Net proceeds
Price-earnings ratio

Risk-adjusted weighted
 average cost of capital
Stock valuation model
Weighted average cost of
 capital
Zero-coupon bonds

Questions

1. Under what circumstances is the coupon rate on a bond issue equal to its cost?

2. Which is the most relevant cost of bonds, before-tax cost or after-tax cost? Discuss.

3. Preferred stock dividends are normally paid how often? Why is it not necessary to calculate an after-tax cost for preferred stock?

4. Of what significance is the weighted average cost of capital?

5. Explain why it is so much more difficult to measure the cost of common stockholder equity than the cost of other forms of long-term financing.

6. How does a corporation's degree of financial leverage influence its weighted average cost of capital?

7. Why do we say that the cost of retained earnings is really an opportunity cost?

8. Formulate a weighted average cost of capital formula for a company that is financed with common stock, retained earnings and preferred stock.

Problems

1. Determine the costs (both K_t and K_t') of a $600,000 term loan, for each of the following payment plans. The borrower's tax rate is 40%.
    A. $158,280 per year for five years.
    B. $115,030 per year for ten years.
    C. $133,700 per year for eight years.
    D. $44,150 per quarter for five years.

2. Compute the cost of a $10 million par value preferred stock issue that carries a 12% dividend rate. The issue was sold for par, but $2 million in flotation costs reduced the net proceeds.

3. A $40 million bond issue is sold for $41.5 million. The issue pays a coupon rate of 7% and matures in ten years. Flotation costs amount to $3 million. Given an income tax rate of 50% for the issuing firm, determine: (a) cost of bonds, (b) after-tax cost of bonds.

4. Calculate the sophisticated equivalent annual interest rates for the following:
    A. 5% per quarter.
    B. 1.25% per month.
    C. 8% semiannual.
    D. 2% per month.

5. Dividends per share of Bondex, Inc., common stock have consistently fallen within a range of $1.25 to $1.75 over the last several years (the median was $1.50). The management of Bondex, Inc., believes the stock market is predicting that this DPS will continue for the life of the business. The present market price of Bondex's common stock is $12.80. Measure Bondex, Inc.'s cost of retained earnings by means of the Stock Valuation Model, assuming the firm will be in operation for: (a) twenty years, (b) indefinitely.

6. Given a risk-free interest rate of 8% and an expected market rate of return equal to 12%, find the costs of retained earnings (K_r) for firms with the following common stock Betas:

Firm	β
A	2.25
B	1.50
C	.70

7. Jaymar Enterprises can borrow $1,350,000 from Continental Bank. The loan and interest will be paid in equal, annual installments of $210,350 over ten years. Given that Jaymar's income tax rate is 40%, determine the interest rate on the loan: (a) before taxes, (b) after taxes.

8. Carlisle Brothers had an EPS last year of $.85. The firm's common stock is currently selling on the market for $6 a share. An investment banking firm has informed the company that a stock issue would net Carlisle only $5 a share. Using the price-earnings ratio, determine the company's K_r and K_c.

9. A $60 million bond issue was recently sold by Cooper Manufacturing in a public offering. The bonds carry an 11% coupon rate and a twenty-year maturity. Sales proceeds from the issue were $51,370,000 while the net proceeds came to $48 million. What interest rate (K_b) is Cooper paying on these bonds? What was the RRR of investors in the bonds?

10. A business has been given the choice of two term loans (X and Y) by its banker. Both loans have a face value of $9.2 million and maturity of five years. Loan X has equal, annual payments of $2,433,500. Loan Y requires payments of $1.6 million; $2.1 million; $2.6 million; $3.1 million; $3.6 million. Which of these two loans is the least expensive?

11. Calculate the costs of common stock (K_c) for the following costs of retained earnings (K_r) and flotation cost percentages (F):

	K_r	F
A.	.18	.08
B.	.14	.10
C.	.25	.04
D.	.20	.15

12. A firm's long-term financing is composed of $80 million in bonds, $20 million in common stock and $100 million of retained earnings. If additional funds were obtained today, the costs of capital would be 8% for bonds, 16% for retained earnings, and 18% for common stock. Derive this firm's WACC.

13. Indiana State Retirement Fund has agreed, in private, to purchase all of the zero coupon bonds offered by Telecomp, Inc., for $7,182,000. The issue has a par value of $30 million and matures in fifteen years. Telecomp's income tax rate is 45%. Determine Telecomp's after-tax cost of bonds.

14. Phillis Towers can obtain a $12,500 personal auto loan from her credit union. Installments on the loan are to be $385 a month for forty months. Ms. Towers is also required to pay a premium of $32.80 each month for credit insurance coverage. What interest rate (annual) will Ms. Towers pay on this loan, if she accepts its terms?

15. An office building can be leased from the current owner or purchased for $650,000. If it is leased, the rental payments shall be $166,080 a year for five yeras. The payments would begin immediately. Determine the cost (K_l) of this lease.

16. Terry Marks has applied for a mortgage installment loan with American Savings Bank for the purpose of buying a home for he and his family. The face value of the loan will be $70,000. Under the terms of the loan, Mr. Marks would be required to pay $921.75 per month for twenty years. Determine Mr. Mark's cost (monthly and annual) for this loan.

17. The β of Terrell Industries common stock is estimated to be 1.35. It is also estimated that the stock market, as represented by the Dow Jones Industrial Average, will grow at an annual rate of 15%. U.S. Government bonds are presently yielding an interest rate of 10%. The company wishes to sell $25 million worth of common stock through a public offering. Flotation costs associated with the stock offering would be about $2.5 million. Derive Terrell Industries cost of common stock (K_c) by means of the capital asset pricing model.

18. A small privately owned restaurant chain has relied over the years on only two sources of capital, common stock and leasing. Common stock has been used about 60% of the time and leasing the other 40%. There are only two stockholders in this firm, and they both require a minimum rate of return equal to 22%. The after-tax cost of leasing for the business is 12%. Calculate the restaurant chain's weighted average cost of capital.

19. The management of Reliance, Inc., wishes to retain all of this year's profits, which amount to $20 million. Reliance's EPS and DPS have grown at an average annual rate of 12% during the past eight years. In the opinion of management, investors are counting on this growth to continue for quite some time. Current EPS and DPS are $3.60 and $1.80, respectively. In addition, the market price of the company's common stock is presently $25. Find the cost of retained earnings for Reliance, Inc., in accordance with: (a) price-earnings ratio, (b) stock valuation model.

20. A rapidly growing business needs to raise $50 million and they wish to do so in the following manner: 10% in preferred stock, 40% in bonds, 25% in retained earnings, and 25% through the sale of common stock. These percentages are the current book value proportions of each form of capital. Flotation costs of preferred and common stock will be $500,000 and $1 million, respectively. The bonds shall be placed privately, and, for all practical purposes, the net proceeds will equal par value. A coupon rate of 15% is required on the bonds. The preferred stock will carry a dividend rate of 16%. Given a K_r of 20% and an income tax rate of 48%, answer the following questions:
    A. Determine the dollar amount of funds to be raised, by type of capital.
    B. Compute K_b^*.
    C. Compute K_c.
    D. Compute K_p.
    E. Compute WACC.

21 Kadel Enterprises has decided to acquire the services of a Data Resources Computer. However, the company has not yet determined whether to buy the computer or lease it. The computer can be purchased for $2 million plus $80,000 in installation expense. As the owner, Kadel can depreciate the computer for tax purposes. The depreciation deductions shall be based on a six-year tax life, salvage value of $250,000 and the straight-line method. An investment tax credit of 8% is also allowed by the government. Kadel plans to retain the asset for six years and then sell it for an estimated $400,000. Maintaining the computer will cost the company approximately $100,000 per year. A purchase would be financed by a term loan costing 14% before-taxes. Conversely, Kadel can lease the computer from Data Resources for six years at an annual rental of $490,000. The *rental payments are due at year-end,* and Data Resources shall provide complete maintenance. Kadel's ordinary income tax rate is 40%. Based upon the information presented above, determine which of the two financing alternatives is the least expensive.

22. Interstate Telephone and Electronics (ITE) has decided to replace its fleet of service vans. The cost of replacing the trucks is $45 million. If they decide to purchase the vans, ITE will obtain the necessary funds by means of a bond issue, the cost of which (K_b') would be 10%. ITE's financial manager projects a five year useful life for the vans and a residual value of $2.5 million. For tax purposes, the trucks are to be depreciated over five years, to a $6 million salvage value by the sum-of-the-years-digits method. ITE's ordinary income tax rate is 45%. Furthermore, the vans are eligible for a 7% investment tax credit. However, an alternative is available. A large insurance company has offered to buy the vans and lease them to ITE for five years. The rental payments shall be $12 million per year, and they are *due at the first of the year*. Moreover, all property maintenance costs are to be the responsibility of ITE. Would the company be wiser to buy the vans or lease them?

23. If American Car Rental, Inc., entered the capital markets today to obtain long-term funds, the firm would face the following costs: $K_c = .20$, $K_r = .18$, $K_p = .14$, $K_b = .12$, $K_t = .11$, and $K_l = .10$. The long-term debt and stockholder equity section of American Car Rental's most recent balance sheet is reproduced below:

Long-Term Debt

Leases	$10,000,000
Term loans	18,000,000
Bonds	12,000,000

Stockholder Equity

Preferred stock	$ 5,000,000
Common stock	20,000,000
Retained earnings	15,000,000

Total Long-Term Debt and Stockholders' Equity   **$80,000,000**

American Car Rental's income tax rate is 46%. Assuming the company raises new funds in book value proportions, what is its WACC? Would it be wise for this firm to accept a capital asset proposal that has an IRR of 16%?

24. A St. Louis salesman who travels a great deal in his job has recently become interested in leasing an automobile rather than buying one. The Clayton Auto Sales and Leasing Company has his favorite Buick for lease as well as sale. He can lease a Buick Electra for $5,000 per year. The term of the lease is four years, and rental payments must be made at the *beginning of the year*. The lessee is required to pay for all maintenance, insurance and license fees, the combined value of which equals $800 a year. (You may assume that all of these expenses occur at the beginning of each year.) The salesman's accountant has informed him that the entire rental payment is deductible for income taxes. He is in a 40% income tax bracket. Should he decide to buy the car outright, it would cost him $16,225. Determine the salesman's approximate after-tax cost of leasing (K_l').

25. Under a sale and leaseback arrangement, Georgia Benefit Life Insurance Company has agreed to purchase Ferguson Steel's Atlanta Foundry. The insurance company will pay $28 million for the facility and then lease it back to Ferguson Steel for fifteen years, at a quarterly rental of $1,011,700. Assuming that Ferguson's income tax rate is 40% and the rental payments are made at the end of each quarter, compute the approximate annual after-tax cost of leasing the foundry.

Selected References

Anderson, Paul F., and John D. Martin, "Lease vs. Purchase Decisions: A Survey of Current Practice," *Financial Management* (Spring 1977), pp. 41–47.

Beranek, W., "The Weighted Average Cost of Capital and Shareholder Wealth Maximization," *Journal of Financial and Quantitative Analysis* (March 1977), pp. 17–31.

Bierman, Harold, Jr., *The Lease versus Buy Decision,* Englewood Cliffs, N.J.: Prentice-Hall, 1982.

Henderson, G. V., Jr., "Shareholder Taxes and the Required Rate of Return on Internally Generated Funds," *Financial Management* (Summer 1976), pp. 25–31.

Lewellen, W. G., *The Cost of Capital,* Belmont, Calif.: Wadsworth Publishing Co., 1969.

Kalotay, A., "Sinking Funds and the Realized Cost of Debt," *Financial Management* (Spring 1982), pp. 43–54.

McConnell, J. J., and C. M. Sandberg, "The Weighted Average Cost of Capital: Some Questions on Its Definition, Interpretation, and Use: Comment," *Journal of Finance* (June 1975), pp. 883–86.

McDonald, John G., "Market Measures of Capital Cost," *Journal of Business Finance* (Autumn 1970), pp. 27–36.

Soloman, Ezra, *The Theory of Financial Management,* New York: Columbia University Press, 1963.

Van Horne, James C., *Financial Management and Policy,* 6th ed. Englewood Cliffs, N.J.: Prentice-Hall, 1983, chapters 7 and 8.

Special Topics

Business Acquisitions

Overview

A rather specialized and important topic is considered in this chapter: the principles of business acquisitions. Why do corporations buy other firms? What are the various forms of business acquisition? How does one value a firm that is to be acquired? What is involved in the negotiations leading to a business acquisition? How can one company buy another company, when the management of the latter does not wish to sell?

Objectives

By the end of this chapter the student should be able to:

1. Understand the reasons for business growth
2. Distinguish between internal and external business growth
3. Understand the reasons why one business acquires another business
4. Measure the value of a business acquisition
5. Explain the terms of exchange in a business acquisition
6. Distinguish between a friendly business takeover and an unfriendly business takeover

Introduction

Companies can grow in two ways: internally and/or externally. Internal growth or expansion is accomplished by acquiring additional assets (e.g., purchase land, produce inventory, construct plants, and buy equipment). External growth is achieved by purchasing other businesses, in whole or in part. Chapters 5–7 were concerned with the acquisition and holding of current assets. Chapters 8–10 dealt with the purchase, modification, and sale of capital assets. This chapter is concerned with the external growth of a business. We will explore the different facets of external growth, such as: the variety of ways in which one corporation can acquire another; the reasons behind business acquisitions; and the procedures that are followed when one business purchases another. This subject is of more than passing interest. Business acquisitions have always been an important avenue for expansion, and the pace of activity has picked up considerably in the last few years.

How, you might ask, can one corporation buy another corporation? In most cases, an acquisition is made through purchasing a firm's outstanding common stock. At other times, only the assets of a firm are acquired. Our discussion will be directed toward the stock purchase method of acquisition.

In order to simplify the forthcoming discussion, a few terms should be defined at the outset: a *suitor* is the term used to describe a company that is looking to purchase another firm; a *target* is the selling firm, or the object of the suitor's advances; a *takeover candidate* is a business with one or more characteristics that make it ripe to become a target company ▪

Business Growth

In as much as business acquisitions are closely tied to corporate growth, it would be well to examine the matter of corporate growth at the outset of this discussion. Corporations grow or expand for many valid reasons. Expansion normally follows one of three paths: horizontal, vertical, or conglomerate. Each of these is briefly described below.

Horizontal Growth   Horizontal growth is expansion in a company's present or similar line of business. An example of horizontal expansion would be for Anheuser Busch to expand its beer production capacity. Horizontal growth can be justified on a number of grounds. A firm may decide to enlarge the size of its present operations simply to meet a growing demand for its products. In other instances, a company will increase the number of facilities in an effort to tap new markets for the same products. An example of the latter situation would be a grocery chain locating additional stores in a neighboring state. Horizontal expansion can also be employed to take advantage of any economies of scale that might be available, such as: quantity discounts on the purchase of goods or services, specialization of labor, and more efficient usage of large capital assets. In addition to these reasons, a firm might wish to grow horizontally so as to monopolize its market or to defend against being dominated by another corporation.

Vertical Growth   Vertical expansion occurs when a company moves forward and/or backward in the product chain flowing from raw materials to the final consumer. An auto manufacturer would be expanding vertically backward if it began producing tires, and further still if it decided to mine iron ore. Expanding forward in the auto industry might lead an automobile manufacturer into the auto dealership business. A major reason why many corporations grow vertically is the desire to exert greater control over suppliers and/or customers. If just one link in the product chain is disrupted (e.g., a prolonged work stoppage) the entire system can break down. By expanding vertically, a firm will not be at the mercy of as many uncontrollable elements, or at least that is the desired consequence. Economies of scale can also be forthcoming from vertical expansion, although to a lesser extent than with horizontal growth.

Conglomerate Growth   Conglomerate growth refers to expansion into unrelated lines of business. An example of conglomerate expansion would be for IBM to manufacture airplanes. The major motivation behind conglomerate growth is diversification which, as we saw in chapter 4, can be used to reduce a company's risk exposure. The idea is to combine firms whose earnings exhibit low covariances vis-a-vis one another.

Lastly, larger businesses, regardless of whether they are the result of horizontal, vertical, or conglomerate growth, are usually able to obtain financing at a lower cost. For one thing, big companies have lower per-dollar flotation costs on their security sales. In addition, large firms are less risky than small firms, all other things being the same.

Types of Business Acquisitions

Most business acquisitions can be classified in one of three ways: mergers, consolidations and holding companies.[1] When one firm acquires another through a *merger,* the identity and common stock of the target company cease to exist and it becomes a *subsidiary* of the acquiring firm. The assets and liabilities of the acquired firm are merged with those of the suitor. As an illustration of a merger, in 1982 U.S. Steel Corporation purchased Marathon Oil. The common stock and name of Marathon ceased to exist, and the new larger company was named after the buyer, U.S. Steel Corporation. A *consolidation* differs from a merger in that the identities and stocks of both buyer and seller cease to exist once the consolidation is completed. A new company will be formed from the combined firms, with both a new name and a new issue of common stock. For instance, in 1983 Sante Fe Industries combined with the Southern Pacific Company. The stock in both firms was cancelled, new shares were issued to the owners, and the new firm was called Sante Fe Southern Pacific. Generally speaking, mergers and consolidations are related to the acquisition of an entire company.[2] A *holding company* is a nonoperating firm that owns (holds) significant amounts of common stock in operating firms. Rather than buying an entire business, a holding company usually elects to purchase a controlling interest of another firm's common stock. The control of a corporation does not necessarily require 51% ownership. Ownership of a mere 20% of the shares in a widely held company may constitute effective control over the firm's operations.

---

[1]Small stock purchases, say less than 5% of a firm's outstanding shares, are simply classified as investment holdings.

[2]Occasionally, a minority group of stockholders will hold out and refuse to sell their shares.

The holding company is often referred to as the *parent* and its operating firms are subsidiaries.[3] UAL, Inc., for example, is a holding company with ownership interests in several other corporations, including United Airlines, Westin Hotels, and GAB Business Services.

A business acquisition, whatever form it may take, can usually be categorized as *friendly* or *unfriendly*. Under the former arrangement, the managements of the suitor and target companies sit down and negotiate in a friendly, albeit tough, manner over the terms of sale. Under these circumstances, both parties are favorably disposed to make a deal. However, friendly acquisitions may become unfriendly if the parties fail to agree on terms. Then, too, there are many instances in which a target company is strongly against being acquired by another firm, regardless of who the suitor is. Should the suitor persist, the acquisition will be unfriendly and may get downright nasty. We shall examine unfriendly acquisitions at the end of this section, under the heading *tender offers*. It will be assumed for now that we are dealing entirely with friendly situations.

The financial negotiations and legal intricacies of mergers and consolidations can be very complicated, and errors may be quite costly. Therefore, the parties to these transactions often turn to investment banking firms for help. Most of the large investment bankers have mergers and consolidation departments that specialize in business acquisitions.

Method of Payment

One of the more intriguing things about business acquisitions is the method of payment. While many firms are purchased with cash, a large number are paid for with an exchange of securities (e.g., stocks and bonds); the suitor exchanges its securities for the common shares (or assets) of the target company. As an illustration, a suitor might exchange 1½ shares of its common stock for each target company common share. Not only does such a transaction do away with the need to raise funds for the purchase, but there may also be certain tax advantages.[4] There are many instances, too, when both cash and securities are used to pay for a business acquisition. A company might offer $20 in cash plus one share of its preferred stock for each target company common share.

Accounting Treatment

When two corporations are combined via a merger or consolidation there must be an accounting of the transaction. This can be complicated if the target company is purchased for a price other than its book value, which happens most of the time. When accounting for a business acquisition, the balance sheets of the buyer and seller are consolidated or combined. This simply means that the book values of assets and liabilities are summed. Generally accepted accounting practices prescribe two alternative accounting treatments for business acquisitions.

---

[3]Technically speaking, at least 51% ownership in a business is required before it can be called a subsidiary.

[4]Stockholders in the target company can avoid capital gains taxes on their shareholdings, if they are paid with shares of stock in the new corporation. This is classified as a like-kind exchange.

Under the *purchase method,* if the common stock of a firm is acquired for more than book value, the premium is listed on the consolidated balance sheet under the heading, *goodwill.*[5] The goodwill is then written off (i.e., amortized) on the consolidated income statement, over a future prescribed period of time, thereby reducing net income. With the *pooling of interest method,* goodwill is simply ignored. Consequently, there will be no impact on the consolidated income statement. To avoid the lower earnings that result from the amortization of goodwill, many firms prefer the pooling of interest method of accounting. However, this alternative may not be available. The appropriate accounting treatment depends upon the specifics of the acquisition.[6]

Reasons for Business Acquisitions

Earlier in the chapter we discussed the reasons why companies expand. Briefly stated, there are advantages associated with horizontal, vertical, and conglomerate growth. It was also said that expansion can occur internally or externally through business acquisitions. We shall now examine the reasons why external growth may be preferred to internal growth. As one studies the reasons for business acquisitions, it is important to keep in mind that an alternative to the purchase of another business is the creation of a totally new one. Consider, for instance, a drug manufacturer with a desire to move into the drugstore business. This firm has the choice of either acquiring an existing chain of drugstores, or constructing, equipping, and staffing an entirely new chain of stores.

A company may find it preferable to acquire another firm rather than create its own, for any one or a combination of the following reasons.

Attributes of a Going Concern   By acquiring a business that is already in operation (i.e., a going concern), the buyer is gaining access to several attributes. For one thing, a market can be entered in a much shorter span of time, since there is no need to locate, design, and construct facilities.[7] The degree of savings will depend upon the type of business involved and how smoothly the transition to new ownership takes place. A going concern also brings with it a trained labor force, which can be a real asset for a business requiring large amounts of skilled labor. Another potential advantage of a going concern is an experienced management team. This can be especially important when the target firm is in a field of endeavor significantly different from the suitor's (e.g., shoes and pharmaceuticals).

Reduce Competition   It is not at all unusual for a company to acquire or attempt to acquire a competitor. While ethical ramifications may be associated with mergers and consolidations of this sort, there are real profit incentives that are difficult to ignore. Briefly stated, by attempting to monopolize its market a company can achieve greater control over

---

[5]The word goodwill is frequently being replaced today with terms like "Premium in excess of net assets required."

[6]The Financial Accounting Standards Board has established a set of criteria that must be met before a firm can use the pooling of interest method of accounting.

[7]This can be offset somewhat by the fact that the assets obtained in a business acquisition may not be the most desirable.

its product pricing and, therefore, profits. There is also less risk facing a firm under these conditions. Moreover, it may be less expensive to buy out one's competitors rather than trying to run them out of business. However, business acquisitions of this sort are limited by the antitrust laws, which are administered by the U.S. Federal Trade Commission.

Special Situations   In certain situations a corporation may find it necessary to buy another business, rather than start one of its own. As one illustration of this, there are cases when a government license is required to deliver a product or service. To complicate matters the number of licenses may be restricted by law. Television stations fit this description. A firm wishing to enter one of these restricted markets must acquire, if possible, a company that possesses a license. Then, too, some raw materials are controlled by a few firms. In order to gain an ownership interest in these particular raw materials, a company must purchase one or more of the controlling businesses.

Tax Advantages   Paradoxical though it may seem, businesses that have accumulated substantial losses are often prime candidates to be acquired. The reason for this unusual state of affairs is the income tax break accorded the buyer of such a company. The specifics of this tax break are spelled out in the loss *carry-over provisions* of the internal revenue code. The carry-over provisions state that corporate losses from unprofitable years can be used to offset the taxable income of profitable years (the losses are carried over to past and future years).[8] Of immediate concern to us, is the fact that the losses and carry-over rights of one firm can be transferred to another firm in an acquisition. Therefore, a profitable firm can purchase a company with sizable losses and use these losses to reduce its (the profitable firm's) income taxes. Consider the following simplified example.

Example: Over the last five years Regy, Inc., has suffered losses totaling $4,200,000 and sees no hope of a turn around. On paper, this firm is practically worthless. Kayro Corporation, on the other hand, is and has been quite profitable. If it acquires Regy, Kayro can reduce its taxable income with Regy's losses to the tune of $4,200,000. Assuming Kayro's income tax rate is 45%, this purchase will translate into a tax savings for the buyer of .45 $\times$ $4,200,000 = $1,890,000 ∎

Despite the tax breaks associated with the acquisition of unprofitable companies, one should use caution in these situations. For one thing, there are limits to the use of this tax break, and various restrictions can be placed on firms that do take advantage of it. Of a more serious nature is the possibility that a buyer could get saddled with substantial debts when an unprofitable business is acquired.

Undervalued Businesses   An undervalued firm is one whose common stock is selling on the market at a bargain price in relation to the *replacement cost* of assets and level of indebtedness. Replacement cost is defined here as the cost of duplicating a given company's assets, which may or may not be equal to the assets' book values.[9] A firm is undervalued, if

---

[8]Unused tax credits can also be carried over and applied against income tax liabilities of past and future years.

[9]For a discussion of replacement cost see Eldon S. Hendriksen, *Accounting Theory* 3d ed., Homewood, Ill.: Richard D. Irwin, 1977, pp. 271–72, 321–24; and Halbert C. Smith, *Real Estate Appraisal,* Columbus, Ohio: Grid, Inc., 1976, chapter 7.

the market price of its stock is lower than the replacement cost per share. *Replacement cost per share can be found by subtracting the total amount of liabilities from the replacement cost of assets and dividing the result by outstanding common shares.* The market price of a given corporation's common stock might be thought of as undervalued for a number of reasons. To begin with, the general stock market could be severely depressed. Secondly, poorly managed firms will have disappointing records and, therefore, lower stock prices. Finally, due to imperfect information, there will always be some very good businesses that are overlooked by the investment community, and, thus, underpriced. *For whatever the reason, ownership of an undervalued company can be acquired for less than the cost of creating an equivalent new firm.*

Example: Esborne Corporation's 800,000 shares of common stock are currently selling on the market for $22 per share. The firm's assets can be replaced for $40 million and it has outstanding debts of $16 million. Accordingly, the replacement cost per share of Esborne stock is found as follows:

$$\text{Replacement Cost Per Share} = \frac{\$40,000,000 - \$16,000,000}{800,000 \text{ Shares}} = \$30$$

Thus, the market price of Esborne's common stock is $8 less than the replacement cost of the firm. Based upon this information, we could say that Esborne Corporation is undervalued in the amount of $8 × 800,000 Shares = $6,400,000 ∎

Undervalued companies are often labeled as takeover candidates, since they make up a large proportion of all business acquisitions. This is evidenced by the surge in merger activity that usually accompanies a depressed stock market.

Valuing a Business Acquisition

Once a suitor has found a takeover candidate suitable to its needs, the acquiring firm must then determine what ownership of the takeover candidate is worth. That is to say, *what is the maximum price the suitor is willing to pay for the target company's common stock.* An approach similar to that used in the evaluation of capital assets (chapters 8 and 9) can be employed to answer the question: what is a company worth?

Acquiring the ownership of an entire business means essentially two things: (1) the buyer is "entitled" to use a group of assets in the quest of additional profits; (2) the buyer is "obligated" for the target company's outstanding debts, if there are any. By placing a value on the target company's assets and deducting the liabilities, a suitor can determine the value of a takeover candidate's common stock. Accordingly, the key to valuing a business is determining what its assets are worth. As we saw in chapter 9, the value of a capital asset is defined as the present value of the proposal's future, incremental net cash flows (recurring and terminal). This same principle can be applied to a group of assets, in this case the combined assets of a going concern. The first step in this evaluation process is to perform a cash flow analysis: identification, estimation, and income taxes. It is in the identification phase of cash flow analysis that such factors as economies of scale, increased market power, and tax loss carryovers are brought into the analysis. For example, if one benefit of buying a business will be to allow the acquiring firm to raise its prices and, thus, revenues, this impact should be taken into account. Having identified the incremental cash flows associated with an acquisition, these cash flows must then be estimated. Following the estimation process, incremental income taxes are measured.

The second step in the valuation process is concerned with finding the appropriate required rate of return (RRR). The RRR will consist of the risk-free interest rate and a risk premium corresponding to the target company's degree of risk. Should the proposed acquisition confer diversification benefits upon the buyer, this must be accounted for in the RRR; the RRR should be appropriately reduced. Let us now turn to a simplified example showing the valuation process for a business.

Example: Textra Corporation wishes to merge with Movark, Inc., by acquiring all one million of Movark's outstanding common shares. Movark is one of Textra Corporation's major competitors in the electronics industry. The president of Textra Corporation is interested in acquiring this firm because he believes the operating costs of the combined establishments can be reduced substantially, as the result of economies of scale. On their own, Movark's assets will produce recurring net cash inflows of approximately $6.5 million per year for thirty years. However, Textra expects to obtain additional recurring net cash inflows of $2.5 million, if it acquires Movark. The additional expected benefits are to be brought about by the aforementioned economies of scale. There is no terminal net cash flow forecasted for Movark's assets. In addition to its assets, the target company will bring $24 million in liabilities to the merger. Based upon the risk aspects of the acquisition, Textron's financial manager feels that an RRR of 15% is appropriate. Given the preceding information, the value of Movark, Inc., common stock is found as follows:

$$\text{Value of Movark's Assets} = \frac{\$9,000,000}{(1.15)^1} + \frac{\$9,000,000}{(1.15)^2} + \ldots + \frac{\$9,000,000}{(1.15)^{30}}$$

Using the annuity discount factor table, we proceed as follows:

$$\text{Value of Movark's Assets} = \$9,000,000 \ ADF_{.15/30} = \$9,000,000(6.5660)$$

Therefore:

$$\text{Value of Movark's Assets} = \$59,094,000$$

Next, we determine the value of the company:

$$\text{Value of Movark Common Stock} = \text{Value of Movark's Assets} - \text{Movark's Debt}$$

Substituting:

$$\text{Value of Movark Common Stock} = \$59,094,000 - \$24,000,000 = \$35,094,000$$

The per share value of Movark's common stock is determined as follows:

$$\text{Value of One Movark Common Share} = \frac{\$35,094,000}{1,000,000 \ Shares} = \$35.09$$

This says that Textra Corporation should not pay in excess of $35.09 per share of Movark common stock ■

Terms of Exchange

Negotiation   Both parties to a business acquisition should attempt to derive the best possible terms for their respective common stockholders. This is in line with the goal of stockholder wealth maximization. The acquiring firm wishes to exchange as little as possible for the target company's common stock. The seller, on the other hand, wants it shareholders to receive as much as possible from the suitor. Quite often there will be a substantial difference between the maximum price a buyer is willing to offer and the minimum price a seller is willing to accept. Not surprisingly, then, there can be considerable latitude in which to negotiate the terms of exchange. Let us say that firm A wishes to acquire firm B. A's management has determined that B's common stock is worth, at most, $45 per share.[10] The management of B, however, will not accept less than $36 per share. Final terms of exchange will fall somewhere between these two values, the precise location depending upon the relative bargaining strengths of the two parties. Given that the negotiations are friendly, there are at least two reasons why such negotiations may fail to reach agreement. In the first place, the suitor may not feel that the target company is worth the target's minimum asking price. This would occur in the preceding example if the figures were reversed. A further reason why negotiations can fail, would be if either party found a better offer somewhere else, and it cannot be matched.

Market Value Exchange Ratio   Given the importance attached to the principle of stockholder wealth maximization, a market value exchange ratio is computed in order to analyze a business acquisition's effect on the two parties' respective stockholder wealth. The market value exchange ratio is found by dividing the market value of the target company's common stock into the market value of securities and/or cash offered by the suitor.

Equation 17.1

$$\text{Market Value Exchange Ratio} = \frac{\text{Market value of securities and/or cash offered by the suitor}}{\text{Market value of target company's common stock}}$$

Example A: CBE Company acquired the ownership of Murphy Motors, Inc. Under the terms of the deal, CBE exchanged one-half share of its common stock for each Murphy Motor's share. At the time of the purchase, CBE common stock was selling on the market for $65, while Murphy Motors stock traded for $25. The market value exchange ratio in this situation is:

$$\text{Market Value Exchange Ratio} = \frac{.5 \times \$65}{\$25} = \frac{\$32.50}{\$25} = 1.3 \ \blacksquare$$

Example B: Bemer Manufacturing acquired Wilson Enterprises in a cash transaction. Bemer exchanged $50 in cash for each of Wilson's outstanding common shares, which at the time were selling for $40 on the stock market. The market value exchange ratio amounted to:

$$\text{Market Value Exchange Ratio} = \frac{\$50}{\$40} = 1.25 \ \blacksquare$$

---

[10]The methodology used in determining one business's value to another was described in the preceding segment.

Example C: Super X, Inc., purchased McIntyre and Company with cash and bonds. In exchange for each of McIntyre's 1,350,000 shares, Super X offered $50 in cash and one-tenth of a Super X bond. The bonds were valued at $1,000 apiece and McIntyre common stock had a market price of $90. Therefore, the market value exchange ratio came to:

$$\text{Market Value Exchange Ratio} = \frac{\$50 + (.1 \times \$1,000)}{\$90} = \frac{\$150}{\$90} = 1.67 \blacksquare$$

In each of the preceding examples, the market value exchange ratio was greater than one. This signifies that the acquiring firms each paid a *premium* over the market price of the target firm's common stock. In example C, for instance, a 67% premium was paid. The owners of a business that is acquired at a premium will gain an increase in wealth at the expense of the acquiring firm's shareholders. Premiums are the norm in business acquisitions primarily because buyers see something of value in takeover candidates that the stock market fails to see. On the other hand, no one would sell their stockholdings to another company at a price below what can be obtained on the market. This in itself would rule out market value exchange ratios less than one. However, while it is true that suitors are often willing to pay premiums for businesses because they expect them to contribute that something extra (e.g., economies of scale), it is in the buyer's interest to keep the premium as low as possible.[11] Under no circumstances is it wise to pay more for a business than its maximum value to the buyer.

Tender Offers

Up to now we have assumed that business acquisitions are basically friendly affairs. That is, while the parties to an acquisition may not agree on the terms, they are nonetheless interested in making a deal, and work toward that end in a determined but agreeable manner. However, on many occasions the negotiations surrounding the marriage of two companies can be unfriendly, some decidedly so. This is brought about by a target firm who, for one reason or another, resists the suitors advances, and a suitor who will not take no for an answer. The management of a takeover candidate might work against a merger or consolidation for several reasons: the management style of the acquiring firm is all wrong for the target company; the offering price is insultingly too low; it will never be allowed to take place, because it violates antitrust laws; the seller will lose a measure of independence, which is highly prized in certain lines of business (e.g., newspaper publishing); experienced managers who have served the firm for years may be replaced. Whether or not such arguments are primarily concerned with protecting shareholders as opposed to the target company's top management, is a frequent subject of debate. The fact of the matter is, these reasons are often used by a takeover candidate's management to justify their opposition to being acquired. When faced with a management team that is hostile to its overtures, a suitor can bypass them and appeal directly to the target company's stockholders. This practice is called a *tender offer.* Cut to its essentials, it is a procedure whereby shareholders are asked to tender

---

[11]One might ask why a target firm's common stock is not simply purchased on the secondary stock market at market prices? First of all, many owners will not wish to sell their shares at the market price, because they think it's worth more. Secondly, the mere fact that another firm wants to take their firm over will make all of the owners tougher to deal with.

(i.e., sell) their shares to the acquiring firm. The appeal is usually made through mailings and advertisements in the financial press. If the offer is unsuccessful, a new appeal will be made with improved terms of exchange.

As one might expect, the bypassed management of a target company is unlikely to stand by idle during a tender offer. Various defensive maneuvers are often employed against a hostile suitor. Court injunctions may be sought based on antitrust or securities law violations. However, legal actions such as these are likely to provide only a temporary defense. In the event that certain assets are especially attractive to the suitor, these might be sold off, thereby making the target less appealing. By repurchasing a significant portion of outstanding common shares, the target company's management can reduce the number of shares available for tendering. One of the more popular defensive actions is to recruit an acceptable suitor who is willing and able to rescue the business. Such third party companies are referred to as "white knights." A perfect example of this occurred in 1982, when Allied Corporation rescued Martin Marietta from the unwanted affections of Bendix. Despite any or all of these actions, a target company could still be taken over by a determined suitor. Finally, a takeover candidate may go deeply into debt so as to become less attractive to potential buyers.[12]

Summary

Corporations seek growth for many reasons: to gain economies of scale; to increase market power; to obtain diversification benefits; or to tighten controls over suppliers and/or distributors. Acquiring a business can be an effective means to achieve growth, whether of the horizontal, vertical, or conglomerate variety. Business acquisitions usually fall into one of three categories: mergers, consolidations, and holding companies. Determining the value of a target firm is a key element in any business acquisition. This value will set the upper limit on the price a suitor will be willing to pay for a target company's common stock. The terms of exchange in a business acquisition are measured with the market value exchange ratio, which is the market value of securities and/or cash offered by a suitor, divided by the market price of a target company's common stock.

A business acquisition is usually described as friendly or unfriendly. A friendly acquisition is characterized by cordial, but tough negotiations between two interested parties. In an unfriendly acquisition, the target company's management does not wish to sell out, but the suitor persists by means of a tender offer to the target's shareholders.

Acquiring an ongoing business can be a superior means of achieving corporate growth. Nevertheless, mergers and consolidations frequently prove to be costly mistakes, especially for the buyer and its owners who paid a premium for the acquisition. Business acquisitions can turn sour for a suitor for many reasons: in some cases the purchase price is simply too high to overcome; hoped for benefits never materialize; the purchase was not well thought out in advance; the chemistry between the buyer and seller turns out to be bad, possibly because of differing management styles. For whatever the reason, business acquisitions often fail to meet expectations. When a purchase turns out to be especially bad, it may be disposed of, thereby becoming what is commonly referred to as a divestiture ■

---

[12]For additional insight into tender offers see David P. Baron, "Tender Offers and Managerial Resistance," *Journal of Finance* (May 1983), pp. 331–43 and Michael Bradley, "Interfirm Tender Offers and the Market for Corporate Control," *Journal of Business* (October 1980), pp. 345–76.

Key Terms/Concepts

Carry-over provisions
Conglomerate growth
Consolidation
Going concern
Holding company
Horizontal growth

Market value exchange ratio
Merger
Parent company
Replacement cost
Subsidiary
Suitor

Takeover candidate
Target company
Tender offer
Terms of exchange
Undervalued business
Vertical growth

Questions

1. What is the major difference between a consolidation and a merger?

2. List the reasons why it might be better to buy a going concern, rather than building a company from the ground up.

3. Do you see a potential conflict of interest between the management of a target company and its stockholders? Explain.

4. Define the following terms: takeover candidate, economies of scale, white knight, and holding company.

5. What is the market value exchange ratio?

Problems

1. Gyro Industries recently became a takeover target of Beechem Enterprises. Gyro's common stock is currently selling on the market for $38, while Beechem's stock is trading at $52. Calculate the market value exchange ratio for Gyro Industry's common stock under each of the following terms:
   A. Beechem offers $20 in cash and one-half share of its stock for each Gyro share.
   B. Beechem offers one share of its stock for each Gyro share.
   C. Beechem offers a $1,000 bond for twenty Gyro common shares.
   D. Which offer is the best from a Gyro shareholder viewpoint?

2. Shown below are relevant premerger financial data for two firms.

	ABC Corporation (Suitor)	XYZ Corporation (Target)
Net income	$15,000,000	$10,240,000
Common shares outstanding	6,000,000	8,000,000
Earnings per share	$2.50	$1.28
Market price of common stock	$24	$15

ABC Corporation acquired XYZ Corporation by exchanging seven-eighths of one of its shares for each outstanding XYZ share. Based upon this information, determine the following:
   A. Market value exchange ratio.
   B. The number of outstanding shares in the postmerger consolidated corporation.
   C. The earnings per share of the postmerger consolidated firm. You may assume that the combined net income of the two companies will not change because of the merger.

3. Amos, Inc., common stock is currently trading on the market for $30. According to the firm's most recent audited financial statements, total assets have a combined book value of $45 million and total liabilities amount to $25 million. In the opinion of an outside consulting firm, the current cost of duplicating Amos' assets would be approximately 50% greater than their book value. Given that Amos, Inc., has 1.25 million shares of common stock outstanding, answer the following two questions:
   A. What is the replacement cost per share of Amos, Inc., common stock?
   B. Is Amos, Inc., undervalued, and if so, by how much?

4. Bemis Industries wishes to merge with Carter-Bulge, Inc., by purchasing all of Carter's three million outstanding common shares. The financial manager of Bemis Industries believes that by combining, these two firms can achieve significant economies of scale. Such savings will amount to approximately $15 million per year, after taxes. Since these companies are competitors, a merger would also allow them to raise their prices, resulting in an additional $9 million of after-tax cash revenues each year. Bemis' financial manager expects both of these benefits to exist for twenty-five years. In the absence of a merger, Carter-Bulge will more than likely remain a viable firm for the next twenty-five years, producing an annual recurring net cash flow of $35 million just as it has for the past ten years. Bemis will use what it considers to be a very low RRR of 15% to value Carter-Bulge's common stock. One of the major reasons for such a low RRR is the fact that Carter has no outstanding liabilities. Based on the preceding information, what value will Bemis place on Carter-Bulge's common stock, both on a total and per share basis?

5. Like many fledgling companies, Tiger National has had a rough start. The firm has never made a profit, having accumulated losses over the last four years of $8 million. Word is out that Tiger National is interested in being acquired by a financially strong business with marketing expertise. Remy, Inc., a firm fitting that description, on hearing of Tiger's intentions, has decided to pursue the matter. After looking into the situation, Remy feels that with proper management and financial backing, Tiger National's assets will produce after-tax cash flows of $5 million annually for the next five years and $10 million annually for the following five years. At the end of ten years, Tiger National would be sold, thereby bringing in a terminal net cash flow of about $25 million. Furthermore, Remy's taxable income for the current year will be reduced by Tiger's entire tax loss carryover, thereby immediately reducing Remy's income taxes in the amount of $4,000,000. At the moment, Tiger National's balance sheet shows $12 million in liabilities and 50,000 outstanding common shares. Remy considers this acquisition to be a rather risky venture. Accordingly, an RRR of 24% will be used in the valuation process. Determine the value Remy will place on Tiger National's common stock.

Selected References

Asquith, Paul, and E. Han Kim, "The Impact of Merger Bids on the Participating Firms' Security Holders," *Journal of Finance* (December 1982), pp. 1209–28.

Bernstein, Peter W., "Who Buys Corporate Losers," *Fortune* (January 26, 1981), pp. 60–62.

Fischer, Paul M., William James Taylor, and J. Arthur Leer, *Advanced Accounting*, 2d ed. Cincinnati, Ohio: South-Western, 1982, pp. 160–285.

Lewellen, Wilbur G., "A Pure Financial Rationale for the Conglomerate Merger," *Journal of Finance* (May 1971), pp. 521–37.

Lewellen, Wilbur G., and Michael G. Ferri, "Strategies for the Merger Game: Management and the Market," *Financial Management* (December 1983), pp. 25–35.

Stapleton, Richard C., "The Acquisition *Decision* As a Capital Budgeting Problem," *Journal of Business Finance and Accounting* (Summer 1975), pp. 187–202.

Finance in the News

Should a corporation change its capital structure by going into debt so as to prevent a takeover? What are the results of such an effort? These were questions facing Phillips when it tried to resist an unfriendly takeover by corporate raiders such as Carl Icahn and T. Boone Pickens. The following article discusses the consequences.

The High Price of Freedom

Joy! It cascaded down Frank Phillips Boulevard and rushed along the corridors of the Jane Phillips Episcopal Hospital and the Phillips Hotel. It spilled over into Frank Phillips Airport and gushed through every Phillips 66 station in town. In Bartlesville, Okla., last week, there was good reason for jubilation. Phillips Petroleum, the eighth largest U.S. oil producer, had succeeded in stopping New Yorker Carl Icahn's bid to take over the company after earlier beating back a similar attempt by Texan T. Boone Pickens. A three-month siege by corporate raiders had ended, and worries for the future were replaced by good feelings. "Hallelujah!" declared Joe Seward, general manager of Martin's department stores. "This town is three feet off the ground." Chamber of Commerce Director Sam Cartwright was ecstatic: "Now that Phillips is saved, Bartlesville is saved, and the tumbleweeds won't take over after all."

Although the end of the dramatic struggle for Phillips (1984 sales: $15.7 billion) came as a relief to many local residents, others remained nervous. Phillips' 7,800 employees in Bartlesville, mostly white-collar professionals who make up 40% of the town's work force, were assured that their company would remain under local control; yet some jobs will probably be lost. Shareholders saw the price of their Phillips stock rise from less than $40 when the battle began to the mid-50s in December and close last week at 49⅜. The clearest winners were the raiders. Centimillionaires already, they became richer still. Pickens and his partners walked away with an $89 million pretax profit, while Icahn will gain at least $50 million for 30 days of high-pressure maneuvering. Said he: "I'm happy the shareholders benefited. But I'm no Robin Hood. I enjoy making the money."

By any measure, Phillips paid a high price for independence. It emerged intact but badly bruised. Just one humiliating item on the tab: payments of $25 million to each to reimburse the two raiders for the expenses they ran up while trying to take over the company. All told, Phillips Chairman William Douce estimated that the back-to-back assaults will cost the company $150 million. The ordeal will leave Phillips smaller and heavily in debt.

The battle for Phillips was so complex and changed so often that even the raiders at times grew confused amid the offers and counteroffers. It all began on Dec. 4, when Pickens, who had been buying Phillips stock since last October at an average price of $43, announced that he had acquired a 5% stake in the company and was going for more. That assault ended just before Christmas, when Phillips agreed to buy back Pickens' stock for $53 a share. Under the agreement, Phillips also consented to a financial restructuring to make the value of all stockholders' holdings equal to what Pickens received.

Not all shareholders were pleased with that arrangement. The most disgruntled of all was Icahn, who rode into town on Feb. 12 with a $4.2 billion offer to buy 45% of the company for $60 a share. When added to the more than 5% he already had, that would have given him majority control of the company. Residents of Bartlesville, who had held prayer vigils to ward off Pickens, quickly set about trying to exorcise the new threat. They burned a pile of blue proxy cards that Icahn was using to solicit shares. Women baked heart-shaped cookies with the Phillips 66 logo, sent off a batch to Icahn and stuck in the message "Have a Heart." The Leighton Venn Photography Studio posted a sign: I CAHN/ YOU CAHN/ WE ALL CAHN/ LICK ICAHN.

It was mostly for naught. Pounded almost daily by Icahn's newspaper ads, Phillips shareholders became convinced that they were being shortchanged. In a vote last month on the plan to restructure the company's finances, they rejected the deal that Phillips management had struck with Pickens. Icahn was thus able to pursue his bid for the company.

Backed into a corner, the Phillips board huddled on Sunday, March 3, and came up with a sweetener that finally satisfied Icahn. It offered to swap IOUs with a face value of $62 each for half of Phillips' outstanding shares. The plan would add $4.5 billion to Phillips' corporate debt, raising it to $7.3 billion. That would equal 75% of the firm's total worth, well above the typical 40% to 50% level for American industry.

Although analysts predicted that the debt package would be worth only about $55 a share once the securities started trading, Icahn declared victory and withdrew. "We're delighted about the outcome," he said. "Now I think it is a fair deal." Pickens chose to sell his 8.9 million shares back to the company at the $53 price that he had been promised last December. It was about time, said Pickens, that Phillips came around, instead of acting like a "mother handing a lollipop to her children one piece at a time."

Phillips Chairman Douce conceded that the debt is "higher than what's comfortable, based on the way we were raised around here." He stressed that the company had assumed a "manageable" burden. To cut debt, Phillips plans to sell about $2 billion worth of assets. Among the possibilities: the company's stake in the Ekofisk field in the North Sea, worth as much as $1.5 billion.

As the winners picked up their chips last week, there were judgments about what the Phillips drama meant not only to the oil business but to corporate America. To William Higgins, a Value Line oil stocks analyst, the fight for Phillips reflected profound changes in the U.S. economy. The raiders, he says, "are prying money loose for better investment. This has happened in every mature industry as long as there has been a stock market." To Icahn, the biggest winners were ordinary Americans, whose pensions are managed by the institutional investors who voted against the initial Phillips offer. That showed, he said, that shareholders "can stand up to the corporate establishments and get a better deal."

Takeovers in the oil industry are likely to go on "as long as you have undervalued assets," according to Joseph Fogg III of the New York investment banking firm Morgan Stanley. For its part, Phillips can rest easy. Pickens promised not to launch a new battle for the company for at least 15 years, and Icahn agreed to stay away for eight. But those may be meaningless pledges. With all its new debt, Phillips has lost much of its luster as a takeover target.

—By John S. DeMott. Reported by Lee Griggs/Bartlesville and Frederick Ungeheuer/New York

18

International Financial Management

Overview

In this chapter we shall examine the international aspects of financial management. Much of this discussion will be focused on the importance of foreign exchange rates. What are foreign exchange rates? How are foreign exchange rates determined? Why are foreign exchange rates the foremost issue in international financial management? How can management deal with the problems caused by exchange rates? A number of other international financial management topics will also be considered ∎

Objectives

By the end of this chapter the student should be able to:

1. Describe the importance of international business to the United States
2. Understand the role of the financial manager in international business
3. Explain foreign exchange rate risk exposure
4. Arrange ways to hedge foreign exchange rate risk exposure
5. Explain the basic elements that are involved in a foreign trade transaction
6. Describe the rewards and risks facing multinational corporations
7. Discuss the major types of foreign investment and financing
8. Understand the reasons for and determinants of foreign exchange rates

Introduction_____

United States corporations are more heavily involved in international business today than at any time in the country's history. Foreign products are to be found everywhere and articles on America's international competitiveness abound. More and more U.S. companies are aggressively pursuing foreign markets. Financial markets and institutions from around the world are becoming more integrated and open, due to government deregulation and improvements in communications technology. Even words like "Eurodollars" are becoming household names. We will study the important role of financial management in international business. We will also examine the prominent institutional arrangements and organizations that affect international financial management■

International Business

U.S. international business transactions fall into one of two categories: *foreign trade* and *foreign capital flows.*

Foreign trade consists of *imports* and *exports.* U.S. imports are purchases of foreign-made goods and services by U.S. residents. U.S. exports are sales of American-made goods and services to residents of foreign countries. American imports and exports are recorded in *Balance of Payments Accounts* by the U.S. Department of Commerce. We are said to have a balance of payments *trade deficit* when imports exceed exports. Conversely, a balance of payments *trade surplus* exists whenever exports are greater than imports. An indication as to the size and direction of foreign trade is shown in figure 18.1.

Exports have grown from $44 billion in 1971 to over $220 billion in 1984. During that same period, imports have increased from $46 billion to $327 billion. Exports constituted about 6% of gross national product at the end of 1984. Clearly, the U.S. has had few trade surpluses since 1970. Not only are trade deficits the order of the day, but they have been growing, to a record $107 billion in 1984.

Foreign capital flows are comprised of investments in foreign countries and fund-raising abroad. U.S. corporations invest directly abroad when they: (1) construct new facilities outside the U.S.; (2) acquire existing foreign businesses by merger or consolidation; (3) enter into joint ventures with foreign-based corporations. Foreign investment by American corporations since 1971 is revealed in figure 18.2. U.S. corporations also invest abroad when they purchase securities in foreign money markets.

U.S. firms acquire financing from foreign nations when they: (1) sell stocks and bonds in foreign capital markets; (2) arrange loans with foreign banks; (3) receive an injection of funds from a foreign parent company or joint venture partner based abroad. Although composite statistics on foreign-fund raising are sparse, all indications point to an increasing reliance on it by American businesses.

Figure 18.1   United States exports and imports, 1971–1984

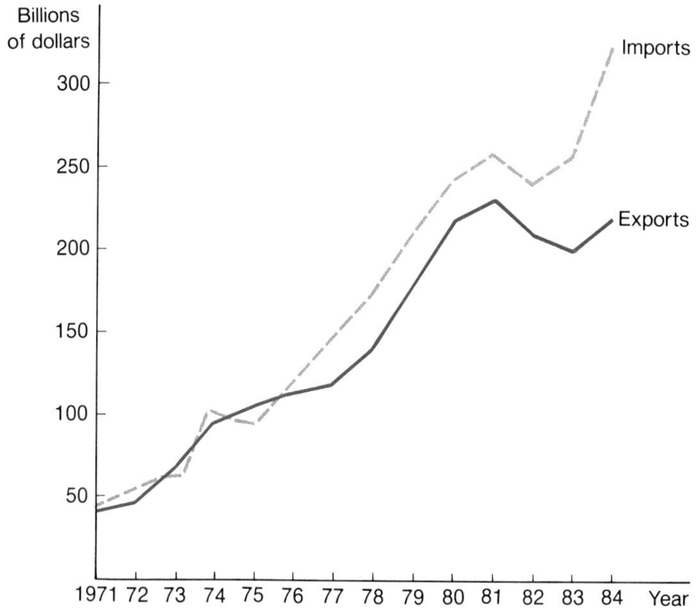

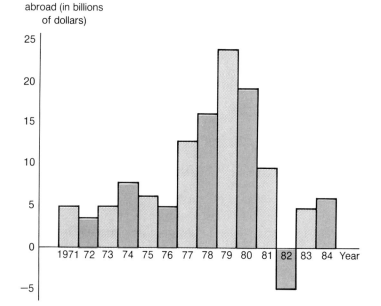

Source: Various issues of the *Federal Reserve Bulletin*, Board of Governors of the Federal Reserve System, Washington, D.C.

Figure 18.2   Direct investments by U.S. corporations in foreign countries, 1971–1984

Source: Various issues of *Survey of Current Business*, Bureau of Economic Analysis, United States Department of Commerce, Washington, D.C.

The Study of International Financial Management

Foreign trade and capital flows can involve a corporation in the standard kinds of financial management activities, such as: capital budgeting, cash management, credit management, financial forecasting, and fund raising. However, international financial management must contend with several complicating factors, which are not found when dealing with purely domestic financial matters. The most widespread complication revolves around the fact that each country has its own monetary system and monetary standard (i.e., currency). That is, the United States has the Federal Reserve System and the dollar; West Germany has the Bundesbank and the mark; and Great Britain has the Bank of England and the pound. As a group, all of these monies are referred to as foreign currencies or foreign exchange. The fact that the supply of each currency is controlled independently of the others usually results in the monies having different values. Consequently, foreign currencies are normally not on a par with one another. That is, one dollar ≠ one pound ≠ one mark. This gives rise to the need for exchange rates between foreign currencies. As we shall discover in the ensuing discussion, exchange rates can be quite troublesome. Another unique aspect of international business is the complicated process by which goods are traded, when the parties are in different nations. Financial management on the international level must also contend with the laws and politics of foreign nations. We shall return to the latter two issues later in the chapter. For now our attention will be centered on the all-important subject of foreign exchange rates.

Foreign Exchange Rates

Most international business transactions give rise to currency exchanges.[1] For example, U.S. dollars are exchanged for French francs, West German marks are exchanged for Japanese yen, and so forth. Other international transactions are priced out in terms of one currency for another. All such foreign currency exchanges and translations are carried out at specified rates, thus the term foreign exchange rates. *An exchange rate is the price of one currency in terms of another currency.* Table 18.1 contains several foreign exchange rates as of January, 1985. This particular quotation sheet gives foreign currency prices in terms of one United States dollar. Take, for example, the exchange rate between the Indian rupee and U.S. dollar (rupee/dollar) of 12.612. This means that in January 1985, 12.612 rupees equaled 1 U.S. dollar. Accordingly, the dollar/rupee exchange rate is the inverse of 12.612, or .079. Notice the extreme variation in exchange rates that are shown in table 18.1. At one extreme is the South African rand/U.S. dollar exchange rate of .4634. At the other extreme is the Brazil cruzeiro/U.S. dollar exchange rate of 3346.67. This is not a misprint, in January 1985 it required 3,346.67 cruzeiro to buy one dollar. From these figures we can solve for the cruzeiro/rand exchange rate, since the dollar is a common denominator. Thus, 3,346.67 cruzeiro equal .4634 rand, which is a cruzeiro/rand exchange rate of 7,222.

From a financial management standpoint, the wide disparity in exchange rates is not nearly as important as the fact that they change over time. For instance, the yen/dollar rate of

---

[1]The word currency is used in the broad sense here to include checking accounts denominated in a particular nation's money.

**Table 18.1   Selected Foreign Exchange Rates: January 1985
(Currency units per U.S. dollar)**

Country/Currency	Exchange Rate
Australia/dollar	.8151
Austria/schilling	22.2670
Belgium/franc	63.4550
Brazil/cruzeiro	3346.6700
Canada/dollar	1.3240
China, P.R./yuan	2.8160
Denmark/krone	11.3300
Finland/markka	6.6368
France/franc	9.7036
Germany/mark	3.1706
Greece/drachma	129.3800
Hong Kong/dollar	7.8110
India/rupee	12.6120
Ireland/pound	.9823
Israel/shekel	n.a.
Italy/lira	1948.7600
Japan/yen	254.1800
Malaysia/ringgit	2.4804
Mexico/peso	227.5600
Netherlands/guilder	3.5819
New Zealand/dollar	.4704
Norway/krone	9.1765
Phillipines/peso	n.a.
Portugal/escudo	172.5600
Singapore/dollar	2.2011
South Africa/rand	.4634
South Korea/won	832.1600
Spain/peseta	175.1300
Sri Lanka/rupee	26.3920
Sweden/krona	9.0716
Switzerland/franc	2.6590
Taiwan/dollar	39.2090
Thailand/baht	27.3300
United Kingdom/pound	1.1271
Venezuela/bolivar	n.a.

Source: *Federal Reserve Bulletin*, Board of Governors of the Federal Reserve System, Washington, D.C. (April 1985), pp. A68.

exchange might be 250 on one day and 280 a month later. Before we examine the implications of fluctuating exchange rates, it is well to review the major determinants of foreign exchange rates.

Determinants of Foreign Exchange Rates   The rate of exchange between one nation's currency and another's is determined largely by supply and demand in the *foreign exchange market*.[2] The foreign exchange market is a loosely knit trading system made up of exporters, importers, speculators, foreign investors, and international bankers. These individuals buy and sell foreign currencies for themselves as well as others. Most of the trading is carried

[2]Government interference in foreign exchange markets can disrupt the forces of supply and demand.

out in the big money centers of the world, such as Paris, New York, Tokyo, London, and Zurich. Each of these markets, in turn, is connected electronically. There are a number of factors that underlie the supply of and demand for a particular country's money in relation to another nation's money.

The most important factor underlying an exchange rate is the relative price level of goods and services between two countries. Let us assume, for example, that a representative basket of goods and services sells for 80,000 rupees in India. The same basket of goods and services sells for 2,500 dollars in the United States. All other things the same, the exchange rate of rupees for dollars should be 32 since this rate corresponds to the price level ratio of 80,000 rupees to 2,500 dollars. Supply and demand can be expected to react if the rupee/dollar exchange rate is not 32. A rate of 40, for example, would mean that Indian goods and services are now cheaper than American products (the dollar is said to be overvalued). In an effort to buy more of the relatively less expensive Indian products, Americans must purchase more rupees with dollars. Thus, the increased demand for rupees (increased supply of dollars) will raise the price of the former and reduce the price of the latter until the bargains disappear, which will occur at an exchange rate of 32.[3] Should the relative price levels of these countries change, so should the exchange rate. If the inflation rates in two nations are unequal, the exchange rate will move against the country with the highest inflation.

Interest rate differentials between two countries can also have a sizable effect on the exchange rate.[4] The reason being that differences in interest rates can influence capital flows between two countries. Capital will flow from the low interest rate nation to the high interest rate nation. The additional demand for investments in the high interest rate country will be accompanied by an increased demand for that nation's currency. The exact opposite takes place in the low interest rate country. These demand-supply shifts should move the exchange rate to a point where there is no longer an advantage to invest in the high interest rate nation. However, any further changes in relative interest rates can be expected to produce additional exchange rate movements.[5]

Foreign Exchange Rate Risk Exposure   Earlier it was pointed out that foreign exchange rates fluctuate over time, often dramatically so. Two examples of this can be seen in figure 18.3. Shown here are the French franc/American dollar and German mark/American dollar exchange rates during the year 1984. The franc/dollar exchange rate not only trended upward during the year, but also fluctuated considerably from month to month. It hit a low of 8.0022 (i.e., eight francs to the dollar) in March and a high of 9.5083 some nine months later. On a percentage basis, the high point was 18.8% above the low figure. Although not as visually apparent, the mark/dollar exchange rate exhibited even more variation. From a low of 2.5973 marks to the dollar in March, it rose to 3.1044 in December, for a percentage increase of 19.5%.

---

[3]Transportation costs between nations as well as government trade restrictions (i.e., quotas and tariffs) can prevent an exchange rate from achieving parity with relative price levels.

[4]We are referring here to equivalent interest rates. Interest rates, that is, that have been adjusted for income taxes, expected inflation, and risk.

[5]For a more comprehensive discussion of the theory underlying exchange rates, see Milton Friedman, "The Case for Flexible Exchange Rates," in *Essays in Positive Economics,* University of Chicago Press, Chicago, Ill., 1953.

Figure 18.3   Movements in the French Franc/U.S. Dollar and West German Mark/U.S. Dollar exchange rates during 1984

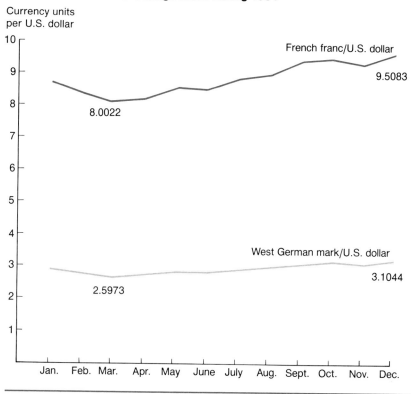

Source: Various issues of the *Federal Reserve Bulletin*, Board of Governors of the Federal Reserve System, Washington, D.C.

Foreign trade and capital flows are exposed to a certain amount of risk, because of foreign exchange rate fluctuations and the inability to accurately forecast these movements. Importers are uncertain as to what they will pay, exporters are uncertain as to how much they will receive and likewise for foreign borrowers and investors. We will now investigate foreign exchange rate risk exposure through the use of examples.

Example A: Texacom, Inc., is one of America's largest manufacturers of television sets. The firm made its own picture tubes up until three years ago at which time it began purchasing them from lower cost Japanese companies. On April 15, 1986, Texacom's purchasing department contracted to buy 230,000 picture tubes from Kyguo Electronics, Ltd., at a unit price of 400 Japanese yen, or a total cost of 92,000,000 yen. Based on the April 15 yen/dollar exchange rate of four, the dollar cost of the shipment amounts to 92,000,000 ÷ 4 = $23,000,000. According to the terms of the contract, payment is to be made in yen and it is due sixty days after the shipment is received by Texacom. Given that it will take approximately thirty days to produce and ship the tubes, there is a time lapse of ninety days from the April 15 signing of the contract until payment is to be made. Let us assume that during this ninety day interval the yen/dollar exchange rate falls, and on July 15 (the payment date) rests at 3.2 yen to the dollar. At the lower rate, 92,000,000 yen will cost Texacom

92,000,000 ÷ 3.2 = $28,750,000, not the $23,000,000 as originally expected. The additional expense of $5,750,000 could create a real hardship for Texacom. If, on the other hand, the exchange rate rises, to say 4.6, the American importer would end up paying less than $23,000,000. Not knowing what the exchange rate will be in ninety days is the source of Texacom's risk exposure[6] ■

Example B: Virginia Southern, a U.S. railroad freight company, has $10,000,000 of cash on hand which will not be needed for about six months. One possible outlet for these funds is a six month certificate of deposit (CD) in a U.S. bank, currently yielding 8%. Alternatively, banks in France are offering six month CDs paying 10%. Virginia Southern's treasurer opts for the higher yielding French CDs. He converts the $10,000,000 into francs at the current franc/dollar exchange rate of eight and buys French CDs worth 80,000,000 francs. When the CDs mature in six months, Virginia Southern will receive 88,000,000 francs (i.e., principal plus interest of .10 × 80,000,000 = 8,000,000). If the exchange rate is unchanged, the firm will be able to convert the francs back into 88,000,000 ÷ 8 = $11,000,000. However, should the exchange rate increase to, say, nine, Virginia Southern will realize only 88,000,000 ÷ 9 = $9,777,777 from the 88,000,000 francs. In the latter case, the firm would not even get a full return of its principal, let alone any interest. Such an adverse outcome can be avoided if Virginia Southern invests in American marketable securities ■

As the two examples above clearly indicate, foreign exchange rate fluctuations add an element of risk to international business dealings that is not found in one's own country. Several methods are available to help manage this risk exposure, and it is to these we now turn.

Hedging Foreign Exchange Risk Exposure   In many cases, foreign exchange rate risk exposure can be hedged. *Hedging* is the process of insuring against adverse price changes, and it is employed in those areas where prices fluctuate dramatically, such as: agricultural commodities, interest rates, petroleum, and foreign exchange. A failure to protect against such price fluctuations is termed *speculation. A perfect hedge can be defined as follows: simultaneously taking opposite and equal positions in the same item.* The item in this case happens to be a foreign currency. Opposite positions means that one is both *long* (has acquired an item or agreed to acquire it at a later date) and *short* (has delivered an item or agreed to deliver it at a later date). Simultaneous means that the opposite positions should be taken on the same day or even same minute, in order to achieve a more perfect hedge. Finally, the opposite positions must be in exactly the same item and for precisely the same quantities, or a perfect hedge will not exist. For one reason or another, a perfect hedge may not be possible. But even with a less than perfect hedge, considerable protection can be afforded.

Referring back to example A of the previous section, a U.S. importer agreed on April 15, 1985, to deliver (i.e., go short) 92 million Japanese yen in ninety days. In order to hedge this commitment, the importer should simultaneously arrange to acquire (go long) 92 million yen. By taking opposite positions such as this, the importer is insured against the risk of a

---

[6]The Japanese firm in this example is not exposed to foreign exchange rate risk, simply because the contract is written in its currency.

significant decline in the yen/dollar exchange rate over the next ninety days. The trick to hedging is being able to find an equal, opposite, and identical position at a reasonable cost. Fortunately, there are a number of hedging vehicles available in the foreign exchange area. The three most commonly used are forward exchange rate markets, foreign money markets, and currency swaps.

Hedging in the Forward Exchange Rate Market

Most foreign currency conversions are handled by the foreign currency trading departments of large international banks. These institutions are concentrated in the financial centers of the world (e.g., Paris, New York, London, and Tokyo). Exporters, importers, foreign investors, and speculators use these facilities to exchange foreign monies. International banks also trade with one another in an interconnected, world-wide, foreign exchange market. It is in this arena that the forces of supply and demand come to bear most heavily on foreign exchange rates. As a rule, the exchange rates quoted by one bank will be identical to those quoted by other banks. If this is not the case, *arbitragers* will move in to profit from the discrepancies, and in the process bring about market equilibrium.

International banks offer two types of exchange rates, spot and forward.[7] Current day trading is done at *spot market exchange rates*. Future trading is done at *forward market exchange rates*. Forward exchange rates are nothing more than contracts to trade currencies on some future day, but at a prearranged rate. Table 18.2 contains selected spot and forward exchange rates in terms of the U.S. dollar, as quoted by New York–based Banker's Trust Company on May 1, 1985. The 30, 90, and 180-day periods for forward rates are fairly standard. The differentials among spot and forward rates can be attributed to market expectations as to what spot rates will be on a future date. In this instance, the market apparently feels that the yen, Swiss franc, and mark will appreciate against the dollar over the next six months, while the pound, Canadian dollar, and French franc should depreciate. Forward markets can be used to hedge exchange rate risk exposure, as the following example illustrates.[8]

Example: An American movie producer (exporter) agrees on May 1, 1985, to sell some movie rights to a British chain of theaters (importer). The selling price is 5 million pounds. According to the sales contract, payment will be made in British pounds, and it is due in three months. The exporter is clearly exposed to foreign exchange rate risk for two reasons: it will receive payment in a foreign currency (long in pounds), and the payment is not due for ninety days. Based on the spot pound/dollar exchange rate shown in table 18.2, the exporter would receive 5,000,000 ÷ .8170 = $6,119,951, if paid on May 1. However, it is difficult to say how many dollars will be obtained from the 5 million pounds in three months. Fearing an adverse movement in the spot exchange rate, the exporter can hedge its risk by entering into a ninety-day forward contract to exchange pounds for dollars (go short in pounds) at the pound/dollar rate of .8251. This transaction would assure the receipt of 5,000,000 ÷ .8251 = $6,059,872 on August 1, 1985. The difference between what could be obtained

[7]Forward rates may not be offered for inactively traded currencies.
[8]Foreign exchange futures markets are also used to hedge certain foreign currencies. One of the more important futures markets is the International Monetary Market, located within the Chicago Mercantile Exchange.

Table 18.2   Selected Spot and Forward Foreign Exchange Rates in Terms of U.S. Dollar May 1, 1985

British Pound	dollar/pound	pound/dollar
Spot	1.2240	.8170
30-day forward	1.2197	.8199
90-day forward	1.2120	.8251
180-day forward	1.2040	.8306

French Franc	dollar/franc	franc/dollar
Spot	.1045	9.5700
30-day forward	.1043	9.5845
90-day forward	.1040	9.6120
180-day forward	.1036	9.6490

Japanese Yen	dollar/yen	yen/dollar
Spot	.003957	252.70
30-day forward	.003965	252.18
90-day forward	.003982	251.15
180-day forward	.004010	249.33

Swiss Franc	dollar/franc	franc/dollar
Spot	.3791	2.6375
30-day forward	.3803	2.6296
90-day forward	.3826	2.6136
180-day forward	.3865	2.5870

German Mark	dollar/mark	mark/dollar
Spot	.3179	3.1460
30-day forward	.3186	3.1388
90-day forward	.3202	3.1234
180-day forward	.3227	3.0985

Canadian Dollar	U.S.$/Can.$	Can.$/U.S.$
Spot	.7310	1.3680
30-day forward	.7303	1.3693
90-day forward	.7289	1.3719
180-day forward	.7264	1.3767

in the May 1 spot market and what will be received in the forward market, or $6,119,951 − $6,059,872 = $60,079, is the cost of hedging. On an annualized percentage basis, the cost is as follows:

$$\text{Cost of Hedging} = \frac{\$60,079}{\$6,119,951} \times \frac{360 \text{ days}}{90 \text{ days}} = .0393 \text{ or } 3.93\%$$

The significance of this computation is described below ■

Hedging in the Foreign Money Markets   Foreign money markets are a hedging alternative to the forward exchange markets. The U.S. exporter of the previous example could have hedged its exchange rate risk exposure in the foreign money markets, as follows.

A ninety-day loan for 5 million pounds is obtained on May 1 from a British bank. The pounds are immediately converted into dollars by the exporter at the May 1 spot exchange rate. The next step is to invest the $6,119,951 in U.S. three-month money market securities. The exporter will then repay the British bank loan in three months with the 5 million pound proceeds from the movie rights sale. Here we have equal and opposite positions in British pounds that will offset one another. The exporter is left with the U.S. money market security. There is only one real problem with this hedging procedure, and it concerns the differential in money market interest rates between the two countries. If interest rates in Great Britain exceed those in the U.S., the exporter will suffer as a result, simply because the firm is borrowing in the high interest rate country and investing in the low interest rate country. Let us assume that May 1 money market rates are 12% in Great Britain and 9% in the United States. The 3% differential is the cost of this hedge, and it should be compared to the percentage cost of hedging on the forward exchange market, shown earlier to be 3.93%. In this example, the money market hedge is cheaper than the forward market hedge. As a matter of fact, the costs of these two alternative hedging techniques will seldom be so far apart. Arbitragers will see to it that spot-forward exchange rate differentials maintain *parity* with interest rate differentials.[9]

Hedging with Foreign Currency Swaps   An increasingly popular hedging technique is the *currency swap*. At its simplest level, two parties agree to exchange two different currencies at a later date. For instance, an American exporter is due to receive German marks in two months, while an American importer is obligated to deliver marks in two months. On learning of their asymmetrical needs, the importer agrees to swap dollars for the exporter's marks some sixty days hence. They both get what they want.

Foreign Trade Transactions

The general characteristics of a foreign trade transaction are best explained by means of an example.

Ameritech Corporation, a U.S. electronics firm, produces telephone equipment for sale to the American and European telecommunications industry. On June 20, 1985, Ameritech arranges to sell $6 million worth of telephone equipment to a British firm, Brit, Ltd. The key terms of the contract are as follows: (1) the goods will be shipped on July 5, 1985; (2) payment is to be made in British pounds at the spot exchange rate prevailing on June 20, 1985; (3) payment is due within ninety days after receipt of the goods; (4) the importer must provide the exporter with a letter of credit from a reputable bank; (5) the importer will pay all shipping, handling, and insurance costs.

Given a June 20, 1985, pound/dollar exchange rate of .75, Brit, Ltd., is obligated to pay Ameritech .75 × 6,000,000 = 4,500,000 pounds under the terms of the contract. (Note: All foreign exchange risk exposure rests with the exporter in this example.) The importer must also apply for a *letter of credit* from its bank, London National. In the letter of credit, the bank agrees to provide Brit, Ltd., with the necessary funds to pay Ameritech at the end of the credit period. Having a bank endorsement such as this reduces the credit risk for the

---

[9]The concept of parity, as used in international finance, is described with considerable detail in J. L. Stein, "The Forward Rate and the Interest Parity," *Review of Economic Studies*, April, 1965, pp. 113–26.

exporter. Assuming all goes well, London National will send the letter of credit to Ameritech's bank, First Chicago, which then forwards it to Ameritech. Upon receipt of the document, the exporter can confidently ship the goods to Great Britain. Ameritech will receive a signed *bill of lading* from the shipping company as receipt for the goods. This document controls the right to claim the goods at their destination. The exporter could send the bill of lading to Brit, Ltd., thereby enabling the importer to claim the goods on their arrival, and wait to be paid. More than likely, however, Ameritech will create a *draft* on London National using the letter of credit as authorization. A draft (also called a bill of exchange) is really nothing more than a specialized check. It orders a bank to pay a specified sum of money, to a certain party, on a given date. Ameritech's draft orders London National Bank to pay 4,500,000 pounds to Ameritech Corporation in ninety days (i.e., equal to the credit period). Ameritech will have First Chicago forward the draft, bill of lading, and a copy of the letter of credit to London National. Brit, Ltd., is then notified by its bank when the documents arrive. In order to obtain the bill of lading from London National, Brit must promise to pay for the goods ninety days after they arrive, as stipulated in the original contract. Assuming everything is in order, London National will accept the draft, thus making it a *banker's acceptance.* In the form of a banker's acceptance, a draft becomes a marketable security and is treated much like commercial paper. Should Ameritech want its money now, rather than wait ninety days, the firm can sell the acceptance in the British money market. Assuming an annual interest rate of 12%, the acceptance could be sold immediately, at a discounted price of:

$$\text{Value of Banker's Acceptance} = \frac{4{,}500{,}000 \text{ pounds}}{1.03} = 4{,}368{,}930 \text{ pounds}$$

If not sold, the acceptance will be sent to Ameritech, via First Chicago Bank. Once the goods arrive in England, Brit, Ltd., will use the bill of lading to take delivery. The entire transaction is completed ninety days later when the banker's acceptance is paid by London National, which in turn collects from Brit, Ltd.

From the foregoing example, it is clear that banks are heavily involved in foreign trade. Moreover, three documents loom very large: letter of credit, bill of lading, and bank draft. A schematic diagram of the preceding example is shown in figure 18.4.

Foreign Investment

American corporations invest huge sums of money abroad. A portion of this capital flow consists of money market investments in such things as foreign bank certificates of deposit and foreign government treasury bills. Yields on foreign marketable securities often exceed the yields on comparable U.S. marketable securities. However, as we saw earlier, exchange rate risk exposure is inherent in such investments, unless hedging is employed. *Eurodollars* are another avenue for foreign investment, but without the exchange rate risk. Eurodollars are dollar-denominated deposits held in commercial banks located outside the U.S., principally in Europe. By and large, these banks are correspondents or branches of U.S. banks. Yields on these short-term investments are quite attractive, because the market for them is very competitive and, for the most part, unregulated by any government. Eurodollars are discussed briefly in chapter 6.

Figure 18.4   Typical steps that are taken in a foreign trade transaction, beginning with the sales contract

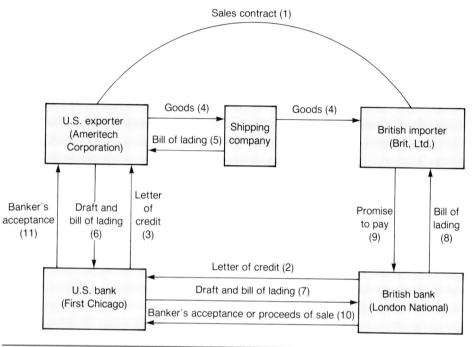

In addition to money market capital flows, there are also the direct investments of *multinational corporations*. A multinational corporation is one with commercial or manufacturing subsidiaries located in more than one country. The parent corporation will have its headquarters in one nation.

Benefits of Multinational Corporations   Corporations expand internationally for many reasons:

1. A labor-intensive business might set up operations in a nation having an abundant supply of relatively cheap labor.
2. It is difficult to export goods and services into some nations, because of tariffs or quotas. In order to circumvent these trade restrictions, a company may decide to produce its product inside the protected nation. Take, for example, the location of Japanese auto plants in the U.S.
3. In an effort to escape government regulation of an activity, a company may be able to form a subsidiary that can perform the task in a nation with less-stringent regulations.
4. Although rarely a determining factor in its own right, transportation costs can certainly contribute to a company's decision to expand overseas.

5. A firm may be accorded diversification benefits by strategically locating subsidiaries around the world. The reasoning runs as follows: national economies are not alike, and no two of them experience identical business cycles. Thus, an internationally diversified company could benefit from a situation where the economic troubles of one nation are offset by the economic fortunes of other nations.

Risks Facing Multinational Corporations   Multinational corporations are exposed to special risk factors in addition to those faced by purely domestic corporations. The most common of these risk factors are:

1. The customs, mores, and laws of each nation are different, sometimes dramatically so. A company that wishes to do business in foreign lands must be prepared to experience the problems brought about by unfamiliar surroundings.
2. Multinational companies must contend with political changes in their host countries, particularly with regard to those nations whose recent history is replete with political instability. For instance, a multinational's South American subsidiary might awaken one morning to discover that, for exchange rate reasons, it can no longer transfer money back to headquarters. In the worst case scenario, a subsidiary might be nationalized (i.e., seized) by a host country, which has experienced a radical change in government.
3. American accounting rules require U.S.-based multinational parent companies to translate their subsidiaries' assets and liabilities into dollars, when constructing consolidated financial statements. The translation is made at the prevailing spot exchange rate. Given the variability of exchange rates, translation gains or losses are likely to occur. These gains and losses must be reported on a multinational's consolidated income statement.

Example: A French subsidiary of a U.S.-based multinational presently has assets with a book value of eighty million francs and liabilities with a book value of sixty-four million francs. Translating at the current franc/dollar exchange rate of eight, the respective values would be as follows: assets = \$10 million and liabilities = \$8 million, for a net worth of \$2 million. Let us assume the exchange rate rises to ten francs equal one dollar by the next reporting period. Accordingly, the newly translated values will be lower, thus: assets = \$8 million and liabilities = \$6.4 million, for a net worth of \$1.6 million. The \$.4 million loss of net worth (i.e., 2 million minus 1.6 million) since the last reporting period must be recorded on the consolidated income statement. On the other hand, a fall in the exchange rate would produce a translation gain. Such gains and losses, even though they tend to average out over time, are very disturbing to multinational companies. In particular, they dislike the fluctuations in reported net income that are brought about by foreign exchange translations[10] ■

[10]For a discussion of the issues and remedies surrounding foreign exchange translations in relation to multinational companies see Janice M. Westerfield, "How U.S. Multinationals Manage Currency Risk," *Business Review*, Federal Reserve Bank of Philadelphia, March–April, 1980, pp. 19–27.

Foreign Financing

Many American companies, both multinational and others, raise funds in the international money and capital markets. Commercial banks located outside of the United States, principally Europe, are the major foreign lenders to U.S. businesses. They extend commercial and term loans denominated in dollars as well as foreign currencies. The principal source of dollar-denominated loans are the Eurodollar deposits described earlier. Many of these foreign banks are branches of U.S. banks, while others are affiliated with U.S. banks.

A number of large, well-known U.S. corporations have discovered over the last several years that an international market exists for their bond issues. Although not large by U.S. standards, this market is important and growing. Firms have found they can often obtain lower interest costs on foreign bond issues, primarily due to the lack of government regulation in this market sphere. International investment banking syndicates are formed to sell these bond issues, not only in Europe, but throughout the world. A distinction is usually made between U.S. corporate bonds sold for foreign currencies—*Eurobonds,* and those sold for dollars—*Eurodollar Bonds.*

Before leaving this section, some mention should be made of the *Export-Import Bank.* The Export-Import Bank is an independent agency of the U.S. Government, whose major purpose is to facilitate the financing of American exports. Also known as the EX-IM Bank, this organization extends and guarantees loans in connection with the export of American goods and services. Most of its loans are used to finance the foreign customers of certain qualified U.S. exporters.

Summary _____

American corporations are more heavily involved in international business today than at any time in the country's history. U.S. international business transactions fall into one of two categories: foreign trade and foreign capital flows. Foreign trade and capital flows can involve a business in a variety of financial management activities, including: capital budgeting, cash management, and fund raising.

International financial management must contend with several complicating factors that are not found with domestic financial matters. The most widespread complication concerns foreign exchange rates, or to be more specific, fluctuations in foreign exchange rates. The rate of exchange between one nation's currency and another's is determined largely by the forces of supply and demand in the foreign exchange market. Fluctuations in exchange rates increase the risk of foreign trade, investment, and fund raising. Although financial managers have at their disposal a number of methods to manage this risk, these procedures are costly and require a great deal of time to implement. Another unique aspect of international business is the complicated process by which goods are traded between quite distant and sovereign nations. Financial management on the international level must also contend with the laws, customs, and politics of foreign countries. Without question, two of the major participants in the international business community are international bankers and multinational companies ▪

Key Terms/Concepts

Arbitrage
Balance of payments
Banker's acceptance
Bill of lading
Currency swap
Draft
Eurobonds
Eurodollars
Exchange rate risk exposure

Export-Import Bank
Exports
Foreign capital flows
Foreign exchange market
Foreign exchange rates
Foreign trade
Forward foreign exchange
 market

Hedging
Imports
Letter of credit
Multinational Corporation
Parity
Speculation
Spot foreign exchange market

Questions

1. What is meant by the term parity?

2. Describe the relationship between a country's inflation rate and the exchange rate of its currency.

3. Your family is planning a trip to France in about six months. Presently, the dollar is relatively strong versus the French franc, thereby implying that French products and services are relatively good bargains. How can you lock in the high-dollar exchange rate for six months, without using the foreign exchange forward markets?

4. How do commercial bank letters of credit contribute to foreign trade?

5. Interest rates in a country fall dramatically in a short time period. All other things the same, what would you expect to happen to the exchange value of this nation's currency?

6. Describe the U.S. balance of payments from 1976 through 1984.

7. Briefly define the following terms: Eurodollars, banker's acceptance, and hedging.

Problems

1. Shown below are several foreign exchange rates:

    mark/guilder = 6, lira/rupee = .850, yen/guilder = 45

    Using the exchange rates shown above, determine the following exchange rates:
    A. guilder/mark
    B. rupee/lira
    C. guilder/yen
    D. mark/yen

2. Using the exchange rates shown in table 18.1, work the following problems:
    A. How many Swedish krona can be acquired for 150,000 U.S. dollars?
    B. An Olivetti typewriter is selling for 585,000 lira in a Rome department store. What would an American tourist pay for this product in dollars?
    C. What is the German mark/Mexican peso exchange rate?
    D. How many U.S. dollars can be purchased for one million French francs?

3. West Germany based Gerhardt's, Ltd., is a wholly owned subsidiary of Micro Tech, Inc., a large computer products firm headquartered in the United States. Gerhardt's most recent balance sheet is displayed below:

Gerhardt's, Ltd., Balance Sheet (figures are in thousands of marks)

Cash	225,000	Accounts payable	650,000
Accounts receivable	800,000	Accrued wages	150,000
Inventory	750,000	Notes payable	400,000
Property, plant &		Bonds	1,200,000
equipment	1,650,000	Common stockholder equity	1,025,000
Total assets	3,425,000	Total liabilities and stockholder equity	3,425,000

Required:
  A. Given the spot mark/dollar exchange rate of four, translate Gerhardt's asset and liability accounts into dollars.
  B. Retranslate the assets and liabilities, assuming that the spot mark/dollar exchange rate rises to 4.5 in a short period of time.
  C. As a result of the exchange rate movement in B, what impact will there be on Micro Tech's consolidated earnings report.

4. Is there an opportunity for arbitrage profit in the following set of spot exchange rates, which were taken from selected markets on the same date.

Tokyo market	yen/rupee	1.497
Bombay market	mark/yen	.545
London market	dollar/pound	2.820
Paris market	rupee/franc	.663
Zurich market	franc/mark	1.669

5. An American importer of Toyota automobiles has contracted with several U.S. auto dealers to sell them the next shipment of cars, which are due to arrive in three months. Assuming the importer will pay for the shipment at the time of delivery, how could the firm protect itself against exposure to foreign exchange rate risk.

6. Pomark Manufacturing has just received a banker's acceptance in connection with an export sale to West Germany. The acceptance has a face value of 80 million marks and matures in ninety days. Given a current money market interest rate in Germany of 18%, how many marks would Pomark receive if it sold the acceptance on the market today?

7. Loomis Corporation, an American-based pharmaceutical firm, is looking to invest $5 million in excess cash for six months. Money market interest rates in New York and London are 10% and 14%, respectively. The spot dollar/pound exchange rate is 1.25. Assuming the $5 million is invested in the London market, work the following problems:
  A. How will the investment fare if the spot exchange rate is 1.32 in six months? Show all calculations.
  B. How will the investment fare if the spot exchange rate is 1.15 in six months? Show all calculations.
  C. Solve for the 180-day forward exchange rate that Loomis could use to hedge the London interest rate such that the two of them combined equaled the New York interest rate.

8. An American importer is scheduled to pay a Japanese supplier 850 million yen in three months. Current yen/dollar exchange rates are shown below:

Spot rate	245
30-day forward rate	240
90-day forward rate	230
180-day forward rate	225

A. How many dollars would the American company spend if payment were due today?
B. How many dollars will the American company spend if the spot rate in ninety days is 220 and the exchange rate risk exposure is not hedged.
C. What is the cost of a ninety-day forward hedge, in both dollar and percentage terms?
D. Discuss the possible reasons for the forward decline in the yen/dollar exchange rate.

Selected References

Aliber, Robert Z., *Exchange Risk and Corporate International Finance.* New York: Wiley 1978.
Davis, Steven I., "How Risky is International Lending?" *Harvard Business Review* (January–February 1977), pp. 135–43.
Eiteman, D. K., and A. I. Stonehill, *Multinational Business Finance,* 3d ed., Reading, Mass.: Addison-Wesley, 1982.
Folks, William R., Jr., and Ramesh Advani, "Raising Funds with Foreign Currency," *Financial Executive* (February 1980), pp. 44–49.
Kolde, Endel-Jokob, *Environment of International Business,* 2d ed. Boston: Kent Publishing, 1985.
Sangster, Bruce F., "International Funds Management," *Financial Executive* (December 1977), pp. 46–52.
Starr, Danforth W., "Opportunities for United States Corporate Borrowers in the International Bond Markets," *Financial Executive* (June 1979), pp. 50, 52–59.

Finance in the News

One of the most important factors affecting the rate of exchange between one nation's currency and another's is the relative price level of goods and services. In addition, interest rate differentials affect the exchange rate. Recently the price of American goods that compete with imports has been held down and American interest rates have been higher than those abroad. As a result, the American dollar has been strong. Unfortunately, this has been a mixed blessing for Americans as is explained in the following article.

Bullish about the Buck

Every American tourist planning a summer swing through Europe or a fall trek through the Himalayas has to be anxious about one thing: the value of the dollar. Many booked the trip of a lifetime because the dollar was so strong, and they are afraid that the great bargain might turn into a budget buster.

In recent years the American currency has been on a joyride on world money markets. During the late '70s, foreign-exchange traders nicknamed the dollar "the downhill racer" because it was slipping and sliding so fast. Since 1980, however, it has been on a march upward. The dollar reached its peak in late February, when it was worth 10.59 French francs, 3.46 West German marks and 2,164 Italian lira; just $1.03 bought a British pound. In recent weeks the dollar has fallen from those dizzy heights, and last week it slid some more. It averaged 9.49 francs, 3.11 marks and 1,988 lira; the price of a pound rose to $1.23.

If tourists are confused by the dollar's ups and downs, they are not alone. World financiers and economists do not fully understand what has been happening either. Moreover, the so-called experts have been almost uniformly wrong in predicting the dollar's course during the past four years. When they were saying that it would certainly soon fall in value, the dollar kept right on rising.

The American currency has been strong for the past few years basically because foreigners see the U.S. as a good place to put their money. Economic growth in this country has been high (6.8% in 1984) and inflation low (4%) at a time when much of the rest of the world trailed anemically behind and faced more rapidly rising prices too. In addition, American interest rates have been higher than those abroad because of the large U.S. budget deficit. Since foreigners can earn 2 to 4 percentage points more after inflation by investing their money in the U.S. rather than in, say, France or West Germany, they have been selling francs and marks to buy U.S. Government securities or to make other American investments.

The dollar's strength has been a mixed blessing for the U.S. economy. On the positive side, it not only has been a boon for tourists but has also helped reduce inflation by holding down the price of American goods that compete with imports. Howard Rosen, an associate at the Institute for International Economics in Washington, calculates that inflation for last year alone would have been 7% if the dollar had not been strong; instead prices rose only 4%. In addition, foreign funds attracted by the strong dollar have helped the Administration finance its $200 billion budget deficit. Without all that imported money, the U.S. would now have much higher interest rates.

But there is a dark side to the strong dollar. American tourists frolicking in London's Piccadilly Circus or Rome's Via Veneto will get no good wishes from Midwestern farmers or machine-tool producers in the East. The strong dollar has made American goods more expensive on foreign markets and hurt U.S. employment by depressing export sales of everything from Iowa corn to film made by Rochester's Eastman Kodak.

Many economists believe that the dollar is now overvalued by as much as 50%. And while the American currency could fall just as far and just as fast as it has risen, experts do not foresee rapid changes. Says Edward Yardeni, chief economist for Prudential-Bache: "It is quite possible that the 1980s will prove to be the dollar's decade to move up, just the way the 1970s was the dollar's decade to move down."

The future of the dollar rests largely in the hands of the Federal Reserve Board. The power of Fed Chairman Paul Volcker to influence the dollar on exchange markets has been clearly demonstrated in recent weeks. When he said last month that he thought that European central bankers should intervene in world currency exchanges more aggressively to keep the dollar's value down, the dollar began weakening. The currency then slid sharply when central banks started actively selling dollars, as he had recommended.

Despite such periodic interventions during the past few years, the dollar has been rising more or less steadily since the Federal Reserve switched to a much tighter money policy in 1979. As long as the American central bank continues to follow that tactic, the dollar is likely to remain strong. Jitters that hit foreign-exchange markets in recent months all have one thing in common: the fear that the Fed would ease up on money policy. Following last month's temporary closing of 69 savings institutions in Ohio, the dollar took a beating in money markets. Reason: fear that the Federal Reserve would be forced to loosen its grip on the money supply and lower interest rates to protect the U.S. banking system. Last week's dollar slide was due in part to worries stemming from the bankruptcy of Bevill, Bresler & Shulman Asset Management, a small New Jersey investment firm dealing in Government securities. The Federal Reserve, though, has given no signs of moving to a much looser monetary policy.

For the moment at least, tourists can plan their travels with some confidence that their bargains will not slip away before they start shopping in boutiques. While the dollar may decline a bit more, it is unlikely to drop sharply or to go back to its days as a downhill racer. Like most American tourists, the dollar is having a good trip.

—By John S. DeMott. Reported by Frederick Ungeheuer/New York and Gregory
H. Wierzynski/Washington

Compound Factor Table

$CF = (1 + i)^t$

Period	1%	1¼%	1½%	2%	3%	4%	5%	6%
1	1.0100	1.0125	1.0150	1.0200	1.0300	1.0400	1.0500	1.0600
2	1.0201	1.0252	1.0302	1.0404	1.0609	1.0816	1.1025	1.1236
3	1.0303	1.0380	1.0457	1.0612	1.0927	1.1249	1.1576	1.1910
4	1.0406	1.0509	1.0614	1.0824	1.1255	1.1699	1.2155	1.2625
5	1.0510	1.0641	1.0073	1.1041	1.1593	1.2167	1.2763	1.3382
6	1.0615	1.0774	1.0934	1.1262	1.1941	1.2653	1.3401	1.4185
7	1.0721	1.0909	1.1098	1.1487	1.2299	1.3159	1.4071	1.5036
8	1.0829	1.1045	1.1265	1.1717	1.2668	1.3686	1.4775	1.5938
9	1.0937	1.1183	1.1434	1.1951	1.3048	1.4233	1.5513	1.6895
10	1.1046	1.1323	1.1605	1.2190	1.3439	1.4802	1.6289	1.7908
11	1.1157	1.1464	1.1779	1.2434	1.3842	1.5395	1.7103	1.8983
12	1.1268	1.1608	1.1956	1.2682	1.4258	1.6010	1.7959	2.0122
13	1.1381	1.1753	1.2136	1.2936	1.4685	1.6651	1.8856	2.1329
14	1.1495	1.1900	1.2318	1.3195	1.5126	1.7317	1.9799	2.2609
15	1.1610	1.2048	1.2502	1.3459	1.5580	1.8009	2.0789	2.3966
16	1.1726	1.2199	1.2690	1.3728	1.6047	1.8730	2.1829	2.5404
17	1.1843	1.2351	1.2880	1.4002	1.6528	1.9479	2.2920	2.6928
18	1.1961	1.2506	1.3073	1.4282	1.7024	2.0258	2.4066	2.8543
19	1.2081	1.2662	1.3270	1.4568	1.7535	2.1068	2.5270	3.0256
20	1.2202	1.2820	1.3469	1.4859	1.8061	2.1911	2.6533	3.2071
21	1.2324	1.2981	1.3671	1.5157	1.8603	2.2788	2.7860	3.3996
22	1.2447	1.3143	1.3876	1.5460	1.9161	2.3699	2.9253	3.6035
23	1.2572	1.3307	1.4084	1.5769	1.9736	2.4647	3.0715	3.8197
24	1.2697	1.3474	1.4295	1.6084	2.0328	2.5633	3.2251	4.0489
25	1.2824	1.3642	1.4509	1.6406	2.0938	2.6658	3.3864	4.2919
30	1.3478	1.4516	1.5631	1.8114	2.4273	3.2434	4.3219	5.7435
40	1.4889	1.6436	1.8140	2.2080	3.2620	4.8010	7.0400	10.286
50	1.6446	1.8610	2.1052	2.6916	4.3839	7.1067	11.467	18.420
60	1.8167	2.1072	2.4432	3.2810	5.8916	10.520	18.679	32.988
120	3.3004	4.4402	5.9693	10.765	34.711	110.66	348.91	
180	5.9960	9.3563	14.584	35.321	204.50			
240	10.893	19.716	35.633					
300	19.789	41.544	87.059					

CF = (1 + i)^t

Period	7%	8%	9%	10%	11%	12%	13%	14%
1	1.0700	1.0800	1.0900	1.1000	1.1100	1.1200	1.1300	1.1400
2	1.1449	1.1664	1.1881	1.2100	1.2321	1.2544	1.2769	1.2996
3	1.2250	1.2597	1.2950	1.3310	1.3676	1.4049	1.4429	1.4815
4	1.3108	1.3605	1.4116	1.4641	1.5181	1.5735	1.6305	1.6890
5	1.4026	1.4693	1.5386	1.6105	1.6851	1.7623	1.8424	1.9254
6	1.5007	1.5869	1.6771	1.7716	1.8704	1.9738	2.0820	2.1950
7	1.6058	1.7138	1.8280	1.9487	2.0762	2.2107	2.3526	2.5023
8	1.7182	1.8509	1.9926	2.1436	2.3045	2.4760	2.6584	2.8526
9	1.8385	1.9990	2.1719	2.3579	2.5580	2.7731	3.0040	3.2519
10	1.9672	2.1589	2.3674	2.5937	2.8394	3.1058	3.3946	3.7072
11	2.1049	2.3316	2.5804	2.8531	3.1518	3.4785	3.8359	4.2262
12	2.2522	2.5182	2.8127	3.1384	3.4985	3.8960	4.3345	4.8179
13	2.4098	2.7196	3.0658	3.4523	3.8833	4.3635	4.8980	5.4924
14	2.5785	2.9372	3.3417	3.7975	4.3104	4.8871	5.5348	6.2613
15	2.7590	3.1722	3.6425	4.1772	4.7846	5.4736	6.2543	7.1379
16	2.9522	3.4259	3.9703	4.5950	5.3109	6.1304	7.0673	8.1372
17	3.1588	3.7000	4.3276	5.0545	5.8951	6.8660	7.9861	9.2765
18	3.3799	3.9960	4.7171	5.5599	6.5436	7.6900	9.0243	10.575
19	3.6165	4.3157	5.1417	6.1159	7.2633	8.6128	10.197	12.056
20	3.8697	4.6610	5.6044	6.7275	8.0623	9.6463	11.523	13.743
21	4.1406	5.0338	6.1088	7.4002	8.9492	10.804	13.021	15.668
22	4.4304	5.4365	6.6586	8.1403	9.9336	12.100	14.713	17.861
23	4.7405	5.8715	7.2579	8.9543	11.026	13.552	16.626	20.362
24	5.0724	6.3412	7.9111	9.8497	12.239	15.179	18.788	23.212
25	5.4274	6.8485	8.6231	10.835	13.585	17.000	21.230	26.462
30	7.6123	10.063	13.268	17.449	22.892	29.960	39.115	50.950
40	14.974	21.725	31.409	45.259	65.000	93.051	132.78	188.88
50	29.457	46.902	74.358	117.39	184.56	289.00	450.73	700.23
60	57.946	101.26	176.03	304.48	524.05	897.60		
120								
180								
240								
300								

15%	16%	18%	20%	24%	28%	32%	36%
1.1500	1.1600	1.1800	1.2000	1.2400	1.2800	1.3200	1.3800
1.3225	1.3456	1.3924	1.4400	1.5376	1.6384	1.7424	1.8496
1.5209	1.5609	1.6430	1.7280	1.9066	2.0972	2.3000	2.5155
1.7490	1.8106	1.9388	2.0736	2.3642	2.6844	3.0360	3.4210
2.0114	2.1003	2.2878	2.4883	2.9316	3.4360	4.0075	4.6526
2.3131	2.4364	2.6996	2.9860	3.6352	4.3980	5.2899	6.3275
2.6600	2.8262	3.1855	3.5832	4.5077	5.6295	6.9826	8.6054
3.0590	3.2784	3.7589	4.2998	5.5895	7.2058	9.2170	11.703
3.5179	3.8030	4.4355	5.1598	6.9310	9.2234	12.166	15.917
4.0456	4.4114	5.2338	6.1917	8.5944	11.806	16.060	21.647
4.6524	5.1173	6.1759	7.4301	10.657	15.112	21.199	29.439
5.3503	5.9360	7.2876	8.9161	13.215	19.343	27.983	40.037
6.1528	6.8858	8.5994	10.699	16.386	24.759	36.937	54.451
7.0757	7.9875	10.147	12.839	20.319	31.691	48.757	74.053
8.1371	9.2655	11.974	15.407	25.196	40.565	64.359	100.71
9.3576	10.748	14.129	18.488	31.243	51.923	84.954	136.97
10.761	12.468	16.672	22.186	38.741	66.461	112.14	186.28
12.375	14.463	19.673	26.623	48.039	85.071	148.02	253.34
14.232	16.777	23.214	31.948	59.568	108.89	195.39	344.54
16.367	19.461	27.393	38.338	73.864	139.38	257.92	468.57
18.822	22.574	32.324	46.005	91.592	178.41	340.45	637.26
21.645	26.186	38.142	55.206	113.57	228.36	449.39	866.67
24.891	30.376	45.008	66.247	140.83	292.30	593.20	1178.7
28.625	35.236	53.109	79.497	174.63	374.14	783.02	1603.0
32.919	40.874	62.669	95.396	216.54	478.90	1033.6	2180.1
66.212	85.850	143.37	237.38	634.82			
267.86	378.72	750.38					

Discount Factor Table

$$DF = \frac{1}{(1 + i)^t}$$

Period	1%	1¼%	1½%	2%	3%	4%	5%	6%	7%	8%	9%
1	.9901	.9877	.9852	.9804	.9709	.9615	.9524	.9434	.9346	.9259	.9174
2	.9803	.9755	.9707	.9612	.9426	.9246	.9070	.8900	.8734	.8573	.8417
3	.9706	.9634	.9563	.9423	.9151	.8890	.8638	.8396	.8163	.7938	.7722
4	.9610	.9515	.9422	.9238	.8885	.8548	.8227	.7921	.7629	.7350	.7084
5	.9515	.9398	.9283	.9057	.8626	.8219	.7835	.7473	.7130	.6806	.6499
6	.9420	.9282	.9145	.8880	.8375	.7903	.7462	.7050	.6663	.6302	.5963
7	.9327	.9167	.9010	.8706	.8131	.7599	.7107	.6651	.6227	.5835	.5470
8	.9235	.9054	.8877	.8535	.7894	.7307	.6768	.6274	.5820	.5403	.5019
9	.9143	.8942	.8746	.8368	.7664	.7026	.6446	.5919	.5439	.5002	.4604
10	.9053	.8832	.8617	.8203	.7441	.6756	.6139	.5584	.5083	.4632	.4224
11	.8963	.8723	.8489	.8043	.7224	.6496	.5847	.5268	.4751	.4289	.3875
12	.8874	.8615	.8364	.7885	.7014	.6246	.5568	.4970	.4440	.3971	.3555
13	.8787	.8509	.8240	.7730	.6810	.6006	.5303	.4688	.4150	.3677	.3262
14	.8700	.8404	.8118	.7579	.6611	.5775	.5051	.4423	.3878	.3405	.2992
15	.8613	.8300	.7999	.7430	.6419	.5553	.4810	.4173	.3624	.3152	.2745
16	.8528	.8197	.7880	.7284	.6232	.5339	.4581	.3936	.3387	.2919	.2519
17	.8444	.8096	.7764	.7142	.6050	.5134	.4363	.3714	.3166	.2703	.2311
18	.8360	.7996	.7649	.7002	.5874	.4936	.4155	.3503	.2959	.2502	.2120
19	.8277	.7898	.7536	.6864	.5703	.4746	.3957	.3305	.2765	.2317	.1945
20	.8195	.7800	.7425	.6730	.5537	.4564	.3769	.3118	.2584	.2145	.1784
21	.8114	.7704	.7315	.6598	.5375	.4388	.3589	.2942	.2415	.1987	.1637
22	.8034	.7609	.7207	.6468	.5219	.4220	.3418	.2775	.2257	.1839	.1502
23	.7954	.7515	.7100	.6342	.5067	.4057	.3256	.2618	.2109	.1703	.1378
24	.7876	.7422	.6995	.6217	.4919	.3901	.3101	.2470	.1971	.1577	.1264
25	.7798	.7330	.6892	.6095	.4776	.3751	.2953	.2330	.1842	.1460	.1160
30	.7419	.6889	.6398	.5521	.4120	.3083	.2314	.1741	.1314	.0994	.0754
40	.6717	.6084	.5513	.4529	.3066	.2083	.1420	.0972	.0668	.0460	.0318
50	.6080	.5373	.4750	.3715	.2281	.1407	.0872	.0543	.0339	.0213	.0134
60	.5504	.4746	.4039	.3048	.1697	.0951	.0535	.0303	.0173	.0099	.0057
120	.3030	.2252	.1675	.0929	.0288	.0090	.0029	.0009			
180	.1668	.1069	.0685	.0283	.0049						
240	.0918	.0507	.0281								
300	.0505	.0241	.0115								

$$DF = \frac{1}{(1 + i)^t}$$

Period	10%	11%	12%	13%	14%	15%	16%	18%	20%	24%	28%	32%	36%
1	.9091	.9009	.8929	.8850	.8772	.8696	.8621	.8475	.8333	.8065	.7813	.7576	.7353
2	.8264	.8116	.7972	.7832	.7695	.7561	.7432	.7182	.6944	.6504	.6104	.5739	.5407
3	.7513	.7312	.7118	.6931	.6750	.6575	.6407	.6086	.5787	.5245	.4768	.4348	.3975
4	.6830	.6587	.6355	.6133	.5921	.5718	.5523	.5158	.4823	.4230	.3725	.3294	.2923
5	.6209	.5935	.5674	.5428	.5194	.4972	.4761	.4371	.4019	.3411	.2910	.2495	.2149
6	.5645	.5346	.5066	.4803	.4556	.4323	.4104	.3704	.3349	.2751	.2274	.1890	.1580
7	.5132	.4817	.4523	.4251	.3996	.3759	.3538	.3139	.2791	.2218	.1776	.1432	.1162
8	.4665	.4339	.4039	.3762	.3506	.3269	.3050	.2660	.2326	.1789	.1388	.1085	.0854
9	.4241	.3909	.3606	.3329	.3075	.2843	.2630	.2255	.1938	.1443	.1084	.0822	.0628
10	.3855	.3522	.3220	.2946	.2697	.2472	.2267	.1911	.1615	.1164	.0847	.0623	.0462
11	.3505	.3173	.2875	.2607	.2366	.2149	.1954	.1619	.1346	.0938	.0662	.0472	.0340
12	.3186	.2858	.2567	.2307	.2076	.1869	.1685	.1372	.1122	.0757	.0517	.0357	.0250
13	.2897	.2575	.2292	.2042	.1821	.1625	.1452	.1163	.0935	.0610	.0404	.0271	.0184
14	.2633	.2320	.2046	.1807	.1597	.1413	.1252	.0985	.0779	.0492	.0316	.0205	.0135
15	.2394	.2090	.1827	.1599	.1401	.1229	.1079	.0835	.0649	.0397	.0247	.0155	.0099
16	.2176	.1883	.1631	.1415	.1229	.1069	.0930	.0708	.0541	.0320	.0193	.0118	.0073
17	.1978	.1696	.1456	.1252	.1078	.0929	.0802	.0600	.0451	.0258	.0150	.0089	.0054
18	.1799	.1528	.1300	.1108	.0946	.0808	.0691	.0508	.0376	.0208	.0118	.0068	.0039
19	.1635	.1377	.1161	.0981	.0829	.0703	.0596	.0431	.0313	.0168	.0092	.0051	.0029
20	.1486	.1240	.1037	.0868	.0728	.0611	.0514	.0365	.0261	.0135	.0072	.0039	.0021
21	.1351	.1117	.0926	.0768	.0638	.0531	.0443	.0309	.0217	.0109	.0056	.0029	.0016
22	.1228	.1007	.0826	.0680	.0560	.0462	.0382	.0262	.0181	.0088	.0044	.0022	.0012
23	.1117	.0907	.0738	.0601	.0491	.0402	.0329	.0222	.0151	.0071	.0034	.0017	.0008
24	.1015	.0817	.0659	.0532	.0431	.0349	.0284	.0188	.0126	.0057	.0027	.0013	.0006
25	.0923	.0736	.0588	.0471	.0378	.0304	.0245	.0160	.0105	.0046	.0021	.0010	.0005
30	.0573	.0437	.0334	.0256	.0196	.0151	.0116	.0070	.0042	.0016	.0006	.0002	.0001
40	.0221	.0154	.0107	.0075	.0053	.0037	.0026	.0013	.0007	.0002	.0001		
50	.0085	.0054	.0035	.0022	.0014	.0009	.0006	.0003	.0001				
60	.0033	.0019	.0011	.0007	.0004	.0002	.0001						

Annuity Compound Factor Table

$$ACF = \frac{(1 + i)^n - 1}{i}$$

Number of Periods	1%	1¼%	1½%	2%	3%	4%	5%	6%
1	1.0000	1.0000	1.0000	1.0000	1.0000	1.0000	1.0000	1.0000
2	2.0100	2.0125	2.0150	2.0200	2.0300	2.0400	2.0500	2.0600
3	3.0301	3.0377	3.0452	3.0604	3.0909	3.1216	3.1525	3.1836
4	4.0604	4.0756	4.0909	4.1216	4.1836	4.2465	4.3101	4.3746
5	5.1010	5.1266	5.1523	5.2040	5.3091	5.4163	5.5256	5.6371
6	6.1520	6.1907	6.2296	6.3081	6.4684	6.6330	6.8019	6.9753
7	7.2135	7.2680	7.3230	7.4343	7.6625	7.8983	8.1420	8.3938
8	8.2857	8.3589	8.4328	8.5830	8.8923	9.2142	9.5491	9.8975
9	9.3685	9.4634	9.5593	9.7546	10.159	10.583	11.027	11.491
10	10.462	10.581	10.702	10.950	11.464	12.006	12.578	13.181
11	11.567	11.713	11.863	12.169	12.808	13.486	14.207	14.972
12	12.683	12.860	13.041	13.412	14.192	15.026	15.917	16.870
13	13.809	14.021	14.236	14.680	15.618	16.627	17.713	18.882
14	14.947	15.196	15.450	15.974	17.086	18.292	19.599	21.015
15	16.097	16.386	16.682	17.293	18.599	20.024	21.579	23.276
16	17.258	17.591	17.932	18.639	20.157	21.825	23.657	25.673
17	18.430	18.811	19.201	20.012	21.762	23.698	25.840	28.213
18	19.615	20.046	20.489	21.412	23.414	25.645	28.132	30.906
19	20.811	21.296	21.796	22.841	25.117	27.671	30.539	33.760
20	22.019	22.563	23.123	24.297	26.870	29.778	33.066	36.786
21	23.239	23.845	24.470	25.783	28.676	31.969	35.719	39.993
22	24.472	25.143	25.837	27.299	30.537	34.248	38.505	43.392
23	25.716	26.457	27.225	28.845	32.453	36.618	41.430	46.996
24	26.973	27.788	28.633	30.422	34.426	39.083	44.502	50.816
25	28.243	29.135	30.063	32.030	36.459	41.646	47.727	54.865
30	34.785	36.129	37.538	40.568	47.575	56.085	66.439	79.058
40	48.886	51.489	54.267	60.402	75.401	95.026	120.80	154.76
50	64.463	68.881	73.682	84.579	112.80	152.67	209.35	290.34
60	81.670	88.574	96.214	114.05	163.05	237.99	353.58	533.13
120	230.03	275.21	331.28	488.25	1123.7	2741.5	6958.2	
180	499.58	668.50	905.63	1716.0	6783.4			
240	989.25	1497.2	2308.9					
300	1878.8	3243.5	5737.3					

$$ACF = \frac{(1 + i)^n - 1}{i}$$

Number of Periods	7%	8%	9%	10%	11%	12%	13%
1	1.0000	1.0000	1.0000	1.0000	1.0000	1.0000	1.0000
2	2.0700	2.0800	2.0900	2.1000	2.1100	2.1200	2.1300
3	3.2149	3.2464	3.2781	3.3100	3.3421	3.3744	3.4069
4	4.4399	4.5061	4.5731	4.6410	4.7097	4.7793	4.8498
5	5.7507	5.8666	5.9847	6.1051	6.2278	6.3528	6.4803
6	7.1533	7.3359	7.5233	7.7156	7.9129	8.1152	8.3227
7	8.6540	8.9228	9.2004	9.4872	9.7833	10.089	10.404
8	10.260	10.637	11.028	11.436	11.859	12.300	12.757
9	11.978	12.488	13.021	13.579	14.164	14.776	15.415
10	13.816	14.487	15.193	15.937	16.722	17.549	18.419
11	15.784	16.645	17.560	18.531	19.561	20.655	21.814
12	17.888	18.977	20.141	21.384	22.713	24.133	25.650
13	20.141	21.495	22.953	24.523	26.211	28.029	29.984
14	22.550	24.215	26.019	27.975	30.094	32.393	34.882
15	25.129	27.152	29.361	31.772	34.405	37.280	40.417
16	27.888	30.324	33.003	35.950	39.189	42.753	46.671
17	30.840	33.750	36.974	40.545	44.500	48.884	53.739
18	33.999	37.450	41.301	45.599	50.395	55.750	61.725
19	37.379	41.446	46.018	51.159	56.939	63.440	70.749
20	40.995	45.762	51.160	57.275	64.202	72.052	80.947
21	44.865	50.423	56.765	64.002	72.265	81.699	92.469
22	40.006	55.457	62.873	71.403	81.214	92.503	105.49
23	53.436	60.893	69.532	79.543	91.147	104.60	120.20
24	58.177	66.765	76.790	88.497	102.17	118.16	136.83
25	63.249	73.106	84.701	98.347	114.41	133.33	155.61
30	94.461	113.28	136.31	164.49	199.02	241.33	293.19
40	199.64	259.06	337.88	442.59	581.82	767.09	1013.7
50	406.53	573.77	815.08	1163.9	1668.7	2400.0	3459.5
60	813.52	1253.2	1944.8	3034.8	4755.0	7471.6	
120							
180							
240							
300							

14%	15%	16%	18%	20%	24%	28%	32%	36%
1.0000	1.0000	1.0000	1.0000	1.0000	1.0000	1.0000	1.0000	1.0000
2.1400	2.1500	2.1600	2.1800	2.2000	2.2400	2.2800	2.3200	2.3600
3.4396	3.4725	3.5056	3.5724	3.6400	3.7776	3.9184	4.0624	4.2096
4.9211	4.9934	5.0665	5.2154	5.3680	5.6842	6.0156	6.3624	6.7251
6.6101	6.7424	6.8771	7.1542	7.4416	8.0484	8.6999	9.3983	10.146
8.5355	8.7537	8.9775	9.4420	9.9299	10.980	12.136	13.406	14.799
10.730	11.067	11.414	12.142	12.916	14.615	16.534	18.696	21.126
13.233	13.727	14.240	15.327	16.499	19.123	22.163	25.678	29.732
16.085	16.786	17.519	19.086	20.799	24.712	29.369	34.895	41.435
19.337	20.304	21.321	23.521	25.959	31.643	38.593	47.062	57.352
23.045	24.349	25.733	28.755	32.150	40.238	50.398	63.122	78.998
27.271	29.002	30.850	34.931	39.581	50.895	65.510	84.320	108.44
32.089	34.352	36.786	42.219	48.497	64.110	84.853	112.30	148.47
37.581	40.505	43.672	50.818	59.196	80.496	109.61	149.24	202.93
43.842	47.580	51.660	60.965	72.035	100.82	141.30	198.00	276.98
50.980	55.717	60.925	72.939	87.442	126.01	181.87	262.36	377.69
59.118	65.075	71.673	87.068	105.93	157.25	233.79	347.31	514.66
68.394	75.836	84.141	103.74	128.12	195.99	300.25	459.45	700.94
78.969	88.212	98.603	123.41	154.74	244.03	385.32	607.47	954.28
91.025	102.44	115.38	146.63	186.69	303.60	494.21	802.86	1298.8
104.77	118.81	134.84	174.02	225.03	377.46	633.59	1060.8	1767.4
120.44	137.63	157.41	206.34	271.03	469.06	812.00	1401.2	2404.7
138.30	159.28	183.60	244.49	326.24	582.63	1040.4	1850.6	3271.3
158.66	184.17	213.98	289.49	392.48	723.46	1332.7	2443.8	4450.0
181.87	212.79	249.21	342.60	471.98	898.09	1706.8	3226.8	6053.0
356.79	434.75	530.31	790.95	1181.9	2640.9	5873.2		
1342.0	1779.1	2360.8	4163.2	7343.9				
4994.5	7217.7							

Annuity Discount Factor Table

$$ADF = \frac{1 - \dfrac{1}{(1 + i)^n}}{i}$$

Number of Periods	1%	1¼%	1½%	2%	3%	4%	5%	6%
1	0.9901	0.9877	0.9852	0.9804	0.9709	0.9615	0.9524	0.9434
2	1.9704	1.9631	1.9559	1.9416	1.9135	1.8861	1.8594	1.8334
3	2.9410	2.9265	2.9122	2.8839	2.8286	2.7751	2.7232	2.6730
4	3.9020	3.8781	3.8544	3.8077	3.7171	3.6299	3.5460	3.4651
5	4.8534	4.8178	4.7826	4.7135	4.5797	4.4518	4.3295	4.2124
6	5.7955	5.7460	5.6972	5.6014	5.4172	5.2421	5.0757	4.9173
7	6.7282	6.6627	6.5982	6.4720	6.2303	6.0021	5.7864	5.5824
8	7.6517	7.5681	7.4859	7.3255	7.0197	6.7327	6.4632	6.2098
9	8.5660	8.4623	8.3605	8.1622	7.7861	7.4353	7.1078	6.8017
10	9.4713	9.3455	9.2222	8.9826	8.5302	8.1109	7.7217	7.3601
11	10.3676	10.2178	10.0711	9.7868	9.2526	8.7605	8.3064	7.8869
12	11.2551	11.0793	10.9075	10.5753	9.9540	9.3851	8.8633	8.3838
13	12.1337	11.9302	11.7315	11.3484	10.6350	9.9856	9.3936	8.8527
14	13.0037	12.7706	12.5434	12.1062	11.2961	10.5631	9.8986	9.2950
15	13.8651	13.6005	13.3432	12.8493	11.9379	11.1184	10.3797	9.7122
16	14.7179	14.4203	14.1313	13.5777	12.5611	11.6523	10.8378	10.1059
17	15.5623	15.2299	14.9076	14.2919	13.1661	12.1657	11.2741	10.4773
18	16.3983	16.0295	15.6726	14.9920	13.7535	12.6593	11.6896	10.8276
19	17.2260	16.8193	16.4262	15.6785	14.3238	13.1339	12.0853	11.1581
20	18.0456	17.5993	17.1686	16.3514	14.8775	13.5903	12.4622	11.4699
21	18.8570	18.3697	17.9001	17.0112	15.4150	14.0292	12.8212	11.7641
22	19.6604	19.1306	18.6208	17.6580	15.9369	14.4511	13.1630	12.0416
23	20.4558	19.8820	19.3309	18.2922	16.4436	14.8568	13.4886	12.3034
24	21.2434	20.6242	20.0304	18.9139	16.9355	15.2470	13.7986	12.5504
25	22.0232	21.3573	20.7196	19.5235	17.4131	15.6221	14.0939	12.7834
30	25.8077	24.8889	24.0158	22.3965	19.6004	17.2920	15.3725	13.7648
40	32.8347	31.3269	29.9158	27.3555	23.1148	19.7928	17.1591	15.0463
50	39.1961	37.0129	34.9997	31.4236	25.7298	21.4822	18.2559	15.7619
60	44.9550	42.0346	39.3803	34.7609	27.6756	22.6235	18.9293	16.1614
120	69.7005	61.9828	55.4985	45.3554	32.3730	24.7741	19.9427	16.6514
180	83.3217	71.4496	62.0956	48.4530	33.1704			
240	90.8194	75.9423	64.7957					
300	94.9466	78.0743	65.9009					

$$ADF = \frac{1 - \frac{1}{(1 + i)^n}}{i}$$

Number of Periods	7%	8%	9%	10%	11%	12%	13%
1	0.9346	0.9259	0.9174	0.9091	0.9009	0.8929	0.8850
2	1.8080	1.7833	1.7591	1.7355	1.7125	1.6901	1.6681
3	2.6243	2.5771	2.5313	2.4869	2.4437	2.4018	2.3612
4	3.3872	3.3121	3.2397	3.1699	3.1024	3.0373	2.9745
5	4.1002	3.9927	3.8897	3.7908	3.6959	3.6048	3.5172
6	4.7665	4.6229	4.4859	4.3553	4.2305	4.1114	3.9976
7	5.3893	5.2064	5.0330	4.8684	4.7122	4.5638	4.4226
8	5.9713	5.7466	5.5348	5.3349	5.1461	4.9676	4.7988
9	6.5152	6.2469	5.9952	5.7590	5.5370	5.3282	5.1317
10	7.0236	6.7101	6.4177	6.1446	5.8892	5.6502	5.4262
11	7.4987	7.1390	6.8052	6.4951	6.2065	5.9377	5.6869
12	7.9427	7.5361	7.1607	6.8137	6.4924	6.1944	5.9176
13	8.3577	7.9038	7.4869	7.1034	6.7499	6.4235	6.1218
14	8.7455	8.2442	7.7862	7.3667	6.9819	6.6282	6.3025
15	9.1079	8.5595	8.0607	7.6061	7.1909	6.8109	6.4624
16	9.4466	8.8514	8.3126	7.8237	7.3792	6.9740	6.6039
17	9.7632	9.1216	8.5436	8.0216	7.5488	7.1196	6.7291
18	10.0591	9.3719	8.7556	8.2014	7.7016	7.2497	6.8399
19	10.3356	9.6036	8.9501	8.3649	7.8393	7.3658	6.9380
20	10.5940	9.8181	9.1285	8.5136	7.9633	7.4694	7.0248
21	10.8355	10.0168	9.2922	8.6487	8.0751	7.5620	7.1016
22	11.0612	10.2007	9.4424	8.7715	8.1757	7.6446	7.1695
23	11.2722	10.3711	9.5802	8.8832	8.2664	7.7184	7.2297
24	11.4693	10.5288	9.7066	8.9847	8.3481	7.7843	7.2829
25	11.6536	10.6748	9.8226	9.0770	8.4217	7.8431	7.3300
30	12.4090	11.2578	10.2737	9.4269	8.6938	8.0552	7.4957
40	13.3317	11.9246	10.7574	9.7791	8.9511	8.2438	7.6344
50	13.8007	12.2335	10.9617	9.9148	9.0417	8.3045	7.6752
60	14.0392	12.3766	11.0480	9.9672	9.0736	8.3240	7.6873
120							
180							
240							
300							

14%	15%	16%	18%	20%	24%	28%	32%	36%
0.8772	0.8696	0.8621	0.8475	0.8333	0.8065	0.7813	0.7576	0.7353
1.6467	1.6257	1.6052	1.5656	1.5278	1.4568	1.3916	1.3315	1.2760
2.3216	2.2832	2.2459	2.1743	2.1065	1.9813	1.8684	1.7663	1.6735
2.9137	2.8550	2.7982	2.6901	2.5887	2.4043	2.2410	2.0957	1.9658
3.4331	3.3522	3.2743	3.1272	2.9906	2.7454	2.5320	2.3452	2.1807
3.8887	3.7845	3.6847	3.4976	3.3255	3.0205	2.7594	2.5342	2.3388
4.2883	4.1604	4.0386	3.8115	3.6046	3.2423	2.9370	2.6775	2.4550
4.6389	4.4873	4.3436	4.0776	3.8372	3.4212	3.0758	2.7860	2.5404
4.9464	4.7716	4.6065	4.3030	4.0310	3.5655	3.1842	2.8681	2.6033
5.2161	5.0188	4.8332	4.4941	4.1925	3.6819	3.2689	2.9304	2.6495
5.4527	5.2337	5.0286	4.6560	4.3271	3.7757	3.3351	2.9776	2.6834
5.6603	5.4206	5.1971	4.7932	4.4392	3.8514	3.3868	3.0133	2.7084
5.8424	5.5831	5.3423	4.9095	4.5327	3.9124	3.4272	3.0404	2.7268
6.0021	5.7245	5.4675	5.0081	4.6106	3.9616	3.4587	3.0609	2.7403
6.1422	5.8474	5.5755	5.0916	4.6755	4.0013	3.4834	3.0764	2.7502
6.2651	5.9542	5.6685	5.1624	4.7296	4.0333	3.5026	3.0882	2.7575
6.3729	6.0472	5.7487	5.2223	4.7746	4.0591	3.5177	3.0971	2.7629
6.4674	6.1280	5.8178	5.2732	4.8122	4.0799	3.5294	3.1039	2.7668
6.5504	6.1982	5.8775	5.3162	4.8435	4.0967	3.5386	3.1090	2.7697
6.6231	6.2593	5.9288	5.3527	4.8696	4.1103	3.5458	3.1129	2.7718
6.6870	6.3125	5.9731	5.3837	4.8913	4.1212	3.5514	3.1158	2.7734
6.7429	6.3587	6.0113	5.4099	4.9094	4.1300	3.5558	3.1180	2.7746
6.7921	6.3988	6.0442	5.4321	4.9245	4.1371	3.5592	3.1197	2.7754
6.8351	6.4338	6.0726	5.4509	4.9371	4.1428	3.5619	3.1210	2.7760
6.8729	6.4641	6.0971	5.4669	4.9476	4.1474	3.5640	3.1220	2.7765
7.0027	6.5660	6.1772	5.5168	4.9789	4.1601	3.5693	3.1242	2.7775
7.1050	6.6418	6.2335	5.5482	4.9966	4.1659	3.5712	3.1250	2.7778
7.1327	6.6605	6.2463	5.5541	4.9995	4.1666	3.5714	3.1250	2.7778
7.1401	6.6651	6.2492	5.5553	4.9999	4.1667	3.5714	3.1250	2.7778

Normal Curve Areas

Normal Curve Areas

Z	.00	.01	.02	.03	.04	.05	.06	.07	.08	.09
0.0	.0000	.0040	.0080	.0120	.0160	.0199	.0239	.0279	.0319	.0359
0.1	.0398	.0438	.0478	.0517	.0557	.0596	.0636	.0675	.0714	.0753
0.2	.0793	.0832	.0871	.0910	.0948	.0987	.1026	.1064	.1103	.1141
0.3	.1179	.1217	.1255	.1293	.1331	.1368	.1406	.1443	.1480	.1517
0.4	.1554	.1591	.1628	.1664	.1700	.1736	.1772	.1808	.1844	.1879
0.5	.1915	.1950	.1985	.2019	.2054	.2088	.2123	.2157	.2190	.2224
0.6	.2257	.2291	.2324	.2357	.2389	.2422	.2454	.2486	.2517	.2549
0.7	.2580	.2611	.2642	.2673	.2704	.2734	.2764	.2794	.2823	.2852
0.8	.2881	.2910	.2939	.2967	.2995	.3023	.3051	.3078	.3106	.3133
0.9	.3159	.3186	.3212	.3238	.3264	.3289	.3315	.3340	.3365	.3389
1.0	.3413	.3438	.3461	.3485	.3508	.3531	.3554	.3577	.3599	.3621
1.1	.3643	.3665	.3686	.3708	.3729	.3749	.3770	.3790	.3810	.3830
1.2	.3849	.3869	.3888	.3907	.3925	.3944	.3962	.3980	.3997	.4015
1.3	.4032	.4049	.4066	.4082	.4099	.4115	.4131	.4147	.4162	.4177
1.4	.4192	.4207	.4222	.4236	.4251	.4265	.4279	.4292	.4306	.4319
1.5	.4332	.4345	.4357	.4370	.4382	.4394	.4406	.4418	.4429	.4441
1.6	.4452	.4463	.4474	.4484	.4495	.4505	.4515	.4525	.4535	.4545
1.7	.4554	.4564	.4573	.4582	.4591	.4599	.4608	.4616	.4625	.4633
1.8	.4641	.4649	.4656	.4664	.4671	.4678	.4686	.4693	.4699	.4706
1.9	.4713	.4719	.4726	.4732	.4738	.4744	.4750	.4756	.4761	.4767
2.0	.4772	.4778	.4783	.4788	.4793	.4798	.4803	.4808	.4812	.4817
2.1	.4821	.4826	.4830	.4834	.4838	.4842	.4846	.4850	.4854	.4857
2.2	.4861	.4864	.4868	.4871	.4875	.4878	.4881	.4884	.4887	.4890
2.3	.4893	.4896	.4898	.4901	.4904	.4906	.4909	.4911	.4913	.4916
2.4	.4918	.4920	.4922	.4925	.4927	.4929	.4931	.4932	.4934	.4936
2.5	.4938	.4940	.4941	.4943	.4945	.4946	.4948	.4949	.4951	.4952
2.6	.4953	.4955	.4956	.4957	.4959	.4960	.4961	.4962	.4963	.4964
2.7	.4965	.4966	.4967	.4968	.4969	.4970	.4971	.4972	.4973	.4974
2.8	.4974	.4975	.4976	.4977	.4977	.4978	.4979	.4979	.4980	.4981
2.9	.4981	.4982	.4982	.4983	.4984	.4984	.4985	.4985	.4986	.4986
3.0	.4987	.4987	.4987	.4988	.4988	.4989	.4989	.4989	.4990	.4990

From Taylor, Bernard W., III, *Introduction to Management Science.* © 1982 Wm. C. Brown Publishers, Dubuque, Iowa. All Rights Reserved. Reprinted by permission.

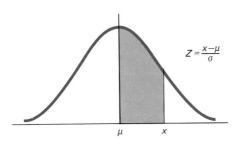

$$Z = \frac{x - \mu}{\sigma}$$

Careers in Finance

Financial Analyst—Revenue

Basic Function   Project future revenues for budgetary purposes and analyze past revenue performances.

Primary Responsibilities and Duties

Forecast company revenue for the annual budget.
Forecast company revenue for the rolling 3 month budget.
Provide an interface between controller and revenue accounting system.
Report company revenue in forms usable by other departments.
Provide a post analysis of last month's revenue performance and what caused deviations.
Respond to revenue questions raised by senior management.

Types of Decisions

Choice of methodology.
Judging results of analysis as to the degree of reasonableness of any variance.
Important methodology questions must be reviewed by superiors.
Problems with data gathering are handled by superiors.

Consequences of Error

If forecasts understate revenue to a large degree, serious cash flow problems can occur.

Organizational Relationships

No subordinates.
Work progress is discussed with supervisor daily.
Revenue Accounting is contacted for data.

Education and Experience

BA minimum; MBA preferred.

Representative Skills and Knowledge

Must have:

An understanding of variance calculations.
A knowledge of company procedures on information gathering and presentation.
An understanding of company and industry structure and terminology.
A knowledge of company data bases.
Presentation skills.
Writing skills.
The ability to use computers.
The ability to deal with others.
The ability to put things in their proper perspective.

Other

There is considerable stress associated with meeting deadlines in this position.

Securities Analyst—Publicly Traded Bonds

Basic Function   Analyze publicly traded industrial and utility bonds to determine their acceptability to company standards, prepare recommendations regarding such offerings, and monitor the condition of the firms whose bonds are purchased.

Primary Responsibilities and Duties

Review the company's portfolio on an on-going basis to assure continued acceptability to company standards.
Recommend sales or additional purchases.
Analyze bids received for the purchase of public bonds, determine impact, and recommend course of action.
Evaluate corporate managements, compile information obtained, and prepare and submit recommendation to senior investment officers.
Prepare periodic reports on the status of the bond portfolio for the Finance Committee.
Act as a back-up for investment/research activities.

Types of Decisions

Determine quality of corporate managements and financial standings of companies offering bonds.
Recommend purchase or sale of public bonds in response to unanticipated changes in public offerings.
Identify specific problems with the public bond portfolio and recommend appropriate course of action.
Evaluate market and industry trends and recommend purchase/sale strategies.

Consequences of Error

Errors in analysis or judgment can result in financial loss or lost investment opportunities.

Organizational Relationships

The incumbent reports to the Senior Investment Officer.

Work Relationships

Occasionally work with:
>   Outside managements.
>   Brokers.

Education and Experience

>   At the first level, a college degree with some business courses in accounting, finance, and/or economics; some prior experience in a financial environment.
>   At the middle level, approximately 2 years directly related experience.
>   At the top level, approximately 4 years directly related experience; an MBA desirable.

Representative Skills and Knowledge

Should have:
>   A knowledge of finance, investments, accounting, and economics.
>   A knowledge of company policies and practices regarding the public bond market.

Must:
>   Continually increase knowledge of the public industrial and utility bond market.
>   Have strong analytical skills, good judgment, and good oral and written communication skills.
>   Be good at human relations.

General Credit Manager

Basic Function   Establish and administer the broad credit and collection policies of the company as they apply to domestic and export customer sales of the manufacturing divisions and specialized distribution and service units. This receivables management is carried out through all company credit and collection units on both a direct and non-direct basis as required to optimize the company's receivables turnover.

Primary Responsibilities and Duties

>   Approve all extraordinary lines of credit, including those that exceed delegated field authority.
>   Visit key customers to maintain good commercial relationships and determine financial liability.
>   Work with appropriate division and field sales personnel to coordinate and communicate terms of payment, credit decisions, and disputed or uncollectible billings.
>   Prepare monthly cash collection forecasts and monitor and report daily cash receipts.
>   Coordinate all legal matters pertaining to receivables management with company and outside attorneys.
>   Establish objectives for domestic and export treasury managers.
>   Supervise the maintenance and safekeeping of special customer records, files, reports, and ledgers.
>   Represent the company at financial professional association meetings and seminars.
>   Keep informed of legislation and changes in laws and regulations which affect financing, credit, and collection policies and procedures.
>   Sign documents as necessary as an authorized officer of the company.
>   Direct the preparation of periodic reports on receivables and analyze customer's accounts and reserve requirements; report unusual trends in developments to management along with corrective action needed.
>   Develop policy and procedures for recruiting and soliciting professional personnel to staff the credit and collection offices.

Administer the department salary program and provide for direct and indirect training of department personnel.

Supervise the effective utilization of funds allocated for the operations of domestic and export credit collection units.

Supervise the booking and collection processing of domestic and export customer's notes and trade acceptances.

Prepare and formulate, within prescribed time limits, various data and reports as may be required by the Vice President-Treasurer.

Develop budgets for domestic and export credit and collection units.

Types of Decisions

Final decision-making responsibility exists in credit/collection problems and procedures, personnel decisions, reporting unit structure, budget and merit increase considerations, and establishment of department/receivables objectives. (All major aspects of the preceding are reviewed with the Vice President-Treasurer.)

Recommendations concerning bad debts are submitted to the Vice President-Treasurer for final approval.

Objectives are established for domestic and export credit and collection units.

Organizational Relationships

The incumbent directly supervises four zone treasury managers, three directors of treasury services, one subsidiary vice president and treasurer, one manager of international collections, and one credit manager of international standard sales. Approximately 150 employees report through these positions.

The incumbent reports directly to the Vice President and Treasurer.

Work Relationships

Work with marketing management to increase both domestic and export sales volume through financing plans designed to accomplish this goal with minimum risk.

Supervise the counseling of both domestic and export customers as to better financing arrangements and more effective control of internal operations.

Enhance the company's image among customers by providing appropriate credit and collection activities conducive to continuing and broadening the commercial relationships that exist.

Education and Experience

BS or BA required with a major in accounting or finance.

Should have five years minimum in direct handling of open account credit and secured transactions, ten years minimum of direct supervision of this type of activity in a management capacity, five years minimum as a zone, regional manager, or director of treasury services.

Representative Skills and Knowledge

Requires a working knowledge of corporate finance, banking, commercial finance, and international credit policies and procedures.

Must be:

A disciplined and determined negotiator.

A leader and motivator of people.

Skilled in selling programs and policies to customers and company units.

Objective in thinking and open to new ideas.

Able to size up a situation and act decisively.

Skilled in short- and long-range planning and reorganization.

Mortgage Analyst—Production

Basic Function　To handle all matters related to the production, analysis, and negotiation of applications for the acquisition of conventional mortgage loans and real estate investments.

Primary Responsibilities and Duties

Negotiate terms, conditions, interest rates, etc. to obtain a flow of acceptable applications for conventional loans and opportunities to purchase real estate.

Analyze client's financial status and past performance, type of property, nature of offer, property location, facilities and access, and competition.

Inspect properties under consideration.

Prepare detailed analyses of proposed loan or purchase and recommend action on offerings.

Prepare mortgage committee memoranda in conjunction with supervisor and present recommendations to the officer in charge or the mortgage committee.

Prepare commitment letters on those investments which have been approved by the committee.

Assist in the negotiation of the final commitment terms and conditions.

Work with clients to help resolve problems which may jeopardize company's rights under a mortgage.

Prepare correspondence under own signature or for signature by supervisor on all aspects of application processing.

Types of Decisions

Must determine pertinent details necessary for proper analysis of loan/purchase offerings.

Responsible for negotiating terms, conditions, interest rates, etc.

Make accept/reject recommendations to supervisor and the mortgage committee.

Consequences of Error

Negotiations conducted to the best advantage of the company will result in the acquisition of high-yield investment opportunities and the addition of sound investments to the mortgage and real estate portfolio; error will result in low yield properties and/or unsound investment decisions.

Organizational Relationships

This is one of three non-officer mortgage analyst positions which can be differentiated by the amount of experience required, the complexity of the duties performed, and the degree of independence with which the duties are performed.

All positions report directly to mortgage officers.

The incumbent has no direct supervisory responsibilities.

Work Relationships

Work regularly with developers, brokers, servicers, and mortgage bankers.

Recommend actions to senior mortgage officer.

Reports are made to the officer in charge and to the mortgage committee.

Work is done with the staff of the administrative and closing units of the divisions of Investment Law and Accounting regarding closings and modifications.

Work is performed within the confines of management specifications, legal requirements, and within the scope of authority granted.

Education and Experience

No specific educational requirements.
Two to three years in mortgage analysis is required.

Representative Skills and Knowledge

Requires:

A knowledge of economics, business, mortgage banking, and real estate.
A command of accounting principles and practices.

Must:

Have sound analytical abilities in order to judge the acceptability of offerings.
Be a strong negotiator.
Be able to appraise the potential of a given investment where past performance criteria are not available.
Know legal requirements and restrictions affecting acquisition of investment properties.

Other

The ability to be tactful and discreet is essential, especially when informing a developer with whom future dealings are desired that a particular transaction must be declined. Strong human relations skills are essential.

Manager—Income Tax Compliance

Basic Function   Supervise the income tax compliance activities of the company and its subsidiaries in a way that will meet the statutory requirements of all taxing jurisdictions and protect the company's interest against excessive taxation. The primary responsibility is to control tax costs and compliance costs. This involves developing ways of saving and/or deferring taxes wherever possible.

Primary Responsibilities and Duties

Supervise the operation and filing of the consolidated Federal income tax and all state and local income tax returns of the company and its affiliates.
To review all returns and make decisions concerning the treatment of all transactions included in the returns.
Establish challenging work performance standards for staff members and develop their professional competence through instruction.
Maintain a good working knowledge of the internal revenue code and related regulations, rulings and cases as well as state income tax laws, etc.
Analyze various transactions and procedures in order to develop ways of saving or deferring taxes and to reduce or eliminate compliance costs.
Coordinate the efforts of various group, division, and subsidiary company controllers to assure proper administration of the income tax function.
Develop the information system necessary to assure proper and timely submission by subsidiaries and divisions of the financial data necessary for preparing tax returns.
Assist the company's independent accountants in their annual audit of the income tax provision and liability accounts.
Supervise the handling of state and local income tax audits to assure proper settlement and make recommendations for appeals or possible litigation.
Assist in the preparation of responses to questions from the Internal Revenue Service.

Types of Decisions

Determine who performs various work assignments.

Establish work priorities.

Select which information is to be filed with income tax returns.

Determine what information is required to assure proper preparation of income tax returns.

Approve employee requests for time off, vacations, etc.

Subject to approval of the Director of Tax Compliance and General Tax Council:

        decide basis for preparation of income returns.

        select applicants to fill open positions within income tax compliance section.

        make salary and other recommendations resulting from the evaluation of the performance of subordinates.

Organizational Relationships

Directly supervise one supervisor, one senior tax accountant, four tax accountants, and one tax report typist.

Directly (or through subordinates) instruct and train headquarters and field personnel with respect to income tax requirements pertaining to the company's activities or policies and provide guidance for conforming with such requirements.

Report directly to the Director of Tax Compliance.

Work Relationships

Advise the Accounting Department as to the tax implications of accounting entries, procedures, and policies.

Examine the records of various businesses whose acquisition is contemplated to ascertain potential tax liabilities and recommended measures to minimize such liabilities.

Extensively read the tax literature in order to keep abreast of developments in income tax laws, court cases, and administrative interpretations which may impact the company.

Education and Experience

BS or BA required.

A minimum of eight (8) years experience either in the field of corporate taxation, public accounting, internal auditing, or general accounting or any combination thereof is required.

Representative Skills and Knowledge

Must have working knowledge and understanding of federal and state income tax laws, regulations, and court cases.

Must have the ability to analyze financial data from an income tax viewpoint.

Must have a complete understanding of basic accounting.

Must understand the company's financial and organizational structure.

Must be able to persuade other department personnel to cooperate with the Tax Department in matters relating to income tax compliance.

Must be able to motivate subordinates to work toward achievement of the same task.

Other

A high degree of administrative ability is required in directing the staff and organizing and planning functional work assigned.

Consultant: Mergers and Acquisitions

Basic Function   To analyze the clients of the firm in order to prepare an in-depth paper for use as a blueprint for raising funds through (or for) mergers and acquisitions.

Primary Responsibilities and Duties

Analyze the need for funds.
Seek out available sources of funds.
Help clients prepare necessary documentation for obtaining these funds.
Coordinate client activities and use the expertise of the Management Advisory Services (MAS) Department to accomplish clients' goals.
Explore the business scene; make proposals to potential clients for using the Management Advisory Services Department and its expertise.

Types of Decisions

Made only after preparation of complete work papers by MAS staff, edited and discussed with supervisory management.

Consequences of Error

Can be very costly.
Firm may be liable to suit should work fall below professional standards.
Position with firm is at stake.

Organizational Relationships

All work performed is subject to review by the partners of the firm; the partner in charge of the MAS Department provides the final review.
Work progress is discussed with supervisor on a daily basis.
The incumbent has authority to direct and control activities of subordinates in analysis of clients' business organization and goals.
The incumbent does not handle grievances, hire or fire personnel but does prepare detailed work performance analysis for each subordinate; this analysis is transmitted to the personnel manager.

Work Relationships

Frequently work with people outside of the firm who are in banking, finance, and investment banking.
Meet with clients' personnel on daily basis.
Co-work with colleagues within the firm in systems analysis, internal control, and computer systems analysis.
Participate in several community, business, and charitable organizations.

Education and Experience

BA from a school of business administration from a recognized university.
MBA is essential for further advancement (GPA—3.5 or better). (Either or both degrees should stress finance, accounting, and computers.)

Representative Skills and Knowledge

Must be able to analyze:
Financial statements.
Capital budgets.
Corporate organizational charts.

Systems of internal control.
Proposed mergers and acquisitions.
Must also:

Understand funding and timing.
Possess a good accounting background.
Have a good understanding of corporate finance, cost of capital, capital budgeting, and various financial decision/analytical models.
Possess the ability to work well with others.
Understand FASB and AICPA policies.
Possess self-confidence, a high degree of intellectual capability, and a desire to progress in your work at the expense of personal life.
Be able to assume responsibility.
Never stop the pursuit of knowledge.

Other

Services are usually rendered at clients' place of business. This job requires extremely long hours, frequent work on weekends. Severe time pressures exist with completion deadlines.

Staff Assistant—Corporate Reporting

Basic Function   Assist in the monthly consolidation of the corporate books in order to prepare accurate and timely financial reports to management, the government, and stockholders. Coordinate the timely and accurate preparation of all Securities and Exchange Commission financial filings.

Primary Responsibilities and Duties

Assist operating units in interpreting and implementing new accounting policies and concepts which are meaningful to local management.
Interpret financial reports.
Create new formats and reports to aid management's decision-making, and review current reports to see if they are still beneficial.
Advise division controllers of problems and solutions involved in booking new acquisitions.
Assist in the financial reporting of international subsidiaries.
Supervise the preparation of monthly balance sheet forecasting reports prepared for corporate treasury.
Maintain a current knowledge of accounting theories and practices as established by the American Institute of Certified Public Accountants and by the Securities and Exchange Commission.
Develop and implement new accounting practices at the corporate level.
Coordinate the timely and accurate preparation of financial data to be included in the annual report to stockholders.
Assist the manager of corporate reporting in managing and utilizing a major computer program for corporate data collection.

Types of Decisions

Provide answers to questions raised by operating units based on corporate financial policies and generally accepted accounting practices.
Participate in decisions with the Manager of Financial Reporting and the Director of Corporate Accounting as to financial matters on the corporate level.
Guide and make operating decisions for technically proficient accounting professionals.
Select and train subordinates.
Report results and unusual situations to immediate supervisor.
Plan and schedule work load and assign work.

Organizational Relationships

The incumbent reports directly to the Manager of Corporate Reporting.
The incumbent must maintain a close relationship with the Law Department for continuous communication of financial information.
The incumbent reviews the performance of subordinates.

Education and Experience

BS degree in Accounting.
Should have three to five years in public accounting or three to five years in the general accounting areas of the company or its divisions.

Representative Skills and Knowledge

Must have:
A thorough understanding of accounting theory and practices. (A CPA certificate, although not mandatory, is very desirable.)
The ability to communicate financial matters clearly to financial as well as non-financial management.
The ability to inspire employees to do a consistently accurate and timely job on all reports required.

Corporate Banking Officer

Basic Function   To maintain and expand existing relationships with clients by marketing all of the bank's services and to develop new client relationships.

Primary Responsibilities and Duties

Call on Fortune 500 companies headquartered near the bank's offices.
Maintain existing clients in the face of product innovations, constant competition, and the fact that many products have specified terms.
Identify opportunities for all of the services offered by the bank, including credit, cash management, pension management, foreign exchange and interest rate exposure management, tax questions, and merger and acquisition activities.
Perform administrative follow-up on overdrawn deposit accounts, loan documents, rate information, memo writing for credit approvals, credit analysis, etc.
Bring in the appropriate specialists to discuss technical products with clients.
Stay current with the technical aspects of new products.
Get to know customers better through personal calls.
Review files and annual reports.

Types of Decisions

Overdraft approval.
Extension of credit to a client (including how much and at what pricing).
Whether or not a specialist should be introduced.
Determining the best approach to take in convincing the bank's management that a deal is right.
Credit extensions require approval at higher levels.
Often the toughest decisions are about prioritizing activities.

Consequences of Error

A poor recommendation will either not get approved and make the person recommending it look foolish in front of superiors or be approved at the risk of losing significant funds/income for the bank and the department.

An unsuccessful recommendation of a good deal will result in a loss for my client.

The dollar amounts involved can be in the $100M's.

What is said to a customer or a superior can make or break a relationship (and a reputation).

Organizational Relationships

Informal discussions are held with the immediate supervisor at least monthly.

There is an annual review of performance which is written and included in the personnel file.

Most work is performed as half of a two-person team.

Work Relationships (contacts)

In-house communications take place with everyone from senior vice presidents to clerks.

External communications occur with chief financial officers, treasurers, assistant treasurers, and other financial officers.

Education and Experience

People with BA's are often successful as bankers as there is a good opportunity to learn the necessary skills on the job; however, it takes longer to develop skills that way.

The bank has an intensive six-month training program followed by regular seminars and "product knowledge" sessions while on the job.

Representative Skills and Knowledge

Must:

Be well versed in the bank's structure, function, capabilities, etc.

Be knowledgeable of new products and people who have knowledge of them.

Know how to use the telephone, a calculator, dictating equipment, and a word processor/personal computer.

Understand present value analysis, international trade transactions, foreign exchange, swaps, and other finance techniques.

Be familiar with tax law, FASB rulings, and maintain a general familiarity with current market conditions.

Be able to use ratio analysis/financial analysis/credit analysis.

Be able to read and understand financial statement footnotes.

Be able to digest information in a credit file to get a feel for relationship.

Understand the regulations governing lending limits relative to total exposure, reserve requirements, federal reserve bank effects on float times, and documentation (as tedious as it is).

Other

The job hours are of an 8:30 to 6:00 P.M. type with occasional late hours for specific jobs. Weekends are often used for review. This is a rare opportunity to see the workings of many different kinds of companies.

Glossary

A

Acceleration clause A provision requiring the immediate payment of an unpaid loan balance upon breach of contract.

Accounts payable Amount due to trade creditor; usually refers to short-term debts for goods and services.

Accounts payable turnover The ratio of credit purchases to accounts payable.

Accounts receivable Amount due from credit customer; usually refers to short-term receivables.

Accounts receivable turnover The ratio of credit sales to accounts receivable.

Accruals Services that have been provided to a business, but have not been paid for (e.g. accrued wages).

Acid test ratio The ratio of total cash, accounts receivable, and marketable securities to current liabilities.

Active resale market A market with a great number of buyers and sellers in a continuous trading fashion.

Activity ratios Activity or turnover ratios that management needs for internal control purposes. They include accounts receivable turnover, inventory turnover, and accounts payable turnover.

After-tax cost of debt The cost of debt financing adjusted for the tax deduction accorded interest expense.

Aging schedule A schedule that shows the collectibility of outstanding receivables with regard to a particular time frame.

Analysts Specialists in capital budgeting who examine all proposals in an effort to evaluate their profitability and risk.

Announcement date The date on which a corporation announces the payment of dividends.

Annuity Equal cash flows that follow consecutively from period to period. There are two kinds of annuities: ordinary and deferred.

Annuity compound factors Tabled values of the computation: $((1+i)^n - 1)/i$.

Annuity discount factors Tabled values of the computation:

$$\frac{1 - \frac{1}{(1+i)^n}}{i}$$

Arbitrage A simultaneous purchase and sale of identical commodities, currencies, and securities in different markets in order to profit from the price differences.

Asset management The management of cash, property, or other tangible or intangible items.

Automatic liabilities Occur as a company's sales and production grow, spontaneously employing more workers, using more energy, and purchasing more materials and supplies.

Average collection period The duration of days in which the average credit customer pays a bill; also, 360 days divided by receivable turnover.

Average cost of debt The ratio of interest charges to total debts.

Average daily credit sales Annual credit sales divided by 360 days.

Average daily production rate Annual production divided by 360 days.

Average daily purchases on account Annual credit purchases divided by 360 days.

Average holding period Average number of days an inventory item is on hand; also, 360 days divided by inventory turnover.

Average payment period Average number of days to pay off a debt; also, 360 days divided by payables turnover.

Average rate of return A simplified method in approximating internal rate of return.

B

Bad-debt expense Accounts receivables that are uncollectibles.

Bad-debt proportion of credit sales Amount of uncollectibles relative to credit sales.

Balance sheet A statement of the assets, liabilities, and equities of a business entity on a given date.

Bank commercial loans Short-term (less than one year) loans extended by commercial banks to business.

Banker's acceptance An obligation of a firm, guaranteed by a bank.

Benefit-cost ratio The profitability index used in capital budgeting.

Best-effort basis Condition under which an investment banker does not guarantee a security issue, but merely sells as much as possible for the issuing company.

Beta (B) A widely used method of measuring risk that encompasses the concept of diversification.

Bid-ask quote Prices at which security dealers agree to buy at wholesale (bid) and sell at retail (ask).

Bill of lading A document executed by a common carrier acknowledging the receipt of goods.

Bond indenture A contract describing the collateral, sinking fund date and other important terms under which bonds are issued.

Bond ratings Credit appraisals by a recognized financial organization (e.g. Standard & Poor's).

Bond value The value of a bond on the open market.

Book value The amount at which an item appears on the accounting records, normally equal to original cost.

Book value per share The amount of net assets applicable to each share of outstanding common stock.

Book value weights A weighting scheme used to calculate the weighted average cost of capital.

C

Call premium Price above face value when a corporation decides to redeem a bond prematurely.

Call price The price at which an obligor is permitted to redeem securities.

Call provisions Benefit the issuing company, which may want to retire the debt in advance.

Capital asset pricing model (CAPM) Describes the relationship between risk and required rate of return.

Capital budget The formal schedule of anticipated sales and purchases of capital assets.

Capital budgeting The process of analyzing and evaluating proposals for investment in capital assets.

Capital gains Excess of proceeds over original cost from the sale of capital assets.

Capital market Market in which long-term securities, both debt and equity, are bought and sold.

Capital rationing Allocation of capital due to limited supply of funds.

Carry-over provision A provision in which a company can have its current losses carried over as tax deductions to prior and future years.

Carrying cost Cost of carrying one unit of inventory for a year.

Cash budget A schedule of expected cash receipts and disbursements for a business.

Cash conversion cycle The process of going from cash to inventory to receivables and back to cash again.

Cash discount Reduction in payment allowed for the prompt settlement of debt arising from a credit sale.

Cash equivalent curves Curves that represent cash flows at different points in time that are equally good.

Cash flow analysis Identifying the relevant cash flows associated with a capital asset and measuring them.

Cash flow identification Identifying the cash flows associated with a capital asset proposal.

Cash flow profile A net cash profile reveals the impact that a capital asset has on a firm's cash flow.

Cash management The management of cash and marketable securities.

Cash profit Net cash flows from a capital asset over its life.

Checking accounts Claims of depositors against a financial institution that are payable on demand.

Cleanup period A provision written into most commercial bank lines of credit that requires the borrower to be out of debt to the bank for a minimum period of time during the year.

Clearing float The time interval involved during which outstanding checks are being cleared through the banking system.

Collateral Securities or other valuable assets pledged to secure an agreement (such as payment of a loan).

Collection agency An individual or organization in the business of collecting debts for others.

Collection effort Actions taken to collect debts.

Commercial finance companies Issue short-term loans to finance temporary buildup of accounts receivable and inventory.

Commercial paper A short-term unsecured promissory note issued by a well-known corporation.

Commitment fee Required by banks of companies needing written assurance that the funds in a line of credit will be available upon request.

Common size statement Converts financial statement dollar amounts to percentages.

Common stockholder equity Assets minus liabilities (or common stock par value plus paid-in capital in excess of par plus retained earnings); also called *net worth* and *owner's equity.*

Compensating balance Money left on deposit in a bank account as a requirement of a loan or services rendered.

Compound factor Calculations of a specific interest rate—number of time periods combination: $CF = (1+i)^t$.

Compound interest Interest calculated on accumulated interest, as well as on the remaining balance of a loan or investment.

Compounding An alternative way of working compound interest problems; related to future value.

Conglomerate growth Corporate growth in unrelated lines of business.

Consolidation Combination of two or more organizations into one, forming a new entity.

Consumer finance companies Institutions that make secured loans to individual consumers for the purchase of consumer products.

Continuous compounding Interest compounded continuously; must be calculated with the use of logarithms.

Contribution margin Sales minus variable expense.

Conversion price The price a convertible bondholder effectively pays for each share of common stock that is obtained through conversion.

Conversion privilege Entitles investors to convert preferred stock/bonds to common stock.

Conversion ratio The ratio that specifies the number of shares of common stock that can be obtained with a single convertible bond.

Conversion value The market value of stock into which a bond is convertible.

Convertible securities Securities that can be converted to common stock.

Corporation A business entity with limited liability empowered to do business under state law.

Cost of bonds The compound interest rate that equates the future semi-annual coupon payments and par value (cash flows) to the net proceeds (present value) of a bond.

Cost of capital The interest rates that a business agrees to pay to investors in its bonds and other forms of long-term financing.

Cost of carrying accounts receivable The interest cost of financing accounts receivable.

Cost of common stock The RRR of those investors who are willing and able to be part-owners of a corporation.

Cost of financing Interest rates as a cost of the corporation; same as the required rate of return.

Cost of leasing The compound interest rate that equates the future rental payments (cash flows) to the value of leased assets (present value).

Cost of preferred stock The compound interest rate that equates a perpetual stream of future dividend payments (cash flow) to the net proceeds (present value) of an issue.

Cost of retained earnings The RRR demanded by owners from any profits that are retained in a business, or what they could earn elsewhere (i.e. opportunity cost).

Cost of term loans The compound interest rate that equates the future installment payments (cash flows) to the loan face value (present value).

Coupon rate The stated rate of return on bonds.

Couriers Used to transport checks internationally so as to minimize negative float.

Covariance A measure of the interrelationship of two variables.

Credit analysis The process of measuring a credit applicant's ability and desire to pay.

Credit information sources Places to obtain information about a credit applicant's capacity, capital, and character.

Credit information system Provides data that would help credit analysis, collection, and control.

Credit limits Maximum dollar amount of credit that a customer may have outstanding at any given point in time.

Credit management Policies, procedures, and controls over all aspects of a credit program.

Credit period Number of days that customers are given to pay their debts.

Credit policy Credit terms, credit standards, and collection effort that a company must determine once it has decided to sell on credit.

Credit policy guidelines Determine the company's credit standard, credit terms, and collection efforts.

Credit program evaluation System of making sure that credit policies and procedures are carried out in an efficient and effective manner.

Credit standards Guidelines that determine potential credit customers.

Credit terms Arrangements under which credit will be extended (e.g. credit period and cash discounts).

Cumulative preferred stock Dividends cannot be paid on common stock until all unpaid dividends on preferred stock are paid.

Currency swap An increasingly popular hedging technique in which two parties agree to exchange two different currencies at a later date.

Current ratio Current assets divided by current liabilities.

D _____

Dealer compensation Commissions earned through working as a middleman by trading stocks and bonds for customers.

Dealer spread The profit a security dealer would make in a transaction by offering different buying (bid) and selling (ask) prices.

Debenture An unsecured corporate bond.

Debt limit Maximum amount that can be borrowed, often included in loans and bond issues as a protective covenant.

Debt maturity The date on which the last payment of the debt is due.

Debt-to-assets Total liabilities divided by total assets.

Debt-to-equity Total liabilities divided by total stockholders' equity.

Decision maker A person who has authority to make decisions on capital asset proposals.

Decomposition analysis Breaking down of financial ratios into individual components for detailed analysis.

Deductible expenses Expenses that can be subtracted from gross income in determining taxable income.

Deferred annuity An annuity under which payments are due to begin immediately (i.e. at the beginning of each period).

Depreciable base Original cost less salvage value.

Depreciation fraction Depreciation method combined with tax life.

Depreciation, accounting Conveys useful information to users of a financial statement; the decline in book value of a capital asset due to use or obsolescence.

Depreciation, economic The decline in market value of a capital asset from one period to the next.

Depreciation, tax Government-mandated depreciation for tax purposes.

Diluted market value The reduction in the market price of common stock due to the issuance of additional shares at below market prices.

Discount factor Calculation for a specific interest rate—number of time periods combination: $DF = \dfrac{1}{(1+i)^t}$

Discounted cash flow The present value of expected future cash flows.

Discounting The process of determining the present value of future cash flows.

Distribution date The date on which dividends are sent out to the stockholders.

Diversification A program of acquiring assets or businesses in industries other than that in which a company is currently engaged.

Dividend reinvestment plan Gives shareholders the opportunity to have their cash dividends automatically reinvested in newly issued shares at the going market price.

Dividend relevancy The dividend payout rate has an effect on the market price of a company's stock.

Dividend restriction Limits a company in paying dividends during the life of a loan in order to maintain the asset level (conserve cash).

Dividend yield (DY) Dividend per share divided by market price per share of common stock.

Dividends Cash payments of a portion or all of profits to shareholders.

Dividends per share Dividends divided by number of common shares outstanding.

Dollar profitability analysis Includes analysis of net income, earnings per share, dividends per share, and dividends.

Dow Jones Industrial Average A popular stock market index used to measure stock market movements and trends.

Draft An instrument directing a depository to make payments to a payee or bearer.

DuPont System A system designed by DuPont to help analyze a firm's overall performance.

E _____

Earnings before interest and taxes (EBIT) The earnings of a business as opposed to earnings of stockholders or net income.

Earnings per share (EPS) A corporation's net income for a period divided by the number of common shares outstanding.

Earnings-price ratio (E/P) The ratio of market price per share to the annual earnings per share.

Economic order quantity (EOQ) Order quantity associated with the lowest total cost of carrying and ordering inventory.

Electronic Funds Transfer System (EFTS) The transfer of funds from the bank account of one depositor to the account of another without the use of checks.

End-of-month (EOM) System in which suppliers who make numerous credit sales to the same customers allow them to start the credit and discount period at the end of the month in which goods are received. It helps to extend the payment period for the customers.

Equity dilution The potential reduction in earnings per share that would occur if convertible securities were converted. This is due to the increase in the number of shares of common stock outstanding.

Equivalent interest rates Converting from annual interest rates to less than annual interest rates and vice versa.

Escape clause A provision allowing one or more parties of a contract to withdraw when stipulated conditions exist.

Eurobonds Bonds released by U.S. a company for sale in Europe.

Eurodollar deposits Dollar denominated deposits held in commercial banks located outside the United States.

Eurodollars U.S. dollar-denominated deposits held in banks outside the United States.

Ex-dividend date Four business days prior to the holder-of-record date for dividend payments on common stock. Anyone who buys stock on or after that date is not entitled to the dividend.

Ex-rights date The date that a stock trades ex-rights. It is four business days prior to the holder-of-record date.

Exchange rate risk exposure The instability of the exchange rate in the international market, which leads to uncertainty on the part of foreign traders and investors.

Exchange ratio Specifies the number of shares of common stock that can be acquired with a warrant.

Exercise price The price an investor must pay for each share of stock that can be acquired with the warrant.

Expected value A weighted average of a random variable where probabilities are the weights.

Expiration date Date on which a warrant expires.

Export-Import Bank A governmental agency organized to engage in lending to certain qualified U.S. exporters and their customers.

Exports Merchandise that is sold and shipped to foreign countries.

Extra dividends Dividends declared and paid in addition to the regular dividends.

F

Factor A lender, usually a commercial finance company, that specializes in the acquisition of accounts receivable.

Factoring A means of advancing credit, whereby a factor purchases another firm's accounts receivable at a discount.

Federal Reserve Communications System (Fedwire) A system that allows debits and credits of bank accounts through computers.

Field warehousing An approach for monitoring inventory collateral pledged in business loans.

Financial forecasting Methods used to prepare plans for future financing.

Financial lease A non-cancelable lease.

Financial leverage Process in which companies attempt to use low, fixed-cost debt funds as a lever to generate higher earnings per share and returns on owner equity.

Financial management The management of assets, liabilities, and stockholders' equity.

Financial statement analysis (FSA) Determines a company's earnings performance and the soundness and liquidity of its financial situation.

Financial structure The mix of financing for a business between debt and equity and short-term and long-term debt.

Fixed costs Relatively stable expenses not affected by the level of production or sales.

Fixed payout rate policy A dividend policy calling for a fixed payout rate.

Float The time interval that exists between when a check is written and when the funds are removed from the checking account.

Flotation costs Various expenses that are encountered in public fund-raising: legal fees, paperwork, underwriter spread, etc.

Floor plan A contract in which a lender may offer to finance the wholesale value of certain dealer's inventory (e.g. automobiles, heavy duty trucks, etc.).

Forecasting errors Difference in actual outcome and predicted outcome.

Forecasting techniques Techniques used to predict market potential, sales volume, stock prices, funding requirements and interest rates.

Follow-up An examination conducted after a capital asset has been purchased.

Foreign capital flows Investments in foreign countries and fundraising abroad.

Foreign exchange market A market involving trading in the currency of one country for the currency of another.

Foreign trade Exports and imports of goods and services.

Forward exchange market A market that deals in the future trading of foreign exchange.

Four C's of credit analysis *Capacity:* Measures the applicant's financial ability to pay the debt. *Capital:* Difference between the applicant's assets and liabilities or debt-to-asset ratio. *Character:* Measures the applicant's willingness and desire to pay. *Conditions:* Unusual circumstances that would affect the decision on a customer's credit application.

Future value Related to compound interest, but more specifically compounding.

G

Generally accepted accounting principles (GAAP) The accounting concepts, measurement techniques, and standards of presentation used in financial statements.

Going concern A business that is currently in operation.

H

Hedging One type of economic insurance used by dealers in commodities and securities in order to prevent loss due to price fluctuation.

Holder-of-record date Stockholders on a firm's records as of a specific date.

Holding company A corporation whose primary purpose is owning common shares of one or more corporations.

Holding period The period during which a capital asset is owned.

Horizontal growth Business expansion in a particular field.

I

Implementation Covers all the arrangements that need to be taken care of from when a capital asset proposal has been selected until it is actually used.

Imports Merchandise that is purchased from foreign countries.

Income tax rates The rates that apply to different levels of taxable income. *Average:* The proportion of total taxable income paid in taxes. *Marginal:* Apply to changes in taxable income; they are determined by a firm's current taxable income or tax bracket.

Industry averages Ratio standards for comparing the performance of companies in the same industry.

Inflation premium Rates of return that would counterbalance the effect of inflation on investment.

Initial cash flows All the cash expenses and receipts that accompany the acquisition of capital assets.

Insider trading The trading of securities on the basis of inside information about a firm's prospects, information that is not available to the investing public.

Institutional investor An organization, such as an insurance company, pension fund, or mutual fund, which invests large sums of money in securities.

Interest rate Price paid for the use of another's money.

Internal rate of return (IRR) The compound annual interest rate earned on capital assets.

Intrayear compounding Interest compounded more often than once a year.

Inventory Merchandise on hand at any given period of time, applicable to raw materials, goods in process, or finished products.

Inventory control The control of merchandise on hand by accounting and physical methods.

Inventory management The management and control of inventory.

Inventory turnover Cost of goods sold divided by inventory balance.

Investment banking Firms that sell corporate securities in the public market.

J

Joint probabilities The probability that two variables will simultaneously take on given values.

K

Key-man insurance Life insurance on a key employee or partner wherein a lender is the beneficiary under the policy.

L

Lead time The time between ordering goods and actually receiving it.

Lessee The tenant or company obtaining the use of property under a lease.

Letter of credit A bank document issued on behalf of a buyer, which gives the buyer the financial backing of the issuing bank.

Liability and equity management Decisions regarding a company's financing.

Limited liability Legal exemptions of stockholders from financial liability for the debts of a firm beyond the amount they have individually invested.

Line of credit A prearranged loan under which a bank (or a group of banks) agrees in writing to lend up to a given amount of funds for one year.

Liquidating dividends The declared dividends in the closing of a firm.

Liquidity The convertibility of assets into cash or the ability to pay bills as they come due.

Liquidity analysis Analysis of a firm's ability to convert assets into cash or pay bills on time.

Loan amortization A systematic process to divide term loan installments into principal and interest portions.

Loan face value The initial proceeds of a term loan.

M

Mail float The time that a check is in the mail.

Managed dividend policy A policy in which dividends are administered in order to achieve continuity and stability.

Margin requirements The amount of debt that can be used to purchase securities as regulated by the SEC and Federal Reserve.

Marginal benefit The extra gain attributable to an additional amount of a current asset.

Marginal cost The amount of money one extra unit of a current asset will add to a firm's cost.

Market value exchange ratio Found by dividing the market value of the target company's common stock into the market value of securities and/or cash offered by the suitor.

Marketable securities Securities that can be easily sold at low cost and with little risk.

Matching A term used to describe the process of equating asset lives to debt maturity.

Maturity date The date on which a financial obligation comes due for payment.

Maturity matching A conservative approach whereby debt maturities equal asset lives. There is no risk associated with this strategy.

Merger The combination of two businesses, usually through the purchase of one by the other.

Modigliani and Miller model States that in a perfect financial environment, unfettered by laws, taxes, transaction cost, and investors' ignorance, it is not possible to reduce a firm's average financing cost by the use of debt financing.

Money market Market for short-term loans and marketable securities.

Mortgage A conveyance of real property as security for the payment of debt.

Mortgage bond Bond secured by a pledge of real property.

Multinational corporation A corporation that has investments and business activities in a number of countries.

Mutually exclusive assets Capital assets that can perform essentially the same service or same work, but only one of which will be selected.

N

Negative float The interval from when a customer writes a check until it is added to the firm's checking account.

Negotiable certificates of deposit Marketable deposit receipts issued by commercial banks, bearing specific rates of interest for specific periods of time.

Negotiable warehouse receipt A document showing title to commodities that is endorsed over to the creditor for the life of a loan. The bank can use this document to seize the property should the borrower default on the debt.

Net cash flows Cash inflows minus cash outflows.

Net income (NI) Net profit, or revenue minus all expenses including interest and taxes; the owner's share of a business's profit.

Net present value The excess present value of the net cash inflows expected from an investment over the amount to be invested.

Net proceeds The net cash receipts from a bond issue or any other public security offering. It is sales proceeds minus flotation costs.

Net working capital The net amount of liquid resources available to a business. It equals current assets minus current liabilities.

New York Stock Exchange (NYSE) The most prominent secondary financial market for common stock. All the rules set by the NYSE are to be observed before securities can be traded.

O

Objective cash flow estimates The estimation of cash flow in the form of a probability distribution.

One-hundred percent payout rate A very high dividend payout rate is found with businesses whose stockholders have a strong desire for current consumption. A high payout rate is often accompanied by a dividend re-investment plan.

Open account A method to facilitate the purchase of goods on credit.

Operating lease A short-term cancelable lease.

Operating leverage The presence of fixed operating costs can magnify changes in a firm's earnings whenever sales rise and fall.

Optimal level of current assets Current assets are optimal when stockholders would not gain in terms of profit or risk from a change in their amounts.

Optimal level of debt The level of debt that produces the lowest weighted average cost of financing.

Option The right to buy or sell a given quantity of an item for a fixed price and predetermined period of time.

Option leverage The magnification of profits that is made possible by common stock warrants.

Order point The quantity of inventory that triggers an order for more units.

Order quantity Number of units ordered; used with economic order quantity (EOQ) model.

Ordering cost Cost of placing one order; used with economic order quantity (EOQ) model.

Ordinary annuity An annuity under which cash flows are due to occur at the end of each period.

Ordinary gross income Taxable revenue before deduction of expenses.

Original cost The cost associated with the acquisition of a capital asset. It would include installation and delivery charges.

Original cost rule Resources used in the production and sale of a product are recorded at historical cost for financial reporting purposes.

Outside credit manager Credit specialist that handles credit programs for manufacturing and commercial enterprises.

Over-the-counter market (OTC) A group of security dealers acting as market makers in certain securities, along with a communication network to tie them together. Trading rules are minimal; listing is not required.

P _____

Par value The face amount of a bond or a preferred stock.

Parity The relationship between exchange rates and interest rates of two countries.

Participating preferred stock Preferred stock that shares with the common stock in any dividends paid after the common stock has received dividends at a rate equal to the preferred rate.

Partnership An unincorporated business owned by two or more persons.

Payback period The length of time necessary to recover the initial cost of an investment from the resulting annual recurring net cash flows.

Payment date The date on which dividends are paid.

Payment period The time interval from when goods are received by a credit customer until they are paid for.

Payout rate The percentage of earnings paid out in dividends.

Permanent financing Funding that is used to acquire and hold capital assets and permanent levels of current assets.

Perpetuity An infinite-lived annuity.

Personal property Movable assets of a more personal nature.

Pledging accounts receivable Accounts receivable used as collateral for bank commercial loans and finance company loans.

Pledging inventory Inventory used as collateral for bank commercial loans and finance company loans.

Portfolio risk The risk associated with a portfolio or grouping of assets.

Positive float The elapsed time from when a payment is made by check until the funds are deducted from a firm's checking account.

Precautionary demand The demand for money because of future uncertainties with regard to cash receipts and disbursements.

Preemptive right Rights of present stockholders to be the first to purchase a proportionate amount of additional common shares offered for sale.

Prepayment clause The privilege of repaying part or all of a loan in advance of its maturity date.

Prepayment penalty A penalty placed on a borrower for paying off a term loan before its maturity date.

Present value The discounted value of future cash flows, assuming a given rate of interest.

Price-earnings ratio The market price per share divided by the annual earnings per share.

Price guarantee An investment banker's commitment to obtain a specific price for a firm's stock in a public offering; also applies to bond interest rates.

Primary financial markets Markets in which companies acquire funding.

Prime rate The benchmark interest rate charged by banks to their best loan customers.

Private placement The private sale of securities or acquisition of loans whereby a company deals with only one or a few investors.

Processing float The period during which checks are being processed after being received by a firm.

Profit margin Return on sales.

Profitability analysis The ratio analysis used to study the ability of a business to earn a profit.

Profitability index A discounted cash flow measure used to study the relationship between benefits and cost of a capital asset.

Promissory note An unconditional written promise to pay a certain sum of money at a determinable interest rate.

Proprietorship An unincorporated business owned by one person; sole proprietorship.

Prospectus Summarizes the information contained in an SEC registration statement.

Protective covenants Provisions required by banks in regard to their business loans, both commercial and otherwise, in order to reduce the chances of default.

Proxy A signed statement that authorizes a third party to vote for an absent owner at the annual stockholders' meeting.

Public market A market in which all investors have an opportunity to purchase a firm's securities.

Purchase option The right that enables the lessee to purchase leased property from the lessor in the future.

Q _____

Quantity discounts A purchase-price discount offered when customers order in large quantities.

Quick ratio The ratio of current assets minus inventory divided by current liabilities.

R _____

Real property Land, buildings, and other improvements to property that may legally be classified as real in contrast to personal property.

Receipt of goods (ROG) The day that goods are received by the credit customer; it begins the credit period.

Recurring cash flows Annual cash flows generated by the use of a capital asset.

Refinancing The situation in which new funding is needed when debt maturities are shorter than asset lives.

Refunding Retirement of a bond issue or term loan prior to the scheduled maturity date.

Regional banking A decentralized banking system devised to minimize negative check float.

Registration of securities A process in which the company involved has to provide all the material information and facts relating to an issue of securities before they can be sold.

Reinvestment The situation in which new investment is needed when debt maturities are shorter than asset lives.

Reinvestment rate Internal rate of return earned on future capital assets; used in capital rationing.

Remaining loan balance Remaining balances of term loans are needed for financial statements and refunding analysis; reflects the present value of the remaining payments.

Renewal option The right to extend a financial lease beyond the initial term.

Replacement cost Cost in today's market for new equipment to replace equivalent existing equipment.

Replacement financing Funds used to replace maturing debt obligations, such as bank loans and bonds.

Repurchase agreements Banking arrangements designed to provide corporations with a flexible, safe, and convenient investment.

Required rate of return (RRR) The interest rate demanded by investors; comprised of premiums for time preference, expected inflation, income taxes, and risk.

Residual dividend policy In an effort to minimize the flotation cost associated with the sale of common stock, dividends will be whatever is left from net income after all equity financing requirements have been met.

Return on assets (ROA) The ratio of earnings before interest and taxes to total assets.

Return on equity (ROE) One way to measure profitability; the ratio of net income divided by stockholders' equity.

Return on investment (ROI) One way of testing management's efficiency in using available resources; also called *return on assets*.

Return on sales (ROS) The ratio of earnings before interest and taxes to sales.

Rights of common stockholders The legal rights of common stockholders, such as the right to vote for the board of directors.

Rights offering An alternative to a public or private sale of common stock in which present stockholders are provided with rights to buy new shares at a given price.

Risk Any chance of monetary loss in regard to business decisions.

Risk averse The psychological description of the fact that the typical investor is averse to risk and must be compensated for it.

Risk premium Return that investors demand from risky investments over and above the risk-free return.

Risk screening An attempt to identify assets with unmanageable risk.

Risk-adjusted weighted-average cost of capital The required rate of return used in capital budgeting.

Risk-free interest rate The basic interest rate, as represented by the yields on U.S. government securities.

Risk-profit ratio A risk measure divided by profit measure, such as SD(IRR)/E(IRR).

Risk-return trade-off The amount of risk that is exchanged for a given amount of profit.

S

Safety from default The backing by strong businesses and governments such that the repayment of principal and interest is guaranteed on a security.

Safety stock A minimum inventory that provides a cushion against unexpected increases in demand and variations in lead time.

Sales finance companies Specialize in financing the inventories and customers of certain retail businesses, such as auto dealers.

Seasonal dating Normally used by manufacturers that have a strong seasonal pattern to their sales, and prefer to shift the burden of carrying inventory to wholesalers and retailers in exchange for an extended credit payment period.

Secondary financial markets Markets consisting of organized exchanges, such as the New York Stock Exchange, and informal markets, such as the O.T.C.

Secured loans Loans that are made secure of payment by pledging valuable property to be forfeited in case of default.

Securities Financial instruments (e.g. stocks and bonds).

Securities & Exchange Commission The agency that governs the initial public sale and trading of securities.

Security agreement The formal agreement between the lender and the borrower that grants the lender an interest in certain goods.

Security dealers Professionals that trade securities on their own accounts, hoping to make a profit through buying and selling price differentials. They dominate the over-the-counter market.

Security market line (SML) A graphical representation of the trade-off between expected rate of return and systematic risk (Beta).

Security valuation The process of pricing securities in the financial market place.

Sensitivity analysis One way to measure the amount of risk associated with an asset. It is done by asking "what-if" questions with regard to net cash flow outcomes different from the most likely estimates.

Separation of ownership and control Most corporations are run by professional managers, rather than by stockholders.

Shelf registration Allows a company to obtain a security registration that is good for two years and can sell its securities to the public during the specified time period.

Short-Term Agency Securities Issued by agencies sponsored by the Federal government.

Simple interest Interest calculated on the principal sum, but not on any interest that has been earned by the sum.

Sinking fund A systematic method to retire a bond issue over its life.

Small Business Administration (SBA) A U.S. government agency that guarantees bank loans to eligible small businesses.

Solvency analysis The financial statement analysis of a firm's ability to service debt.

Speculation Going either long or short in an investment that is very risky.

Sponsors Individuals responsible for submitting proposals concerning capital assets.

Spot foreign exchange market The setting in which current day trading is done in foreign exchange.

Standard and Poor's Stock Index A popular stock market index based on 500 stocks in a multitude of industries.

Standard deviation The square root of variance; a measure of dispersion.

Statement of changes in financial position A record of changes in a company's accounts over one year.

Stock broker A middleman who facilitates the purchase and sale of securities.

Stock dividends The distribution of profit in the form of shares of common stock.

Stock exchange A formal security trading facility, such as the NYSE.

Stock repurchase A corporation's open market purchases of its own common stock.

Stock split Artificially increasing the number of outstanding common shares so as to lower their market price.

Stock valuation model States that the market price or market value of a share of common stock is equal to the present value of estimated dividends per share, discounted by the required rate of return.

Stockholder A person who owns part of the corporation.

Stockholders' equity Total assets minus total liabilities; also called *net worth*.

Stockout costs Deficiency in materials and shortages of products that lead to missed sales and production delays.

Straight line depreciation The allocation of the cost of an asset to expense is spread uniformly over its useful life or tax life.

Stretching the payables A way to obtain credit by delaying payments as long as possible.

Subjective cash flow estimates Estimation based on mathematical forecasting techniques, studying the underlying economic factors, and personal intuition; often referred to as *most likely cash flows*.

Subordinated bonds Bonds that are stated to be junior to other specified securities.

Subscription price The price at which the new shares will be sold in a rights offering. By setting the price lower than the market price, a firm can increase the chances that all new shares will be sold.

Subsidiary A self-contained business acquired by a parent company and administered under its direction.

Suitor The term used to describe a company that is seeking to purchase another firm.

Sum-of-the-years digits depreciation The method of allocating a large portion of the cost of a capital asset to the early years of its life.

Systematic risk Risk that an asset has in common with the market portfolio; measured by the statistic *Beta*.

T

Takeover candidate A business with characteristics that make it ripe to be purchased (target company).

Target company Selling company, as opposed to suitor.

Tax life The period of time over which capital assets are depreciated for income tax purposes.

Tax premium An interest rate premium necessary to compensate investor for income taxes on interest earnings.

Tax salvage value A government-stipulated deduction from the original cost of a capital asset to arrive at the depreciable tax basis.

Tax-free notes Short-term notes and bonds offered by state and local government.

Temporary financing Used to fund seasonal and transitory increases in working capital, primarily accounts receivable and inventory.

Tender offer An offer to purchase a business that is made to stockholders rather than management.

Term loans Long-term installment loans that could run up to twenty years.

Term of the lease   The life of the lease; that interval of time during which all rights and obligations of the lessor and lessee are in force.

Term structure of interest rates   The relationship between yield and maturity.

Terminal cash flows   Final cash flows that are associated with capital assets.

Terms of exchange   Negotiations between a suitor and target company so as to arrive at a compromise for their stockholders.

Third market   Unusually large transactions in listed stocks away from the exchange floor.

Time lag   The time lapse between a decision and when it is actually carried out.

Time preference premium   The interest rate reward associated with the postponement of consumption.

Time value of money   The process of adjusting cash flows for time differences by the use of the risk-free interest rate.

Times interest earned   The ratio of earning, before interest and taxes, to annual interest expense.

Total asset turnover   The ratio of sales divided by total assets.

Trade credit   Credit generated when a company acquires supplies, merchandise, or materials and does not pay immediately.

Trade credit terms   Terms under which trade credit is extended (e.g., credit period, cash discounts).

Tradeoff between profit and risk   The phenomenon in which a higher level of profit will be associated with a higher level of risk, and vice versa.

Trading activity   The frequency and volume of trading that is done in a particular security.

Trading costs   Includes paper work, registration fees, and dealer compensation with respect to a transaction.

Transactions demand   Businesses hold money for the purpose of daily transactions.

Treasury stock   A corporation's own common stock that has been issued and then repurchased, but not canceled.

Trustee   The third party overseer of a bond indenture.

U _____

U.S. Treasury Bills   A short-term obligation of the U.S. government to pay the bearer a fixed sum on a specified date.

Undervalued business   One whose common stock is selling on the market at a bargain price in relation to replacement cost of assets and level of indebtedness.

Underwriter's spread   The difference between the gross proceeds from a sale of securities and the amount that the company actually receives; the investment banker's compensation.

Underwriting   The assumption of risk, as in investment banking and insurance.

Unsecured loans   Loans that do not require the pledging of valuable property.

Unsystematic risk   The kind of risk that can be eliminated by investors through diversification.

Useful life   The depreciable life of an asset for accounting purposes.

Users of financial statements   Short-term creditors, long-term creditors, stockholders, management, and others.

V _____

Value of a right   The price of a right on the market as determined by the subscription price and market price of stock.

Value of warrants   Equal to the market price of common stock less the exercise price, multiplied by exchange ratio.

Variable costs   Expenses that are directly related to the volume of business conducted.

Variable interest rates   Interest rates that fluctuate with the prevailing market rates.

Variance   The statistical measure of dispersion of a random variable.

Vertical growth   A situation when a company moves forward/backward in the product chain flowing from raw materials to the final consumer.

W _____

Warrant   An option to buy a specified number of shares of common stock at a fixed price for a predetermined period of time.

Weighted average cost of capital   The average cost of new, long-term, corporate financing.

Weighted average cost of financing   The average cost of debt and equity financing for a firm that should be minimized.

Wire transfers   Electronic transfers of credits and debits to checking accounts stored in computers.

Work-in-process   All goods that have begun the manufacturing process, but have not been completed.

Working capital behavior   The movement of a firm's current assets under different (economic) conditions.

Working capital cyclical behavior   Changes in working capital because of business cycles.

Working capital seasonal behavior   Changes in working capital because of changes in seasonal demand and production.

Working capital trend behavior   Changes in working capital with regard to business growth.

XYZ _____

Yields   Interest rates; frequently used with marketable securities.

Zero payout rate   Instead of paying out dividends, rapidly growing companies usually retain all or a large portion of profits.

Zero-coupon bonds   Securities that sell at very deep discounts from par value and have no interest payments associated with them.

Index